ISLAMIC REFORM IN TWENTIETH-CENTURY AFRICA

This book is dedicated to my teacher,
Jamil M. Abun-Nasr

ISLAMIC REFORM IN TWENTIETH-CENTURY AFRICA

Roman Loimeier

EDINBURGH
University Press

Edinburgh University Press is one of the leading university presses in the UK. We publish academic books and journals in our selected subject areas across the humanities and social sciences, combining cutting-edge scholarship with high editorial and production values to produce academic works of lasting importance. For more information visit our website: edinburghuniversitypress.com

© Roman Loimeier, 2016

Edinburgh University Press Ltd
The Tun – Holyrood Road
12 (2f) Jackson's Entry
Edinburgh EH8 8PJ

Typeset in 11/15 Adobe Garamond by
Servis Filmsetting Ltd, Stockport, Cheshire

A CIP record for this book is available from the British Library

ISBN 978 0 7486 9543 0 (hardback)
ISBN 978 0 7486 9544 7 (webready PDF)
ISBN 978 1 4744 1491 3 (epub)

The right of Roman Loimeier to be identified as author of this work has been asserted in accordance with the Copyright, Designs and Patents Act 1988 and the Copyright and Related Rights Regulations 2003 (SI No. 2498).

CONTENTS

GLOSSARY OF ARABIC TERMS

ʿāda	customary law, tradition
adhān (*muʾadhdhin*)	call to prayer (Muezzin)
ahl	people
ʿālim, pl. *ʿulamāʾ*	religious scholar
amīr	commander (*amīr al-muʾminīn*: commander of the faithful)
anṣār	supporters
ʿaqīda	confession (of the faith), catechetic theology, doctrine
ʿaṣr	afternoon prayer
ʿawrah	intimate (parts), pudenda
baraka	blessing power
bāṭin	hidden, inner meaning
bidʿa, pl. *bidaʿ*	(un-Islamic) innovation
bikāʾ	wailing, weeping
dāʾira	recitation/study circle
dalīl, pl. *dalāʾil*	guide
dār	land, house
daʿwa	cause, message, propaganda (*dāʿiya*: a person who represents a cause, pl. *duʿah*)
dhikr	Sufi meditation exercises, ceremony, ritual

dīn	religion
diya	blood money
duʿāʾ	supplication, supererogatory prayer
fajr (*ṣubḥ*)	morning (prayers)
fatwā, pl. *fatāwā*	formal (yet, not binding) legal opinion
fiqh (*uṣūl al-*)*fiqh*	law, jurisprudence (Islamic legal theory)
fitna	chaos, disorder, disunity
ghawth	succour (*ghawth al-zamān*: succour of the age)
ḥadd, pl. *ḥudūd*	qurʾānic regulations and punishments
ḥadīth, pl. *aḥādīth*	the (discipline of) Prophetic traditions
ḥajj (*ḥājj*)	pilgrimage (pilgrim)
ḥaqīqa	truth
ḥaraka	movement, speed (in terms of the rules for the recitation of the Qurʾān, *tajwīd*)
ḥawāla	cheque, bill of exchange, money transfer
ḥijāb	amulet, protection, veil
hijra	(e)migration
hilāl	new moon, crescent
ḥirāba	robbery
ḥisba	guarding (public order), (*muḥtasib*: a person who guards)
ḥizb, pl. *aḥzāb*	group, part (one of sixty recitational sections of the Qurʾān)
ʿibādāt (pl.)	acts of devotion, religious obligations
ibtilāʾ	trial, visitation
ʿīd, pl. *aʿyād*	festival day (such as *ʿīd al-kabīr/al-aḍḥā* and *ʿīd al-fiṭr*)
iḥyāʾ	revivication, revival
ijāza	authorisation (to represent and/or to teach a text)
ijtiḥād	effort
ikhwān, sg. *akh*	brothers (*al-ikhwān al-muslimūn*: 'the Muslim Brothers')
ʿilm, pl. *ʿulūm*	discipline (of learning), science
ʿilm al-falak	astrology, numerology, astronomy
īmām	leader (of prayers)

īmān	faith
ʿiqāl	headband (to hold the headcloth)
irshād	right, correct, proper guidance
irtidād	apostasy
isbāl	wearing of garments below one's ankle, trailing of garments
ʿishāʾ	night prayer
iṣlāḥ	reform, purification
isnād, pl. *asānīd*	chain (of transmission, of authorities)
iʾtilāf	coalition
iʿtiṣām	preservation, adherence
iʿtizāl	withdrawal
ittiḥād	union
jāhiliyya	(time of) ignorance, heathendom
jamāʿa	community
jihād	exertion
jumʿa	(Friday, communal) prayers
juzʾ, pl. *ajzāʾ*	part, portion (thirtieth part of the Qurʾān)
kāfir, kuffār	unbeliever
kalām	theological disputation
khalīfa	successor, deputy
khalwa	(spiritual) seclusion
khaṭīb, pl. *khuṭabāʾ*	preacher (of the Friday sermon: khuṭba)
khawārij	dissidents, the Kharijites
kūfiyya	headcloth for men (also ghuṭra)
madhhab, pl. *madhāhib*	school of Islamic jurisdiction and legal thinking
madrasa, pl. *madāris*	school
maghrib	evening prayer, west; sunset
maʿhad, pl. *maʿāhid*	institute
manhaj	programme, strategy
maʿrifa	knowledge, insight
markaz, pl. *marākiz*	centre
mawkib	procession
mawlid (*al-nabī*)	(the celebration of the) Prophet's birthday

muʿāmalāt	obligations regarding human mutual relations (Islamic law)
muftī	legal expert, official expounder of Islam law
munāfiqūn	hypocrites
munkirūn	deniers
muqriʾ	reciter (of the Qurʾān)
mustaḍʿafūn	the ‘weak’, the ‘oppressed’
nahḍa	renaissance
naḥw	grammar
nasab	descent
niqāb	(full facial) veiling
niyya	intention (*ḥusn al-niyya*: good intention)
qabḍ	position of arms during prayers (crossed)
qāḍī, pl. *quḍāh*	judge
qaṣīda, pl. *qaṣāʾid*	poem
qirāʾa	reading, recitation, punctuation and vocalisation of the Qurʾān
qiyām	upright, standing position during prayers
qunūt	supererogatory prayers
rakʿ, pl. *rakaʿāt*	bending position during prayers
rātib	litany of prayers, prayers in honour of someone
ruʾyā	vision (of the Prophet)
sadl	position of arms during prayers (outstretched)
ṣaḥāba	companions (of the Prophet)
ṣaḥwa	awakening
salaf	forefathers (*al-salaf al-ṣāliḥ*: the ‘venerable forefathers’)
ṣalāt	prayer
ṣariqa	theft
shabāb	youth
shahāda	confession of the faith
sharḥ, pl. *shurūḥ*	commentary
sharīʿa	(the principles of) Islamic law
sharīf, pl. *ashrāf*, *shurafāʾ*	noble (person), descendant of the Prophet
shirk	polytheism

shūra	council, consultative assembly
shurūṭ, sg. *sharṭ*	conditions
silsila	chain (of transmission)
sīra	(the) life (of the Prophet)
siyāsa	politics
sukr	consumption of alcohol (also: *shurb al-khamr*)
sunna	tradition (of the Prophet)
sūra, pl. *suwar*	chapter, sūra of the Qurʾān
(al-)tabiʿūn	the followers of the *ṣaḥāba*
tafsīr	exegesis (translation and interpretation) of the Qurʾān
taḥfīẓ	memorisation (of the Qurʾān)
taḥrīf	distorted
tajammuʿ	meeting, gathering
tajdīd	reform, rejuvenation (*mujaddid*: reformer)
tajwīd	the rules of recitation (of the Qurʾān)
takfīr	expiation
takyīf	shaping, formation
ṭalab al-ʿilm	the quest for knowledge
talqīn	catechism
taqlīd	emulation, pej.: blind imitation
taraqqi, *taqaddum*	progress
tarāwīḥ	supererogatory prayers
tarbiya	education, formation
ṭarīqa, pl. *ṭuruq*	Sufi order
taṣawwuf	Sufism
taṣfiyat al-ʿaqīda	purification of the faith
taṣḥīḥ al-ʿaqīda	rectification of the faith
tashrīk	communal feasting
taʿṭīl	empty
tawassul	plea, intercession
tawḥīd	dogmatic theology
taʾwīl	metaphorical (interpretation)
tayammum	ritual ablution with sand
tazkiyat al-ʿaqīda	purification of the faith

^{c}*urf*	customary law, tradition
ustādh, pl. *asātidha*	professor
uṣūl	the basics (of faith, for instance)
waqf, pl. *awqāf*	charitable foundation
wa^{c}*ẓ*	exhorting sermon (the person who exhorts is a *wā*^{c}*iẓ*, pl. *wu*^{cc}*aẓ*)
witr	supererogatory prayers
ẓāhir	outward, visible
zāwiya, pl. *zawāya*	Sufi convent, centre
zinā$^{\circ}$	extramarital sex
ziyāra, pl. *ziyārāt*	local pilgrimage, shrine pilgrimage
zuhd	ascetism
ẓuhr	noon prayer

FOREWORD

This book is the result of almost thirty years of fieldwork and travels in Africa and beyond, and of reading and teaching the history and development of African Muslim societies to students at the universities of Bayreuth (Germany), Bamberg (Germany), Vienna (Austria), Helsinki (Finland), Göttingen (Germany), and Florida (Gainesville). This work in the field resulted in three monographs on Muslim movements of reform in northern Nigeria (1997), Senegal (2001) and Zanzibar (2009). A further monograph on the history of Muslim societies in sub-Saharan Africa (2013) brought me into the twentieth century, and the present volume will round up my work on the dynamics of Islamic reform in sub-Saharan Africa.

My work on Muslim societies in sub-Saharan Africa started in 1981 in the context of a first field trip to Senegal, where I worked in a farmers' cooperative in Bamba Thialène. The farmers happened to be Muslim, yet Islam was so much a part of their everyday life that I did not even realise that I was naturally living in a Muslim community. Islam became a theme only when I moved on to Dakar, Senegal's capital and largest city, and was then confronted with the fact that Islam could indeed become a vehicle of political debates, as well as, of course, a platform for the mobilisation of hundreds of thousands of followers in the guise of the Murīdiyya or Tijāniyya Sufi orders. My acquaintance with Muslims deepened in the course of fieldwork in northern Nigeria (mostly Kano, but also Sokoto, Jos, Kaduna, Maiduguri and Zaria) between 1986 and

1988. In northern Nigeria, I enjoyed integration into the *zāwiya* of Nasiru Kabara in Kano, but also came in contact with outspoken representatives of Nigeria's Salafi-oriented movement of reform, such as Abubakar Gumi, Ismaila Idris and Ibrāhīm Sulaimān. The study of Salafi-oriented movements of reform continued in the context of research in Senegal between 1990 and 1993, where I met Cheikh Touré, the founding father of Salafi-oriented reform in Senegal, as well as members of the jamāᶜat ᶜibād al-raḥmān. In Senegal, the development of Islamic education turned out to be a major focus in my research, and this was intensified in the context of my third regional case study, Zanzibar (and, by extension, Tanzania), where I spent several research periods from 2001 onwards. Shorter research trips to Egypt, Morocco, South Africa and Ethiopia have complemented my regional expertise.

After the conclusion of my research work in Senegal, northern Nigeria and Zanzibar/Tanzania, I continued to follow events, read relevant publications and stay in contact – as far as possible – with my local interlocutors, either by inviting them to Germany for conferences or as visiting scholars or by communicating with them by way of letters and, more recently, modern social media such as the Internet. In addition, I expanded into the history of movements of reform in Chad, Sudan, Mali, Kenya, Ethiopia and Somalia by following the literature and the debates and by meeting colleagues from these countries, in their European or North American exile or in the context of conferences and workshops. The Internet has had a tremendous impact on research and communication, as time has been (almost) eclipsed as a factor in communication: while a surface mail letter took weeks to reach an address in northern Nigeria in the 1980s, and while telephone communication was notoriously unreliable in those times, the Internet has created a worldwide community of scholars, and has contributed to the democratisation of research work, giving scholars from sub-Saharan Africa direct access to research institutions in the 'north'.

Due to the fact that I have been working on movements of reform in sub-Saharan Africa for such a long time, some of the material in this text has already been presented to academic audiences in the context of conferences and has also been published in earlier work, in particular, in articles for the *Journal of Religion in Africa*, the *Journal of Islamic Studies* and *Die Welt des Islams*, as well as in a number of articles for edited volumes (see, for example,

Loimeier 2007a, 2007b, 2010). Chapter 1 has been discussed in the context of the Africa study group at Göttingen's Max Planck Institute for the Study of Multiethnic and Multireligious Societies, while Chapter 2 has been discussed twice (in a preliminary form and in a largely revised form) in the context of workshops at the University of Bergen. For constructive comments in the context of these workshops, I would like to thank Anne Bang, John Bowen, Gøran Larsson, Ismael Moya, Abdul Sheriff, Martin Slama, Terje Østebø, and Knut Vikør. For the present book, I have updated, developed and expanded my data, and also revised, where necessary, my concepts of thought and argumentation.

More than thirty years of research in sub-Saharan Africa have taught me a lot about the factor of time: not only have I turned personally from being a young 'rebel', but my interlocutors have aged as well, and, sadly, many of them have died: John Lavers, John Hunwick, Abdurrahman Doi, Maalim Idris, Cheikh Touré, Nasiru Kabara and Abubakar Gumi, to name just a few. I would like to dedicate this text to them and their memory. Time has also taught me another important thing, namely that, as Nigerians are accustomed to say, 'no condition is permanent'. Muslim reformers and Muslim movements of reform have changed so much in the last thirty years (as well as in the years and decades before) that it has become very hard to come to general conclusions that will remain valid for an extended period of time and/or a larger region. Rather, variability and change have to be regarded as constant factors when looking at movements of reform, as well as context, the importance of locality and situational negotiability of positions. In the context of my encounters and conversations with African Muslims, the dynamics of generational change became particularly obvious to me and informed the argumentation in this book.

For assistance and advice, I would like to thank Amīnu d-Dīn Abūbakar (Kano), the late ^{c}Abd al-Wahhāb ^{c}Alawī ^{c}Abd al-Wahhāb Jamal al-Layl (Zanzibar), Dr Usman Bugaje (Zaria), Jābir Ḥaiḍar Jābir al-Farsy (Zanzibar), the late Abūbakar Gumi (Kaduna), the late Isma^{c}ila Idris (Jos), Mwalimu Isḥāq (Zanzibar), Dr Muḥammad Hārūn (South Africa), Dr ^{c}Abd al-Qādir Ḥāshim (Zanzibar), Dr Thierno Kā (Dakar), the late Shaykh Nasiru Kabara (Kano), Dr Shehu Usman Kabara (Kano), Prof. Dr Ousmane Kane (New York), Tidiane Kassé (Senegal), Ibrāhīm Ado Kurawa (Nigeria), Mwalimu

Ramadhani Kututwa (Zanzibar), ᶜAbdoulaye Lô (Dakar), Dr Dahiru Maigari (Kano), Hamad Kassim al-Mazrūᶜī (Mombasa, Berlin), Prof. Khadim Mbakke (Dakar), Cheikh Saliou Mbakke (Senegal, Kenya), Dr Tijānī al-Miskīn (Maiduguri), Prof. Ebraheem Moosa (USA), the late Mwalimu Muḥammad Idrīs Muḥammad (Zanzibar), Saidi Musa (Dar es Salaam), Dr Ḥasan Mwakimako (Kenya/Berlin), ᶜAbdillāhi Nassir (Mombasa/Berlin), Sidi Lamine Niass (Dakar), Muḥammad Sall (Thies), Yunus A. Sameja (Zanzibar), Dr Ibrāhīm Sulaimān (Zaria), Shaykh Ibrāhīm Ṣāliḥ (Maiduguri), Masᶜūd Aḥmad Shani (Zanzibar), ᶜUmar Sheha (Zanzibar), Yūsuf b. Sulaimān (Zanzibar), the late Cheikh Touré (Senegal), Prof. Muḥammad Sani ᶜUmar (Nigeria), the late Bilkisu Yūsuf (Nigeria) and Dr Issa Ziddy (Zanzibar), as well as numerous Muslim activists. In addition, this work has profited from the archival collections of the Nigerian National Archives in Kaduna, the Zanzibar National Archive in Zanzibar and the Public Record Office in London, as well as the Materialsammlung Islam in Afrika at the University of Bayreuth. Finally, I would like to thank Markus Höhne, Rüdiger Seesemann, Abdoulaye Sounaye, Terje Østebø and Julia Vorhölter who have either read the whole manuscript or individual chapters. Without their advice, this text would have been considerably poorer. If I have persisted in error, the responsibility is mine alone. Last but not least, I would like to thank the editorial team at Edinburgh University Press, in particular Ellie Bush, Eddie Clark and Nicola Ramsey, and copy-editor Laura Booth, for their meticulous work on my manuscript.

In this book, I will look at the development of Muslim movements of reform in sub-Saharan Africa in the twentieth century and address the question of how we can develop an understanding of processes of reform that considers both the dynamics of movements of reform and the constant change in the meaning of reform. In an introductory chapter, I will present the historical and social context for the development of movements of reform in sub-Saharan Africa, that is, the processes of social, political and religious change that continue to inform African societies in the twentieth and twenty-first centuries. In a second chapter I discuss terminology, concepts of reform and the question of how 'reform' may be grasped analytically. I then turn to a number of empirical case studies, starting with Senegal in Chapter 3. After presenting the general historical context, I will introduce the reader to the legacy of Sufi-oriented reform in Senegal, and then switch to the emergence in the 1950s of a new mode of reform that I regard as Salafi-oriented, in the guise of the Union Culturelle Musulmane and the jamāᶜat ᶜibād al-raḥmān. Subsequently, I will show how both traditions of reform started to counter-influence each other in the 1970s, in their efforts to mobilise popular support, and how such efforts informed the trajectory of reform as such. Finally, I will contrast the case study of Senegal with the development of Islamic reform in neighbouring Mali. I follow this pattern in the same way when discussing the trajectories of Islamic reform in Nigeria (and Niger) in Chapter 4, in Tanzania (and Kenya) in Chapter 6 and in Zanzibar (and the Comoros) in Chapter 7. Chapter 5 has a different structure: in this chapter, I present the trajectories of Islamic reform in Chad, Sudan, Ethiopia and Somalia in a somewhat shorter form, concentrating on a comparison of Salafi-oriented movements of reform. In sum, these twelve countries not only form an 'Islamic core belt' across sub-Saharan Africa, but are also home to more than 80 per cent of sub-Saharan African Muslims (in the region of 240 out of 300 million). In Chapter 8, the concluding chapter, I will again address the question of what 'reform' actually means to Muslims in Africa. The intake of data for this book was stopped on 31 May 2016.

In my analysis, I will omit one major movement of reform, namely, the jamāᶜat al-tablīgh (or tablīghī jamāᶜat), due to the fact that this movement, although present today in most African states and among most African Muslim societies, is still under-researched as far as its activities in sub-Saharan Africa are concerned. For a general history of this missionary movement of Indian origin, see Masud (2000). Unfortunately, his volume contains only one article (by Ebrahim Moosa) on the jamāᶜat al-tablīgh in sub-Saharan Africa, namely, in South Africa. The work of the jamāᶜat al-tablīgh in The Gambia has been covered by Marloes Janson (2009), while Terje Østebø (2008b) has written about the jamāᶜat al-tablīgh in Ethiopia. Originally, I also planned to include a chapter on South Africa. But in recent years a number of excellent studies on the development of Muslim societies and the development of Islamic reform in South Africa have been published and others are forthcoming. I would thus refer the reader to the work of Bangstad (2007), Koch (2014), Mahida (1993), Niehaus (2008), Sadouni (2011), Solomon (2013), Tayob (1995, 1999) and Vahed (2009).

A NOTE ON ISLAMIC TRANSNATIONAL ORGANISATIONS

Since the 1960s, Islamic transnational organisations have been active in Muslim societies in sub-Saharan Africa, providing charity, education, health services and disaster relief. In many ways, these Islamic organisations have provided career perspectives and employment for Muslims who have gone through an Arabophone education in Senegal, Nigeria or Tanzania and a higher Arabophone education at al-Azhar University in Cairo or at the Islamic University of Madinah. In addition, such organisations have funded many Islamic development projects, as well as mosques and Islamic propagation centres. Instead of presenting these organisations again and again in each chapter, I will briefly introduce here the most important players and provide some preliminary orientation:

1. The rābiṭat al-ᶜālam al-islāmī (short: rābiṭa) (Muslim World League) can be regarded as the 'mother' of all Islamic transnational organisations. It was founded in Mecca in 1962, represents pro-Saudi doctrinal positions and has developed a plethora of sub-organisations for *daᶜwa*, Islamic law, propaganda and publishing, such as the kulliyat al-daᶜwa wa-uṣūl al-dīn at the Islamic University of Madinah or the al-majlis al-aᶜlā al-ᶜālamī li-l-masājid (the World Supreme Council of Mosques). For an extensive discussion of the rābiṭa, see Schulze (1990: 181–313, 1993: 21ff).
2. The jamᶜiyyat al-daᶜwa al-islāmiyya (Islamic Call Organisation) was

set up by Mu^cammar al-Qadhdhāfī in 1972 as a Libyan Islamic transnational organisation in order to counter-balance the activities of the rābiṭat al-^cālam al-islāmī. For the jam^ciyyat al-da^cwa al-islāmiyya, see Mattes (1986).

3. The lajna muslima ifrīqiyya (Africa Muslim Agency (AMA)) is a Kuwait-based charitable foundation established in 1981 by a Kuwaiti medical doctor and a member of the Kuwaiti branch of the ikhwān al-muslimūn, ^cAbd al-Raḥmān b. Ḥammūd Sumayṭ (Ahmed 2008: 139ff). AMA spread rapidly in Africa and employed teachers and medical doctors from a broad spectrum of Muslim countries such as Morocco, Libya, Sudan, India and Malaysia. AMA has tried to present itself as a humanitarian, non-governmental organisation. Although established in Kuwait and funded by Kuwait, its headquarters were based in Sudan. AMA stressed its policy of not interfering with local politics and cooperating with local administrations. AMA started its activities in Africa in Malawi in 1981, as a basis for Islamic *da^cwa* in Southern Africa, at the invitation of the Southern Africa Islamic Youth Conference (SAIYC), which was supported by Kuwait. As a result, a first Islamic Africa Committee was created and then transformed into the Africa Muslim Agency. After Malawi, other African countries such as Mozambique followed suit and became target countries for AMA. AMA started to work in Zanzibar in 1998, and gave grants to Zanzibari students for studies abroad. In particular, AMA financed the College of Education that was connected with the Jam^ciyyat Ifrīqiyya al-^cĀlamiyya fī-l-Khartūm. AMA also paid the salaries of more than eight professors at this college (Ziddy 2002: 16). In 2003, the Zanzibar headquarters of AMA were directed by Aḥmad Ṭālib and ^cAbdallāh Nagy, both Moroccans. In Zanzibar, apart from the kulliyat al-tarbiya al-jam^ciyya (College of Education), AMA supported other *madāris*, health centres and mosques (on AMA in general, see Ahmed 2008; Sadouni 2002: 107; Morier-Genoud 2002: 134).
4. The al-nadwa al-^calamiyya li-l-shabāb al-islāmī (World Association of Muslim Youth (WAMY)) was founded in 1972 by a long-time member of the Muslim Brotherhood, Kamāl Ḥilwābī, under the auspices of King Faisal of Saudi Arabia. The headquarters were set up in al-Riyādh, Saudi Arabia. The association is a Salafi-oriented non-governmental organisa-

tion (NGO) close to the Saudi religious establishment and cooperates with the rābiṭat al-ᶜālam al-islāmī. Today, WAMY has branches in fifty-six countries and is affiliated with more than 500 Muslim youth associations. WAMY focuses on *daᶜwa*, humanitarian relief and education. WAMY organises national Muslim youth and student camps and Scout groups, organises conferences and workshops and produces Islamic literature. On WAMY and other Islamic charities, see Lacey and Benthall (2014).

5. Al-muntadā al-islāmī (The Islamic Assembly) is a Saudi-financed NGO that became a major target in the US-led 'war on terror' after 2001. Al-muntadā al-islāmī was founded in 1986 by Saudi students in London. Its headquarters were based in Parsons Green, West London. This charity focused on development projects (water, sanitation, health or social affairs) and followed a 'Wahhābī' agenda (Benthall 2007: 168). Al-muntadā al-islāmī was a staunchly Sunni- and Salafi-oriented organisation. In Africa, al-muntadā al-islāmī was active in, among other places, Chad, Nigeria, Kenya, Tanzania, Somalia, Ethiopia, Niger, Ivory Coast, Mali and Senegal where it started to develop a network of modern schools that combined Islamic and Western education. Al-muntadā al-islāmī cultivated close links not only with Saudi Arabia but also with a series of Saudi-financed charities and organisations, such as al-ḥaramayn, WAMY, Islamic Relief and the rābiṭat al-ᶜālam al-islāmī.
6. ḥayāt al-ighātha al-islāmiyya al-ᶜālamiyya (International Islamic Relief Organisation or Islamic Relief (IIRO)) was founded in 1978 by the Saudi Government but shifted its basis to Birmingham in 1984. Since then, IIRO has become the largest Islamic charity globally. Islamic Relief is a signatory of the Red Cross/Red Crescent code of conduct and fully integrated in the international development community. Islamic Relief was not affected by financial or political problems after 9/11 (Benthall 2007: 169). Islamic Relief works in more than thirty countries worldwide, among them South Africa, Kenya, Somalia, Ethiopia, Sudan, South Sudan, Chad, Niger and Mali (see Benthall and Bellion-Jourdan 2003: 78; Kaag 2014).
7. Al-ḥaramayn was established in Peshawar, Pakistan, in 1988 by a Saudi citizen, ᶜAqil b. ᶜAbd al-ᶜAzīz al-ᶜAqil, but established its headquarters

in al-Riyādh as a Saudi-based and -funded Muslim charity in 1991. It was supervised by the Saudi Arabia Ministry of Islamic Affairs (Ahmed 2008: 175ff). It was similar to AMA in its objectives, but focused almost exclusively on religious education and *da^cwa*. Also, al-ḥaramayn was closer to a Saudi- (that is, 'Wahhabi') oriented programme of religious education. Its personnel was almost exclusively Saudi and was often not familiar with African social realities. The organisation stagnated considerably after 9 September 2001 and was eventually dissolved by the Saudi state on 5 October 2004 (see Ahmed 2008: 165ff; Rabasa 2009: 45; Bokhari et al. 2014: 199ff).

8. Al-mu'assassa al-islāmiyya (the Islamic Foundation (IF)) is a Muslim charity established in the 1960s by Abū l-Aʿlā Maudūdī, which established its central seat in Leicester, UK, in 1963. The IF worked in Africa (Lagos and Nairobi) from 1963 but suffered a decline after 9 September 2001. This Muslim charity was supported by Saudi Arabia and had a focus on school and mosque building, as well as *daʿwa* (Ahmed 2008: 197ff).
9. The International Institute of Islamic Thought was founded in Pennsylvania in 1981 with financial and personal support from the International Muslim Brotherhood, of which it was a branch. Its headquarters were set up in Herndon, Virginia, close to Washington, DC.
10. The Makka al-Mukarrama Charity Trust for Orphans is another Saudi-based Islamic charity, founded in 1990 and linked (like al-ḥaramayn and IIRO) with the rābitat al-ʿālam al-islāmī. In its objectives it is comparable to WAMY and the African Muslim Agency (AMA), but it focuses on charitable work for orphans (see Kaag 2014: 79ff).
11. The munaẓẓamat al-daʿwa al-islāmiyya was founded in May 1980 in Khartoum in the context of an international conference on *daʿwa*. The munaẓẓamat al-daʿwa al-islāmiyya was linked with WAMY and developed a charitable branch in 1981, the Islamic African Relief Agency (IARA), which became active in a number of African countries. In the 1980s, both organisations came under the increasing influence and control of Ḥasan al-Turābī's Islamic Movement (see Benthall and Bellion-Jourdan 2003: 114–27).

1

INTRODUCTION: THE CONTEXT OF REFORM

In the nineteenth and twentieth centuries, Muslim societies in Africa had to face a plethora of challenges: European colonialism and the development of secular nation states, processes of urbanisation and the social transformation of many African societies. Processes of social transformation have created new spaces and new forms of social life, as well as new modes of organising time. National and international efforts have contributed to increasing literacy and a subsequent explosion of text production for local consumers. Processes of change have also enhanced the spread of new media such as the Internet and have introduced global issues into local discussion contexts. Today, sub-Saharan Africa's most prominent place is no longer a shade tree in the village, but the central bus station, and time in Africa's Muslim societies is not primarily marked by the *adhān*, the call to prayer of the local *muʾadhdhin*, but by the daily programmes of a multitude of radio and TV stations. Also, in many sub-Saharan Muslim societies, the *khuṭba*, the Friday sermon, is rendered today in the local vernacular languages and broadcast in these languages on national radio and TV (Tamari 1996: 49), even though Islamic prayers and the ritual are still recited and enacted in Arabic: Africa, including Muslim Africa, has thus become modern in multiple, yet often inconspicuous ways.

Processes of change have often been seen as having an adverse impact on communities and societies. This applies not only to modern Europe, but also to modern North Africa, western Asia and sub-Saharan Africa. In response, Muslim scholars have tried to find answers to the challenges of modernity (and globalisation) and find a place for religion in different local, regional and national contexts. In their responses to processes of change, Muslim scholars of different orientations have sometimes developed rejectionist answers and sought self-isolation, or supported movements of radical opposition against processes of change (perceived as Westernisation). But Muslim reformers have also incorporated features of modernity, such as new media technologies. In their efforts to translate modernity into an Islamic code, they have contributed to the emergence of new ways of viewing both their own communities and the world. Muslim reformers have thus been at the forefront of African modernity and have translated modernity into Islamic codes in many different ways, developing a multitude of Muslim expressions of modernity, as well as corresponding contestations of modernity. These Muslim expressions of modernity are negotiated in specific local contexts and reflect the dynamics and dialectics of these local settings.[1] The emergence of movements of reform has been intrinsically linked to processes of change since the nineteenth century: as such, movements of reform are not only an answer to processes of change but are themselves part of modernity. What is resisted by Muslim reformers is not modernity as such but Western-defined modernity and the loss of hegemony of definition.

When looking at the broader frame conditions for reform in sub-Saharan Africa in the nineteenth and twentieth centuries, before going into more detail, two general observations have to be made: first, all Africans, including Muslims, had to learn to live with and within the boundaries of modern (European-style) nation states in this period. Other and earlier forms of government, such as emirates or sultanates, became obsolete. The political framework of modern nation states has informed the development of Muslim movements of reform to a considerable extent, and has to be considered accordingly. In this book, the terms 'modern' and 'modernity' are thus linked to a historical era, namely, a period of time marked by accelerated change and dynamics of social and economic transformation originating in and radiating from Britain from the eighteenth century, which informed (and eventually transformed) societies worldwide. Processes of change were expressed in many different fields, including technologies of transport (such as steam ships, trucks and airplanes); technologies of communication (for instance, the telegraph, telephone, radio, TV, computer and Internet); modes, places and times of sociability; the re-assessment of gender relations; and different ways of organising labour. With respect to Muslim societies in sub-Saharan Africa, three distinct historical stages of modernity can be differentiated: the pre-colonial era, when Africans still had the power to define processes of change (as, for instance, in nineteenth-century Egypt and Zanzibar, or late nineteenth-century Ethiopia); the colonial era, when Africans mostly lost the power to define processes of change; and the post-colonial era, when Africans (partially) regained the power to define processes of change.

Second, movements of reform in the Islamic world have not developed in thin air: since the eighteenth century at least, the 'Islamic world' has been marked by far-reaching processes of social and economic change. Social and economic dynamics of change in the nineteenth and twentieth centuries have produced new social groups that are often regarded today as 'middle-class'. Such new social groups have been a major driving force in processes of political democratisation in a number of 'Muslim' countries such as Tunisia and Senegal in recent years. New social groups have supported processes of social change and have been looking for new religious leaders and new religious orientations that reconcile their consumerist aspirations with religion. The corresponding process of 'embourgoisement' (Haenni 2005: 9; Luckmann 1991: 68) has supported the development of new modes of religiosity that reflect the social and religious aspirations of the new social groups. These processes of change have also led to the destabilisation of established religious authority. The refusal to submit to the authority of the established *ᶜulamāʾ*, in particular, those linked with Sufi orders, resonates with the critique of Sufism as propagated by contemporary reform movements, yet does not necessarily mean that Muslims wholeheartedly accept the anti-esoteric dimension of reformist ('Islamist') criticism: rather, they rebel against authority and concur with the Islamists' critique of modes of conspicuous consumption in marriage ceremonies, for instance, or other seemingly obsolete (and mostly local) Islamic practices.

Due to its association with European social history and due to the fact that the term 'middle-class' sponges up so many different meanings, I hesitate to describe Africa's new social groups as middle-class. Yet, other terms, such as 'intermediary social groups', are not only clumsy, but also don't contribute much to solving the problem of defining Africa's new social groups. Equally, while most African societies know terms in their own languages for the very rich, the 'fat cats', as they have been called in Egypt, and for the utterly poor and weak ('subalterns'), the *mustaḍ*^{c}*afūn* in Arabic,[2] emic terms for the middle-class are lacking, some exceptions granted: in Hausa, middle-class groups, that is, those who are affluent and able to spend beyond their immediate needs, are called *masu kudi* ('masters of money').

Efforts to define the 'middle-class' in African contexts through the magic of statistics are also not very helpful: according to the 2011 report of the African Development Bank, approximately 323 million Africans (or 34 per cent of Africa's population as a whole) were regarded as being middle-class in 2010, and were able to spend from two to twenty US dollars a day, based on purchasing power parity (Lofchie 2015: 42). The term 'middle-class' was defined as comprising three sub-categories, namely, first, the so-called 'floating class' that was able to spend from two to four US dollars a day and that was most in danger of falling back into the category of the 'poor'; second, the lower middle-class (able to spend from four to ten US dollars a day); and, finally, the upper middle-class (able to spend from ten to twenty US dollars a day) (Ncube and Lufumpa 2015: 2). 'Middle-class' was equally defined by the ability to acquire consumer goods, such as cell phones, cars, fridges and other durable household goods; access to electricity (and the Internet); access to health services and education; as well as (mostly) urban residence (in small families). Such a statistical definition of the term 'middle-class' is not only too rigid and does not consider significant differences in development between different African countries, but it is also highly unrealistic as an income horizon for most intermediary social groups, a broad array of heterogeneous social groups with vastly different incomes and aspirations. Intermediary social groups are characterised, however, by the fact that they are able to consume beyond immediate vital needs, and are, thus, affluent to a certain degree. In addition, middle-class groups tend to invest more (than farmers and pastoralists) in health care and education, not only for children, but also for adults. Also middle-class families tend to shrink in size, not only due to the fact that such families are increasingly nuclear families, but also due to the fact that middle-class families cultivate strategies that serve to exclude the extended family and the 'clan': they no longer practise a culture of reciprocity.

Another important marker of middle-class groups is aspirations and the capacity to translate aspirations into social realities and lifestyles, in terms, for instance, of the ability to send children to (good) schools, provide adequate health care for family members, acquire modern housing and buy ('conspicuous') consumer goods such as fridges, TV sets, cars, tablet computers and/or journeys abroad. Such middle-class aspirations are also characterised by the fact that they are not (necessarily) inspired any more by local concepts of living well, but by mass-media mediated global standards, which are expressed in new types and fashions of dress, food consumption and the organisation of leisure, in short new lifestyles that imply, for instance, shopping in supermarkets and shopping malls (instead of the market) and visiting coffee shops that are consciously designed as global places and, thus, devoid of markers of locality.

In the colonial period, middle-class groups in most African countries were still small, mostly recruited among employees (such as clerks, teachers and bureaucrats) in the public sector and those working in the transport sector, such as drivers, mechanics and craftsperson of all kinds, that is, a plethora of professions with a mostly urban background. Middle-class groups were not involved in primary production (such as agriculture, pastoralism, mining and fishing), while most trade and retail activities, as well as small- and medium-scale production, were dominated by either Indian or Lebanese traders-cum-entrepreneurs. Since the 1960s, middle-class groups have grown considerably in sub-Saharan Africa, from 5 per cent or 10 per cent to 40 per cent, 50 per cent and 60 per cent of the population, or even more today, and thus form a considerable and growing market in many respects. In the post-independence period, the process of formation of middle-class groups has acquired additional force due to the fact that the independent states and their respective administrations invested an over-proportionate amount of national income in ever-growing bureaucratic apparatuses and thus stimulated the emergence of a growing group of functionaries and bureaucrats who have come to form the backbone of African governments. African governments used their position of power not only to feed their own clientele, however, but also to domesticate opposition by integrating opposing groups into the state apparatus. Both public and private sector employees, such as teachers and doctors, other employees in the education and health sectors, employees in banks, NGOs and insurance companies, traders, mechanics, drivers and craftsmen, state functionaries and bureaucrats formed a growing array of (mostly) urban middle-class groups. Many African countries have also seen the emergence since the 1980s of African traders and small- or medium-scale entrepreneurs who have partially replaced Indian and Lebanese competitors (Lofchie 2015: 42). And although the new social groups suffered due to the economic readjustment crises in the 1980s and early 1990s, remittances and economic recovery have helped to overcome these crises and have contributed to strengthening social groups that are visibly better off than the poorer sections of African societies.

A major feature of contemporary Muslim social, religious and political movements in Africa (as well as in other parts of the Islamic oikumene) is their striving to develop new forms of social organisation, in particular with respect to seemingly banal features of everyday life such as sports and the general organisation of leisure time. Thus, virtually every major *madrasa* in Zanzibar is home today to a football team of its own, and the football team of Zanzibar's biggest reformist *madrasa*, the madrasat al-nūr, won Zanzibar's first league national football championship in the 1990s (Penrad 1998: 308). Football is also a major feature of the social organisation of the reformist movement on the Kenyan coast, in particular Lamu, where the local Sufi orders have quickly reacted by setting up teams of their own. The same is true for northern Nigeria, where the 'Yan Izala reform movement has encouraged the formation of football teams and managed to gain a foothold in the old city of Kano, controlled until recently by the scholars of the Qādiriyya and Tijāniyya, to the extent that many young people tend to take part in the activities of the football clubs rather than attending the *dhikr* groups of the Sufi scholars (see Haruna and Abdullahi 1991). However, football has repeatedly led to hostile reactions on the part of conservative *ᶜulamāʾ* who point out that Umayyad soldiers committed a sacrilege when they played 'football' with the head of al-Ḥusayn after the massacre of Karbala in 680. This incident often serves as a historical analogy to condemn sports as un-Islamic. And although football may not be a major topic for Senegalese reformists, they cultivated their own forms of social organisation by setting up theatre groups in the 1950s, and by actively supporting the organisation of scouting activities. Today, holiday camps and scouting have become major features of the social programme of the jamā^{c}at ^{c}ibād al-raḥmān in Senegal.

The emergence of Muslim sports and Islamic football clubs reflects another and rather spectacular aspect of change, not only with respect to the way in which such new ways of organising leisure time are expressed, but also with respect to the fact that sports clubs reproduce new forms of organisation. In Senegal, for instance, football clubs are often Associations Sportives et Culturelles and belong to a spectrum of associations such as associations de quartier, amicales, dahiras, groupements d'interêt économique (gie) or tontines. As such, football clubs (and Islamic NGOs) belong to a larger range of associational organisations that have been called *Kassenwart-Vereinigungen* ('treasurer associations') by the German sociologist Dieter Neubert, as they reproduce organisational structures that are defined by the 'President, Secretary General, Treasurer' set-up of modern functional associations (communication Dieter Neubert, 2 January 2002). Efforts to restructure social activity, social space and time had already been made by early Muslim movements of reform, such as the Algerian jamā^{c}at al-^{c}ulamā$^{\circ}$ al-muslimīn al-jazā$^{\circ}$iriyīn or the Egyptian ikhwān al-muslimūn. The third annual conference of the ikhwān al-muslimūn in 1935, for instance, supported athletic training, and later, scouting, as an essential feature of social organisation. The major slogan of the ikhwān al-muslimūn defined the movement as 'a Salafiyya message, a Sunni way, a Sufi truth, a political organization, an athletic group, a cultural-educational union, an economic company, and a social idea' (Mitchell 1993 [1969]: 14).

Another major feature of Muslim movements of reform is their educational efforts and the emphasis they put on modern (Islamic) education, a process that has been described by Robert Launay as a move from the social skills acquired in the established traditions of Islamic learning, to the marketable skills offered by Muslim reformers in modern Islāmiyya schools (Launay 1992: 93).[3] In fact, most African Muslim movements of reform have been, from their very beginning, movements of education: this is not only true of contemporary movements such as the jamā^{c}at izālat al-bid^{c}a wa-iqāmat al-Sunna (Hausa: 'Yan Izala) in Nigeria and Niger, the jamā^{c}at ^{c}ibād al-raḥmān in Senegal or the different groups of the anṣār al-sunna in East Africa, but also of earlier generations of reform as represented by al-Amīn b. ᶜAlī al-Mazrūᶜī (d. 1947) and ᶜAbdallāh Ṣāliḥ al-Farsy (d. 1982) in East Africa, Abubakar Gumi (d. 1992) in Nigeria and Cheikh Touré (d. 2005) in Senegal, or the ahl al-sunna movement in Mali and the ḥarakat al-falāḥ li-l-thaqāfat al-islāmiyya as founded by Maḥmūd Bā in both Senegal and Mali. Equally, Muslim reformers have started to write for a mass-market and have realised the opportunities offered by modern media for propagating their ideas. Muslim movements of reform have produced thousands of pamphlets and both polemical and didactic texts in the vernacular languages, as well as in French and English. The endeavours of Muslim reformers to popularise and to implicitly also commercialise religious discourses and knowledge is not confined to texts but may also be observed with respect to other media, such as public or semi-public sermons, cassettes, videos, radio and TV programmes and Internet discussions, in both African and non-African languages such as French and English.[4]

Today, all major Islamic movements have media groups of their own. They usually record on video important events such as the procession of the Qādiriyya in the streets of Kano on the *mawlid ᶜAbd al-Qādir*, and use TV for propaganda purposes, most spectacularly in the case of Usāma b. Lādin's al-qāᶜida network. Muslim scholars also use the media, both radio and TV, to broadcast religious sermons, such as the *tafsīr* in the month of Ramadan, or the *khuṭba* during *jumᶜa* prayers on Friday. Some Muslim reformers, such as the South African Aḥmad Deedat, have, in fact, become Internet and video *duᶜah* (sg. *dāᶜiya*). Thus, it has been possible to observe the development of a new class of intermediaries, of new *ᶜulamāᵓ* who try to mediate between modern contexts and Muslim communities and recompose history from a modern perspective (Coulon 1993a: 29, 63), even if the charisma of these modern *duᶜah* is a virtual charisma due to the fact that it is video- and Internet-based.

This development has to be seen as a major break with the past when Muslim scholars wrote for a comparatively small audience, mostly other scholars, even if these traditions of learning acquired considerable recognition in sub-Saharan Africa and beyond. In the twentieth century, African Muslim authors started to write and publish texts in African vernacular languages for numerically much larger and predominantly non-scholarly audiences on fundamental issues such as *ᶜaqīda*, *īmān* and *talqīn*, that is, catechisms and confessions, the interpretation of the holy texts, as well as banal questions of everyday life, in addition to polemics against Sufi orders, the Aḥmadiyya movement, capitalism, zionism, imperialism and crusaderism, or, again, specific popular practices such as the celebration of the *mawlid al-nabī* or funeral ceremonies, which are often connected with local traditions of conspicuous consumption and popular festivities, or, finally, a plethora of *fatāwa*, legal opinions on questions of everyday life. In addition, texts of a non-religious character have become increasingly important. For instance, since the 1950s a religious scholar from Zaria, ᶜUmar b. Ibrāhīm b. Aḥmad b. ᶜUmar al-Wālī (b. 1922), has published poems of praise on the achievements of Charles Darwin, William Shakespeare and the astronomer Edmond Halley, while ᶜIsāᵓ Alabi Abūbakar from Ilorin has written about diverse topics such as the crash of an airliner carrying pilgrims near Kano in 1977, or the contents of Colonel Muᶜammar al-Qadhdhāfī's 'green book'. ᶜAbd al-Salām Alkinla from Ilorin (b. 1960) wrote a poem in the *lāmiyya* verse-style on the work of the BBC, while in 1989 ᶜAbd al-Raḥmān ᶜAbd al-ᶜAzīz al-Zakawī (b. 1965) wrote a *yāᵓiyya* poem entitled *qaṣīda ᶜalā l-ᶜuṭla* on the importance of leisure times and holidays (see Hunwick 1995: 532). This development towards non-religious themes in text production (beyond the 'academic' topics mentioned above) started relatively early in East Africa, probably in the late nineteenth century, while in northern Nigeria the first non-religious texts (mostly poems) were published only in the 1930s.

Muslim reformers began to translate classical and sacred Arabic texts into vernacular languages in order to popularise religious knowledge and enlarge the popular basis for reform, as well as to offer individual, easy and autonomous access to the sources of the faith to any Muslim capable of reading. This created the basis for a new interpretation and understanding of the faith. Today, mediation by the established *ᶜulamāᵓ* is becoming increasingly superfluous, a development that is likely to influence their future social role and position in society. Yet, again, this popularisation of texts is not really new to African Muslim societies: texts in Fulfulde and Hausa were written in northern Nigeria in the context of the Sokoto *jihād*, and texts in Kiswahili on the East African coast are recorded at least as far back as the eighteenth century. What is new, however, is the size and volume of this movement of popularisation of (sacred) texts, or, in abstract terms, of the sacred as such.

Muslim initiatives of reform have not remained confined to urban agglomerations but have also reached the rural areas. Robert Launay (1992: 192) was able to witness the impact of a Muslim preacher and reformer in Koko, northern Ivory Coast, in the mid-1980s:

> One such man passed through Koko in 1985 and delivered a sermon. Local Dyula, particularly those educated in French, were impressed. It was pointed out to me that he could pronounce Arabic in the way Arabs do – the mass media have familiarized Dyula with 'Arab' Arabic pronunciation – and not with the heavy accent of locally trained scholars. He read texts fluently out loud – rather than reciting them from memory – and could comment readily on the meanings of different words, glossing them in Dyula with greater ease, in the opinion of his audience, than could local scholars.

However, the processes of social, economical and cultural change in Africa have not only brought the mobile phone or shortwave radio sets into the remotest areas of the continent, but have also changed the character and outlook of religious movements, Christian and Muslim alike, in urban as well as rural Africa. These changes are not only due to the media revolution, but to the interface between the media revolution and the movement towards mass alphabetisation and mass education. This movement is unprecedented in African history, and has had considerable repercussions on religious culture, as it has led to new approaches to texts and translations of texts.

In recent decades, this process of change has also led to a significant change in the role of Arabic. Through the intensification of trade contacts between sub-Saharan Muslim societies and Arab countries, the increasing number of students in Arab countries and the impact of modern media such as satellite-operated TV programmes like al-Jazīra, familiarity with the Arab language has indeed acquired a new significance: Arabic has become, particularly in the eyes of many young Muslims, a profane language. At the same time, it has retained some vestiges of sacrality: Muslims still appreciate the importance of Arabic as an intrinsic part of 'proper' Islamic education, and schools that provide Arabic language skills are still popular, even in modern urban contexts. In addition, Arabic has kept some of its talismanic usages in modern contexts such as sports, especially football, when *imāms* are asked to recite the *sūrat al-naṣr* (the *sūra* of victory) before a match starts,[5] or in the widespread acceptance of amulets, which are even exported to Saudi Arabia by African pilgrims (Robinson 2004: 44f). Despite the growth of Muslim reformist movements, established religious scholars have thus been able to retain part of their authority in important niches of social development.

Processes of change and efforts to Islamise modernity have also informed Sufi-oriented movements of reform. The dā᾿irat al-mustarshidīn wa-l-mustarshidāt (DMM) in Senegal has adopted new modes of organisation and hybrid forms of education that were initially cultivated by the Union Culturelle Musulmane (UCM) or the jamāᶜat ᶜibād al-raḥmān (JIR). Movements such as the JIR in Senegal, the 'Yan Izala in northern Nigeria or the anṣār al-sunna in Tanzania were inspired in their own organisational development by Western colonial and post-colonial modes of organisation. Similarly, in epistemological terms, movements of reform have adopted features of the ritual such as the communal and solemn recitation (*tajwīd*) of the Qur᾿ān that was formerly cultivated by religious movements identified with what Louis Brenner has termed the 'esoteric episteme' (Brenner 2001: 7).

In fact, we encounter hybrid forms in many spheres of everyday life. Most of these hybridities are quotidian and scarcely visible, but some are more spectacular. In general, the phenomenon of hybridities links up with the debate on processes of syncretisation and bricolage. Yet, while these debates tend to focus on the different aspects and processes of métissage, or mixing, they remain confined to a descriptive presentation of the hows, that is, the different manners in which material goods, for instance, are incorporated into local cultures and the question as to how people deal with, for instance, Western consumer products. The questions as to why processes of hybridisation occur and what kind of role they have in a specific local context, often remains unanswered. One answer could be, of course, that people appreciate what is new, modern and trendy. Yet, this does not explain why Islamic religious movements have adopted new modes of organisation, why 'fundamentalist' groups accept a female wing, or why Muslims adopt Pentecostal ways of preaching.

Processes of hybridisation, bricolage, métissage and syncretisation could, however, be linked with the desire to form new spaces for agency (Förster 2005: 33), to generate order and community as well as differences, to practice or dissolve inclusion or exclusion (Weissköppel 2005: 331). Processes of hybridisation also occur because people adopt new forms of organisation or new ways of addressing the public in order to position themselves in a specific local context, or, more generally, to find a place for themselves in a changing world. By adopting, translating and cultivating hybridities in terms of language, music, sports and leisure time, fashion, organisation, ritual or education, Muslims try to expand their say in local politics or assert claims for hegemony of interpretation. The question of hybridities is consequently bound up with questions of power and empowerment.

While some of these re-mixes of Western modes of culture in Muslim contexts may appear spectacular or even un-orthodox, they represent efforts to translate modernity into Muslim contexts. From Muslim perspectives these efforts at translation and re-mixing are not ridiculous, funny or peculiar, but an ongoing effort to Islamise Western influences in order to make them digestible. Processes of hybridisation in Muslim contexts should thus be seen as an effort to conserve a certain degree of Muslim identity in a quickly changing world. Thus, hybridities are not only a fascinating aspect of contemporary life in Muslim societies but a crucial aspect of an ongoing process of negotiation and positioning of different social, political and religious groups.

As a result of processes of hybridisation, contemporary Muslim societies present us today with a multitude of re-mixes of specific features and concepts of modern Muslim culture that are trans-local, trans-religious and trans-traditional in character and outlook. At the same time, the protagonists of these new modes of expression of Muslim modernities are still involved in a dialogue with the past within Islamic religious and historical traditions, and try to draw legitimising inspiration from the authoritative sources of Islam: Muslims insist on being modern while stressing their distinct Islamic identity. The formation of hybridities can be observed on many different levels: within a specific religious tradition such as a Sufi order, among different Sufi orders, between Sufi orders and contemporary reformist movements, as well as between different religions. Different forms of saint veneration or the way in which holy places are preserved and cultivated attest to numerous epistemic parallels between Jews, Christians and Muslims.[6] In the confrontation with evangelical churches, Muslim *du^{c}ah* have adopted evangelical styles of preaching, as, for instance, in the *mihadhara* (public lecture) meetings in Tanzania, that started in 1982 after a visit of Aḥmad Deedat as a reaction to Christian *mihadhara* meetings (Njozi 2000: 11). In Zanzibar, Muslim and Christian (evangelical) *mihadhara* meetings started in 2003 only, but quickly became popular, as the preachers openly attacked the government as well as the other religion. In their attacks on the other religion, both Muslims and Christians use stereotype sources and similar strategies of argumentation: in the case of Muslim (mis)representations of Christianity, where the (apocryphal) gospel according to Barnabas[7] is often quoted to show the falseness of Christianity, while Christian preachers in Tanzania go back to a text by Canon Godfrey Dale to show the erroneous nature of Islam.[8] As a response to the preaching and missionary efforts of evangelical churches, Muslims have developed counter-strategies of preaching that look strikingly similar and have even been called 'Pentecostal Islam' on account of these similarities (communication André Mary, 5 April 2004). Due to these variegated dynamics of change, Muslims in different parts of Africa, in northern Nigeria, Senegal and Zanzibar have even portrayed contemporary Muslim movements of reform as being 'Protestant' in character.

Processes of social change and hybridisation have also informed gender relations and the role of women in modern Muslim societies, as well as in Islamic movements of reform. Muslim associations have established their own female branches and women have become outspoken in Muslim associations: they have become a vanguard in Muslim politics. The changing role of women and processes of hybridisation are also expressed in terms of fashion, in particular, Islamic fashion, and the multiple ways of expressing positions through different ways of veiling-up or veiling-down. Dress codes are in fact another pool from which women (and men) may quote in order to express specific positions. Fashion thus has to be seen as a major way of social, religious and political positioning and empowerment. *Ḥijāb* and *niqāb* dress codes allow Salafi-oriented Muslim women to keep a social and symbolic distance between themselves and a polluting environment when leaving their houses and moving beyond codes of spatial segregation. On the other hand, it has to be stressed that neither *ḥijāb* nor *niqāb* should automatically be seen as manifestations of Salafi-mindedness among Muslim women (see Herrera 2000; King 2006; Masquelier 2009). A specific kind of *ḥijāb* may not only point to a specific religious orientation, but may also hide economic constraints that prevent women from acquiring a more varied wardrobe; in addition, as Nyamnjoh has pointed out, a *ḥijāb* may be used as a way to fish for pious (rich) men (Nyamnjoh 2005). In Zanzibar, women have adopted the *niqāb* in order to be able to move incognito in the narrow streets of Zanzibar's 'Stone Town'. Last but not least, women may use a *ḥijāb* to legitimise their arguments in favour of women's rights in Islamic contexts (communication Fatou Sow, 15 October 2005).

However, when considering phenomena of hybridisation and trying to figure out why they occur, we have to be careful not to over-interpret what we see: many features of contemporary Muslim life do not transport explicit religious meaning, even if, from an outside perspective, we perceive the unknown or odd as being part and parcel of Muslim culture. Also, Muslims have developed ingenious ways of accommodating new contexts and have reconciled established norms and values with the challenges of modernity. Processes of accommodation have been important for Muslims since the beginning of colonial rule, as David Robinson and Muhammad Sani Umar have shown in their work on the different paths of accommodation to colonial rule in Senegal and northern Nigeria respectively (Robinson 2000; Umar 2002, 2006). Strategies of accommodation should not only be interpreted as a form of collaboration with the respective colonial (alien) power, but also as an effort to develop new forms of resistance to and contestation of colonial (alien) rule. When the first Senegalese reformist groups of the early twentieth century adopted associationist modes of organisation, they were not only recognised quickly by the French colonial administration as modern French-style religio-political associations, but also as compatible partners for the negotiation of disputes in the colonial context.

The processes of positioning, accommodation and hybridisation involve everybody, young and old, men and women, religious scholars and rap musicians, as every single actor, every single group that develops new positions will sooner or later defend, justify, sanctify or reject these positions. With globalisation, the possibilities of hybridisation have expanded tremendously and so has the scope of (mis)interpretation, the possibilities of orientation and dis-orientation and the range of possible bones of contention. In this maze of hybridities, symbols and icons may change meaning quickly and contribute to creating polyphony. Being a result of processes of positioning and social change, hybridities are intrinsically bound up with questions of local and global power. As a consequence, local affairs increasingly cease to be local affairs and, should need and wish arise, may become an issue of discussion in far-away places. At the same time, global affairs may easily turn into local affairs and acquire new and unforeseen notions in local contexts. Muslim movements of reform cannot escape these dynamics: they are an intrinsic part of local and global processes of positioning and of negotiating modernity.

Notes

1. For similar expressions of Muslim modernity in Arab, Near or Middle Eastern contexts, see Eickelman and Piscatori (1996) or Eickelman and Anderson (2003).
2. In Hausa, the respective terms would be '*talakawa*' for the poor and weak, and '*masu sarauta*' for the powerful and rich. In Kiswahili, the poor and weak are labelled '*maskini*', while the rich are known as '*tajiri*'.
3. For the development of modern Islamic education in Mali, see Brenner (2001); for Nigeria, see Reichmuth (1998); for Senegal, see Loimeier (2001); for Zanzibar, see Loimeier (2009).
4. On the role of modern media in religious discourse in Mali, see Schulz (2003, 2012).
5. In Tanzania, football clubs have started to travel with their own spiritual healers, 'sorcerers' (waganga) and talismanic experts of the Qurʾān, and have triggered a nationwide competition between 'spiritual advisors' (communication Mohamed Saleh, 3 April 2005).
6. On interfaces between Jewish and Muslim traditions, see Weingrod's saint map of Jewish saints in Morocco (Weingrod 1990: 229) or Stauth's presentation of ᶜAbdallāh b. Salām (d. 664), a Jewish convert to Islam, whose tomb has become a major focus of saint veneration for Muslims in the Nile delta (Stauth 2005). Similarly, Stefan Wild has pointed out the hybrid character of Muslim, Christian and Jewish festivals (Ramadan, Easter, Pass-Over, Christmas) among these different religious groups (Wild 2005: 406).
7. The gospel according to Barnabas began to spread in the sixteenth century only (that is, in the period of the Reformation). It insinuates that Jesus responded to a question by Caiphas, a Jewish high priest, by saying that he was not the Messiah

and that God would eventually send a messenger, who would come from the south and take away all evil. This response came to be interpreted by Muslim *du^cah*, such as Aḥmad Deedat, as a biblical reference to Muḥammad.

8. This text is Canon Dale's '*Khabari za dini ya Kiislamu kwa mukhtasari pamoja na maelezo ya ikhtilafu zilizopo kati ya dini ya Kiislamu na ya Kikristo*' ('Summary of the religion of Islam with an explanation of the differences between Islam and Christianity') (Loimeier 2009: 113).

2

WHAT IS REFORM?

On Definition and Terminology

Academic research in the humanities has been interested in processes of reform in Muslim societies for some time, often assuming that movements of reform reflect structural social, political and economic changes in Muslim societies that are linked to the process of enlightenment or secularisation in Europe. Approaches of this kind express the hope that Muslim societies will sooner or later be able to liberate themselves from the chains of tradition and open up to Western modernity. Apart from the fact that European or Western debates on movements of reform in Muslim societies usually depart from Western and not from Muslim imaginaries (Haj 2009: 1ff), etic approaches often use the term 'reform' in indiscriminate ways. The term 'reform' has thus come to describe a large array of different processes of change.

In order to understand reform, we thus have to ask a whole set of questions on the very nature of processes of reform and their structural features before being able to apply the term, at least as a working definition, to Muslim contexts: how is reform presented; who supports a movement of reform; how do reformers address audiences; what are the specific characteristics of a movement of reform in a specific period of time; are there patterns of agency, of development and success (or failure) of movements of reform (even of different orientations) in different regional settings and in different times; are similarities between movements of reform accidental or part of larger social processes that lead to similar results in other contexts and at different times; why do movements of reform acquire social relevance (*Wirkmächtigkeit*) in some specific historical contexts and not in others; what are the historical chances of a movement of reform; how strongly are movements of reform influenced by other movements of reform and adopt aspects of such reform movements; and how are internal religious dynamics of movements of reform informed by such trans-religious interfaces? By studying movements of reform in their historical context, by identifying the specific dynamics of movements of reform as well as their social and religious relevance, we will eventually be able to unfathom the true nature of religious movements of reform.

In order to be able to answer these and other questions, some conceptual and methodological problems have to be approached first, and the term 'reform' has to be defined in conclusive ways. In dictionaries of comparative religion, such as *Die Religion in Geschichte und Gesellschaft*, the term 'reform' is presented in impressive detail.[1] Similarly, the semantic field of 'reform' has been understood in Arabo-Islamic contexts (but not only there) as *tajdīd* (renewal) and *iṣlāḥ* (return to the pure values of early Islam), *iḥyāʾ* (revival, revitalisation and revivification) or *ṣaḥwa* (awakening). In more secular contexts, one also finds the terms *nahḍa* (renaissance), *taraqqī* or *taqaddum* (progress).[2] 'Reform' thus stands for many different notions and ideas and may have conservative, modernising, liberal, progressive, egalitarian, activist[3] or revolutionary connotations.

In sub-Saharan Africa the term *tajdīd*, for instance, dominated discourses on reform until the early twentieth century. This term usually meant the renewal of existing Muslim societies with respect to a number of established, yet seemingly un-Islamic, ways of life or government. However, in response to processes of modernity, we can observe not only the emergence of movements of reform from within the existing esoteric episteme in a first stage of reform, which could be described as being linked with the established concept of reform as *tajdīd* (renewal), but also, in a second step, the emergence of movements of reform that react against the esoteric episteme and that could be described as being linked with a new concept of reform as *iṣlāḥ* (purification). Reform is in fact deeply embedded in the Islamic tradition. Human history is often conceived as a continuum of renewal (*tajdīd*), revival (*iḥyāʾ*) and reform (*iṣlāḥ*) (Haj 2009: 7). In the twentieth century, new generations of Muslim reformers, however, have come to use the term *iṣlāḥ* to claim a return to the pure ways of the Prophet. The shift from *tajdīd* to *iṣlāḥ* thus signals a programmatic re-orientation of Muslim reformers in sub-Saharan Africa. It is also interesting here to note that other terms that are used with respect to reform in Arab countries are not, or only rarely, used in sub-Saharan Africa. To my knowledge, the term *nahḍa* (renaissance), for instance, was used only among Arab intellectuals in Zanzibar in the 1950s, and the term *iḥyāʾ* (revivication) had a prominent role in Sokoto in the nineteenth century, but remained confined to Sufi milieus; *taraqqī* (progress) was introduced into debates in the 1990s only in Senegal in the context of the emergence of a new group of Sufi reformist movements. One of these movements, affiliated with the Murīdiyya, was called ḥizb al-tarqiya.

It is important to look not only at the terminology of reform, however, but also at the terminology and language of social organisation: Why are particular movements of reform known as a *jamāʿa* (union, group), a *ḥizb* (party), *ahl* (people), *anṣār* (supporters) or as a *ḥaraka* (movement) while fighting for a specific concept of *tajdīd*, *iṣlāḥ* or *nahḍa* and pointing out the centrality of the sunnah (as in the case of the anṣār al-sunna in East Africa) or God (Allāh, as in the case of the ḥizb allāh in Lebanon)? Each of these terms proclaims difference to other groups and signals both a specific programme of inclusion (that is, only those Muslims who are defined as 'proper Muslims') and exclusion (that is, all other Muslims): 'sacred injunctions are matters of struggle, of competing readings . . . we thus need to examine the conditions that allow social forces to make a particular reading of the sacred texts hegemonic' (Bayat 2007: 4–6). At the same time, terminology signals change in the political agenda or in the religious orientation of a group. In Sudan, for instance, a branch of the influential Umma Party, which, in contrast to the leader of the party, Ṣādiq al-Mahdī, was prepared to cooperate with the regime of Ḥasan al-Turābī in the late 1980s, split from the Umma Party in the 1990s and formed a ḥizb al-umma li-l-iṣlāḥ wa-l-tajdīd (Seesemann 2006b: 29). In northern Nigeria, a group of dissidents split from Ibrāhīm al-Zakzakī's *iṣlāḥ*-oriented Brothers (*ikhwān*) that had turned to shīʿism in

1994. The dissidents chose to call themselves jamāᶜat al-tajdīd, in opposition to al-Zakzakī's group (Loimeier 2007a: 57).

When considering reform, it is thus necessary to look at the emic representation of Muslim reformers and the way in which they represent themselves to other Muslims and the outside world: specific terms signal a specific cause (*daᶜwa*). It consequently makes a difference whether a group chooses the term *tajdīd* or *iṣlāḥ* (or any other term)[4] to describe its cause. However, despite their different orientations, all religious reformist movements advocate some form of social change and criticise, at the same time, specific aspects of their respective societies. Most importantly, religious movements of reform are characterised by the fact that they have a programme for the kind of change they propagate. In a first step of analysis, I thus define the term 'reform' for the purpose of my argument, as *any transformation that is linked with an implicit or explicit programme* (manhaj)[5] *of change*, or in short, I see reform as *change with a programme*. This definition understands reform to be informed, first, by a normative (reformatory) discourse, an ideology, a programme, a will and an intention (*niyya*) and, second, by modes of programme-oriented agency that propose to translate a specific programme of change into social reality in a specific historical context.[6] This theoretical approach is also valid for movements that reject reform. Movements that advocate maintaining the status quo in a society often adopt the programmatic features of movements of reform and, in a dialectical turn, come to represent reform, even if in a conservative mode, due to the fact that their programmes reflect issues of reform.

Such a broad operational definition of the term 'reform' as 'change with a programme' (as informed by the intention and the will to achieve something) triggers, of course, the question of whether there are any social fields that are not covered by 'reform'. Social situations that are characterised by the absence of reform do exist and can be described as situations of stasis and stagnation. Equally, processes of change without a programme are nothing but transformation, routines, processes that 'take place' when an administration enacts a law, a decree or a regulation. Reform starts when such an administration reconsiders the usefulness, effectiveness and/or legitimacy of a law, decree or regulation and discusses possible changes. Thus, reform is a product of conscious agency, a will and an intention, while processes of transformation are responses and reactions, characterised by established (bureaucratic, social, political and so forth) routines, although there is, of course, 'no hard boundary but a continuum between routine practices that proceed with little reflection or planning and agentive acts that intervene in the world with something in mind' (Ortner 2006: 134–6).

Initiatives of reform are linked not only with a programme, an agenda of reform, though, but also with societal movements that try to implement programmes of change, and this fact necessarily creates tension: other social, political or religious forces may oppose agendas of reform. Such tensions have to be negotiated by each movement of reform. The process of negotiation consequently contributes to establishing the unique character of each movement of reform and enables us to identify and analyse different movements of reform in their respective societal and temporal contexts. Equally, reform may fail not only due to the opposition of counter-reformist movements, but also due to society's indifference. In such a case, a movement of reform has not managed to translate its programme into social realities. When considering movements of reform, we thus have to look at the agents of change and their motivations; the specific programme of change they propagate; and both the temporal and social context in which these movements of reform are situated, and how they try to translate their programme of reform into social realities, or, in Asef Bayat's words, how such movements 'mediate between words and worlds' (Bayat 2007: 6).

An inclusive definition of reform has four main advantages. First, it takes into consideration the internally dialectical character that reform programmes display over time. That is, in the name or guise of modernisation, a particular reform programme may seek to modify, completely change or eradicate established social, religious or political traditions, rituals and reforms introduced in the past, or the manner or form by which Muslim scholastic teachings are interpreted or taught. In a subsequent twist, the very same reform programme, even if viewed as possessing a modernising spirit during its own time, sooner or later comes to be regarded as the established tradition and may become, often after one generation only, the target of a new movement of reform: what is modern today will be obsolete tradition tomorrow, becoming history for tomorrow's modernity (see Voll 2005).

Second, the examination of reform as change with a programme (as informed by the intention and will to change something) allows for the study of reform movements that do not have a distinctive modernising mission and rather propose a return to the roots, to the fundamental tenets and teachings of the faith. Such movements of reform inevitably refer to the sacred texts, in order to explain and sanctify their programme of change while at the same time rejecting the allegoric interpretation of the texts. Such movements of reform, like the al-muwaḥḥidūn ('Wahhābiyya') on the Arabian Peninsula in the eighteenth century, are said to represent a scripturalist or, better, a literalist episteme. Movements of reform committed to a literalist episteme often reject supererogatory prayers, in particular certain forms of the *dhikr*, the *mawlid al-nabī*, the veneration of saints, and faith in their power of intercession and a multitude of Sufi practices, while simultaneously putting stress on the centrality of the Qurʾān and the sunnah of the Prophet, advocating, for instance, the reform of particular rituals or the reform of Islamic education.[7]

Third, a broad definition of reform allows for the inclusion of a spectrum of Sufi-oriented traditions of reform, which represent an esoteric episteme. Although Sufi-oriented movements have been the focus of many studies, they are often viewed not as forming part of a greater reformist paradigm, but as being opposed to reformist Islam, as allegedly quietist, or opposed to modernist and/or Salafi-oriented movements of reform.[8] Such an approach ignores the fact that change is not obliged to have a specific orientation; it may in fact be esoteric or literalistic, modernising, traditionalist or activist. A movement of reform may either support processes of change or reject such processes of change, when change comes to be seen, for instance, as a form of unconditional Westernisation of society.

Fourth, an inclusive definition of reform has the advantage of escaping politically biased perceptions of Muslim reform movements that tend to indiscriminately portray such reform movements as basically radical, activist, 'fundamentalist' and militantly Islamist expressions of 'political Islam', while opposing them to allegedly quietist, peaceful and accommodating expressions of 'Sufi Islam'. For example, the events of 11 September 2001 and the subsequent focus on 'fundamentalist' movements have tended to emphasise these dichotomous interpretations of patterns of reform in Muslim societies. This reifies both types of expression and places one in opposition to the other. Ultimately, most external representations of reform movements in Muslim societies fail to account for the multiplicity of expressions that cover the spectrum between activist and quietist poles, and fail to recognise the dynamic character of Muslim societies.

Hence, this book argues that while reform movements have to be understood in terms of how they are situated in a matrix of international networks and media-based representations, they must also be interpreted in terms of how they are situated in local contexts where their advocates attempt to translate their interpretation of reform into reality on the ground. Adopting such an analytical posture thus serves to examine the manner and extent to which a particular reform programme converses with its own history. The success or failure of particular reform movements is consequently defined by processes of negotiation in the local context and not so much by their degree of trans-local integration. It is only if a reform movement manages to translate its programme in a multitude of local contexts and properly addresses the needs, anxieties, frustrations and aspirations of many different local populations by offering viable solutions to the nagging and often banal problems of everyday life, that such a reform movement will gain acceptance in multiple local contexts and become a truly trans-local movement.

Having evoked such a framework of analysis, it can be suggested that Muslim reform movements are characterised by a wide spectrum of expressions that attempt to translate specific interpretations of a 'great tradition' (see Redfield 1956: 41), such as the canon of Islam's sacred texts and rituals as well as legal norms, into multiple local contexts in a constant process of negotiation, contestation and re-interpretation. This process has been defined by Talal Asad as being 'a constitutive part of any Islamic tradition' (Asad 1986: 14). In the process of translation, contestation, negotiation and re-interpretation of a specific interpretation of the canon in different geographic, social, political and religious contexts, reform movements develop distinctive positions both with respect to their contexts but also with respect to other contemporary reform movements and/or historical traditions of reform: such reform movements have synchronic and diachronic dimensions that require careful examination. Thus, each tradition of reform is marked by distinctive contexts, distinctive markers of reform and distinctive positions with respect to other traditions of reform. Such an open definition of the term 'reform' is valid not only for Islamic contexts but also for other religious traditions,[9] in particular, Christianity and Judaism, and this applies not only to contemporary times: it would be perfectly possible to analyse the development of religious traditions as a history of their respective movements of reform.

Such a comparative approach to the history of reform movements in Muslim, Christian and Jewish contexts would enable us to identify not only structural similarities and patterns, but also structural differences between different historical and religious trajectories of reform. Such differences could be rooted in the fact that the term 'reform' refers to different conceptual foundations in Muslim, Christian and Jewish contexts. In Islam, the concept of *tajdīd*, for instance, carries the notion of cyclical renewal, while reform in a Jewish context stands for a more flexible application of the rulings of the Jewish sacred law. In a comparative study of reform and the history of reform movements in Islam, Christianity and Judaism it is thus not possible to simply transfer concepts from one context to another without considering their different conceptual meanings.

Generational Dynamics of Reform and Their Disjunctures

Although the emergence of a Salafi-oriented tradition of reform in Africa has been inspired by external poles of orientation, such as Egypt or Saudi Arabia, such traditions of reform have been informed by local conditions. In fact, the local context has usually been decisive for the success or failure of a specific movement of reform. And although there are a number of success stories as far as Salafi-oriented movements are concerned, such as northern Nigeria, where the 'Yan Izala have gained considerable social as well as political influence, there are also some cases where movements of reform have so far had only marginal influence on the development of Islamic societies. In Senegal and mainland Tanzania, for instance, Salafi-oriented movements of reform have a long tradition, but they have not been able to gain the support of a majority of the Muslim population. Large-scale, even global, structural changes and processes thus do not necessarily lead to similar (political) outcomes: the local context and local dynamics are decisive for the trajectory of a social or religious movement (see Robinson in Wiktorowicz 2004: 115).

In the process of negotiation of programmes of reform in different local (political, religious and historical) contexts, reformist movements develop their specific programmes with respect to the particular context and the particular time. Each movement of reform cultivates its own dialogue with history and the canon of fundamental (key) texts, and thus demonstrates its autonomy and specific character with respect to earlier (and later, or other) movements of reform. Differences between movements of reform, however, may be rooted not only in the different historical experiences of a specific society, but also in the unique regional and cultural entanglements of this society, or in its specific experiences of interaction with other (also non-Islamic) religious traditions. For Muslims in Africa, entanglements with both Christian and Jewish religious traditions (in North Africa, the Nile Valley and Ethiopia), as well as African indigenous religions, have been particularly influential.[10]

There is indeed a dialectical interaction of reform movements with their respective social and political contexts, and between different reform groups, but also between different generations within a particular tradition of reform. With regard to the latter, one generation of reformers follows its predecessor, responding to established norms of thought and practice. Each generation of reformers is equally linked with specific and distinctive markers of reform and may consequently be clearly identified with a particular tradition of reform. The markers of reform are the specific ways in which reform is translated into social contexts and acquires relevance in everyday life. However, the different generations and traditions of reform are also characterised by disputes that contribute to defining the distinct character of a specific generation of reformers. These disputes, whether between contemporary, new or old movements of reform, are shaped by specific strategies of argumentation that are again marked by legitimising references cultivated by the different groups. These legitimising references may assume a trans-local, trans-historical, trans-traditional or trans-generational character. All of which attest to the pluralistic character of reform in Muslim contexts. More specifically:

1. A group of reformers may try to establish (quote, activate) a (new) co-temporal but *trans-local* link with a spiritual centre of the *same* tradition of learning (such as Baghdad for the Qādiriyya or Fes for the Tijāniyya), which had, until then, been unknown, irrelevant or neglected in a specific local context, in order to marginalise competing sub-centres within the same tradition.

2. Reformers may also establish co-temporal *trans-local* links to *other* centres of authority, which represent *other* interpretations or traditions of reform, in order to discredit competing scholars within the same tradition; such a link would have a *trans-tradition(al)* character.[11]
3. Reformers may establish a *trans-temporal* and *trans-tradition(al)* link to an earlier tradition of learning, in order to either discredit or legitimise a specific dogmatic, ritual or political position or to achieve a compromise or a solution in a dispute, based on a new interpretation of the sources. This may lead to a new interpretation of the key texts or to a change of emphasis, for instance, by stressing *ḥadīth* more than *fiqh*.[12]
4. Finally, a group of reformers may establish within the *same* tradition of reform a *trans-generational* (and *trans-temporal*) link to the generation of the fathers or grandfathers to give legitimacy to their cause. Such a trans-generational link not only serves to recall a respected tradition of thought (as with trans-traditional references), but also the memory of a respected personality, a saint or a scholar. In addition, such a trans-generational link within the same tradition may legitimise a rebellion against established leadership.

In disputes between distinctive traditions of reform, trans-generational dialectics are particularly important when a new generation of reformers tries to bring an established tradition of reformers into disrepute by referring to an (allegedly sound) tradition established by a previous generation. The disputes between religious scholars and traditions of reform clearly show, for instance, that interpretation and presentation of a specific ritual as 'orthodox' or 'unorthodox', as 'Islamic' or 'un-Islamic', as 'African' or 'Arab' may be deceptive, when set within a specific context of dispute and linked with the negotiation of claims for leadership and hegemony of definition (*Deutungshegemonie*). As a consequence, the interpretation of the issues at stake and the legitimising references and links may change at any time, if the context changes. The fact that trans-local, trans-historical, trans-traditional or trans-generational links may be cultivated for strategic purposes, such as the legitimisation of claims of superiority of one tradition over another in contexts of conflict, points to the basic instrumentability (*Instrumentalisierbarkeit*) as well as the interpretability of traditions and texts, or the canon of Islamic doctrine as such.

Efforts at the interpretation of canonical texts are again a precondition for the development of 'cultures of interpretation' (*Auslegungskulturen*) (Assmann 2000: 56–7). The strategic *disponibilité* of traditions, texts and the canon disproves essentialist reductions of Islam and Muslim societies as timeless and static.[13] The interpretability of texts (over time) and their strategic *disponibilité* also contradicts the alleged unchangeability of Islam throughout time. This logic extends to Salafi-oriented Muslims who have tried to essentialise traditions and texts and who have advocated a selective reading and interpretation of these traditions and texts in order to instrumentalise such readings for their own purposes: even essentialistic readings of Islam do not escape the dynamics of negotiation and change. As soon as contexts and times change, essentialisations have to be revised and adapted to new situations. Even if specific groups make such essentialisations from time to time, their claims to hegemony of interpretation will be challenged, sooner or later, by new generations of scholars and reformers.

In my case studies from different African countries, I am dealing with a spectrum of reform movements of vastly different orientations, which may be grouped, within certain periods of time, into families. At the same time, it is necessary to consider a large array of markers of reform that are shared in varying degrees by different movements of reform. When regarding movements of reform as a societal field, some movements will share many or even most markers of reform, while those on the extreme ends of the spectrum will share only a few or none. Movements of reform thus differ both by their degree of sharing specific markers of reform, and by the emphasis they put on these markers of reform. Yet, again, this model has to be imagined as being dynamic and evolving all the time; convergences among movements of reform may occur, but are temporary. What is true of the 1930s may already be wrong for the 1950s. In fact, movements of reform seem to evolve in a process of dialectic interaction defined by four major social, religious, political and historical forces: their interaction with other (contemporary) movements of reform (of either local or trans-local orientation); their interaction with historical legacies and earlier movements of reform (of either local or trans-local orientation); their interaction with the local social context that eventually defines the social relevance of trans-local influences; and, finally, their interaction with trans-local sources of authority such as the canon of referential texts, religious authorities or institutions, and the way in which these trans-local sources of authority are translated in the local context.

The situatedness of movements of reform can be shown clearly by taking a closer look at the structure of movements such as the 'Yan Izala in Nigeria, the Union Culturelle Musulmane (UCM) in Senegal or the anṣār al-sunna in East Africa. We can easily identify these religious movements as distinct movements of reform by looking at their programme, organisational set-up, public discourse and so forth and by examining the question of how these movements translate their programmes of reform into societal realities. Often, this is accomplished through the establishment of mosques, schools, youth and women's organisations and the like. Equally, these movements of reform are led by activist elites and we can again ask how these activists reach out and organise the individual movement in practical terms. Finally, movements of reform and activists are inspired by Muslim intellectual leaders and/or charismatic religious scholars, such as Cheikh Touré for the UCM, Abubakar Gumi for the 'Yan Izala, and al-Amīn b. ᶜAlī al-Mazrūᶜī and ᶜAbdallāh Ṣāliḥ al-Farsy for the anṣār al-sunna.

When comparing the historical development of movements of reform, we discover, however, *temporal* disjunctures between movements, activists and intellectual leadership: the rise of the UCM in Senegal in the 1950s, for instance, was closely associated with the rise of Cheikh Touré as a Salafi-oriented reformer and opponent of the Sufi orders. Equally, the rise of the 'Yan Izala was intrinsically linked with the activities of Abubakar Gumi and his efforts to fight the Sufi orders in Nigeria. When looking at East Africa, however, it is easy to see that both al-Amīn b. ᶜAlī al-Mazrūᶜī and ᶜAbdallāh Ṣāliḥ al-Farsy, the major propagators of Salafi-oriented reform in Kenya and Tanzania, acted as individuals, while the anṣār al-sunna movement developed only in the 1980s, after the death of both scholars.

At the same time, the societal context was marked by *structural* disjunctures: while the 'Yan Izala established a broad array of social and religious institutions to bolster their programme of reform, focused on the struggle against the Sufi orders and fought in one single country (Nigeria), often supported by the government, the anṣār al-sunna have not (yet) built a grassroot network of schools and mosques; they are split into numerous fractions in

Zanzibar, Tanzania and Kenya, and fight not only against quietist or loyalist 'government scholars' but also against the respective political administrations and an array of churches, mostly Pentecostal churches. The UCM in Senegal, and its successor, the jamāᶜat ᶜibād al-raḥmān (JIR), have not managed to establish an independent economic basis that would enable them to compete with the Sufi orders on a par. But Sufi orders in Senegal have successfully adopted issues and themes of reform propagated by the UCM/JIR and enjoy the support of the state. This contributes again to the argument that each single movement of reform has to be studied in its own temporal and societal context.

Thus, reform does not connote a specific historical period in the development of Muslim societies. There is no 'before and after' reform, as we can speak about a time 'before Islam' (that is, the time of *jāhiliyya*) and 'since Islam', although some movements of reform have spoken of a relapse into the times of *jāhiliyya*. In order to identify the real character of reform in a specific period of time and a specific societal context, it is necessary to identify the markers of change and to see what specific movements of reform intend to achieve, what reformers criticise, what they aspire to and how specific movements of reform try to translate these programmes of change into the social realities of their time. At the same time, it has to be stressed that movements of reform are not juggernaut-like movements that blaze their way through established traditions. They have to be located in specific contexts, their programmes have to be translated into respective idioms and the respective context has to welcome social support for reformist discourses. Only when these conditions apply may movements of reform have a chance to find support in a specific, or even in several, local contexts.

In order to gauge the character of a specific movement of reform, and in order to overcome any arbitrary usage of the term 'reform', it is necessary to translate the term 'reform' into the language of the Muslim society, the time and the locality that we wish to study: when and where do we encounter what kind of programme of reform, and who propagates such a programme of change with what kind of motivation? What are the identifying markers, the characteristic features of a movement of reform that would help us to define the specific character of a movement of reform? If we endeavour to identify the distinctive 'markers' of each movement of reform we may eventually develop a systematic approach to the study of movements of reform. Identificatory markers of a movement of reform relate to the way in which a programme of change is translated into social realities and to the way in which a programme of change claims relevance for the agency of peoples and communities.

Markers of reform may thus be specific to a movement of reform in a specific context and in a specific period of time. Yet, such markers of reform may sooner or later be adopted by other movements. Such hybridities are a characteristic feature of movements of reform in Senegal, northern Nigeria, Tanzania and Sudan, where Sufi orders adopted forms of associative organisation and even constituted Islamic NGOs in the twentieth century. The same applies to movements of reform that have criticised Sufi orders in the past, but have started to cultivate recitation of the Qurʾān according to the rules of *tajwīd* in a rather *dhikr*-like form. At the same time, Muslim movements of reform may adopt, consciously or otherwise, forms of preaching (*waᶜẓ*), public sermons, usage of the media and modes of addressing public audiences from non-Muslim, often Pentecostal movements. For this reason, the French scholar of comparative religion, André Mary, has called these Muslim reformers Pentecostal or born-again Muslims (see Fourchard et al. 2005; see also Ludwig 1996 for Tanzania; Westerlund 2003 for South Africa; Hock 1996 for Nigeria).

However, the transfer of ideas does not necessarily imply immediate social relevance. This is shown clearly by the false start of the first Salafi-oriented movement of reform in Zanzibar in 1910/11, which was familiar with the reformist thought of Muḥammad ᶜAbdūh, yet did not achieve popular support. The year 1910 may be seen as the one in which the term *iṣlāḥ* turned up for the first time in debates on reform in East Africa, yet these debates remained confined to a small circle of Arabophone intellectuals. The social conditions for the emergence of a larger movement of reform were not yet given. Only in 1930 was al-Amīn b. ᶜAlī al-Mazrūᶜī able to popularise reformist ideas in his journal *Iṣlāḥ* (see Loimeier 2009).

Among the characteristic markers of movements of reform, surprising interfaces and similarities can be identified, as well as numerous parallels between different religious movements, orientations and families of reform, not only in Islamic contexts but beyond.[14] However, similarities, parallels or even identical features in orientation, programme and modes of approaching the public do not necessarily point to common structures in the orientation of such movements of reform.[15] Despite phenotypical similarities in orientation, organisation, argumentation or modes of approaching audiences, the meaning (*Sinnbesetzung*) and function of such characteristic features of reform may be totally different (Stolz 1988: 224). The critique of specific forms of ecstatic saint veneration among Coptic Christians in Egypt in the late twentieth century, as well as among Muslims, should thus not be taken as the one and only indication of the existence of a trans-religious anti-esoteric movement of reform (see Schielke 2007). Rather, there must be many different indicators in many different spheres that document the existence of such a movement, and only the temporal accumulation (*Häufung und Verdichtung*) of these indices in a specific historical context will allow us to identify a true anti-esoteric trans-religious reformist movement.

Salafi-oriented Reform

Having addressed the general theme of reform, I will now focus on the specificities of Salafi-oriented reform in sub-Saharan Africa. In the eighteenth, nineteenth and twentieth centuries sub-Saharan Africa was characterised by far-reaching processes of transformation and corresponding crises of orientation that stimulated movements of reform. These were linked with Sufi orders and a series of movements of *jihād* led by Sufi scholars, such as Usman dan Fodio. In the twentieth century, this tradition of reform was challenged by a number of new movements that essentially followed an anti-esoteric episteme[16] and that have been labelled 'Salafi' or 'Wahhābi'. These Salafi-oriented movements of reform were united in their endeavours by the fact that they combined religious and doctrinal patterns of explanation with programmes of social reform that essentially tried to translate Islam into modern contexts. For the first time in the history of its Muslim societies, sub-Saharan Africa thus saw the emergence of a tradition of reform that developed a distinct critique of saint veneration, Sufism and a number of local practices that were condemned as un-Islamic innovations (*bid^{c}a*, pl. *bida^{c}*), superstition and magic. The new movements of reform criticised shrine pilgrimages (*ziyārāt*), the *dhikr* and *mawlid* celebrations of the Sufis, their claims to spiritual superiority and the faith of the common believers in the power of the saints to intercede (*tawassul*). This critique constituted an anti-iconic turn in the history of Muslim societies in sub-Saharan Africa and has sometimes led to violent reactions on the part of those attacked. The turn against the esoteric episteme may also be seen as being part of a larger process of religious change, a process that was characterised by Max Weber as a process of 'disenchantment of the world' and a process of gradual rationalisation of religion and society, in which 'all forms of magic are rejected as superstition' (Weber 1988 [1920]: 94–5).

However, the critique of specific aspects of Sufism was not only directed against magico-religious practices and aspects of Islamic mysticism such as the belief in the hidden or inner (*bāṭin*) meaning of texts and a corresponding initiatic access to a higher truth (*ḥaqīqa*), which allowed for considerable interpretative freedom regarding canonical texts and their meaning for everyday life, it was also directed against the Sufis' claim to *irshād* (guidance, here: hegemony of interpretation) based on their alleged exclusive knowledge of the hidden meaning of texts, and, thus, a claim to religious and spiritual superiority over other Muslims, a claim that implied access to prophetic visions (*ruʾyā*) and revelations. By contrast, the new reform movements supported a literalist approach to the interpretation of the Qurʾān, as expressed in the statement 'in Islam, nothing is secret'.[17] Such statements essentially limit interpretative freedom regarding canonical texts and offer an opportunity to define the correct faith and proper behaviour clearly. Indeed, a major element in the agenda of Salafi-oriented movements was their wish to reform Muslims by calling them to enjoin what is right and to forbid what is wrong, the classical task of *al-amr bi-maʿrūf wa-l-nahy ʿan al-munkar*.[18] However, Salafi-oriented reform movements stressed not only the paramount importance of the Qurʾān, but also that of Qurʾān-related disciplines, such as *tawḥīd* and *ḥadīth*, while de-emphasising established disciplines of Islamic learning such as *fiqh* (jurisprudence) as well as the different schools (*madhāhib*) of law. The emphasis on new disciplines was connected with the fact that any movement of reform stressing the importance of the sources of the faith and the example of the Prophet for the renewal (*tajdīd*) of Islamic society has to de-emphasise and de-legitimise disciplines linked with post-prophetic developments in Islam, such as *taṣawwuf* (sufism) or *fiqh* (jurisprudence), as well as the schools of law and institutions entrusted with interpretation of the law.

The new reform movements in sub-Saharan Africa were influenced by movements in North Africa, especially in Algeria and Egypt. The North

African reformers were united by the fact that they did not describe their efforts as *tajdīd* (renewal), a term that referred to earlier generations of reformers and, in particular, to the idea of a *mujaddid*, a 'reformer of the era', who would appear in cyclical periods. Rather, they used the term *iṣlāḥ* (purification), with reference to the pure foundations of the faith laid at the time of the Prophet and his followers, the 'venerable forefathers', *al-salaf al-ṣāliḥ* (see Merad 1967; Meijer 2009), that is, the first (three) generations of Muslims, namely, the companions of the Prophet, the *ṣaḥāba*, the following generation of the *al-tābiᶜūn* and the generation following the *tābiᶜūn*, the *tābiᶜ al-tābiᶜūn*. They saw the *al-salaf al-ṣāliḥ* as the 'chosen qurᵓānic generation' (*jīl qurᵓānī farīd*). For this generation, revelation had allegedly taken the character of a 'daily command' (*al-amr al-yaumī*) 'under the eyes of God' (*taht ayni allāhi*) (Quṭb 1981 [1966]: 19).

The stress on *iṣlāḥ* by recent Muslim reformers can thus be understood as a form of distantiation from earlier generations of scholars, as well as from established social structures and religious customs. Earlier generations were accused of *taqlīd* – 'blind imitation' – of established authorities. The *taqlīd* of earlier generations of scholars was contrasted with the *ijtihād* of the reformers who offered solutions for contemporary problems by establishing a direct link to the *sunnah* of the forefathers, the very foundations of the faith (*uṣūl al-dīn*), Qurᵓān and *sunnah*. The stress on the sources of Islam by way of *ijtihād* and on 'purification' of the faith (*taṣḥiḥ al-ᶜaqīda*) also meant that reformers tried to liberate themselves from the burden of earlier interpretations and to open new spaces for their own interpretations (Haj 2009: 36f). Purification (*iṣlāḥ*) and purity (*ṭahāra*) was a major aspect of the social and religious programmes of the new movements of reform, in both North Africa and sub-Saharan Africa. The example of the *salaf al-ṣāliḥ* was understood to be a trans-temporal model of societal organisation, a model of a 'pure' Islamic society that eclipsed centuries of history contaminated by *bidaᶜ* and 'un-Islamic' rulers. Due to the trans-temporal reference to the *salaf*, I call these movements of reform Salafi-oriented movements.

However, since the late nineteenth century, the term 'Salafi' has taken on multiple meanings (see Ch. Ahmed 2015; Gauvain 2013; Griffel 2015; Haykel 2009; Hegghammer 2009; Lauzière 2010, 2016a and 2016b; Meijer 2009; Østebø 2015a). While it originally described the efforts at reform of late nineteenth century Muslim scholars such as Muḥammad ᶜAbdūh, 'Salafi' can denote Islamist, jihādist, modernist and strict literalist orientations today (Triaud and Villalon 2009: 30). This means that the term has acquired different and often confusing connotations in different local contexts (Hodgkin 1998: 205; Griffel 2015: 186ff; Lauzière 2016a: 89–96 and 2016b). Contemporary texts on Salafi-oriented reform movements differentiate, for instance, between three different 'schools or trends of Salafi thought, namely, the 'purist' (quietist), the 'politicos' and the 'jihādis' (militant) (see Wiktorowicz 2006; Meijer 2009). Østebø has argued for a slightly different categorisation of Salafi-oriented movements of reform in the Ethiopian context, where he differentiates between the Salafi, the Tablīghī and the intellectualist movements (2008b: 417). For the sake of convenience, I stick to a broad understanding and to an operational definition of the term 'Salafi' for an array of non-Sufi oriented reformers, who call themselves Salafi-oriented and who describe their endeavours to reform their societies as *iṣlāḥ*: their aim is to repair what hundreds of years of decadence have destroyed and to counter European imperial influence (Triaud and Villalon 2009: 29).

A broad understanding of the term 'Salafi' corresponds to an equally broad understanding of Sufi-oriented movements of reform in this book: Salafi-oriented movements of reform must be seen as complementary to Sufi-oriented movements. For this reason, I will avoid terms that have often been used to explicitly label Salafi-oriented movements of reform as 'fundamentalist' or 'Islamist'. Due to their rootedness in the basic texts of Islam and their claim to speak for all Muslims, Sufi-oriented movements of reform can also be seen in terminological terms as 'fundamentalist' and Islamist. It has to be kept in mind that the stark contrast between Sufi and Salafi should be regarded with caution, due to the fact that 'each of these terms has (historically) covered a number of shifting positions' (Asad 2015: 4). For this reason, I use a more cautious approach and speak about Sufi- and Salafi-*oriented* or Sufi- and Salafi-*minded* movements of reform.

In the light of the case studies in the present volume, it is possible to differentiate between two major orientations within the Salafi-oriented episteme of reform, namely, first, those groups that seek political power or, at least, a major role in politics (*siyāsa*), in order to eventually build an Islamic state, and second, those groups that regard doctrinal purity and the purification of the faith (*tazkiyat al-ᶜaqīda*) (Salomon 2009a: 152) and, consequently, the education (*tarbiya*) of Muslims as being more important than political power. Such *tarbiya*-minded groups want to reform Muslims by calling them to enjoin what is right and forbid what is wrong, heeding, thus, the classical task of *al-amr bi-maᶜrūf wa-l-nahy ᶜan al-munkar*. Such groups are much more concerned with the aberrations of other Muslims than with questions of political strategy, and are consequently willing to criticise other Salafi-oriented movements for the sake of doctrinal purity. *Siyāsa*-oriented groups try to bring about Muslim unity and are willing to ignore doctrinal differences. For the sake of Muslim unity, *siyāsa*-minded groups are even prepared to modify their rejection of the esoteric episteme. Opposition to the esoteric episteme is thus formulated in different degrees of radicality in Salafi-oriented movements.

Apart from *siyāsa*- and *tarbiya*-minded Salafi-oriented movements of reform, some sub-Saharan African countries have seen the emergence of *jihād*-minded activists who do not care much about doctrine and who are also not willing to cultivate paths of accommodation with the state. In Saudi Arabia, the jamāᶜat al-salafiyya al-muḥtasiba around Juhaymān b. Muḥammad al-ᶜUtaybī that stormed the Grand Mosque in Mecca in November 1979 represented such a *jihād*-oriented group of Salafis (Lacroix 2009: 74) that can also be labelled 'Quṭbī' or 'takfīrī' due to their oppositional activist stance regarding the state, their closeness to Sayyid Quṭb's ideas and their willingness to declare other, allegedly deviant, Muslims 'unbelievers' (kuffār) (Griffel 2015: 189; Salomon 2009a: 147ff). The anṣār al-sharīᶜa in Tunisia (Werenfels 2015: 65ff), the Boko Haram movement in north-eastern Nigeria and the ḥarakat al-shabāb al-mujāhidīn in Somalia represent a similar orientation.

Last but not least, it is possible to identify a fourth group of Muslims who have left (mostly) *siyāsa*-oriented organisations such as the jamāᶜat ᶜibād al-raḥmān in Senegal, the 'Yan Izala in northern Nigeria or the *sunnance* in Niger, and who stress the value of individual religiosity, the pious self, beyond organisation. The northern Nigerian scholar Jaᶜfar Maḥmūd Adam has summarised this position by contending that, according to Islamic law, some obligations were individual and some were collective. Muslims should thus know 'which individual struggles they should wage, and which collective struggles they need to pursue as a group'. He continued by saying that 'an individual who practices *shirk* (polytheism) . . . would be punished in hellfire even if he does so under an Islamic government; conversely, if an individual does the right thing even under a non-Islamic government, the individual will be saved and rewarded with a blissful life in paradise' (quoted in Anonymous 2012: 133). Due to this stress on individual piety, piety-minded Muslims are prepared to accept (again) local practices of Islam that have been condemned as *bida*ᶜ by both *siyāsa*- and *tarbiya*-minded reformers.[19] Such piety-minded groups can also be labelled 'Madkhālī' due to their accommodationalist stance regarding the state and their closeness to the ideas of Muḥammad Nāṣir al-Dīn al-Albānī and Rabīᶜ al-Madkhālī (Griffel 2015: 189).[20]

An important feature of the exegetical wars between different Salafi-oriented reformist groups was the insistence of piety-minded reformers on the importance of the personal faith (*īmān*) of believers. Consequently, all believers had to be regarded as equally faithful or even 'holy': *īmān* yielded the 'promise to paradise' for each single believer, as it was an inner act of the heart (Salvatore 1997: 21). In his programmatic text *al-ᶜaqīda al-ṣaḥīḥa bi-muwāfaqat al-sharīᶜa* (1976) the Nigerian reformer Abubakar Gumi consequently stressed that 'each believer is a saint' (*fa-kull muᵓmin walī*) (Gumi 1976 [1972]: 9), even if he conceded that there were degrees of saintness: 'saintness belonged to those who believe and guard themselves against evil practices' (. . . *fa-l-wilāya li-man kānū min alladhīna āmanū wa kāna yattaqūna*). At the same time, faith was not connected with the question as to 'how many fasts' or how many prayers a believer performed, nor were constant adulation (praising of God) or religious exercises a marker of saintness (. . . *wa-laisat bi-kathratī ṣaumin wa-lā ṣalātin wa-lā tamalluqin wa-lā riyādhatin*) (Gumi 1976 [1972]: 10). *Imān* was not an expression of visible acts of piety but of an exclusive relationship between each single believer and his Lord, and this relationship was a secret between such a believer and God: '*wa-man āmana, bi-kulli mā jāᵓ bihi al-rasūl (S.A.W.), fi-qalbihi, fa-huwa muᵓmin, idhan lā sabīl lanā ilā maᶜrifati dhālika: fa-huwa sirr fi-mā baina al-ᶜabd wa-rabbihi*' ('anybody who has faith, in his heart, in all that came unto the Prophet [in form of revelations], is a believer, as there is no way for us to know otherwise: and it [this faith] is a secret between him and his Lord') (Gumi 1976 [1972]: 17).

While it is possible to identify and differentiate Salafi-oriented movements by their epistemic orientation, it is also possible to talk about a historical evolution of movements of reform since the late nineteenth century: from different modes of Sufi-oriented reform (that continue to exist and develop today) to a first (late nineteenth century and early twentieth) Salafi-oriented generation[21] of reform characterised by Muḥammad ᶜAbduh's efforts to Islamise modernity; to a second (mid-twetienth century) generation of Salafi-oriented organisations such as Ḥasan al-Bannā's ikhwān al-muslimūn in Egypt, Rashīd al-Ghannūshī's al-nahḍa-movement in Tunisia or the 'Yan Izala in northern Nigeria characterised by their pragmatic approaches to reform that equally proposed to Islamise modernity; to a third (and almost co-temporal) generation of *tarbiya*-minded reformers such as the Sudanese anṣār al-sunna al-muḥammadiyya or the different groups of ahl al-sunna in Mali, Niger, Nigeria, Kenya and Tanzania who have been influenced by scholars such as Muḥammad Nāṣir al-Dīn al-Albānī and Abū Muḥammad al-Maqdīsī (see Lacroix 2009: 63ff; Wagemakers 2012); to a fourth generation of piety-minded Muslims who still heed Salafi positions, yet stress the importance of individual piety.

In between these ideal types of Salafi-oriented movements of reform one can find (mostly smaller) groups that follow a different programmatic cocktail, such as the Islamic Movement of Ibrāhīm al-Zakzakī in northern Nigeria. All of these movements of reform are characterised (and united) by at least four major doctrinal issues, namely, their rejection of the esoteric episteme, their rejection of the idea of intercession (*tawassul*), their rejection of local *ᶜurf* and *ādat* practices and their rejection of *taqlīd*, that is, the practice of following a chain of established authorities (*muqallidūn*) in a specific field of Islamic learning. In contrast, Salafi-oriented Muslims stress the central role of the *sunnah* of the Prophet, the central role of the text (Qurᵓān), the direct access of Muslims to the text without intermediaries and the need to practice *ijtihād* in order to overcome *taqlīd* and achieve change. A major problem remains, though, namely the fact that such ideal types are valid for a limited period of time only: Salafi-oriented groups develop over time and move from one position to another. In addition, the ideas of Salafi-oriented thinkers regarding their *ᶜaqīda* (doctrinal position) as well as their *manhaj* (programme) have often been broader than the definitions mentioned above. The dynamics of social, political and economic change that inform religious change can be grasped best if we imagine that Sufi- and Salafi-oriented movements of reform navigate in a constellation of three major social and political forces: the state, society at large and other Muslims. The development of Sufi- and Salafi-oriented movements of reform can thus be viewed as an effort to find a position in an ever-changing constellation of social and political forces and actors.

Doctrinal Distinction, Symbolic Distantiation, Social Separation and Spatial Segregation

In general terms, it is possible to read Salafi-oriented movements of reform through at least four different lenses, namely, doctrine, symbolism, the social field and geopolitics. These lenses represent processes and dynamics of doctrinal distinction, symbolic distantiation, social separation and, ultimately, spatial segregation, often linked with a declaration of withdrawal and emigration (*hijra*) from the land of unbelief. The processes that may eventually lead to the establishment of spatially segregated communities are again not confined to Salafi-oriented movements of reform, but can also be found among Sufis, as, for instance, in the community of Madina Gounass in Senegal, or in virtually all Sufi-led movements of *jihād* in eighteenth, nineteenth and early twentieth century sub-Saharan Africa (see Loimeier 2013).[22] The Salafi concept of spatial segregation or 're-location' (Last 2014: 47) is not based, however, on the Sufi concept of the *khalwa*, spiritual seclusion, but on the principle of *al-walāʾ wa-l-barāʾa*, that is, loyalty towards God and the *sunnah* of the Prophet as well as disavowal and withdrawal from everything that is not in conformity with the *sunnah* of the Prophet[23] (Wagemakers 2014: 70). When Salafi-oriented movements of reform took such a path towards spatial segregation, especially radical ones such as the jamāᶜat al-muslimīn in Egypt in the 1970s, colloquially known as the jamāᶜat takfīr wa-l-hijra,[24] they saw segregation not as being limited in time, but as something permanent, a precondition, in fact, for the establishment of the ideal and pure Islamic community. But Salafi-oriented movements do not necessarily start out with the idea of seeking spatial segregation. Rather, they stress distinctness, purity (*ṭahāra*) and dissent in less radical ways by doctrinal distinction, by symbolic distantiation and by social separation:[25]

> Symbolic boundaries are conceptual distinctions made by social actors to categorize objects, people, practices, and even time and space . . . Symbolic boundaries also separate people into groups and generate feelings of similarity and group membership . . . Social boundaries are objectified forms of social differences manifested in unequal access to unequal distribution of resources (material and nonmaterial) and social opportunities . . . At the causal level, symbolic boundaries can be thought of as a necessary but insufficient condition for the existence of social boundaries . . . Symbolic boundaries are often used to enforce, maintain, normalize or rationalize social boundaries . . . symbolic boundaries, however, are also employed to contest and reframe the meaning of social boundaries. (Lamont and Molnár 2002: 168–9, 186)

Salafi-oriented movements of reform verbally criticise or condemn established practices, attack such practices as *bida*ᶜ and proclaim their own orthodoxy (and orthopraxy) as well as their own purity. In the process of radicalisation, other Muslims are condemned as hypocrites (*munāfiqūn*), ignorant (*jāhil*) or even unbelievers (*kuffār*), and this escalation may eventually lead movements of reform to declare a *jihād* against other Muslims.[26] In this respect, 'words', that is, doctrinal arguments, are of basic importance, because they serve to legitimise radicalisation and respective action. It is important, however, to point out the differences between Salafi-oriented groups regarding doctrine: while *tarbiya*-minded groups grant doctrine a primary role and insist on doctrinal purity, *siyāsa*-minded groups have been willing to neglect doctrinal issues in order to enhance political unity among Muslims. *Jihād*-minded activists are characterised by the fact that doctrinal issues are deemed marginal for their agenda, while piety-minded groups are prepared to accept doctrinal flexibility.

Symbolic and social boundaries thus have to be based on texts and related arguments that establish doctrinal distinctions between true believers and the others. Markers of doctrinal distinction are, for instance, specific patterns of interpretation and argumentation (scholastic, modern, literalistic, allegoric, exclusive, inclusive), especially with respect to the Qurʾān: Muslim reformers are characterised by their stress on the paramount importance of the sources of the faith, in particular the Qurʾān (on the level of scriptures), the authority of the *salaf* and the corpus of *ḥadīth*. Muslim movements of reform also tend to stigmatise their opponents and have become notorious for proclaiming *takfīr* against dissidents, on the basis of Muḥammad b. ʿAbd al-Wahhāb's principle *man lam yukaffir al-kāfir fa-huwa kāfir* ('he who does not declare an unbeliever an unbeliever is an unbeliever himself'), a principle that triggers, of course, the (old) question as to what constitutes unbelief. Consequently, Muslim movements of reform have developed a rich polemical literature that is specifically directed against the Sufi orders and the widespread practices of popular religion. However, doctrinal arguments (and polemics) may also be turned against competing groups in the heat of a debate. The inherent dynamic of doctrinal argumentation has stimulated processes of fragmentation and othering even within the Salafi-oriented movement of reform. Movements of reform try to legitimise their endeavours by referring to scripture and also try to claim hegemony of interpretation of scripture. Due to the fact that the Qurʾān is seen as the ultimate authority, exegetical wars have been fought.

Other markers of doctrinal distinction are specific texts that are seen by reformers as key texts. Often linked with such key texts are disciplines that acquire different interpretative importance in different historical contexts. Equally, historical references to earlier and other traditions of reform, to the Prophet, to saints or events, can be used in a doctrinal argumentation as a marker of distinction: each movement of reform cultivates a specific dialogue with the past. The same applies to specific positions on the language of texts and discourses (such as translations, Arabic, and vernacular languages) or on terminology (for instance, stress on *iṣlāḥ* or stress on *tajdīd*), as well as a plethora of other issues such as the role of women, the role of modern media, the issue of the secular state, the way in which other states (such as Saudi Arabia) are presented as a model (or not), specific concepts of education, specific modes of teacher–student relations, specific school models and syllabi, other reformist groups, social and political opponents and earlier generations of reform, as well as social questions in general. All of these issues may become the focus of a doctrinal debate and trigger, for instance, the production of *fatāwa* that serve as a basis for doctrinal distinction. This implies that texts may wax and wane in importance depending on their function and role in conflicts and the temporal dynamics of such conflicts.

In the fields of symbolic distantiation and social separation, Salafi-oriented movements of reform cultivate outwardly visible signs and symbols of distinction, such as *ḥijāb* or *niqāb* (or gloves) for women, or their complete seclusion, or even the question of whether a woman's voice is part of her *ᶜawrah*, and must be 'covered' (hidden), just like her body.[27] Women play a major role in Salafi-oriented movements of reform and express their support for such movements of reform by dressing in a Salafi way: dress is not only a marker of membership of women in such a movement, but also a marker of general support for Salafi reformist issues (Hodgkin 1998: 211).[28] Men also adopt a specific way of dressing, a particular beard and a certain hairstyle, or remaining shod when entering a mosque for prayer, a practice that has raised much controversy among Muslims (Meijer 2009: 16; Lacroix 2009: 72).[29] For instance, the practice of wearing shortened trousers is a typical Salafi dress code and is subsumed under the term *isbāl* (from the Arabic root s-b-l and meaning to let down; to wear one's garments below one's ankles; to trail one's garments). *Isbāl* is based on a series of *ḥadīth*, such as the one related by al-Nawāwī in his *sharḥ* (commentary) of the ṣaḥīḥ Muslim: *wa-innahu la yajūz isbāluhu taḥt al-kaᶜbayn* (and it is not permissible to lower [the garment] below the ankles), which is based on an interpretation of Qur'ān 17: 37: 'And walk not upon the earth with conceit and arrogance.' Similarly, a *ḥadīth* related by al-Bukhārī states: 'Allah will not look, on the day of resurrection, at the person who drags his garment (behind him) out of conceit' (Scharrer 2013: 113; see also the Internet debates on *isbāl*). All of these habits contribute to the public visibility of Salafi-oriented Muslims. The fact that followers of Salafi-oriented movements of reform create symbols of distantiation on so many different levels (including language) has also created a specific Salafi habitus that signals difference.[30]

Other markers of symbolic distantiation and social separation are specific positions on questions of ritual, purity, the veneration of saints and shrine pilgrimage;[31] different ways of performing prayers; the timing of Islamic festivities; and the ritual complex of death, burial and mourning. The critique of extensive burial rites has been an important part of anti-esoteric discourses in many Muslim societies. In Sudan, for instance, Salafi-oriented Muslims started a campaign against the ritual of wailing (*bikāʾ*) in 1989 and not only condemned this practice as such but also the length of the ritual and the respective delay in the execution of the proper Islamic ritual (Seesemann 2005a). In Senegal, Cheikh Touré focused in a whole chapter of his programmatic text – *Le vrai et le faux: L'Islam au Sénégal* (Loimeier 2001: 198–9) – on the issue of burial rites and a critique of local burial practices. Similar condemnations of local burial rites and rites of mourning can be found in the discourse of the 'Yan Izala in northern Nigeria and of Salafi-oriented reformers such as ᶜAbdallāh Ṣāliḥ al-Farsy in East Africa.[32]

Other fields of symbolic confrontation are the celebration of the birthday of the Prophet, the widespread practice of *ruqya* (spirit possession) in Muslim societies (van de Bruinhorst 2007: 187) and the production of and faith in amulets. Faith in amulets and, generally, any form of intercession (*tawassul*), such as the consultation of Sufi saints, are seen as violating the principle of *tawḥīd* (the uniqueness of God). At the same time, Salafi-oriented movements of reform cultivate other forms of religious practice, such as the sober recitation of the Qurʾān according to the rules of *tajwīd*,[33] which has become a major discipline in reformist education as well as a feature of Salafi-oriented religious practice in all of sub-Saharan Africa (Kane 2003: 89, 109, 117 and 144). Prayer has been another field of symbolic dispute, for instance over the question of when to perform *qunūt*[34] (van de Bruinhorst 2007: 325ff) or how to hold the hands during prayers (in the upright, *qiyām*, position), that is, *qabḍ* (arms crossed) or *sadl* (arms outstretched) (Loimeier 1997a: 79ff). Supererogatory prayers, such as *tarāwīḥ* prayers in Ramadan, have been criticised as a waste of time.[35] Equally, the times for the call to prayer, the *adhān*, have been a matter of dispute: for instance, in northern Nigeria, the commonly agreed time for noon (*ẓuhr*) prayers was from 1pm to 3pm, although most Muslims prayed at about 2pm. In order to express their dissent to such established practices, the 'Yan Izala movement insisted on the earliest possible time for *ẓuhr* prayers at 1pm. The 'Yan Izala also changed the temporal sequence of the *fajr* (morning) prayer: while the phrase *al-ṣalāt khayrun min al-nawm* ('prayer is better than sleep') usually concludes the second and final call for the morning prayer, the 'Yan Izala transferred this phrase to the first *adhān* (Mustapha and Bunza 2014: 65–6).

Salafi-oriented Muslims also create social segregation by forms of participation or non-participation in communal ritual and communal social life or by organising their groups in specific ways, often in the form of bureaucratic associations. Salafis equally often refuse to join other Muslims in prayer; they set up their own mosques and schools, settle in their own communities and – if they refuse to join their path – keep at an (increasing) social distance from non-Muslims, fellow Muslims, members of their own communities and, finally, their families (such as fathers, mothers, husbands and wives). Their polemics and attacks on established practices necessarily lead to hostility and to *fitna* (strife) and support dynamics of mutual exclusion among Muslims: 'Collective identity is constituted (thus) by a dialectic interplay of processes of internal and external definition' (Lamont and Molnár 2002: 170).

Social separation and symbolic distantiation may also be established by a specific way of organising time. The way in which utopias are imagined and constructed may become markers of symbolic distantiation and social separation: one of the most important arenas for the symbolic and social negotiation of conflict among Muslims is time, and the Islamic regime of time, as manifested, for instance, in the times for daily prayer, the Friday prayer, the times for feasting (as informed by the sighting of the moon) and fasting, in particular in Ramadan, the feast at the end of Ramadan *ᶜīd al-fiṭr* on the first day of Shawwāl, the pilgrimage (*ḥajj*) and the *ᶜīd al-aḍḥā* (also *ᶜīd al-ḥajj*, *ᶜīd al-kabīr*) on 10 Dhū l-Ḥijja. Exact timing is also important for other Islamic feast days, such as the New Year on 1 Muḥarram, 10 Muḥarram (*ᶜāshūrā*), the birthday of the Prophet (*mawlid al-nabī*) on 12 Rabīᶜ al-Awwal or the *lailat al-qadr*, the 'night of providence' when the first qurᵓānic revelation was 'sent down', an occasion that is celebrated annually on the night of 27 Ramadan.

On a larger scale, the *hijra* has created a dividing line between the time of Islam and the time of *jāhiliyya*, the time of ignorance before Islam. The Prophet used his final pilgrimage in 632 to proclaim the new Islamic calculation of times on the day of the gathering of the faithful at mount ᶜArafa, on 10 Dhū l-Ḥijja, when the pre-Islamic moon calendar had turned full cycle. For the exact determination of the beginning (and the end) of the Islamic months and the festival days related to them, in particular, the feast of sacrifice (*ᶜīd al-ḥajj*) on 10 Dhū l-Ḥijja and the feast (*ᶜīd al-fiṭr*) to end the month of fasting, the question of the sighting (*ruᵓyā*) of the crescent (*hilāl*) of the moon plays a central role. As the Islamic moon calendar comprises 355 days, the beginning of each month and thus the exact number of days (29 or 30) depends on the sighting of the new moon. Depending on each sighting of the new moon the month of fasting (like any other month) may have twenty-nine or thirty days.[36] Should the *hilāl* of the following month not be sighted in the night from the twenty-ninth to the thirtieth day, the thirtieth day is regarded as a 'day of doubt' and will be taken as another day of fasting.

This rule is important as the communal ritual defines the religious identity of all Muslims. Thus, all Muslims are called upon to fast in Ramadan. However, there are also days when fasting is prohibited. Such days are Friday, the day of communal prayer; *ᶜīd al-fiṭr*, the day of the communal breaking of the fast at the end of Ramadan; the festival of sacrifice and the days of communal feasting (*tashrīk*) after the feast of sacrifice (11–13 Dhū l-Ḥijja); and, finally, the 'day of doubt' at the end of Shaᶜbān when the crescent of the new moon, announcing the month of Ramadan, has not yet been sighted reliably, thus extending the month of Shaᶜbān by one day to a length of thirty days. Equally, there is an obligation to continue the fast on the thirtieth day of Ramadan if the crescent moon for the next month (Shawwāl) has not been sighted reliably. Violations of these rules of communal feasting and fasting on the basis of different local sightings of the new moon are regarded as serious violations of the rule of Islamic communality and are condemned accordingly.

Today, astronomical calculations, satellite data and the clock have rendered the calculation of months much easier, but they have not replaced the actual (local) sighting of the moon. As a result, there are repeated conflicts over calculation of the months and their festival days. In all of these conflicts between different Muslim groups the central question is what kind of validity the local sighting of the new moon has for the translocal community of the Muslim *ummah*. Salafi-oriented activists and universalists, such as Zanzibar's anṣār al-sunna, for instance, propose to replace the local sighting of the new moon (as well as the method of counting the days since the last *hilāl*) by a new regulation based on an astronomical calculation of the new moon. This idea is founded on the consideration that local sighting of the *hilāl* may be based on the *sunnah* of the Prophet and related texts, but that astronomical regulation would effectively strengthen the more important rule of co-temporal fasting, non-fasting and feasting of the ummah as a whole. Muslim universalists such as the anṣār al-sunna thus basically recognise the validity of the local sighting of the new moon as being part of the *sunnah* of the Prophet, yet they subordinate local sighting of the new moon to the concept of Islamic communality that stresses the rule that there should be only one *ᶜīd al-ḥajj* and one *ᶜīd al-fiṭr* for all Muslims. This requirement of communality in praying and feasting, in fasting and non-fasting is violated by multiple local sightings of the new moon. In the context of the increasing technological entanglement of the world, multiple local sightings of the *hilāl* bring about an anachronistic multiplication of religious feasts and fasting days that are no longer acceptable in view of the contemporary speed of exchange of information regarding the sighting of the new moon.

To strengthen this universalist argument, Salafi-oriented activists point out that many communities that had diverging local sightings of the *hilāl* in the past were situated in the same time zone. They argue that it should be possible to assume and accept the 'congruence of times of dawn' (*ittiḥād al-maṭāliᶜ*) and a single sighting of the new moon within a given time zone. This argument basically concerns the fundamental question of whose *ruᵓyā* will be accepted locally (van de Bruinhorst 2007: 195ff). This question is set in the centre of numerous local conflicts, as the question of the sighting of the new moon is one of those basic questions that reflect the conflict between established traditions of Islamic learning and movements of reform that like to demonstrate their universal orientation through symbolic issues such as the sighting of the new moon. Behind Salafi-oriented activists such as the anṣār al-sunna in Zanzibar is Saudi Arabia's claim to represent, as 'protector of the two holy places', Mecca and Medina, a universal claim to *irshād* for the *ummah* as a whole.[37] The dispute over control of the calendar and the regulation of the religious feasts and festival days thus expresses basic social conflicts and mirrors different positions on issues of the ritual.

Feasting, or not feasting, at the 'wrong' time signals deviation, the violation of communality, and dispute (*fitna*). The exact times for praying, fasting and feasting constitute a public declaration with regard to the ideal of community of each Muslim society and thus have been a central feature of the Islamic identity of each local community (van de Bruinhorst 2007: 221). It is no wonder that Muslim movements of reform often express both their programme of reform as well as their distinctness in aspects of the Islamic time regime. Time thus has to be regarded as a central factor in the formulation of doctrinal distinction, the demonstration of symbolic distantiation and the development of social separation and spatial segregation. Time constitutes the hidden sub-structure underlying these categories: both doctrinal distinction and symbolic distantiation are expressed in categories of time (and respective texts) and the ways in which Muslims 'live time' reflect both doctrinal distinctions and modes of symbolic distantiation: social separation and spatial segregation may be limited or unlimited in time. However, Salafi arguments regarding time and the need to stick to one single concept of time in order to strengthen the *ummah* of Muslims are in complete contradiction to the Salafi stress on doctrinal distinction, symbolic distantiation and social separation, which stress difference. This contradiction has rendered Salafi arguments about the unity of the *ummah* and the value of communality highly problematic.

Doctrinal distinction, symbolic distantiation, social separation and spatial segregation exist not only side by side, but may also be part of a historical escalation and intensification of distinction, identity building and segregation, although the move from doctrinal distinction to symbolic distantiation and social separation and finally to spatial segregation is neither predestined nor inevitable. Doctrinal, symbolic, social and spatial distinctions serve to preserve and construct purity in a social context that is seen as being polluting. In order to understand Salafi-oriented movements of reform, it is thus necessary to look at the way in which doctrinal, symbolic, social and spatial boundaries and distinctions are formulated and established. Processes of mutual exclusion and the fact that Salafi-oriented movements of reform stress doctrinal distinction, symbolic distantiation, social separation and even spatial segregation, also impact, however, on the very concept of the Muslim public sphere that has been described as a 'sphere of discourse that combines religious, social and political messages' (Bowen 1993: 325). What happens to such a public sphere if participants refuse to talk and live with one another? Salafi-oriented movements of reform seem to work against their participation in the public sphere by establishing boundaries and by creating distinctions. However, due to the fact that Salafi-oriented movements of reform stress doctrinal, symbolic, social and spatial distinctions, they, haphazardly, become visible (and audible) and thus part of the public sphere.

In order to be able to identify structural similarities among different movements of reform, I therefore propose to not only check the meaning of specific markers of reform in their respective contexts, but also to document the temporal intensification and accumulation of specific markers of reform in a given historical context. We still have to be careful, however, as specific markers of reform may have different interpretative weight and value in different contexts. Also, some markers of reform may be adopted sooner or later by other and competing movements of reform. Finally, programmes of reform may acquire relevance for both individual agency and social reality. Yet, not each movement of reform is successful: the failure of programmes of reform consequently constitutes an important field for research.

On the basis of the case studies discussed here, it can be suggested that traditions of reform evolve not only in a dialectical process of interaction with the particular context of time and region (space) and with one another, but also in a generational mode of interaction with preceding traditions of reform, in a dialogue with the past. Such preceding traditions of reform may be quoted (and activated for a contemporary context) in trans-traditional, trans-historical, trans-generational and trans-local terms. As a consequence, distinctive generations and traditions of reform can be identified and analysed only after having analysed the programmes and markers of reform in their respective discursive, spatial and historical contexts. The interplay between traditions, texts and the canon through space and over time disproves essentialist reductions of Islam and Muslim societies, confirming Talal Asad's basic assumption of the contested and pluralist nature of Islam and Muslim traditions and enabling us to overcome obsolete yet convenient binary constructions of Muslim societies.

Constructions of Muslim Societies

The discussion above of the term 'Salafi' has already shown the difficulties of definition, demarcation and differentiation. Such epistemological problems are intensified by efforts to construct Muslim societies in binary ways. Muslim constructions of society in contexts of conflict have most particularly informed Western constructions of Muslim societies. Muslim societies have thus been presented as being divided into 'peaceful' Sufis versus 'militant' reformers. This dichotomy was essentially informed by the idea that there was a cosmos of local, allegedly tolerant forms of 'Sufi' Islam, often characterised by the cult of saints as well as a plethora of (pre-Islamic) survivals in local practices (see Osella and Soares 2010: 59), and, on the other side, one monolithic, 'fundamentalist', 'puritan', 'orthodox', 'scripturalist' and usually 'outlandish', reformist Islam. Such a construction of Muslim societies in sub-Saharan Africa (and beyond) was not only much too simplistic, but also omitted the fact that Muslim societies in sub-Saharan Africa had a long history of militant reform movements associated with Sufi scholars and Sufi orders: consider, for instance, the *jihāds* led by Usman dan Fodio, Aḥmad Lobbo and al-Ḥājj ᶜUmar Taal. Equally problematic is Louis Brenner's concept of the 'esoteric' and the 'rationalistic' paradigms (Brenner 2001: 17ff). On closer investigation, we see that such an academic construction is misleading due to two major factors: first, even if they are committed to an esoteric paradigm, Sufis are at least as rationalistic, in the logic of their own thinking, as Salafi-oriented reformers and vice versa. Second, there is never one single expression of Sufism or Salafi-oriented reform, but a spectrum of different manifestations of reform, including Sufi-oriented reform. Virtually all catchwords that have been identified as markers of difference between Sufis and Salafis such as their alleged 'scripturalist' (or 'non-scripturalist') and 'fundamentalist' (or 'non-fundamentalist') character have thus turned out to be less than convincing when scrutinised properly, and consequently dissolve into thin air.

However, binary constructions of Muslim societies have also been an intrinsic part of Muslim constructions of society, especially in contexts of conflict, as a way of de-legitimising other Muslims for being 'less orthodox' or 'bad' Muslims, as *munāfiqūn* (hypocrites), as *munkirūn* (deniers), as *khawārij* (dissidents) or even as *kuffār* (unbelievers).[38] These dynamics of othering and the respective construction of binary oppositions can be shown clearly in the development of conflict among Muslims in sub-Saharan West Africa, where there was opposition between the Qādiriyya and the Tijāniyya Sufi orders from the mid-nineteenth century, then, from the 1930s, a dispute within the Tijāniyya over the issue of *qabḍ* and *sadl* (Loimeier 1997a: 79ff)[39] and, finally, from the late 1970s, a conflict between the Sufi orders and the Salafi-oriented 'Yan Izala in northern Nigeria. In each of these conflicts, the other was depicted in the respective emic view and in the respective 'orientalizing grammar' (Baumann 2005: 18ff) as being distinctly different (that is, 'unorthodox' and so forth). Yet, binary constructions of society may also become obsolete when the context of conflict vanishes in the course of time. In Baumann's 'segmentary grammar' of conflicts, former enemies, such as eleven and twelve bead Tijānis, the Qādiriyya and the Tijāniyya in northern Nigeria or both Sufi orders and the 'Yan Izala, may become (temporary) allies when new enemies appear on the horizon and produce a new context of conflict (Loimeier 1997a: 309).[40]

Dichotomous representations of reform thus constitute an important means of 'othering' opponents. It is important to examine such processes of othering in so far as they reflect emic perceptions of reality. Dichotomous representations are relational, however, and the result of negotiation processes in a local context. They are often made operational or articulated for specific purposes and consequently change ascription when the context changes. Binary constructions of society may conserve their vitality as a grammar of conflict because Islam and its canonical texts still play an important role in at least two ways in Muslim societies: first, as a central source of authority in questions and debates on the 'moral order' (*Moralordnung*) of a society (touching on questions such as marriage, divorce, inheritance or social and moral conduct) and, second, as an identifier in contexts of conflict, that is, as a source and an authority that is activated in order to define specific positions and perceptions and to create distinctions with respect to other Muslims, as well as non-Muslims. Although they are highly diverse, contexts of conflict (and debates on the moral order of a given society) are extremely conducive for the construction of binarities among Muslims. Binary constructions in fact function as a tool in local strategies of identifying and othering purported outsiders and/or enemies (Loimeier and Seesemann 2006: 9). As such they are essential to the production of meaning. Understanding binary oppositions thus helps us to understand the negotiated and situated character of dispute in Muslim societies and to answer the question of how far binary oppositions are constitutive of Sufi- and Salafi-oriented movements of reform or, better, how far they are useful for differentiating between Sufi- and Salafi-oriented movements of reform.

For instance, a major marker for the construction of a binary opposition between Salafi-oriented reformers and other Muslims has been the difference between metaphorical (*taʾwīl*) and literalist (*ẓāhir*) approaches to texts. While Sufis follow the paradigm of metaphorical interpretation, Salafi-oriented reformers are said to be literalists. Yet, even though Salafi-oriented reformers represent a 'literalist' approach to texts, such a clear-cut take on Salafi doctrine turns out to be less clear-cut at a second glance: although Salafi-oriented scholars reject the metaphorical interpretation and understanding of the Qurʾān, such scholars would also reject a purely anthropomorphic interpretation that would claim that God's face, hands and eye are identical with those of humans. Salafi-oriented scholars rather advance a 'literalist' approach to the holy text that is not distorted (*taḥrīf*) by metaphorical interpretation (*taʾwīl*). Such an approach does not empty (*taᶜṭīl*) the conception of God, does not associate specific 'shaping' (*takyīf*) with God's attributes and does not compare God with his creation. In this sense, Salafi doctrinal positions reject a metaphorical interpretation of those verses of the Qurʾān that mention a face, a hand, an eye of God and that refer to him as sitting on a throne. At the same time, Salafis stress that there are similarities (*mushābahāt*) but no complete identity (*mumāthala*) between God and humans: *laisa ka-mithlihi shayʾun* (Qurʾān 42: 11: 'There is nothing that is equal to him'). God has settled on his throne, yet the revelation is silent about the concrete way in which he has done that (Gharaibeh 2014: 113): 'he settled on the throne in his own way' (C. Ahmed 2015: 128). As a consequence, Salafi-oriented scholars do not have an anthropomorphic concept of God, but prefer to argue that the true shape of God's attributes exceeds human powers of imagination and should thus not be described; they are 'transcendental anthropomorphists', believing in a God with a human-like shape, while the concrete form of this shape is unknown (Gharaibeh 2014: 123). Salafi-oriented scholars such as ᶜAbdallāh Ṣāliḥ al-Farsy or Abubakar Gumi have thus rejected a literalistic translation of the Qurʾān and stick to the position that only God knows the meaning of the ambiguous verses; they must be accepted without asking questions (*bilā kaifa*).

Despite such analytical problems, academics have repeatedly tried to come up with new categories to describe religious movements, often in binary terms. Noah Salomon, for instance, has offered a set of categories for differentiating between Sufi and non-Sufi ('postmodern') epistemologies (Salomon 2013: 821). His argument is based on debates on the 'theory of Islamic knowledge' in contemporary Sudan, where Ḥasan al-Turābī's *mashrū*ᶜ *al-ḥaḍarī* (civilisational project) implies an attempt at 'Islamisation of knowledge' (*islāmiyyat al-ma*ᶜ*rifa*). Such a 'scientific' and text-as-authority-oriented approach was rejected by followers of the Sufi episteme who supported, in Louis Brenner's words, 'a hierarchical conceptualization of knowledge . . . (in which) knowledge is transmitted in an initiatic form and is closely related to devotional practice' (Brenner 2001: 19). Such an initiatic approach that assumes the spiritual authority of a master over his student relies on a 'theory of knowledge' that is based on the idea of the secret and hidden (*bāṭin*) meaning of texts. It stresses the elusiveness of knowledge, that is, its remaining eternally secret to the common adept (Salomon 2013: 824), rather than its *Erkennbarkeit* or *Erlernbarkeit*, that is, that it is possible to grasp the hidden meaning of a text. Such a concept of knowledge violates the idea of the basic openness of texts and the certainty of knowledge about the meaning of things in the modern period as represented by Salafi-oriented scholars in Sudan (and elsewhere) (Salomon 2013: 824). Salafi-oriented scholars would come back, in their respective 'discourses of certainty' (Salomon 2013: 826), to their basic ᶜ*aqīda* (conviction), namely, that 'the Qur'ān is clear. Any person can understand it . . . There is nothing called hidden knowledge.'[41] Although Salomon has identified here an important epistemological divide between Sufi- and Salafi-oriented concepts of knowledge, the reality of exegesis of the Qur'ān by Salafi-oriented scholars such as Abubakar Gumi or ᶜAbdallāh Ṣāliḥ al-Farsy shows that such thinkers refrain from a crude literalistic interpretation of texts and accept metaphorical interpretation to a certain extent.

Other scholars have maintained that Sufis and Salafi-oriented reformers can be distinguished by their different approaches to authority: while Salafi-oriented reformers are said to reject *taqlīd* (here: 'the blind imitation of both former and established authority') and favour a direct link with the very sources of Islam without recourse to a chain (*isnād*, pl. *asānīd*)[42] of intermediaries, Sufis are said to accept *taqlīd* (here: 'the respectful emulation of earlier authorities') through such a chain of intermediaries that ultimately link contemporary scholars with the Prophet Muḥammad.[43] The importance of an unbroken chain of tradition can be called an '*isnād* paradigm', which can be summarised as

> the overt . . . predilection in diverse strands of Islamic life for recourse to previous authorities, above all the prophet and companions, but also later figures (whether an Abū Ḥanīfah, Jalāl al-Dīn Rūmī, Shaykh Walī Allāh ad-Dihlāwī or Ibn ᶜAbd al-Wahhāb) who are perceived as having revived (jaddada), reformed (aṣlaḥa) or preserved (ḥafiẓa) the vision and norms of true, pristine Islam, and thus as being in continuity and connection with the original community or ummah. (Graham 1993: 500)

Such intermediaries are seen as the interpreters of God's revealed word, rejecting all *bidaᶜ* and having a sense of connectedness 'across the generations with the time and personages of Islamic origin' (Graham 1993: 501). Truth in fact lies not in documents but in authentic human beings and their personal connections with one another (Graham 1993: 507). The central role of the *silsila* – the unbroken chain of transmission – is particularly important for four different orientations in Islam, namely, the Sufis and the different Sufi orders; the followers of the different shīᶜī groups that claim descent (*nasab*) from ᶜAlī; the *shurafāʾ*, the physical descendants of the Prophet (Graham 1993: 514ff); and, last but not least, numerous traditions of learning, especially in Islamic law (*fiqh*), that transmit learning by *ijāzāt* from teacher to student. Chains of transmission may thus be of very different character.

While not being completely wrong, this concept is also not quite true if we consider that even the most radical 'fundamentalists' or literalists like to refer to earlier authorities such as Muḥammad Rashīd Riḍā, Muḥammad ᶜAbduh, Muḥammad b. ᶜAbd al-Wahhāb or Ibn Taimiya (see Fuchs 2013: 216ff).[44] The concept of *al-walāʾ wa-l-barāʾa*, that is, the command to follow the *sunnah* of the Prophet as lived and expounded by the *salaf*, in fact leads to a Salafi *isnād*, consisting, for instance, of those scholars and Muslim reformers of the nineteenth century and early twentieth who fought popular customs and who tried to revive the *sunnah* of the Prophet, especially Muḥammad ᶜAbduh (1849–1905) and Rāshid Riḍā (1865–1935), as well as contemporary Muslim reformers such as Sayyid Quṭb (1906–66), Abū l-Āᶜla Maudūdī (1903–79), ᶜAbd al-ᶜAzīz b. ᶜAbdallāh b. Bāz (1912–99), Muḥammad Nāṣir al-Dīn al-Albānī (1914–99), Dr Rabīᶜ b. Hādī ᶜAmīr al-Madkhālī (b. 1931) or Muḥammad b. Ṣāliḥ b. al-ᶜUthaimin (1929–2000), who claim – in divergent ways – the legacy of the *salaf* as interpreted by scholars such as Aḥmad b. Muḥammad b. Ḥanbal (780–855), Ibn Taimiyya (1263–1328), Muḥammad b. ᶜAbd al-Wahhāb (1703–92) or Muḥammad al-Shawkānī (1760–1834) (Haj 2009: 57). The fact that even scholars with well-known roots in Sufi traditions, such as Ibn Taimiyya or, in Nigeria, Usman dan Fodio, have become part of contemporary Salafi *asānīd* points to a process in which Salafis expand the Salafi canon by 'retroactively salafizing' historical thinkers of Islam who may not have understood themselves in the way that contemporary Salafis do (Thurston forthcoming: 19) in order to enlarge their historical basis and legitimacy. This process of 'retroactive Salafisation' has an inclusive thrust and rebels against co-temporal tendencies within Salafi-oriented movements of reform to exclude 'dissident' thinkers from the Salafi canon in order to preserve, for instance, doctrinal purity. These processes are mutually exclusive and create tension within Salafi-oriented movements of reform regarding the question of who is regarded to form part of a Salafi *isnād*.

However, Salafi *asānīd* are still characterised by the fact that they do not constitute 'unbroken chains' of transmission (of, for instance, *baraka*) from teacher to teacher and from scholar to scholar back to the times of the Prophet. And there is another difference: for Sufis, an unbroken *isnād* of authorities is not only an unbroken chain of teachers in a tradition of learning going back to the Prophet Muḥammad, it is also a chain of *dalāʾil* (guides) who transmit the blessing (*baraka*) of the Prophet and a specific and highly spiritual message that sanctifies all those who belong in the circle of the chosen few of such a tradition. As a consequence, rebellion among Sufis against established authorities is fairly problematic: such a rebellion is not just a rebellion against one specific authority but a rebellion against a whole tradition based on the blessings of the Prophet. Salafi-oriented reformers, by contrast, reject such chains of authority and blessing and seek to (re)define Islam on the basis of their own *ijtihād* of the key sources, that is, Qurʾān and the *sunnah* of the Prophet.

As a consequence, disputes among Salafi-oriented reformers are comparatively easy: their dissent is directed against human authority and not against a chain of blessing. This fact may help to explain processes of rapid fragmentation among Salafi-oriented movements of reform, as, for instance, in the case of the 'Yan Izala in northern Nigeria, which not only split into two competing organisations immediately after the death of Abubakar Gumi in 1992, but have also seen the development of numerous dissident groups since the 1980s, that is, even within the very first generation of organisational development. By contrast, conflict among Sufis who essentially accept *taqlīd* (that is, the 'respectful emulation of accepted authorities') and the importance of the *isnād* leading to the Prophet through a chain of venerable ancestors, is comparatively difficult: their dissent is directed against a tradition of learning and blessing. Yet, rupture happened, as in the case of Aḥmad al-Tijānī in the late eighteenth century, who tried to eclipse or bracket a long chain of authority by claiming to have gained a direct link to the Prophet. In addition to such radical breaks with an *isnād*, there is a series of cases of milder breaks with earlier authorities when young scholars rebel against the authority of the elders by rejecting authority in partial ways only: while still accepting the respective *isnād* and tradition of learning, young rebels reject, for instance, the political or social programme of their fathers, while accepting the programme (and spiritual legacy) of their grandfathers. Such a partial break has happened in the context of a number of splits within the Tijāniyya in sub-Saharan Africa in the twentieth century (Loimeier 2001: 120ff; 2010: 144ff).[45]

Following the partial failure of the *taqlīd-isnād* argument or the argument of the metaphorical or literalistic interpretation of texts, we could resume the search for ultimate epistemic criteria to differentiate Sufi- and Salafi-oriented reformers. On the other hand, we could also ask ourselves whether analytical categories such as Sufi- and Salafi-oriented reformers are just too general and should thus be abandoned altogether. But how would we then grasp religious movements that claim to be different, to be 'true Muslims', for instance? A way out of this dilemma could be to accept emic categories of symbolic and ritual distinction (such as *qabḍ* and *sadl* in sub-Saharan West Africa) and to respect, for the time being, emic categories of doctrinal qualification (such as *Salafī* and *Uṣūlī*). However, such an acceptance of emic qualifiers and emic categories of distinction should not lead us to overstretch the analytical power of such categories with respect to

- their rootedness in a local context: that is, even if valid in one local context, such categories must not be taken to be automatically valid for other local contexts,

- their situatedness in religious and/or political debates: that is, while emic categories such as *qabḍ* and *sadl* may allow us to distinguish between a clear-cut group of followers of *qabḍ* and an equally clear-cut group of followers of *sadl*, other religious or political debates may lead us to assume completely different social formations[46] and
- their boundedness in time (*Zeitgebundenheit*): that is, even if valid for a particular period of time, they should not be taken as being valid for all times.

As conflicts, societies and contexts change with time, so do emic categories of distinction. In our analysis we should follow such changes and revise our academic categories, if necessary, from time to time without reifying them: *qabḍ* and *sadl* were valid emic categories of distinction for many Muslims in sub-Saharan West Africa in the 1930s, 1940s and 1950s, but stopped being significant (or primary) qualifiers for conflict, even within the Tijāniyya, in the 1960s and 1970s. In addition, we have to consider that binary constructions of society dissolve into thin air not only when the local context of conflict changes, but also when we leave the local context of dispute, such as the *qabḍ-sadl* discussions in sub-Saharan West Africa, and try to gain a larger picture.

We usually then find that Muslim societies as a whole are characterised by a large spectrum of different positions on almost everything. Categorisations such as 'orthodox' or 'less orthodox' or even 'unorthodox', 'literalist', 'fundamentalist', 'moderate' or 'pietist' are consequently not only highly biased and often influenced by particularistic interests, but such categorisations also omit the fact that Muslims worldwide are rooted in multiple local traditions of Islam that produce their own categories of distinction. Such traditions of Islam are the result of specific historical dynamics. Interaction with local Christianities or with African (Indian, Southeast Asian) religions has further contributed to generating specific local practices of Islam. As a result, any tradition of Islam may appear to be particularly 'orthodox' or 'unorthodox' from the perspective of another tradition of Islam, or from the perspective of another age. This is not only true of Muslim societies in Africa, but also applies to those in Arabia, Turkey, Central Asia, Europe, India and Southeast Asia. In such diverse geographic, historical and social contexts, categories are necessarily relational, situational and time-bound. They may make sense for a certain period of time, but will most probably become obsolete sooner or later when the context changes. In the end, we will probably have to live with 'quotation marks' and the concluding words 'for the time being', as well as two problems: binary constructions of society in contexts of conflict, and an amazing array of ways of living Islam in the past, present and future.

Notes

1. In *Die Religion in Geschichte und Gesellschaft*, reform is broadly situated in the linguistic field of the terms 'renovare, innovare, restituere, instituere, regenerare, reviviscere, suscitare, resuscitare, surgere, renasci' (RGG 1986: 858–9) and is seen, in its strictest sense, as a 'return to a norm'.
2. For an extensive discussion of this question, see the article by ᶜAlī Merad (n.d.) in the *Encyclopaedia of Islam* (second edition).
3. I use the term 'activist' to denote an array of movements, ranging from extremely radical and even militant to moderate positions (in both religious and political terms). Muslim activist groups and organisations have a distinct religious, social and/or political agenda in society and (in contrast to piety-minded groups) try to propagate their message/cause (*daᶜwa*) and programme of reform in active ways, often, but not always, in opposition to existing regimes. In Western political analysis such groups have (sometimes misleadingly) been labelled *intégriste*, 'Islamist' or 'fundamentalist'. Such labels suffer from the fact that they usually exclude activist Sufi-oriented movements of reform.
4. Other terms in the semantic field of 'purification' that are often quoted by Salafi-oriented reformers are *taṣfiya* and *tazkiya*, as well as *taṣḥīḥ* (rectification).
5. The term 'programme' (*manhaj*) is not understood here in the narrow sense of the word (for example, a list of things that should be changed), but in a broad sense as a platform, a basic text (such as Sayyid Quṭb's *maᶜālim fi-l-ṭarīq* or Yūsuf al-Qaraḍāwī's *minhāj al-muslim*) and/or a social consensus that is informed by the will to achieve change. Such a programme of change may be based on an (idealised) projection of the past, but is aimed at the future. I would like to thank Anne Bang and Terje Østebø for comments on this definition.
6. Østebø (2008b: 418) has proposed a similar definition: 'As the name implies, the main object for any reform movement is to initiate change. This involves evaluative perceptions of the existent reality, a determined agenda and a strategy for change and reflections on an idealized future.'

7. Such understandings of reform that advocate a renewed understanding of the faith translate particularly well into Arabo-Muslim contexts, where reform is often presented as *tajdīd* (renewal) or *iṣlāḥ* (improvement). The Wahhābiyya of the eighteenth and twentieth centuries, the jamāᶜat al-tablīgh, the ahl i-ḥadīth and the nadwat al-ᶜulamāᵓ may be regarded as such movements of reform (see Masud 2000; Zaman 2002). Even a number of Sufi-oriented movements of reform did have such an orientation as, for instance, those linked with the teaching of Aḥmad b. Idrīs and the Sanūsiyya (see O'Fahey 1990; Triaud 1995).
8. John Voll takes such a position in his 'Renewal and Reform in Islamic History' (Voll 1983: 32–47).
9. When referring to the term 'religious tradition', I rely on Riesebrodt who has defined religions as 'concrete systems of practices that refer to supernatural forces and that are manifested in a "cult" as well as in a respective promise of salvation' (*Heilsversprechen*). He defines 'religious traditions' in a wider sense as 'cultural forms of life that include but also transcend religious practices' (Riesebrodt 2007: 13ff).
10. There is a vast body of literature on this issue. See, for instance, Braukämper (2004), Cuoq (1981), Faulkner (2006), Kaplan (1992) or Stauth (2005).
11. Activist and associationist groups in northern Nigeria such as the 'Muslim Brothers' of Ibrāhīm al-Zakzakī or the Daawa group of Amīnu d-Dīn Abūbakar have become famous for having switched, since the late 1970s, from Iranian to Saudi Arabian, to Kuwaiti, to Libyan and back to Iranian or Saudi Arabian sources of inspiration and funding, while cultivating, at the same time, a plethora of less conspicuous links with Sudan, Egypt, Malaysia and Pakistan, as well as the activist diaspora in Great Britain (Loimeier 1997a: 291ff).
12. An example of a virtual, imagined link is the case of ᶜAbd al-Muḥyī, a Javan scholar of the seventeenth century, who in his dreams established a trans-historical connection with the eleventh-century founder of the Qādiriyya, ᶜAbd al-Qādir al-Jīlānī (Kraus 2000: 298ff).
13. I am grateful to Réné Otayek for this remark. Manipulations or interpretations of traditions and texts are mostly confined to contexts of dispute, though. The instrumentalisation of trans-local, trans-historical, trans-traditional or trans-generational references for legitimatory aims is less visible in quotidian contexts.
14. Due to phenotypical similarities of religious movements, scholars of comparative religion such as Fritz Stolz, sociologists such as Pierre Bourdieu and historians such as Jürgen Osterhammel have accepted the basic possibility of trans-temporal

and trans-religious comparisons of religions and their movements of reform (see Bochinger 2003; Bourdieu 1970; Hodgson 1960; Osterhammel 2001; Stolz 1988). In principle, I follow Stolz and Osterhammel who have argued that the comparison of religions is possible because human beings and cultures have developed similar basic structures and strategies to solve specific problems on different continents and in different civilisations (Osterhammel 2001: 62; Stolz 1988: 182).

15. This is also true of trans-religious take-overs: the introduction of ecstatic *mawlid* celebrations in East Africa, especially the *maulidi ya hom*, which implied the use of drums and that was celebrated first in Brawa, Lamu and Zanzibar, cannot be interpreted as a Muslim reaction to Pentecostal services that are also characterised by ecstatic ritual and music. New forms of the *mawlid al-nabī* developed in the context of rivalries between different branches of the Qādiriyya and the ᶜAlawiyya since the mid-1880s, that is, eighty years before the first appearance of Pentecostal churches in East Africa, and must thus be seen as an internal Muslim development.
16. The term 'episteme' is not understood here in its literal sense, as 'knowledge' (*Wissen*, *Erkenntnis*, in contrast to a 'doxa', an opinion, a dogma), but in a wider sense, to include those aspects of the ritual and the religious sphere that are associated with a particular epistemic tradition, such as, in the case of the esoteric episteme, veneration of the Prophet, celebration of the *mawlid al-nabī* (the birthday of the Prophet), faith in saints and their baraka and their power to intercede, the allegoric interpretation of the Qurᵓān and a multitude of Sufi rituals, in particular the *dhikr*. For a discussion of different meanings of the term 'episteme' in the Malian context, see Brenner (2001: 17ff).
17. ᶜUmar ᶜIsā Sulaimān, a 'Yan Izala leader in Niger, quoted in Sounaye (2012a: 442). I have heard similar statements made by a number of Salafi-oriented scholars in the context of my own research in Senegal, northern Nigeria and Tanzania. This idea is supported by a number of verses in the Qurᵓān, such as 34: 4, which describe the Qurᵓān as a 'clear book' (*al-kitāb al-mubīn*), while being contradicted, for instance, by Qurᵓān 3: 7 on *clear* (categorical, *muḥkamāt*) and *unclear* (allegorical, *mutashābihāt*) revelations. Salafi-oriented scholars also point to sūra 12: 2 ('We have revealed the Qurᵓān in the Arabic tongue so that you may grow in understanding': *innā anzalnāhu qurᵓānān ᶜarabiyyan la-ᶜalakum taᶜaqiluna*).
18. Qurᵓān 3: 104 (and other verses) call on each Muslim to 'enjoin what is right and to forbid what is wrong' (*al-amr bi-l-maᶜrūf wa-l-nahy ᶜan al-munkar*). This

duty is a well-established principle in Islamic theology and has been discussed by religious scholars since the early days of Islam (see Cook 2000). A major issue in these discussions was always the question what defined and limited the individual duty to 'command right and to forbid wrong', such as being suitably qualified, putting oneself to rights before commanding others and taking care not to bring calamity upon oneself worse than the evil one was forbidding (Cook 2000: 43f).

19. I would like to thank Terje Østebø and Ismael Moya (both 7 March 2015) for empirical evidence regarding such piety-minded Muslims in both Senegal and Ethiopia.
20. On both al-Madkhālī and al-Albānī, see Lacroix (2009: 58ff); on their major source of inspiration, Muḥammad al-Shawkānī, see Haykel (2003); on the disputes between 'Quṭbīs' and 'Madkhālīs', see Gauvain (2013).
21. The term 'generation' is not understood here in its purely biological dimension. A generation of reform may comprise two or even more biological generations of reformers, if the issues of reform and the orientation of a movement of reform are not modified substantially. A shift to an epistemological new generation of reformers implies a significant break with an established episteme (see Mannheimer 1984; Fietze 2009).
22. For an analysis of Sufi-inspired dissidence, withdrawal and *jihād* in the context of early nineteenth-century Hausaland, see Last (2014).
23. For an extensive discussion of the concept of *al-walāʾ wa-l-barāʾa*, see Wagemakers (2009: 81ff; 2014: 70), and Meijer (2009: 10ff).
24. On the ideology of the jamāᶜat al-muslimīn, see Kogelmann (1994: 123ff). In the late 1960s, the jamāᶜat al-muslimīn led by Shukrī Muṣṭafā (b. 1942), propagated 'complete separation' (*al-mufāṣala al-kāmila*) from Egyptian ('*jāhilī*') society and started to live in caves in Upper Egypt (Hegghammer 2009: 246f).
25. For multiple ways of expressing dissent in the northern Nigerian context, see Last (2014: 39–50). Last specifically mentions mosques as venues of dissent, as well as rituals and the times of rituals as focal points of disputes. Last but not least, he mentions dress and body styles as symbolic markers of dissent.
26. Such dynamics were also at work in the context of movements of *jihād* in eighteenth- and nineteenth-century sub-Saharan Africa that were led by religious scholars who belonged to a Sufi order (Loimeier 2013: 108ff).
27. This notion was based on the assumption that a 'woman's voice can nullify an act of worship because it is capable of provoking sexual feeling in men' (Mahmood 2005: 65). This position was rejected by Yūsuf al-Qaraḍāwī on the

basis of Qurʾān 33: 32 (*fa-lā takhḍaʿna bi-l-qawlī*: 'and be not submissive when talking').

28. In a text titled *ḥijāb al-marʾa al-muslima*, Muḥammad Nāṣir al-Dīn al-Albānī has rejected the *niqāb* for women. His male supporters have equally rejected the *ʿiqāl*, the headband used to fasten the headcloth, the *ghuṭra* or *kūfiyya*. Al-Albānī's male followers have also started to wear their hair long, in the fashion of the Prophet (Lacroix 2009: 72).
29. The practice of keeping shoes on when entering a mosque for prayer has been defended prominently by Muḥammad Nāṣir al-Dīn al-Albānī in a text titled *ṣifāt ṣalāt al-nabī* ('attributes of the Prophet's prayer') (see Lacroix 2009: 63ff). On the historical development of the practice of shedding one's shoes when entering a mosque, see Lecker (1995).
30. On the concept of habitus, see Bourdieu (1982: 277ff).
31. Muslims who visit shrines to pray at the tombs of saints are polemically attacked as *qubūriyyūn* (grave worshippers) by Salafi-oriented Muslims (Haykel 2009: 41).
32. The critique of local burial rites was an issue for earlier Muslim reformers as well. Chapter 17 (pp. 130–47) in Usman dan Fodio's (d. 1817) *iḥyāʾ al-sunna wa-ikhmād al-bidʿa* is devoted to un-Islamic innovations in the context of burials (*maqābir*) and rites of burial and mourning (*janāʾiz*), including the custom of wailing (here: *bukāʾ*) that is criticised as a *bidʿa muḥarrama* (dan Fodio n.d.: 136).
33. The solemn recitation of the Qurʾān according to the rules for the recitation of the Qurʾān, especially the different *ḥarakāt* (speeds). The recitation of the Qurʾān and competition over memorisation (*ḥifẓ*) of the Qurʾān has seen a boom in sub-Saharan Africa in recent years. Today, Qurʾān recitation and memorisation tournaments have acquired showbiz character and are linked with considerable price monies as well as scandals. Thus, a four-year-old Tanzanian *ḥāfiẓ* of reputedly prodigious knowledge who toured sub-Saharan Africa in April and May 1999 was eventually unmasqued as a fraud (see Villalon 1999: 137).
34. *Qunūt* is a supplicatory prayer performed (by most adherents of the four Sunni schools of law) after the first (or the second *rakʿ*) of the *salāt al-fajr* and after *witr* prayers (in the *qiyām* position), but there have been debates about the question of whether *qunūt* should be prayed at all: while Ibāḍis reject *qunūt*, Ithnāʿsharis do *qunūt* during all of the five daily prayers. Members of Salafi-oriented groups often reject *qunūt* prayers (see Ware 2014: 230).

35. In Ramadan 2003, Muslims in Zanzibar discussed the question of whether *tarāwīḥ* prayers should have twenty *raka^{c}āt* (according to the Shāfi^{c}ī tradition) or only eight (as practised in the Ibāḍī tradition). Personal communication Masoud Ahmed Shani (6 August 2003) and ^{c}Umar Sheha (7 August 2003), confirmed by Muḥammad Haron for South Africa (15 April 2004) and Ḥassan Mwakimako for Kenya (10 March 2005).
36. In concrete terms, the Muwaṭṭa of Imām Mālik b. Anas, the basic text of the Māliki school of law, has the following references regarding the Sunna of the Prophet with respect to the sighting of the new moon (see Chapters 18: 1 and 20: 13, 14, 15 and 32): 'Yaḥyā transmitted from Mālik and Mālik from Nāfi^{c}, Nāfi^{c} from ^{c}Abdallāh and ^{c}Abdallāh from ^{c}Umar, that the messenger of God had said: "Do not start the fast, as long as you have not seen the new moon and do not stop the fast as long as you see the moon. If the moon is hidden, then do the calculation"' (18.1.1.). This *ḥadīth* has been accepted by both al-Bukhārī and Muslim on the authority of Abū Huraira who said: 'Start and stop fasting as soon as you see the new moon. And if the sky is clouded and a sighting of the new moon is not possible then complete the days in Sha^{c}bān until you arrive at thirty' (Ferchl: Ṣaḥīḥ al-Buḫārī, 233). The question of the sighting of the new moon in the case of a cloudy sky was discussed in a *fatwā* of the Muslim World League, the rābiṭa al-^{c}ālam al-Islāmī in 1981. This *fatwā* advised believers to 'follow the next Islamic town'.
37. The Saudi claim to hegemony of interpretation with respect to the sighting of the new moon has encountered opposition by scholars who argue that the *hilāl* is sighted first in the eastern parts of the Islamic oikumene, namely, Indonesia, and not in Saudi Arabia. Thus, the Indonesian sighting of the new moon should be acknowledged when stressing the importance of the universal unity of the *ummah* (van de Bruinhorst 2007: 224).
38. Such claims to religious hegemony and the corresponding will to condemn others may be quite radical. One day in Zanzibar, Mufaddal Karimji, the owner of the Hatimi Secretarial Services copy shop, and a proud Bohora, representing thus a religious community with about 700,000 believers worldwide, told me: 'Roman, let me tell you, all these Muslims that you study as a historian, they have left the true path and the true guidance, the *da^{c}wat al-hādiya*. The only Muslims who follow the *da^{c}wat al-hādiya*, are we, the Bohoras. All the others are unbelievers.'
39. Another issue of dispute within the Tijāniyya from the 1930s was the question of whether the prayer *jawharat al-kamāl*, which forms a central part of

the Tijānī *dhikr*, should be recited eleven or twelve times. The respective positions were expressed symbolically in Tijānī rosaries that contained either eleven or twelve beads for this section of the *dhikr* (see Hanretta 2009; Soares 2005a).

40. The question arises, however, of whether the duration and the intensity of a conflict and respective binary constructions of society depend on factors such as the degree of mobilisation and the number or weight of those who remain outside a context of conflict. See Baumann (2005: 18ff) and what he calls the 'ternary challenge'.
41. A representative of the Sudanese anṣār al-sunna al-muḥammadiyya quoted in Salomon (2013: 831).
42. Literally, the term *isnād* signifies support and in Islamic scholarship and history means a 'chain' of individual trustworthy transmitters who span the generations (Graham 1993: 502).
43. *Taqlīd* can be understood as a consensual precedent espoused by established religious authority as well as blind acceptance of religious authority (Haj 2009: 37). At the same time, *taqlīd* can mean the acceptance of legal procedure and adherence to a legal authority, a *madhhab* of an intelligent application of principles (Haj 2009: 81), that is, *taqlīd* is not always set in opposition to *ijtihād*: *taqlīd* can also be the result of *ijtihād* (communication Knut Vikør, 7 March 2015).
44. Equally, we can observe that even Salafi-oriented reformist scholars strive to multiply their *salāsil* and seek to acquire links with prestigious networks of Salafi-oriented scholarship, either by studying at a renowned institution (such as the Islamic University of Madinah) or by establishing contact with a respected scholar (such as ᶜAbdallāh Ṣāliḥ al-Farsy, with regard to the East African context).
45. In addition, there are the endeavours of scholars to shorten an *isnād* (of *ijāzāt*) to acquire a more direct link to the Prophet. Nasiru Kabara, the leader of the Qādiriyya in Kano since the late 1950s was particularly successful in such an endeavour when he visited the supreme shaykh of the Qādiriyya in Baghdad in the early 1950s, and acquired an *ijāza* from him, thus circumventing a number of intermediary authorities who had until then linked Qādirī scholars in northern Nigeria with Baghdad by way of Tunisian or Libyan shaykhs (Loimeier 1997a: 52ff).
46. If we were to establish, for instance, how many Muslims accept the *bāṭin* character of the Qurʾān (and equally accept doubt as far as the literal understanding

of the Qur'ān is concerned), and how many Muslims stick to the *ẓāhir* character of the Qur'ān, we would get quite a different idea of social formations within a Muslim society. See Bauer (2011) for an extensive discussion of the factor of doubt in Muslim religious debates.

3

REFORM IN CONTEXT I: SENEGAL (AND MALI)

In the following chapters, I will present the emergence and dynamics of Muslim movements of reform in their local and national contexts. I will start out with Senegal, where Sufi orders were largely able to maintain their social and religious influence in the twentieth century, and then contrast Senegal with Mali, where Sufi orders have been less prominent historically than in Senegal. I will continue with northern Nigeria, where one specific movement of reform, namely the jamāᶜat izālat al-bidᶜa wa-iqāmat al-sunna (Hausa: 'Yan Izala), was extremely successful as a social and religious movement. The northern Nigerian case study will be contrasted with Niger, where the development of the 'Yan Izala met a different local context. I will then proceed to a number of case studies, namely, Chad, Sudan, Ethiopia and Somalia, where different movements of reform, both within and beyond what Louis Brenner (2001: 7) has called the 'esoteric episteme', had different trajectories. Subsequently, I will discuss Tanganyika (since 1964 Tanzania) and Kenya, where neither Sufi orders nor Salafi-oriented movements of reform managed to gain the kind of social and political support they enjoyed in northern Nigeria or Senegal. I will conclude with Zanzibar and the Comoros, where specific local contexts stimulated the development of influential Salafi-oriented movements of reform in different ways. In each case study, I will focus on several modes of reform, beginning with different Sufi-oriented traditions of reform that developed in the late nineteenth and early twentieth century and were followed, often in a competitive manner, by more recent Salafi-oriented movements of reform. These Salafi-oriented movements of reform were characterised by their distantiation from the 'esoteric' paradigm, their activist and often confrontative approach to social, religious and political questions and their rejection of established authorities. Where possible, I will sketch the biographies of Salafi-oriented scholars and provide some background to their thinking.

Introduction

In the nineteenth century, Senegal witnessed the emergence of a distinct Sufi-oriented movement of reform that branched out into many different orientations in the twentieth century. These traditions of reform span several generations and include reformers who attempted to translate multiple colonial and post-colonial modernities in their own context, by adopting, among others, associationist forms of organisation and expression, while remaining true to Sufi modes of organisation and expression. It is important to note that each tradition of reform and its respective chain of reformers developed in constant interaction and dialogue with one another; 'associationist' and Salafi-oriented movements of reform have influenced Sufi-oriented movements of reform and vice versa.[1] Equally, the development of these traditions in Senegal was not only influenced by particular programmes of reform but also by the way in which the representatives of a specific generation of reformers articulated their position in relation to another tradition of reform and/or a preceding generation of reformers. Finally, it has to be kept in mind that many families of scholars in Senegal are related to one another in multiple ways. Thus, clear distinctions are often difficult and Salafi-oriented reformers are related to families of well-known Sufi scholars and vice versa: the influence of the Sufi orders on the development of Salafi-oriented reform movements is persistent (Gomez-Perez 1997: 287) and must thus be seen as a major, even if hidden, force. Thus, Senegal's development in the twentieth century was characterised by the emergence of an array of Muslim reformist orientations, both within and beyond the esoteric episteme. Yet, even if Salafi-oriented reformers have not been able to come close to the social, religious and economic importance of the established Sufi orders in Senegalese society, Salafi-oriented ideas of reform and modes of expression have been adopted by the Sufi orders. Salafi-oriented movements of reform, on the other hand, have accepted established rules of Senegal's civil society, despite some 'loud' protests against specific features of Senegal's social and political development, such as the *code de la famille.* The question thus arises of whether the multiplication of religious and political actors, the fragmentation of religious and political fields and the emergence of an array of activist Muslim movements and associations has produced new contexts for the negotiation of religion and politics.

Sufi Reform in the Nineteenth Century and Early Twentieth Century: From Jihād to Accommodation

In the nineteenth century, Senegal's political and social development was characterised by far-reaching processes of change connected with the rise of groundnut cultivation, the end of the slave trade and the corresponding fragmentation of political authority, along with increased instability and resistance to the rule of the established aristocracies. This situation stimulated the development of local *jihād* movements directed against established forms of rule labelled 'pagan' by Muslim scholars. Most leaders of Senegalo-Gambian *jihād* movements were linked with the Tijāniyya, a Sufi order that claimed spiritual superiority over all other Sufi orders. The best known Tijāni scholar and *jihād* leader in the Senegalo-Gambian region was al-Ḥājj ᶜUmar Taal (*c.* 1796–1864). Although he came from the Fuuta Tooro region in the Senegal River valley, he established his empire further east, in Kaarta and Segou, in contemporary Mali. Al-Ḥājj ᶜUmar recruited followers in Senegal, however, who either followed him east or supported his reform policies (and resistance against colonial expansion) in Senegal proper. Shaykh Mā Bā Jaxu ('Diakhou', 1809–67) was thus able to establish a small *imāmate* on the Gambia and Saloum rivers in 1860, which was capable of withstanding French military advances, while Shaykh Aḥmad Bā or 'Amadou Sexu' (Shaykh, d. 1875), another Tijāni *jihād* leader, established an *imāmate* in the Jolof region of central Senegal in 1869 (see Loimeier 2013).

The long wars against these *imāmates* disturbed French colonial policies considerably, and informed French views of seemingly rebellious religious scholars, such as Aḥmad (Amadou) Bamba (1850–1927). He refused to acknowledge French colonial authority by withdrawing into the wilderness of

Bawol in central Senegal in the 1890s. To prevent escalation, Aḥmad Bamba was imprisoned in 1895 and exiled to distant Gabon. His followers, the 'Murīds', tried to rescue their spiritual leader, eventually discovering a way to do so in the very set-up of the French colonial system: starting in 1848, France had granted French community status to four coastal settlements – St Louis, Gorée, Dakar and Rufisque – the Quatre Communes. This status implied equal political rights as French citizens for all residents of the Quatre Communes, including Muslims. Muslim citizens subsequently came to play a vital role in the political dynamics of the Quatre Communes, which were entitled to send one *député* to the French Parliament (Johnson 1991: 65ff). The candidates for this seat campaigned in the local electorate, a process that in the nineteenth century usually implied an *échange de services*[2] between candidates and prospective voters. This arrangement encouraged Murīd leaders such as Cheikh Ibra (Ibrāhīm) Fall, one of Aḥmad Bamba's first disciples, to use the money earned by Murīd farmers from groundnut cultivation to finance the electoral campaign of François Carpot, a *métis* candidate for the National Assembly, in exchange for Carpot's promise to do something, if elected, for Aḥmad Bamba's release from exile. Carpot indeed won the 1902 elections with Muslim support and kept his promise, enabling Aḥmad Bamba's return, first to Mauritania, in 1902, and then to Senegal, in 1907. His return was celebrated by the Murīds as a manifestation of Aḥmad Bamba's powers as a saint, even over non-Muslim France. Aḥmad Bamba realised, however, that times had changed and in 1912 accepted French rule over Muslims, asking his followers in a letter to tolerate French rule, which had brought peace, stability and equality to Senegal. This perspective on Franco-Murīd cooperation largely holds true for the Tijāniyya and the smaller Sufi orders in Senegal, the Qādiriyya and the Layènes.

Although linked by spiritual chains (*salāsil*) with the founder of the *ṭarīqa*, Aḥmad al-Tijānī (1737/8–1815), the Tijāniyya disintegrated in Senegal in the twentieth century into a number of competing branches and family networks that cultivated internal rivalries. Essentially, the Tijāniyya was represented by the Taal, Sy and Niass family branches, as well as a number of smaller families such as the Dème family in Sokone established by al-Ḥājj Ceerno (Thierno) Aḥmad Dème (1885–1973), the Sall family in Louga as established by al-Ḥājj ᶜAbbās Sall (1909–90) (Loimeier 2001:

403), the community of al-Ḥājj Muḥammad (Mamadou) Ceerno (Thierno) Seydou (Sayyid) Bā (*c.* 1900–80) in Madina Gounasse (Casamance) or the community of Cheikh Hamallāh and his disciple Yacouba Sylla in Soudan (Mali), Mauritania and Côte d'Ivoire (see Soares 2005a; Hanretta 2009), both of which represented, for some time at least, a walk-out option on the colonial state. The Tijānī community of Madina Gounass (approximately 85 km southwest of Tambacounda) was formed in 1936 and became famous for its self-isolation, a position often understood and described as a conscious distantiation from both the colonial and the post-colonial secular state, and thus, as a form of spatial segregation. After the death of the founder, Ceerno (that is, teacher) Muḥammad Sayyid Bā in 1980, who had come to Madina Gounass from the Fleuve region in northern Senegal, the community disintegrated into two fractions, one led by a son of Ceerno Muḥammad Sayyid Bā, Ceerno Aḥmad Tidiane Bā. The disintegration of the Madina Gounass community reflected not only a dispute over succession but also disputes over questions of political and social orientation, such as the end of politics of isolation and the question of how to deal with state development politics. In addition, there was a conflict between local FulBe adherents of the community and immigrant Tukulóór, as well as other trans-regional issues, such as Madina Gounass' increasing importance as a centre of regional and trans-border smuggling activities between Senegal, The Gambia and Guinea-Bissau (Smith 2008: 29; van Hoven 1999: 25). In contrast to the role played by Tijāni scholars in the *jihād* movements of the nineteenth century and communities such as Madina Gounasse, most Tijānī families became collaborators of the colonial government in the twentieth century. This was particularly true for the family of al-Ḥājj ʿUmar Taal, and his grandson Seydou Nourou Taal, who was regarded by the French colonial administration as an *africain sûr* (Johnson 1991: 183) and who, in the context of his journeys through French West Africa, contributed to the acceptance of French colonial rule.

A second major Tijāni family was represented by al-Ḥājj Malik Sy (1855–1922) in Tivaouane, the first prominent scholar of the Tijāniyya to support French colonial rule publicly, in 1912, in a statement similar to that of Aḥmad Bamba, proclaiming France a government 'blessed by God' (Robinson 1993: 189). In contrast to the Murīds and the Niass family, Sy economic activities did not focus on groundnut cultivation so much as on commerce. Traders, entrepreneurs and notables subsequently became the major clientele of the Sy network. This legacy was continued by al-Ḥājj Malik Sy's successors, especially Abūbakar Sy (1890–1957) and ᶜAbd al-ᶜAzīz Sy (1905–97), who managed to transform the Sy branch of the Tijāniyya into the most prominent urban Sufi movement in Dakar and the greater Cap Vert region.

The Niass branch of the Tijāniyya, based in Kaolack, developed a different approach to colonial rule that was characterised by greater caution, although never going so far as to advocate active opposition to French rule. ᶜAbdallāh Niass (1845–1922), the founder of this branch of the Tijāniyya, developed groundnut production in the Saloum area on a scale comparable to Murīd cultivation projects in Bawol, which earned him the respect of the French colonial administration. His successors, Muḥammad Niass (1881–1959) and Ibrāhīm Niass (1900–75), continued along these lines, contributing to the transformation of the Saloum region into a major zone of groundnut cultivation. Ibrāhīm Niass, who had provoked a first split within the family in 1930 by refusing to accept the authority of his elder brother,[3] became an opponent of colonial rule for a short period, and even joined a group of dissident Murīd sheikhs and Salafi-oriented reformers who demanded immediate independence in 1958, only to return to moderate positions when their endeavours misfired (see Gray 1988).

Senegal thus saw the emergence of a system of 'exchange of services' between the French colonial administration and the Sufi orders from the early colonial period. This system of 'exchange of services' not only cemented the paramount role of religious leaders in the political and economic life of the country, but was also an important factor for Senegal's stability in colonial and post-colonial times, when social and political changes such as independence were negotiated, and not achieved by armed struggle, as for instance in Algeria. Due to the paramount role of marabouts in Senegalese politics and social life, Salafi-oriented reformist scholars such as Cheikh Touré and movements that criticised the collaboration of the marabouts with the colonial system, such as the Union Culturelle Musulmane (UCM), founded by Cheikh Touré, never had a real chance to acquire popular support on the scale of the Sufi orders. As such, the *contrât social sénégalais* (Cruise O'Brien 1992: 9) has to be seen as a rather unique development within the French colonial realm. Although relationships based on an 'exchange of services' also developed in other French colonial territories, such as Soudan (Mali), Niger, Ivory Coast and Guinea, Sufi orders never acquired the same paramount religious, political, social and economic role as in Senegal.

When looking at the question of what reform actually meant in concrete terms for the first generation of Sufi-oriented reformers, two major aspects of Sufi-driven reform can be identified: education and ritual. In religious terms, the leaders of both the Murīdiyya and the Tijāniyya stressed respect for Islamic legal norms in everyday life and the importance of Islamic law as an ethical principle. The writings of Aḥmad Bamba were manuals for teaching the principles of Islamic law, in particular the ritual and the *ᶜibādāt*, as well as Sufism, to a largely ignorant Muslim rural population. In addition, some leaders of the Murīdiyya and Tijāniyya stressed specific ritual aspects: while Ibrāhīm Niass introduced *qabḍ* instead of *sadl* as a ritual identifier and as a symbolic distinction for his reform endeavours, the Murīdiyya became famous for their practices of *qaṣīda*-recitation in recitation circles (*dāʾira*). In their self-perception, Senegal's Sufi-oriented reformers made a conscious break with pre-Islamic religious practices that were still a dominant feature of Muslim societiy in Senegal in the late nineteenth century (see Babou 2007). At the same time, the development of Sufi-oriented movements of reform was characterised by disputes over leadership and hegemony of interpretation that could acquire a transnational character.

When Ibrāhīm Niass, a leader of the Niass branch of the Tijāniyya in Kaolack, claimed in the 1930s to be the supreme Sufi saint, the *ghawth al-zamān* ('succour of the age'), he was attacked not only by his own family as represented by his brother Muḥammad Niass, but also by leading scholars of the Qādiriyya in northern Nigeria. The leaders of the Qādiriyya rejected Ibrāhīm Niass' claim to spiritual supremacy as false on account of his well-known 'love for money' and accused him of just being a 'successful farmer'. In the debate that ensued between the Tijāniyya and Qādiriyya, Abūbakar Atiku, a Tijāni scholar from Kano, took up Ibrāhīm Niass' defence by arguing that the *ghawth al-zamān* always assumes the character of his time (Tahir 1975: 515): a *ghawth* was not defined by specific behavioural features or his *zuhd* (ascetism), a conventional measure of a man's piety. Rather, the veracity of his claim was demonstrated by his material success, a measurement of success more commensurate with contemporary times: the greater his wealth, the greater would be his *baraka*. The major argument in this dispute, namely, that saints assume the character of their times, can be translated into the larger context of movements of reform in Muslim societies in Senegal (and beyond) so far as movements of reform always assume the character of their times.

Struggles over questions of succession and leadership were informed by 'dialectics of positioning' within the different maraboutic families (Villalon 1999: 134). These dialectics of positioning used religious, social and political issues to negotiate between marabouts, the maraboutic clientele and the colonial administration, and often became paramount in the context of disputes over succession in the leadership of a specific maraboutic family. Muhammad Niass' (d. 1959) succession to ᶜAbdallāh Niass (d. 1922) was thus opposed by Ibrāhīm Niass (d. 1975), while Manṣūr Sy's (d. 1957) and later, ᶜAbd al-ᶜAzīz Sy's (d. 1997) succession to Abūbakar Sy (d. 1957) was opposed by Cheikh Tidiane Sy (Samson 2005: 146–54). Within the Murīdiyya, Muḥammad Muṣṭafā Mbakke's (d. 1945) succession to Aḥmad Bamba was opposed by Cheikh Anta Mbakke (d. 1941), while Falilou Mbakke's (d. 1968) succession to Muḥammad Muṣṭafā was opposed by Cheikh Aḥmad Mbakke Gainde Fatma (d. 1978). In the context of internal rivalries and other matters of dispute, such as dislike of Senegal's first president, L. S. Senghor, or support for Senegal's struggle for independence, some of these marabouts were even willing to cooperate with the Salafi-oriented UCM. This shows that Sufi orders did not form monolithic blocks but were divided by internal fissures (see Cruise O'Brien 1971; Behrman 1970).

Cheikh Tidiane Sy's aborted succession to his father, Abūbakar Sy, in 1957, attests to the longevity of family disputes in Senegal (and beyond) over several generations and their religious and political implications. Cheikh Tidiane Sy (b. 1925) was the son of the second Khalifa Général of the Sy branch of the Tijāniyya, Abūbakar Sy (d. 1957), through al-Ḥājj Mālik Sy's first wife, Rokhaya N'Diaye and Abūbakar Sy's third wife, Astou Kane. Abūbakar Sy, however, had two half-brothers, Manṣūr (d. 1957) and ᶜAbd al-ᶜAzīz (d. 1997), by a different mother, namely Safiétou Niang, al-Ḥājj Mālik Sy's second wife, who had come to dominate the house of the family in Tivaouane. In the dispute over the succession to Abūbakar Sy in 1957, first Manṣūr and then ᶜAbd al-ᶜAzīz managed to divert succession away from the direct patrilineage, that is, from Abūbakar Sy to his son Cheikh Tidiane Sy, and established the dominance of the Niang branch of the Sy family as against the N'Diaye branch. In order to show his protest, Cheikh Tidiane Sy introduced a different date for the Gammu, the annual family pilgrimage to Tivaouane in the late 1950s, and he was willing to cooperate with Cheikh Touré and the UCM in order to fight the second branch of the family in both religio-symbolic as well as political terms.[4] The family dispute within the Sy branch of the Tijāniyya has continued since and is today in the hands of the third generation of sons, grandsons, nephews, great-grandsons and grand-nephews of al-Ḥājj Mālik Sy. Thus, Cheikh Tidiane Sy and Sérigne Muṣṭafā Sy currently represent the N'Diaye branch of the family, while Manṣūr Sy (1925–2012), a son of ᶜAbd al-ᶜAzīz Sy and his successor as the Khalifa Général of the Sy family, has represented the Niang branch since 1997. Manṣūr Sy's death in 2012 and the fact that he was followed by Cheikh Tidiane Sy, the leading representative of the N'Diaye branch, may be read as an indication that this old family dispute has been resolved. This dispute shows, however, that politics (of reform) may be subordinated in substantial ways to family history and that political and/or religious disputes may mask other agendas.

The Origins of the Salafi-oriented Movement of Reform

The emergence of a Salafi-oriented tradition of reform in Senegal is usually associated with Cheikh Touré and the UCM (Arab. al-ittiḥād al-thaqāfī al-islāmī (ITI)), and, to a lesser degree, the ḥarakat al-falāḥ (HF). Salafi-oriented ideas of reform and modes of organisation are much older, though, and go back to the mid-nineteenth century, namely, the Muslim civil rights movement in the Quatre Communes of St Louis, Gorée, Dakar and Rufisque. This Muslim civil rights movement fought for public recognition of Muslim norms, customs and rites, and the use of Islamic personal (family) law in courts of law. It was connected with the activities of Muslim intellectuals and scholars such as Aḥmad Ndiaye Hann, Muḥammad Seck and Ndiaye Sarr (Loimeier 2001: 90). These *ᶜulamāʾ*-citoyens (scholar-citizens) were the first to cultivate what David Robinson has called 'paths of accommodation' (Robinson 2000), seeking a modus vivendi with French colonial rule by agreeing to work within the institutional parameters as established and defined by the French colonial administration, in particular, tribunaux musulmans and écoles franco-arabes.

In the early twentieth century, the Muslim civil rights movement in the Quatre Communes acquired a new character and developed the typical features of modern French political associations. These associational forms of organisation were not only better suited for translating Muslim aspirations in the colonial context, but they were also close to French conceptions of organisation and thus easily identifiable for French colonial administrators as 'modern' religio-political movements. In order to improve the conditions of the *ḥajj*, a Union Fraternelle des Pèlerins Musulmans de l'A.O.F was established, for instance, in 1922, followed by many other pilgrims' associations. In 1936, the French colonial administration estimated the number of these associations to be more than fifty in Dakar alone (Loimeier 2001: 168). Most of them were confined to urban areas, however, and fought for limited goals, such as the improvement of the pilgrimage, Islamic personal law or a distinctive Muslim code of dress. In addition, these associations, and in particular their leaders, were still affiliated with a Sufi order, mostly the Tijāniyya (Loimeier 2001: 168). The vanguard of this new form of organisation was the liwāʾ taʾakhi al-muslim al-ṣāliḥ (Brigade de la Fraternité du Bon Musulman, or Fraternité Musulmane (FM)), established in 1934 by ᶜAbd al-Qādir Fall and ᶜAbd al-Qādir Diagne, which started to campaign for a more encompassing programme of reform, such as modern concepts of Islamic education. The dynamic growth of Muslim associations was seen with some misgivings by the French authorities, though: France wanted to remain in control of this development and the FM was not granted official recognition (Gomez-Perez 1997: 57). In 1941, at the onset of the Vichy regime in Senegal, ᶜAbd al-Qādir Diagne (b. 1900), who had been president of the FM since 1934, was even sentenced to two years of imprisonment for being 'a risk for the external security of the State' (Gomez-Perez 1997: 109). After his release in 1942, Diagne and the FM continued their struggle against 'obsolete' social practices (see Gomez-Perez 1991; 1997: 111).

The establishment of the UCM in 1953 under the leadership of Cheikh Touré[5] may thus be seen as a watershed in the development of Salafi-oriented reformist organisations in Senegal insofar as it was the first organisation to develop an encompassing programme of reform that had a distinctively anti-Sufi character. The UCM had a much more encompassing programme of reform than the urban associations of the 1920s and the 1930s and was characterised by its rejection of the Sufi orders and their practices of maraboutage as well as popular ritual and customs. The UCM specifically attacked the leaders of the Tijāniyya and Murīdiyya for their collaboration with the colonial power. Equally, the UCM demanded immediate independence, which was again a reaction against the moderate positions of the leading marabouts, who, with the exception of Ibrahim Niass (d. 1975) and Cheikh Aḥmad Mbakke (d. 1978), supported French temporal schedules regarding independence. The UCM's programme of reform has influenced all subsequent movements of reform in Senegal and has exerted considerable influence on Muslim movements of reform in neighbouring countries, in particular, Mali, Ivory Coast and Burkina Faso.

A Biography: Cheikh Toure and the UCM

Cheikh Touré was born in July 1925 in Fass Touré in the region of Louga. His father Muḥammad Touré belonged to a family of well-known religious scholars linked with the Tijāniyya. In Fass Touré he directed a qurʾānic school. Both village and school had been established by Cheikh Touré's great-grandfather, Cheikh Sidi (Sayyid) Cissé Touré, in 1894. Until his nineteenth birthday, Cheikh Touré lived in Fass Touré and studied the Qurʾān with his uncle Hady Touré. At the age of ten he recited the Qurʾān by heart. At the same time, he studied Arabic, *kalām*, *māliki fiqh*, *sīra* and *ḥadīth* (communication Cheikh Touré, 13 April 1992). In Fass Touré, Cheikh Touré also experienced the system of maraboutage, which he described in his own words as 'there was a marabout who was regarded as being a little god to whom one did not dare to ask questions, while his students behaved like sheep with respect to him' (quoted in *Le Musulman*, No. 26, 1989). In contrast to other families of the Tijāniyya in Senegal, the Touré family never practised the system of maraboutage, the complete submission of the students to the authority of their teachers. The Touré family was thus regarded by other prominent Tijānī families as 'dissident' (Cheikh Touré in *Le Musulman*, No. 26, 1989).

In 1944, Cheikh Touré left Fass Touré and went to St Louis, Senegal's administrative centre, where he continued his studies in a number of Islamic schools. Among others, he studied with a Mauritanian scholar, Mukhtār uld Ḥamidūn, an influential scholar of the Tijāniyya who worked for the Institut Français de l'Afrique Noire (IFAN). Mukhtār uld Ḥamidūn introduced Cheikh Touré to the writings of Muḥammad ᶜAbduh and other Salafī thinkers and he gave him access to old issues of the first Salafi-oriented journal in the Arab world, *al-ᶜurwa al-wuthqā*. In St Louis, Cheikh Touré also heard for the first time of the existence of Muslim reformist organisations in Senegal, in particular, the FM. In 1949, Cheikh Touré stayed for a short period of time at the Institut d'Études Islamiques in Boutlimit in Mauritania, where he received his *brevet d'études franco-arabes*. After his return from Boutlimit, he again lived in St Louis and established his first *école arabo-islamique*. In addition, he became secretary of the Saint Louis section of the FM (Gomez-Perez 1997: 126–7). In 1952, he shifted his activities to Dakar, the capital city of French West Africa. In Dakar, he came in contact with a number of Senegalese politicians, such as Lamine Gueye, the mayor of Dakar, who represented the interests of Muslims in their struggle against French colonialism. Lamine Gueye was also able to organise six grants for Senegalese students in Algeria. Among the six students were Cheikh Touré and Alioune Diouf,[6] who became the first president of the jamāᶜat ᶜibād al-raḥmān (JIR), Senegal's most influential Salafi-oriented organisation from the 1980s (communication Cheikh Touré, 27 March 1993). Other members of the group were Sérigne Same Mbaye, Amadou Baky Dia, Diaware Ndiaye and Cheikh Tidiane Ba.

Although these study grants were cancelled by Leopold Sédar Senghor, at that time the president of the Commission d'Éducation de l'Assemblée Territoriale du Senegal (Gomez-Perez 1997: 130), under French pressure, the six Senegalese students were eventually invited to Algeria by Algeria's major reformist organisation, the Association des Ulémas Musulmans Algériens (AUMA) (jamāᶜat al-ᶜulamāᵓ al-muslimīn al-jazāᵓiriyīn) (see Merad 1967), to study at the Institut Bin Bādīs in Constantine. The trip to Algeria, which took place in 1952/3, informed Cheikh Touré's thinking decisively as he came in contact not only with a number of Algeria's Salafi-oriented scholars, such as Abū l-Qāsim al-ᶜArabī al-Tebessī, but also with the ideas of Rashīd Riḍā, Ḥasan al-Bannā and Sayyid Quṭb (communication Cheikh Touré,

13 April 1992; Kane 2005: 2). At the Institute Bin Bādīs in Constantine, Cheikh Touré witnessed the efforts of the AUMA to reform Algerian society. These efforts of reform had not only weakened the social role of the Algerian Sufi orders that had already been discredited due to their cooperation with the French colonial administration, but had also brought about the establishment of a network of Salafi-oriented schools that constituted one of the backbones of the Algerian struggle for liberation after 1954.

After his return to Senegal in March 1953, Cheikh Touré established a new organisation, the UCM (communication Cheikh Touré, 27 March 1993), together with Saliou Kandji[7] and Muḥammad Cissé, on 6 September 1953. Other rebels such as Amadou Ka, Thierno Diallo, Alioune Diouf, Djogo Doro, Mustafa Thiam, Sidya Mbaye, Mame Bara Mbakke, Mane Cissé, Omar Hady Dieng, Assane Fall, Bachirou Ly,[8] Mamadou Ka, Makhtar Thiam and Ousmane Diop joined later and took part in the first general meeting in late 1954 (Gomez-Perez 1997: 128). Cheikh Touré's split from the FM and the foundation of the UCM after his return from Algeria may be explained by the fact that in this period of time the FM had drifted into a generational conflict over questions of leadership between its founding fathers, such as ᶜAbd al-Qādir Diagne who represented moderate political positions, and a group of young scholars such as Cheikh Touré (Gomez-Perez 1997: 126f). In concrete terms, Diagne supported a reformist education programme (an *école experimentale*) developed with French support by Amadou Hampaté Ba and ᶜAbd al-Wahhāb Doukouré in Bamako, Mali (see below), and he argued publicly against *études arabes* as part of the French-sponsored programme of médersa-building, while Cheikh Touré supported an arabophone orientation (Gomez-Perez 1997: 126).

The new organisation soon started to build Franco-Arab schools in Dakar, Thiès, St Louis and Kaolack. In 1962, the UCM already had twenty-eight schools in Senegal: ten in Thiès, six in St Louis, three in Dakar, two in Rufisque, two in Louga and one each in Coki, Khombole, Bambey, Mbacke and Touba (Gomez-Perez 1997: 211). The building of mosques and schools has been of utmost importance for the development of the UCM (and later, the JIR) and underlined its efforts to insist on social separation from the polluting government schools as well as the qurᵓānic schools of the marabouts. At the same time, the UCM propagated the theatre as a new form of expression of religious and political thought in Senegal. The UCM in fact set up a Muslim theatre group and performed plays such as *L'heure de la verité* and *Le cadeau politique* that attacked the collaboration between marabouts and colonial administration. As these plays were performed in Wolof, they attracted considerable audiences (Loimeier 2001: 183). Equally, the UCM established Senegal's first Salafi-oriented journal, *Le réveil islamique*. In the 1950s, Cheikh Touré and *Le réveil islamique* became famous for their anti-Sufi and anti-colonial agitation, as summarised in Cheikh Touré's programmatic text *Afin que tu deviennes croyant* (published in 1957; for an analysis see Loimeier 2001: 192–200). The UCM's use of these modern mass media indicates that it sought to sever links with the local esoteric tradition and its leadership who ruled through personal networks and maintained authority through genealogical ties and personal charisma. The new forms of expression cultivated by the UCM also show that the UCM was trying to woo the urban and Western-educated Muslim populations that started to grow in size in the 1950s.

In December 1957, the first federal congress of the UCM took place in Dakar, and attested to the spread of the UCM beyond Senegal to Guinea, Ivory Coast, Haute-Volta (today's Burkina Faso), Mali and Ghana. Cheikh Touré was elected federal president, while Bachirou Ly replaced Cheikh Touré in 1958 as the president of the Senegalese section of the UCM. From 1958, Bachirou Ly took the political initiative, while Cheikh Touré focused on regional and international issues. Bachirou Ly was followed as president of the Senegalese section by Alioune Diouf (1960–4), was again in office from 1964–78, to be followed finally by Iyane Thiam (since 1978), who not only was a member of the Niass family, but was also related to the Sy family (Gomez-Perez 1997: 213). In these years, the UCM cultivated a religio-political discourse that was not only critical of the French colonial administration policies but also attacked the Senegalese Sufi orders, especially those marabouts who cooperated with the colonial administration. Polemics against alleged acts of *bid^{c}a makrūha* (reprehensible innovation), such as excessive spending on marriage ceremonies and burials, the practice of the *dhikr* and specific features of local ritual practices such as the wearing of 'gris-gris' (amulets), became another important element of the UCM's public discourse. In these ways, the UCM represented the first tradition of reform in Senegal that turned against the 'esoteric episteme' and thus symbolised an 'anti-iconic turn'.

Yet, when taking a closer look at Cheikh Touré and the programme of the UCM, we discover that neither Cheikh Touré nor the UCM categorically refused to cooperate with the (colonial) state or condemned Sufism as a whole. Thus, Cheikh Touré, who followed the career of a typical *ᶜālim*, never relinquished his links with the Tijāniyya. In a personal communication he maintained that 'concerning my affiliation with the Tijāniyya, I never really renounced it, neither in the 1950s, nor earlier, or later. It is only that my numerous activities have prevented me from practising the ritual regularly'.[9] Although the UCM took up some of the issues of the Algerian reformers and cultivated an anti-*ṭarīqa* as well as an anti-colonial discourse, as may be gleaned, for instance, from Cheikh Touré's, *Afin que tu deviennes un croyant*, the UCM also cooperated with marabouts such as Ibrāhīm Niass or Cheikh Aḥmad Mbakke who were known for their critical positions towards the colonial administration.

Cheikh Touré and his followers were also prepared to work with the state, when specific issues of reform such as the struggle against obsolete social and religious customs could be linked with state policies of reform. Thus, the UCM was closely affiliated with the Mamadou Dia wing of the Union Progressiste Sénégalaise (UPS). Mamadou Dia rose to political power after 1958 as Prime Minister of Senegal and advocated reforms that were at least in part inspired by the programme of the UCM. Among others, he advocated the reform of Islam and fought against the dominant role of the marabouts. He essentially wanted to create a secular state inspired by Islamic law and morals (Diouf 2013b: 17). As a consequence, both Tijānī and Murīd marabouts supported Senghor's deposition of Prime Minister Mamadou Dia in late 1962. This led to the demise of Dia's programme of structural reforms, which may have broken the power of the marabouts, as Sekou Touré's reforms did in Guinea in the late 1950s.[10] From 1962, Senghor could thus rely on an alliance with the 'grands marabouts' such as Falilu Mbakke and was subsequently able to domesticate the UCM. However, Cheikh Touré, who had become Chef de la section de presse arabe in the Ministry of Information under Mamadou Dia, was allowed to keep this position until he retired in 1980 (Loimeier 1994b: 61). Salafi-oriented reformers supported the development strategies propagated by colonial or postcolonial administrations, in particular, when these strategies were presented as a kind of Islamic state reformism. Such Islamic state reformism was characterised by its modernising orientation, as for instance in Mamadou Dia's development policies in Senegal in the early 1960s, and was often directed against established religious scholars, in particular the marabouts of the Sufi orders (see Dia 1985). Still, the majority of the demands of the UCM such as the reorganisation of the pilgrimage were rejected by the administration at that time and the UCM became 'une sorte de syndicat pour arabisants en quête de statut' (Gomez-Perez 1997: 197).

From 1958, the year when Senegal achieved political autonomy, the UCM was increasingly haunted by political splits that were associated with divisions in Senegalese politics. In the context of the 1958 referendum, Cheikh Touré and the UCM supported the 'no' campaign against the foundation of a Communauté Franco-Africaine and demanded immediate independence, a demand that was defeated in the referendum. While some UCM members sympathised with the Union Progressiste Sénégalaise (UPS), led by Mamadou Dia and Leopold Sédar Senghor, others sided with Senghor's major rival, Lamine Gueye, or even the Marxist Parti Africain de l'Indépendence (PAI) (Gomez-Perez 1997: 203). These internal disputes were possibly linked with an offer to the UCM by Mamadou Dia to assume a position in Dia's cabinet. Although this position had been offered to the UCM as such and not to an individual, Cheikh Touré seems to have claimed this position for himself personally without having discussed the matter with the UCM leadership (Gomez-Perez 1997: 206).

The Jamāᶜat ᶜIbād al-Raḥmān (JIR) and the Ḥarakat al-Falāḥ (HF)

In the 1960s and 1970s, Salafi-oriented organisations such as the UCM were domesticated by the state and were incorporated into state-controlled associations such as the Fédération des Associations Islamiques du Sénégal (FAIS). Associations such as FAIS were controlled by young marabouts of the Tijāniyya and Murīdiyya who were closely associated with the ruling party, Senghor's UPS. In this period of time, loyalist Muslim civil servants came to dominate both Muslim and state-informed developmentalist discourses. As a result, leading members of Sufi orders, such as the late Khalifa Général of the Sy-branch of the Tijāniyya, ᶜAbd al-Azīz Sy (d. 1997), labelled Muslim reformers who came to support these state-informed policies of reform as 'Islamologues fonctionnariés', as Islamists in the pay of the state (ᶜAbd al-ᶜAzīz Sy, in: *Wal Fadjri*, No. 258, 25 April 1991; see also Fall 1993: 197ff). Only in the late 1970s were Muslim activists able to free themselves of state control and to establish new and independent organisations, such as the jamāᶜat ᶜibād al-raḥmān (JIR) or the ḥarakat al-falāḥ li-l-thaqāfat al-islāmiyya (HF) (Gomez-Perez 1994: 79ff).

The time from 1962 to 1977, when Muslim opposition became possible again, was characterised by Cheikh Touré as 'une sorte de traverse du désert' (Loimeier 1994b: 62). The first protest against 'the Islam of the functionaries' ('L'Islam des fonctionnaires') was voiced by Sidi Khaly Lô, the future president of the JIR, in October 1974, in the context of elections for the members of the bureau of the FAIS, when he accused the nomenclatura of these loyalist organisations, including the UCM, of being agents of the state. After October 1974, the UCM rebels and Cheikh Touré started to regroup as the young members of the Fraternité Musulmane had done in the early 1950s, before establishing the UCM. The young activists united in the Thiès office of the UCM called for a new UCM strategy (Gomez-Perez 1997: 243). The process of re-formation intensified in 1976 in the context of a *semaine culturelle* in honour of Aḥmad Bamba. In 1977, the UCM section at Thiès, now controlled by the young activists, refused to take part in a similar *semaine culturelle* in honour of Leopold Sédar Senghor. Yet the impending split of the UCM was not simply a generational conflict: some older members of the UCM, such as Cheikh Touré and Alioune Diouf, participated in the rebellion of the young members, while others, such as Bachirou Ly, Oumar Dieng, Saliou Kandji and Iyane Thiam, who continued to lead an increasingly inactive UCM, maintained their loyalist position and prepared to exclude the dissident group (Gomez-Perez 1997: 252ff). In this context of internal disputes, the Thiès section of the UCM eventually split from the mother organisation, expressing broad dissatisfaction with government policies in the 1970s, and support for government policies by Muslim loyalist organisations such as the UCM (Gomez-Perez 1997: 256): 'In order not to be compromised, we left the UCM. Thus, the jamāᶜat ᶜibād al-raḥmān came into being. It was a reaction to the treason [committed by the majority of the UCM]' (Cheikh Touré in *Le Musulman*, No. 27, 1989). The JIR, better known in Senegal under the name 'Ibadou', has been variously labelled reformist, islamist, 'fundamentalist', 'integrist' or salafist (Seck 2010: 42).

The JIR was formally established in Thiès on 7 January 1978, and on 8 February 1978 Alioune Diouf, an old friend of Cheikh Touré, was elected the first 'guide' of the JIR. The chairperson of the first congress of the JIR was Cheikh Touré (Gomez-Perez 1997: 263). The organisation was officially recognised by *récipissé no. 3470* published in the 'Bulletin d'État' of 24 March 1979 (*Le Musulman*, No. 37, 1990). Alioune Diouf led the JIR until 1983 and was succeeded by Bamba Ndiaye (communication Cheikh Touré, 27 March 1993). In 1979, a new Muslim oppositional journal, *Études Islamiques*, which saw forty editions up to 1990, was also established, inspired again by Cheikh Touré, to be followed by *Le Musulman* (published in French with a version in Arabic – *al-Muslim*), JIR's most important journal to this day. In the 1980s, Cheikh Touré established his own centre, the Centre Islamique Sérigne Hady Touré, in the Liberté III quarter of Dakar, which became an Islamic information centre and a school where Cheikh Touré taught tafsīr (communication Cheikh Touré, 13 April 1992). Despite Cheikh Touré's polemics against the marabouts and a series of Sufi practices in the 1950s and early 1960s, Cheikh Touré slowly changed his radical positions and abandoned anti-Sufi polemics in the 1980s. By the 1990s, Cheikh Touré had become a widely respected scholar even beyond Salafi-oriented circles. He passed away on 28 September 2005, mourned as an outstanding Muslim scholar who had considerably informed the development of Senegal's religious field for a period of more than fifty years.

In 1989, Sidi Khali Lô took over the leadership of the organisation as president (*amīr*), assisted by Muhammad Sall, who was elected Secretary General in 1981 and who also acted as *inspecteur de l'enseignement* of the JIR. The headquarters of the JIR was the Markaz Bilāl in Thiès. In 1991, the Executive Committee of the JIR had a total of fifteen members (*Le Soleil*, 9 February 1991). Since 1987, the JIR has been closely linked with the World Association of Muslim Youth (WAMY) and in 1993, Sidi Khaly Lô, the *amīr* of the JIR, even became the regional representative of WAMY West Africa. In 1994 he was replaced as *amīr* of the JIR by Malick Ndiaye (Gomez-Perez 2005: 217), who has recently been replaced by Cheikh Tidiane Fall. Since 1994, JIR has become more accomodatating with respect to its relationship with the Senegalese state: Muḥammad Mustafa Wane became a member of the Commission Technique National de l'Éducation, while Serigne Babou and Marietou Dieng were appointed members of the Commision du Pèlerinage in 2002:[11] JIR has thus been subject to a process of 'domestication' like numerous other Islamic associations and organisations before it (Gomez-Perez 2005: 219).[12]

Since the early 1980s, the JIR has spread nationwide (Seck 2010: 141; Cantone 2012: 294). Its administrative centre, directed by Muhammad Sall,[13] remained in Thiès and was not transferred to Dakar. The national expansion of the movement has been expressed in three ways: the building of mosques, the proliferation of 'reformist' schools (écoles franco-arabes) and the spread of the *ḥijāb* among women. The building of mosques and schools as well as hospitals was not confined to Dakar or the Cap Vert region, but has become a national phenomenon. Known as 'Ibadou' mosques, these mosques were open to all Muslims, although Sufi ritual was banned (Cantone 2012: 237). Many 'Ibadou' mosques were funded by Saudi Arabia, Kuwait and the rābiṭat al-ᵉālam al-islāmī,[14] but also by rich Senegalese businessmen or the Senegalese state. 'Ibadou' mosques have acquired an image of being multi-functional. In contrast to mosques controlled by a Sufi order, 'Ibadou' mosques also provide a place for women (Cantone 2012: 293–6).

Up to 1991, the JIR set up branches in all regions of Senegal, especially in Cap Vert, Thiès and Kaolack. The basic unit of the organisation was a cell comprising up to thirty members. Should a certain area have more than thirty followers, a sub-section was founded. In 1991, the JIR had twenty-six cells and eight sub-sections in the country (*Le Musulman*, No. 37, 1991). During the fourth congress, which took place on 31 December 1988 and 1 January 1989, the organisation set up autonomous youth sections and a female wing. The organisation's most important institution was the general conference that convened every three years. During such conferences, JIR's policies were discussed and adopted for the next three-year period. In addition, the leading representatives of the organisation's regional sections, the Assemblée Nationale, met once every six months, whereas the Comité Directeur, comprising forty members and elected by the general conference for a period of three years, met every two months. The direction of the JIR consisted of the Bureau Exécutif Permanent, which organised the day-to-day work of the JIR and executed the decisions of the general conference, the Assemblée Nationale and the Comité Directeur (*al-Muslim*, No. 1, 1991).

In the sphere of Islamic education, the JIR established schools that taught Arabic and Islamic disciplines as well as the subjects taught at government schools. By the mid-2000s, the *écoles franco-arabes* of the JIR had been re-structured to adopt the Senegalese Government school syllabus completely, in addition to some classes in Arabic and Islamic sciences (Gomez-Perez 2005: 204). In addition, JIR schools and mosques offered seminars and weekend classes for adults and *tables rondes* as well as *causeries* (open discussions) on specific topics. During the annual holiday camps of the JIR, literacy campaigns, pedagogical seminars and continuing education courses were organised. In all sections of the JIR, Arabic courses were instituted and local school libraries were established. Members of the JIR visited the schools of other Islamic organisations and cultivated the exchange of ideas with these organisations. The JIR also organised examinations for the Certificat d'Études Primaires Élémentaires (CEPE), the state primary school examination, as well as the Brevet de Fin d'Études Moyennes (BFEM), the secondary school examination. Gifted children were encouraged to participate in the national competitions organised by the Ministry of National Education (*Le Musulman*, No. 37, 1991).

The network of mosques, nursery schools and schools was of utmost importance for the development of the JIR and its ability to mobilise public support: from 1988 to 1991, three nursery and infant schools were built in Dakar, Thiès and Diamaguène, in addition to a primary school in Diamaguène. The existing primary-school complex in Dakar was extended. In 1991, the JIR's most important primary schools were the École Franco-Arabe Bilal in Thiès, the École Imām Malick in the Medina quarter of Dakar and the École ᶜAbdallāh bin Yassin in Diamaguène near Mbao/Cap Vert. The Institut al-Ḥājj ᶜUmar in Thiès, which was regarded as an École de l'Enseignement Moyen Franco-Islamique, completed the picture. Another primary school with nursery school and artisan workshops opened in Sébikhotane in 1991 (*Le Musulman*, No. 37, 1991). Since the early 1990s, the number of JIR schools has grown continuously. The JIR was particularly successful in the Cap Vert region, and there especially in Pikine, in the Parcelles Assainies quarter and in Thiaroye, where the JIR acquired or built more than 300 schools in the 1990s and early 2000s (Piga 2007: 23). According to Sidi Khali Lô, these schools were intended to support the pupils of qurʾānic schools by providing them with a chance to continue their education after leaving qurʾānic school (*Le Soleil*, 9 February 1991). From the very beginning, the syllabus of the JIR schools stressed bilinguality, enabling pupils to take examinations equivalent to the CEPE, the primary-school examination at government schools (see Gomez-Perez 2005: 204ff).

From the 1990s, the educational efforts of the JIR led to the establishment of numerous Salafi-oriented schools that not only taught Islamic disciplines but that also stressed the importance of 'marketable skills' (see Launay 1992: 92), as well as female education.[15] Although the JIR was known as a movement of 'arabisants', it supported bi-lingual education, arguing that 'former toute une jeunesse à l'arabe et aux matières religieuses ne suffit pas à garantir son intégration dans la société sénégalaise' (Gomez-Perez 1997: 354). At the same time, the Sufi orders have increased the stress on Arabic in their own schools, a clear sign of rapprochement between the different movements of reform. The success of the new JIR schools has forced the Sufi orders to follow suit with educational programmes of their own that reproduce this trend in the development of Islamic education.

Today, the JIR is Senegal's most important Salafi-oriented movement of reform, and the JIR is able to address and mobilise Muslims in considerable numbers, including women (see Sieveking 2005; Augis 2003, 2005, 2009a and 2009b), at least in some urban agglomerations, even if the JIR has not yet acquired the economic resources that would be necessary to develop a social network and a power basis comparable to that of the Sufi orders (communication Ndiouga Benga, 5 April 2006). Still, since the late 1970s the JIR has managed to find adherents among the urban middle-class groups and to slowly broaden its social basis. In the early 1980s, the JIR also started a process of mobilising women. A women's wing of the JIR was established in 1989, led by Hajja Binta Thiaw. In the 1990s, the mobilisation of women by the JIR became visibly manifest in a turn towards the *ḥijāb* (Augis 2009b: 88). Not all veiled women were JIR members, but the movement towards the *ḥijāb* can be seen as a distinct marker of symbolic distantiation and social separation (see Cantone 2005: 121, 2012: 343; Augis 2009a, 2009b; Villalon 2007: 178). The development of the JIR has been symbolically expressed in a number of distinctive bodily representations and practices. For women these include wearing a veil, refusing to shake hands with men (and vice versa), praying *qabḍ* and taking part in prayers; for men these include growing a beard and wearing shortened trousers (Seck 2010: 160). As a result, the JIR, and those who sympathise with the 'Ibadou' movement, have become highly visible in Senegal.

In its programme and orientation, the JIR has been influenced by the Iranian revolution and contacts with a number of northern Muslim countries, as well as reformist organisations of Saudi Arabian, Libyan and Egyptian extraction. In Senegal, the JIR initially continued the tarbiya-oriented discourse of the UCM and condemned so-called un-Islamic innovations such as excessive spending on marriage ceremonies and burials, or the practice of *dhikr*, as well as specific features of local Islamic ritual and religious concepts such as the wearing of amulets (gris-gris). These are produced in Senegal in vast amounts and are exported, interestingly enough, to Saudi Arabia where Senegalese amulets enjoy great popularity among Muslims. In the late 1980s, the JIR seems to have realised, however, that the struggle against the marabouts and the Sufi orders was largely counter-productive on account of the ongoing popularity of the Tijāniyya and Murīdiyya. Since the early 1990s, the JIR has participated in the major celebrations of the great marabouts (Piga 2007: 28). A significant symbol of rapprochement between the Sufi orders and the JIR, as well as related organisations such as AEMUD (see below), was the fact that the JIR started to praise the 'grands marabouts' of the early colonial period, in particular, Aḥmad Bamba, as fighters against colonialism (Gomez-Perez 1997: 342).

After its third national congress, the JIR, which had originally planned to form an organisation of the Muslim vanguard, began becoming more open towards other organisations and Muslim personalities. This reorientation was confirmed at the JIR's fourth congress. A number of religious dignitaries in Senegal were contacted in order to signal the JIR's willingness to cooperate with them. From then on, the JIR leaders took part in the religious festivities of the country, that is, Tabaski, Korité and Tamkharit (*ᶜīd al-fiṭr*, *ᶜīd al-kabīr* and the Islamic new year festival), as well as the great celebrations and festivities of the Sufi orders. Privileged relationships were established with ᶜAbd al-ᶜAzīz Sy and Saliou Mbakke, the leaders of the Tijāniyya and Murīdiyya, but also with other prominent religious scholars, such as Mountaga Tall, Cheikh Muḥammad Bounama Kunta of Ndiassane, Sérigne Mamadu Ly Seck of Thienaba, ᶜAbd al-ᶜAzīz Sy junior, Djili Mbaye and the family of Amadou Sakhir Mbaye, ᶜAbass Sall in Louga and the Touré family in Fass Touré (*Le Musulman*, No. 37, 1991). Contacts were also established with the embassies of Kuwait, Saudi Arabia, Algeria, Libya and Sudan. In letters to the President of the Republic and to a number of ministers, the JIR's activities were presented and contacts with other Islamic organisations, political parties and trade unions in Senegal were set up (*Le Musulman*, No. 37, 1991).

A gradual rapprochement between Sufi orders and the JIR could thus be observed from the early 1990s (Gomez-Perez 1997: 321), although some JIR *imāms* maintained the view that those who followed a marabout could not be admitted in their mosques (Cantone 2012: 236). At the same time, while the Murīdiyya and the Tijāniyya and other Sufi orders were rejected as Sufi institutions (Aḥmed Kante quoted in Cantone 2012: 256). Equally, the JIR was not prepared to recognise hereditary *baraka* or hereditary religious authority, although historical religious authorities such as Aḥmad Bamba were accepted as model personalities. Despite these reservations, the JIR has modified its critique of the marabouts since the early 1990s, and has redirected its polemics against the secular state. Thus, most times at least, the JIR has escaped the dilemma of being accused of creating *fitna* by fighting against fellow Muslims. However, the *siyāsa*-informed turn towards incorporation into Senegalese mainstream society and politics (as well as the decreasing critique of Sufism) has driven members of the JIR to leave the movement in recent years. The JIR dissidents criticise the 'brotherhoodification' of the JIR and claim to follow 'Salafism without an organization' (communication Ismael Moya, 6 March 2015).

At the same time, the JIR has started to cultivate a public discourse that concentrate on topics such as the unity of the *ummah*, the 'moral decay' of contemporary Senegalese society and issues such as drug abuse, prostitution and other undesirable effects of modernisation that may easily be pinned on the secular state and its inability to provide for balanced social development. Thus, *bida*ᶜ, marabouts and Sufi orders have no longer been the major target of criticisms by the more recent reformist organisations in Senegal since the early 1990s (for details, see Loimeier 2000b, 2001). This development points to an 'essouflement de l'islam radical' since the 1990s (Gomez Perez 2005: 215), a development confirmed by Tidiane Kassé, the editor-in-chief of *Wal Fadjri*, Senegal's most successful Muslim newspaper in the 1980s, who once remarked: 'L'Islam ne se vend plus' ('Islam does not sell any more') (communication Tidiane Kassé, 17 April 1991, quoted in Loimeier 2000b: 169). Political themes and the struggle for true democracy have become more important for many Senegalese, while the Senegalese also criticise 'l'esprit concurrentiel et individualiste de chaque association' (Gomez Perez 2005: 217).

Despite the 'brotherhoodification' of the JIR in recent years, doctrinal divisions continue to exist between the Sufi orders and the JIR, as attested by the proliferation of Islamic festival days (Korité and Tabaski, that is, *ᶜīd al-fiṭr* and *ᶜīd al-kabīr*) and annual disputes over the sighting of the moon, that are used by Murīds, Tijānīs and Salafi-oriented reformers as occasions to signal difference. As a consequence of such disputes over the sighting of the moon and the proper beginning and end of festival times, Senegal has had to live with at least three different Korités and Tabaskis in recent decades. This proliferation of religious holidays has been criticised, among others, as a major problem for the national economy. In 2013, for instance, an announcement that parts of the JIR would not celebrate Korité on the same day as other religious movements in Senegal, was greeted with remarks such as 'c'est du pur cinéma', 'ah, ces barbus, toujours en train de réveiller fitna qui dort', 'vraiment, ces gens nous fatiguent' and 'ces gens sont des anarchistes, ils trouvent toujours un moyen de jeûner ou de fêter un jour différent des autres' (*rewmi.com*, 19 December 2013). Such statements can be read as a sign of Senegalese passion fatigue.

Closely linked with the JIR and founded by JIR members, yet independent from the JIR in organisational terms, was and is the Association des Étudiants Musulmans de l'Université de Dakar (AEMUD), established in 1984, with its centre at the university's mosque (Cantone 2012: 255; 1986 according to Gomez-Perez 2005: 200). The AEMUD was led by two outspoken *imāms* in the 1990s and 2000s, Aḥmad Kante and Muḥammad Niang, and it publishes the journal *L'Étudiant Musulman*. Although AEMUD follows a similar code of dress and bodily representation as the JIR, AEMUD has been more radical than the JIR and has continued to cultivate anti-Sufi positions, although, over time, moderation has also been observable, especially in the 2000s. Nevertheless, violent clashes with Murīd students occurred in 2004 (Thurston 2009: 8). Despite its conspicuous presence on the campus, most student activities are secular, and AEMUD does not play a national role, even though AEMUD has been quite active in the building of new mosques (see Cantone 2012: 258ff.).

The moderation of AEMUD positions was expressed in corresponding changes of position on the part of the two major AEMUD leaders, Aḥmad Kante and Muḥammad Niang. Muḥammad Niang, who is a former JIR youth wing president, has today abandoned the call for full application of the *sharīᶜa* and for an Islamic state in Senegal, while Aḥmad Kante has entered a 'phase of spiritual reflection, a phenomenon that occurred for many other reformists in Senegal. According to Kante, initial enthusiasm about the Iranian revolution diminished as disagreements arose over questions such as the depth of difference between Sunnism and Shiism' (Thurston 2009: 9). Kante still supported implementation of the *sharīᶜa*, though, and favoured a bottom-up process of Islamising Senegal. Both Kante and Niang, as *imāms*, have moved from the university to the nearby Point E mosque, an elite mosque that caters for the businessmen, intellectuals and politicians living in this part of Dakar, a sign of their incorporation into the Senegalese mainstream (Thurston 2009: 10).

While the JIR has been comparatively successful as a Salafi-oriented movement of reform in Senegal, the ḥarakat al-falāḥ (HF) has had a different trajectory: the HF was established by al-Ḥājj Maḥmūd Bā (1905–78), a religious scholar who was born in Diowol near Matam on the Senegal River (for his biography, see Kane 1997: 431ff). After some years of advanced Islamic studies in Mauritania, Maḥmūd Bā went on pilgrimage in 1928 and studied at the Madrasat al-Falāḥ in Mecca from 1933 to 1939. He returned to Senegal in 1940 and established a school in Diowol in 1941, but transferred his school to Dakar, where the new school flourished despite French colonial bureaucratic 'tracasseries' (Kane 1997: 444). Due to constant problems with the French colonial administration, Maḥmūd Bā eventually decided to move to Kayes in Mali in 1945, where he founded the jamᶜiyyat tadrīs al-qurʾān wa-mabādīʾ al-dīn (association for the teaching of the Qurʾān and the basics of the faith). He also established a school named madrasat al-falāḥ that had 300 students in 1948. Due to the success of this school and Maḥmūd Bā's 'militantisme' (Kane 1997: 451), the French authorities closed the school in 1953. Al-Ḥājj Maḥmūd Bā subsequently travelled to Egypt to find support for his ideas at al-Azhar University and returned to Mali in 1954, trying in vain to reopen his school in Kayes. In 1955, he undertook another effort, acting now under the auspices of the UCM. The new madrasat al-falāḥ was eventually registered by the French authorities in 1956, under the condition that he must not become the director of this school (Kane 1997: 454). In these years, al-Ḥājj Maḥmūd Bā travelled widely in West Africa and continued to spread his educational ideas, settling in Mauritania in 1962, where he was appointed Inspecteur de l'Enseignement Arabe. In 1964 he was appointed advisor to the president (Ould Daddah), a position he occupied until his death in 1978 (Loimeier 2001: 388–9; Brenner 2001: 65ff).

Although the HF took root in Kayes (Mali), it eventually became more important in Senegal, in particular among the Soninke-speaking groups of Upper Senegal, where in the 1960s Salafi-oriented Muslims became known under the term '*sunnadunko*' (Soninke for 'ahl al-sunna') (Rialland 1998: 77ff). Based on graduates and students of the first school of Maḥmūd Bā in Dakar and the mouvement culturel et social musulman, the Senegalese section of the Association al-Falāḥ in Mali, which was created by Maḥmūd Bā in 1956, the movement slowly formed in the 1960s and 1970s and was officially registered in 1975 as ḥarakat al-falāḥ li-l-thaqāfat al-islāmiyya. The first Président was Cheikh Ndiaye (b. 1933), in office from 1968 to 1991 and originally a member of the UCM; he was followed by Khalil Marega from the Fuuta Tooro region, a scion of a family of religious scholars, who had become a rich trader in the 1950s.[16] Under his leadership, and that of the vice-president, Sadio Cissé,[17] the HF essentially became a traders' organisation (Gomez-Perez 2005: 215). However, a series of internal disputes, allegations of mismanagement of funds and critique raised against Khalil Marega and Sadio Cissé with respect to their style of leadership led to a serious crisis within the HF in 1993. Since 1993, the HF has been plagued by internal disputes between old and new members, representing different social groups, merchants, 'arabisants' and 'francisants' (Gomez-Perez 2005: 197ff; see also Cantone 2012: 261f; Loimeier 2001: 276ff; Ware 2014: 204ff). In 1998, the HF split into two groups, manifested by two conferences in Dakar: a *congrès extraordinaire* in Dakar's grand mosquée convened by Khalil Marega who had directed the HF for twenty-five years, and a meeting of the National Executive Committee in the HF headquarters in Colobane/Dakar. During these meetings both groups voted to exclude each other from the organisation (Rialland 1998: 78).[18]

Sufi Reform Reloaded

While Sufi scholars started to establish associationist modes of organisation in the 1960s, such as the Fédération des Associations Islamiques Sénégalaises (FAIS) on the model of the UCM, Sufi-oriented associations essentially served as mediating organisations between the state and the ordinary population. In the early 1980s, however, new religious mass movements emerged from the orbit of the Sufi orders and addressed both the discourse and programme of the UCM and its successor organisations, as well as modern forms of Islamic education and orders. These religious mass movements contributed to the opening of the Sufi orders to global influences, and the transformation of Senegal under their spiritual guidance. The most active organisations were the dāʾirat al-mustarshidīn wa-l-mustarshidāt (DMM) for the Tijāniyya, and the ḥizb al-tarqiya (HT) and the Mouvement Mondial pour l'Unicité de Dieu (MMUD) for the Murīds.

In the first decades of the twentieth century, the 'grands marabouts' had fostered a system of 'exchange of services' with the Senegalese (colonial) state, as has been mentioned above. Despite some exceptions, this system of cooperation between state and religious leaders provided social and economic stability and political recognition of the Sufi orders. The sons and nephews of the 'grands marabouts', the 'marabouts-fils', developed a spectrum of different positions that ranged from being close to power and mere acceptance of the state's role, to withdrawal from the state, or active and militant opposition to the state. For instance, ᶜAbd al-ᶜAzīz Sy junior, a leading marabout of the Tijāniyya and a son of the Khalifa Général of the Sy branch of the Tijāniyya, came to assume a leading role in state-controlled Islamic associations, while many marabouts of the Murīdiyya, including the Khalifa Général, Abdou Lahatte (ᶜAbd al-Ahad) Mbakke, adopted attitudes of conspicuous indifference with respect to the affairs of the state. In this regard, the Tijānī community of Ceerno Muḥammad Sayyid Bā in Madina Gounass, Casamance, became famous for its policy of self-isolation. Equally,

Sidi Lamine Niass or Abdoulaye Khalifa Niass gained notoriety for their spectacular critique of Leopold Sédar Senghor's development policies, and their call, in the late 1970s, for a *jihād* in the context of the foundation of new religio-political party, the Hisbollah (Coulon 1981: 280). Marabouts were prepared to adopt Salafi-oriented positions from time to time and thus, for instance, demonstrated their political independence with respect to the Senegalese state. In the 1950s, Sufi leaders were thus willing to enter into alliances of convenience with the UCM. In 1989, the Khalifa Général of the Tijāniyya, ᶜAbd al-ᶜAzīz Sy, expressed his support for Khomeiny's *fatwā* against Salman Rushdie, and in 1985 he opposed the visit of Pope John Paul II to Senegal (Thurston 2009: 5).

In the 1960s, new Muslim associations were created by the state in order to cultivate a new elite of Muslim functionaries. These associations were controlled by the Sufi orders, in particular, the Tijāniyya, and even more specifically, the generation of the sons of the 'grands marabouts' of the 1920s to 1940s. Generational conflicts and questions of positioning vis-à-vis the state, as well as competing family branches, also led to the emergence in the 1980s of a generation of grandsons, 'marabouts petit-fils',[19] who not only disputed the claim to leadership of their own fathers or elder brothers, but also started to create new associationist movements that were no longer controlled by the state, as the Muslim associations of the 1960s were. While the second generation of 'marabout-fils' dominated Sufi-oriented discourses from the 1930s to the 1970s, a new generation of 'marabouts-petit-fils' emerged in the 1980s. This new generation of 'grandson-marabouts' has also been described as 'marabouts mondains',[20] a term that refers to the worldly nature of the activities and appearance of a number of third-generation marabouts, such as Aḥmad 'Modou' Kara Mbakké (b. 1954), a grandson of Mame Thierno Birahim Mbakke (a younger brother of Aḥmad Bamba) who established a Murīd youth movement in 1995, the Mouvement Mondial pour l'Unicité de Dieu (MMUD). In fact, the 'marabouts-petit-fils' who emerged as a new generational group of marabouts in the 1980s, as well as a number of young Muslim activists, developed new movements within both the Tijāniyya and the Murīdiyya. These movements, such as, the dāʾirat al-mustarshidīn wa-l-mustarshidāt (DMM) (the group of rightly guided men and women) for the Tijāniyya, and the ḥizb al-tarqiya (HT) (the group for advancement), the Maam Jaara Buso (see Babou 2007; Evers-Rosander 2003; Sieveking 2005),[21] the Matlaboul Fawzaïni[22] (MF), or the Mouvement Mondial pour l'Unicité de Dieu (MMUD) for the Murīdiyya, were marked by their associationist character and their new style of approaching audiences. While Maam Jaara Buso was a Murīd women's association based in Porokhane, Matlaboul Fawzaïni was established by Dame Ndiaye in 1990 as a Murīd initiative in the European diaspora, and has been recognised in Senegal as an NGO. The organisation was often seen as a 'dahira of the émigrés', but has gained considerable support among intellectuals and academics of Murīd inclination (see Gueye 2002: 249ff). MMUD claims to have approximately 500,000 supporters (see Audrain 2004: 110), among them 15,000 to 20,000 active core members (Samson 2007: 43). It was also known in Senegal as Diwaan or Diwanou Silkoul Jawahir Fi Akh Bari Sarahir (vernacular for dīwān silk al-jawāhir fī-akhbār ṣaghā°ir). MMUD was established in 1995 for the unemployed and often destitute urban youth.[23]

The DMM, the MMUD and the HT have passed through different stages of development that reflect their efforts to negotiate specific religious, political and social issues as well as personal disputes within the Sufi orders. The DMM was established in the middle of the 1970s as a youth movement of the Tijāniyya and has been led since 1976 by its *responsable moral*, Sérigne Mustafa Sy. In the 1980s, the DMM became a major movement of support for President Abdou Diouf (Samson 2005: 38, 2009b: 151ff). According to Mustafa Sy (b. 1952), son of Cheikh Tidiane Sy, a major contender for leadership within the Tijāniyya, the DMM had in the region of 500,000 members, a claim that has been made frequently by various religio-political movements in Senegal, such as the HT and the MMUD (Samson 2005: 48; Audrain 2004: 99ff). In 1993, Mustafa Sy organised a complete political *volte-face* and switched support to Abdoulaye Wade, Abdou Diouf's challenger in the 1993 presidential elections. In a short period of time, the DMM became one of the most outspoken movements opposing Abdou Diouf. DMM protests against Abdou Diouf triggered riots in Dakar that led to Mustafa Sy's imprisonment in 1993, while the DMM was interdicted in early 1994. In 1995, the movement was rehabilitated and subsequently renewed its support for Abdou Diouf in late 1996, albeit for a short period of time only. When the Khalifa Général of the Tijāniyya, ᶜAbd al-ᶜAzīz Sy, died in 1997,

Cheikh Tidiane Sy's efforts to rise to the position of the supreme leader of the family misfired again, as it had in the 1950s, and the old feud reopened between the two branches of the Sy family, represented by Cheikh Tidiane Sy and Mustafa Sy, and the new Khalifa Général, Manṣūr Sy, who continued to support Abdou Diouf. As a consequence, Mustafa Sy and the DMM decided to support Abdoulaye Wade's call for *sopi* (Wolof: 'change'). However, in the run-up to the elections in 2000, Mustafa Sy decided to switch political allegiance yet another time, and to support a religious party, the Parti de l'Unité et du Rassemblement (PUR), established by Khalifa Diouf.[24] In the electoral campaign, Mustafa Sy quickly withdrew his candidature for the office of the president, and PUR, as well as all other 'religious' candidates, failed to score a significant number of votes. The elections of February and March 2000 brought about the victory of Abdoulaye Wade and a coalition of the opposition (Villalon 1999: 142ff; Samson 2002: 164ff).

While the DMM dominated the development of a reformist youth movement within the Tijāniyya, the ḥizb al-tarqiya (HT) had a similar role within the Murīdiyya. The HT, which has gained attention by promoting new projects and concepts of Murīd development, was actually founded in 1975 (1978 according to other sources) in Dakar as a Murīd students' *dāʾira* (circle), namely, the Dahira des Étudiants Mourides de Dakar (DEM) (in Wolof, *dem* means 'to go'; my translation), under the patronage of the Khalifa Général of the Murīdiyya, Abdou Lahatte Mbakke (communication Cheikh Gueye and Cheikh Anta Babou, 12 September 2004; see also Cruise O'Brien 2003: 76, 89ff.). After some formative years, DEM was able to establish a first *daara* (centre) in Sicap Rue 10 in Dakar, which was transferred to Sicap Amitié 3 in 1989 (see the journal of the HT, *L'Abreuvoir des Assoiffés*, 3, 2008). When the rival Association des Jeunes Mourides was dissolved in 1986 by Abdou Lahatte Mbakke, for being too outspoken, the *dāʾira* became even more important for the organisation of the Murīd youth as well as, more recently, the Murīd diaspora, and in 1992 it was finally renamed ḥizb al-tarqiya (HT) (in Senegal: 'Hizbut-Tarqiyyah') by the new Khalifa Général, Saliou Mbakke. After 1989, DEM started to spread on a nationwide level and emerged as a major youth organisation of the Murīdiyya, led by Atou Diagne, the 'responsable moral' of the movement. In the 1990s, the influence of the HT grew to such an extent that in 1995 it was asked to organise the annual

Magal (shrine pilgrimage) in Touba in 1996. In 1995, the new national centre of the HT was completed in Touba (Gueye 2002: 245; see Gueye 2002: 239ff. and *L'Abreuvoir des Assoiffés*, 3, 2008, for the development of the HT).

The HT thus acquired a growing role in the management of the order, not only with respect to the organisation of the annual Magal, but also in the representation of the Murīdiyya in Senegal's public sphere. Due to privileged access to the Khalifa Général, the HT was about to exclude all other forms of legitimacy within the Murīdiyya in the mid-1990s. The increasing prominence of the movement was resented, however, and regarded as a form of disrespect by a number of 'marabouts petit-fils' of the Mbakke family, who objected to the rise of a non-Mbakke group to leading ranks within the order (Gueye 2002: 248). These 'marabouts-petit-fils' also criticised 'Hizbu' proclamations which publicly rejected the authority of the younger generation of Mbakke marabouts, and, thus, implicitly, the authority of inherited power. The leader of HT, Atou Diagne, even dared to challenge third generation marabouts of the Mbakke family by claiming that leadership within the Murīdiyya must not necessarily be linked to the Mbakke family, that any Murīd disciple could become the Khalifa Général and that direct allegiance to Ahmad Bamba was more important for Murīds than loyalty to his grandsons (Villalon 1999: 139). When members of HT eventually refused to grant Sérigne Mustafa Saliou Mbakke, the son of the Khalifa Général, Saliou Mbakke, access to his own father, the Khalifa Général disowned the group in July 1997 (Villalon 1999: 138f; Gueye 2002: 239ff). The HT had in fact eclipsed Mustafa Saliou's leading role in the order in the context of the organisation of the Magal of 1996. Until 1996, Mustafa Saliou Mbakke had led the order, represented it in the context of international conferences and been in charge of major projects of development in Touba due to his managerial qualities (Gueye 2002: 233). In recent years, HT seems to have been able to recover and to reclaim its important role in the organisation of the Magal (communication Mamadou Diouf, 17 November 2006).

The new Sufi-oriented mass movements such as the DMM, the HT and the MMUD are characterised, among other things, by the fact that they started to use new spaces, and in particular public spaces (such as stadiums and squares) and new media (for example, loudspeakers, radio, TV and the

Internet), as well as organising public campaigns (such as to remove waste, to visit and repair hospitals and schools or to clean cemeteries) on the model of the community-based *set setal* (clean-up) campaign of the 1980s, in order to gain and cultivate public support (Samson 2009b: 154). Two groups set up political parties and have become active in partisan politics: while Mustafa Sy supported the Parti de la Vérité pour le Développement (PVD) for a short time before switching his support to Abdoulaye Wade in the context of the 2000 elections, and to Idrissa Seck in the 2007 elections, Aḥmad 'Modou' Kara Mbakke, the leader of the MMUD, campaigned for Abdou Diouf in 2000 (Samson 2009b: 157). In 2004, Sérigne Modou Kara Mbakke created his own political party, the PVD or Hizbul Hakh (Arab.: ḥizb al-ḥaqq) as a political wing of the MMUD, yet still supported Abdoulaye Wade in the 2007 elections (Samson 2009b: 151ff). The leaders of the new Sufi-oriented mass movements may thus also be regarded as a new generation of 'marabouts politiques' (Samson 2009b: 151). Yet, despite Modou Kara Mbakke's (and Cheikh Tidiane Sy's) support for Abdoulaye Wade in the 2007 presidential elections, Wade lost the Thiès seat to his competitor, Idrissa Seck, who was supported by Mustafa Sy (Samson 2009b: 163, 2007: 43ff; Thurston 2009: 12).

The new Sufi-oriented movements of reform, such as the DMM, the MMUD or the HT, were also characterised by the fact that they adopted modern types of organisation and expression that had been the domain of Salafi-oriented movements of reform, such as the UCM. In addition, the DMM, the MMUD and the HT came out in support of modern expressions of youth culture through music and sports, and Senegal's popular bands and musicians, such as Youssou Ndour, Baba Maal and Ismail Lô, as well as the plethora of Dakar's rap bands, reflected this turn to the youth in their texts, which have since assumed a remarkably religious character (see Loimeier 2001: 315ff). A paradigmatic example of new forms of addressing religious crowds was presented by Sérigne Mustafa Sy. In a famous speech made in Thiès in 1993, he addressed his young followers and disciples in the outfit of a rocker and music-star, while showing off his worldliness in diatribes against the moral decay of the Senegalese Government in Wolof, French and Arabic. The usage of these three languages served to prove his rootedness in three frames of reference: the scholastic (Arabic), the modern (French) and the local (Wolof) (see Kane and Villalon 1995).[25] When Mustafa Sy started his speech, he pointed out the hybrid character of his public appearance by quoting from the Qurʾān (sūra 3: 140), thus sanctifying his discourse: '*wa-tilka al-ayām: nudāwiluhā baina al-nās*'.[26] In the context of the time, this statement could be understood as a comment on contemporary events in Senegal or, more particularly, the surprising shift of alliance of his religio-political movement, the DMM, from Abdou Diouf to Abdoulaye Wade. More particularly, however, Mustafa Sy explained his unconventional 'Western', rock-star garb, with leather cap, leather trousers and waistcoat, in political terms:

> Pardonnez moi. Si je suis vêtu comme je le suis aujourd'hui c'est parce que je suis en campagne électorale. Comme les hommes politiques nous ont emprunté nos gros grands boubous, nos châles, nos chapeaux, nos cannes, nos versets du Coran et nos hadith(s), moi aussi je leur emprunte leur pantalon, leur versets, leur casquette: ces jours, nous les faisons alterner parmi les hommes. (Kane and Villalon 1995: 139)

Mustafa Sy's public speech expressed hybridity not only in terms of language, but also in dress-codes and fashion, while conveying, at the same time, a political and a religious message. As such, the speech manifests the influence of new modes of approaching public audiences and the growing influence of Salafi-oriented reform in Senegal, as well as that of a globalised media-scape.

The generation of grandson marabouts has thus cultivated independent strategies with respect to politics, and seems to be increasingly willing to question the authority of the fathers, as expressed, for instance, in the *ndiggël* of the Khalifa Général of the Murīdiyya. The *ndiggël* may be defined as a command issued by the supreme religious leader of the Murīdiyya, the Khalifa Général and, in extension, by any religious leader in Senegal. The *ndiggël* is regarded as binding for all Murīds as it expresses the ultimate submission of each individual Murīd to the supreme authority of the Khalifa Général. In Senegal's political history, the different Khalifa Général of the Murīdiyya have proclaimed a *ndiggël* to vote for the ruling party since independence. The *ndiggël* of the Khalifa Général, in particular the 'ndiggël politique' (Cruise O'Brien 1992: 18), was questioned for the first time in 1988, though, when a number of young Murīd marabouts such as Sérigne Khadim Mbakke, as well as many of the Murīdiyya youth, were no longer prepared to follow the *ndiggël* of Khalifa Général Abdou Lahatte Mbakke and to vote for the Socialist Party in the presidential elections of that year. Rather, they supported the leader of the opposition, Abdoulaye Wade (see Loimeier 2001: 328–9). Abdou Lahatte Mbakké's successors, Abdulkhadre (ᶜAbd al-Qādir) Mbakke (1989–90) and Saliou Mbakke (1990–2007) have since abstained from proclaiming a 'ndiggël politique' and more recent efforts to impose a 'ndiggël politique' have failed, as in the case of Modou Kara Mbakke's effort, in 1999, in the context of a public rally with Tanor Dieng in a stadium in Dakar, to ask his followers to vote for the Socialist Party in the 2000 presidential elections. Although Gueye claims that the *ndiggël* has been over-emphasised in the political analysis of the past as a spectacularly visible symbol of religious authority in the political domain, the failure of the 'ndiggël politique' since the late 1980s supports the argument of the factual fragmentation of the Murīdiyya as a religio-political movement (Gueye 2002: 280ff).

The fragmentation of established modes of authority within the Tijāniyya and Murīdiyya in Senegal since the 1980s can be attributed to the merging and blending of different modes of organisation and expressions of reform over several generations. It cannot be said that such processes are confined to either Sufi- or Salafi-oriented traditions, but they clearly inform a range of Muslim traditions and groups at various junctures in their respective histories. At the same time, references across both generations and traditions emerge as a pattern of religious disputes in the Senegalese context. Contemporary reformers thus fight the 'islamologues fonctionnariés' by referring to the first generation of non-Sufi-oriented reformers, in particular Cheikh Touré, who followed a similar argumentative pattern: in order to attack the marabouts of his time, espcially those who collaborated with the colonial state, he established legitimising links not only with the dissident marabouts, but also with the generation of fathers of the 'marabouts-fils', namely Aḥmad Bamba and al-Ḥājj Mālik Sy. A major element of Cheikh Touré's discourse was to present contemporary marabouts as corrupt, while depicting the founding fathers of both Tijāniyya and Murīdiyya in Senegal, that is, the 'grand marabouts', as good Muslims whose straight path had been abandoned by their own sons. Not surprisingly, trans-generational legitimising references may also be identified within both the Tijāniyya and the Murīdiyya.

'Loud' and 'Silent' Politics

Neither Salafi-oriented reformist groups nor Sufi orders form homogeneous movements in Senegal. Rather, they have to be viewed as an array of competing networks that negotiate their relations with the state on an individual basis and consequently also develop different 'paths of accommodation' with the state. Aḥmad Bamba's return from exile in 1903, for instance, not only pacified relations between his supporters and the French colonial system, but also established a pattern of understanding that proved to be profitable for both sides: Murīd farmers would continue to produce Senegal's major cash crop, groundnuts, support the colonial system, pay taxes and support French war efforts during World War I and World War II, while France, and later the Senegalese state, would grant the Murīds a certain degree of internal autonomy, particularly with respect to religious affairs, a privilege that found expression in French support for Murīd projects such as the construction of a railway line from Dakar to the seat of the Khalifa Général in Touba (Cruise O'Brien 1971: 58ff; Behrman 1970: 50ff). The acceptance of these unwritten rules of *échange de services* constituted a basic pillar for the development of post-colonial Senegal. Efforts to modify or even abolish this basic understanding between state and Murīdiyya (or the Tijāniyya), for example under Prime Minister Mamadou Dia in the late 1950s and early 1960s, were strongly countered, in Mamadou Dia's case by his deposition as prime minister by President Senghor in late 1962.

However, when the state or a religious group were unable to deliver the goods that formed the material basis of their relationship, Murīd and Tijān leaders were willing to shift gears and voice critique, even to the extent of non-obedience. This was true for the economic crisis in the 1970s in the aftermath of the Sahel drought and the collapse of the national groundnut marketing board, or for President Abdou Diouf's gradual and silent withdrawal in the 1990s from established traditions of mutual recognition and the increasing unwillingness of the bureaucratic elite to respond to maraboutic demands. In 1973, following the economic failure of the state in the Sahel drought, Abdou Lahatte Mbakke, the Khalifa Général of the Murīdiyya in the 1970s and

1980s, denounced the Senegalese state as a manifestation of 'Satan' (Coulon 1981: 276) and started a movement of symbolic distantiation from the state. After 1993, his successor, Khalifa Général Saliou Mbakke,[27] abstained from directing his followers to cast their votes for Abdou Diouf, due to increasing dissatisfaction with both the government's economic policies and Murīd support for these policies.

Still, we have to make an important differentiation here: while the Murīds have so far managed to conserve internal unity, despite a number of conflicts over succession and other family disputes, and have followed the supreme religious guidance of their Khalifa Général, the Tijāniyya has been split, in religio-political terms, into a number of family networks that do not accept the authority of one Khalifa Général. At the same time, the Murīds appear to have been almost unanimously supporting the state, while the Tijāniyya has brought forth a number of dissident personalities and movements and were prepared to form alliances of convenience with associationist reformist organisations. As the Murīds have been successful in recent decades in getting their goods delivered, they also appear to be the more successful group in political terms, while the Tijāniyya seems to have been handicapped by their internal religious divisions, an impression that has led to assumptions of Murīd political and demographic superiority over other Sufi orders in Senegal, in particular the Tijāniyya.

The resulting 'mouridocentrisme' (Villalon 1995: 68) is vastly misleading: while Murīds have been an essentially rural movement for a large part of their history, the branches of the Tijāniyya have effectively been able to conquer the urban areas since the early twentieth century.[28] As a consequence, the Tijāniyya has evolved to become the order of the political elite and the intelligentsia, as well as urban middle-class groups, in particular the bureaucracy, and employees in the education and health sectors and virtually all state-related agencies and institutions: the state became Tijānī a long time ago, and followers of the Tijāniyya have been sitting in government offices for decades, silently ensuring the proper distribution of their goods. The Murīds, by contrast, have been aloof, rural and proud of their separate, autonomous identity, symbolised by their holy city, Touba. Also, Murīds have been practically non-existent in state bureaucracies and the political nomenclatura of the country until very recently. Thus, Murīds have had to ask for their goods rather loudly. However, loudness of claims and politically conspicuous presentation should not automatically be associated with corresponding political power, while discreetness of claims and inconspicuous political presentation do not necessarily point to political weakness: until 2000, Tijānis were not forced to resort to Murīd strategies as they were already in power (Loimeier 2001: 323).

The scenario of a monolithic Murīdiyya far removed from power in spatial terms, and a Tijāniyya close to power, yet split into many family networks, changed dramatically in 2000, when Abdou Diouf and the socialist party (Parti Socialiste) (PS) lost the elections and Abdoulaye Wade and the Sopi coalition of opposition parties became the first democratically elected non-socialist government of Senegal. An analysis of this change of power, which was unprecedented in Senegal's post-colonial history, shows that Abdou Diouf and the PS lost the 2000 (and 2001) elections partly because they had been virtually unable 'to deliver the goods' in the economic crisis of the 1980s and 1990s, and to provide sustained economical development, in particular with respect to the growing urban populations, especially the youth. But Abdou Diouf and the nomenclatura of the PS had also become increasingly wary of the established system of *échange de services*, as Leonardo Villalon has shown in his study of Fatick (Villalon 1995: 219; see also Cruise O'Brien 2003: 197). Dissatisfaction with maraboutic whims was not confined to the ranks of the Socialist Party, though: for two consecutive days in 1995, the independent daily paper *Sud Quotidien* published the headline 'Terrorisme spirituel: Ces petits marabouts qui nous tiennent en ôtage', with articles that criticised the 'little marabouts' who took advantage of their descent to profit personally (see Villalon 2000: 495). The shaykhs of the Murīdiyya, however, felt increasingly neglected by the political nomenclatura and started to think about political alternatives, especially when Abdoulaye Wade stressed that he would become 'their' president. When the Khalifa Général of the Murīds (again) did not proclaim a *ndiggël* in favour of Abdou Diouf in the elections of 2000, and the leaders of the Tijāniyya, except for Cheikh Tidiane Sy, who had performed another political U-turn, remained rather vague with respect to their political preferences, the voters, and especially the rural electorate, turned their back on the PS in masses.[29]

The 1990s thus witnessed a redefinition of the relationship between state and Sufi orders. This redefinition was due not only to a certain disenchantment of government functionaries with the established system of *échange de services*, but also to the fact that economic conditions have changed considerably since the 1970s: an ongoing economic crisis has forced the state to follow a policy of far-reaching economic liberalisation. As a consequence, the state has lost direct control over the goods to be allocated to marabouts. On the other hand, the marabouts long ago started to diversify their economic activities: groundnut production has ceased to be the major asset of the Murīdiyya, while in the informal sector, transport, large-scale import–export and retail trade, real-estate development, building and cement, as well as the organisation of considerable expatriate activities (and respective remittances) have been largely conquered by Murīd (but also by a number of Tijāni) marabouts and their followers in recent decades. The Murīd diaspora, in particular, has become so important since the 1990s that the Senegalese state is no longer able to top diaspora remittances by way of its own development politics. As a result, Murīds have become increasingly independent of the state and disciples consequently claim a greater say in Murīd internal debates. They have gained bargaining power and are particularly critical of marabouts who are perceived to be too close to the government. As a result, Murīd–state relations have been in a process of re-evaluation in recent years (Babou 2013a: 139).

In addition, Murīds have gained increasing control over markets, not only Ocass in Touba, but also Sandaga and HLM in Dakar, and the Murīdiyya has also developed it's own *ḥawāla* money transfer networks such as Kara International Exchange (Buggenhagen 2012: 75). Murīd marabouts, in particular, are thus no longer constrained to pass 'through politics' in order to gain access to resources (Mamadou Diouf in Samson 2005: 185). This may be one of the reasons why politics have not assumed a religious character. In the presidential elections of February and March 2000, as well as the parliamentary elections of 2001 that brought about the victory of Abdoulaye Wade and a coalition of forty opposition parties, religious candidates and parties such as PUR or PVD failed to score a significant number of votes. The outcome of these elections confirmed the 'defeat of the ndiggël politique' (Villalon 1999: 142ff; Samson 2002: 164ff), a process that can also be described as a weakening (*affaiblissement*) or breaking-away (*effritement*) of the *ndiggël*.[30] The failure of the religious candidates may also be explained, however, by the fact that a majority of (young) voters did not want to jeopardise the victory of Abdoulaye Wade by voting for a religious party. By following a political rationale, they wanted *sopi* to prevail.[31] This should not be interpreted as a vote against religion. However, not a single protest movement in Senegal since the mid-1990s has had a religious motivation: major issues of protest have been access to resources, social services and infrastructure, sanitation and environmental problems, communal rights and political participation (Ndiaye 2013: 471).

Since 2000, the administration of Abdoulaye Wade has returned to the established rules of 'échange de services' that were neglected by Abdou Diouf, and appears to be increasingly dominated by Murīd interests, a perception enhanced by repeated visits of Abdoulaye Wade to Touba, claiming to be 'le Président Mouride' (communication Cheikh Anta Babou, 12 September 2004; Wane 2003: 120; Gervasoni and Gueye 2005: 632ff), and his promises with respect to Murīd development. The reallocation of bonds that started after 2000 has consequently triggered 'loud' protest among the Tijāniyya, who were afraid of losing established pastures (see Wane 2003: 45ff, 115ff). As a consequence, Tijānis have become increasingly outspoken, while Murīd public declarations have become more 'silent' and less conspicuous in their public presentation. Thus, a reversal of roles and positions can be observed in the relationship between the Sufi orders: Tijānis, removed from power, have become increasingly outspoken in public, while Murīds, closer to power, have become increasingly silent (*muet*) (communication Mamadou Alassane Bā, 10 May 2005). Thus, the change of power in 2000 and 2001 did not lead to a fundamental change in the social matrix of the Senegalese political system (Seck 2007: 47).

The reversal of roles in the 2000s was not unanimously greeted by the Murīds, however. Some Murīds seemed to be rather torn with respect to their relationship with *le Président Mouride*: while one group was proud that the state had acquired a more visible Murīd character, a second group dreaded too close a relationship with the state and rather hoped to continue a policy of neutrality and aloofness, as expressed in the past by Khalifa Général Abdou Lahatte Mbakke. To his great surprise, the Khalifa Général of the Murīdiyya found himself leading the PDS list for Touba in the local government elections in 2002. This list was immediately withdrawn after publication, but by then it had fulfilled its obvious purpose, namely to gain Murīd popular support for the PDS (Coulibaly 2003: 133). Most Murīds were afraid, however, that the new character of their links with the state may become embarrassing, particularly in the case of the political and economic failure of the Wade administration. The family of the successor to Saliou Mbakke, Muḥammad al-Amīn Bara Mbakke,[32] thus limited contact with Wade as far as possible (Cheikh Anta Babou, 14 November 2004). Saliou Mbakke rejected Wade's efforts to claim his support for his politics by refusing to accept the ranch of Doli as a gift; this was a *réserve sylvo-pastorale* east of Touba that had been transferred to his domain by Wade. He also ended the debate about the special legal status of Touba by declaring that Touba was a 'partie intégrante du Sénégal' (Seck 2007: 38). Wade's efforts to favour the Murīds and even force his ministers to consult Murīd leaders before forming state policies were reversed in 2012 by Macky Sall, Wade's successor as president, who insisted that 'there are no special laws for some marabouts. I say clearly: we are in a secular, democratic republic, where religious liberty is guaranted for all religions, for all brotherhoods' (quoted in Buckley 2013: 176).

Thus, Senegal's 'specific social and political stability', based on the *contrat social sénégalais*, does not depend on the *ndiggël* of the marabouts, and it cannot be assumed that the *contrat social* implies nothing but unfettered obedience of disciples to marabouts and 'unlimited marabout control over disciples' (Babou 2013a: 125). Disciples have been notoriously unruly, and marabout–state relations have been less stable than is generally assumed, at least since the 1950s. The Murīdiyya, in particular, is not a monolithic organisation but should be seen as a religious movement organised in numerous families ('houses') that have followed their own interests. Both disciple–marabout and marabout–state relations are a temporary result of ongoing processes of mutual adjustment that eventually led to a modus vivendi between marabouts and the state, as well as between marabouts and their disciples (Babou 2013a: 127). In the course of the twentieth and twenty-first centuries, these processes of adjustment have led to variegated results: while the founder of the Murīdiyya, Aḥmad Bamba, established a first model characterised by mutual acceptance, implying Murīd support for French colonial politics and French acknowledgement of Murīd internal autonomy, Falilou Mbakke, the second Khalifa Général, who had to fight against the internal opposition of Cheikh Mbakke 'Gainde Fatma', unconditionally supported President Léopold Sédar Senghor, for instance in the 1958 referendum on immediate independence, in the 1962 crisis regarding the deposition of Mamadou Dia and in the student riots of 1968. In exchange, Senghor supported the building of the great mosque in Touba and was present at its opening ceremony in 1963. According to Babou, this was the 'golden age of the contrât social' (Babou 2013a: 130).

Under Falilou Mbakke's successor, Abdou Lahatte Mbakke (Khalifa Général 1968–89), this *modus vivendi* changed considerably: not only was Abdou Lahatte Mbakke much more critical of Senghor, he also reacted to the economic crisis of the 1970s and to increasing farmer pressure and became an outspoken advocate of the rural populations vis-à-vis the state. This situation changed again with Abdou Diouf's rise to presidency in 1981. Not only was Abdou Lahatte Mbakke now in control of formerly dissenting fractions, he also found Abdou Diouf more willing to compromise and consequently supported him publicly in both the 1983 and the 1988 elections. Under Sérigne Saliou Mbakke (Khalifa Général 1990–2007), state–marabout relations experienced a 'new chill', though (Babou 2013a: 135): Saliou Mbakke opted out of open involvement with politics and refused a 'ndiggël politique' in favour of any political party, while Abdou Diouf and the Socialist Party became increasingly unhappy with the role of marabouts in politics. The fact that state–marabout relations became increasingly strained in the years after 1990 contributed to Abdoulaye Wade's electoral victories in 2000 and 2001: he was obviously the candidate not shunned by the leadership of the Murīdiyya. After his electoral victory, Abdoulaye Wade went to Touba and personally thanked the Khalifa Général of the Murīdiyya for his support in a way that symbolised de facto submission to the Khalifa Général of the Murīdiyya: he removed his headgear, sat on the floor at the feet of the Khalifa Général and kissed his hands, thus creating the impression that he was a 'Président Mouride' who enjoyed the support of the Khalifa Général (Babou 2013a: 135). Abdoulaye Wade's prostration in front of the Khalifa Général of the Murīdiyya was even described as a symbol of 'la République couchée', 'the republic lying down', by Ousseynou Kane (Walfadjri, 8 May 2001). Although the Khalifa Général and the leading families of the Murīdiyya always kept their distance from Abdoulaye Wade, Wade was nevertheless able to create and sustain the public impression that the Murīdiyya as such was supporting him (Babou 2013a: 137). As a result, Wade gained the electoral support of both the rural and diaspora Murīd communities until the local government elections of 2009, when the context changed again.

Abdoulaye Wade's Mouride policies have been characterised by their highly erratic and manipulative character: although Wade's family had been in contact with the Murīdiyya since the 1920s, Abdoulaye Wade established closer links with the Murīdiyya in the 1960s only and chose Cheikh Aḥmad Mbakke 'Gainde Fatma' as his 'guide spirituel', that is, Falilou Mbakke's, Abdou Lahatte Mbakke's and Senghor's major opponent within the Murīdiyya. In 1988, he shifted his loyalties to Abdoulkhadre Mbakke, who became the new Khalifa Général of the Murīdiyya after Abdou Lahatte Mbakke's death in 1989. When Abdoulkhadre Mbakke died in 1990, Abdoulaye Wade quickly shifted his allegiance again to Saliou Mbakke, the new Khalifa Général. Saliou Mbakke kept his distance from Abdou Diouf and the Socialist Party, however, and stayed aloof from politics.[33] Yet, even though Saliou Mbakke never declared his support for Abdoulaye Wade, his declared distance from Abdou Diouf allowed Wade to profit most from this position of the Khalifa Général (Babou 2013b: 304). After his electoral victory, Wade continued to stress his close and good relations with Touba and supported investment in Touba in multiple ways. As a result, the Murīdiyya suddenly appeared to be the most privileged religious movement in Senegal, although leading Murīd families did their best to counter that impression by evading both Wade and his gifts (Babou 2013b: 314). Many Murīd families in fact saw Wade's pro-Murīde positions both as an effort to instrumentalise the Murīdiyya for his policies and as a violation of Murīd ethics that require loyalty to one's spiritual guide (and his family):

> Lorsqu'un disciple se soumet à un lignage, une règle non écrite, mais strictement respectée, exige que lui-même ainsi que sa descendance perpétuent leur loyauté à ce lignage . . . Le Président Wade, qui a changé quatre fois de Cheikh depuis 1988, n'a pas respecté cette règle . . . ce nomadisme spirituel est fustigé par certains mourides qui y voient la preuve de son mépris des valeurs de la Mouridiyya et son opportunisme politique. (Babou 2013b : 315)

. . . *Wa-Tilka al-Ayām: Nudāwiluhā Baina al-Nās*

Senegal thus changed vastly from the early 1980s onwards, particularly in urban areas: Abdou Diouf's *sursaut national* led the country into post-colonial modernity and it was possible to sense the hopes of many that the future would bring a better life. Groundnuts ceased to be Senegal's dominating product and were replaced by income from tourism and fisheries and the remittances of an increasing number of Senegalese migrants. Senghor's ghost faded and the Senegalese political arena opened up to a number of opposition parties. The Sufi orders had to fight against the polemics of Salafi-oriented reformist groups, in particular the jamā^cat ^cibād al-raḥmān. Senegal underwent a process of national *set-setal* (clean-up) that was supported by a number of new newspapers, such as *Wal Fadjri* and *Sud Hebdo*. The political field was still dominated by Abdou Diouf and the Socialist Party, even if the call for '*sopi*' was becoming more and more audible.

In the early 2000s, *sopi* occurred and passed by: the elections of 2000 brought about some political change, yet Abdoulaye Wade, the new president, quickly disappointed great expectations:[34] *sopi* brought about a change in persons but not in structure. Wade's erratic style of politics was referred to satirically as 'www.ttt.sn', that is, *wade wax weddi* (meaning 'Wade talks and disclaims at the same time') and *tukki touba télé*, pointing out Wade's favourite activities, namely, 'travelling, going to Touba and appearing on TV' (Coulibaly 2003: 224). In fact, Wade proclaimed numerous plans for national development, such as a new airport in Ndiass, southeast of Rufisque, a car factory in Dakar, a bus factory in Thiès, a *réseau hydrographique national*, a *université du futur*, a new public transport system called *Dakar Dem Dikk*, an express motorway *à péage* in Dakar, a trans-continental road to Tanger, a heliport for Touba or a *bassins de rétention d'eau* scheme that, however, by early 2003 had produced only 28 instead of 13,000 water reservoirs (see Coulibaly 2003: 150ff; Villalon 2004: 64; Gervasoni and Gueye 2005: 621ff).

At the same time, a young generation had replaced the old, which had experienced colonial times, and the population had grown considerably:[35] a majority of Senegal's population now lived in the Dakar-Cap Vert agglomeration and a series of secondary cities, as well as an ever-growing Touba, the capital of the Murīdiyya. Senegal was now suffering from the sobering effects of fading hopes and new questions as to how the immediate future would develop in a globalised economy. The devaluation of the Franc Communauté Financière Africaine (CFA) in 1994 and an economic crisis had only recently been overcome in a precarious recovery, essentially based on remittances by the Senegalese migrant worker diaspora in Europe and the USA, which found expression in an impressive building boom in Dakar. This building boom reflected basic changes in the social structure of Senegalese families, in particular the demise of the *kër* (the compound that housed extended families) in urban areas and the rise of privacy and the Western nuclear family (communication Babakar Lô, 31 March 2006).

Also, the number of daily newspapers and periodicals has increased tremendously since the late 1980s. In addition to *Le Soleil*, four periodicals have managed to find acceptance in the market: *Sud Hebdo*, *Wal Fadjri*, *Le Témoin* and *Le Cafard libéré*. Some of these periodicals have become dailies, while a number of additional papers, journals and periodicals such as *Le Politicien*, a whole series of fashion journals such as *Thiof* or religious periodicals such as *Mouride* were published on a weekly, bi-weekly or monthly basis. Since 1993, these press media have been complemented by about forty radio stations, such as *Matin*, *Com7*, *SUD FM* and *Wal Fadjri FM*, or radio stations that specialise in programmes for the youth, such as *Oxy-Jeunes* in Pikine, established in 1999 (Gellar 2005: 83). A closer look at Senegal's weekly papers and journals (*Mouride*, *Nouvel Horizon*, *Le Jour*, *La Voix du Touba*, *L'Espace*, *Zenith*, *Thiof*, *Le Soleil*, *Wal Fadjri*, *Sud Hebdo* and *Focus*) shows, however, that religion has not played a significantly larger role in the 2000s as compared to the 1990s and late 1980s, except, of course, at the times of Senegal's religious festivals (*Korité* and *Tabaski*), as well as the well-established ritualised 'religious news' in the context of the annual *Magal* to Touba and the *Gammu* to Tivavouane.

At the same time, the new constitution of 2001 continues to define Senegal as a *laïque* state. The fact that Senegalese citizens, even if Muslim, do not necessarily view political and social processes from an Islamic perspective became particularly clear in the context of the 'Senegalese spring' in 2011/12, when considerable parts of the population protested against the re-election of President Abdoulaye Wade for another term of office. The 'Senegalese spring' was prepared from 2008 onwards by debates in the so-called 'assises nationales' (national congress) convened by the former UNESCO Secretary-General Amadou Makhtar Mbow. The debates in the 'assises nationales' brought together a huge coalition of diverse social and political forces that started a nationwide discussion on the development of the country. These debates dominated the 2012 elections and forced politicians and parties to voice a position with respect to the demands of the 'assises nationales'. A major issue was the sanctity of the constitution, leading to the anti-Wade slogans of 2012, *non au troisième mandat* and *touche pas à ma constitution*: Senegalese citizens wanted to prevent the succession of Abdoulaye Wade's son Karim in the case of Abdoulaye Wade being re-elected.

As such, the *assises nationales* constituted a remarkable development of Senegal's 'secular' public sphere, enhanced by the fact that religious leaders again refrained from a 'ndiggël politique' in the context of the 2012 elections (see Diop 2013b: 83; Gellar 2013: 127ff). Equally, protests, as organised most prominently by the *Y'en a marre* (we are fed up) movement from January 2011, never assumed a religious character but reflected the largely secular or civilian agenda of a broad array of opposition groups, both spontaneous and organised, namely, the will to defend the constitution. Considering the fact that Senegal is a Muslim majority country (95 to 96 per cent of the population is Muslim) and that Islam is an important part of Senegal's political, social and economic life, the a-religious character of the 2012 protest is remarkable. As a result of these protests, Abdoulaye Wade, who had tried to present himself as a religious candidate, had to abandon his plans to bend the constitution in his favour and eventually lost the presidential elections.[36]

The introduction of optional religious instruction in government primary schools in 2002 does not challenge this perspective because this meant the introduction of both Muslim and Christian religious instruction (see D'Aoust 2012: 230; Bodian and Villalon 2015: 74ff) and was a decision not met by any substantial opposition.[37] Also, female circumcision had been banned by law (in 2000) even before the introduction of religious education at government schools (see Augis 2013). In contrast, the debate over the *code de la famille* was renewed in 2002 and 2003, and mobilised supporters as well as opponents. While an initiative to limit the permitted number of wives to two had failed in 1996 (Brossier 2004: 82), the new initiative to reform the *code de la famille* in 2002 created much more discussion. This initiative of reform aimed at creating a *code de statut personnel* for Muslims on the basis of the *sharīᶜa*, while Christians would continue to rely on the existing *code de la famille*. The organisation responsible for the new debate over the *code de la famille* was the Comité Islamique pour la Réforme du Code de la Famille (CIRCOFS) as established in 1996 and led by Maître Babacar Niang (1930–2007). Niang, who had studied at the University of Dakar and at the Sorbonne in Paris, was a member of the Marxist Parti Africain de l'Indépendence (PAI) up to 1963, then joined Cheikh Anta Diop's Rassemblement National Démocratique (RND), and finally, in 1983, established his own party, the Parti pour la Libération du Peuple. In the course of time, he increasingly became a devout Muslim and eventually created CIRCOFS in 1996, which seems to have been a rather personal project, yet for a short period of time it gained the support of a number of 'grands marabouts', as well as Senegal's 'élite musulmane non-confrérique' (Brossier 2004: 93).

A major aim of the 2002/3 reform initiative, as supported by seventeen Islamic associations and as expressed in a 276-article *Code du Statut Personnel Islamique*, was to limit the right of women to make decisions without the consent of their husbands. This aim was vehemently opposed by a *camp laïc*, consisting of well-known personalities, women's associations such as Siggil Jigeen, an umbrella organisation for eighteen women's NGOs, human rights organisations and the trade unions. In 2003, these groups formed a Collectiv pour la défense de la laïcité et de l'unité national au Sénégal. Under attack, CIRCOFS disintegrated, some members even turning against its initial aims, and President Wade eventually rejected the CIRCOFS initiative for good in the context of a state visit to Japan (Brossier 2004: 91; Augis 2013: 86).

Religious and political debates in Senegal's public sphere have thus evolved in a long tradition of political debates since the mid-nineteenth century. These debates have changed in content but have kept a clear political character: religion has so far not become a defining issue of political debates in Senegal. Senegal's secular system, inherited from France, has thus never come under serious attack, at least until today, despite the critique of Salafi-oriented reformers in the 1980s and despite recurring critiques of the *code de la famille*. In addition, the Senegalese state has not only defined clear spheres of influence and thus provided space for different religious movements, it has also defined its obligation 'to protect religion' (Loimeier 2001: 375). Sufi orders consequently never had to fight hard for acceptance. They were seen by the state as indispensable 'translators' and brokers between the state and the population, providing religious legitimacy to the state. Equally, Salafi-oriented movements of reform have emerged in a political context in which they were accepted as political players, despite their at times radical character. In addition, the different religious movements in Senegal, marabouts, reformers and activist associations, have usually expressed clear political positions and, with a few exceptions, never asked for Islamisation of the state. Rather, they regarded the secular state as a body that, under the established rules of accommodation and cooperation, provided space for religious expression and autonomy. Keeping this development in mind, we will now focus on the question of how Salafi-oriented reform has developed in Mali, a country that has not had Senegal's tradition of 'exchange of services' between secular state and religious movements.

. . . and Mali?

A comparison between Senegal and Mali demonstrates the importance of the local context for the development of Salafi-oriented movements of reform: while such a movement originated in Senegal in the early 1950s and was informed by the dominating role of the Murīdiyya and the Tijāniyya, the emergence of a Salafi-oriented movement of reform in Mali (and in Guinea, Ivory Coast, Sierra Leone, northwestern Ghana and western Burkina Faso, that is, the greater Mande region) started in the mid-1940s and was associated with the network of Mande-speaking Juula traders in these countries. Sufi orders had a comparatively weak social and political position in the greater Mande region, although different branches of the Tijāniyya and the Qādiriyya had been present in these countries for some time and had developed a number of well-known centres of learning, such as Timbuktu, Jenne and Kankan (see Loimeier 2013: 77ff). Contacts between Senegal and the Juula–Salafiyya network in Mali, Guinea, Ivory Coast, Ghana and Burkina Faso increased in the late 1950s with the expansion of the Union Culturelle Musulmane and Cheikh Touré's efforts to unite the Salafi-oriented movements of reform in these countries. In the 1960s, the UCM was 'domesticated' in Senegal and re-surfaced in the late 1970s only, in the guise of the jamāᶜt ᶜibād al-raḥmān. In Mali, Ivory Coast, Ghana and Burkina Faso, Salafi-oriented movements of reform prospered in the 1960s and 1970s and continued to grow in the 1980s. In particular, they expanded their social basis beyond students, functionaries and traders and started to gain support among middle-class groups. In the following pages, I will concentrate on the development of Salafi-oriented reform in Mali, which has been a key country for the development of Salafi-oriented reform in the greater Mande-Juula region.

The first propagators of Salafi-oriented ideas of reform were al-Ḥājj Muḥammad ᶜAbdallāh Ag Maḥmūd al-Madanī (d. 1951) and al-Ḥājj Tiekodo Kamagaté. Al-Ḥājj Muḥammad ᶜAbdallāh Ag Maḥmūd, a Kel es-Suq Tuareg from Gao, had walked to Mecca (together with his father) and had lived in the Ḥijāz since 1906 (Ch. Ahmed 2015: 28). In 1924, he was appointed *imām* of the Prophet's mosque in Medina, but he resigned in 1934 and went on a journey to India. In 1938, he returned to Mali via Medina to introduce Salafi-oriented ideas of reform in the region of Gao, where he earned his living as a trader and a scholar (Kaba 1974: 30; Brenner 2001: 141; Ch. Ahmed 2015: 28ff). Al-Ḥājj Tiekodo Kamagaté, a Juula trader from Bouaké (Ivory Coast), had gone on pilgrimage in the 1930s and returned in 1944 to propagate Salafi-oriented ideas of reform in Sikasso (Mali), Bouaké and Bobo Dioulasso (in Haute-Volta, later Burkina Faso) (Kaba 1974: 34). Although he was imprisoned in 1947, his ideas continued to spread in the Juula-trader network in Mali, Guinea, Ivory Coast, northwestern Ghana and western Burkina Faso. These two early propagators of Salafi-oriented ideas of reform established a pattern of regional expansion of such ideas that remained valid until the early twenty-first century, namely, the separation between a Juula-dominated network of reformers in southern and western Mali, Guinea, Ivory Coast, western Burkina Faso and northwestern Ghana and a Songhay-Tuareg-dominated network of reform in northern and eastern Mali, western Niger and northern Ghana. These networks of reform were complemented by a third network, namely that of Hausa-oriented traders and scholars who gained influence in northern and southern Ghana, Benin and eastern Burkina Faso.[38]

For all of these networks, pilgrimage to Mecca was of paramount importance. The colonial period saw a rapid increase in the number of pilgrims, and pilgrims inevitably brought back new ideas from Mecca and Medina. From 1948, the pilgrimage was organised by the French colonial administration. In 1948, twenty-two Muslims from Mali went on pilgrimage, in 1950 thirty-two and in 1952 eighty-five (Hock 1999: 33). In Saudi Arabia, pilgrims from West Africa were supported by a small group of West African Muslims living in Mecca and Medina. These people were important intermediaries and helped pilgrims from West Africa to contact Saudi dignitaries, scholars, businessmen and politicians (Brenner 2001: 146; see also Schulze 1990). For pilgrims from Mali, ᶜAbd al-Raḥmān b. Yūsuf 'al-Ifrīqī' (1908–57), a Songhay from Ansongo, was of particular importance (for his biography, see Ch. Ahmed 2015: 45ff; Triaud 1986: 162ff). ᶜAbd al-Raḥmān b. Yūsuf 'al-Ifrīqī' arrived in Mecca in 1926 and started to study at the feet of the most eminent scholars of his time in the Ḥijāz, in particular Alfa Hāshim and Aḥmad b. Muḥammad al-Dihlāwī. After completing his studies, he taught at the Mosque of the Prophet in Medina. In a *fatwā* of 1937, he declared followers of the Tijāniyya to be 'unbelievers'. From 1945 to 1957, he was a teacher at the Dār al-Ḥadīth Institute in Medina that had been established in 1931 (Hock 1999: 34). From 1955 to 1957, he directed the Institute after the death of the founder, Aḥmad b. Muḥammad al-Dihlawī (Lacroix 2009: 73). After ᶜAbd al-Raḥmān b. Yūsuf 'al-Ifrīqī's death in 1957, the Institute was directed by his student, ᶜUmar b. Muḥammad al-Fallāta (1926–98), whose grandparents had emigrated from Masina, Mali, to northern Nigeria in the early twentieth century. His parents had settled in Medina in 1927 (for his biography, see Ch. Ahmed 2015: 115ff). In 1964, the Dār al-Ḥadīth Institute was attached to the Islamic University of Medina where it functioned as a department of *ḥadīth* (Lacroix 2009: 73ff). Another influential Malian scholar in Mecca was Muḥammad ᶜAlī Ag Ataher, a Kel Intassar Tuareg from Goundam, who returned to Mali in 1952 (Brenner 2001: 101).[39]

An equally important pillar for the spread of Salafi-oriented ideas of reform was studying in Mecca and Medina[40] and in Egypt (al-Azhar University): from the mid-1930s, the number of West African students in Egypt and Saudi Arabia increased considerably and after their return these students formed the core of the nascent Salafi-oriented movement of reform.[41] In Egypt and Saudi Arabia these students witnessed the rise of Arab nationalism, as well as the rise of the ikhwān al-muslimūn and the jam^ciyyat al-shubbān al-muslimīn (JSM) reform movements.[42] The JSM became even more important for the life of early students from West Africa than the ikhwān al-muslimūn due to the fact that Shubbān leaders Dr Aḥmad Yaḥyā Dardir and Professor Maḥmūd Shaltūt, a later rector of al-Azhar University, actively supported the first students from West Africa.

The first West African students had come to al-Azhar in 1935 and completed their studies in 1943. Due to World War II, their return to West Africa turned out to be rather complicated, but it was eventually organised by the French consulate in Cairo (Kaba 1974: 83). In 1944, the first six students were able to return to West Africa, and they became the founders of the first Salafi-oriented movement of reform in Mali, Ivory Coast and Guinea: al-Ḥājj Muḥammad Lamine Tunkara (b. 1915) and al-Ḥājj Muḥammad Sanusi Jabi (Diabi, b. 1912) arrived first, to be followed by al-Ḥājj Kabiné Kaba (b. 1918), al-Ḥājj Muḥammad Fode Keita (b. 1918), al-Ḥājj Sanusi Tura (Turé) Gassama and al-Ḥājj ᶜAbd al-Raḥmān Dramé from the Gambia (Kaba 1974: 85; Hock 1999: 37). After stop-overs in Bouaké, which became the centre for the spread of Salafi-oriented ideas of reform in Ivory Coast (Launay 1992: 85), and in Kankan, these students settled down in Bamako, which was not only a major centre of the Juula trader network, but also a major urban agglomeration and the railway head for the Bamako–Dakar railway line.[43] The early supporters of the Azhar students were almost exclusively traders. These traders were not learned in the Islamic sciences, but pious Muslims and, at the same time, cosmopolitan, that is, part of a larger world of trade that extended far beyond local or regional contexts. One of them, al-Ḥājj Muḥammad Kaba, offered his courtyard to the Azharis for their lectures, which quickly attracted an interested audience. Important for the early success of the Azharis were their oratory capabilities and their perfect knowledge of Arabic (Kaba 1974: 175). Another aspect of the nascent ahl al-sunna movement was their propagation of a new Islamic fashion, the *ḥijāb* for women and the white *galabiyya* for men that represented 'Egyptian elegance' (Kaba 1974: 175) and established symbolic distinction.

Although the Azhar students and their followers started to call themselves ahl al-sunna, or Salafis who followed the *ᶜaqīda al-salafiyya* (Brenner

2001: 147), they were soon labelled 'Wahhabis' by the director of the Bureau des Affaires Musulmanes in Bamako, Michel Cardaire, who opposed 'Wahhabis' whereever he could.[44] Michel Cardaire and the French saw the ahl al-sunna as representing 'un Islam de combat' (Brenner 2001: 164). The derogative term 'Wahhabi' was also adopted by the Muslim opponents of the ahl al-sunna, such as Shaykh Muḥammad Sharīf. In Mali (as well as in the wider Mande region), Salafi-oriented reformers became known as 'bras croisés' due to their practice of praying with their 'arms crossed' (*qabḍ*). In Ghana and Benin they were labelled *munkiri* or *munkirai* (Hausa, from the Arabic *al-munkirūn*, those who reject/deny, that is, those who deny, for instance, the ability of Sufi to 'see' God) (Abdoulaye 2007: 160; Hiskett 1980: 132).

Central to the early activities of the ahl al-sunna, apart from their critique of Sufism, in particular the Tijāniyya and Sufi-oriented practices such as saint veneration ('maraboutisme'), were their attacks against both Islamic and pre-Islamic religious traditions, such as the Kònò mask society,[45] divination, faith in amulets, therapeutic usage of the Qurʾān, local funeral practices, costly marriage and naming ceremonies and highly symbolical issues such as the sighting of the moon. The first dispute over the sighting of the moon took place in 1948 in Bamako in the context of the *ᶜīd al-kabīr* (*Tabaski*) of that year (Brenner 2001: 69). Another important element of ahl al-sunna critique was their rejection of established social traditions: while the Suwarian tradition in the greater Mande region basically accepted ethnic, social and communal differences among Muslims, the ahl al-sunna denied 'the religious salience of such distinctions . . . for them, there were only "pure" Muslims . . . and ignorant Muslims' (Launay 1992: 89). Such a position was perceived as being rather exclusivist, yet it attracted newcomers to Islam as well as casted people: true Muslims were to be known not through their birth and descent but from their behaviour. Authority did not come through inherited social status, but through years of studies at al-Azhar or in Mecca and Medina (Launay 1992: 90). In addition, followers of the ahl al-sunna regarded other Muslims as impure and refused to marry outside ahl al-sunna circles: all others were regarded as unbelievers (Kobo 2012: 145). The doctrinal critique expressed by the ahl al-sunna was complemented by their refusal to take part in festivities, both on the family level as well as on the communal level: their doctrinal critique was thus embedded in a general social and political discourse that advocated profound reform of existing ways of living Islam (Brenner 2001: 145). The combination of doctrinal critique, symbolic distantiation, social segregation and the rejection of established and well-respected ways of living Islam inevitably created animosity on the part of those who were rejected and who felt insulted by the ahl al-sunna.

A major reason for the success of the ahl al-sunna in Mali was that they offered emancipation from social conventions and structures, in particular social hierarchies,[46] hierarchies of age ('les vieux') and religious hierarchies based on the authority of Sufi scholars. The refusal of ahl al-sunna to participate in social events and religious celebrations that were linked with high costs enhanced the puritanic image of the ahl al-sunna, but also created the impression that they were people who wanted to get rich. This impression was fed by the ahl al-sunna slogan 'if you don't pray, you cannot earn any money' (Brenner 2001: 149). By working hard and by spending little, the ahl al-sunna were able to accumulate capital and to become successful traders and entrepreneurs. Another important element of ahl al-sunna activities was their critique of the colonial system and their endeavours to establish a new system of Islamic education. These efforts began in the guise of evening classes in the houses of supporters of the ahl al-sunna. In 1946, the ahl al-sunna tried to register their first school in Bamako. Their request was granted in 1947, but construction did not start until 1949 and the school was finally opened in 1950 (Brenner 2001: 55). They also tried to open a school in Kankan (Guinea) in 1945/6 but were opposed by Kankan's leading religious scholar, Shaykh Muḥammad Sharīf (Chérif, d. 1955; see Kaba 2004). In subsequent years, the ahl al-sunna in both Mali and Guinea clashed repeatedly with Shaykh Muḥammad Sharīf and eventually were forced to apologise to him, before they were allowed to open their first school in Bamako (Brenner 2001: 58). Shaykh Muḥammad Sharīf continued, however, to denounce the ahl al-sunna as 'Wahhabis' or 'Wahhabi heretics' (Brenner 2001: 62). The showdown with Shaykh Muḥammad Sharīf led to a reaction by the French colonial administration: from 1950, the French started a policy of 'containment' (*politique d'endiguement*). The officer to implement this policy was Michel Cardaire, who also organised a counter-reform movement around Amadou Hampaté Bā and ᶜAbd al-Wahhāb Doucouré (Brenner 2001: 87).[47] A major element of this counter-reform movement was the establishment of Sufi-oriented 'médersas' in Bamako, Segu and Kankan (Kaba 1974: 163). The school established by ᶜAbd al-Wahhāb Doucouré in Bamako, *raḍīᶜ al-ᶜilm*, compared rather badly, however, with the first 'Subbanu' school in Bamako and had only ninety students in late 1951 (Hock 1999: 44).[48]

After four years of fighting with the French administration, which was unwilling to accept a new type of 'médersa', the ahl al-sunna eventually succeeded in getting their first *madrasa* registered in Bamako. At the same time, they registered their movement as the jamᶜiyyat al-shubbān al-muslimīn (JSM) (Kaba 1974: 139), or, colloquially, the 'Subbanu' movement. Meanwhile, the reformers continued their evening courses and public lectures. In order not to create conflict with established religious authorities, these meetings were held outside mosques and in private courtyards. Despite the efforts of the ahl al-sunna not to provoke disputes with established religious authorities, a first dispute occurred in November 1948, when scholars of the ahl al-sunna groups met with established scholars from Bamako following an invitation by Marije Niarè, Bamako's 'chef'. In the public dispute, the local scholars were humiliated because not one of them was able to answer questions on the basics of the faith of the ahl al-sunna, and because they demonstrated their lack of knowledge of the Arabic language (Hock 1999: 41). This dispute boosted the image of the ahl al-sunna as proper religious scholars and was central to their demand for the opening of a school in 1949. This school was officially registered on 22 July 1950 (Hock 1999: 41), but was closed again in 1951. At the same time, the French authorities interdicted the JSM. Subsequently, the four Malian Azharis, al-Ḥājj Muḥammad Lamine Tunkara, al-Ḥājj Muḥammad Sanusi Jabi, al-Ḥājj Kabiné Kaba and al-Ḥājj Muḥammad Fode Keita left Bamako and settled in Bouaké in Ivory Coast, which now became the major centre of the ahl al-sunna in the greater Mande region (Hock 1999: 44).

The first ahl al-sunna school in Bamako and the schools that were established in Segu, Bouaké and Sikasso in the early 1950s were characterised by their Western outlook and structure, for instance in terms of curricula and timetables, as well as equipment (such as desks and blackboards). As such, they responded to a demand for modern Islamic education among a growing number of urban Muslims, often the families of traders, who were no longer affiliated to a Sufi scholar. The first students of the 'Subbanu' school in Bamako came from Bamako, but also from Guinea, Ivory Coast and Burkina Faso. In October 1951, the school had 300 students, in December 1951, 400, and was subsequently closed down by the French authorities in order 'to avoid trouble' (Kaba 1974: 158).

The confrontation between the ahl al-sunna and the French-supported movement of counter-reform as led by scholars such as ᶜAbd al-Wahhāb Doucouré and Amadou Hampaté Bā, both affiliated with the Tijāniyya-Ḥamāwiyya,[49] was intensified by the fact that the ahl al-sunna supported the independence movement in Mali, Guinea and Ivory Coast, in particular the Rassemblement Démocratique Africain (RDA) led by Mamadou Konaté (d. 1956) and Modibo Keita in Mali. In the late 1950s, conflicts between the ahl al-sunna and their opponents intensified due to the fact that ahl al-sunna started to dispute existing claims to religious leadership. Paradigmatic was the conflict over control of the Bamako Friday mosque in 1957 (see Kaba 1974: 211ff). Although Bamako had only one Friday mosque (built in 1948), the local scholarly establishment had ordained that Muslims practising *qabḍ* (which meant all ahl al-sunna) should be excluded from Friday prayers. On 17 May 1957, the situation escalated when ahl al-sunna followers announced that they would pray in their own new mosque. A gathering of loyalist Muslims tried to prevent this, and when a single 'Wahhabi' tried to enter the mosque to pray, the situation escalated into a riot (Brenner 2001: 123–4). As a result, 278 houses and the new ahl al-sunna mosque were plundered and burned down. In the aftermath of the 1957 riots in Bamako, a rich trader, Moriké Mankané, offered the ahl al-sunna his mosque as a new centre, and in March 1958, the new RDA-dominated administration registered the new ahl al-sunna school (Hock 1999: 46).

Despite French repression in the early and mid-1950s, the ahl al-sunna continued to spread along the coffee and kola trade routes 'à la vitesse des camions de transports inter-territoriaux' (Kaba 2004: 240) from the urban centres of the greater Mande region into smaller market towns, in particular, Mopti, San, Buguni, Sikasso and Kayes (all in Mali), Kayrawan, Macenta, Belya, Kissidougou, Conacry and Boke (all in Guinea), to Bo and Sefadu (in Sierra Leone), Bouaké, Danane, Man, Daloa, Gagnoa and Treichville/ Abidjan (all in Ivory Coast) as well as Bobo Dioulasso (Burkina Faso) (Kaba

1974: 149). The ahl al-sunna were less successful, however, in places such as Nioro, Kankan, Jenne, Timbuktu and Gao, where Sufi orders ruled supreme (Brenner 2001: 148; see also Soares 2005a; Mommersteeg 2012).

When the RDA eventually won the elections in Mali in 1956, the situation changed again. The Bureau des Affaires Musulmanes was closed in 1958 and the RDA hit out against the 'chefferie' system, that is, the established local political authorities, and in this endeavour they sought the support of the ahl al-sunna. Equally, the RDA-led government ceased its support for the movement of 'counter-reform' (Brenner 2001: 125). In late 1956, the ahl al-sunna were allowed to register again, now as a branch of the UCM, and in 1957, they applied for permission to construct a new school and a first mosque of their own. In 1958, the ahl al-sunna also set up their first women's branch, Silama Jama, led by al-Ḥājja Binta Sall, the daughter of an *imām*, which rapidly spread to Keyes, Segu and Gao (Hock 1999: 47). The women's branch of the ahl al-sunna became very successful in the 1960s and 1970s and acquired particular fame due to its efforts to organise pilgrimages for women in the 1970s (Hock 1999: 47). In January 1959, the ahl al-sunna movement acquired a second school in Bamako that was accommodated in the house of another rich reformer, Issa Yattasaye. This school was led by 'Cheikhna' Ḥamāllāh Yattabari (b. 1920), who became Mali's leading ahl al-sunna scholar in the 1960s and 1970s (Hock 1999: 46, 67). 'Cheikhna' Ḥamāllāh Yattabari had studied in Nioro and had gone on pilgrimage in the mid-1940s. He stayed in Saudi Arabia, was appointed *imām* in Medina and taught at the 'maᶜhad al-ᶜulūm wa-l-sharīᶜa'. In 1958, he returned to Mali via Sudan, Congo and Ivory Coast and opened the school mentioned above. In 1962, he was imprisoned because he attacked Mali's socialist government in a letter to a member of Saudi Arabia's royal family. He was released in 1964 and was appointed *imām* of the Nuurumissiri mosque of Moriké Mankané (Hock 1999: 67). 'Cheikhna' Yattabari died in 1985 and was followed by his son ᶜAbd al-ᶜAzīz Yattabari, who had studied Islamic law in Benghasi (in Libya) (Hock 1999: 101).

In 1957, ahl al-sunna delegates from Mali, Guinea, Burkina Faso and Ivory Coast took part in the first transnational congress of the UCM in Dakar. Although local JSM branches in Mali, Guinea, Ivory Coast and Burkina Faso joined the UCM, the UCM never became a centralist organisation. Regional particularities prevailed and the congress revealed first splits within the Salafi-oriented movement of reform in West Africa: while the Senegalese UCM advocated a moderate and modernist approach to reform, the JSM branches from Mali, Guinea, Ivory Coast and Burkina stuck to their radical positions (Kaba 1974: 243ff).

After independence, Mali's ahl al-sunna experienced a period of marginalisation under Modibo Keita's socialist regime (1960–8). The Keita regime also hit out against traders who were branded as 'parasites'.[50] In 1962, the UCM was prohibited, and ahl al-sunna schools were put under state control as *écoles franco-arabes*, in the context of the nationalisation of the 'colonial' school system (Brenner 2001: 186). As a consequence, many ahl al-sunna moved to Ivory Coast within the Juula traders' network and strengthened the Salafi-oriented movement of reform there, or stayed in Mali and became increasingly radical (Hock 1999: 68). The 1962 educational reforms defined 'médersas' as primary schools, where the study of Arabic started in the first year. The goal was to secularise education in the 'médersas' and to integrate them into the government school system (Brenner 2001: 212). Due to the fact that the Keita regime was not able to translate its plans for educational reform into social realities, the Malian Government school system deteriorated, while the Muslim 'médersas' flourished (Hock 1999: 65).

The general situation in Mali changed again in 1968, when the Keita regime was ousted in a military coup and replaced by the regime of Moussa Traoré (r. 1969–91). Both traders and ahl al-sunna were rehabilitated and were even sought after as allies of the new military regime. The Islamic 'médersas' were now basically ignored by the state and could develop on their own. In subsequent years, the ahl al-sunna movement spread widely in Mali, established a number of new schools and even found support in some rural areas. In 1968, the new regime liberalised regulations for Friday prayers; Friday afternoons were declared a national holiday (Hock 1999: 94) and new Friday mosques were established in Bamako and beyond.[51] The first ahl al-sunna Friday mosque in Bamako was opened in 1971. 'Cheikhna' Yattabari became its first *imām*. In 1974, the old Friday mosque in Bamako was torn down and replaced by a larger one that was opened in 1976. First religious programmes on the national radio were broadcast in 1968 (from 1983 also on TV) (Soares 2005a: 233). In 1970, the new regime registered the UCM, although it was prohibited again in 1972, in the context of the efforts of the military regime to impose political hegemony. Still, reformist activities were supported by the state: from 1969 to 1971, for instance, twelve Malian students who had returned from studies in Egypt were appointed functionaries of the state and quickly rose in rank (Hock 1999: 82).[52] From 1970, Air Mali conducted weekly flights to Mecca that were highly subsidised by the state and were used by the Juula trader network in Mali, Ivory Coast and Guinea. After an air crash in 1974, these flights were cancelled, but by this time thousands of Muslims from the region had used this opportunity to perform the pilgrimage (and to do business). Their experiences, and the fact that Saudi Arabia started a policy of generous funding of Islamic activities in countries such as Mali with income generated by the oil boom since 1973, led to a re-orientation of the ahl al-sunna movement in Mali away from Egyptian influence and towards Saudi Arabia. Saudi financial support resulted, for instance, in the building of a new *madrasa* for 'Cheikhna' Yattabari in Bamako and the building of numerous new ahl al-sunna mosques and 'médersas' all over Mali from 1973/4, often mediated by ahl al-sunna-oriented traders (Hock 1999: 85).[53] At this time, some 'médersas' were better equipped than government schools and were able to attract more and more students. The numerical growth of 'médersas' also provided employment for second-generation ahl al-sunna followers (Brenner 2001: 214).

The influx of funds from Saudi Arabia as well as the crisis of the Malian education system led to a considerable increase in the number of ahl al-sunna-led schools: in 1981, Mali had in the region of 170 'médersas', in 1983 288, in 1989 318 and in 1992 358. These schools had more than 67,000 students and more than 1,800 teachers (Brenner 2001: 210; Cissé 1992: 130).[54] In 1983, Mali also had 1,233 qur'ānic schools with about 5,000 students.[55] In 1991, about 28 per cent of all children of school age were actually attending school and 20 per cent of these children were attending 'médersas' (Brenner 2001: 197; Zobel 2013: 77). As a consequence of the educational efforts of the ahl al-sunna, Arabic continued to spread as Mali's second language of communication and as the primary language of scholars. As a result, established scholars gradually lost their hegemony of interpretation of Arabic texts (Hock 1999: 102). When Mali's system of education collapsed in the late 1980s due to lack of funds, ahl al-sunna schools recruited in the region of 25 per cent of all students in Mali (Hock 1999: 125). The major ahl al-sunna school in Bamako was 'Cheikhna' Yattabari's Wahhabiyyamissiri, which had been led since 1985 by ᶜAbd al-ᶜAzīz Yattabari (Hock 1999: 126). Apart from Cheikhna Yattabari's school there was the Institut Islamique Narou Joliba led by Amadou Kansai, and the Institut Khāled b. ᶜAbd al-ᶜAzīz led by al-Ḥājj Baba Cissé (Amselle 1985: 347).

Saudi support for the ahl al-sunna in Mali became manifest in the visit of the first *imām* of the mosque of Medina, ᶜAbd al-ᶜAzīz b. Ṣālaḥ in 1974, who gave a sermon in Bamako's major Friday mosque, preaching against Sufi ideas, the concept of intermediaries and faith in amulets. He also defended the practice of *qabḍ* during prayer (Hock 1999: 89). Mali cultivated close connections with Saudi Arabia in the 1970s for political reasons: it was seen as a convenient (and profitable) way to boost the regime's policies as Islamic. In that sense, Moussa Traoré's regime started a policy that eventually led into a piety trap as the gap between the regime's public announcements and its will to translate such announcements into social realities grew wider and wider. At the same time, the regime needed the ahl al-sunna as allies in its fight against the chefferie and established Sufi scholars who were seen as opponents of the regime's policies of reform (Hock 1999: 91). In order to coordinate (and to control) government Islamic policies, a Bureau des Oulémas was established in 1975. This institution was initially controlled by pro-government Sufi-oriented scholars such as Muḥammad uld 'Cheikhna' Ḥamāllāh from Nioro and Salif Tall from Segu, both affiliated with the Tijāniyya. Later, some ahl al-sunna-oriented scholars joined the Bureau des Oulémas and came to be seen as 'marabouts de gouvernement' (Hock 1999: 91).

This development continued in the 1980s, the period of Mali's second republic under President Moussa Traoré: the state tried to organise Islam and to maintain control over Muslim activities. In Ramadan 1983, the regime of Moussa Traoré closed all bars and discotheques, a rather cosmetic measure to boost the Islamic legitimacy of the regime (Hock 1999: 118). In order to organise and administer Muslim activities, the Traoré regime established the Association Malienne pour l'Unité et le Progrès de l'Islam (AMUPI) in 1980, although this organisation made its first public appearance in 1983 and held its first congress in 1987 only (Hock 1999: 112). Its first director was Oumar Ly, un *islamologue fonctionnarisé*. In effect AMUPI was nothing but a branch of the *section religieuse* of Mali's Ministry of the Interior and as such part of the ruling Union Démocratique du Peuple Malien (UDPM), duplicating its national, regional and local cadre structure. Due to its closeness to the ruling party, leading representatives of both the ahl al-sunna movement and the Sufi orders refused to join (Hock 1999: 112). At the same time, AMUPI monopolised access to external funds: all requests for external funds had to pass through AMUPI, which also controlled the distribution of funds and acquired an aura of corruption (Hock 1999: 117).

Despite the support of the Malian state, AMUPI failed to impose its own concepts in the field of education against the resistance of a multitude of 'médersas' which had been asked to adopt the new 'médersa' curriculum (*al-manhaj al-rasmī li-l-madāris al-ahliyya al-^{c}arabiyya: al-marḥala al-ibtidāʾiyya*), developed by AMUPI in 1987 (Hock 1999: 117) as an effort of the Malian state to integrate the 'médersas' in the government school system and to thus domesticate ahl al-sunna schools (Brenner 2001: 258). This decision was adopted officially by decree 112/PG-RM on 30 April 1985 and declared that all 'médersas' were subordinate to the Ministère de l'Éducation Nationale (MEN) as represented by AMUPI (Brenner 2001: 260; Magassa 2006: 145). The section of the MEN responsible for AMUPI as well as the new education policy was the Centre pour la Promotion de la Langue Arabe (CPLA), created in 1979, which was led by a son of Sa^{c}d ^{c}Umar Touré, ^{c}Umar Sa^{c}d Touré (Brenner 2001: 261). In 1981, the CPLA conducted a first census of 'médersas' and started to develop the legislation that led to the 1985 decree. In 1986, ^{c}Umar Sa^{c}d Touré resigned from his position and went to Morocco. At the same time, protest against the new 'médersa' curriculum started, led by Sa^{c}d ^{c}Umar Touré, and resulted in a national boycott of the 1986/7 examinations that had been declared to be optional while the 1987/8 examinations were meant to be obligatory. The opposition against the new curriculum was based on the argument that it did not provide enough space for religion (Brenner 1993b: 170). The boycott of the *madāris* led the Ministère de l'Éducation Nationale to exclude all those students from grants who did not participate in the examinations, a policy that encouraged opposition. In 1988, the minister of national education ordered the CPLA to compromise. This decision led to a stalemate in government 'médersa' development (Brenner 2001: 267–8). In 1989, a new minister of national education accepted the demands of the *madāris* as a basis for negotiations (Brenner 1993b: 170). At the same time, the CPLA became responsible for control of the administration of the *madāris*, although not a single employee of the CPLA spoke Arabic apart from the director (Brenner 1993b: 179).

Although AMUPI tried to co-opt representatives of all religious orientations, in particular the ahl al-sunna, it failed in this effort as ahl al-sunna representatives continued to criticise state policies with respect to Islam as insufficient (Hock 1999: 119). In the context of the economic crisis of the 1980s, the ahl al-sunna gained further popular support, especially in the urban centres: they were increasingly able to provide those social services that the state failed to provide, particularly in the fields of education and health. The ahl al-sunna also supported people in finding accommodation and work, and at the same time fought against cost-intensive social practices such as marriages, funerals and naming ceremonies that an increasing section of the Malian population was unable to afford (Hock 1999: 121). In the 1980s, the ahl al-sunna even financed the building of hospitals of their own that competed with the increasingly derelict institutions of the state. Traders and entrepreneurs affiliated with the ahl al-sunna opened new supermarkets (often combined with a mosque and a *madrasa*) and thus opened new business venues. The saying 'whoever turns Wahhabi will become rich' reflected the increasing wealth of ahl al-sunna entrepreneurs in Bamako in the 1980s (Hock 1999: 125) and mirrored the popular perception of the ahl al-sunna as a religious movement that taught an Islamic 'gospel of prosperity'.

In the 1980s, the ahl al-sunna were in the vanguard of the fight for democracy, assuming that a government elected democratically would not be able to resist popular demands for Islamisation: a democratic state would express the will of a Muslim majority. By demanding implementation of the government's promises regarding the Islamisation of state and society, the ahl al-sunna unmasked the Moussa Traoré administration. These demands were often supported by representatives of the Sufi orders (Hock 1999: 139). As the government was not able or willing to fulfil the demands of the Islamic opposition, the regime lost all remaining vestiges of legitimacy: the Malian state had fallen into its own piety trap. In March 1991, the regime of Mousssa Traoré was deposed in a peaceful revolution cum military coup, supported prominently by the ahl al-sunna, to be followed by the introduction of a democratic multi-party system in 1992 and the election of first Alpha Oumar Konaré (1992–2002) and then Amadou Toumani Touré (2002–12) as presidents of Mali. With the liberalisation of the political system, the number of political and religious associations exploded and brought about an increasing fragmentation of the ahl al-sunna movement, a development that continued well into the 2000s. In 2000, Mali had 106 associations; in 2010, it had 146 different Islamic associations. The proliferation of Mali's Islamic associations has been manifested, for instance, in annual disputes (since the 1990s) over the sighting of the moon (Holder 2012: 389; Holder 2009b: 277ff).[56]

Due to the fact that AMUPI supported the Moussa Traoré administration to its very end, AMUPI was discredited. As a consequence, a plethora of newly established associations fought over the spoils and tried to gain institutional influence in post-Traoré Mali. On 18 September 1991, nine Islamic groups eventually formed the Comité de Coordination des Associations Islamiques du Mali (CCAIM). Some of them represented ahl al-sunna ideas, while others were close to Sufi orders. The first leader of the CCAIM was Mory Sidibé, a follower of the Niass branch of the Tijāniyya. One of the strongest associations within the CCAIM was the Association Islamique pour le Salut (AIS) led by ᶜAbd al-ᶜAzīz Yattabari and Modibo Sangaré (Hock 1999: 141). This coalition of Islamic associations shows that alliances of convenience against the Traoré regime had led to the emergence of a working relationship between Sufis and moderate ahl al-sunna.[57]

At the same time, AMUPI lost its monopoly as the only officially registered Islamic association in Mali (Soares 2005a: 233). The crisis of the ahl al-sunna, often due to disputes over authority between second- and third-generation representatives of the group, became manifest when initial demands for further Islamisation of the Malian state and society were rejected by the democratically elected government of President Alpha Oumar Konaré that stressed that Mali was to remain secular and that religious parties would not be tolerated. In 1992, the Konaré administration even lifted the ban on alcohol during Ramadan and brought back Fridays as full working days. In the end, even ahl al-sunna resistance to the visit of the German evangelist Reinhard Bonnke and his plan to conduct an 'evangelisation crusade' in Bamako misfired in September 1993 due to lack of mass support for ahl al-sunna protests. Although radical Muslims protested against the *laïcité* of the

Malian state, the reversal of Traoré's closure of bars and nightclubs during Ramadan, the popular habit of betting on horses (PMU), the reforms of the *code de la Famille* since 2001 and the Miss Communauté Économique des États de l'Afrique Occidentale (CEDAO) beauty pageant, the majority of Muslims in Mali were not mobilised by such opposition and supported the democratic process (at least up to 2002). This process was supported by a vast majority of Malians who hoped that the new democratic system would eventually master all crises (Hock 1999: 144).

Due to the fact that AMUPI was unable to recover lost ground in the 1990s and was no longer acceptable as a national Muslim umbrella organisation, President Konaré established the Haut Conseil Islamique in 2000 in order to accommodate Muslims who rejected AMUPI policies. In 2000, there was a new debate in Mali on the *code de la famille et des personnes*, in which the ahl al-sunna advocated greater conformity with the *sharīᶜa* (Holder 2012: 390). These discussions referred to the *code de la famille et de la tutelle* of 1962. Presidents Konaré and Touré both endorsed the secular character of Mali and supported, for instance, the campaign against female circumcision (Schulz 2012: 36ff). In 2009, the new *code de la famille* was ratified by the parliament, but was sent back to a committee of inquiry by President Amani Toumani Touré due to protests from a plethora of religious associations, including the Haut Conseil Islamique, and was finally accepted as law in December 2011 (Zobel 2013: 80).[58]

Debates on the reform of the 1962 *code de la famille* had actually started in 1991/2 and involved efforts by President Konaré (and his wife) to reform laws that were adverse to women. These endeavours turned into a real commitment in the context of the fourth global conference on women in Beijing in 1995. In 1997, a ministry for the promotion of women, children and the family was created, but efforts to draft the new legislation took a lot of time due to the fact that public meetings (*concertations regionales*) were organised throughout the country to hear the opinion of the people. In 2002, the draft version of the new legislation was published, but was withdrawn again after several weeks of controversial debates (Soares 2009: 418). Under President Amani Toumani Touré, efforts to introduce new legislation subsided and were opposed by a broad coalition of Muslim associations. These groups have proposed substantial changes to the proposed legislation since 2002, in particular because the new (and old) *code de la famille* did not accept the validity of religious marriages. In 2004, religious associations and *imāms* even started to issue their own marriage certificates that were immediately declared 'not legally valid' by the government (Soares 2009: 427).

While the 1990s were a period of crisis for the ahl al-sunna, other Muslim movements rose to prominence and developed into true mass movements. The most conspicuous movement of reform at this time was founded by Sharīf ᶜUthmān Madani Haidara (b. 1955) under the label Ansar Dine (or Association Malienne pour le Soutien de l'Islam) (AMSI)) (see Holder 2009b: 277, 2012, 2013a, 2013b; Soares 2005a: 234ff, 2013: 76ff; Schulz 2012). Sharīf Haidara was born in Tamani, 70 km south of Segu, into a family of Tijānī scholars. As a child, he attended the médersa of Saᶜd ᶜUmar Turé. After the death of his father, he returned to Tamani, and in 1976 continued his *ṭalab al-ᶜilm* in Ivory Coast, where he started a career as a *dāᶜī*. In 1981, he returned to Mali and lived for some time in Tamani and Mopti. Due to a conflict with a local religious scholar, Lassana Konaté, in 1981/2, he was banned from religious activities in 1983 and moved to Bamako, where he restarted his 'iconoclastic' preaching activities in 1984 (Holder 2012: 393). In 1989, he was again banned from preaching due to two controversial statements, namely, that 'prayer was not Islam' and that 'Jesus had died (on the cross) and would not return at the end of time to assist the Mahdi' (Holder 2012: 394).[59]

Due to his controversial statements and his open critique of habits of corruption in both Malian society and government, 'moral decay' and 'false saints', Sharīf Haidara became the most popular scholar and preacher in Mali in the 1990s (Mommersteeg 2012: 145). His Ansar Dine movement consequently became a religious mass movement in democratic Mali in a short period of time. Although Sharīf Haidara came from a Sufi background, his movement of reform had many ahl al-sunna features: it found most supporters in urban centres, was highly popular among women and advocated modern Islamic education, as well as a modern way of living Islam, beyond established religious practices. Equally, Sharīf Haidara defended the translation of the Qurᵓān into Bambara, Mali's national language of communication (Soares 2005a: 234). In 1992, the Ansar Dine movement held its first national congress and elected a bureau national, while Sharīf Haidara became its *guide spirituel*. In subsequent years, the Ansar Dine movement spread to Ivory Coast and Burkina Faso and was renamed Ansar Dine International in 2004 (Holder 2012: 403). The success of the Ansar Dine as an Islamic reform movement in the 1990s and 2000s mirrors the failure of the ahl al-sunna to develop a correspondingly popular programme of reform: in many ways, the ahl al-sunna were too radical and too puritanical for a majority of Malian Muslims, while the Ansar Dine responded better to everyday aspirations.[60]

The region of Gao became another centre for the development of Salafi-oriented reform from the 1970s, attesting to the fragmented character of the ahl al-sunna movement in Mali. Apart from the mainstream ahl al-sunna group that recruited most of its followers among functionaries, traders and artisans, there also was a more radical group that became known as jamāᶜat anṣār al-sunna. This movement had 5,000 to 8,000 followers in several communities in the early 1990s. While the jamāᶜat anṣār al-sunna chose to settle in distinct and separate quarters or villages, the more moderate ahl al-sunna remained integrated into Gao's urban milieu. The jamāᶜat anṣār al-sunna movement was marked by its conscious adoption of rural settlements in order to stress its segregation from *jāhilī* urban society (Nietzen and Bankson 1995: 404). This move towards spatial segregation was possibly informed by experiences of Muslim migrant workers in Ghana, where migrant workers had lived in separate quarters. Migrant workers had been the first to convert to Islam (beyond the circles of the religious scholars and their families) in the colonial period in Mali, and later were often among the first to support the ahl al-sunna movement (Peterson 2011: 204).

The jamāᶜat anṣār al-sunna started to gain a foothold in Gao in the early 1970s, due to the return of migrant workers from Ghana, where these workers had been living in 'zongos'.[61] In 1969, however, the Ghanaian Government ordered the expatriation of about 200,000 migrant workers without a valid residence permit. Some of these migrant workers returned to Gao and established their own community there. The leader of this group was Abū ᶜAmr Saᶜīd b. Idrīs, colloquially known as Seydou Idrissa (Nietzen 1990: 406), who had been educated by local scholars in Kumasi and Tamale in the 1960s. In Tamale, one of the major centres of the ahl al-sunna movement in Ghana (see Weiss 2008; Ihle 2003), he had become *imām* of the 'Songhay' mosque in 1967/8. Back in Mali, Seydou Idrissa established the jamāᶜat anṣār al-sunna in Kadji near Gao and continued his *da^{c}wa* among migrant workers in Niger, Burkina Faso, Togo, Ghana and Ivory Coast (Nietzen 1990: 407). Seydou Idrissa's deputy, Sa^{c}d ^{c}Abd al-Raḥmān, eventually started to address Seydou Idrissa as *amīr al-mu$^{\supset}$minīn*, that is, supreme leader of all Muslims, a claim that was rejected by a majority of Muslims in Gao, including the ahl al-sunna. A break with the larger community occurred in 1973, when a stone disappeared that had allegedly been set up by Askia Muḥammad Turé in 1497 on the outskirts of Gao and that had become a centre of veneration. A majority of Muslims in Gao thought the followers of Seydou Idrissa were responsible (Nietzen and Bankson 1995: 410). The crisis was aggravated by the 1973/4 Sahelian drought. Seydou Idrissa was deposed as *imām* of the Kadji village mosque, and consequently left with his followers to establish a new settlement near Kadji, a move that was called a *hijra*. Malian authorities were not prepared to accept this and forced Seydou Idrissa to return to Kadji, where he established himself in a new quarter, Dar al-Salam. Due to his violent attacks against established Islamic practices, Seydou Idrissa was seen by a majority of villagers as a 'slanderer of tradition' (Nietzen 1990: 409), yet his movement continued to gain followers and created many splits, even within families, when new members rejected their own families. This social dynamic created much bitterness and Seydou Idrissa, as well as some of his followers, were eventually arrested in 1974 and 1975 for stirring up unrest (Nietzen 1990: 409). They were sent to Kidal prison, and released in 1977. After their return to Kadji, the situation remained tense but did not escalate into physical confrontation.

Despite its spatial segregation from the majority of Muslims in Gao, the jamā^{c}at anṣār al-sunna continued to grow, especially among women, for it provided security in a local context that was characterised by the precarity of living conditions and the absence of men who had gone to Ghana as migrant workers. Also, the practices of *niqāb* veiling and seclusion that were adopted by jamā^{c}at anṣār al-sunna women were associated with high social status: secluded and veiled women were not expected to labour in the fields (Nietzen and Bankson 1995: 426): to this day, wealthy people are those 'who can afford to seclude their wives', while the poor cannot afford the loss of female labour, especially in the fields, that results from seclusion (Warms 1992: 497). Also, jamā^{c}at anṣār al-sunna settlements introduced communal work, kitchen gardens and labour cooperation, and Tuesdays became community project days. These new forms of organisation effectively increased agricultural production and the physical living conditions of the jamāᶜat anṣār al-sunna (Nietzen 1990: 415). The jamāᶜat anṣār al-sunna stressed punctuality, proper ritual and religous piety and rejected, for instance, the practice of tayammum (Nietzen 1990: 412). However, jamāᶜat anṣār al-sunna members also stopped participating in communal rituals and ceremonies, such as burials, and even established separate burial grounds (Nietzen and Bankson 1995: 404). While veiling was adopted as a mode of personal seclusion for women, separate settlements were chosen in order to stress spatial segregation. The jamāᶜat anṣār al-sunna communities in the region of Gao can be regarded thus as 'closed communities' (Nietzen 1990: 414); they represent a particular path within the wider movement of Salafi-oriented reform leading from symbolic distantiation, doctrinal distinction and social separation to spatial segregation.

In sum, it is possible to differentiate four generations of ahl al-sunna in Mali since independence: the founding fathers of the 1940s and 1950s, mostly traders and students who had been to al-Azhar; the generation of their sons and followers in the 1960s and 1970s, still mostly traders and their families as well as students who had been to Saudi Arabia; the generation of grandsons in the 1980s who witnessed the expansion of the ahl al-sunna movement into new social circles beyond traders and students: state functionaries, teachers and Western-educated intellectuals, but also artisans and workers who had recently migrated to the larger urban centres (Hock 1999: 127); and, finally, the generation of 'crisis' in the 1990s and 2000s that witnessed not only the failure of the ahl al-sunna as a mass movement, but also its fragmentation into many different associations, and the rise of Sharīf Haidara's Ansar Dine movement. The only Muslim association that has achieved grass roots support since the 1990s was Ansar Dine (Soares 2007: 222).

'Tuareg' Rebellion and *Jihād*

In 2012, Mali's uneasy development towards a democratic nation was rocked by yet another Tuareg rebellion. This time, the war did not remain confined to the north but threatened to engulf the whole nation (see ICG 2012c). While seen by many outside observers as being part of the general destablilisation of the Sahara after the collapse of Libya in 2011, the Tuareg rebellion of 2012 was the result of social dynamics that had transformed Mali since at least the 1990s.[62] Both Mali and Niger can look back on a long tradition of rebellion (by Tuareg groups) against colonial and post-colonial central administrations. In addition, from the 1960s Tuareg emigrated to Algeria and Libya, looking for work, either as refugees following the failure of the 1963/4 rebellion, or due to a series of drought years in the 1970s and 1980s. These *Ishumaren* (from the French term *chômeur*, vagabond) started to return to Mali (and Niger) in the 1990s and contributed to social change. In exile, many 'Ishumaren' had received military training (for instance, in the Libyan Islamic Legion) and were prepared to revenge the massacres carried out by the Malian Army during the suppression of the 1963/4 rebellion.

The second rebellion against the central government started in mid-1990 and quickly defeated a demoralised and badly equipped Malian Army. Negotiations led to a peace agreement in mid-1991 and Mali's new interim government granted ample rights of autonomy to its three northern regions.[63] Still, the war continued, due to the fact that the Tuareg split into several competing factions (four in Mali, ten in Niger). In addition, sedentary populations in the Niger valley formed self-defence militias, the Ganda Koy ('lords of the land') that openly called for the extinction of Mali's 'white' (Tuareg and Arab) minorities.[64] In the civil war between the different rebel groups, the Mouvement Populaire de l'Azawad (MPA – or MPLA, Mouvement Populaire pour la Libération de l'Azawad) eventually defeated the competing Armée Révolutionaire pour la Libération de l'Azawad (ARLA), the Front Populaire de Libération de l'Azawad (FPLA)[65] and the Front Islamique Arabe de l'Azawad (FIAA)[66] in 1995. The victory of the MP(L)A, which represented the noble Ifoghas and the religious families (the *Inesleman*), as well as their 'slaves' (the *Iklan*, sg. *Akli*, better: 'freed slaves', *Iderfan*, sg. *Edaref* in Tāmashāq), simultaneously constituted a defeat for the vassal groups among the Ifoghas, the *Imghad* (sg. *Amaghid*), as well as the *Inaden* (sg. *Inad*), the socially ostracised artisan groups, organised in both ARLA and FPLA, which had tried to gain emancipation from supremacy of the Ifoghas. The military leader of the MPA, Iyād ag Ghālī, was a nephew of the paramount chief, the *Amenokal* of the Ifoghas federation, Intallah ag Ataher. Iyād ag Ghālī's second in command had been an *Akli*, Bilāl Salūm, who was killed by ARLA units on 25 February 1994 (Klute 2013a: 186f, 573).

This political development hides a second important development in the 1990s, namely the rise of the vassal groups, or *Imghad*, among both Tuareg and Arabs (in particular, the Kunta) in the spheres of trade and salaried employment. Until the 1990s, trade in the Sahara between Algeria, Libya, Niger and Mali had been organised and controlled by networks of trading families who were often linked with the religious families of the Kunta (or the Tuareg *Inesleman*) and their vassals and 'slaves' in Algeria and northern Mali. These trader dynasties had managed to protect their economic hegemony in the colonial period and survived the shift from camels to trucks in Saharan trade after World War II, even when trade goods changed. In 1962, Saharan transit trade was declared illegal by both Algeria and Mali, and turned into smuggling, causing the gradual demise of the Algerian trading dynasties. In the 1990s, Malian Tuareg and vassals of the Kunta increasingly assumed control over 'legal smuggling' with consumer goods, cigarettes, petrol and dates (Scheele 2012: 95). At the same time, 'illegal smuggling' (*al-frūd al-ḥarām*) of guns (from China via Mauritania) and drugs (from Colombia via Guinea Bissau, Togo, Benin and Burkina Faso) gained in importance and was controlled almost completely by new trader networks among the *Ishumaren* and the vassal groups, the *Imghad*, even if the patrons of this trade, which also switched from slow trucks to fast four-wheel pick-ups, were again based in Algeria and often employed Tuareg *Imghad* and Kunta vassals as drivers only (Scheele 2012: 98). At the same time, the *frūd al-ḥarām* generated those resources (money, vehicles and guns) that gave the *Imghad* (and the *Ishumaren*) among the Tuareg the ability to rebel against their noble and saintly overlords in the early 1990s. Although this rebellion eventually collapsed in 1995, it pointed to the basic change in social and economic structures that informed the rebellions in northern Mali from 2006 to 2009 and from 2012 to 2015.

With their victory over ARLA in 1995, the political elite of the Ifoghas and the religious families managed to consolidate their social and political paramountship in the region that had existed since the colonial period. The major argument that decided the 1990–5 civil war among the Tuareg was the question of which of the major rebel groups was able to protect the civilian population most effectively (for instance, against attacks by the Malian Army or massacres by the Ganda Koy militias). The military victory of the MPLA was thus not only a result of their superior strategy and numbers, but also due to the fact that the MPLA was able to provide better security for civilian populations than ARLA or FPLA. The military victory of the MPLA was turned into a series of electoral victories in the context of Malian parliamentary, local and regional elections in 1997. These elections were won almost exclusively by Ifoghas candidates supported by *Iklan*. A most remarkable episode was the electoral campaign for the position of the mayor of Kidal in 1999, when the ruling Alliance pour la Démocratie au Mali (ADEMA), representing the established elites, was forced to choose between two competing candidates, namely, Gamny, an *Akli*, and Nina walat Intallu, an *Inad* lady, who had organised the Tuareg diaspora (that is, the *Ishumaren*, mostly *Imghad* and *Inaden*) in Abidjan and who was supported by the *Inaden* in Kidal. In the end, the *Amenukal* of the Ifoghas federation spoke out against Nina walat Intallu who was subsequently supported by the opposition party Congrès National pour la Démocratie au Mali (CNID) and won the election in Kidal (Klute 2013a: 600).

In 2006, a third rebellion started, and lasted until 2009. This rebellion was initially led by Ibrāhīm ag Bahanga (d. 2011) and the Alliance Démocratique du 23 Mai pour le Changement (ADC) that soon disintegrated, however, and broke up into several factions that represented different social and political aspirations among the Tuareg groups. A major factor of the 2006–9 rebellion was the struggle for control of trans-Saharan trade, especially in drugs like cocaine. The government of Amadou Toumani Touré has been accused of tolerating the establishment of AQMI in the region as a counterforce to existing drug trafficking networks, and has also been accused of being involved (ICG 2012c: 5).

The Tuareg rebellion of 2012 can essentially be seen as a continuation of the quest for socio-political emancipation among the *Inaden* and *Imghad* and, in response to such aspirations, as an effort by the established groups and families to preserve the status quo in northern Mali. The conflict acquired a complicated character due to the unprecedented intervention of outside forces, as well as the proliferation of arms from a disintegrating Libya. First of all, the Mouvement National de Libération de l'Azawad (MNLA) (*al-*

ḥaraka al-waṭaniyya li-taḥrīr Azawad), established in 2011, which opened the rebellion on 17 January 2012, can be seen as a successor to both ARLA and FPLA: the MNLA represented the interests of the Ifoghas *Imghad* and *Inaden* groups, as well as the Kel Antessar who opposed Ifoghas' claims to political supremacy, and was led by Bilal ag Chérif (b. 1977), a cousin of Ibrāhīm ag Bahanga, Hama ag Sid'Aḥmad, Ibrāhīm ag Bahanga's father-in-law, and Nina walat Intallu. The political (and secular) aspirations of the MNLA, namely, independence for the region, were opposed by an alliance of the established elites and religious families, represented by Iyād ag Ghāli, the leader of the MPLA during the 1990s, in the guise of the anṣār al-dīn group that was established in early 2012. In October 2011, Iyād ag Ghālī had claimed the position of secretary-general of the MNLA, but was rejected by a majority of *Imghad* fighters in the MNLA (Klute 2013b: 12).

The MNLA of early 2012 represented a broader social spectrum than ARLA in 1991. However, after the emergence of the anṣār al-dīn as the dominant force in mid-2012, many MNLA fighters, including some with an *Imghad* background joined the anṣār al-dīn that paid better salaries (ICG 2012c: 17, 26). Other *Imghad* of the Ifoghas federation preferred to remain loyal to Mali. They were led by Colonel al-Ḥājj ag Gamu (b. 1964), an *Amaghid* from the Menaka region, who had been appointed an officer of the Malian Army in 1996. In 2012, he led his troops (mostly *Imghad* and 'black' Malians) into Niger when he realised that he could not hold Kidal against the MNLA. Al-Ḥājj ag Gamu had fought as an ARLA fighter against Iyad ag Ghali and the MPLA in the 1991–5 war in northern Mali and he had also fought as an officer of the Malian Army against Ibrāhīm ag Bahanga from 2007 to 2009 (Klute 2013b: 12). In Mali, al-Ḥājj ag Gamu has been accused of covering up the government's involvement in the trans-Saharan drug traffic.

In early 2012, the well-equipped fighters of the anṣār al-dīn entered an alliance with both *al-Qā*ᶜ*ida fi-Gharb Ifrīqiyya*/al-Qāᶜida au Maghreb Islamique (AQMI) and the Mouvement pour l'Unicité de Dieu et le Jihād en Afrique Occidentale (MUJAO) (Arab.: *ḥarakat al-tawḥīd wa-l-jihād fi-gharb Ifrīqiya*) forces. This coalition succeeded in pushing aside MNLA forces until June 2012 and taking over control of the rebellion, which now turned into a *jihād* (Bourgeot 2013: 120). The goal of AQMI and MUJAO was to establish an Islamic state in Mali as a whole and they were the major force behind the military offensive into the south in January 2013. Both AQMI and MUJAO were organisations that relied on Arab rather than Tuareg fighters. MUJAO had split from AQMI in 2011 and represented mostly Arab vassal populations in Mali, in particular the Lamhar of the Tilemsi valley east of Timbuktu and north of Gao, as well as *jihād*-minded FulBe in the Gao region and a number of Mauritanians (see Klute and Lecocq in print; Lacher and Steinberg 2015: 82). In addition, MUJAO was supported by the jamāᶜat anṣār al-sunna villages near Gao, in particular, Kadji (Lebovich 2013: 3). AQMI, in contrast, was dominated by North Africans, mostly Algerians, as well as Barābīsh Arabs. AQMI forces had been able to establish a base in the Timétrine mountains, that is, in Kunta territory, and west of the Ifoghas-controlled Adrar in 2007, and were tolerated there by the Malian Army, possibly in order to counterbalance Ibrāhīm ag Bahanga's rebel fighters (Bourgeot 2013: 117ff). AQMI forces in northern Mali were led by Mukhtār b. Muḥammad Belmukhtār (b. 1972 in Ghardaia), an Algerian activist who had fought in Afghanistan and who had become a member of the Algerian Groupe Islamique Armée (GIA) after his return from Afghanistan. In 2002/3, he established himself in northern Mali and led an AQMI commando, the katībat al-mulaththimīn ('the brigade of the veiled ones') that claimed control over the trans-Saharan cigarette trade. In December 2012, Mukhtār b. Muḥammad Belmukhtār split from AQMI and formed a new organisation, the katībat al-muwaqqiᶜīn bi-l-dam ('those who sign with blood') (ICG 2013b: 2; 39). In August 2013, the katībat al-muwaqqiᶜīn bi-l-dam, searching for local support, merged with MUJAO and formed a new organisation, al-murābiṭūn. Since 2013, the murābiṭūn have suffered serious losses against French troops and their African allies in northeastern Mali and northern Niger, but have been able to survive by retreating into Libya.[67]

After the French military victory over this coalition of *jihād*-minded groups by means of Operation Serval, the MNLA was able, with French support, to re-occupy important positions in northern Mali, especially in Kidal (see ICG 2013d: 8ff; Olivier de Sardan 2013: 15ff; Soares 2012: 1–2). The come-back of the MNLA implied the possibility of political emancipation for the *Imghad* and *Inaden* groups as well as the *Ishumaren* that had supported the MNLA. In order to counter such a development, the Ifoghas political elites and Ifoghas religious families reacted in a well-established manner: the anṣār al-dīn split and Iyād ag Ghāli as well as some of the anṣār al-dīn fighters went into exile to Algeria. Those who stayed behind formed a new organisation on 24 January 2013, namely, the Mouvement Islamique de l'Azawad (MIA), led by Alghabass ag Intalla, a son of the *Amenokal* of the Ifoghas federation, Intalla ag Ataher. Another son of Intalla ag Ataher, Muḥammad ag Intalla, founded the Haut Conseil de l'Azawad (HCA) that represented the intelligentsia of the Ifoghas and the religious scholars. The HCA also led the negotiations with the Malian Government in Ouagadougou, Burkina Faso, which resulted in a peace agreement in June 2013. These negotiations aimed at the exclusion of the competing MNLA and thus of the *Imghad* and *Inaden* groups, from a political solution in Mali (Bourgeot 2013: 125).[68] At the same time, they were meant to show that only the noble Ifoghas and the religious families were able to assure security and stability in the region. This strategy turned out to be successful in the elections for Mali's new legislative assembly in autumn 2013. For these elections, the HCA fronted three candidates on the ticket of the Rassemblement pour le Mali (RPM), the party of Ibrahim Boubacar Keita, who became Mali's new president in September 2013 (ICG 2014d: 15), namely Muḥammad ag Intalla, Aḥmada ag Bibi, who had fought for anṣār al-dīn, and Inawlène ag Aḥmad who was close to Iyād ag Ghāli. While Muḥammad ag Intalla and Aḥmada ag Bibi won two of the three seats reserved for the Kidal region, Inawalène ag Aḥmad lost his seat to an independent *Imghad* candidate, Aḥmoudene ag Iknass, who had been opposed by the HCA (ICG 2014d: 19, 24).

Despite this partial set-back, the Ifoghas-dominated alliance in the HCA was able to demonstrate that it could still organise peace and stability most effectively (ICG 2014d: 25), even if competing Arab and Tuareg alliances, as well as the *Imghad*, proved to be increasingly important players. As a result of these political manouvres, the MNLA split into two groups on 18 March 2014, namely, die-hard MNLA followers who still advocated independance, and a more moderate Coalition du Peuple de l'Azawad (CPA), which was prepared to accept autonomy. On 21 May 2014, the MNLA resumed the armed struggle, but re-entered negotiations only two days later. Since then, periods of truce and low-intensity warfare have characterised developments in northern Mali. On 20 June 2015, the major rebel groups finally signed a peace agreement with the Malian Government that promised limited autonomy for the Azawad (*Neue Zürcher Zeitung*, 20 June 2015).[69] The events of 2012 show that Tuareg and Arab populations in northern Mali continue to be fragmented into competing factions and that actors continue to regroup strategically, political considerations being paramount. It would thus be misleading to interpret events in northern Mali since 2012 from a religious perspective only and regard all groups involved as exclusively *jihād*-minded. Rather, a series of issues was at stake, such as the social and political emancipation of the *Imghad* and *Inaden* groups, the preservation of Ifoghas and Kunta paramount rule, control over trade routes and trade in the Sahara, including control of the lucrative trade in arms and drugs, the assertion of Mali's sovereignty in the northern regions, as well as a series of competing 'imperial' interests: France, the US and Algeria all tried to profit from Libya's collapse as a political player in the Sahara in 2011.

Conclusion

Despite their geographical closeness, the cases of Senegal and Mali show that local conditions were paramount for the development of both Sufi- and Salafi-oriented reform and led to the emergence of different trajectories of Salafi-oriented reform in the two countries. Although traders, religious scholars and students formed the initial social basis for the UCM (and the HF) in Senegal, as well as the ahl al-sunna in Mali, the UCM and, later, the JIR, had major difficulties in gaining popular support in Senegal. The Sufi orders in Senegal were, by contrast, successful in their efforts to establish their own movements of reform and to deny UCM and JIR popular support. This situation changed slightly in the 1990s, when the JIR decided to abandon outright critique of Senegal's Sufi-oriented families and to offer a model of Islamic education that has started to attract popular support among middle-class groups due to its combination of established Islamic sciences and secular marketable skills. In contrast to Senegal, Mali's Salafi-oriented movement of reform had a better head-start in the 1940s and 1950s, and grew beyond the clientele of traders, scholars and students in the 1970s and 1980s. This success was based not only on the fact that Mali's ahl al-sunna offered a new educational model that was attractive to Mali's small but growing middle-class groups, but also on the fact that Sufi orders in Mali, when compared with Senegal, had a weaker social, political and economic basis and were not really seen as partners by Malian governments. Despite better conditions for the development of Salafi-oriented reform, Mali's ahl al-sunna proved unable to profit from the process of democratisation in the early 1990s, and lost out to a new Sufi-oriented movement of reform, the Ansar Dine movement of Chérif Haidara. In contrast to the JIR in Senegal, Mali's ahl al-sunna movement, which has never been a homogeneous movement, has suffered from a process of fragmentation since the 1990s and the shock of *jihād*-minded rebellion in northern Mali since 2012. In both Senegal and Mali, Salafi-oriented movements of reform have not really won popular social support beyond traders, scholars and students, and some urban middle-class groups.

Notes

1. These dynamics have been diagnosed with respect to Senegal by Leonardo Villalon, as 'mutualities of position' (Villalon 2004: 69) and 'hybrid' features of organisation (Villalon 1999: 142), and by Monika Salzbrunn as a 'hybridization of religious and political practices' (Salzbrunn 2002).
2. The expression 'échange de services' was coined by Christian Coulon (1981: 174). D. B. Cruise O'Brien called the 'échange de services' a 'social contract' (Cruise O'Brien 1992: 9).
3. For Ibrāhīm Niass's biography see Seesemann (2011); for succession disputes within the Niass branch of the Tijāniyya see Hill (2013) and Seesemann (2011). Ibrāhīm Niass's role as *imām* of the Madina Baay mosque community in Kaolack was assumed by Cheikh Ḥasan Cissé (1945–2008) and Ḥasan Cissé's son, Aḥmad Tijānī ᶜAlī Cissé (b. 1955, *khalīfa* since 2008) (Hill 2013: 106ff.) Ḥasan Cissé established close links with the diasporic communities of the Tijāniyya in the West, especially London and New York, but also in Cape Town.
4. On Cheikh Tidiane Sy's political career, see Behrman (1970), Villalon (2000), Loimeier (2001) and Samson (2005).
5. For Cheikh Touré's biography, see Gomez-Perez (1997), Kane (2005) and Loimeier (1994b, 2001).
6. For his biography, see Gomez-Perez (1997: 436).
7. For Saliou Kandji's (1924–2006) biography, see Gomez-Perez (1997: 442).
8. For Bachirou Ly's (b. 1927) biography, see Gomez-Perez (1997: 444).

9. Communication Cheikh Touré, 13 April 1992; letter Cheikh Touré, 23 May 1995; see Loimeier (2001: 340).
10. Loimeier (2001: 151); see also Lô (1985) and Coulibaly (1999) for a discussion of Mamadou Dia's politics and Senghor's take-over of power in 1962.
11. Pilgrimage has expanded considerably in Senegal since the 1990s, in particular, the participation of *pèlerins commerçants*, mostly women. In 2008, approximately 10,500 Senegalese were able to perform the pilgrimage, and 80 per cent of Senegalese pilgrims were women (Hardy and Semin 2009: 141). The nomination of JIR representatives to the Commission de Pèlerinage reflects the growing importance of the JIR in Senegal.
12. See Loimeier (2001: 269ff), Augis (2005: 309ff), Cantone (2005: 119ff) and Gomez-Perez (2005: 193ff, 219).
13. Muḥammad Sall graduated from school in 1964 and became a teacher, and then, in 1977, inspector of education, until he became, in 1983, 'responsable' of the JIR in Thiès (Gomez-Perez 2005: 196).
14. While most founding fathers of Salafi-oriented reform in the 1950s and 1960s had studied either in Senegal or in some North African countries, in particular, Algeria and Egypt, many second-generation 'Salafis' got the chance to pursue studies in Libya, Sudan and Saudi-Arabia since the 1970s. In addition, the number of graduates from Arab universities has increased, at least until 2001, when grants for studies in Saudi Arabia dried out. In addition, many second-generation 'arabisants' realised that their education at an Arab university did not provide them with job opportunities in Senegal beyond the 'écoles franco-arabes' (Gomez-Perez 2005: 196f).
15. For the development of Islamic education in Senegal in the twentieth century see Loimeier (2001: 227ff, 349ff).
16. A significant number of leading personalities and 'militants' within HF (as well as within the UCM) in fact had a Sufi background, mostly families of scholars associated with the Tijāniyya (see Gomez-Perez 2005: 202).
17. Sadio Cissé from St Louis was Khalil Marega's son-in-law. He joined HF in 1980, was appointed Senegalese ambassador to Kuwait in 1986 and became vice-president of HF in 1991 (Gomez-Perez 2005: 216).
18. At the same time, it has to be stressed that efforts to unite Senegal's different Salafi-oriented associations under one roof, such as the Organisation de l'Action Islamique (OAI) (est. 1985), the Association de Soutien et de Coordination des Activités Islamiques (1997), the Collectif des Associations Islamiques du Sénégal or the Comité Islamique pour la Réforme du Code de la Famille du Sénégal

(CIRCOFS), have failed, so far, due to numerous disputes over questions of leadership, orientation and strategy (Gomez-Perez 2005: 213f).

19. Gueye (2002: 248); both Cheikh Gueye (2002) and Leonardo Villalon (1999. 2000: 477f) have pointed out the importance of generational dynamics of development within Senegalese Sufi orders and have stressed the role of the 'marabouts petit-fils' (grandson marabouts).
20. Audrain (2004: 99). The term 'marabouts mondains' was coined by A. Diaw, M. C. Diop and M. Diouf (see Audrain 2004: 99).
21. For female Islamic activism on a broader scale see Gomez-Perez and Ba (2015: 175ff) and Sow (2005).
22. The term Matlaboul Fawzaïni, literally 'the quest for both kinds of accomplishment', referring to success and accomplishment (*fawz*) in this world as well as the hereafter, indicates the far-reaching ambitions of this Sufi-oriented movement of reform.
23. On the MMUD, see Audrain (2004: 99ff), Samson (2005: 48, 2007: 46ff, 2009a: 257ff, 2009b: 151ff) and Seck (2010: 72ff).
24. Khalifa Diouf's father was a secretary of Abūbakar Sy, Cheikh Aḥmad Tidiane Sy's father, and worked with Cheikh Aḥmed Tidiane Sy in the 1960s (Samson 2005: 120).
25. For a detailed analysis of heteroglossia in Senegal, see Hill (2011).
26. Literally: '. . . and such days (of varying fortunes) we give to men and men by turns' (Qur'ān 3: 140, translation ᶜAbdallāh Yūsuf ᶜAlī).
27. For a recent presentation of the different Khalifa Général of the Murīdiyya, see the bi-monthly journal *Mouride*, No. 40, February 2006, a special issue on *Le Khalifat 1927–2006* that was published for the annual magal to Touba.
28. According to the 1994 census, Murīds had a share of 85.5 per cent of the population in Diourbel (Tijānīs 9.5 per cent, Qādirīs 3.7 per cent), 44.7 per cent in Thiès (T.: 40.3 per cent, Q.: 7.4 per cent) and 45.9 per cent in Louga (T.: 37.3 per cent, Q.: 15.1 per cent), while in all other regions, Murīds constituted a minority: Dakar (M.: 23.4 per cent, T.: 51.4 per cent, Q.: 6.9 per cent), Ziguinchor (M.: 4.0 per cent; T.: 22.9 per cent; Q.: 32.9 per cent), St Louis (M.: 6.4 per cent; T.: 80.2 per cent; Q.: 8.4 per cent), Tambakounda (M.: 7.5 per cent; T.: 54.1 per cent; Q.: 25.2 per cent), Kaolack (M.: 27.2 per cent; T.: 65.4 per cent; Q.: 4.9 per cent), Fatick (M.: 38.6 per cent; T.: 39.5 per cent; Q.: 12.4 per cent) and Kolda (M.: 3.6 per cent; T.: 52.7 per cent; Q.: 26.0 per cent). On the national level, the Murīdiyya accounted for 30.1 per cent of the population, the Tijāniyya for 47.4 per cent, the Qādiriyya for 10.9 per cent,

while other groups (Layènes, Christians and so on) represented 11.3 per cent of the population. See Piga (2002: 35).

29. In a first round, Diouf scored 42.3 per cent of the votes, while Wade gained 28.1 per cent, Mustafa Niass 18 per cent and Djibo Ka 6 per cent. In the second round Wade united most opposition votes and gained 58 per cent, while Diouf lost with a score of 42 per cent. In the parliamentary elections of 2001, SOPI, an electoral alliance of PDS and forty other parties won 89 out of 120 seats, while the PS was left with 10 seats. In 1998, the PS had garnered 93 seats (50.12 per cent of the vote) as against 23 for the PDS (in a parliament of 140 seats). In the 1993 elections, the PDS had won 27 seats (PS: 84, 56.24 per cent), in the 1988 elections 17 (PS: 84, 71.05 per cent) and in the 1983 elections 9 (PS: 111, 79.6 per cent). These results show a constant increase of votes for the opposition and almost present the victory of the opposition in the 2000 and 2001 elections as being inevitable. The rise of the opposition was due, however, to the simultaneous fatigue, constant in-fights and a structural crisis of the PS that was not resolved in the next round of elections in 2007: the 2007 elections confirmed Abdoulaye Wade as president of Senegal (with 56 per centof the votes), while his opponents Idrissa Seck, Tanor Dieng and Moustapha Niass garnered 15 per cent, 14 per cent and 6 per cent of the electorate, respectively. In the parliamentary elections of 2007, the ruling 'SOPI' coalition won 131 of 150 parliamentary seats, and 19 went to twelve small opposition parties. The bigger opposition parties boycotted these elections (see Dahou and Foucher 2004; Diop 2013a; Havard 2004).
30. For an analysis of the 'ndiggël electoral' and the failure of the *ndiggël*, see Audrain (2004: 99ff); Dione (2013: 111ff); Diaw, Diop and Diouf (2000: 167–8 ff); Gomez-Perez (1997); Gueye (2002: 280ff); as well as Samson (2002, 2005: 326ff).
31. For an analysis of the presidential elections of 2000, see Audrain (2004: 99ff).
32. Muḥammad al-Amīn Bara Mbakke (1925–2010, also Sérigne Mouhamadou Lamine Bara Mbakke or Cheikh Bara Mbakke), the eldest son of the second Khalifa Général, Falilou Mbakke (1945–68), became the new Khalifa Général of the Murīdiyya when his uncle Saliou Mbakke died on 28 December 2007. His succession was quickly accepted by all major leaders of the Murīdiyya, including Sérigne Moustapha Saliou Mbakke. When Muḥammad al-Amīn Bara Mbakke died in 2010, he was followed by his son, Sérigne Cheikh Makhtar 'Maty Leye' Mbakke.
33. Abdou Diouf refused to extend the special territorial and legal status of the city of Touba that had been established by the French colonial authorities in 1928 (Babou 2013b: 304).

34. For a resumé of Abdoulaye Wade's administration, see Diop (2013a), and especially the articles by Diop (2013b), Diagne (2013) and Gellar (2013).
35. In 2014, Senegal had a total population of approximately 12.5 million.
36. In a first round of the elections, Abdoulaye Wade received 34.8 per cent of the vote (Macky Sall 26.5 per cent and Mustafa Niass 13.2 per cent). In the decisive second round on 25 March 2012, Abdoulaye Wade received only 34.2 per cent, while Macky Sall (b. 1961 in Fatick) received 65.8 per cent. Macky Sall, a geologist and engineer, had been a politician in Wade's PDS; he was appointed minister in Abdoulaye Wade's government and became prime minister from 2004 to 2007. In 2009, he left the PDS and joined a broad oppositional coalition that eventually won the 2012 elections. He has so far kept an equal distance from both Mūridiyya and Tijāniyya.
37. The introduction of optional religious (Islamic and Christian) education in government primary schools in 2002 was complemented by the creation of public franco-arab schools in 2003 and a general law on national education in 2004 (see Bodian and Villalon 2015: 74).
38. On the development of Salafi-oriented movements of reform in West Africa in general, see Triaud (1981); for Ivory Coast, see Launay (1992), LeBlanc (2005, 2009), Lebovich (2005), Miran (1998, 2006a, 2006b) and Savadogo (2005); for Ghana, see Hiskett (1980), Ihle (2003), Kobo (2012), Miran (2005), Pontzen (2014) and Weiss (2006, 2008); for Benin, see Abdoulaye (2007) and Brégand (2007, 2009); for Burkina Faso, see Cissé (1998), Kobo (2012), Kone-Dao (2005), Kouanda (1998), Otayek (1993b) and Traoré (2005, 2010).
39. For details of the role of Malian scholars in Saudi-Arabia, see Ch. Ahmed (2015).
40. The Islamic University of Medina was founded in 1961. Its first rector was the Grand Mufti of Saudi Arabia, Muḥammad b. Ibrāhīm Āl al-Shaykh, followed by his deputy ᶜAbd al-ᶜAzīz b. ᶜAbdallāh b. Bāz, who acted as rector until 1975 (Schulze 1993: 25). The Islamic University of Medina was extremely important as a centre for the formation of Salafi-oriented networks among African students, and challenged the leading role of al-Azhar in Cairo as a centre of study for African students from the 1970s. In contrast to the Umm al-Qurā University in Mecca, the Islamic University of Medina had a distinct Islamic syllabus. On the Islamic University of Medina, see Schulze (1990: 156ff), Lacroix (2009: 73ff), Meijer (2009: 20) and Ch. Ahmed (2015: 132ff).
41. In 1952, 105 students from French West Africa were studying at al-Azhar (Kaba 1974: 77).

42. The jamᶜiyyat al-shubbān al-muslimīn was founded in 1927 by ᶜAbd al-Ḥāmid Sard and was more a 'literary club' than an activist movement like the ikhwān al-muslimūn, although the programme and orientation of these two Salafi-oriented groups was virtually identical (Kaba 1974: 81).
43. Bamako grew from a population of approximately 130,000 in 1960 to about 236,000 in 1972 and in the region of 420,000 in 1976. Many migrants who settled in Bamako and other urban centres were recent converts to Islam or converted to Islam in the city and subsequently became followers of the ahl al-sunna (Hock 1999: 22, 87).
44. Cardaire was director of Bamako's BAM branch from 1950 to 1956. His opposition to the 'Wahhabis' was expressed in his text *L'Islam et le terroir africain* (1954) (Kaba 1974: 102).
45. The fight against the Kònò mask society was a major preoccupation of the ahl al-sunna in southwestern Mali in the 1950s (see Peterson 2011: 228).
46. Many West African societies have rules of social endogamy that prevent marriage across social boundaries between 'free-born' and 'castés' (casted people), that is, smiths, tanners, carpenters, potters and weavers, as well as griots (bards) and slave descendants. These social boundaries extend into politics as well as economics, and have been important for the development of religious movements of reform that rejected social boundaries.
47. Apart from the French-supported counter-reform 'médersas', other scholars also established schools that were neither supported by the French colonial administration nor linked with the JSM. Most important was the school established by al-Ḥājj Saᶜd ᶜUmar Touré (b. 1912) from Segu, a religious scholar affiliated to the Tijāniyya who was opposed to the ahl al-sunna, and developed his own programme of reform. In 1948, he founded the madrasat sabīl al-falāḥ, which was characterised by its new and modern didactics, as well as its inclusion of modern subjects such as mathematics (Hock 1999: 35). On Saᶜd ᶜUmar Touré, see Brenner (2001: 55ff).
48. ᶜAbd al-Wahhāb Doucouré studied at the Zaytuna University in Tunis. His father, Mamadou Doucouré, had been a follower of Shaykh Ḥamāllāh, the founder of a reform movement within the Tijāniyya in Mauritania and Mali's Nioro region the 1930s, but had broken with him in the late 1930s (Soares 2005a: 185).
49. On the Ḥamāwiyya-Tijāniyya which acquired major popular support in Mali, Ivory Coast, Burkina Faso and Ghana from the 1930s, see Brenner (1984, 2001), Hanretta (2009), Hock (1999), Soares (2005a) and Traoré (1983).

50. The Keita regime also hit out against the Tuareg populations in the north who had risen in 1963. The brutality of the suppression of this revolt by the Malian Army in 1963 and 1964 created a fertile ground for revenge and informed the background of the next 'Tuareg' rebellion in 1990 (see Klute 1995).
51. While Bamako had a total of 41 mosques (including one Friday mosque) in 1960, their number grew to 203 in 1983 (including thirty Friday mosques). Twenty-seven or twenty-eight mosques were affiliated to the ahl al-sunna movement in that year (Triaud 1988b: 168). In 1986, Bamako had forty-one Friday mosques (Brenner 2001: 197).
52. These students had studied at Sa^{c}d ^{c}Umar Touré's school in Segu before going to Egypt. Their return and rise in the administration meant a huge success for Touré's *sabīl al-falāḥ* school in Segu (Hock 1999: 82).
53. From 1974 to 1984, Mali received about 600 million US dollars from Saudi Arabia and other Arab countries. These funds were mostly used for the construction of new ahl al-sunna mosques and schools. Saudi Arabia also provided funds for numerous grants for students (Hock 1999: 99). Saudi funding led to a remarkable increase in the numbers of mosques in Bamako: while Bamako had 41 mosques in 1960 and 77 in 1968, their number rose to 203 in 1983. In 1993 80 (out of 230) mosques in Bamako were under ahl al-sunna control (Hock 1999: 103).
54. In 1983, the 288 médersas had 62,203 students and 1,196 teachers; most schools (100) were in Bamako: they had 22,294 students and 476 teachers (Brenner 1993b: 191).
55. Apart from the ahl al-sunna schools, other schools were also quite successful in their endeavours to acquire grants for their students. Particularly successful was the school of Sa^{c}d ^{c}Umar Touré (Hock 1999: 99).
56. On the development of the mostly Salafi-oriented, but still fragmented Islamic printing market in contemporary Bamako, see Zappa (2015).
57. For an extensive list of Malian Islamic associations, see Hock (1999: 154ff).
58. In 2012, Amani Toumani Touré also established a Ministry for Religious Affairs, which had been a major part of HCI demands (Schmid 2014: 65).
59. While the first statement was not particularly controversial, when understood as 'prayer alone is not Islam', the second was: Sura 4 (al-nisā$^{\circ}$): 157 states unequivocally that Jesus had not (!) died on the cross.
60. Sharīf Haidara's Ansar Dine movement was not identical with another movement of that name that surfaced in early 2012 in the context of a rebellion by the Tuareg and Arab populations in northern Mali.

61. Historically, a *zongo* (Hausa) was an abode for traders from Hausaland, but has today come to mean a separate quarter for Muslim migrants in Ghana.
62. Scheele has stressed in this context that the analysis of the rebellions in northern Mali suffers from 'a chronic underestimation of the vastness and complexity of the Sahara (that) sweeps all religiously minded locals into the vast bucket of "Islamism" or even "terrorism"' (Scheele 2012: 234; see also Greven 2013: 89ff).
63. It has to be considered here that the majority of people in northern Mali (Kidal, Gao and Timbuktu regions) were neither Tuareg nor Arab (except in the region of Kidal), but FulBe pastoralists and Songhay-speaking farmers, as well as Marka fishermen and traders.
64. The Ganda Koy militias were dismantled in 1996 but re-emerged in 2007 under the label Ganda Isa (sons of the land). The Ganda Isa militias were led by Amadou Diallo who was killed in a clash with MNLA forces on 25 March 2012 (ICG 2012c: 14).
65. The FPLA was established in 1991 by Ghissa ag Sidi Muḥammad, and recruited most of its fighters among the Shamanamas (Menaka region), a faction of the Iwellemmidan, as well as the Idnān and the Taghat Mellet, *Imghad* factions of the Ifoghas federation. ARLA also recruited support among Tuareg groups that were not willing to accept Ifoghas-Kel Adrar supremacy (see Klute and Lecocq in print).
66. The FIAA was founded in 1991 and recruited most of its fighters among the Lamhar and Barābīsh Arab populations west, northwest and north of Timbuktu, which rejected both Tuareg and Kunta claims to political domination in the region (Bourgeot 2013: 117ff). In response to FIAA attacks on Gao, Ganda Koy forces massacred a group of Kel Essuk *Ineslemen* who had settled around a Qādirī *zāwiya* near Gao on 23 October 1994. In 1995, FIAA fighters led by Zahabi uld Sidi Muḥammad withdrew to Libya (Klute 2013a: 423).
67. The al-murābiṭūn group has been able, however, to organise terrorist attacks against hotels in Bamako (20 November 2015), Ouagodougou (16 January 2016) and Grand Bassam/Ivory Coast (13 March 2016).
68. The MNLA was in a weak negotiation position due to the fact that the MNLA was possibly responsible for the massacre of Aguelhok in mid-February 2012, when eighty-five Malian soldiers who had been taken prisoner were killed in detention (Schmid 2014: 33f).
69. The MAA, led by Aḥmad uld Sidi Muḥammad, took the place of the Front de Libération Nationale de l'Azawad (FNLA) in 2012, which had again replaced factions of the FIAA.

4

REFORM IN CONTEXT II: NORTHERN NIGERIA (AND NIGER)

Introduction

This chapter follows the same pattern as the last one: I will first of all present the general context of reform, and then briefly discuss the different Sufi-oriented reform movements, before focusing on the emergence of Salafi-oriented movements of reform in the 1970s. In contrast to Senegal (and Mali) as well as Niger, Nigeria is not an overwhelmingly Muslim country, and even in northern Nigeria,[1] Christians have come to form a sizeable minority. This is especially so in the so-called Middle Belt regions, that is, the historical slave hunting grounds of the Sokoto Caliphate and its emirates, including Katsina, Kano, Zaria and Bauchi. Muslim–Christian conflicts have played a major role in the political development of northern Nigeria in the twentieth century, and continue to inform Nigerian politics to this day, for instance in the context of northern Nigeria's *sharīᶜa* debates. Since the late 1970s, Muslims in northern Nigeria have also been confronted with the development of a plethora of different reform-oriented movements. Their struggle for popular support has acquired a violent character at times, as seen in the development of the Boko Haram movement since the early 2000s. Interestingly enough, neighbouring Niger has so far escaped most of northern Nigeria's problems and this chapter will thus ask why Niger's development has been so markedly different, despite the fact that Niger's Salafi-oriented movement of reform is close to the Salafi-oriented movement of reform in northern Nigeria.

In northern Nigeria, Salafi-oriented movements were initially split into two different orientations, namely the (politically) conservative jamāᶜat izālat al-bidᶜa wa-iqāmat al-sunna (Hausa: 'Yan Izala), established in 1978 by Abubakar Gumi and Ismaila Idris, and a group of politically radical but smaller groups, such as the ikhwān led by Ibrāhīm al-Zakzakī. Whereas the politically radical groups stressed the struggle against the Nigerian state that was portrayed as being dominated by Western-oriented Christians, the 'Yan Izala focused almost entirely on the struggle against the Sufi orders, at least until the early 1990s. In recent years, these movements of reform have branched out in a number of further directions, often due to internal disputes over questions of leadership or political strategy. Northern Nigeria also shows that the emergence of a Salafi-oriented movement of reform has to be located, in contrast to Senegal, in the late 1970s, almost twenty years after independence. Earlier movements of reform were linked with the Sufi orders and tended to protest against aspects of colonial rule in terms of moral decay, while political parties such as the Northern Elements' Progressive Union (NEPU) were characterised by a socialist ideology that in the 1950s sought to win the support of the peasant-farmers, the *talakawa*, and cultivated some elements of a religious discourse, but lacked other markers of Salafi-oriented movements of reform. Like the associations of the 1920s and 1930s in Senegal, NEPU and similar movements may be regarded as 'precursors' of later movements of reform, but the cumulation and temporal intensification of reform in terms of a Salafi-oriented programme began in northern Nigeria in the late 1970s only.

The Sufi orders in northern Nigeria, in particular the Qādiriyya and the Tijāniyya, thus represented an earlier tradition of reform that in the 1950s was linked with the names of Ibrāhīm Niass (Tijāniyya) and Nasiru Kabara (Qādiriyya) (see Loimeier 1997a). Their reform endeavours were related to the opening of the ritual and popularisation of the esoteric teachings of the respective order. The opening of the ritual was marked by the introduction of new ritual elements such as *qabḍ* instead of *sadl* for the Tijāniyya, or the *bandiri-dhikr* and the procession (*mawkib*) to the graves of Qādirī saints in Kano on ᶜAbd al-Qādir al-Jīlānī's birthday on 11 Rabīᶜ al-Thānī for the

Qādiriyya. These rituals served as markers of identity and symbolic distanciation from established scholars within both Sufi orders. However, the religious leaders of these Sufi orders can also be seen as representatives of an even older tradition of reform, which was linked with the activities of the Tijānī *jihād* leader al-Ḥājj ᶜUmar Taal (d. 1864), whereas the Qādiriyya was inspired by the legacy of the leader of the Sokoto *jihād* (1804–8), Usman dan Fodio (d. 1817). The writings of these earlier reformers had a strong didactic character, focusing on the basics of *tawḥīd*, *fiqh* and *tasawwuf*.

Early Sufi-oriented Reform

In the context of a study of movements of reform it is possible to interpret the Sokoto *jihād* (1804–8) in the early nineteenth century as a distinctive movement, and as a forerunner of northern Nigeria's movements of reform in the twentieth century (see Last 1967). Murray Last has stressed that the *jihād* was primarily a reform movement, 'reforming lax Muslims, not converting pagans' (Last 1979: 273). A major element of *jihādist* discourses was their critique of the *bidaᶜ* that were tolerated by the Muslim rulers of the Hausa states. An important result of the *jihād* was the emergence of an educational movement that tried, for the first time in northern Nigerian history, to address Muslim women, as the efforts of Nana Asmāʾū, Usman dan Fodio's daughter, show. The legacy of the Sokoto *jihād* was so important for the development of Islam in northern Nigeria that Abubakar Gumi, who was known for his pro-Saudi positions, defended it, although the leaders of the *jihād* were known for their affiliation with the Qādiriyya, Yet, Gumi maintained that 'his own efforts of reform would have been meaningless without the achievements of Usman dan Fodio' (communication Abubakar Gumi, 17 September 1987).

The leaders of the *jihād*, in particular Usman dan Fodio, were indeed affiliated with the Qādiriyya and saw ᶜAbd al-Qādir al-Jīlānī as the 'patron saint' of their movement (Brenner 1988: 47). As a consequence, close links were established and cultivated with the regional centres of the *ṭarīqa*, in particular the Kunta in Timbuktu. However, for the time being, affiliation with the Qādiriyya remained an affair of the scholarly elite and although the Qādiriyya was established as a *ṭarīqa* in Hausaland in the early nineteenth century, Sufi activities and teachings did not become an issue in Islamic education. The Qādiriyya thus did not assume the function of an 'official ideology' for the empire (Brenner 1988: 44). Religio-political competition started, however, in 1831, when the Senegalese scholar al-Ḥājj ᶜUmar Taal came to Sokoto and subsequently won a number of followers for the Tijāniyya, which claimed spiritual supremacy over all other Sufi orders. The ruling elite in Sokoto saw the Qādirī legacy of Usman dan Fodio and the *jihād* endangered by the growth of a competing *ṭarīqa*. In the context of this struggle for spiritual hegemony, the Sultan of Sokoto deposed local rulers, such as the Emir of Zaria, Abdulkadir, who in 1854/5 had dared to publicly proclaim his affiliation with the Tijāniyya and to reject the supreme spiritual authority of the Sultan. Only when the Sokoto caliphate was integrated into the British colonial realm in 1903, and became part of the colony of Nigeria as Northern Nigeria, were Tijānī scholars free to publicise their affiliation.

After the disruption of the wars of conquest, colonial rule came to mean a greater degree of peace and stability, fostering travel and exchange among Muslim communities in West and North Africa. Although both British and French authorities remained nervous about alleged Mahdist or *jihādist* (and later 'Wahhābī') activities, and consequently tried to control religious activities in their respective colonial domains, the number of travelling scholars increased considerably in the twentieth century. As a consequence, a multiplication of orientations took place, even if still confined to different variations of the esoteric episteme. In particular, the religious scholars connected with the Tijāniyya strove to intensify their network links with the centres of their *ṭarīqa*, a move that was answered by corresponding initiatives by the Qādiriyya. In the case of the Qādiriyya, a great number of traders based in the commercial emporium of the north, Kano, helped to establish new links with Qādirī centres in the trading communities of northern Africa, in particular Ghāt and Ghadāmis, but also Tripoli, Tunis and the Fazzan, where centres of the Qādiriyya-Arūsiyya and the Qādiriyya-Salamiyya existed.

With respect to the Tijāniyya, the first *silsila* of the Tijāniyya as introduced by al-Ḥājj ᶜUmar Taal in the mid-nineteenth century was quickly complemented by a number of new *salāsil* that established links with the centres of the *ṭarīqa* in Fes (Morocco) and ᶜAyn Māḍī (Algeria). Of particular importance was the link with the centre of the Tijānī diaspora in the Ḥijāz, led by Alfa Hāshim al-Fūtī (d. 1931), a nephew of al-Ḥājj ᶜUmar Taal, who had emigrated to the Ḥijāz in 1903, after the collapse of al-Ḥājj ᶜUmar Taal's Tukulóór Empire in the late 1890s.[2] Pilgrims from northern Nigeria, in particular, made a point to renew their *salāsil* through Alfa Hāshim, who thus became the hub of Tijānī activities in the Ḥijāz. One of the first Tijānī scholars to come to Nigeria after 1903 was the Mauritanian scholar ᶜAbd al-Wahhāb Ujdūd, also known in northern Nigeria as 'Sharīf Ujdūd'. He came to northern Nigeria in 1909 and was instrumental in renewing spiritual links for the ᶜUmarian branch of the Tijāniyya. This process was characterised as *tajdīd*, the renewal of spiritual allegiances through personal contact with a respected shaykh of the *ṭarīqa*. The latter would claim possession of a specific *silsila* within the *ṭarīqa*, a link that was preferably not known before or shorter than all other known *salāsil*, and thus came to mean an increase in *baraka* for the 'holder' of such a *silsila*. Competition for prestigious *salāsil*, and the diversification of *salāsil*, became a respected activity for scholars of both the Tijāniyya and the Qādiriyya in northern Nigeria in the twentieth century. These activities by Tijānīs as well as Qādirīs were still characterised, however, by the fact that they were restricted to only a small group of scholars and students.

Sufi Reformers of the Twentieth Century: Ibrāhīm Niass and Nasiru Kabara

This kind of *ṭarīqa* affiliation was to change, however, through the activities and teachings of Ibrāhīm Niass (1900–75) and, later, Nasiru Kabara (1925–96) who opened up the teachings of Tijāniyya and Qādiriyya respectively for all Muslims, transforming both Sufi orders into religious mass movements. These mass movements, which may be seen as an expression of the changing political, economic and social conditions of the colonial era, were to influence northern Nigeria's religio-political development decisively. From the 1950s, *ṭarīqa* networks became conveyor belts for political activities, the mass mobilisation of voters, and thus primary tools of power in the hands of increasingly influential scholars.[3] The leaders of these networks consequently started to compete for followers. Great numbers of disciples of the network in the 1950s increased the buying and selling power of religious scholars. The movements of reform that were first started by Ibrāhīm Niass in Senegal in the 1930s and Nasiru Kabara in Kano in the 1950s, were again connected with a renewed quest for spiritual *tajdīd* and the establishment of new transnational links with the centres of the respective order (Loimeier 1997a: 33ff).

Despite widespread critique of processes of change in northern Nigeria, Muslim reformist scholars such as Ibrāhīm Niass and Nasiru Kabara were also willing to defend features of modernity such as the radio. Debates over the radio were part of a general critique of processes of change in northern Nigeria in the 1940s that came to a climax in the 1950s, when both Emir Jaᶜfar of Zaria and Emir ᶜAbdullahi Bayero of Kano protested against the use of the radio for recitation of the Qurʾān, arguing that this constituted a *bidᶜa*. Ibrāhīm Niass retorted that one had to differentiate between recommended and reprehensible *bidaᶜ*, and that the use of the radio for the propagation of Islam was a recommendable innovation, like the use of the aeroplane for transporting pilgrims to Mecca, as it was useful for the dissemination of Islam (Loimeier 1997a: 44; Larkin 2008: 55). However, the different networks of the Sufi orders were not only characterised by their respective endeavours to reform established modes of teaching within both the Tijāniyya and the Qādiriyya. Other traits also intervened, such as the way in which they approached teaching and audiences, their doctrinal argumentation and their stress on specific features of the ritual such as praying with arms crossed, *qabḍ*, and arms out-stretched, *sadl*. These features of the ritual were central to the politics of identity of these different religious groups. As a result of intra-*ṭarīqa* disputes in the 1930s, the further expansion of different realisations of the esoteric episteme can be attested. The move towards the fragmentation of religious authority, which had started with competition between the Qādiriyya and the Tijāniyya in the nineteenth century, was accentuated by competition between the different networks and family branches of the individual Sufi orders.

The success of the Tijāniyya-Ibrāhīmiyya as a religious mass movement in northern Nigeria in the 1950s had a number of consequences for the development of this branch of the *ṭarīqa*. As membership in the Tijāniyya-Ibrāhīmiyya came to mean membership in a network that was open to any Muslim willing to join without being constrained to undergo the time-consuming process of religious learning, the Tijāniyya-Ibrāhīmiyya became a network for traders and entrepreneurs who saw this affiliation as a channel to further economic activities within a transnational religious network. Such a network could provide important political and economic contacts as well as spiritual protection by virtue of shared membership in a spiritual family. In fact, the network of Ibrāhīm Niass was to become so important, not only in religious but also in economic and political terms, that in 1962 he was invited to become a member of the rābiṭat al-ᶜālam al-islāmī, the Saudi-based Muslim World League. Ibrāhīm Niass remained a member of the *rābiṭa* until his death in 1975. The inclusion of Ibrāhīm Niass shows that the rābiṭa was willing, at times, to sideline doctrinal considerations for the sake of political interests (Loimeier 1997a: 33ff; Schulze 1990: 157ff).

The spiritual activities and rituals of the Tijāniyya-Ibrāhīmiyya were effectively used by politicians, traders and entrepreneurs to discuss and advance their worldly and spiritual affairs, both inside and outside the mosques of the *ṭarīqa*. Since the 1950s, these networks of trust have become an umbrella for all kinds of religious, economic and political activities. They focus not only on northern Nigeria but also on Kaolack, Senegal, where Ibrāhīm Niass' residence, Medina-Kaolack, has turned out to be a major centre for regional shrine pilgrimages, as well as a centre of studies in search of knowledge and recognition. These activities did not stop with the demise of Ibrāhīm Niass in 1975, but continued under the leadership of Ibrāhīm Niass' successors, in particular Ḥasan Cissé (see Kane 1989: 27ff).

What has been said for the development of the Tijāniyya-Ibrāhīmiya may be repeated, with a slight difference in emphasis, for the Qādiriyya-Nāṣiriyya. In the 1950s, Nasiru Kabara[4] started to develop the Qādiriyya after the model of Ibrāhīm Niass. In order to be able to claim leadership of the local networks of the Qādiriyya, he began in the early 1940s to collect the *salāsil* of the different local branches of the Qādiriyya. In 1949, he established a direct link to the Sammāniyya in the Sudan. Finally, he made a *ziyāra* to Baghdad in 1953, visiting the grave of ᶜAbd al-Qādir al-Jīlānī and establishing a direct link with the leader of the Qādiriyya, Sharīf Ibrāhīm Saif al-Dīn al-Jīlānī. Nasiru Kabara thus acquired the largest number of *salāsil* of all Qādirī scholars in Kano, as well as in northern Nigeria, and he was the only one to have established a direct link with Baghdad, shortcutting all other *salāsil* in northern Nigeria. This link with Baghdad was to help him enormously to establish his spiritual supremacy within the Qādiriyya in the ensuing years, first in Kano, then in northern Nigeria. In 1978, the Sultan of Sokoto, who had until then been regarded as the supreme leader of the Qādiriyya in Nigeria, recognised Nasiru Kabara's ascendance by asking him to lead the struggle against the 'Yan Izala.

In addition to his success in northern Nigeria, Nasiru Kabara renewed scholarly ties with Libya and established a link with Muᶜammar al-Qadhdhāfī. In late 1986, Dr Sālim Warfallī, a leading member of the Libyan jamᶜiyyat al-daᶜwa al-islāmiyya, visited Nasiru Kabara in Kano and started negotiations in respect of closer ties, as well as the publication of Nasiru Kabara's Hausa translation and *tafsīr* of the Qur^ᵓān. Dr Salim Warfalli's visit was followed by another visit in 1987, when a Libyan delegation took part in the celebrations of the *mawlid* of ᶜAbd al-Qādir al-Jīlānī in Kano and opened a Nigerian office of the jamᶜiyya. In spring 1988, Nasiru Kabara responded to these Libyan initiatives and met Muᶜammar al-Qadhdhāfī in Libya. In February 1988, the links between northern Nigeria and Libya were strengthened when Bayero University Kano (BUK) conferred an honorary doctorate on al-Qadhdhāfī. The alliance between al-Qadhdhāfī and the Qādiriyya-Nāṣiriyya was of mutual interest: Nasiru Kabara acquired not only a donor prepared to publish his *tafsīr* of the Qurᵓān and recognition of his links with the Qādiriyya in Libya, but also support for his struggle against the 'Yan Izala. Al-Qadhdhāfī, for his part, won a local ally for his struggle against the Saudi regime as represented, locally, by the 'Yan Izala and Abubakar Gumi. In 1981, after a series of polemics, Saudi Arabia had declared al-Qadhdhāfī a heretic. In 1982, this *takfīr* led al-Qadhdhāfī to call upon Muslims to 'liberate the Kaᶜba' (Loimeier 1997a: 289).

Nasiru Kabara was eventually able to defend the Qādiriyya against the attacks of the 'Yan Izala and to provide it with a high degree of internal cohesion. This unity survived his death in 1996 and the succession of Qarīb Allāh b. Nasir Kabara (b. 1960), who continued to cultivate links with Libya (Bari 1997: 45ff). By contrast, after the demise of Ibrāhīm Niass in 1975 and the rise of the 'Yan Izala in the late 1970s, the Tijāniyya experienced a serious crisis due to 'Yan Izala attacks. This crisis was accentuated by the recrudescence of local networks of the *ṭarīqa*. To this day, these networks cultivate their own links with centres of spiritual authority such as Fes, ᶜAyn Māḍī, Cairo and the Ḥijāz, but also Kaolack and Tivaouane in Senegal. The Tijānī networks also developed distinctive positions as far as the attacks of the 'Yan Izala on the doctrinal tenets of the Tijāniyya were concerned. Thus, there was a 'die-hard' faction led by Dahiru Bauchi (b. 1929) who simply refused to discuss the tenets of the Tijāniyya for the sake of a de-escalation of intra-Muslim religious disputes and Muslim political unity, and there was an 'accommodating' faction led by Ibrāhīm Ṣāliḥ (b. 1939) from Maiduguri.[5] As the major spokeperson for the 'die-hard' faction within the Tijāniyya, Dahiru Bauchi managed to establish contacts with Iran, hoping to win an external ally against the 'Yan Izala movement that profited from support by Saudi Arabia. In 1988, Dahiru Bauchi visited Iran and gave interviews to *Sakon Islam* (The Message of Islam, an Iranian-sponsored newspaper in Hausa) (Loimeier 1997a: 289).

At the same time, Ibrāhīm Ṣāliḥ emerged as a leading figure of the 'accomodating' faction within the Nigerian Tijāniyya. He earned widespread recognition on account of his prolific writing, as well as his efforts to defend the Tijāniyya against the attacks of the 'Yan Izala. In addition, he became famous for his efforts to collect as many *salāsil* of the Tijāniyya as possible, thus repeating the earlier efforts of Ibrāhīm Niass and Nasiru Kabara. He established links with, first, the scholars of the Tijāniyya in Bornu, in particular Shaykh Abū l-Fātiḥ, and then the leading scholars of the *ṭarīqa* in Cairo, especially Muḥammad al-Muṣṭafā and Muḥammad al-Ḥāfiẓ al-Miṣrī, who were the most prominent scholars of the Tijāniyya in Egypt in the 1950s and 1960s. In 1970, Ibrāhīm Ṣāliḥ also formed a personal link with Ibrāhīm Niass in Kaolack. Last but not least, he acquired a direct link with Mawlā Idrīs al-ᶜIrāqī in Fes and thus had links with virtually all major centres of the *ṭarīqa*. Ibrāhīm Ṣāliḥ's fame was also due to the fact that Nigeria's head of state at the time, General Ibrāhīm Babangida, regarded him as his personal spiritual guide (Hausa: malam). In addition, he established a network of spiritual and economic links with Chad, the Central African Republic, Sudan and Saudi Arabia, where he became known for his powerful amulets. In 1985, Ibrāhīm Ṣāliḥ rose to become the Nigerian chairman of a transnational initiative of the Tijāniyya. Supported by the Kingdom of Morocco, this movement strove to re-evaluate Tijānī writings so as to present an acceptable interpretation of the most controversial doctrinal positions of the *ṭarīqa*, as derived from the teachings of Aḥmad al-Tijānī (Loimeier 1997a: 273). This Moroccan connection had been established in the context of a conference on the Tijāniyya in Fes. Organised by the Moroccan Minister of Religious Affairs, it convened hundreds of scholars of the Tijāniyya from all over Africa. The conference resulted in the subsequent establishment of an Association of ᶜUlamāᵓ of Morocco and Senegal, as well as a corresponding Association of ᶜUlamāᵓ of Morocco and Nigeria. Both were supplied with Moroccan funds. This move may have been connected, as in the case of Libya, with a Moroccan political agenda in sub-Saharan Africa, such as winning local allies for its annexation of the Western Sahara.

A Biography: Abubakar Gumi

Before starting to portray the development of northern Nigeria's first Salafi-oriented movement of reform, it is necessary to delve into the historical context from which this movement emerged. Movements of reform do not develop out of the blue, they emerge in a context that is conducive to the development of new social and religious movements, and they need charismatic religious scholars who are able to inspire such a movement of reform. In the case of the 'Yan Izala, this charismatic scholar was Abubakar Gumi (1924–92),[6] who became famous in the 1960s as an outspoken and radical critic of the esoteric paradigm in general, and the Sufi orders in particular. Central to his *daᶜwa*, which was also to become the paramount aspect of his *tafsīr*, was his statement that

> Sufi teachings are contradictory to Islam, especially as regards the powers attributed to their leaders, the canonisation of individuals as saints, the elaborate initiation rites and the observance of special prayers and chants determined for the individual follower by his authorised Sheikh. There is no mysticism in Islam. Everything has been laid out clearly and the individual Muslim never stands in need of anyone else's intercession between him and God. (Gumi and Tsiga 1992: 135)

Yet, if we take a closer look at Abubakar Gumi we see that he was initiatially rooted in the established esoteric episteme, just like Cheikh Touré in Senegal. Born into a family of religious scholars and initially educated by his own father, the *alkali* (*qāḍī*) of Gummi in Sokoto, he attended the school of Malam Musa in Ambursa (Sokoto), where he was trained in Islamic law (*fiqh*). In 1930, Abubakar Gumi began his secular (*boko*)[7] education at the Dogondaji Primary School, where he was soon appointed *hakimin salla* (leader in prayer) for the pupils, due to his extraordinary knowledge of religious matters for his young age. On account of his quick progress, he was transferred to the Sokoto Central Elementary School in 1933 and to the Sokoto Middle School in 1936. After completing his education at the Sokoto Middle School in 1942, he passed the entrance examinations for Katsina College. Nevertheless, he decided to continue his studies at the Kano Law School that was to become the School of Arabic Studies in 1947. At this school, Gumi was trained as *alkali* from 1942 to 1947. In 1947, he obtained a job as a scribe to *alkali* Attahiru in Sokoto. This position did not meet his expectations, though, and he soon returned to Kano and began to teach at the Kano Law School in late 1947. At this time, he was also in close contact with the Qādiriyya. In fact, he nurtured a life-long relationship of competition and critical dialogue with Nasiru Kabara, the leader of the reformist movement within the Nigerian Qādiriyya, who also happened to be one of his teachers (Loimeier 1997a: 150). In contrast to Nasiru Kabara, who remained an independent *ᶜālim* throughout his life, Gumi became a *qāḍī* in the British colonial system of jurisdiction.

Abubakar Gumi's first public appearance took place in 1949 in the small settlement of Maru in central Sokoto in 1949. Gumi had accepted a position as teacher at the Teachers' Training College at Maru in that year. In Maru, he also met one of the co-founders of the Northern Teachers' Association, Aminu Kano.[8] In the rural seclusion of Maru, a friendly relationship developed between the two teachers. Their conversations and discussions repeatedly centred on the development of Islam in northern Nigeria, the distortion of the faith as a result of mixing with Hausa traditions and the toleration of these *bidaᶜ* by the Sufi orders. Gumi, influenced by his discussions with Aminu Kano, seems to have found in Maru the aim that was to shape his later life decisively: the struggle against un-Islamic innovations and against the Sufi orders as the most prominent agents of such *bidaᶜ*. The bone of contention in Gumi's first doctrinal dispute with existing authorities was the practice of *tayammum* that was practised by the *imām* of Maru, although there was no scarcity of water in Maru. Gumi argued that according to the established interpretation of law, *tayammum* was acceptable only if no water was available for the ritual ablutions. Such conditions did not apply in Maru. He therefore appealed to the students of the college to boycott the obligatory Friday prayers until the *imām* of Maru abandoned *tayammum*. The appeal to rebel against the authority of the *imām* would probably never have had any consequences if the Sultan of Sokoto had not taken up the case himself. However, Gumi had already criticised the Sultan of Sokoto in a personal letter in which he questioned the Sultan's last *salla* (*ᶜīd al-fiṭr*) speech, when the Sultan of Sokoto had indiscriminately mentioned God, the Prophet, Usman dan Fodo and the King of Britain, that is, the spiritual head of the Anglican Church, in the same opening lines (Gumi and Tsiga 1992: 49). For this criticism, the Sultan obviously wanted to revenge himself on Gumi by attacking him directly and demanding that he explain his protest concerning *tayammum*. In the following inquiry, Gumi carried the day by a purely doctrinal argument. The commission of inquiry that had been set up by the Sultan acquitted Gumi and even urged the Sultan in his function as *amīr al-muʾminīn* to come to Maru and to stop the practice of *tayammum* in person (Shanono 1976: 10). Although the Sultan did not comply with this appeal, his dignity had suffered as a result of Gumi's acquittal. Gumi, on the other hand, was able to profile himself as a renowned scholar in northern Nigeria.

After these clashes with representatives of the local administration and the Sultan of Sokoto, Gumi returned to Kano to complete his studies. From 1950 to 1953 he took courses at the School of Arabic Studies (SAS) and then took up a teaching assignment at this institution until 1954. Most teachers at the SAS had been recruited in the Sudan since 1934 and the 'Sudanese shaykhs' had also introduced a new model of education that encouraged students to ask critical questions and to discuss problems with their teachers (Gumi and Tsiga 1992: 33). It is therefore no surprise that the majority of outspoken critics of the Sufi orders in northern Nigeria in the 1970s and 1980s were one-time students of this school (Umar 1988: 170). In 1954, Abubakar Gumi applied for a grant to continue his studies at al-Azhar University in Cairo, but his request was refused by the British colonial authorities, who were obviously afraid that he would come under the influence of the ikhwān al-muslimūn in Cairo (Gumi 1976 [1972]: 4). Instead, Abubakar Gumi was sent to the Bakht al-Rawḍa College of Education in Sudan. From here he went on his first pilgrimage to Mecca, where he met Ahmadu Bello and assisted him in his negotiations with Saudi Government representatives. After his return to Nigeria, Bello not only appointed Abubakar Gumi to become northern Nigeria's first Pilgrim's Officer in Jidda, but also appointed him, in 1960, to the highly influential office of Deputy Grand Kadi of the northern region.[9]

In the early 1950s, Gumi had joined the party of the modernisers of the north, the Northern People's Congress (NPC), led by Prime Minister Ahmadu Bello.[10] Bello's policies of reform, as well as Abubakar Gumi's endeavours, led to the emergence of a first generation of Muslim reformers who rejected Sufi influences and sought to establish their own transnational links. Bello's reform policies were not only conceived as policies for the economic development of the north. His administrative, political and religious reforms essentially sought to end the established political and religious authority of both emirs and Sufi scholars. He aimed to replace accepted forms of political and religious authority with a modern administration that would bring about far-reaching judicial reforms as well as social change. On the religious level, Ahmadu Bello found support for his policies in Abubakar Gumi who, like Ahmadu Bello in the 1930s, had fought a personal struggle against the Sultan of Sokoto in the 1940s (Loimeier 1997a: 106ff). As deputy, and since 1962 as Grand Kadi of the Northern Region, as personal adviser to Ahmadu Bello, and as holder of an array of other official functions, Abubakar Gumi was able to form a small but growing group of Salafi-oriented Muslim reformers in the 1950s and 1960s.

The original organisational framework of the Muslim reformers in the new religio-political set-up of the north was the jamāᶜat naṣr al-islām (JNI, 'The society for the success of Islam'), established in 1962. The JNI was supposed to support the policies of reform of the new elites of the north in religious terms, as well as to act as an umbrella organisation for all religious groups in the north, irrespective of their religious affiliation. As such, the JNI not only legitimated the reform policies, but was also asked to coordinate the building of mosques and schools, to organise the *ḥajj* and Islamic *daᶜwa*, and to enhance religious unity in order to overcome the spiritual authority of the Sufi scholars. In order to achieve these goals, Abubakar Gumi, who had established contacts with Saudi Arabia in the context of a number of pilgrimages to the holy places since 1955, organised links with Saudi Arabia, Kuwait and other Gulf states. These soon started to channel money into Islamic development projects. In 1956, Gumi became the first Nigerian Pilgrims' Officer in Jidda. In the early 1960s, Gumi also played an influential role in the rābiṭat al-ᶜālam al-islāmī. In 1962 he was a founding member of the rābiṭa. In the ensuing year he rose in the rābiṭa to become a member of the Supreme Council for the Islamic University of Medina, where in the 1970s many graduates from Nigeria continued their studies. He also became a member of the World Supreme Council for the Affairs of Mosques, and a member of the Legal Committee of the rābiṭa. A major success in Gumi's efforts to use Saudi capital (spiritual and financial) was the reorganisation of the *ḥajj*. In 1974, Nigerian members of the heterodox Aḥmadiyya movement were banned from taking part in the pilgrimage. Efforts to tighten control over mosques in Nigeria misfired, however. Not all Muslims were prepared to accept Abubakar Gumi's ideas and supreme guidance with respect to administration and organisation of their mosques, even when presented as advice by the Supreme Council for the Affairs of Mosques. In addition, transnational links multiplied, and Egypt, which had its own political agenda, started to support the JNI in 1962. This took the form not only of funds but, more importantly, of grants for studies at al-Azhar University. In the quest for the diversification of external sources of support, new contacts were cultivated. From 1974 on, Sudan, Pakistan, India and Malaysia entered the donor scene. With the erosion of Abubakar Gumi's monopoly of access to external sources of funding, his role as a national player suffered as well.

Of central importance for the erosion of Abubakar Gumi's power as the major spokesperson of official Islam in Nigeria, however, was the assassination of Aḥmadu Bello in the context of the military coup in 1966, and the subsequent rise of the Nigerian Army as the major political player. In the years to come, Abubakar Gumi lost exclusive access to power in Kaduna. With the death of Ahmadu Bello, Gumi had lost his political mentor and had to continue his struggle against the Sufi-oriented scholarly establishment on his own. Yet, his efforts to acquire public support for his ideas of reform largely failed, as his texts, in particular his polemic against Sufism, *al-ᶜaqīda al-ṣaḥīḥa bi-muwāfaqat al-sharīᶜa* (The right faith according to the regulations of the *sharīᶜa*) (1972) (for an analysis see Loimeier 1997a: 186–96), were written in Arabic. Gumi thus changed his strategy in the 1970s and started a commentary translation of the Qurʾān into Hausa, which was published in 1978 under the title *Tarjamar Ma'anonin Alkurani Maigirma zuwa harshen Hausa* (The translation of the meaning of the glorious Qurʾān into Hausa). At this time he also began publishing articles in the northern Nigerian daily newspaper *Gaskiya Ta Fi Kwabo*, and in 1978, he translated his programmatic text *al-ᶜaqīda al-ṣaḥīḥa bi-muwāfaqat al-sharīᶜa* into Hausa under the title *Musulunci da abinda ke rushe shi* (Islam and the Things that Lead to Its Destruction), triggering a broad public debate on the deviations of the Sufi orders. The Sufi orders responded by publishing their own pamphlets, defending themselves against Gumi's literary attacks (Loimeier 1997a: 197–206).

Meanwhile, leaders of the Sufi orders had been able to reassert their public influence and even to take over control of the management of the JNI in the late 1960s and early 1970s. As a consequence, Gumi could no longer rely on the institutions of the state in his efforts to fight *bidaᶜ* in the guise of the Sufi orders. Rather, he turned to other means of struggle: public sermons, pamphlets and the radio. In 1967, after five years of delivering a public *tafsīr* in the Sultan Bello Friday mosque in Kaduna, Gumi started to broadcast his Ramadan *tafsīr* through Radio Kaduna in order to reach a larger audience all over northern Nigeria (see Brigaglia 2004, 2005, 2007, 2009; Larkin 2015). The shift to a *tafsīr* transmitted by radio had a tremendous effect on Gumi's popularity and role as a public figure in northern Nigeria, and was commented by him accordingly:

> When I addressed only my immediate audience in the mosque, I could say my understanding freely without fear. The people would sit right in front of me, and any one of them who wanted further explanation could ask me . . . Once my readings were being broadcast to the entire region, however, I lost this privilege. My audience were now no longer in my reach. (Gumi and Tsiga 1992: 132)

In 1977, Sufi scholars reacted by starting to broadcast their own radio *tafsīr* programmes and thus again retaliated in kind. In order to overcome this stalemate, Gumi resorted to the establishment of a new Muslim mass organisation in his struggle for reform of Islam and in 1978 he initiated the foundation of the 'Yan Izala under the official tutelage of Ismaila Idris (d. 2000), a former army *imām* (for his biography, see Ben Amara 2014: 129ff; Loimeier 1997a: 210ff). With their headquarters in Jos and the moral backing of Gumi, as well as financial support from local and Saudi donors, the 'Yan Izala became the first Salafi-oriented mass organisation in northern Nigeria to seriously disrupt the activities of the Sufi orders, especially the Tijāniyya. The 'Yan Izala immediately started to fight against a broad range of 'un-Islamic innovations', such as amulets, saint veneration, supererogatory prayers, conspicuous consumption and customary funeral ceremonies.[11]

The 'Yan Izala

Competition between the Qādiriyya and the Tijāniyya was superseded in the 1970s by the rise of the 'Yan Izala movement. This movement came to stand for a *sharīᶜa*-minded and Salafi-oriented type of reform that fought against all kinds of un-Islamic innovations. The success of the 'Yan Izala as a religious mass movement in northern Nigeria in the 1970s and 1980s was related to the transformation of northern Nigerian society in the colonial and post-colonial period. It was also tied to the emergence of a Western-educated and urban Muslim population, mostly identifying with the growing number of middle-class groups that were no longer willing to accept seemingly obsolete, costly and time-consuming social and religious customs. The development of the 'Yan Izala in northern Nigeria must thus be situated in a wider socio-political context connected to the policies of change introduced by the British colonial administration and continued in the 1950s and 1960s by the first prime minister of the Northern Region, Aḥmadu Bello.

From 1978, the 'Yan Izala movement became the most powerful Salafi-oriented movement of reform in northern Nigeria and the most outspoken opponent of the established Sufi orders. Sufi orders were fought by violent means, such as the occupation of their mosques. Becoming a member of the 'Yan Izala meant breaking with society, including relatives, and rejecting all manifestations of allegedly un-Islamic character, including social customs such as the bride price, extensive mourning (Arabic: *bikāᵓ*) and supererogatory prayers, often in the context of Sufi ritual. Thus, in reference to a sermon given by Abubakar Gumi, Ismāᶜīla Idris condemned the Sufi orders in a speech in Jos on 20 October 1978. He appealed to the followers of the 'Yan Izala not to give their daughters away in marriage to members of the Sufi orders as these must be regarded as unbelievers (quoted in Loimeier 1997a: 253). In Kano (as in other places in northern Nigeria and in Niger) the followers of the 'Yan Izala refused to eat meat that was slaughtered by *mushrikūn*, that is, other Muslims not affiliated with the 'Yan Izala (Kane 1990: 18), a powerful marker of both symbolic distanciation and social separation. Many clashes between the 'Yan Izala and the Sufi orders have erupted in the context of the socio-religious sermons of the 'Yan Izala. These conflicts were carried over into the fabric of family life. The appeal by the 'Yan Izala to their followers that they dissociate themselves from members of their families who were still affiliated with a Sufi order led to serious crises of authority in many families. However, the development of the 'Yan Izala in Kaura Namoda and Argungu shows that the appearance of the 'Yan Izala movement in these towns had a socially liberating effect (Loimeier 1997a: 232ff): many youths and women were enabled to voice protest against their fathers or demand emancipation from their husbands on the basis of religious arguments. The 'Yan Izala gave their protest the necessary organisational backing by offering alternatives and by establishing a new social network with the help of their schools (Loimeier 1997a: 254). The protest of the 'Yan Izala thus led to a revolution of the existing models of explanation. This new social development was characterised by its unwillingness to compromise. The followers of the 'Yan Izala did not want to preserve parts of the old value system they had condemned as un-Islamic but rather rejected this system outright. For the 'Yan Izala, the process of reorientation could contain no half-truths. A system of explanation was either right or wrong. The rejection of former social and religious values is also an explanation for the aggressive and militant character of the actions of the young 'Yan Izala in their struggle against the representatives of the established system. This brutality also characterised the reactions of the Sufi orders to the attacks by the 'Yan Izala (Loimeier 1997a: 259). The conflict between the 'Yan Izala and the Sufi orders has thus led to a deepening division within the Muslim community. Many families – in the countryside as well as in the cities, in professional groups and at all levels of society – were affected by this split: 'The two sides cannot interact religiously, they are incompatible and regard each other as non-Muslim' (Umar 1988: 86).

However, the 'Yan Izala not only fought against seemingly un-Islamic features of northern Nigerian society, but also advocated substantial reforms, for instance by establishing modern Islamic schools even in rural areas, and by calling for the political and religious mobilisation of women. The 'Yan Izala movement thus represented an emancipatory programme of Islamic reform that offered Muslim women,[12] youth and usually urban, Western-educated Muslims an alternative vision of Islam no longer mediated by established religious authorities.[13] In more general terms, the 'Yan Izala fought against the esoteric episteme symbolised in the position of the Sufi shaykh as the mediator between the faithful and the Prophet. Instead, the 'Yan Izala insisted on direct access to the sources of the faith without an intermediary, on the ritual in its pure and simple form and a modest style of living. The 'Yan Izala thus came to represent a new religious path that not only broke with established forms of religiosity but that also constituted a new and comprehensive socio-religious programme. It thus incarnated the aspirations of Western-educated Muslims in the north who sought doctrinal blessing for a process of distanciation from established forms of religiosity and seemingly obsolete forms of ritual. On the other hand, the educational reforms propagated by the 'Yan Izala also triggered reform initiatives within both the Tijāniyya and the Qādiriyya. As a consequence, the level of formal education among Muslims in northern Nigeria has risen significantly since the 1980s.

An important pillar of the 'Yan Izala campaigns was its preachers, the *masu waʾazi* (Hausa: 'masters of *waᶜẓ*),[14] who in 1978 started to challenge the *ᶜulamāʾ* hegemony of interpretation of Islam in the public sphere.[15] These new preachers formed a key group in the movement, who translated its message and programme to large audiences. In their preaching activities, the *masu waʾazi* were caught in a constant dilemma, however: on the one hand, they despised ordinary Muslims as 'ignorant' (Arabic: *jāhil*); on the other hand, they wanted to (and had to) teach and convince the same people to join the 'Yan Izala movement (Hassane 2009: 104). The ignorant popular masses in fact constituted the mass of potential followers of the 'Yan Izala and thus had to be treated with respect. This logic, and the will of the *masu waʾazi* to spread the *daᶜwa* of the 'Yan Izala, contributed to the commodification of religious preaching and religious activities in northern Nigeria, and later in Niger, Benin, Cameroon[16] and Chad. The *masu waʾazi* had to sell their message to the popular masses and thus applied, consciously or not, the laws of the market. For this reason, the sermons of the *masu waʾazi* never acquired the scholarly character of sermons by established religious scholars: the *masu wa'azi* did not care to expound on certain intricate details of Islamic law, for instance, but wanted to popularise their message of social liberation and religious rebellion against the established authorities. Due to this logic, action was at the very core of 'Yan Izala preaching: the *masu wa'azi* communicated through action. An implication of this dynamic was that the message of Islam was discussed in new arenas, beyond the realm of mosques and schools, and consequently acquired an increasingly public and popular character, rejecting established rules of protocol and conventions of respect based on seniority, as maintained by the established religious authorities. At the same time, the *masu wa'azi* were forced to remain open to voices from the public and to present themselves as amiable and accessible. As a result, they developed a personal touch and cultivated specialisations in terms of the themes, style or presentation of their *waʿẓ* sermons (Hassane 2009: 109). While some *masu wa'azi* specialised in themes such as marriage, Islamic law or Islamic ritual, others became famous for their political polemics or their moralistic diatribes. As itinerant *masu wa'azi,* they travelled through the ever-expanding realm of the 'Yan Izala, contributing to the perception of the movement as being highly mobile (Hassane 2009: 110). The *masu wa'azi* also had to renew their products from time to time in order to make them attractive, to conquer new markets and to satisfy demand. The communicative speed and the transnational character of the movement were other important elements of the *masu wa'azi*'s agency. Ideology and the techniques of a liberal market economy fed this new form of preaching, while the 'consumers' of their sermons experienced the boons of participation. In this way, Islamic knowledge was not only transmitted in a more direct way than ever before, it was also handed out liberally to the masses and contributed thus to the democratisation of religious debates. Due to the fact that the product of the 'Yan Izala was essentially religious, social relationships within the 'Yan Izala movement transcended particularistic identities, social hierarchies and even gender for the profit of both a fraternity and a sorority within the movement that was the foundation of a 'communauté d'émotion' (Hassane 2009: 114).

The disputes between the 'Yan Izala and the Sufi orders were expressed not only in political, social or economic terms, but also in doctrinal terms. Sound doctrinal argumentation was the precondition for legitimization of the reformist programme of the 'Yan Izala, as well as the de-legitimization of its opponents. Both groups presented their doctrinal positions in public sermons, radio programmes, pamphlets and programmatic texts such as Gumi's *al-ᶜaqīda al-ṣaḥīḥa* and the respective responses of Nasiru Kabara and Sani Kafanga. As a result of the disputes between the 'Yan Izala and the Sufi orders, different schools of *tafsīr* developed in northern Nigeria in the 1970s, representing different readings of the Qur°ān, and expressing different doctrinal positions. Until the early 1970s, northern Nigerian traditions of *tafsīr* had been dominated by a scholastic tafsīr. This *tafsīr* achieved prominence during the month of Ramadan, when recitation of the Qur°ān and the respective *tafsīr* assumed a particularly sacred character. In Kano, Nasiru Kabara dominated the scholastic *tafsīr* of the Qādiriyya: since 1953 he had held the Ramadan *tafsīr* in the palace of the Emir of Kano. The Tijāniyya, by contrast, brought forth a number of their own *masu-tafsiri*, masters of *tafsīr*, such as Sani Kafanga (d. 1989), Tijani Usman (d. 1970), Dahiru Bauchi (b. 1927) and Ustadh Yusuf Ali (b. 1949). In 1977, other religious scholars followed suit: in 1977, Umar Sanda Idris (d. 2002) started a radio *tafsīr*, and Dahiru Bauchi took over in 1980. The scholarly character of the *tafsīr* was abandoned in the 1970s, however, on account of the activities of scholars such as Abubakar Gumi or Dr Ibrāhīm Datti Aḥmad. When Abubakar Gumi died in 1992, Lawal Abubakar and Aḥmad Muḥammad Sanusi Gumbi, leading representatives of the 'Yan Izala, took over from him in Kaduna, while Dr Ibrāhīm Datti Aḥmad and Jaᶜfar Maḥmūd Adam came to represent an ahl al-sunna-oriented radio *tafsīr* in Kano and Maiduguri in the mid-1990s. These activists have contributed to politicisation of the *tafsīr* by linking their *tafsīr* to religio-political contexts. The exegesis of the Qur°ān thus acquired a new direction and an object, and so did the master of *tafsīr*, the scholar who presented his interpretation. Dahiru Bauchi, for instance, used his *tafsīr* to fight against the 'Yan Izala. He consequently developed a polemic style that aimed at delegitimising his opponents as religious entrepreneurs. The same was valid for the *tafsīr* of Abubakar Gumi and, in more general terms, all public *tafsīr*. The burgeoning of radio *tafsīr* in the 1970s has since led to 'exegetic duels' (see Brigaglia 2005).

The 'Yan Izala in Crisis

From the late 1970s, the development of the 'Yan Izala was dominated by issues of a predominantly Nigerian national, social, economic and political nature. Only in the early 1990s did local branches of 'Yan Izala start to develop in neighbouring countries. Translocal and transnational affiliations seem to have played a comparatively minor role for the 'Yan Izala. Ousmane Kane, in fact, describes the 'Yan Izala as a religious movement that was characterised by its national agenda and its identification with the Nigerian federal state (Kane 2003: 237). It almost seems as if Abubakar Gumi's role as a mediator of Saudi Arabian influences was sufficient as an external link for the 'Yan Izala. Indeed, its preoccupation with education and the development of a reformed Muslim society in northern Nigeria appears paramount, while political questions came second. The 'Yan Izala thus stuck to an accommodating position in their relationship with the state and did not attack the state like other Muslim activist groups. This pragmatic orientation of the 'Yan Izala may be attributed, at least until Abubakar Gumi's death in 1992, to the fact that the 'Yan Izala saw themselves as a primarily religious and social movement. The 'Yan Izala worked with the implicit support of state institutions, or at least the support of the political nomenclatura of the north: it was not a movement of political opposition. The 'Yan Izala were tolerated and even actively supported by both the Shagari (1979–83) and Babangida (1985–93) administrations, and experienced adverse treatment only during the short regime of General Buhari (1984–5). The 'Yan Izala were always willing to tolerate northern Nigeria's conservative political status. They also supported the consolidation of the modernist northern elites, a position that was again compatible with Gumi's close affiliation with Saudi Arabia and its conservative politics. The 'Yan Izala thus became the most important Muslim movement of religious, social and educational reform in contemporary northern Nigeria, and a major force of religious opposition to the Sufi orders. They did not aspire to become a Muslim revolutionary organisation in political terms.

From their foundation in 1978,[17] the 'Yan Izala became famous for their harsh critique of any kind of *bid*^{c}*a* and of the practices of the Sufi orders, the Tijāniyya in particular. However, the struggle of the 'Yan Izala against the Tijāniyya and, to a lesser extent, against the Qādiriyya, which was the major concern of 'Yan Izala strategies from 1978, was stopped in the late 1980s due to strategic considerations: the leaders of the 'Yan Izala realised that their constant attacks on the Tijāniyya and the Qādiriyya effectively split the northern Nigerian Muslim *ummah* and thus brought about *fitna*. This was seen to be highly problematic in the context of the growing influence of Pentecostal Churches in the mid-1980s. In 1987, Christian candidates won a surprising number of local government seats, even in Muslim-majority areas in northern Nigeria, because the Muslim vote was split between 'Yan Izala, Tijāniyya and Qādiriyya candidates. Christian local government electoral victories raised the spectre of Christian domination over Muslim northern Nigeria, and eventually forced the 'Yan Izala, Tijāniyya and Qādiriyya to shelve their disputes and form an alliance of convenience. As a consequence, the 'Yan Izala movement had to stop its attacks against Sufi orders and become moderate. This strategic re-orientation led to a major, but silent, protest within the 'Yan Izala and stifled the development of the movement until 2000, when the introduction of 'political *sharīʿa*' allowed it to again assume a more activist role in society.[18]

In fact, Sufi polemics in the 1980s focused on the *fitna* the 'Yan Izala had started among the Muslims by their constant attacks against the Sufi orders, and raised the question of why the 'Yan Izala abstained from fighting the increasing influence of Christian mission organisations. The rapid expansion of Christian churches and mission organisations in northern Nigeria in the 1980s, as well as the need to achieve Muslim unity in order to enhance the chances of Muslim politicians in national elections, eventually forced Abubakar Gumi to come to terms with his opponents among the Sufis. As a consequence, in a famous interview with the northern Nigerian daily *Gaskiya* in 1987, he proclaimed that 'politics was more important than prayer (*siyasa tafi muhimmanci da salla*)', and that Muslim men should allow their women to vote and 'to mix' in public, especially at election times: 'if this is not done, even to the point of letting unbelievers predominate, then what is our position? . . . It is a necessity that every man takes his women and children above the age of eighteen to register so that we can predominate over the Non-Muslims' (quoted in Christelow 1987: 323–4). In 1990, in order to achieve Muslim unity, Abubakar Gumi finally overcame his opposition to Nasiru Kabara and visited his former teacher in his house in Kano, an event commented on by Bature Idris Gana, reporter of the Kano daily *The Triumph*, with the words '*Dare daya Allah kanyi Bature*' (if God wishes, he may turn [a black man] into a white man) (quoted in Loimeier 1997a: 309).

At the same time, the 'Yan Izala experienced regional divisions, since many outspoken representatives of the movement, while accepting the overall spiritual leadership of Abubakar Gumi, rejected the authoritarian style of Ismaila Idris. A first rebellion occurred in Sokoto in about 1985, when the local 'Yan Izala leaders, Abubakar Jibril and Abubakar Tureta, joined Ibrāhīm al-Zakzakī's ikhwān movement and took control of Farfaru, the most important 'Yan Izala mosque in Sokoto. The remaining followers of the 'Yan Izala under the leadership of Sidi Attahiru Ibrāhīm had to resettle in a new mosque on Ali Akilu Street. Yet, Sidi Attahiru soon also broke with the 'Yan Izala, and established a new organization, ahl al-sunna. It failed, however, to gain more than regional importance (Loimeier 1997a: 244). As a result of these splits, the 'Yan Izala lost influence in Sokoto.[19]

Another hotbed of rebellion against the central leadership of the movement was Kano, where an influential businessman, A.K. Daiyyabu, had managed since 1986 to marginalise the existing leadership of the movement under Shaykh Sulaimān (Kane 2003: 112ff). Daiyyabu particularly criticised the loyalist attitudes of the 'Yan Izala movement with regard to the Nigerian government under General Babangida: both Abubakar Gumi and the 'Yan Izala leadership were highly supportive of the Babangida government, despite its agenda of economic liberalisation and its conservative foreign policies. Daiyyabu's authoritarian style, however, triggered his own deposition by the central committee in Jos in 1990. However, Daiyyabu's demise did not put an end to the internal disputes. The 1990s saw a growing number of rebellions against the Jos leadership, which was accused of financial mismanagement and embezzlement of funds, and of colluding with Nigeria's corrupt political elites. A number of regional sections of the 'Yan Izala under the leadership of either Alhaji Musa Mai Gandu (1930–2011), the chairman of the national Committee of Patrons, or Rabiu Daura, the chairman of the Council of ᶜUlamāᵓ of the 'Yan Izala for Kaduna State, advocated either neutrality or a critical position with respect to the Nigerian state without openly attacking Nigerian politicians. They criticised Ismaila Idris, however, and questioned the sources of his income. In June 1991, Musa Mai Gandu suspended the national steering committee of the 'Yan Izala in Jos, accusing it of embezzlement of funds.

In direct reaction to this, Ismaila Idris and the 'Yan Izala national steering committee removed Musa Mai Gandu and his supporters from all official functions. As a result, the Ismaila Idris ('Jos' or 'Izala A') faction, dominated by the 'old brigade' and the Musa Mai Gandu ('Kaduna' or 'Izala B') group of the 'Yan Izala, dominated by younger activists, started a bitter dispute that continued to divide the 'Yan Izala movement despite repeated efforts at reconciliation. Each 'Yan Izala faction published its own constitution and established markers of doctrinal distinction and symbolic distantiation: while the Kaduna group, for instance, started to stress the importance of *ḥadīth* and *ijtihād* and stuck to the practice of *qabḍ*, the Jos faction stressed the primordial role of Māliki law and switched to the practice of *sadl* (Mustapha and Bunza 2014: 68–9). In the 1995 constitution of the Kaduna group, Abubakar Gumi was named as founder of the movement, while the 2004 constitution of the Jos group refered to Ismaila Idris in that context.[20] Even after Ismaila Idris' death in 2000, his successor, Muḥammad Sani Yahya Jingir (b. 1950) continued to fight the Musa Mai Gandu group, although both factions advocated the introduction of 'political *sharīᶜa*' in twelve northern Nigerian states in 2000. The dispute within the 'Yan Izala acquired a rather bitter note due to both factions' stubborn adherence to doctrinal arguments, in particular, the mutual accusation of unbelief, in order to discredit the other side (Ben Amara 2011: 108ff.). In December 2011, the two 'Yan Izala factions managed to reunite, however, in the context of a summit in Abuja (Brigaglia 2012: 7). Since 15 December 2011, Abdullahi Bala Lau has been acting as the National Chairman of the 'Yan Izala, replacing al-Ḥājj Musa Muḥammad Mai Gandu, who died in 2011. Muḥammad Sani Yahaya Jingir was replaced as National Chairman of the Council of ᶜulamāᵓ of the 'Yan Izala by Dr. Ibrāhīm Jalo Jalingo, while Muḥammad Kabiru Gombe was appointed National Secretary.[21]

An exemple of a successful reformist career outside the 'Yan Izala movement was Amīnu d-Dīn Abubakar (b. 1947 in the Sheshe quarter in Kano).[22] Amīnu d-Dīn Abubakar originally started higher education at the School of Arabic Studies in Kano in 1967, where he graduated in 1970. For a short period of time, he became a student of Nasiru Kabara. In 1971, he started to study at Bayero University Kano (BUK), intermittently working as a teacher. He graduated in 1979 with a BA. From 1975 he acted as the leading spokesperson of the Muslim Students' Society (MSS) at BUK. At the same time he used to translate the Friday sermon into Hausa. It was during this period that he became familiar with the writings of the Egyptian Muslim Brothers, in particular Sayyid Quṭb. Still, like many young Muslims, he was drawn towards the Iranian revolution. In 1979, he moved to Kaduna where he came into contact with Abubakar Gumi, who apparently convinced Amīnu d-Dīn Abubakar to change his affiliation. As a consequence, Aminu d-Din Abubakar turned against Iran and in 1982 he accepted Saudi support for the construction of his own mosque in Sulaiman Crescent in Nasarawa, Kano. In 1983, he was appointed principal of the Gwale Arabic Teachers College. In addition, he became a major leader of the 'Yan Izala in Kano: however, he was never as outspoken against the Sufi orders as other 'Yan Izala leaders.

In the mid-1980s, Amīnu d-Dīn Abubakar shifted affiliations yet again, breaking ties with Abubakar Gumi and the 'Yan Izala. While accepting Kuwait and Emirates support for a short period of time, he rejected that of the Saudis. The new organisation that Amīnu d-Dīn Abubakar set up, *Daawa*, soon became an important group in Kano. It refused to adopt the radical position of 'Yan Izala towards the Sufi orders, but still propagated a Salafi-oriented agenda. In 1987 Amīnu d-Dīn Abubakar once again shifted alliances, this time establishing links with Libya. Amīnu d-Dīn Abubakar's biography may thus be presented as a showcase for the rapid change of affiliations and the games Nigerian Muslim scholars were willing to play. At the same time, Amīnu d-Dīn Abubakar's example shows that Nigerian religious scholars were keen on remaining the masters of their own career. When 'political *sharī^ca*' was introduced in Kano State in 2000, Amīnu d-Dīn Abubakar became chairman of the Kano State 'Hisba Committee' in 2001, which supervised the implementation of *sharī^ca* law in Kano (Peters 2003: 49). The debate over the implementation of *sharī^ca* law in twelve northern Nigerian states in fact created major opportunities for 'Yan Izala activism: numerous second-generation 'Yan Izala followers became militant supporters of *sharī^ca* legal reforms and formed a majority among the 'Yan Hisba[23] militia members (Brigaglia 2004: 243). For many young 'Yan Izala members,

'Yan Hisba activities meant a welcome return to militant activism, which had been ended for strategic reasons in the late 1980s. Boko Haram pressure has also helped 'Yan Izala to regain a sense of unity and vigour in recent years. In 2013, 'Yan Izala launched its own satellite TV programme, *Sunnah TV*, a YouTube channel, a Twitter account and its own website[24] (Thurston forthcoming: 319).

One of the most outspoken 'Yan Hisba groups in Kano consisted of activist Muslims who had been socialised as 'Yan Izala activists in the 1980s. After the split of the organisation in 1991 and Abubakar Gumi's death in 1992,[25] these second-generation 'Yan Izala activists, often graduates of the Islamic University of Medina, refused to pledge allegiance to either the 'Kaduna' or the 'Jos' faction of the 'Yan Izala. They remained independent and formed a new Salafi-oriented group under the name ahl al-sunna that came to be led by a number of charismatic 'Medina graduates', such as Ja^cfar Maḥmūd Adam, and were thus labelled *Yan Medina* (Mustapha and Bunza 2014: 69). This new ahl al-sunna group was not identical with the aforementioned Sokoto-based ahl al-sunna. However, all ahl al-sunna groups adopted basic 'Yan Izala ideas, such as the struggle against un-Islamic innovations. At the same time, they stressed the need for Muslim unity and the need to participate actively in politics. The link between the ahl al-sunna and politics was most obvious in Zamfara State: the governor, Ahmad Sani Yerima, was closely linked with the 'Yan Izala movement and was the first northern Nigerian state governor to introduce 'political *sharī^ca*', in 1999. In Kano State, this link was less obvious: 'Yan Izala members had been marginalised in the 1980s and were insultingly referred to as *yan shege* (Hausa: bastards). 'Yan Izala positions in Kano were consequently adopted by both Amīnu d-Dīn Abubakar's Daawa group and the new ahl al-sunna group, which gained support due to their split from the main 'Yan Izala group. The Kano ahl al-sunna group was also less radical than other 'Yan Izala groups on a number of doctrinal issues: they accepted eating the meat of an animal slaughtered by a follower of a Sufi order, regarded followers of Sufi orders not as 'unbelievers', but as mere 'innovators' (Arabic: *mubtadi^cūn*) and allowed prayers behind an *imām* affiliated with a Sufi order under certain circumstances, such as the absence of a 'Yan Izala or ahl al-sunna *imām* (see Brigaglia 2012: 8).[26]

The most outspoken representatives of the ahl al-sunna in Kano in the late 1990s, Yakubu Musa, Dr Ibrāhīm Datti Aḥmad and Jaᶜfar Maḥmūd Adam, became 'Yan Hisba leaders in the 2000s. Dr Ibrāhīm Datti Aḥmad (b. 1962) was a medical doctor and *imām* of the Bayero University Kano (BUK) Friday mosque. In addition, he chaired the Supreme Council for Sharīᶜa in Nigeria (established in 2000) (Brigaglia 2004: 153, 360). Both Dr Ibrāhīm Datti Aḥmad and Jaᶜfar Maḥmūd Adam were also highly active in Kano State policies and opposed Kano State Governor Rabiu Kwankwaso (in office 1999–2003), who was accused of being far too timid with respect to the implementation of *sharīᶜa* penal laws. At the same time, they supported Ibrāhīm Shekarau, a more radical politician from the All Nigerian People's Party (ANPP) in the 2003 state government elections.

Jaᶜfar Maḥmūd Adam (b. 1961)[27] from Daura, Katsina state, had gone through both qurʾānic school and *boko* education in Kano and Hadejia, and was a 'Yan Izala follower in the 1970s and 1980s (initially the Kaduna, later the Kano faction). In 1987, he won the Nigerian Qurʾān recitation competition, got a grant for studies at the Gwale Arabic Teachers' College in Kano and subsequently (1989) went to Saudi Arabia in order to continue his education at the Islamic University of Medina, where he acquired a BA in qurʾānic studies. In 1993, he returned to Nigeria and became director of the ᶜUthmān b. ᶜAffān mosque and school complex in Unguwar Gadon Kaya in Kano. At the same time, he entered a master's programme at Bayero University Kano (BUK), only to leave again for Sudan in 1993, where he continued his studies at the Africa International University in Khartoum. In 1996, he returned to northern Nigeria and became *imām* of the Dorayi Friday mosque in Kano and a leading ahl al-sunna representative. He also enrolled for a PhD at Usman Danfodio University in Sokoto. When Ibrāhīm Shekarau was elected governor of Kano State in 2003 and started to implement a more rigid interpretation of *sharīᶜa* penal laws, Jaᶜfar Maḥmūd Adam was appointed to a leading position in the Kano State 'Hisba Board' that screened the implementation of *sharīᶜa* penal laws.[28] Yet, over time, Jaᶜfar Maḥmūd Adam seems to have become increasingly critical of the ways in which *sharīᶜa* penal laws were implemented and eventually refused to support Ibrāhīm Shekarau when the latter stood for re-election in the 2007 Kano State Government elections (Brigaglia 2012: 16). Disenchantment with Ibrāhīm Shekarau started in about 2005 when it became clear that Ibrāhīm Shekarau had started to turn for political support to Kano's established *ᶜulamāʾ*, in particular the Tijāniyya (Thurston forthcoming: 199, 225). Jaᶜfar Maḥmūd Adam also became a leading representative of the London-based al-muntadā al-islāmī foundation. In Kano, the activities of al-muntadā al-islāmī were opposed not only by the leading representatives of the Sufi orders but also by a small but growing group of radical Muslims who rejected Western education even in a Saudi guise. Jaᶜfar Maḥmūd Adam was assassinated in his Friday mosque on 13 March 2007 during *fajr* prayers, possibly by a Boko Haram killer commando.[29]

As a consequence of these processes of change and their effects on strategy, the 'Yan Izala underwent a serious crisis of orientation in the 1990s. This crisis was connected with Abubakar Gumi's death in 1992 and the fact that the organisation was not able to find a new *murshid ᶜamm* (spiritual guide) who would be acceptable to the different wings of the movement. These developed in the 1990s in the context of questions of strategy with respect to the organisation's position regarding the Nigerian state as well as the Sufi orders. In addition, the 'Yan Izala had not managed to monopolise the field of Islamic reform in northern Nigeria. In the 1970s the Muslim Students' Society (MSS) had already won considerable support among the student population on account of its radical political positions and since the 1980s, other, though smaller, and often MSS-related movements of reform started to form, introducing a decisively political discourse into public debates in northern Nigeria. In the 1990s a number of these recent reformist organisations, such as the ikhwān, and later the Islamic Movement under the leadership of Ibrāhīm al-Zakzakī, were able to gain considerable popularity on account of their consequent opposition to the series of military regimes that were supported at the same time by Abubakar Gumi and the 'Yan Izala (Loimeier 1997b: 298ff). However, these recent and radical movements of reform cultivated a political (oppositional) discourse and have (so far) not developed programmes of social reform.

The Activists: The Muslim Students' Society, the 'Ikhwān' and the Islamic Movement

As a consequence of the politically accommodating position of the 'Yan Izala, radical and revolutionary political positions developed outside the 'Yan Izala movement. Politically radical groups were originally often linked with the Muslim Students' Society (MSS) and were primarily characterised by their activist attitudes with respect to political issues; socio-religious or economic issues came second. These politically radical groups may thus be seen as representing a *siyāsa*-minded orientation of Muslims in northern Nigeria: doctrinal questions were de-emphasised, for the sake of political unity among Muslims. Groups that emerged from an MSS background were the Daawa group, led by Amīnu d-Dīn Abubakar; the Umma group; the 'Brothers' (ikhwān); and, later, the Islamic Movement in Nigeria of Ibrāhīm al-Zakzakī. For a long time, these groups were confined to the campuses of the universities, in particular Bayero University Kano (BUK), Usman dan Fodio University Sokoto and Ahmadu Bello University (ABU) Zaria. Founded in 1962, ABU Zaria was northern Nigeria's first university, and a fertile breeding ground for all kinds of radicals, both religious and political. It was often the first public platform for Marxists such as Dr Bala Usman, and later Muslim activists like Ibrāhīm al-Zakzakī. The MSS and the Umma group, as well as the ikhwān, the Islamic movement and Daawa, rejected the conservative political positions of the 'Yan Izala and its affiliation with Saudi Arabia. They also condemned the Nigerian military regimes of the 1980s and 1990s as corrupt and pro-Western. After the Iranian revolution in 1978–9 they advocated radical political solutions for northern Nigeria.

Some of these groups were stigmatised as 'Shiites' on account of their sympathies towards Iran and the fact that the Iranian Government actively supported these groups. In the mid-1980s, Iranian efforts to rally support among Muslims largely misfired, however. War with Iraq, non-implementation of social reforms in Iran and massive rioting of Iranian pilgrims in Mecca in the 1987 *ḥajj* season led to disenchantment with the Iranian revolution among Nigeria's pro-Iranian activists. Some activist groups turned to Libya, others to Saudi Arabia. Still others, especially the Muslim intellectuals connected with the Umma group, came to stress the historical legacy of Nigeria's indigenous revolutionary models, notably the Sokoto *jihād*. As a consequence, Iran began to diversify its links with other Nigerian Muslim groups and, for instance, established a link with a leading scholar of the Tijāniyya, Dahiru Bauchi. Subsequently, Iranian influence seems to have increased, especially among the younger generation of Muslim radicals led by Ibrāhīm al-Zakzakī.

For them, the Iranian revolution represented the only Muslim polity to effectively resist US imperialism and Westernisation. In the 1990s, these groups were able to gain support outside university campuses. This constituency enabled them to challenge the military regime, beginning with the military governors of some northern states.

Ibrāhīm al-Zakzakī (b. 1953 in the Kwarbai quarter in Zaria) was educated at a local (provincial) Arabic School, then moved to the School of Arabic Studies in Kano and finally began to study political science at ABU Zaria in 1976. He soon became the local chairperson of the MSS and the leading organiser of a number of campus riots in the late 1970s and early 1980s. After a return from a journey to Iran in 1980, he became a staunch supporter of the Iranian revolution. As a consequence, his supporters, the ikhwān, were labelled by an unsympathetic press 'Yan Brothers', 'Yan Shia', 'Shiawa' or 'mini-ayatollahs'. Ibrāhīm al-Zakzakī denied any religious connections with Shīᶜism and stressed that there were 'no shiites (*sic*) in Nigeria, but only Islam' (West Africa, 26 May 26 1991). This statement was supported by Abubakar Gumi who claimed that the supporters of the ikhwān were not Shīᶜites but 'only admire what happened in Iran' (Sulaiman 1993:11). Due to his radical positions during his time studying economics at ABU Zaria, Ibrāhīm al-Zakzakī was imprisoned several times between 1981 and 1989 (in Enugu, Lagos and Port Harcourt). After his release from the Port Harcourt prison in 1989 he was put under constant surveillance. He was imprisoned again (in Port Harcourt and Kaduna) throughout most of the period of office of General Abacha (r. 1993–8) (Isa and Adam 2013–14: 61ff). Although he seems to have rejected violent means of political struggle after 1987, al-Zakzakī was still seen as the mastermind of northern Nigerian politically radical Islam. He continued to attack established rulers. The Sultan of Sokoto, for instance, was attacked by him as *sarkin gargajiyan sokoto*. The term '*gargajiya*' explicitly refers to the un-Islamic character of rule by the kings of Hausaland before the *jihād* of 1804. He called for a *jihād* against the 'system' from which every Muslim should withdraw, giving rise to the appellation 'Yan System' for his followers. The appeal to withdraw from an un-Islamic system was publicly represented as a long tradition in Islam, from the Prophet Muḥammad to Usman dan Fodio to Ayatollah Khomeini. In 1994, Ibrāhīm al-Zakzakī made his attachment to shīᶜism public, triggering a crisis within the ikhwān movement, which now became the Islamic Movement in Nigeria. Bunza confirms that members of the ikhwān openly acknowledged their 'shīᶜite inclination' in the 'late' 1990s and celebrated *ᶜAshūra*, the tenth of Muḥarram, the anniversary of the massacre of Karbalāᵓ and Faṭima's birthday (Bunza 2005: 231). In the mid-1990s, the Islamic Movement became a well-organised activist and shīᶜī-oriented movement in northern Nigeria, organised in a number of regional branches, such as Kano led by Muhammad Mahmoud Turi (b. 1963 in Zaria) and Katsina led by Yakubu Yahaya (on the development of the Kano branch, see Isa and Adam 2013–14: 65ff). In December 2011, the Islamic Movement managed to mobilise more than 20,000 Muslims for *ᶜAshūra* celebrations in Zaria (Mustapha and Bunza 2014: 73). They also started to ritually curse Abū Bakr, ᶜUmar and ᶜUthmān, the first three caliphs of Islam before ᶜAlī (Bunza 2005: 231).[30] As a result of Ibrāhīm al-Zakzakī's turn towards shīᶜism, a faction of Ibrāhīm al-Zakzakī's followers established the jamāᶜat al-tajdīd al-islāmī under the leadership of Abubakar Mujāhid.[31] This group had its headquarters in the Yakasai quarters of Kano, and declared itself to be close to the Egyptian Muslim Brotherhood, meaning it was rooted in Sunni Islam. Since 2000, the jamā'at al-tajdīd al-islāmī has also been one of the most outspoken supporters of 'political *sharīᶜa*' (Brigaglia 2012: 22; Ben Amara 2011: 52ff.).

Yakubu Yahaya, Ibrāhīm al-Zakzakī's major ally in Katsina, was born in 1954 in Unguwar Madawaki in Katsina. He studied Arabic and the Qurᵓān with his father, and then continued his studies in Kaduna and at Bayero University Kano, where he acquired a diploma in Arabic studies. Until 1983, he taught Arabic at the Katsina Teachers' College (see Sulaiman 1993; Falola 1998: 195). In 1983, he joined Ibrāhīm al-Zakzakī and in 1994 he established the Islamic Movement's branch in Katsina. In the early 1990s, the Islamic Movement in Katsina took the lead in a number of highly politicised conflicts with military governors of northern states, such as Colonel Madaki in Katsina. Due to his authoritarian style of government, Madaki had become a symbol for the arbitrary character of the Nigerian military regime that the Islamic Movement sought to fight (Falola 1998: 195–202). In the aftermath of a number of clashes with the Nigerian security forces in 1990 and 1991, Yakubu Yahaya was imprisoned and sentenced to death. To date, however, the verdict has not been executed. Serious clashes between followers of the

Islamic movement and security forces also occurred in 2002 in the Pindiga emirate of Kaduna state and in Yauri emirate. Under the leadership of Malam Tukur, Abdullahi Bello, Shuaibu Tela and Abubakar Danfulani members of the Islamic movement interrupted Friday prayers and abused the established rulers.

The Clash of Religions and the 'Muslim Internationale'

The dynamics of religious and political change in northern Nigeria were not only influenced by intra-*ṭarīqa* disputes. Nor does the struggle of the Sufis against the 'Yan Izala tell the rest of the story. Christian Churches, mostly Pentecostal Churches, united under the umbrella of the Christian Association of Nigeria (CAN), have also become a source of unrest in northern Nigeria from the 1980s.[32] Christian Churches were particularly successful in the so-called Middle Belt areas, the territories of the north that were not central lands of the Sokoto caliphate but that were used as slave raiding areas in the nineteenth century. In the twentieth century, the populations of the Middle Belt region continued to feel threatened by claims of political supremacy as formulated by the Hausa–Fulani administrative elites, as well as encroaching Hausa–Fulani settlement. They consequently joined Christian churches in considerable numbers and thus shook northern Nigeria's self-image of being a *dār al-islām*. In fact, major areas of the north became religiously mixed. Some areas in the Middle Belt even became predominantly Christian. Many Muslims consequently feared that their role as the major religious group in the Federation of Nigeria was under jeopardy.

The rise of this inter-religious conflict scenario became particularly visible in the Kafanchan riots of 1987, probably the first violent disturbances in northern Nigeria that were interpreted in a Christian–Muslim conflict paradigm as a manifestation of 'Muslim jihādism' or 'Christian crusaderism' (Loimeier 1997a: 295ff). This Muslim–Christian crusade–*jihād* conflict paradigm resurfaced more and more frequently in the 1990s and the early years of the twenty-first century with a number of serious riots and clashes in Plateau and Kaduna states (see Ibrahim 1991; Loimeier 1992; Paden 2005; Higazi 2007).[33] It has brought about the emergence of what Klaus Hock has called an 'Islam complex', an almost paranoid obsession that tends to portray the respective 'other' as the ultimate source of all things evil. It is a syndrome of feeling threatened by the 'other', and is easily activated in periods of crisis (Hock 1996: 6–7). The refusal of *ṭarīqa* candidates to support 'Yan Izala candidates (and vice versa) in the 1987 local government elections contributed to some spectacular victories of Christian candidates in Muslim majority areas. The neutralisation of the Muslim vote also paved the way for Christian majorities in some local councils. As a consequence, *ṭarīqa* and 'Yan Izala leaders eventually shelved their disputes and in 1988 they agreed to form a coalition of convenience in order to better resist the Christian 'crusade' in the north. These alliances of convenience have led to a considerable pacification of intra-Muslim disputes. Still, they should be seen as temporary, subject to revocation at any time. Change in the political context may again lead to a re-definition of religio-political discourses and disputes. Inasmuch as religious movements in northern Nigeria became mass movements from the 1950s, they also became more susceptible to the dialectics of social and political change. This includes the social, political and economic aspirations of their clienteles.

The rise of activist Christian groups to political prominence had far-reaching effects on the positioning of the different Muslim factions in the north and put renewed stress on the need to overcome religious disputes for the sake of political unity. Muslim re-positioning, expressed in meetings of reconciliation between Abubakar Gumi and Nasiru Kabara in 1990, led to the emergence of new Muslim national umbrella organisations. Foremost among these were the Council of ᶜUlamāᵓ and the Nigerian Supreme Council of Islamic Affairs (NSCIA). These organisations pressed for the introduction of the Islamic calendar, the establishment of *sharīᶜa* courts of appeal, the introduction of Islamic religious education for all Muslim school children and the introduction of Muslim school uniforms. A group of Muslim intellectuals and functionaries, often affiliated with the Umma group, soon came to dominate these new Muslim bodies. They stressed the need for unity of the Muslims in the north as a precondition for political success. The constant propagation of the ideal of Muslim political unity became a major problem for the 'Yan Izala in its efforts to fight the Sufi orders. Religious argumentation inherently implies the othering of Muslim religious opponents as unbelievers. Accordingly, it strengthened those groups that argued in primarily political terms while accepting the basic nature of all Muslims as faithful believers (*muᵓminūn*). In the early 1990s, these changes in the religious set-up of northern Nigeria became even more accentuated, as many representatives of the old generation of scholars, such as Abubakar Gumi, Sani Kafanga and Nasiru Kabara, died and were replaced by a younger generation of Muslim religious and political leaders, who were confronted with a social, political and economic context different from that of the 1970s. The return to civilian rule in 1999 after the authoritarian rule of General Sani Abacha saw the rise to power of General Obasanjo from Abeokuta in southwestern Nigeria. He was the first born-again Christian to win democratic elections in the Federation with 62 per cent of the vote, which forced Muslims in the north to rethink their legacies of internal competition and dispute. At the same time, the pressure to achieve Muslim unity was kept alive by activist and radical Muslim groups such as the MSS and the Islamic movement. These groups continued to point out to Muslims that internal disputes, as cultivated by the 'Yan Izala and the elder generation of Sufi leaders, would lead to *fitna* and promote the spread of Christianity. The shift from intra-Muslim rivalries to a larger conflict between Muslims and Christians was complicated, however, by the fact that religion was not the only motivation for dispute. Questions of land distribution, political rule and ethnic rivalry continued to contribute to the cocktail of potential conflict.

It is noteworthy that a considerable number of Muslim–Christian clashes occurred in Plateau state, where *sharīʿa* was not applied (see Hock 1992; Loimeier 1992; Paden 2005). Conflicts in Plateau state were mostly linked with disputes over land and access to resources between old populations and 'immigrant settlers' (see Ostien 2009; HRW 2012: 27ff). Conflicts in Nigeria, if registered at all beyond the local level, are interpreted in many different ways on different levels of political negotiation and instrumentalised for a variety of reasons. As a consequence, an economic conflict over access to land between FulBe pastoralists and Birom farmers in a Plateau state local government area may assume an ethnic character on the Plateau state level and be presented as a conflict between 'invading northerners' (FulBe) and 'indigenous local populations' (Birom), but then acquire a religious character on the Nigerian national level by being presented as a conflict between Muslims (FulBe) and Christians (Birom). Conflict in northern Nigeria should thus be seen as an ever-changing cocktail of ethnic, economic, political and religious motivations that may be easily remixed.

In the mid-1980s, Muslims started to move beyond old Sufi–'Yan Izala dichotomies by stressing the need for Muslim unity in the face of Christian 'crusaderism' in the north. By doing so, they implicitly deprived the 'Yan Izala of their own legitimation in their struggle against Sufi orders. The most notable leaders were Muslim intellectuals such as Ibrāhīm Sulaimān (ABU Zaria), Dr Umar Bello (Centre of Islamic Studies, Sokoto), Usman Muḥammad Bugaje (Islamic Trust of Nigeria, Zaria), Muḥammad Ṣādiq al-Kafawī (Centre of Islamic Legal Studies (CILS), ABU Zaria), Ibrahima Na'iya Sada (CILS, Zaria), Aliyu Dauda and Danjuma Maiwada (both BUK). All were more or less closely affiliated with the Umma movement, in addition to a younger generation of Muslim students who graduated from northern Nigeria's universities in the 1990s. These Muslim activists became outspoken local leaders of the MSS and their affiliated organisations. They started to de-emphasise the importance of affiliations with national players such as Saudi Arabia, Iran, Kuwait, the Gulf States, Pakistan, Libya, Egypt or Sudan, and stressed the legacy of the Sokoto *jihād* as a model for Islamic revolution in Nigeria. Outside support was still welcome, but the younger generation did not develop close ties with any country.

Much more important for the development of Muslim political discourse in northern Nigeria than affiliations with countries such as Saudi Arabia was the development of a Muslim Internationale. This arose in the context of a number of international conferences organised by Muslim organisations, such as the Organization of Islamic Cooperation (OIC). One example was a conference on Islam in Africa at the Islamic University of Uganda in Mbale in December 2003. This new form of organisation and networking seems to have started with a first 'Islam in Africa' conference in Abuja in December 1989. The Abuja conference attracted delegations from all over Africa. In attendance were well-known Muslim opposition leaders and intellectuals, such as Rashīd al-Ghannūshī from Tunisia, the Shaykh al-Azhar from Egypt and delegations from Iran, Saudi Arabia and Great Britain.

Networks and ties between Muslim internationalists were largely formed in the context of their studies at al-Azhar, the Islamic University of Medina, the Universities of Khartoum and Umdurman and the Islamic University of Mbale in Uganda. Teachers from these countries, in particular Sudan, were often employed by the Africa Muslim Agency (AMA). Other transnational

Muslim organisations of importance for the Nigerian context (and beyond) were al-muntadā al-islāmī, Islamic Relief, the al-ḥaramayn Foundation, the Islamic Foundation, the International Institute of Islamic Thought and the World Assembly of Muslim Youth (WAMY). Local and national networks of Muslim intellectuals, including members of local and national Muslim organisations such as the MSS and the Islamic Movement, are also linked globally through the 'old boys' networks' of the different universities and colleges.

Networking through academic and bureaucratic institutions was not entirely new to the Nigerian context, however. Indeed, it began in the colonial period when the first modern Islamic institutions were established. These institutions were closely connected, not only in structure and scope or with respect to their religious and political tasks, but also with respect to the personal links that were to develop among the graduates of these institutions. In Nigeria, the first modern Islamic institution was the Northern Provinces Law School (or Kano Law School, established in 1934 in Kano), which became the School of Arabic Studies in 1947. Its purpose was to train teachers, *qāḍīs* and clerks for the modern colonial administration, education and legal services. From 1954, the SAS offered an expanded *madrasa* curriculum and went on to become northern Nigeria's first college for higher Islamic education. It was a model for the Sokoto Arabic Teachers' College in 1963, as well as a whole series of Arabic colleges established after 1979: one in Gombe, two in Kano, one in Maiduguri, one in Katsina and others elsewhere in the north (Umar 2004: 99ff). Again, modern Islamic institutions of higher learning in northern Nigeria followed the earlier, colonial-era development of Islamic institutions modelled on the Bakht al-Rawḍa College near al-Du^{c}aym in the Sudan (about 190 km south of Khartoum on the White Nile), which had been planned since 1931 and was opened in 1937. The Bakht al-Rawḍa College was inspired by still earlier British Indian models of modern Islamic education and professional training. In its turn, the Nigerian SAS served as a model for the Zanzibari Muslim Academy, established in 1952, as well as Islamic colleges in The Gambia, Brunei and Malaysia. A central feature of modern Nigerian institutions was the mediating role of the Sudan, first in the form of the Bakht al-Rawḍa College and then through the Universities of Khartoum (Gordon College) and Umdurman, as well as the Africa Muslim

Agency, and finally in the guise of Sudanese teachers who came to teach in northern Nigeria or contributed, as directors of schools and in other administrative functions, to the development of modern Islamic institutions in northern Nigeria. These academic links were cultivated in the context of conferences. In 1960, a first African conference on Islamic education united a number of Muslim scholars from northern Nigeria, Sudan and Zanzibar in Kano to discuss issues of educational reform. Since the 1960s, these ties have become an important factor in intra-African Muslim academic networks that have today moved into the second or third generation.[34]

New forms of Muslim organisation on the non-governmental level have at times been denounced by Christian organisations as manifestations of an 'Islamic threat' or 'proof of Islamist internationalist networks of terror'. This is a convenient strategy to delegitimise Muslim political positions and discourses in a climate of mistrust and rumour. A few months after the 1989 Abuja 'Islam in Africa' conference, for instance, a fake communiqué from this conference was published that presented a number of 'Muslim demands' for the development of the 'member nations' of the 'Islam in Africa' conference. Among other things, the communiqué said that Muslims demanded that Nigeria be declared a member of the OIC as a 'Federal Islamic Sultanate' and that all Western legal and judicial systems should be replaced by *sharī*^{c}*a* (quoted in *The Reporter*, 11 June 1990). In an aborted military coup in April 1990, the coup leaders, mostly army officers of Middle Belt origin under General Gideon Orkar, proclaimed in their radio announcement the 'excision of five northern states, Sokoto, Katsina, Kano, Bauchi and Bornu' from the Federation in order to stop the discrimination of non-Muslim populations in the rest of the Federation (*Newswatch*, 7 May 1990). Muslim–Christian disputes have thus characterised the religio-political development of northern Nigeria to a considerable extent since the late 1980s. As a consequence, any kind of event is likely to trigger responses in the form of Muslim–Christian accusations and counter-accusations based on mutual perceptions of marginalisation. In such a climate of suspicion, everything is necessarily subject to political and religious interpretation. Such interpretations tend to confirm the paradigm of mutual fear of the 'other'.

'Political *Sharīᶜa*' v. 'Complete *Sharīᶜa*'

Since 2000, a new field of conflict has been added to the long list of northern Nigeria's religious and political problems: the introduction of *sharīᶜa* penal laws in twelve of the northern states, namely, Zamfara (January 2000), Niger (spring 2000), Sokoto (spring 2000), Gombe (May 2000), Kano (June 2000), Kebbi (July 2000), Jigawa (August 2000), Katsina (August 2000), Yobe (August 2000), Bauchi (February 2001), Bornu (June 2001) and Kaduna (November 2001, but confined to the Muslim areas of northern Kaduna).[35] Four other states are preparing *sharīᶜa* penal codes of their own but have not yet enacted them. The announcement to introduce *sharīᶜa* penal laws by the Governor of Zamfara state, Aḥmad Sani Yerima, an ABU graduate and a supporter of the 'Yan Izala movement and, more recently, of the ahl as-sunna, on 27 October 1999, and the enactment of the new *sharīᶜa* legislation in Zamfara on 27 January 2000, triggered a wave of enthusiasm for *sharīᶜa* and forced other politicians to follow suit. Yerima was regarded as a hero who had re-established the rule of Islamic law in 1420 (2000), 100 *hijrī* years after the end of the Sokoto empire in 1320 (1903).

The introduction of *sharīᶜa* penal laws in twelve northern Nigerian states was called 'political *sharīᶜa*' by many Nigerians, due to the fact that it had an obvious political goal, namely, to legitimise the political agenda of northern Nigerian politicians and to de-legitimise the Obasanjo administration, while the supporters of an extended *sharīᶜa* legislation, mostly members of the 'Yan Izala, preferred the term 'complete *sharīᶜa*'. The introduction of *sharīᶜa* penal laws (Arab. *ḥadd*, pl. *ḥudūd*)[36] was supported by a plethora of Muslim groups and organisations and a majority of the Muslim population of northern Nigeria. They saw it as a chance to re-establish justice where all other systems of law had failed. It must be stressed here that other aspects of *sharīᶜa*, in particular Islamic personal (family) law, were always in force in northern Nigeria, in colonial and post-colonial times. Only the Islamic penal laws were abolished or modified by the British after 1903. According to Last, the introduction of *sharīᶜa* penal laws can thus be seen as a form of decolonisation of the legal system, and a return to a system of law as recommended by God. At the same time, it was seen by the population as a way of fighting corruption and bad government, immorality and ostentatious wealth: *sharīᶜa* was seen as a new option where all others had failed (Last 2000: 141).

However, the introduction of *sharīᶜa* penal laws was criticised by a number of Muslim personalities and organisations in northern Nigeria. These critics included those with a record of opposition to the northern Nigerian religio-political establishment going back to the 1970s. They also included those who had fought, for different reasons, against the religious and political programme of the 'Yan Izala. Ibrāhīm al-Zakzakī, for instance, argued that, inasmuch as it was politically motivated and not introduced in a proper Islamic way, the introduction of *sharīᶜa* penal laws was illegal (Brigaglia 2012: 22; Ben Amara 2011: 52ff.). This argument was shared, if for different reasons, by Dahiru Bauchi, and Muslim women's associations such as the Federation of Muslim Women's Associations in Nigera (FOMWAN).[37] When looking at other opponents of the introduction of *sharīᶜa* penal laws, we encounter familiar faces. One is the Sultan of Sokoto, Muḥammad Maccido, who had replaced the controversial former Sultan, Ibrāhīm Dasuki, a close associate of Abubakar Gumi, who had been deposed in 1996 by the military government. Sultan Muḥammad Maccido remained conspicuously neutral in 2000 when *sharīᶜa* penal laws were introduced in Zamfara state. All he said was that 'adequate enlightenment on *sharīᶜa* should have been carried out by its proponents before its full adoption' (Danfulani 2005: 28, 52). Yusuf Bala Usman, a leading representative of a Marxist tradition of thought at ABU Zaria, rejected the introduction of *sharīᶜa* penal laws, as did Sanusi Lamidu Sanusi, an outspoken Muslim intellectual and Governor of the Nigerian Central Bank.[38] BAOBAB, a women's rights group in Lagos led by Dr Ayesha Imam, also joined the club of 'opponents'.

The introduction of *sharīᶜa* penal laws in Zamfara state, incidentally Abubakar Gumi's state of origin, added to existing anxieties among the non-Muslim populations of the north, particularly in those states, such as Kaduna and Niger, where Christians formed a considerable part of the population. These anxieties were fed by the fact that the most outspoken supporters of the introduction of 'complete *sharīᶜa*' were well-known members of the northern political and economic establishment. It was they who had influenced the political and economic development of the north from the 1960s until General Obasanjo's accession to power in May 1999, and they included former presidents Shehu Shagari and Muhammad Buhari; JNI leader Usman Jibrin; secretary-general of the Nigerian Supreme Council of Islamic Affairs (NSCIA) Alhaji Lateef Adegbite; and the wealthy businessman Alhaji Ahmed Chanchangi, a well-known patron and financer of the 'Yan Izala and a relative of the former Sultan of Sokoto. Backing by these politicians supports the claims of those who argue that the introduction of *sharīᶜa* penal laws was essentially a political manoeuvre as well as highly unconstitutional. The impression that 'complete *sharīᶜa*' was instrumentalised for many purposes is supported by the fact that a number of Muslim groups, or 'Yan Hisba, saw the introduction of *sharīᶜa* penal laws as a chance to enforce their own concepts of Islamic law and order, often in a rather arbitrary way.

Since 2000, the actions of the 'Yan Hisba have opened up a wide field for the misuse of power that has led to recurrent civic dispute, killings and riots in the Middle Belt areas and Christian diasporic communities in the far north. First riots occurred in Kaduna and Kano on 20 February 2000, in Gombe in May 2001, in Bauchi and Jigawa states in June and July 2001, and again in Kaduna in 2002 and resulted in hundreds of deaths (see Paden 2005). Since the introduction of *sharīᶜa* penal laws, at least ten people have been sentenced to death (even if only a few cases, such as those of Amina Lawal and Safiya Hussayni, have gained notoriety), dozens have been sentenced to amputations and floggings have been a regular occurrence. Defendants usually had no access to legal representation. Badly trained judges of quickly established (lower) *sharīᶜa* courts often failed to inform defendants of their rights and have even accepted confessions extracted under torture. Almost all of the convicted were poor and often female, with little knowledge of legal procedures in general and *sharīᶜa* penal laws in particular. Many trials before (lower) *sharīᶜa* courts were also linked with 'Yan Izala or Salafi-inspired accusations of allegedly un-Islamic Sufi ritual practices, spirit possession (bori) and spirit exorcism practices (Hausa *rukiyya*, Arab. *ruqya*, 'to use magic') as cultivated by religious scholars (mostly) affiliated with the Tijāniyya (O'Brien 2007: 60–4). Such trials showed that the conflict between Salafi-oriented groups and the Sufi orders, in particular the Tijāniyya, was ongoing, even if in a new disguise. According to many Nigerian Muslims, these trials have violated the principles of *sharīᶜa* itself and, in addition, one of the basic popular assumptions regarding *sharīᶜa* penal laws, namely, that all Muslims, including the rich, should be punished on equal terms. As a result, many Muslims have started to say that the *sharīᶜa* penal laws in application today are not *sharīᶜa* proper but 'political *sharīᶜa*'. They furthermore point to the politicians' failure to implement economic and social reforms that would alleviate poverty in northern Nigeria.

By 2005, the application of *sharīᶜa* penal laws had lost steam. Although *sharīᶜa* penal laws were still in place in twelve states, no other state introduced them. Political will to enforce *sharīᶜa* penal laws was waning, especially when it came to the application of *ḥadd* punishments. With one exception, all death sentences and numerous other penalties for criminal offences imposed by lower *sharīᶜa* courts were cancelled by *sharīᶜa* courts of appeal for procedural reasons. Of dozens of amputation sentences, only three were executed, and none since mid-2001. By 2005, only one case of a verdict of amputation for theft had reached the Federal Court of Appeal (FCA), the first non-Islamic level of appeal beyond the upper *sharīᶜa* court of appeal and the last level of appeal before the Supreme Court (HRW 2004: 89). Even cases of 'Yan Hisba harassment seem to have decreased, perhaps because male adulterers now visited prostitutes in non-*sharīᶜa* states or acquired Christian identities (and identity cards) in order to be able to drink alcohol.[39] As a result, a majority of Muslims came to think that *sharīᶜa* may no longer be a viable option. A local Muslim voice from Kaduna asserted that 'Muslims are fed up with *sharīᶜa*' (HRW 2004: 89). According to Sanusi Lamido Sanusi, 'the euphoria seems to have fizzled out. After the initial sensational sentences of amputation, caning and even stoning to death, the people have come to realise that nothing in reality has changed and that the poor seem to be the only ones facing the wrath of the law' (Sanusi 2007: 185). At the same time, Muslims were ashamed to say 'we don't want *sharīᶜa*. Challenging the government is like challenging Islam. There is a fear of being misunderstood, so people keep quiet. They would be seen as blasphemous' (HRW 2004: 89).

In sum, people became disillusioned with the way in which *sharīᶜa* had been implemented so far. The state governments of the north that introduced *sharīᶜa* were increasingly perceived as not being sincere in its application. Religion had transparently been instrumentalised for politics. Even religious scholars who had originally supported the introduction of *sharīᶜa* penal laws turned against the way in which they were applied in 2003:

> The penal code of northern Nigeria was working well until some states like Zamfara began agitating for *sharīᶜa*. Their motives were purely political. It had nothing to do with religion. The real needs of the people are health, education etc. The politicians did nothing about that. Instead, they made a big fuss about *sharīᶜa*. There is manipulation by politicians. The call for *sharīᶜa* contributed to violence and social tension between Muslims and non-Muslims, and even among Muslims themselves. (HRW 2004: 90, 94)

The first initiatives to amend *sharīᶜa* penal laws were initiated in March 2002 by the Attorney General of Nigeria and Minister of Justice, Kanu Agabi. Nonetheless, the federal government was reluctant to interfere directly in '*sharīᶜa* states' lest it antagonise the Muslim electorate in the north. These voters had contributed considerably to the victories of President Obasanjo in both the 1999 and 2003 presidential elections. At the same time, politicians and state governments of the north still saw *sharīᶜa* as a way to increase their political legitimacy. Some politicians, such as Ibrāhīm Shekarau of Kano, a former member of the MSS, were able to win elections in 2003 for being 'more principled' than their predecessors or other state governors with respect to the implementation of both full *sharīᶜa* and popular welfare programmes. 'Saying no to implement *sharīᶜa* would have constituted political suicide' (HRW 2004: 92). *Sharīᶜa* thus became a symbol of identity of the Muslim north. Northern Nigerian Muslims felt they should not sacrifice it to national and international pressures or 'Western values'. *Sharīᶜa* thus also became a symbol of resistance to the encroaching Westernisation of northern Nigeria. According to Nafiu Baba Ahmed, the Secretary General of the Supreme Council for Sharīᶜa in Nigeria, '. . . the introduction of the *sharīᶜa* shows the yearning of the people. They are not happy with having a foreign system imposed on them'. A 'Yan Hisba leader from Kano added, 'we have our own value system and religion. Just because the West doesn't agree, it doesn't mean it's wrong' (HRW 2004: 103). Under these circumstances, it seems as if *sharīᶜa* and *sharīᶜa* penal laws will stay for some time and remain a platform for the negotiation of religion and politics.

The *sharīᶜa* debate led to yet another turn in the dialectics of religio-political development in northern Nigeria. A younger generation of 'Yan Izala started mobilising for the implementation of the *sharīᶜa* laws through different 'Yan Hisba groups. The struggle for the implementation of *sharīᶜa* penal laws must be seen as a discourse reflecting local, northern Nigerian, preoccupations and agendas. At the same time, the struggle for the implementation of *sharīᶜa* penal laws stimulated the emergence of a new generation of 'Yan Izala in the guise of the ahl al-sunna that were more at home with local dialectics of development than international agendas. Recurrent experiences of the instrumentalisation of religion for politics had a sobering effect on a growing number of Muslims; the *sharīᶜa* debate was but one recent example. In the end, Muslims in northern Nigeria may reach a stage of disillusion with respect to the different models of an Islamic order as offered by disparate social, religious and political forces. Ultimately, they may turn to societal models that are less defined by religion. One important aspect of the implementation of 'complete *sharīᶜa*' was the basic fact that existing social and political structures in northern Nigeria were not transformed, that is, established power groups remained in power, existing inequalities and social fragmentations were not challenged, 'complete *sharīᶜa*' did not bring about a more just or a more Islamic society. Salafi-oriented Muslims, in particular the 'Yan Izala, realised that although they may have acquired some leverage through the 'Yan Hisba groups, 'complete *sharīᶜa*' was still administered by the established *qāḍī* courts, which were mostly staffed with *qāḍīs* affiliated with the Tijāniyya, especially in Kano, Yobe and Bornu states. Equally, the governors of Kano state, Rabiu Kwankwaso (r. 1999–2003 and again 2011–15) and Ibrahim Shekarau (r. 2003–11), filled central positions and committees with representatives of all influential Muslim groups in Kano state, that is, Tijāniyya, Qādiriyya, 'Yan Izala and ahl al-sunna, as well as independent academics and intellectuals (Thurston 2014: 41ff). 'Complete *sharīᶜa*' thus served to empower established religious forces, to the chagrin of the 'Yan Izala, and led to further disenchantment among Salafi-oriented Muslims regarding 'complete *sharīᶜa*'. This disenchantment may have contributed to the emergence of even more radical groups such as Boko Haram (communication Andrea Brigaglia, 2 June 2014).

The Boko Haram Years

The confusing multifacetedness and increasing fragmentation of northern Nigeria's religio-political spectrum was furthered in recent years by the emergence of yet another group of radical Muslims. Since 2009, this Muslim movement has become widely known in Western media for both its militant actions and its ultra-fundamentalist programme,[40] under the name of Boko Haram, often translated as 'Western education is forbidden' (sometimes even more misleadingly as 'Western education is sin').[41] Boko Haram activities have been reported not only in northern Nigeria, but also in neighbouring Chad, Cameroon and Niger. By 2012, Boko Haram had established a base in Diffa, southeastern Niger, in order to escape Nigerian Army and Nigerian police repression. Other Boko Haram bases in Niger were recorded in Maradi and Zinder. Since 2009, one Boko Haram sub-group, Ansaru (jamāᶜat anṣār al-muslimīn fi-bilād al-sūdān), has been linked with an al-Qāᶜida branch, namely, al-Qāᶜida au Maghreb Islamique (AQMI).[42] However, not all violence in northern Nigeria was and is linked to Boko Haram (see Kukah 2012). It is equally misleading to view Boko Haram exclusively as a terror organisation. Such a narrow-minded approach is not particularly useful in fathoming the true character of the movement and understanding why Boko Haram has managed to attract popular support in northern Nigeria despite harsh police and army repression.

The Boko Haram movement was a result of social, political and generational dynamics within the larger field of northern Nigerian Salafi-oriented Islam, as represented most prominently by the 'Yan Izala movement. In addition to disputes over leadership, authority and regional autonomy, the development of the 'Yan Izala has been characterised since the 1990s by the emergence of a group of younger 'Yan Izala leaders. This led to generational conflicts within the 'Yan Izala and disputes over the question of proper Islamic education. The struggle for modern Islamic education has indeed been one of the major programmatic features of 'Yan Izala development and has led not only to the establishment of numerous 'Yan Izala schools in northern Nigeria but also to the emergence of a second generation of 'Yan Izala leaders and followers who went through this new system of education, only to discover that modern Islamic education 'Yan Izala-style' did not necessarily provide jobs. In particular, the stress on sound training in Arabic in 'Yan Izala schools, as well as 'Yan Izala-sponsored university education in Saudi Arabia, did not provide enough career options in Nigeria. Even positions within the movement were still occupied by first-generation 'Yan Izala who were not keen to retire. Second-generation activists thus found their career paths blocked and were increasingly prepared to dispute existing claims to leadership. Many second-generation 'Yan Izala activists either established their own schools to engineer careers as teachers, or split from the 'Yan Izala movement to carve out a position for their own reformist endeavours by establishing their own mosques, schools and Islamic NGOs (Anonymous 2012: 118ff).

When analysing the Boko Haram movement, it is necessary not only to look at the social framework for the emergence of this militant movement, but also to consider some of the doctrinal dimensions of the disputes between the Boko Haram movement and other Muslim reform movements in northern Nigeria. Taking such a perspective can help to clarify processes of radicalisation and to show that in moments of crisis and rapid social change, doctrinal arguments acquire paramount importance for the self-definition of a new religious movement. Boko Haram is not the first Muslim movement in the region to advocate *jihād* (in the sense of an armed struggle) as a strategy for implementing its reform programme. The movement of *jihād* started by Usman dan Fodio in the early nineteenth century led to the removal of the *Habe*[43] rulers and to the establishment of the rule of religious scholars, who strove to legitimate their rule through doctrinal argumentation. Since then, recourse to doctrinal argumentation has become a precondition for political action in northern Nigeria. A sound education in Islamic law and doctrine has consequently become a sine qua non for participation in public or political debates. The introduction of Western education in the colonial period seriously challenged the hegemonic position of Islamic education and has consequently been seen as both a threat and a symbol of the increasing impact of an alien, colonial, Christian, materialist and corrupt process of Westernisation.

Colonial rule, the establishment of British education, British law and the economic dynamics of the colonial and post-colonial periods have indeed led to a deep crisis in northern Nigerian Muslim society that can be described by the umbrella term 'modernisation shock'. Although religious and political leaders such as Ahmadu Bello and Abubakar Gumi were highly successful in their reform endeavours and their efforts to create a modern, yet still Muslim, northern Nigeria, their policies of reform were contested by representatives of the religious and political establishment, as well as by small but outspoken radical groups who maintained that reform was either not radical enough in political terms or basically un-Islamic, equivalent to another form of Westernisation. A paradigmatic example of such a radical anti-modern movement was Maitatsine, a group that surfaced in a number of violent clashes with the Nigerian Army from 1980 to 1987. The Maitatsine movement was established by the Cameroonian Muslim scholar Muḥammad Marwa, who had settled in Kano in the 1960s and had slowly built a group of followers among Muslim migrants in Kano's Ayagi quarter. Due to his radical rejection of all non-qur᾽ānic innovations such as watches, Western dress, bicycles and even ritual prayers,[44] he became known as the 'master of rejection'.[45] In 1980, the disputes between the Maitatsine movement and state security as well as established scholars escalated, and Muḥammad Marwa and his group were accused of being heretics by Kano's scholarly establishment. On 19 December 1980, Muḥammad Marwa tried to storm Kano's major Friday mosque, close to the emir's palace. This attack triggered massive retaliation by the Nigerian Army, and in the course of several days of fighting approximately 6,000 people, including Muḥammad Marwa himself, were killed. The movement continued to blossom, however, and again rose in rebellion in 1982 (Maiduguri and Kaduna), 1984 (Yola), 1985 (Gombe) and 1993 (Funtua) (Loimeier 1997a: 218ff; Hiskett: 1987: 209ff).[46]

Due to its radical and militant character, along with its ultra-fundamentalist positions, the Maitatsine movement has been compared with the Boko Haram movement. This comparison extends to the social roots of both movements – namely, the *almajirai* (sing. *almajiri*): those young students of qur᾽ānic schools who still move (migrate), as in olden times, from teacher to teacher in order to acquire knowledge. Many *almajirai*, often of rural origin, live in destitute circumstances and are therefore considered easy prey for radical groups. In the 1980s, Muslim religious scholars, the Nigerian press and Western observers and academics such as Lubeck (1985) and Hiskett (1987) saw a connection between Maitatsine and the *almajirai*. Similar allegations have been made in the context of the rise of the Boko Haram movement (Höchner 2012). However, while some *almajirai* may indeed have joined both Maitatsine and Boko Haram, an understanding of the social set-up of the two movements still requires proper research. Indiscriminate allegations are misleading and ignore the ability of established (and respected) qurʾānic teachers to control their students.[47]

Boko Haram as an organisation emerged in the mid-1990s among a group of young and activist Muslims in Bornu. Its first base was in the al-Ḥājj Muḥammad Ndimi Mosque in Maiduguri and it was originally led by Malam Abubakar Lawal. When Malam Lawal left for studies in Saudi Arabia in 1998, Muḥammad Yūsuf took over leadership of the group (Azumah 2014: 8). At that time, the group was known as shabāb al-islām and was regarded as a regional cell of the ahl al-sunna movement in Maiduguri (ICG 2014c: 7). Muḥammad Yūsuf (1970–2009), who stemmed from Girgir in Yobe State, had been one of Jaᶜfar Maḥmūd Adam's students in Kano, but had split from him in 2002 (Brigaglia 2012: 22; Ben Amara 2011: 52ff; ICG 2014c: 9). According to Muḥammad Awwal Adam 'Albani' Zaria, who knew Muḥammad Yūsuf, his father had migrated to Nigeria from Niger and had become a follower of Muhammad Marwa in Kano, but was killed in 1980 in the context of the suppression of the Maitatsine movement in Kano (Higazi 2013: 145). Muḥammad Yūsuf was allegedly also close to Abubakar Mujāhid, founder of the jamāᶜat al-tajdīd al-islāmī, who had split from Ibrāhīm al-Zakzakī in 1994 and chaired the jamā'at al-tajdīd al-islāmī branch in Bornu for some time (Adesoji 2010: 95ff).

After the split from Jaᶜfar Maḥmūd Adam in 2002, Maiduguri's ahl al-sunna group closed its mosques for Muḥammad Yūsuf and his followers, who moved to the 'Markaz' mosque that was renamed masjid Ibn Taimiyyah (Higazi 2013: 147). This mosque was actually built on grounds rented by Baba Fugu Muḥammad, Muḥammad Yūsuf's father-in-law, although he did not become a member of Boko Haram.[48] In this period of time the group also becme known as ahl al-sunna wa-l-jamāᶜa wa-l-hijra. From 2004 (the year of Jaᶜfar Maḥmūd Adam's assassination), bitter doctrinal disputes characterised the confrontation between Jaᶜfar Maḥmūd Adam and Muḥammad Yūsuf. These disputes, often presented in the guise of public sermons, spread by way of pamphlets and cassettes or CDs. In his sermons and pamphlets, Jaᶜfar Maḥmūd Adam criticised Muḥammad Yūsuf's doctrinal positions as 'ignorant' and 'stupid', and as dangerous for the political ambitions of Muslims in Nigeria.[49] Jaᶜfar Maḥmūd Adam advocated the importance of Western and secular education for Muslims, for instance in a taped sermon entitled '*Ilimin boko da aikin gwamnati ba haramun ba ne*' (Western education and work for the government are not forbidden) (Brigaglia 2012: 22): only the conscious adoption of Western and secular boko education would enable Muslims to effectively fight the Western enemy. Jaʿfar Maḥmūd Adam also defended the long-term strategy of slowly Islamising these institutions. The fight against the Nigerian state was seen as counter-productive (Anonymous 2012: 132f.).

Muḥammad Yūsuf, by contrast, rejected the modern Islamic schools of the 'Yan Izala and related groups, as well as Nigeria's secular system of education and allegedly summarised this specific position as '*ilimin boko haramun ne*' (Western education is forbidden).[50] He also turned against the Nigerian state and criticised the arbitrariness of Nigerian institutions – in particular, the security forces. He refused to recognise the Sultan of Sokoto as the nominal head of Nigerian Muslims and called him '*sarkin sokoto*' (Hausa: king of Sokoto). Central to Muḥammad Yūsuf's argumentation was a text written by a Saudi scholar, President of the International Islamic Fiqh Council and a permanent member of the Saudi Arabian Permanent Committee for Islamic Research and Fatāwa, Abūbakar b. ʿAbdallāh Abū Zayd (1944–2008), entitled '*al-madāris al-ʿalamiyya al-ajnabiyya al-istiʿmariyya: taʾrīkhuha wa-makhāṭiruha*' (The Secular, Foreign and Colonialist Schools: Their History and Dangers). This text served as the doctrinal basis for his rejection of a natural science-based (Western and secular) view of the world (Anonymous 2012: 123). In December 2003, the dispute turned into open conflict.

At the time of Muḥammad Yusūf's break with Jaʿfar Maḥmūd Adam, another conflict developed within the ahl al-sunna wa-l-jamāʿa wa-l-hijra: a leader of the group's youth movement, Muḥammad ʿAlī, insisted on a more radical strategy at this early stage in the development of the movement and attacked Maiduguri's Muslim establishment as corrupt. The dissidents criticised in particular Muḥammad Yūsuf's support for Ali Modu Sheriff, the All Nigeria People's Party (ANPP) candidate for the position of governor of Bornu state, who had pledged to implement 'complete *sharīʿa*', yet was known to be highly corrupt: Muḥammad Yūsuf served, in fact, as a member of the Bornu state Sharīʿa Implementation Committee from 1999 to 2007 under governors Mala Kachallah (r. 1999–2003) and Ali Modu Sheriff. Ali Modu Sheriff was voted into power in April 2003 and was even re-elected in

2007, again supported by Boko Haram. When Muḥammad Yūsuf refused to support Muḥammad ᶜAlī's radical plans, this group of dissidents, led by Muḥammad ᶜAlī and Aminu Tashen Ilmi, withdrew to Kanamma, close to the border with Niger, in 2002 or early 2003, according to other sources (Comolli 2015: 47), under pretext of a *hijra.* In Kanamma, they established a *dār al-Islām*, a spatially segregated community of 'Ṭālibān', soon labelled 'Afghanistan', who started to live out their own idea of an ideal Muslim society. From 23 to 31 December 2003, these radicals clashed with Nigerian security forces and most members of the group including Muḥammad ᶜAlī were killed, while the survivors rejoined Muḥammad Yūsuf in Maiduguri in early 2004 (Azumah 2014: 8; Higazi 2013: 150; Mustapha 2014c: 179).[51]

As a consequence, the Nigerian media started to call Muḥammad Yūsuf's followers by a series of nicknames such as 'Yusufiyya', 'Taliban' and 'Boko Haram' (Ben Amara 2011: 55f.; Anonymous 2012: 118ff), labels that were quickly adopted by Western media.[52] After further attacks against police stations in Bornu State in September 2004, the Nigerian Army killed twenty-seven 'Taliban', while others managed to flee into neighbouring Cameroon where they developed a basis for future operations.[53] Muḥammad Yūsuf escaped to Sudan and subsequently went to Saudi Arabia, where he met with the Deputy Governor of Bornu State Adamu Dibal, who eventually organised his return to Nigeria in 2005.[54] His opponents in Nigeria, such as Jaᶜfar Maḥmūd Adam, were quick to point out Muḥammad Yūsuf's 'hypocrisy' in using modern means such as a passport, visa and aeroplanes (provided by corrupt Nigerian authorities) despite his supposed espousal of anti-modern and ultra-fundamentalist ideas. This statement was purely polemical: Muḥammad Yūsuf and his movement had never adopted such a position regarding modern technology, and had in fact claimed that, in contrast to Western education, modern technology, meaning mobile phones, television, motorbikes and even modern medicine (as well as AK-47 machine guns), was completely acceptable in Islamic terms. In this respect, the Boko Haram movement has clearly taken a different view from that of the Maitatsine movement of the 1980s (Last 2009: 10; Pérouse de Montclos 2014: 8).

From 2004 to 2009, Boko Haram largely refrained from military action and instead recruited new followers, not only among the unemployed and *almajirai* in Maiduguri and other cities in north-eastern Nigeria, but also among Kanuri farmers in northern Bornu and Yobe, the region where most leading Boko Haram members came from. In addition, Boko Haram recruited followers among a number of small ethnic groups in southwestern Bornu (Damboa, Biu and Chibok), as well as in the border regions with Cameroon in Bornu and Adamawa states. These recruiting areas were characterised by the fact that they were marginal even within north-eastern Nigeria. Last but not least, Boko Haram recruited support among migrant workers in north-eastern Nigerian cities. Many of these migrant workers had come to cities such as Maiduguri from marginal areas such as the Gwoza Hills close to the border with Cameroon (Higazi 2013: 148f).

Since 11 June 2009, the conflict escalated again and erupted into violent clashes between Boko Haram followers and Nigerian security forces in five northern Nigerian states, including Bauchi and Kano (see Pérouse de Montclos 2015: 276f; Comolli 2015: 54ff). In the course of these clashes from June to September 2009, 1,387 people were killed (Higazi 2013: 153). Among them was Muḥammad Yūsuf, who was killed in a police station after having been taken prisoner (Anonymous 2012: 128; HRW 2012: 35ff). Another prominent victim of the 2009 clashes was one of the most important patrons of the movement, Alhaji Buji Foi, a former Bornu State commissioner for religious affairs, who had sold his properties in order to support Muḥammad Yūsuf. Buji Foi was appointed state commissioner for religious affairs in 2003 by Bornu's new state governor Ali Modu Sheriff and retired in 2007 when it became clear that the Sheriff administration was not willing to implement 'complete *sharīᶜa*' (ICG 2014c: 12; Harnischfeger 2012: 499). The role of Alhaji Buji Foi and that of the Bornu deputy state governor, Adamu Dibal, points to the existence of high-ranking sympathisers of the Boko Haram movement in the Bornu state government. Most of these politicians were voted into office following the political *sharīᶜa* campaigns in 2000.

The June–September 2009 clashes were triggered by a series of Nigerian police raids on Boko Haram camps and against members of the movement in Dutsen Tanshi, Bauchi and Biu on 26 July 2009. Fourteen Boko Haram followers were killed in these skirmishes. By then, Boko Haram fighters had developed new (and modern) violent tactics, including drive-by shootings and hit-and-run attacks against police stations and other targets. At the same time, the authorities imposed a ban on night driving for motorbikes. Wearing a helmet was also made obligatory, and police roadblocks were introduced to enforce these regulations. In June 2009, seventeen motorbike riders were shot by the police (although none died as a result) because they were not wearing helmets (Last 2009: 7). Due to the fact that police roadblocks were often used to extract exaggerated fees from drivers for minor infractions, attacks against police stations earned Boko Haram sympathy among the population. In its public statements, often video messages, Boko Haram stressed that it would fight the rampant corruption, abuse of power and economic injustice of the Nigerian 'system' and thus responded to widespread feelings of resentment in the Nigerian population (see HRW 2012).

After the death of Muḥammad Yūsuf in 2009 and the clampdown on the movement, Boko Haram was seriously weakened. Surviving Boko Haram members fled into neighbouring countries or went underground. They reorganised in 2010, in the guise of a number of semi-autonomous groups, led by a thirty-seven-man council (Arabic: *shūra*) under the leadership of Muḥammad Abūbakar Muḥammad Shekau, a Kanuri from Shekau, Tarmuwa Local Government, in Yobe State on the border with Niger. In April 2010, Boko Haram resurfaced and changed its strategy: Boko Haram not only attacked perceived opponents, in particular police officials and politicians linked with the ANPP, but also started to attack high-profile targets outside north-eastern Nigeria (Mohammed 2015: 5). This escalation brought about a number of internal disputes over questions of strategy (see Pérouse de Montclos 2014: 11ff).[55] Most importantly, the group adopted a new name: jamāᶜat ahl al-sunna li-l-daᶜwa wa-l-jihād ᶜalā minhaj al-salaf. This change of name reflects internal dynamics: the former name, ahl al-sunna wa-l-jamāᶜa wa-l-hijra, may be translated freely as 'the people of the Sunnah (of the prophet) and the community (of Muslims) as well as (those who accept the obligation) to emigrate (from the land of unbelievers, that is, the Nigerian state)'. By choosing this name, Boko Haram claimed authority regarding the interpretation of the Sunnah as well as the question of who could be regarded a Muslim. By analogy, the reference to the term '*hijra*' declared the Nigerian state a heathen state that must be left by way of emigration, as the prophet did in 622 when he migrated from heathen Mecca to Medina. The name ahl al-sunna wa-l-jamāʿa wa-l-hijra thus proclaimed an agenda of both inclusion and exclusion of fellow Muslims.

The new name of the group, jamāᶜat ahl al-sunna li-l-daᶜwa wa-l-jihād ᶜalā minhaj al-salaf, signalled a corresponding shift in the programme of the group and a distinct radicalisation: now Boko Haram claimed to represent 'the community of the people of the Sunnah who fight for the cause (of Islam) by means of *jihād* according to the method of the *salaf*'. The reference to the salaf, the companions of the Prophet Muḥammad, was a clear indication that Boko Haram was propagating a narrow interpretation of the term '*jihād*' – namely, the kind of armed struggle against (Meccan and Arab) unbelievers as fought by the followers of the Prophet. During his lifetime, the Prophet advocated a much broader understanding of the term '*jihād*' and accepted armed struggle against his enemies only after the *hijra* from Mecca to Medina in 622. Again, Boko Haram claimed to be the supreme authority for the definition of both 'Sunnah' and 'Islam', excluding all those who did not meet their own definitions of the terms; in addition, the group's position shifted from advocating emigration to advocating *jihād*, *jihād* being defined as an armed struggle against the enemies of Islam. At the same time, the doctrinal development of Boko Haram reflects the fact that the movement moved from symbolic distanciation and social separation, as well as a *siyāsa*-minded position in terms of strategy that respected doctrinal debates, to spatial segregation and a *jihād*-minded orientation that largely neglected doctrinal debates, building liberated zones in north-eastern Nigeria, in particular in the border regions with Cameroon and Niger.

In 2011, the conflict acquired new dimensions when Boko Haram not only targeted police stations and prisons, but also attacked churches (first ones in 2009), abducted people (see HRW 2012: 96ff; Higazi 2013: 154) and assassinated politicians linked with Bornu's ruling party, the All Nigeria People's Party (ANPP) of Ali Modu Sheriff. Attacks against Christians were a new element and point to a change in strategy that followed a double rationale: Christian churches – in particular, Pentecostal churches – were seen by even moderate Muslims as a threat to Muslim claims of hegemony in northern Nigeria.[56] Attacks against Christians also responded to an argument developed by Sufi leaders in their struggle against the 'Yan Izala movement in the 1980s: they had accused 'Yan Izala followers of attacking fellow

Muslims (Sufi orders) and creating *fitna* among Muslims instead of targeting the 'real enemy', Christians. Attacks against Christians thus acquired an integrative function in political contexts characterised by disputes among Muslims. Boko Haram attacks in Jos, one of the centres of northern Nigerian Christianity, as well as the abduction of 276 (mostly Christian) girls from Chibok (Bornu State) on 14 April 2014 support the impression that Boko Haram had started to target Christians in northern Nigeria and wanted to bring about an exodus of Christians (see Harnischfeger 2012: 493ff; Higazi 2013: 160). In an ultimatum on 1 January 2012, Boko Haram told all 'settlers' from the south to leave the north (Harnischfeger 2012: 497). Since 2011, Boko Haram has repeatedly attacked Christian enclaves (often northern Christians and members of local ethnic minorities, not migrants from the south) in north-eastern Nigeria and forced Christians to return to their home regions in south-western Bornu and Adamawa states.[57] In addition, Boko Haram started to attack targets beyond its home base, Bornu and Yobe, and expanded its activities to Kano, Bauchi, Plateau and Adamawa States, and even to the Federal Capital Territory, gaining control over major parts of Bornu and Yobe in early 2013 (Higazi 2013: 143; for a chronology of events see Pérouse de Montclos 2015: 275ff and Comolli 2015: 167–74).

In 2010, Boko Haram also started to assassinate Muslims who dared to criticise Boko Haram publically. One ardent critic of the Boko Haram movement, Muḥammad Awwal Adam 'Albani' Zaria (b. 1960 in Zaria), a well-known Salafi-oriented scholar in Zaria, was assassinated by Boko Haram on 1 February 2014. Muḥmmad Awwal Adam 'Albani' Zaria attended the 'boko' primary school in Zaria's Sabon Gari quarter, and then moved to Barewa College and the Federal University of Technology in Yola. Finally, he studied for a master's degree in electronic engineering at Ahmadu Bello University in Zaria. While at ABU Zaria, Muḥammad Awwal Adam 'Albani' Zaria seems to have become a follower of Ibrāhīm al-Zakzakī, but he abandoned al-Zakzakī in 1993/4 in the context of the latter's public turn towards shīᶜism. Having turned ahl al-sunna, he established two private Salafi-oriented schools in Zaria and became the director of the Dār al-Ḥadīth Salafiyya School in Zaria. He also gave weekly sermons at the Markaz Salafiyya in Tudun Wada, Zaria (Bunza 2005: 235; Bala 2014: 32; Thurston 2015: 109ff). Despite his Salafi orientation, like Jaᶜfar Maḥmūd

Adam, he openly defended Western education for Muslims. His assassination shows that Boko Haram has been attacked on doctrinal issues by a wide spectrum of both Salafi- and Sufi-oriented religious scholars in northern Nigeria in the recent past. Boko Haram has reacted not only verbally (or visually, by way of YouTube statements) but also by the assassination of Salafi-oriented scholars, as well as representatives of northern Nigeria's Muslim establishment. Since 2010, twenty prominent Muslim scholars have been killed by Boko Haram, while others have escaped assassination attempts, including the Shehu of Bornu and the emir of Fika. Among those killed (apart from Ja^{c}far Maḥmūd Adam and Muḥammad Awwal Adam 'Albani'), were Bashīr Kashara (9 October 2010), Ibrāhīm ^{c}Abdullahi Bolori (13 March 2011), Gani Tijani and al-Ḥājj Abur (9 May 2011), Ibrāhīm Birkuti (6 June 2011) and Malam Dalal (4 September 2011) (see HRW 2012: 53; Pérouse de Montclos 2015: 277; Thurston 2015: 115f). On 28 November 2014, Boko Haram also tried to assassinate the new emir of Kano, Sanusi Lamido Sanusi, who had called on Muslims to actively fight Boko Haram. In a suicide attack on the Kano Central Mosque during *jum^{c}a* prayers, more than 100 Muslims were killed. This shows that the escalation of violence has reached a new level in recent years[58] and that Boko Haram was not only a threat to the Nigerian state, but even more so a challenge to other Muslims in northern Nigeria.

The development of the Boko Haram movement shows that Muslims in Nigeria do not form a homogeneous block but are divided into numerous larger and smaller movements and groups that mirror social, political and religious orientations and divisions. While some of these movements fight against the Nigerian state, others are deeply involved in governmental dynamics and politics of positioning. These differences in orientation and the dynamics of positioning continue to foster competition among Nigerian Muslim movements and produce bitter conflict among Muslims over questions of leadership and over which interpretation of 'Islam' can and should be accepted as a model for Muslims in Nigeria. The Boko Haram movement has not found acceptance for its religious and political programme. Despite having been able to gain some sympathy for its actions against the highly unpopular and corrupt Nigerian police force and army, the movement had numerous enemies and critics among Nigeria's Muslims, including other radical groups.[59] Yet, as long as the basic social and economic context does not decisively change – specifically, Nigeria's ongoing inability to achieve sustained economic growth and some degree of social justice for a large part of the population[60] – *jihād*-minded movements such as Boko Haram are likely to rise again.

. . . and Niger?

From a Nigerian perspective, Niger is an extension of northern Nigeria, not only with respect to the Hausa-speaking communities in central Niger, but also with respect to the Kanuri-speaking populations around Lake Chad, as well as Niger's and northern Nigeria's pastoral FulBe populations. Yet, a closer look reveals significant differences. Thus, western Niger, in particular the Niger River valley and the capital region of Niamey, is dominated by Zarma- (Jerma-)speaking populations that extend deep into northern Mali.[61] Also, Niger is a predominantly Muslim society today, like Senegal and Mali. According to recent estimations (*Fischer Weltalmanach* 2014), 94 per cent of the population was Muslim, while followers of African religious traditions and Christians, who have come to constitute a sizeable minority in northern Nigeria, formed 6 per cent of Niger's population. Like northern Nigeria, Niger can point to a tradition of Sufi-oriented traditions of learning, connected with the Qādiriyya, the Tijāniyya and the Shādhiliyya, and to the emergence of a Salafi-oriented movement of reform in the late twentieth century. In contrast to Senegal or northern Nigeria, however, a majority of Niger's Muslims are not linked with any specific religious group (Sounaye 2009: 482). Equally, in the early nineteenth century northern Nigeria saw the emergence of a movement of *jihād* and the establishment of the Sokoto Empire, while Niger is marked by the fact that it became home in the nineteenth century to a number of Hausa kingdoms such as Kebbi, Gobir, Maradi and Damagaram, which fought against the Sokoto Empire. It is thus possible to identify an Islamic historical legacy in Niger that is both pre- and post-*jihādist*. This legacy still includes a number of vibrant local religious traditions, such as the Bori spirit possession cult. So how can we read the development of Islam in Niger as compared to northern Nigeria, and what are the structural differences between Niger and northern Nigeria with regard to the development of Salafi-oriented movements of reform such as the 'Yan Izala?

It is easy to see that the rise of the 'Yan Izala in northern Nigeria from the late 1970s to the late 1980s was bound up with a confrontation with the Sufi orders, while its crisis in the late 1980s was linked with the emergence of evangelical churches.[62] In the 1990s, the 'Yan Izala were confronted with a series of internal conflicts, and then, in the 2000s, experienced a period of recovery linked with northern Nigerian *sharīʿa* debates. These debates allowed the 'Yan Izala and related ahl al-sunna groups to develop a new form of Islamic activism, as represented by the 'Yan Hisba, who were charged with supervising the implementation of *sharīʿa* rules. In northern Nigeria, the 'Yan Izala movement has thus seen five stages of development: germination, growth, crisis, fragmentation and revival.

In Niger, the development of the 'Yan Izala took a different course and was inscribed into the particular dynamics defined by the historical process of Islamisation of Niger mentioned above. Since the early 1990s, six major, yet competing groups of Muslim activists and scholars representing different social groups can be identified in Niger's public sphere (Hassane 2005: 373ff, 2009): first, the masters of the qurʾānic schools, or *malaman zaure*, who are still mostly linked with a Sufi order; second, the Western-educated state functionaries, who are colloquially known as *malaman gwamnati* (government scholars); third, the established leaders and scholars of the major Sufi orders, Tijāniyya[63] and Qādiriyya; fourth, the small group of Muslim intellectuals, both Western and Arab trained (in French, 'arabisants'), who are colloquially known as *malaman yan boko* (masters of Western knowledge), and who have often emerged from a Marxist background; fifth, the group of wealthy supporters and sympathisers, usually wealthy merchants and *Alhazai* (sg. *alhaji*)[64] traders, colloquially known as *masu taimakon addini* (masters of religious support), who are often linked with the 'Yan Izala; and, finally, the 'Yan Izala activists proper, the *masu waʾazi* (masters of sermons) who represent the rise of a new type of religious activist in Niger and who strive to replace established qurʾānic school teachers as well as other Muslim scholars, in particular those linked with the Sufi orders.

The implantation of the 'Yan Izala movement in Niger started shortly before the death of President Seyni Kountché in 1987, approximately ten years after the foundation of the movement in northern Nigeria. Its first major representative in Niger was Malam Shuʿaibu Ladan, a student of Abubakar Gumi who started to build the movement in Maradi.[65] Malam

Shu^caibu Ladan and his followers found a major group of supporters among the *alhazai*, the wealthy merchants of Niger's bigger towns,[66] who, as in northern Nigeria, became the major donors of the movement, financing its activities (Grégoire 1991: 54). Artisans, functionaries, university and high-school graduates, and some *malaman zaure* linked with the Sufi orders joined the movement and helped to spread it to other towns in Niger. In 1990, the Yan Izala established the Association pour la Diffusion de l'Islam au Niger (ADINI-Islam), an association that was officially recognised in 1992 and registered in 1993, but that already started a first national preaching campaign in 1992, involving 'Yan Izala members from northern Nigeria. Since the early 1980s, 'Yan Izala members from Niger had gone to northern Nigeria seeking higher Islamic learning. These 'Yan Izala students built a network of contacts between Niger and northern Nigeria that was instrumental in boosting 'Yan Izala activities in Niger in the 1990s (communication Abdoulaye Sounaye, 27 January 2015).

In Niger, as in northern Nigeria, the 'Yan Izala established a network of national preachers, the *masu wa'azi*, that was organised in national, regional and local branches and that held monthly preaching campaigns, community meetings and other *da^cwa* activities. The *masu wa'azi* are key to understanding the contemporary dynamics of Islam's development in Niger. They can in fact be identified as the most important 'religious entrepreneurs' in an 'Islam de marché' (Haenni 2005), an Islam that follows market rules: even if the *masu wa'azi* of the 'Yan Izala regard the majority of their 'clientele' as 'ignorant' (*jāhil*), they nevertheless have to respect their Muslim 'customers' in order to convince them of their *da^cwa* (Hassane 2009: 104). For this reason, the *masu wa'azi* have to go out and seek their 'clientele' and circulate in the country. The nationwide spread of the movement in the 1990s was linked with numerous preaching campaigns (Hausa: *wa'azin kasa*). These *wa'azin kasa* not only served to address large audiences, but also to collect donations for 'Yan Izala projects, such as the building of mosques or schools (Sounaye 2009: 483ff).[67] As a result of 'Yan Izala activities, Bori activities in Niger have decreased since the late 1980s and were condemned as un-Islamic by the 'Yan Izala, while non-Muslim Hausa (*Maguzawa*) have converted to Islam. After the early 1990s, there was a rise in the number of publicly visible faithful Muslims, in particular women and youth, and a renewed emphasis on daily prayers, linked with a remarkable growth in the number of mosques in recent decades.[68] These years have seen a multiplication of Islamic associations (more than sixty in 2009) and the establishment of Muslim NGOs as well as an important growth in Islamic education and many new, modern *madāris*, which have contributed to improving standards of qurʾānic and Arabic learning. At the same time, Nigeriens have expressed a general wish to discover or rediscover Islam and the number of pilgrims from Niger to Mecca has increased annually. It has also been possible to observe, as in northern Nigeria, the transformation of fashion and symbols of body language, represented by the *ḥijāb* and the *niqāb* used by female followers of Salafi-oriented movements of reform. In the 1990s symbolic distanciation and social separation became manifest in multiple ways: even in villages, walls between compounds were erected and women stopped working in the fields or outside their compounds (Charlick 2007: 27; Masquelier 2009: XVII). The stress on proper dress has not spared men either: sleeves were buttoned up to hide wrists, heads became turbaned to cover hair and trousers end at shins. Men have also abandoned the expensive and cumbersome *babban riga* robe (Masquelier 2009: 218).

Symptomatic of the degree of social separation between 'Yan Izala and other Muslims is the tale (also recorded in northern Nigeria) of young 'Yan Izala followers who broke with their families by bringing their mothers a calabash of milk to compensate for the milk that had sustained them (Loimeier 1997a: 240). Although this tale must be seen as slander against the 'Yan Izala and was never substantiated, it can be seen as a symbol of the process of social distanciation between 'Yan Izala and other Muslims: 'Yan Izala (allegedly) even violate family obligations and loyalty to their parents (Masquelier 2009: 91). However, as in northern Nigeria, the 'Yan Izala in Niger have indeed rejected elaborate gift-giving traditions in the context of burials, marriage and naming ceremonies. Established gift-giving practices were condemned as 'local practices' (Hausa: *al'ada*, pl. *al'adu*; Arabic: *ʿāda*) and un-Islamic innovations. Also, they attacked a number of magico-religious practices such as the use of amulets, the practice of *sha rubutu* and divination (*ʿilm al-raml*, *ʿilm al-falak*). The 'Yan Izala instead stressed frugality, simplicity and the need to care for immediate dependants rather than neighbours and whole communities. Merchants and entrepreneurs connected with the 'Yan Izala have earned 'a reputation for being tightfisted, selfish individuals who turn their backs on social obligations' (Masquelier 2009: 89).

At the same time, the 'Yan Izala created an opening for merchants and entrepreneurs to break out of existing economic constraints: they became major supporters of the 'Yan Izala in the 1990s, as in northern Nigeria. Young merchants stopped sending their children to qur'ānic schools and enrolled them instead in the new *madāris* established by the 'Yan Izala (Grégoire 1993: 112; see also Meunier 1997). In Maradi, followers of the 'Yan Izala even moved into a quarter of their own, called *Izalawa* and started to set themselves apart in spatial terms (Grégoire 1993: 113). Equally, the 'Yan Izala attacked a number of aspects of the ritual such as the *dhikr* of the Sufi orders, they propagated their own distinct manners of praying and followed their own timetable as far as prayers and Islamic festival days were concerned. Being an ostensibly anti-Sufi movement, 'Yan Izala activities soon led to conflicts with followers of the Tijāniyya. But, as in northern Nigeria, the fight against the Tijāniyya triggered a revival of Tijānī activities, a process that in 1992 led to the establishment of the Association pour le Rayonnement de la Culture Islamique (ARCI), an organisation linked with the Niass branch of the Tijāniyya. The confrontation between 'Yan Izala and Tijāniyya assumed quite violent forms: in Dogondoutchi in 1992 and in a series of other places in 1992 and 1993 some people were killed and mosques were burned down.

In Niger the 'Yan Izala have established numerous modern Islamic schools and introduced modern forms of teaching, symbolised by benches, blackboards, primers and a syllabus, and they have also become open towards youth and women (see Sounaye 2012b). In their social activities, the 'Yan Izala were financed by their donors, mostly wealthy merchants and traders, but also by the contributions of their own members (Zakari 2007a: 51ff). Apart from the costs of the preaching campaigns and other activities, these funds allowed the 'Yan Izala to provide members with some degree of financial and social support, a factor that explains the success of the 'Yan Izala as a social and religious reform movement. But, as in northern Nigeria, the 'Yan Izala in Niger have also seen a number of splits due to disputes over questions of authority, corruption or the management of funds, and these disputes and splits show that the movement is far from being homogeneous. And while the

'Yan Izala movement fought against the Sufi orders, it initially opposed the state of Niger, a feature that distinguished the movement in Niger from the movement in northern Nigeria, where the 'Yan Izala have remained largely loyal towards the state.

In order to understand the social and religious success of the 'Yan Izala movement in Niger in the 1980s and 1990s, it is necessary to look into the political and historical context of development in Niger since the early 1990s. After the collapse of the Soviet bloc in 1989, Niger, like other African countries saw a process of democratisation, of social and political opening that was, however, accompanied by a series of brutal economic reforms under the umbrella of the World Bank, implying structural adjustment, and, in particular, a dramatic devaluation of the national currency, the Franc CFA, in 1994. These economic reforms and a new liberal market economy have brought economic insecurity for a number of marginal social groups. Yet, the 1990s were also the years of globalisation, expressed in the rapid growth of regional and international exchanges and the establishment of a pluralistic political system. There was a liberalisation of Niger's media legislation in the mid-1990s, which brought about the establishment of Islamic radio and TV programmes, and led to a proliferation of Islamic books, brochures, cassettes, CDs and DVDs (see Sounaye 2011, 2013, 2014). This development boosted the *masu waʾazi* of the 'Yan Izala and their *daʿwa* activities, especially in the urban centres.

The processes of structural adjustment in the early 1990s led to a veritable 'shock' regarding religious ideas and practices, opposing both 'Yan Izala and Sufi orders as well as 'Yan Izala and the state. A number of events marked this confrontation of ideas and concepts: the struggle of Muslims against family-planning policies, which became particularly virulent in Zinder in 1992; opposition to the project of a new *code de la famille* in 1993 (that was dropped accordingly); the rejection of the Convention pour l'Élimination des Discriminations à l'Égard des Femmes (CEDEF) in 1999, or opposition to the Festival International de la Mode Africaine (FIMA) in Niamey and Maradi in 2000, a festival that took place for the first time in Tiguidit in the Aïr region in 1988. In a more general way, it was possible to observe increasingly coordinated efforts by the Muslim associations to argue in favour of an Islamisation of the state, in particular with respect to those institutions that were regarded as indispensable for the Islamisation of society. The state of Niger, on the other hand, has been active in building a *politique musulmane*: this policy started under President Seyni Kountché in 1974, when the Association Islamique du Niger (AIN) was established as a loyalist Islamic umbrella organisation that served to employ Niger's growing group of 'arabisants'.[69] In 2007, a Ministère des Affaires Religieuses et de l'Action Humanitaire was created, but lost its autonomy in 2010 when it was integrated into the Ministère de l'Intérieur, de la Sécurité Publique, de la Décentralisation et des Affaires Religieuses; also, a series of 'Islamic advisers' to the state were appointed; the number of pilgrims to Mecca increased considerably; Islamic festival days were recognised as national holidays (Sounaye 2005: 512); the number of religious programmes in the state media increased; a bilateral relationship with Muᶜammar al-Qadhdhāfī's Libya was cultivated (until 2011); and, last but not least, a Conseil Islamique du Niger was created in 2003 – even if it only actually became active in 2007. In April 2004, the Ministry of Justice even proposed to introduce an oath (according to religious convictions) for Niger's magistrates presiding over electoral commissions, a move that was immediately seen as being a conciliatory response to demands for further Islamisation. This proposal was rejected by secular-minded citizens, in particular Niger's bureaucrats, only a few religious scholars supported the move and a majority remained silent, thus expressing their disdain for the state's efforts to instrumentalise religion. And even those religious scholars who spoke out openly criticised the proposal as an effort to manipulate religion (Sounaye 2007: 212f, 232f).

Despite this 'politique d'apaisement' (Sounaye 2005: 512), Niger still has a secular constitution that affirms the separation of state and religion. All rulers of Niger since independance (Diori Hamani 1960–74, Seyni Kountché 1974–87, ᶜAlī Saibou 1987–93, Mahamane Ousmane 1993–6, Ibrahim Baré Mainassara 1996–9, Daouda Malam Wanké 1999, Tandja Mamadou 1999–2010, Salou Djibo 2010–11 and Mahamadou Issoufou, since 2011) have defended the principle of 'laïcité', although they have also, at least symbolically, accepted Islam as Niger's dominant religion, for instance by making Islamic holidays national holidays, by tolerating and supporting Arabo-Islamic schools and education, and by giving financial support to Islamic associations. All constitutions have established the religious neutrality of the state (see Sounaye 2005, 2009: 481ff; Zakari 2013: 13ff), although proposals have been made to develop a new constitution that would end the separation of state and religion, for instance by the Collectif des Associations Islamiques du Niger in 2009 (ICG 2013b). Even if the principle of separation of state and religion has been widely debated and contested among Muslims, especially the 'Yan Izala, it remains an important element of Niger's constitutional set-up. In addition, Niger's secular constitution has been an important asset with respect to the international donor community (Sounaye 2005: 506) that provides substantial support under the condition that the principle of separation of state and religion is maintained. The separation of state and religion was affirmed in constitutional reforms in 1992, 1996 and 1999. Article 8 of the preamble stresses that the republic of Niger 'respects and protects all religions. No religion is allowed to assume political functions or to meddle with the affairs of the state.' Article 9 states that all parties with an ethnic, a regionalistic or a religious character are proscribed. Beyond these formal regulations that are important as a 'show front' for Western and super-national partners, the maintenance of the separation of state and religion is also a tool of interior politics that allows the state of Niger in the name of the constitution to control, exclude and punish, if necessary, any Islamic association that becomes too critical.

In this way, Nigerien governments have not been indifferent to Islamic activities and their social impact. Niger has in fact developed 'paths of accommodation' with Muslim associations, which open up possibilities of arrangement between the state and Islamic associations. Due to this fact, it is possible to ask whether the state of Niger has fallen into a piety trap, like Mali in the 1980s,[70] thinking that it can fight Islam on its own ground (Hassane 2009: 120), yet under-estimating the dynamics of such a policy that tries to draw legitimacy from claiming to be a 'pious state'. In light of the state's failure to impose its own concepts of a secular society on the Convention sur les Droits de la Femme or the *code de la famille*, the state seems to have failed to defeat its Islamic opposition. In addition, divide-and-rule strategies have their own limitations, due to the fact that even loyalist Muslim organisations and Muslim functionaries, the *malaman gwamnati*, who are called upon to guard the state against the 'Yan Izala, have to preserve their own social and religious legitimacy and thus have to demonstrate, from time to time, a certain distance from the state.

Recent years have shown, however, that both state and civil society in Niger have been able to 'domesticate' the activism of Salafi-oriented groups: in 2000, the government of Niger dissolved seven Islamic associations, among them ADINI-Islam. This was a reaction to internal disputes among the members of ADINI-Islam regarding its relationship with the government and the Convention contre l'Élimination des Droits de la Femme: the government of Niger had ordered a stop to this debate and the leadership of ADINI-Islam had accepted this decision. In November 2000, however, the conflict escalated when followers of ADINI-Islam protested against the Festival International de Mode Africaine in Niamey. As a result, a number of 'Yan Izala were arrested, which again triggered protests against these arrests. These protests did not mobilise a significant part of the population in Niamey, however, and thus showed the weakness of ADINI-Islam and related groups. Since their dissolution, Salafi-oriented groups of reform in Niger have suffered a crisis that was also informed by the fact that they were not allowed to organise *wa'azin kasa* tours.

As a result of disputes within ADINI-Islam over questions of leadership and authority, the movement split into two groups in 2000, one following the leader of ADINI-Islam, now renamed iḥyāʾ al-sunna, Yaḥyā Muḥammad (d. 2010), who represented the first generation of 'Yan Izala based in Niger's trading milieu,[71] and a second group called al-Islām kitāb wa-sunna ᶜalā fahm al-salaf al-ṣāliḥ (for short, kitāb wa-sunna) and led by ᶜUmar ᶜIsā Sulaymān, who had studied in Say (Niger), Nigeria and Medina (Sounaye 2012a: 430ff, 2009: 489; Zakari 2007a: 72).[72] The kitāb wa-sunna movement also represented a second generation of young 'Yan Izala followers who increasingly resented the leadership of the first generation 'Yan Izala. The first generation of 'Yan Izala had been trained in Niger, northern Nigeria and al-Azhar University in Egypt (and were influenced by the ikhwān al-muslimūn), while second-generation 'Yan Izala were trained in Niger, northern Nigeria and at the University of Medina in Saudi Arabia (Sounaye 2012a: 430). The split into iḥyāʾ al-sunna and kitāb wa-sunna factions has led to a certain paralysis of the 'Yan Izala movement. Since 2000, 'Yan Izala activism has decreased and their preaching tours have become less aggressive, less polemic and more local. After supporting the development of the 'Yan Izala from the late 1980s, the youth started to turn away from the 'Yan Izala. In Dogondoutchi, for instance, young men were simply fed up with the petty disputes among the 'Yan Izala and other Muslim groups and in 2004 they were reported to 'be less anxious to engage in visible displays of piety' (Masquelier 2007: 246). As a consequence of the disenchantment of Niger's youth with 'Yan Izala concepts, Niger has seen the development of a large spectrum of youth clubs, *clubs des jeunes musulmans*, which still heed Salafi-oriented ideas, but reject the radical (and negative) 'Yan Izala positions in respect of parents and the 'elderly' (Sounaye 2012b: 217ff). The development of the 'Yan Izala in Niger thus more or less seems to follow the northern Nigerian pattern, even if there is a major difference regarding the debates over the introduction of 'complete *sharīᶜa*' in northern Nigeria in 2000, a political development that has remained specifically northern Nigerian. However, northern Nigeria *sharīᶜa* debates and the activities of the northern Nigerian 'Yan Hisba have led to an increase in transborder traffic and a certain boom of Niger's border settlements, where Muslims from northern Nigeria come to consume alcohol, meet with prostitutes and indulge in a new pleasure economy that has largely vanished in northern Nigeria (Hassane 2007: 92).

Beyond the split in Niger's 'Yan Izala movement that mirrored the divide between the 'Yan Izala and the ahl al-sunna groups in northern Nigeria in the 1990s, Niger has seen the emergence, in the 2000s, of a new movement of Salafi-oriented youth, labelled *sunnance* (Sounaye 2011: 3; 2015: 82ff). This development has not only led to the rejuvenation of the Salafi movement in Niger, but has also given it a new direction: while the first generation of 'Yan Izala sought social and economic integration (in terms of positions and employment), the second generation of Salafi-minded Muslims, most particularly, the kitāb wa-sunna group and the *sunnance*, were more 'entrepreneurial' in their approach to society and the state (Sounaye 2015: 94ff): they established their own schools and centres (*marākiz*, sg. *markaz*), started their own shops and media activities and produced their own CDs and DVDs, as well as their own radio and TV programmes. Paradigmatic for the cultivation of the new media is ᶜAbd al-ᶜAzīz Amadou 'Alarama' in Niamey, who has started to pose as a moral guide for Niger's urbanite youth (Sounaye 2013: 95). Salafi-oriented media savvy *masu waᵓazi* such as ᶜAbd al-ᶜAzīz Amadou 'Alarama' reflect the 'entrepreneurial turn' that started with the spread of the 'Yan Izala in the 1990s and that has thoroughly challenged established religious scholars.[73] Second-generation 'Yan Izala and *sunnance* were also prepared, however, to part from their own fathers' generation that was regarded as too conciliatory in many respects and that had taken most of the available jobs in the administration and in the education sector. Equally, second-generation 'Yan Izala and ahl al-sunna have toned down their critique of Sufi scholars and Sufi orders and have abandoned the critique of *mawlid* celebrations in the mid-2000s: 'This is a futile debate and we'll not waste our time speculating on it' (quoted in Sounaye 2015: 108). Second-generation 'Yan Izala and *sunnance* have also reduced their critique of 'un-Islamic' (and costly) social and cultural practices, and have thus sought reintegration into Niger's social life: they have opened up towards other Muslims, in particular, women, and have de-emphasised social segregation (a development that also characterised Senegal's JIR in the 1990s): 'one can follow the footsteps of the Prophet and still celebrate and partake in cultural practices' (quoted in Sounaye 2015: 95). However, even second-generation 'Yan Izala and *sunnance* continue to criticise amulets and bori, spirit possession practices and divination and, thus, follow some core tropes of 'Yan Izala critique (Sounaye 2015: 95).

In comparison with northern Nigeria, it is necessary to stress that the 'Yan Izala movement in Niger is characterised by the fact that it has remained a largely urban movement (among traders and the youth) that has not yet made major inroads into Niger's middle-class groups, while Salafi-oriented concepts of reform have found wide support among northern Nigeria's middle-class groups in the urban areas and beyond: Nigeria is one of the few African countries where Salafi-oriented movements of reform such as the 'Yan Izala were able to touch rural populations. The programme of social reforms, legitimised in doctrinal terms, especially in the spheres of education and social emancipation, has created profound cleavages among Muslims in both northern Nigeria and Niger. Thus, the late 1970s and 1980s (in northern Nigeria) and the 1990s (in Niger) were characterised by numerous religious conflicts, in particular between 'Yan Izala and Tijāniyya. In the early 2000s, the tensions calmed down, at least in Niger. A better knowledge of Islam, due to exhaustive debates about texts and their meaning, and the realisation that different doctrinal positions are possible, may have contributed to this pacification, a dynamic that can also be observed in other countries. The negative example of northern Nigeria may have also contributed to calming the situation in Niger. It seems as if Muslims in Niger were anxious to avoid the hatred, violence and conflict that Muslims in northern Nigeria had been experiencing since the late 1970s. The emergence of the Boko Haram movement in northern Nigeria in the early 2000s led to fears of a similar development in Niger. These factors may have convinced even radical groups in Niger to accept expressions of difference and to tolerate the right of other Muslim groups to express themselves openly (Hassane 2009: 121). In comparison with the 1990s, but also with the situation in northern Nigeria, Niger has thus witnessed a process in which rivalry between different religious groups has become less violent and acid. This may be due to a certain compassion fatigue: the different Muslim actors have shown themselves willing to desist from polemics and sterile debates over themes that have been discussed exhaustively. Perhaps they realised that different doctrinal positions were only interpretations that were acceptable on a scholastic level. And once they accepted the idea that the 'good intention' (*ḥusn al-niyya*) of each Muslim was the only thing that really counted, whatever his or her religious orientation and doctrinal position, doctrinal disputes had the chance to cool down and make room for other debates over social, political and economic questions.

Notes

1. This chapter focuses on northern Nigeria and does not include other parts of Nigeria, due to the fact that Nigeria as a whole is much too diverse: historical legacies and contemporary conditions in southwest Nigeria (historical Yorubaland), for instance, are completely different from those in the north, especially those federal states that have (re-)introduced *sharīʿa* penal laws since 2000, and thus merit separate analysis.
2. On Alfa Hashim, see Ahmed (2015: 24ff).
3. On religious and political development in northern Nigeria in the colonial period see Paden (1973).
4. For Nasiru Kabara, see Bari (1997), Kabara (1981) and Loimeier (1997a).
5. On Ibrāhīm Ṣāliḥ, see Loimeier (1997a); on Dahiru Bauchi, see Brigaglia (2014a).
6. For his biography, see Gumi and Tsiga (1992), Loimeier (1997a) and Shanono (1976).
7. The Hausa term '*boko*', 'false', 'fake', 'deceit', 'deception' has come to mean, in

the course of the twentieth century, 'deceptive education' (*'ilimin boko'*) , that is, Western, colonial education (Hansen and Musa 2013: 288; for a broader discussion of the term *'boko'*, see Higazi 2013: 144).

8. For Aminu Kano, see Paden (1973).
9. When Abubakar Gumi applied for the position of Deputy Grand Kadi, he was only thirty-four years old, but the position required a minimum age of thirty-six years. Gumi's referee, Mervyn Hiskett, then at the School of Arabic Studies in Kano, not only wrote a positive report on Gumi but also changed his date of birth to 1922, feeling that 'the age limit was unfair' (Gumi and Tsiga 1992: 73).
10. For Ahmadu Bello's biography, see Paden (1986).
11. For the development of the 'Yan Izala, see Kane (2003), Loimeier (1997a) and Umar (1988, 1993). The Arabic term *'izāla'* is often used in connection with acts of cleansing and purification: *izālat al-najāsa* would be the 'removal of substantive impurities, of dirt, of filth'. For a discussion of the ritual complex of purity, see Gauvain (2013: 14ff).
12. For an analysis of 'Yan Izala efforts to develop women's education, see Renne's (2012) study on 'Yan Izala schools for women in Zaria.
13. In Kano, the 'Yan Izala established their first foothold in Fagge, a quarter just outside the old 'walled city' (*birni*) dominated by traders and artisans, a social group among which 'Yan Izala found major support (Kane 1990: 11–13; see also Kane 1998: 117ff).
14. The term *'wa*ᶜ*ẓ'* ('warning', 'admonition', 'exhortation') denotes a specific type of sermon characterised by an often polemical and aggressive content and tone.
15. From 1978 to 1988, the 'Yan Izala organized in the region of 700 *wa*ʾ*azin kasa* (preaching tours) (Ben Amara 2014: 131).
16. On the development of Salafi-oriented reform in Cameroon, see Adama (1999, 2004, 2007, 2009 and 2013), Mouiche (2005) and Taguem-Fah (2001, 2007).
17. Formally, the 'Yan Izala were only registered as an Islamic association on 11 December 1985 (Ben Amara 2014: 134).
18. The 'Yan Izala and affiliated Salafi-oriented groups have been so successful in appropriating the application of *sharī*ᶜ*a* politics that Sufi-oriented movements felt eclipsed and preached to. The Qādiriyya in Kano eventually protested against their alleged exclusion from, or underrepresentation in, the state *sharī*ᶜ*a* coucils in a demonstration in Kano in 2005 (Paden 2005: 167). O'Brien has shown, however, that scholars affiliated with the Tijāniyya were well represented in *sharī*ᶜ*a* councils under Kano State Governors Rabiu Kwankwasu (r. 1999–2003) and Ibrāhīm Shekarau (r. 2003–11) (O'Brien 2007: 61ff).

19. Abūbakar Jibril broke with Ibrāhīm al-Zakzakī in 1994 when al-Zakzakī made his affiliation with Shīʿism public and established the Islamic Movement in Nigeria. Abūbakar Jibril subsequently cultivated his position as an independent scholar who spoke out openly against corruption and political mismanagement, in particular in Sokoto state. He defined his doctrinal and political position as 'being with Saudi Arabia in terms of theology and creed' and being with Iran in terms of politics (Mustapha and Bunza 2014: 87f).
20. The Kano 'Yan Izala leader of the Kaduna faction, Dr ʿAbdallāh Ṣāliḥ Pakistan, described the 1991 split of the movement as a split in which the Kaduna faction moved from an orientation towards *takfīr* (expiation) to an orientation towards *taʿlīm* (education) (Thurston forthcoming: 137).
21. On the recent development of the 'Yan Izala, see Ben Amara (2014) and Thurston (forthcoming).
22. For his biography, see Loimeier (1997a: 247–50, 288); and Kane (2003: 75ff).
23. The Hausa term 'yan hisba' refers to the Arabo-Islamic institution of the market overseer, the *muḥtasib* and the practice of *ḥisba* ('guarding, checking or controlling public order'). The 'Yan Hisba justified their activities by reference to Qurʾān 3: 104, which calls on each Muslim to 'enjoin what is right and to forbid what is wrong' (*al-amr bi-l-maʿrūf wa-l-nahy ʿan al-munkar*). The conditions (*shurūṭ*) guiding Muslims with respect to the principles of *al-amr bi-l-maʿrūf wa-l-nahy ʿan al-munkar* have been quoted by critics of the implementation of *sharīʿa* penal laws in northern Nigeria, such as Ibrāhīm al-Zakzakī. Ibrāhīm al-Zakzakī has added an idea based on the thinking of Sayyid Quṭb, namely, that the establishment of a good Muslim society was more important than the righting of 'small scale, personal and individual wrong' (Cook 2000: 528).
24. www.jibwisnigeria.org
25. Abubakar Gumi's son, Dr Ahmad Gumi (b. 1960), replaced Abubakar Gumi as the leading preacher at the Sultan Bello Mosque in Kaduna after his father's death and assumed a leading role within the Kaduna faction of the 'Yan Izala. In internal disputes over leadership, he possibly defeated Jaʿfar Maḥmūd Adam, who subsequently started to build the ahl al-sunna movement in Kano (Thurston forthcoming: 121). On the development of the ahl al-sunna movement in northern Nigeria, see Thurston (forthcoming: 134ff).
26. Alexander Thurston even reports that ahl al-sunna members in Kano cultivated personal links of friendship with Muslims affiliated with Sufi orders, in particular the Qādiriyya (Thurston forthcoming: 132).
27. For his biography, see Thurston (forthcoming: 124ff).

28. He had already been appointed as a member of a Kano state review committee that had been formed in 2000 to draft the new *sharīᶜa* code (Thurston forthcoming: 131).
29. See Weimann (2010), O'Brien (2007) and Anonymous (2012). For a biography of Jaᶜfar Maḥmūd Adam, see Brigaglia (2012). Brigaglia discusses a number of hypotheses regarding Jaᶜfar Maḥmūd Adam's assassination and argues that this murder was committed by Boko Haram followers (Brigaglia 2012: 18–23). Other sources claim that Jaᶜfar Maḥmūd Adam was killed by thugs connected with the governor of Kano, Ibrahim Shekarau, due to the fact that Jaᶜfar Maḥmūd Adam had become increasingly dissatisfied with the Shekarau administration and had started to challenge its religious legitimacy. In 2005, Jaᶜfar Maḥmūd Adam had resigned from the Hisba Board while other ahl al-sunna leaders resigned from the *Sharīᶜa* Commission (Thurston 2014: 46–7).
30. In the context of the annual 'al-Quds' procession in Zaria on 25 July 2014, a conflict over the right of way led to a confrontation between Ibrāhīm al-Zakzakī's followers and an army convoy. In this confrontation, thirty-five followers of Ibrāhīm al-Zakzakī, among them three of his sons, were killed (Mustapha and Bunza 2014: 73).
31. See Ben Amara (2014: 144), Bunza (2005: 231), Harnischfeger (2006: 207), Falola (1998: 194ff) and Isa and Adam (2014: 61ff).
32. On the Christian Association of Nigeria (CAN), see Falola (1998: 107–14).
33. One of the most serious incidents happened in the context of Reinhard Bonnke's visit to Kano in 1991. Bonnke had been invited by the Christian Association of Nigeria (CAN) and was allowed to use the race course grounds for a 'crusade', while some months earlier the South African preacher Aḥmad Deedat had been refused entry. As a result, riots started in Kano on 14 October 1991 (Falola 1998: 211–12).
34. In addition to conferences and educational institutions, missions of *daᶜwa* have to be considered as a third dimension of transnational entanglement. Since 1964, Saudi Arabia (through the rābiṭat al-ᶜālam al-islāmī as well as the Islamic University of Medina) has financed missions of *daᶜwa* by Salafi-oriented scholars (and functionaries) to many sub-Saharan African countries (see Ahmed 2015: 146).
35. See Kogelmann (2006), Last (2000), O'Brien (2007), Ostien (2006), Paden (2005), Peters (2003) and Weimann (2010).
36. The term '*ḥadd*' refers to legal and religious regulations explicitly mentioned and thus 'fixed' in the Qurʾān. In a more narrow sense, the term '*ḥadd*' refers

to punishments for criminal offences as prescribed by the Qurʾān, namely, extra-marital sex (*zināʾ*; punishable by flogging or death by stoning), robbery (*ḥirāba*; death by hanging, amputation or banishment), theft (*sariqa*; amputation), slander in a case of *zināʾ* (*qaḍf*; flogging), apostasy (*irtidād*; death) and the consumption of alcohol (*sukr*, *shurb al-khamr*; flogging). These *ḥudūd* punishments are subject, however, to a set of conditions (*shurūṭ*) and a respective law of procedures. In northern Nigeria, apostasy is not acknowledged as an offence according to the *sharīʿa* penal laws. Critics of *ḥudūd* punishments often stress that basic political and social pre-conditions for the application of *sharīʿa* penal laws are not given, as an ideal Islamic society where theft would indeed constitute a crime (and not just an act of desperation, as in a case of stealing food) does not exist. For a discussion, see Peters (2003).

37. FOMWAN was an umbrella organisation for more than 400 Muslim women's associations in Nigeria, the majority (about 300 associations) being based in the Yoruba region. FOMWAN grew out of the Muslim Sisters' Organization (MSO) (see Paden 2005).
38. Sanusi Lamido Sanusi (b. 1961) is a grandson of the late Emir Muḥammad Sanusi of Kano. He studied at King's College in London and at ABU Zaria, where he seems to have become a follower of the jamāʿat tajdīd al-islām for a short period, and subsequently did a degree in Sharīʿa and Islamic Studies at the African International University in Khartoum in 1997. He then started a career in the Nigerian banking sector, where he became famous for his anti-corruption campaign. In the 1990s and 2000s, he became an outspoken opponent of both Jaʿfar Maḥmūd Adam and the Boko Haram movement. In 2009, he was appointed governor of the Nigerian Central Bank. Following disputes with Nigeria's President Goodluck Jonathan (in office since 2010) over inquiries into massive fraud by some of the subordinates of the new president, Sanusi Lamido Sanusi was suspended from office in early 2014. In June 2014, he was turbaned as the new emir of Kano as successor to Emir Ado Bayero (r. 1963–2014). Following his enthronement, Sanusi Lamido Sanusi led the Friday prayers in Kano's central mosque, a role that only his own grandfather, Muhammad Sanusi, had performed before him (Adam 2014: 80ff). On the disputes over his succession, see Thurston (2014: 39).
39. Equally, the implementation of *sharīʿa* regulations does not seem to have affected Bori spirit possession ceremonies, often led by scholars linked with the Tijāniyya, despite the efforts of Kano State Governor Ibrāhīm Shekarau to follow stricter *sharīʿa* implementation policies since 2003 (O'Brien 2007: 58ff).

40. For a discussion of Boko Haram, see Brigaglia et al. in the 2014 *Annual Review of Islam in Africa* special issue on *Islam in Nigeria*, Brigaglia (2015), Anonymous (2012), Comolli (2015), Higazi (2013), HRW (2012), ICG (2013b, 2014c), Loimeier (2012), Mustapha and Bunza (2014: 79–87), Mustapha (2014c), Pérouse de Montclos (2014, 2015), Rémy (2012), as well as Thurston (2016) and Thurston (forthcoming: 245ff).
41. The Christian concept of 'sin', in particular, 'original sin', does not exist in Islam. While the term '*ḥaram*' has a wide meaning, it can best be translated as 'forbidden, prohibited, interdicted', and thus carries a rather legalistic notion of 'things one should not do'. In colloquial usage, the term '*ḥaram*' also has the connotation of 'shame'. The Arabic term that comes closest to the Christian concept of sin is '*ᶜaṣī*', implying somebody who is 'disobedient, refractory, rebellious, mutinous'.
42. Communication Maikorema Zakari, 13 March 2012. See also Rémy (2012) and Comolli (2015). The leaders of the Ansaru group fled to southern Algeria after the 2009 riots in Bornu state and the subsequent suppression of Boko Haram by Nigerian security forces in August 2009. In southern Algeria, Ansaru members received military training by AQMI (Higazi 2013: 158). In 2011, these 'Yan Sahara ('Sahara guys') returned to northern Nigeria and became notorious for abductions of expatriates working in Kebbi, Kano and Bauchi states. Until his death in 2012, the Ansaru group was led by Abubakar Adam Kambar. He was succeeded in the same year by Khālid al-Barnāwī (Comolli 2015: 66ff).
43. '*Habe*' is a Fulfulde term referring to the pre-*jihādist* (and allegedly pre-Islamic, heathen) rulers of Hausaland.
44. Due to the fact that the Qurʾān mentions only three ritual prayers (not five, as established by the *Sunnah*), the Maitatsine group stuck to only three daily prayers (Loimeier 1997a: 218ff).
45. In proper Hausa: *maiyatsine*, 'the master who picks out [things] one by one, who selects one by one (. . . and condemns)'. '*Maitatsine*' is linguistically incorrect; the infix '*ta*' denotes female gender.
46. Other Maitatsine-like movements in northern Nigeria were the 'Yan Hakika ('people of truth') and 'Kala Kato' groups (see Mustapha and Bunza 2014: 76–9).
47. Hannah Höchner has recently stressed that there is 'no systematic evidence to support such assertions', namely, that Boko Haram recruits its followers mostly among the *almajirai* (Höchner 2015a: 72, 2015b). This position is shared by Virginia Comolli (2015: 74–5).

48. Baba Fugu Muḥammad was shot in 2009 by the Nigerian police, when he presented himself in a Maiduguri police station in order to warn police of impending Boko Haram activities (Higazi 2013: 148).
49. For a detailed presentation of this argumentation and of the dispute between Muḥammad Yūsuf and Jaᶜfar Maḥmūd Adam, see Anonymous (2012), Adamu (2012) and Thurston (2015). The writer who remains anonymous and Adamu were the first scholars to properly study the cassettes and CDs produced by both sides in northern Nigeria up to 2009. Of particular interest is a public recording from 2 June 2006 of a dispute between Muḥammad Yūsuf and a follower of Jaᶜfar Maḥmūd Adam, Mallam Isa Aliyu Ibrahim Pantami (or Fantami), entitled *Muqabala akan mastayin karatun boko da aikin gwamnati a Nigeria tsakakin Mallam Isa Aliyu Ibrahim Pantami da Mallam Muhammad Yusuf Maiduguri* (Debate on the Status of Western Education and Working for the Nigerian Government between Mallam Isa Aliyu Ibrahim Pantami and Mallam Muhammad Yusuf Maiduguri) (see Anonymous 2012: 144; Adamu 2012).
50. Muḥammad Yūsuf laid down his creed in a text entitled *hadhihi ᶜaqīdatunā wa-manhaj daᶜwatinā* (this is our creed and the programme of our cause) (2009). For an analysis, see Mustapha and Bunza (2014: 80–2; Mohammed 2015: 13f; Thurston forthcoming: 280ff.
51. This split was not to be the last one: in July 2011 another group split from Boko Haram under the leadership of Mamman Nūr, a Shuwa (Arab) born in Maiduguri, and established the Yūsufiyya Islamic Movement. This group accused Abubakar Shekau, Boko Haram's new leader since 2009, of privileging his own ethnic group, the Kanuri, and marginalising members of other ethnic groups within Boko Haram (Azumah 2014: 10; ICG 2014c: 19). Both he and Abubakar Shekau had studied at the Bornu State College of Legal and Islamic Studies (BOCOLIS) in Maiduguri.
52. Confusion has characterised reports on Boko Haram by both Nigerian and Western media. In September 2014, for instance, Nigerian military intelligence announced that a major Boko Haram commander, Bashir Muhammad, had been killed in the context of heavy fighting near Kondugu in the region of Maiduguri (Sahara Reporters, 22 September 2014). This information has not been confirmed. Bashīr Muḥammad was the man who was called Abubakar Shekau by both Western and Nigerian media from 2010 to 2013, despite the fact that Abubakar Shekau spoke excellent Arabic, Hausa and Kanuri as well as a bit of FulFude but no English. In one of his Internet appearances in February 2014, Bashīr Muḥammad aka 'Abubakar Shekau' switched into English with

a northern Nigerian intonation but 'impeccable grammar' for about a minute during his announcement. According to Nigerian military intelligence the true Abubakar Shekau had been killed, however, in summer 2013 in the context of a skirmish with the Nigerian Army. This information has again not been commented on or confirmed so far by US, British, French or Israeli intelligence (communication Andrea Brigaglia, 12 September 2014; Brigaglia 2014b: 43ff).

53. See Brigaglia (2004: 240–1); Süddeutsche Zeitung, 25–6 September 2004; *iz3w*, August/September 2004; Paden (2005: 170, 187–8).
54. *The Guardian*, Dar es Salaam, 5 August 2009; Pérouse de Montclos (2014: 32).
55. For Abubakar Shekau's biography, see Pérouse de Montclos (2014: 32). Due to increasing military pressure, Boko Haram has split into several semi-autonomous groups since September 2012, the largest being led by Abubakar Shekau, while smaller groups were led by Kabiru Sokoto, Abdullahi Damasak and Aminu Tashen-Ilmi. The Ansaru group (jamāᶜat anṣār al-muslimīn fi-bilād al-sūdān) led by Khālid al-Barnāwī and Abubakar Adam Kambar (d. 2012) split from Boko Haram in 2012, but allegedly re-united with it in 2013 (ICG 2014c: 21f; see also Pérouse de Montclos 2014: 20 and Mohammed 2015: 25f).
56. Attacks against Christians were also set in a larger political context: in 2007, President Obasanjo, a born-again Christian, had handed over power to Umaru Musa Yar'adua, a Muslim politician from Katsina state who died, however, in 2010, and was followed by another southern Christian, Goodluck Jonathan, from Bayelsa State, who won the 2011 presidential elections.
57. The 'Chibok' girls were used by Boko Haram to demand the release of Boko Haram family members from Nigerian prisons. Boko Haram has repeatedly attacked Nigerian prisons in recent years, in order to liberate its followers and family members from custody. Abubakar Shekau, in particular, justified the Chibok girls' abduction as a response to the detention of women married to Boko Haram members by the Nigerian authorities (see Thurston forthcoming: 271; Comolli 2015: 125).
58. For an overview of Boko Haram activities, see the 2012 Human Rights Watch report 'Spiraling Violence: Boko Haram Attacks and Security Forces Abuses in Nigeria', the 2014 *Annual Review of Islam in Africa* special issue on 'Islam in Nigeria' and Comolli (2015). From 2009 to 2012, more than 2,000 people were killed in Boko Haram attacks (as well as attacks by security forces), most of them in Bornu, Yobe and Kano states. In 2011, Boko Haram started to employ the method of suicide bombings in order to increase chaos and insecurity. Since 2013, Boko Haram attacks have increasingly targeted Nigerian Army

installations, possibly in reaction to a joint Nigerian Army and security forces (Joint Military Task Force) (JTF) campaign against Boko Haram in 2013. In 2013, Nigeria, Niger, Cameroon and Chad started to coordinate military action against Boko Haram across borders and in Bornu (ICG 2013b: 42). While suffering military setbacks due to troops from Niger, Cameroon and Chad, Boko Haram was able to withstand the Nigerian Army until March 2015, when a large-scale offensive drove Boko Haram out of north-eastern Nigeria's cities back into its well-known hideouts such as the Sambisa Forest Reserve close to the border with Cameroon (see Tull and Weber 2015: 2; Hütte et al. 2015: 100ff).

59. Muhammad Buhari's victory in the presidential elections of 28 and 29 March 2015 created a chance for sustained pacification of northern and north-eastern Nigeria: his victory has shown that a Muslim may still win democratic elections in Nigeria and that Nigeria is not inevitably bound to be ruled by Christians (such as Obasanjo and Goodluck Johnson). Buhari was the target of a Boko Haram attack on 23 July 2014 and has promised to resolutely fight Boko Haram.
60. According to the 2012 Human Rights Watch report, nearly 100 (out of approximately 160) million Nigerians were living on less than one dollar a day while the percentage of Nigerians living in absolute poverty increased from 55 to 61 per cent of the population from 2004 to 2011 (HRW 2012: 26).
61. While Hausa-speaking populations account for about 55 per cent of Niger's population, Zarma-speaking populations have been estimated to form about 21 per cent of Niger's population (Idrissa 2005: 352). Both FulBe and Tuareg populations account for another 10 per cent each, while the Kanuri form 4 per cent of Niger's population.
62. On the development of evangelical churches in Niger, see Cooper (2006). Like Senegal and Mali, Niger has so far not seen any confrontation between activist Muslims and evangelical Christians on a scale comparable to northern Nigeria, although 45 churches were attacked and burned on 16 and 17 January 2015 in the context of Muslim protests against depictions of the Prophet Muḥammad by the French satirical magazine *Charlie Hebdo*. In the same context, 10 people were killed and 177 injured (Schritt 2015: 1).
63. A majority of Niger's Tijānis are affiliated with the Niass branch of the Tijāniyya, as in northern Nigeria.
64. The Hausa term '*alhazai*' refers to those who have been to Mecca for the pilgrimage (*ḥajj*).

65. For the development of the 'Yan Izala in Zinder, see Glew (1996, 1998, 2001); for Dogondoutchi see Masquelier (2001, 2009).
66. Apart from Niamey, the capital city with a population of approximately 1 million in 2014, Zinder (approximately 320,000) and Maradi (approximately 270,000) should be mentioned here.
67. In many ways, the *wa'azin kasa* of the 'Yan Izala resemble the *ziyārāt* of the Sufi orders, such as the annual *Magal* of the Murīdiyya to Touba in Senegal (Sounaye 2009: 483). In recent years, Niger's *masu waʾazi* have started to spread into smaller urban centres. Cassettes, CDs and DVDs are now produced in Niger rather than in northern Nigeria (Sounaye 2014: 25).
68. On the increasing visibility of Muslim women (both Salafi- and Sufi-oriented) in Niger's public sphere, as well as in Niger's booming NGO milieus, see Sounaye (2011).
69. In 1957, a first *médersa* had been opened in Say, an important centre of Islamic learning in western Niger. Graduates from this médersa were sent to study at al-Azhar in the 1960s and started to return to Niger in the late 1960s (Souley 1993: 213). In 1986, the Islamic University of Niger was opened in Say (Triaud 1988a: 157ff).
70. The piety trap of Islamic morality and publicly enforced religious norms becomes particularly obvious when Muslim religious scholars, intellectuals and/or politicians are found guilty of having violated their own standards of proper Islamic behaviour and unmasked publicly as hypocrites. I became witness to double standards in Muslim contexts when doing research in Kano, northern Nigeria, in the late 1980s and was surprised to meet well-known pious *birni* (old city) Muslims in bars in 'Sabon Gari' (new city) quarters during weekends. The enforcement of *sharīᶜa* laws in twelve northern Nigeria states has produced short-term 'conversions' to Christianity among Muslims who do not want to abandon their drinking habits (or traditions of extra-marital sex), and consequently pose (with forged identity cards) as 'Christians' during their weekend excursions to northern Nigeria's Sabon Garis in order to escape *ḥisba* controls (see Last 2000; Peters 2003).
71. Shaykh Yaḥyā Muḥammad was a trader based in Niamey's Waddata market. He was trained in Niger and northern Nigeria only (Sounaye 2012a: 437).
72. Both Shaykh Yaḥyā Muḥammad and ᶜUmar ᶜIsā Sulaymān have stressed the importance of the *jihād* of Usman dan Fodio and his texts as a model for their own programmes of reform, thus reproducing 'Yan Izala positions in northern

Nigeria on the *jihād* and Usman dan Fodio's struggle against *bida*ᶜ (see Sounaye 2012a passim for an account of their respective ideas).

73. In 2010, Sounaye counted about sixty young *masu wa*ᵓ*azi* who had programmes on Niamey's ten radio and TV channels. These programmes were broadcast in Hausa, Zarma and French (Sounaye 2013: 96).

5

REFORM IN CONTEXT III: CHAD, SUDAN, ETHIOPIA, SOMALIA

Introduction

In this chapter four African countries that at first glance seem to be vastly different will be compared with respect to the development of Islamic reform: both Chad and Sudan may be seen as countries with a fairly homogeneous Muslim population (like Somalia), yet they are marked by numerous internal divides, such as that between the 'Muslim' north and the 'heathen/Christian' south in Chad,[1] or between the riverain *awlad al-baḥr* (people of the river, that is, the River Nile) and the peoples of Sudan's peripheries: the Red Sea Mountains, Kordofan, the Nuba mountains and Darfur.[2] Somalia, one of Africa's most homogeneous countries in ethnic and linguistic terms, has been torn by a devastating civil war since 1988, while Ethiopia by contrast has a regionally highly fragmented Muslim population with diverse historical backgrounds. Chad, Sudan, Ethiopia and Somalia can all look back on major turning points in their recent history: in Chad, after a series of internal wars from 1965 onwards and a series of changes in government since 1975, the regime of Idriss Déby was able to consolidate its hold on the country since 1990; in Sudan, an Islamic revolution was proclaimed in 1989 that changed the course of the country; in Ethiopia, the existing military regime, the Derg (committee), was replaced by a new government in 1991, leading to a federal structure; in Somalia, the regime of Siyad Barre came to an end in 1991 and was replaced by warlords and clan leaders. Each of these turning points opened up new avenues, chances and threats to respective Muslim populations and forced them to negotiate the challenges of revolution, civil war, state failure, nation building and globalisation in many different guises. Despite their historical differences, Chad, Sudan, Ethiopia and Somalia are intertwined in different ways: thus, Ethiopia has been directly involved in both Sudan's and Somalia's historical development in the twentieth century (and vice versa), while Ethiopia, Sudan and Somalia (as well as its contemporary successor states such as Somaliland and Puntland) form one large northeast African community. Equally, Chad and Sudan have become intertwined in conflict, in particular in the context of the conflict over Darfur since 2003. Chad and Sudan (as well as northern Nigeria) also share a history of slave hunting in their respective southern marches that have become predominantly Christian in the twentieth century and have aspired to political emancipation or even independence (as in Sudan) in the twentieth century.[3] All of the four nations discussed here have a tradition of Sufi-oriented movements of reform that were challenged, at different times and in different intensities, by Salafi-oriented movements. Yet, in all four countries, the trajectories of Salafi-oriented movements of reform were different, and so were the reactions of Muslim populations. Debates on reform have been marked by their focus on reformist critiques that were directed, for instance, at cultural elements of Islam or practices of saint veneration, but have often overlooked the social aspects of reform. This chapter will thus focus on this specific aspect and ask which social groups form the basis of Salafi-oriented movements of reform. Finally, this chapter will address an issue that has already surfaced in the context of Mali and northern Nigeria, namely the emergence of *jihād*-minded groups such as al-shabāb in Somalia.

Chad

Although it is a Sahelian country like Niger, Mali and Senegal, Chad is more comparable in significant ways to Sudan (as it was before the independence of Southern Sudan in 2011). Thus, Chad has a variegated history of Islamisation, which impacted most Chadian populations in the late nineteenth century and early twentieth only and that was linked in the eighteenth and nineteenth centuries with the struggle for regional hegemony between the empires of Bornu (around Lake Chad), Wadai (bordering Darfur in the east) and Bagirmi (northeast of the Chari River) (see Reyna 1990). Due to the influx of Arab pastoralist populations from Sudan in the seventeenth century and Libya in the nineteenth century,[4] as well as its importance in trans-regional trade, Arabic became Chad's major language of communication in the twentieth century. Despite the fact that northern and central Chadian populations adopted Islam in the nineteenth and twentieth centuries only, Islam in the guise of scholars and traders informed the history of 'Chadian' empires to a considerable extent, most prominently in the empire of Kanem-Bornu (from the eleventh century) (see Magnant 1992). Both Wadai and Bagirmi had Muslim ruling elites in the seventeenth century, and Wadai became a major political ally of the Sanūsiyya Sufi order in the mid-nineteenth century, supporting the expansion of the Sanūsiyya towards Lake Chad in the late nineteenth century (see Triaud 1995). In contrast to pre-colonial northern Nigeria, Mali and Senegal, the Lake Chad region was never affected by a movement of *jihād.* Both the kingdom of Bagirmi and the Sultanate of Bornu were devastated in the late nineteenth century by the Sudanese warlord Rābiḥ b. Faḍlallāh (1845–1900) (see Zeltner 1988). Only the Sultanate of Wadai was able to resist Rābiḥ b. Faḍlallāh and to defend its independence against French colonial conquest with the support of the Sanūsiyya up to 1909.

Passive resistance against the imposition of French colonial rule continued in Wadai until 1917 and was finally crushed in a massacre in Abéché. In retaliation for the assassination of a number of French military officers, French troops killed several dozen Wadaians, among them numerous members of the religious establishment, in particular scholars affiliated with the Sanūsiyya. Most of the surviving religious scholars and their families thereupon fled to Darfur. In the aftermath of the Abéché massacre, scholars affiliated with the Tijāniyya filled the gap, but kept their distance from the French colonial administration (Gardinier 1989: 161f; Doutoum 1992: 83).[5] In order to keep control of the situation in Wadai, the French colonial administration established the Service de Renseignement Permanent in Abéché in 1926, which became the Service des Affaires Musulmanes et Arabes in the 1940s (and the Direction des Affaires Religieuses et Coutumières in 1960). 'Suspicious elements' were deported to either Faya or to Fort Lamy, where they could be kept under close supervision. Due to the fact that religious scholars affiliated with the Tijāniyya opposed the expansion of the Salafi-oriented movement of reform in Wadai, the French colonial administration also supported the Tijāniyya wherever possible (Doutoum 1992: 90).

The Abéché massacre of 1917 triggered an anti-colonial and Salafi-oriented reaction in Abéché by a number of students who had gone to Sudan and Egypt in the 1920s and 1930s for higher studies, and who started to come back in the early 1940s (Doutoum 1992: 86). The emergence of a Salafi-oriented reform movement in Chad thus started in Wadai and was linked with the return of students from al-Azhar in the 1940s, most prominently Muḥammad ᶜAwūḍa ᶜUllaysh (1909 or 1919–76) (for details see Gardinier 1989; Seesemann 2005b), a scion of the Ṭaha trading family in Abéché, Wadai. Muḥammad ᶜAwūḍa ᶜUllaysh studied first in the Sudan, then, from 1943 to 1945, at al-Azhar in Cairo, where he passed his examination in Islamic law with distinction. After his return to Abéché in 1946, Muḥammad ᶜAwūḍa ᶜUllaysh established Chad's first modern Islamic *madrasa*, al-maᶜhad al-ᶜilmī, in Abéché in 1947, with the support of local *jallāba* (traders) from the Sudan who had settled in Abéché in the mid-nineteenth century. These traders were based in the Am-Siégo quarter of Abéché. In 1943, during the reign of Sultan Muḥammad Urāda (r. 1934–45), the *jallāba* of Am-Siégo had established their own Friday mosque that acquired a 'Wahhabi' character, and stopped attending the Sultan's Friday mosque (Gardinier 1989: 164). The emergence of a local 'Wahhabi' movement (and its school) was opposed not only by the French colonial administration, but also by the Sultan of Wadai and the establishment of local religious scholars who were mostly linked with the Tijāniyya (Seesemann 2005b: 334). The *maᶜhad* of Abéché quickly grew to more than 100 students in the late 1940s, and to 160 in early 1951, and so did the number of Chadian students at al-Azhar: their number grew from 14 in 1947 to 120 in 1951 (Gardinier 1989: 175). In December 1948, Muḥammad ᶜAwūḍa ᶜUllaysh managed to secure authorisation from al-Azhar University for the *maᶜhad* as an affiliated institution, and from 1950 the Egyptian Government paid a monthly grant of 95 Egyptian Pounds for the *maᶜhad*, mediated by al-Azhar. These funds were used to pay the salaries of eight teachers, including Muḥammad ᶜAwūḍa ᶜUllaysh (Gardinier 1989: 172).

In 1950, in order to balance the growing influence of the Salafi-oriented movement of reform in Abéché, the French colonial administration opened a competing *madrasa*, the collège franco-arabe d'Abéché, on premises provided by the Sulṭān ^{c}Alī Silek (r. 1946–77) (Khayar 1976: 78). This school quickly grew in the years to come at the cost of the ma^{c}had al-^{c}ilmī that suffered a first blow when Muḥammad ^{c}Awūḍa ^{c}Ullaysh was forced to resettle in Fort Lamy in 1952, and a second blow in 1954, when the Sulṭān of Wadai ordered all teachers at the *ma^{c}had* to transfer their respective classes to the collège (Gardinier 1989: 177; Seesemann 2005b: 335). The political background of Muḥammad ^{c}Awūḍa ^{c}Ullaysh's removal to Fort Lamy (renamed N'Djaména in 1972) was the fact that in 1951 he had supported the Parti Socialiste Indépendant Tchadien (PSIT) of Aḥmad Khullamallāh (1912–75), who opposed the Sultan of Wadai and was supported by Abéché's *jallāba* community.[6] From Fort Lamy, Muḥammad ^{c}Awūḍa ^{c}Ullaysh moved to al-Ubayyid in the Sudan in 1952, and then to Cairo, and finally to Umm Durmān, where he taught at the ma^{c}had Umm Durmān until his death in 1976 (Gardinier 1989: 177). After 1960, the ma^{c}had al-^{c}ilmī was rebuilt by Adam Barke, one of the first students of Muḥammad ^{c}Awūḍa ^{c}Ullaysh, who had become the director of the *ma^{c}had* in 1952, and a leading representative of Abéché's Salafi-oriented *jallāba* community. In the 1960s, the *ma^{c}had* recovered and had in the region of 500 students in 1970 (Khayar 1976: 96). In 1981, Adam Barke was assassinated in the context of the Chadian Civil War.

Despite the strong presence of Islam, Christianity became a major religion in Chad under French colonial rule (1900–60), especially in the Sara-speaking southern regions of the country. The growth of Christianity continued after independence and in 1993 Chad had a population of 35.3 per cent Christians against 53.8 per cent Muslims, the remainder being followers of African religions (Ladiba 2011: 114; Roné 2000: 408). Christians have also become increasingly outspoken in recent times, a development linked to the emergence of Pentecostal Churches since 1995. At the same time, Christian politicians have lost their prominent position to Muslims, after being in power from 1960 to 1979. Due to the fact that Muslims in Chad never formed a homogeneous population but were split into numerous competing ethnic groups, Chad's history since 1966 can be compared in significant ways to that of Somalia since 1988, namely, as the efforts of a series of warlords to gain and defend political supremacy. After independence in 1960, Chad's first president, François Tombalbaye (1918–75), a Sara from southern Chad and a protestant Christian, ruled in an increasingly authoritarian way that excluded the Muslim populations of the north, in particular the Teda and Daza of the Tibesti and Borku regions and the different Zaghāwa-speaking groups of the Ennedi region bordering Darfur. In 1966, northern political leaders founded the Front de Libération Nationale du Tchad (FROLINAT) in Nyala (Sudan) that started the struggle for political emancipation of the Muslim populations of Chad. In 1975, François Tombalbaye was deposed by General Félix Malloum who was equally unable to defeat the Muslim rebellion in the north and the east. In 1979, he was forced to cede power to the leader of FROLINAT, Goukouni Weddeye (b. 1944), a son of the *Derdé*, the religious leader of the Teda. In 1980, the alliance between the Teda (Goukouni Weddeye) and the Zaghāwa (led by Hissène Habré, b. 1942) broke up and Habré drove Goukouni Weddeye from N'Djaména, Chad's capital city, in 1982. In 1987, Habré also defeated the Libyan troops that had supported Goukouni Weddeye and that had occupied major parts of Chad, but he was removed from power by Idriss Déby (b. 1952), another Zaghāwa warlord, in 1990.[7]

Although FROLINAT was a movement of rebellion by the Muslim populations of northern, eastern and central Chad, Islam never became an issue[8] and FROLINAT, as well as all Chadian governments since 1979, under Goukouni Weddeye, Hissène Habré and Idriss Déby, have defended the principles of religious tolerance and secular government (Buijtenhuijs 1992: 127ff). Due to the secular orientation of FROLINAT, both Chadian *ᶜulamāᵓ* and Chad's Salafi-minded *jallāba* have been very hesitant to support it (Buijtenhuijs 1992: 129): The Chadian civil war thus never turned religious, but was a struggle for political hegemony in Chad. The only exception to the rule was Muḥammad al-Baghalānī (d. 1977), one of FROLINAT's founders, who was affiliated with the Egypian ikhwān al-muslimūn, and was excluded from FROLINAT in 1970 (Buijtenhuijs 1992: 128)

After independence, President François Tombalbaye initially continued the restrictive policies of the French colonial administration with respect to the Salafi-oriented movement of reform. In 1971, he changed strategy, however, possibly in order to counter the rebellion of the 'Muslim' FROLINAT, an assessment summarised by Buijtenhuijs (1992: 127): 'not all Muslims are rebels, but all rebels are Muslims.' The government started to organise the *ḥajj*, provided grants for studies in Arab countries and invited teachers from Egypt to teach in Chad. In N'Djaména, Saudi Arabia built a huge central mosque. In 1972 the *imām* of this mosque, Mūsā Ibrāhīm, started to form a Comité Islamique that was recognised officially in 1974 as the Comité Islamique d'Arbitrage de la République du Tchad and was asked to coordinate (and screen) all Islamic activities in Chad (Yacoub 1992: 96). After the Khartoum coalition government agreement between General Malloum and the FROLINAT in 1977 and Goukouni Weddeye's rise to power in 1979, the process of Islamisation gathered speed: Arabic was acknowledged as Chad's second national language (apart from French), office hours were redefined to allow time for (Islamic) prayers and mosques and places for prayer were opened in administrative buildings (Roné 2000: 274). Since 1984, Chad has also seen the establishment of Islamic charitable organisations such as the Africa Muslim Agency, al-munaẓẓamat al-daᶜwa al-islāmiyya or Islamic Relief (see Kaag 2007, 2014; Ladiba 2011, 2013), which have supported the construction of mosques, schools and hospitals. Due to their efforts (as well as the efforts of Chadian Salafi-oriented groups), the number of modern *madāris* grew to about thirty nationwide in 1978, and more than fifty in the capital city of N'Djaména alone in 1994 (Ladiba 2011: 120). The number of students in *madāris* and government schools was almost the same in 1994: in the region of 18,200 students in *madāris* against approximately 22,000 students in government primary schools (Ladiba 2011: 120).[9] In 2004, eleven transnational (and about twenty national) Islamic NGOs were active in Chad (one Libyan, three Sudanese, one Kuwaiti and six of Saudi extraction) (Kaag 2007: 89ff; Ladiba 2011: 31). In 1990, with Déby's rise to power, a national Islamic organisation was set up, the Conseil Supérieur des Affaires Islamiques (CSAI), led by the Sudan-born *imām* of N'Djaména's central mosque, Ḥasan Abakar, who has also been nicknamed the 'Sudanese General' (Ladiba 2011: 87; Kaag 2014: 88).[10] The CSAI was not only in charge of the annual pilgrimage, but also in control of all Friday mosques and thus represented government Islam. Until recently, the CSAI was dominated by loyalist scholars affiliated with the Tijāniyya (Kaag 2007: 93). Chad's major religious associations were al-Hūda pour la bienfaisance, a Salafi-oriented organisation, and the Tijāniyya- (Niass branch) oriented association al-faiḍa al-jāriya, as led by Maḥamat Djarma (Ladiba 2011: 108).

While there have been tensions between these two organisations (as well as between Muslims and Christians), Chad has so far not seen open religious conflict among Muslims[11] as in northern Nigeria. This absence of serious conflict among Muslims was due to several factors: first, the Déby administration has always been supported by Chad's major religious movement, the Tijāniyya, and would not have tolerated Salafi-oriented attacks against the Tijāniyya; second, Salafi-oriented NGOs in Chad have so far focused on charitable work and proselytisation among the southern Christian populations as well as 'counter-propaganda' against Christian (often Pentecostal) NGOs; third, the Chadian Government may revoke permission to work in Chad at any time and has done so in the past, as, for instance, in spring 2004, when the Chadian offices of al-ḥaramayn and the Makka al-Mukarrama Charity Trust were closed down due to US pressure, while WAMY, the International Islamic Relief Organization (IIRO) and the Sudan-based al-daᶜwa al-islāmiyya had to cut down their activities considerably (Kaag 2007: 98, 2014: 86).[12] The Idriss Déby administration also dissolved thirty religious associations on 30 July 1996, which were accused of activities 'non conformes à l'idéal de la Répubique' (Ladiba 2011: 143).[13] The government equally called to order all Islamic religious associations that challenged the supreme role of the CSAI, for instance in *circulaire* 015/MAT/DG/2002 that reminded Islamic NGOs in Chad to respect the laws and regulations of the country and confirmed the CSAI as the 'seul et unique interlocuteur' between such associations and the government (Ladiba 2011: 144). In 2008, the Chadian Government and the CSAI accused al-muntadā al-islāmī of 'terrorism' and forced the organisation to leave the country. Despite allegations of terrorism, this conflict was really caused by a personal feud between the CSAI and its president, Ḥasan Abakar, and 'al-muntadā al-islāmī' as an organisation supported by Chadian Muslim intellectuals with strong links to Islamic charities who had started to oppose the policies of the CSAI and to question the authority of Ḥasan Abakar (Kaag 2014: 87–8).

Due to the fact that Chad has so far not seen the development of significant middle-class groups (in contrast to Sudan, Nigeria or Senegal), support for Salafi-oriented organisations has remained confined to students and traders, the classic supporters of Salafi-oriented reform, and to the Chadian employees of Islamic NGOs (Kaag 2007: 91f; Arditi 2003: 56). The demographic and political weakness of these social groups has so far thwarted efforts by Salafi-oriented charities and organisations to develop deeper roots in Chadian society.

Sudan

Like many other sub-Saharan African countries, Sudan can look back on a long history of Sufi traditions of learning. In the nineteenth century, Sudan also saw the development of a number of Sufi-oriented movements of reform, such as the Khatmiyya/Mirghāniyya (see Voll 1969) and the Majdhūbiyya[14], which brought new forms of social and religious organisation and ritual, and that can be seen as a response to the onset of processes of change under Egyptian rule. In the late nineteenth century, these Sufi-oriented movements of reform, in particular, the Khatmiyya, were challenged by a movement of rebellion against rule by Egypt and its allies. This movement, led by the Mahdī Muḥammad Aḥmad,[15] ruled Sudan from 1885 to 1898. Although the Mahdī rejected both Sufism and existing Islamic legal practices, and instead proclaimed the return to the very foundations (*uṣūl*) of Islam, this movement acquired a Sufi-like outlook, not only as far as the veneration of the Mahdī by his followers, the Anṣār, as a 'founding saint' was concerned, but also in ritual practice, in particular in the practice of the *rātib*, a litany of prayers of the Mahdiyya.[16]

British colonial rule triggered a second wave of reform, accompanied by the development of modern media: in 1913, a first newspaper was established, *Rāʾid al-Sūdān* (Leader of Sudan) (el-Affendi 1991: 29). *Rāʾid al-Sūdān* became the medium for two generations of Sudanese 'effendis', was nationalist in outlook and existed until 1938 (Daly 1991: 80). Equally important was *al-Fajr*, created by ᶜArafat Muḥammad ᶜAbdallāh, which only existed from 1934 to 1937, yet captured the aspirations of the educated class (Daly 1991: 80; Sidahmed 1997: 36). Another feature of British colonial modernity was the establishment of a modern administration and modern schools, first the Gordon Memorial College (GMC) in Khartoum in 1902, which became the University College of Khartoum in 1951 and the University of Khartoum in

1956, and later the Bakht al-Rawḍa College of Education.[17] After independence, these were followed by the Omdurman Islamic University and the African International University of Khartoum. British policies of social and economic transformation created a 'new field of action' (el-Affendi 1991: 27) for the Sudanese and led to the emergence of a Sudanese colonial 'intelligentsia' (el-Affendi 1991: 28) in the 1910s.[18] These new elites were an extension of the Egyptian intelligentsia, mostly bureaucrats and teachers in the urban centres, and especially in greater Khartoum. They were taught by Egyptian teachers and instructors and were informed by what was going on in Egypt. In Sudan they were called 'Effendis' ('Sirs') (el-Affendi 1991: 29). Yet, although the Sudanese intelligentsia established the Graduates' General Congress as a first nationalist party in 1938, its members remained affiliated with the established religio-political leaders, the 'Sayyids', that is, the leaders of the Mahdiyya, ᶜAbd al-Raḥmān al-Mahdī, and the Khatmiyya, ᶜAlī al-Mirghānī.

In terms of social support, the Mahdiyya dominated the White and Blue Nile regions, Kordofan, Darfur and Omdurman (Umm Durmān), while the Khatmiyya acquired a strong foothold in Kassala, in the Jazīra, in Khartoum (al-Kharṭūm) and in the northern valley of the Nile (Daly 1991: 72).[19] In the twentieth century, the Mahdiyya and the Khatmiyya influenced religious and political development in the Sudan to the extent that both pre- and post-independence politics were decisively informed by the rivalry of these religious movements. Both movements established their own political parties in order to control the political development of the country. The Khatmiyya thus supported the foundation, in 1938, of the Graduates' General Congress under Ismāᶜīl al-Azharī, a movement representing the young and Western-educated Sudanese intelligentsia, and in 1951 the National Unionist Party (NUP) that supported a form of union with Egypt. In truth, the NUP was an assortment of small political groups competing with one another. The most important among these groups was the Ashiqqāᵓ (that is, 'brothers by the same father and mother') Party established in 1943 and led by Ismāᶜīl al-Azharī who represented the educated urban elites. The Anṣār, by contrast, founded the Umma Party in 1945 with British support, which rejected union with Egypt. In Sudan's first elections for the Legislative Assembly in 1952, NUP won fifty-one of ninety-seven seats and Umma twenty-two. In 1954,

Ismāᶜīl al-Azharī was elected first Prime Minister of the Sudan, yet, despite the pro-Egyptian positions of the NUP, Sudan declared independence on 1 January 1956. When al-Azharī was ousted from power only six months after independence in 1956, the bid of the educated class for power and for an independent stance in politics collapsed (el-Affendi 1991: 37): The intelligentsia had not been able to form an independent power base and had not produced charismatic leaders who would have been able to unite the Sudanese for a non-religious and nationalist political agenda. The failure of the intelligentsia to develop their own political agenda confirmed the dominance of the Umma/Anṣār and Khatmiyya/NUP religious and political blocks (el-Affendi 1991: 37) that continued to inform partisan politics, called *ṭāʾifiyya* (fractionalism) after independence. Post-independence politics in the Sudan oscillated between periods of civilian rule (1954–8; 1964–9; 1986–9) and periods of military rule (1958–64; 1969–86; since 1989). Civilian administrations were characterised by the quick succession of short-lived (mostly coalition) governments representing partisan interests and dominated by either the Umma party or the NUP/DUP.[20]

The emergence of a Salafi-oriented movement of reform was linked with the development of three different groups of Salafi-minded Muslims: first, the foundation of the anṣār al-sunna al-muḥammadiyya by the Egyptian Azhari scholar and disciple of Rashīd Riḍā, Muḥammad Ḥāmid al-Fiqī in 1926. The Sudanese branch of the anṣār al-sunna al-muḥammadiyya was formed in Umm Durman and in Port Sudan in 1939 by Aḥmad Ḥassūn, a postal worker, and al-Fāḍil al-Taqlāwī, a teacher, but traced its origins to a lecture circle in al-Nuhūd (about 700 km southwest of Khartoum in Western Kordofan) led by an Algerian scholar and student of Rashīd Riḍā, ᶜAbd al-Raḥmān Abū Ḥajar (Ch. Ahmed 2015: 40ff; E. Ahmed 2015: 166).[21] Throughout the twentieth century, the anṣār al-sunna al-muḥammadiyya remained independent of the Egyptian organisation and a comparatively small group (el-Affendi 1991: 43; see also E. Ahmed 2015: 170ff; al-Karsani 1993: 146; Salomon 2009a: 146). In the Sudan, they were led by Muḥammad Ḥāshim al-Hadiyya (1910–2007) from 1952 to 2007. In the early 2000s, the anṣār al-sunna al-muḥammadiyya split into two factions over a number of issues, most particularly, cooperation with the al-Bashīr regime. One branch was the al-Hadiyya or '*markaz*'-branch led by Ismāᶜīl ᶜUthmān, which kept control over a majority of mosques, schools and administrative centres, while the '*iṣlāḥ*'-branch, led by Abū Zayd Muḥammad, continued to refuse participation in politics (E. Ahmed 2015: 170ff; Salomon 2009a: 146ff, Salomon 2009b: 453).[22] In Sudan, the anṣār al-sunna al-muḥammadiyya have also been nicknamed *ᶜulamāᵓ al-ḥayḍ wa-l-nifās* due to their insistence on the importance of seemingly minor points of doctrine, such as women's menstruation and questions of childbirth (Salomon 2009a: 164). In political terms, the anṣār al-sunna al-muḥammadiyya have disputed the idea that the revivication of Islam (*iḥyāᵓ*) could be achieved through the mechanism of the state and its institutions (Salomon 2009a: 144).

The second major branch within Sudan's Salafi-oriented movement of reform was linked with the *daᶜwa* of members of the Egyptian Muslim Brothers in Sudan from 1946, when a first delegation of Egyptian Muslim Brothers visited Sudan (Sidahmed 1997: 45). Egyptian *daᶜwa* did not lead to a unified organisation, however, and remained inconsequential for the time being. Sudanese students joined the ikhwān al-muslimūn, however, while studying in Egypt. The first prominent Sudanese 'brother' was Jamīl al-Sanhūrī from Dongola, who went to Egypt for studies in the late 1930s and joined the ikhwān in the early 1940s. He started to form a nucleus of ikhwān sympathisers among Sudanese students in Egypt (el-Affendi 1991: 46) who often became supporters of the Ashiqqāᵓ Party after their return home. In 1947, they founded the League of Sudanese Students (LSS), their own students' association in Cairo, separate from the communist-controlled Sudanese Students' Union. The leading personality in this group was Ṣādiq ᶜAbdallāh ᶜAbd al-Mājid, who had studied in Egypt since 1940 and who had got into contact with both Ḥasan al-Bannā and Sayyid Quṭb. In 1949, the Sudanese returnees established the first Sudanese section of the ikhwān al-muslimūn (Sidahmed 1997: 45). The ikhwān were led at this time by ᶜAlī Ṭalballāh who received a letter of appointment as 'general supervisor' of the ikhwān in Sudan by Ḥasan al-Bannā in 1947 while he was in prison for possessing an unlicensed pistol (el-Affendi 1991: 51). Finally, students at Sudanese secondary schools and students at the Gordon Memorial College (GMC) established the ḥarakat al-taḥrīr al-islāmī (HTI) (Islamic Liberation Movement (ILM)) at the GMC in March 1949 led by Babikir Karrar, a teacher (Sidahmed 1997: 45). The members of ILM claimed that they founded their movement without outside support, as a reaction to the activities of communist students at the Gordon Memorial College, and that the movement was 'unique, coming from nowhere' (Gallab 2008: 36).

Although the followers and members of the anṣār al-sunna al-muḥammadiyya', of ILM and of the ikhwān al-muslimūn represented different historical loyalties, they supported the same Salafi-oriented programme of reform, and have thus been labelled Islamic Movement, al-ḥaraka al-islāmiyya in Sudan. This label should not hide the fact, however, that the Islamic Movement, as well as the groups within the Islamic Movement, were divided over questions of strategy and doctrinal orientation from the very beginning. The Islamic Movement thus never constituted a uniform movement of reform. In the 1950s, for instance, two different orientations emerged within both the ikhwān and the larger Islamic Movement: the political (*siyāsa* or 'pragmatic') wing (later led by Ḥasan al-Turābī) and the educationalist (*tarbiya* or 'ideological') wing that represented a purist approach to politics.[23] The educationalist orientation was shared by a majority of the followers of the anṣār al-sunna al-muḥammadiyya. The different branches of Sudan's Salafi-oriented movement of reform can thus be differentiated on the basis of their inclusivist or exclusivist positions with respect to the state and the Muslim population: while the anṣār al-sunna al-muḥammadiyya as well as factions of the ikhwān cultivated exclusivist educationalist positions and a cautious distance from the state, the larger Islamic Movement, represented by Ḥasan al-Turābī, supported inclusivist positions and the need to develop broad popular support for politics of reform and participation in politics. At the same time, the anṣār al-sunna al-muḥammadiyya and factions of the ikhwān defended the primary role of doctrine and accused Ḥasan al-Turābī of neglecting or ignoring doctrinal issues in order to gather Muslims for a political goal und, thus, compromising the soundness of the religion (Salomon 2009a: 158). In the eyes of the anṣār al-sunna al-muḥammadiyya and factions of the ikhwān, the duty of *al-amr bi-l-ma^{c}rūf wa-l-nahy ^{c}an al-munkar* and the respective 'cleansing' and purification of the faith (*tazkiyat al-^{c}aqīda*) was more important than overcoming doctrinal differences for a 'supposed greater (political) good' (Salomon 2009a: 158).[24]

It is also necessary, however, to stress that neither the anṣār al-sunna al-muḥammadiyya nor factions of the ikhwān advocated complete withdrawal (*i*ᶜ*tizāl*) from politics. Party-based politics and efforts to implement *sharī*ᶜ*a*, as undertaken by Ḥasan al-Turābī and the Islamic Movement, were regarded as secondary to the task of educating Muslims (Salomon 2009: 148). This task not only involved teaching Muslims to 'enjoin what is right and to forbid what is wrong' and to worship correctly, but also the general rectification of doctrine (*taṣḥīḥ al-*ᶜ*aqīda*) and was directed against both the laxness of contemporary society and the 'compromised and faulty doctrines of pious Muslims' (Salomon 2009: 151). The focus on rectifying the doctrine of Muslims who were seen as 'errant' also implies that 'education'-oriented Salafis did not target non-Muslims in their *da*ᶜ*wa*, but were willing to cultivate 'paths of accomodation' with, for instance, Christians. This position is not restricted to Sudan, but can also be identified among Salafi-oriented groups in northern Nigeria: non-Muslims who make no claims regarding the correct interpretation of faith and doctrine pose little threat to 'education'-minded Salafis (Salomon 2009a: 152).

In 1951/2, the students' branch of the ikhwān scored its first victory by winning the elections for the Khartoum University Students' Union (KUSU) that had been under communist control since 1947 (el-Affendi 1991: 52). This victory was an important feat, as the GMC was 'more than just a college, it was the government in person' (Sharkey 2003: 43). In August 1954, a conference was organised in Umm Durmān to unite the different Salafi-oriented trends in Sudan and the participants voted to unite under the name al-ikhwān al-muslimūn. The conference stressed that the Sudanese ikhwān al-muslimūn movement should not be linked with the Egyptian ikhwān organisation (Gallab 2008: 43). At the conference, the pro-Egyptian ikhwān leader, ᶜAlī Ṭalballāh, was deposed and a new executive bureau was elected, led by Muḥammad Khayr ᶜAbd al-Qādir, who represented the 'Sudanese' wing of the ikhwān. However, the conference was not able to resolve existing disputes. As a result, divisions continued to exist within the ikhwān and led to recurring conflicts between the *siyāsa* and the *tarbiya* wings (el-Affendi 1991: 53).

The history of the ikhwān in the Sudan shows that divisions between the different wings could lead to quick reversals of power relations: thus, the repression of the Egyptian ikhwān in 1954 by General Jamāl ᶜAbd al-Nāṣir had immediate repercussions in the Sudan, where a majority of the ikhwān now rejected political union with Egypt and replaced ᶜAlī Ṭalballāh as leader of the ikhwān by Muḥammad Khayr ᶜAbd al-Qādir. Only one year later, however, in 1955, Muḥammad Khayr ᶜAbd al-Qādir was forced to resign by ᶜAlī Ṭalballāh. This development motivated Babikir Karar, the leader of the Islamic Liberation Movement (ILM), to secede from the ikhwān al-muslimūn and to establish a new Salafi-oriented group, al-jamāᶜa al-islāmiyya (Gallab 2008: 43). These developments eventually brought about the emergence of a younger generation of activists as led by al-Rāshid al-Ṭāhir who also led the new executive bureau of the ikhwān al-muslimūn as *murāqib ᶜāmm* (general supervisor) (Gallab 2008: 44). Al-Rāshid al-Ṭāhir had turned against Egypt in 1954 and against close affiliation with the Egyptian ikhwān and had brought the ikhwān and the larger Islamic Movement in Sudan close to the equally anti-unionist Umma Party.

In late December 1955, the different Salafi-oriented groups formed the Islamic Front for the Constitution (IFC), a coalition of groups that were united by the ideal of an Islamic constitution. The IFC produced a model constitution that forced all other political groups to respond (el-Affendi 1991: 58). The history of the Sudan after independence shows that the issue of the constitution (and the legal system) was more central to the development of the Sudan than was the case in other Muslim countries south of the Sahara. With respect to this issue, two basic questions were discussed in the Sudan after independence: first, whether there should be a constitution and a legal system with an Islamic character at all, considering the fact that the south was predominantly non-Muslim. The second question was whether there should be a codified system of Islamic law for the north only and which form such codification could take. The implementation of *sharīᶜa* law in 1983, its reform as from 1989 and re-enactment in 1991, raised the question of whether Sudan should follow the majoritarian Mālikī school of law or the Ḥanafī school of law as introduced by Egypt in the nineteenth century, or whether it should develop a completely new system of Islamic law as advocated by Ḥasan al-Turābī. Due to the fact that all Sudanese governments from independence up to 2011 needed to keep control over the 'Christian' south and were thus forced to compromise on the issue of an Islamic constitution, this question has remained unanswered.

After the 1958 elections and the military coup of General ᶜAbbūd in the same year, the IFC collapsed and the ikhwān were forced to shut down their headquarters and publications (el-Affendi 1991: 61). After the imposition of military rule, the ikhwān called for a return to civilian rule and became increasingly influential in KUSU. On 9 November 1959, al-Rāshid al-Ṭāhir supported a coup against the ᶜAbbūd regime that failed, however, and led to renewed debates within the Islamic Movement over questions of strategy. In the aftermath of the aborted coup, al-Rāshid al-Ṭāhir was imprisoned (until 1963), but was appointed minister in the transitional government after the return to civilian rule in 1964. In the 1965 elections he won a seat for the Islamic Charter Front (ICF) and became the ICF spokesperson in Parliament. In 1965, however, he dissociated himself from the Islamic Movement and turned to the NUP, thus removing the last obstacles to Ḥasan al-Turābī's rise to the top of the Islamic Movement (Warburg 2003: 179; el-Affendi 1991: 78). In 1976, al-Rāshid al-Ṭāhir was appointed deputy president and prime minister by President al-Numayrī.

The rise of Ḥasan al-Turābī as the future leader of the Islamic Movement in Sudan started in this political context: Ḥasan al-Turābī was born in Kassala in 1932. His family represented an old tradition of learning in the region of Kassala. His father, ᶜAbdallāh Dafᶜallāh al-Turābī, had been a *qāḍī* in the British colonial period. Due to the fact that Islamic jurisdiction was confined to personal (family) law and that most cases involved women, *qāḍīs* were not only seen as being subordinate to civil judges but they were also ridiculed as 'women's judges' (Ibrahim 1999: 199). Ḥasan al-Turābī studied law from 1951 at the University of Khartoum. In 1954, he was elected leader of the ikhwān's university branch in KUSU, but then went to London in 1955, where he studied for a master's degree at the University of London. In 1957, he returned and joined the Executive Bureau of the Islamic Movement, but then left again for Paris in 1959 and registered for a PhD in law at Sorbonne University. His PhD thesis was written on the topic of the power of the executive under a state of emergency in constitutional law (Laible 2005: 6). While in London, Ḥasan al-Turābī studied together with al-Ṣādiq al-Mahdī, the future leader of the Anṣār. In 1961, Ḥasan al-Turābī married a sister of al-Ṣādiq al-Mahdī, Wisāl al-Mahdī (el-Affendi 1991: 79), who later became famous in the Sudan for her views regarding the emancipation of women. He returned to Sudan for a short period of time in 1962. Due to the fact that he was one of the first Sudanese to be awarded a PhD, he enjoyed enormous prestige and was appointed Dean of the Faculty of Law at the University of Khartoum after his final return to Sudan in 1964. As Dean of the Faculty of Law, Ḥasan al-Turābī influenced hundreds of students and future members of the Islamic Movement (see el-Affendi 1991; Ibrahim 1999). Due to his 'unauthorised' participation in the 1959 coup, al-Rāshid al-Ṭāhir had been damaged and was deposed as leader of the Islamic Movement in 1962. His demise furthered the rise of Ḥasan al-Turābī. Ḥasan al-Turābī's election as secretary general also 'sidelined al-Rāshid al-Ṭāhir and those who followed the ikhwān of Egypt school' (Gallab 2008: 63), who emphasised the educational approach rather than politics. However, the *tarbiya* wing remained a critical minority within the larger Islamic Movement.

Under the leadership of Ḥasan al-Turābī, the Islamic Movement continued its opposition against the junta until General ᶜAbbūd was forced to step down from power in October 1964. On 6 December 1964, Ḥasan al-Turābī was able to establish another coalition of Islamic groups, called the Islamic Charter Front (ICF) (jabhat al-mithāq al-islāmī) in an effort to cultivate a larger social basis for the Islamic Movement (el-Affendi 1991: 74). Despite the resistance of some (*tarbiya*-minded) ikhwān, the ICF united not only the Islamic Movement but also a section of the *ᶜulamāʾ*, the anṣār al-sunna al-muḥammadiyya, some smaller Sufi groups and a number of tribal notables who were recruited for the ICF by their ikhwān-oriented sons. At the same time, Ḥasan al-Turābī was elected Secretary General (*al-amīn al-ᶜāmm*) of the ICF (el-Affendi 1991: 76). At this time, the ikhwān and the larger Islamic Movement mostly consisted of students or recent graduates. The social basis of the Islamic Movement was still very slim (el-Affendi 1991: 67).

In the 1965 elections, the ICF, which advocated the introduction of an Islamic constitution and the implementation of a codified system of Islamic law, fielded an impressive number of 100 candidates, supported by a new newspaper, *al-mithāq al-Islāmī* (The Islamic Charter) and won seven seats and 5.1 per cent of the vote, mostly in Khartoum, Kassala and the northern Nile valley, while the majority of seats and votes were again divided among the two major religio-political blocks, Umma/Anṣār and NUP/Khatmiyya (el-Affendi 1991: 77) that now formed a coalition government under al-Ṣādiq al-Mahdī. In 1967, the new government formed a fifty-four-member constitutional commission to develop a new constitution. Although the ICF had only three members in this commission, it influenced the work of the commission in decisive ways. In 1968, new elections were held, but this time the ICF was able to win only five seats, a defeat that was interpreted as a failure of Ḥasan al-Turābī's strategy to win a broader social basis for the Islamic Movement. Internal disputes, which had been dormant since 1964, thus came to the foreground again, but were settled in a number of internal meetings in April 1969, in which Ḥasan al-Turābī and his group prevailed over the 'dissidents' and was re-elected leader of both the ikhwān and the ICF (el-Affendi 1991: 87–8). While Ḥasan al-Turābī advocated a flexible 'political' strategy and defended his quest for a broad social basis, the dissidents or 'educationalists' led by Muḥammad Ṣāliḥ ᶜUmar[25] and Jaᶜfar Shaykh Idrīs[26] but also Ṣādiq ᶜAbdallāh ᶜAbd al-Mājid advocated an elitist approach and rejected 'coalitions' that would compromise the 'pure' line (el-Affendi 1991: 87). As a result of the April 1969 disputes, the ICF was able to consolidate its political orientation and its social basis that had grown from approximately 2,000 hard-core supporters in 1964 to more than 45,000 supporters in 1968 (el-Affendi 1991: 89). The social basis of the ICF now consisted not only of students and graduates, but also of some *imāms* and *ᶜulamāʾ* and a growing number of merchants, as well as urban workers organised in the different unions, although a majority of workers still followed the Sudanese Communist Party (SCP). In 1964, the ICF also established a Patriotic Women's Front as the first Salafi-oriented women's organisation. However, by 1969 the Islamic Movement had still not achieved 'a substantial breakthrough anywhere in the modern sector' (el-Affendi 1991: 99), the left being stronger among the intelligentsia, the women and the workers.

The further development of the Salafi-oriented movement of reform was informed by Sudan's second military coup on 25 May 1969, organised by Colonel Jaᶜfar Muḥammad al-Numayrī. The 1969 coup started a trail of violence in Sudanese politics that was intensified in 1984/5 and after 1989. Al-Numayri's coup came as a shock in several respects, not only because al-Numayrī was known as a staunch secularist and a heavy drinker, but also because his government was initially strongly supported by the SCP and committed to a course of social and economic transformation: twelve out of twenty ministers in his first cabinet were either members or sympathisers of the SCP. In the aftermath of the coup, many ikhwān and ICF leaders were imprisoned or fled abroad, or were simply killed, as in the case of the rebellion of a section of the Anṣār under the leadership of al-Hādī al-Mahdī, supported by many ikhwān, which was crushed on Aba island in March 1970 (el-Affendi 1991: 106; Collins 2008: 98). In 1971, however, al-Numayrī eliminated the SCP that challenged his claim to political hegemony, and thus also removed the ikhwān's most important opponent. In late 1971, most ikhwān, including Ḥasan al-Turābī, were freed from prison and were able to resume their work. Still, further crackdowns on the ikhwān occurred in 1973 and 1974 that decimated the Islamic Movement. As a result, the ikhwān again decided to join a larger coalition of opposition forces, the National Front, which eventually staged a major coup on 2 July 1976 with the support of Libya. The coup failed, however, leading to severe repression of the opposition, in particular the ikhwān, who accused al-Ṣādiq al-Mahdī of having abandoned them in the coup (el-Affendi 1991: 110).

The failure of the 1976 coup against al-Numayrī led to a strategic reorientation of the Islamic Movement in the Sudan: while the Islamic Movement had sought to establish coalitions with other political groups in the past in order to enhance its political weight, it now decided to remain independent and to not rely any more on allies such as al-Ṣādiq al-Mahdī. When the al-Numayrī administration started talks with the opposition regarding national reconciliation in 1977, many followers of the Islamic Movement were willing to leave the National Front and to support the al-Numayrī Government for strategic reasons: reconciliation with al-Numayrī offered the Islamic Movement the chance to recover from repression, to create new organisational structures, to implement parts of their religio-programme as part of the government and to recruit new members (Gallab 2008: 73). Nevertheless, on entering al-Numayrī's government in 1977, Ḥasan al-Turābī still felt obliged to declare: 'Our participation in the Socialist Union was against all our instincts, and we would not have ventured into it' if it had not been 'a necessary part of our plan to reach the wider sectors of society in the countryside, in the south and in the popular and labour groups' (quoted in Hamdi 1998: 21). Ḥasan al-Turābī justified his alliance with al-Numayrī with a reference to the 'Joseph paradigm', that is, the idea that it was possible to work for a detested ruler in order to serve a higher cause (Qur'ān 12: 20–111, in particular verse 21). According to Ḥasan al-Turābī, religion could not abandon its duty to educate people in a 'godless' state, it was the responsibility of the time to assume this task (Ibrahim 1999: 205; see also Mahmoud 1996: 167ff).

Ḥasan al-Turābī's reconciliation with al-Numayrī had been facilitated by the latter's turn towards religion: in the mid-1970s, al-Numayrī had started to cultivate relations with a number of smaller Sufi orders in order to gain the support of a social basis independent of the major religious blocks, that is, Anṣār and Khatmiyya (Warburg 2003: 152–5; Collins 2008: 145f). Al-Numayrī's turn towards Islam in the mid-1970s also allowed Ḥasan al-Turābī to win allies among the Sufi groups that supported al-Numayrī. At the same time, Ḥasan al-Turābī's strategy resulted in a marked loss of influence of the Islamic Movement within KUSU.[27] However, Ḥasan al-Turābī could now justify his cooperation with al-Numayrī by arguing that he was not fighting for democracy but for Islam. According to him, al-Numayrī had come to Islam because the activities of the Islamic Movement had shown him its relevance. Whether genuine or not, al-Numayrī's turn towards Islam had given the Islamic Movement 'room to manoeuvre' (Ibrahim 1999: 215). The Islamic Movement now had the chance to use this room and did not let itself be deterred by the divergent ideas of either the 'educationalists' within the Islamic Movement or the established political elites representing the 'effendiyya' class (Ibrahim 1999: 215).

However, the Islamic Movement did not pass into the regime as an organisation, but as individual persons. This process allowed the building of a network for a new organisation (Gallab 2008: 72). In 1977, together with Jaᶜfar Shaykh Idrīs, Ḥasan al-Turābī was appointed member of the *lajna murājaᶜa al-qawānīn li-tatamasha maᶜa al-sharīᶜa* (Prunier 1989: 364; Warburg 2003: 155), which had the task of seeing whether existing laws were in conformity with the principles of the *sharīᶜa*. This enabled Ḥasan al-Turābī to start his work on a comprehensive system of codified Islamic law. In 1978, Ḥasan al-Turābī was appointed secretary of information and foreign relations in al-Numayrī's Sudanese Socialist Union (SSU) and Attorney General of the Sudan in 1979. As a result, the ikhwān diversified their membership beyond student circles, in particular among upper- and middle-class women and businessmen (el-Affendi 1991: 117; Seesemann 2005a: 21).[28] Ḥasan al-Turābī's cooperation with al-Numayrī, however, led to another conflict within the movement, and brought about the defection in 1979 of Ṣādiq ᶜAbdallāh ᶜAbd al-Mājid (el-Affendi 1991: IX) and Mālik Badrī.[29] They established a new organisation by the name of ḥizb al-ikhwān al-muslimīn and formed an alliance with the anṣār al-sunna group (Prunier 1989: 366). Ṣādiq ᶜAbdallāh ᶜAbd al-Mājid, one of the first leaders of the Islamic Movement in the 1940s, represented the 'ideological' tradition in the Islamic Movement (by contrast to Ḥasan al-Turābī's 'pragmatic' line). Although support for the al-Numayrī regime made the Islamic Movement unpopular, and many Sudanese regarded Ḥasan al-Turābī as an opportunist, and although many members of the Islamic Movement were dissatisfied with his policy, Ḥasan al-Turābī and his followers used this chance to infiltrate the army and to win allies in the army (el-Affendi 1991: 120) by way of courses in Islamic ideology for senior army officers at the African Islamic Centre that eventually became the International University of Africa.[30] Four members of the military council that ruled Sudan from 1989, including ᶜUmar ᶜḤasan al-Bashīr, actually attended these courses (Warburg 2003: 189) and seven (out of fifteen) members of the future Revolutionary Command Council (RCC) were 'Islamist' officers (Ahmed 2007: 195).

In May 1983, Ḥasan al-Turābī lost his position as Attorney General of the Sudan in the context of al-Numayrī's decision to introduce *sharīᶜa* penal law in September 1983. Although Ḥasan al-Turābī had been central to the formulation of the 'September' laws since 1979 (Köndgen 1993: 224), the regime was not willing to give Ḥasan al-Turābī the credit for this political move. In May 1983 he was replaced as attorney general by his old rival within the Islamic Movement, al-Rāshid al-Ṭāhir, while his own function in the government was reduced to the role of a legal advisor, later an advisor on foreign affairs (el-Affendi 1991: 126). The implementation of the 'September' laws, in particular, the harsh interpretation of the *ḥudūd* regulations from April 1984, was enacted by an ikhwān sympathiser, al-Mukāshifī Ṭāhā al-Kabbāshī (el-Affendi 1991: 125).[31] In February 1985, Ḥasan al-Turābī was imprisoned by the al-Numayrī regime, a move that turned out to be very helpful for Ḥasan al-Turābī in a context in which al-Numayrī had ordered the execution of Sudan's most conspicuous dissident scholar, Maḥmūd Muḥammad Ṭāhā[32] in January 1985. In April 1985, al-Numayrī was overthrown by General ᶜAbd al-Raḥmān Siwār al-Dhahab who started a process of return to civilian rule (el-Affendi 1991: 128). After his release from prison, Ḥasan al-Turābī and his followers established another Salafi-oriented political party, as successor to the ICF and the Islamic Movement, namely, the National Islamic Front (NIF) (al-jabha al-islāmiyya al-qawmiyya) (Burr and Collins 2010: 8; Warburg 1985: 400ff).[33]

The inclusion of the Islamic Movement in al-Numayrī's government in 1977 had brought it many advantages: it could continue to work semi-clandestinely and infiltrate organisations, especially in administration, where they were able to occupy key positions and subsequently distribute funds, building a growing power base from within the regime. In the 1970s, the Islamic Movement moved from 'campus to community' (Sidahmed 1997: 203). Due to ongoing control of the student organisations, it was also able to influence generations of students in their ideological orientation and thus to transform influence on the campus into influence in society, in particular among the *mughtaribūn*. The *mughtaribūn*, the emigrants to the Arabian peninsula, were central to the emergence of the Islamic Movement as a mass movement in the 1970s: in 1979, 10 per cent of Sudan's male population from the age of 20 to the age of 34, and in 1985 two-thirds of Sudan's skilled and professional workers were working in Saudi Arabia and the Gulf and were responsible for massive remittances (Sidahmed 1997: 195). These remittances remained outside the government-controlled currency exchange system and were often not invested in commercial ventures but hoarded or used for core family issues such as housing (Sidahmed 1997: 197): The *mughtaribūn* effectively refused to feed their remittances into larger clan structures, weakening the extended family, while at the same time strengthening female education and raising the degree of female participation in economic and public life: the absence of their men strengthened women at home (in the Sudan) (Sidahmed 1997: 199). All this led to a gradual breakdown of the old social order and enhanced the chances of the Islamic Movement that responded best to the new times.

Another social group that came to support Ḥasan al-Turabi were the *Fallāta*, that is, immigrants from sub-Saharan West Africa who had settled in the Sudan since the early twentieth century as pilgrims and migrant workers. In the 1970s, Ḥasan al-Turābī started to support the cause of the *Fallāta* in the context of his efforts to expand the social basis of the Islamic Movement. After 1989, West African migrants were granted Sudanese citizenship and thus joined Ḥasan al-Turābī's constituency (Burr and Collins 2010: 298). Equally, the *jallāba*, riverain traders who had come to settle in Sudan's peripheries and who despised both farmers and pastoralists for their rudimentary understanding of Islam and their customs, in particular their craving for millet beer (Beck 1993: 4), came to espouse the ideals of the Islamic Movement. With respect to women, rather than fighting for the *ḥijāb* or the re-domestication of women, the Islamic Movement tried to rationalise the prevailing situation, accepting their 'Islamic garb' but endorsing their rights in education and work and their engagement in public life, provided that they abide with *sharīᶜatic* regulations of modest dressing, decent behaviour and a measure of religiosity (Sidahmed 1997: 205–6).

Sudan's Salafi-oriented movement of reform thus emerged in Sudan's institutions of higher learning and was cultivated slowly by Sudan's educated urban middle-class groups that espoused the 'sober' mode of life of the ikhwān and their critique of established Sufi and Mahdist milieus as being essentially corrupt and un-Islamic (Beck 1993: 1). As bureaucrats, this social group inevitably came to control the state and thus had a real chance to implement politics of reform that were formulated by the ikhwān and that criticised established Sudanese religious and social practices (Seesemann 2005a: 21). The NIF most prominently gained the support of Sudan's rising urban middle-class groups in the riverain regions, the *awlād al-baḥr* (Fluehr-Lobban 2012: 303), and thus realised Ḥasan al-Turābī's strategy of expanding the social constituency of the Islamic Movement. Ḥasan al-Turābī's tactics were rewarded in October 1985 when the Islamic Movement was able to recapture control over KUSU (el-Affendi 1991: 139). In the general elections of April 1986, the NIF scored a remarkable victory: while the established blocks, Umma (now NNUP) and NUP (now DUP – Democratic Unionist Party) re-emerged as the two leading political fractions, gaining 100 and 63 seats in the new Parliament respectively, the NIF not only gained almost 20 per cent (18.47 per cent) of the vote (that is, in the region of 625,000 votes out of approximately 3.5 million, a remarkable rise since 1968), but also 51 seats[34] in the Parliament, and thus clearly emerged as a third political force in the Sudan (el-Affendi 1991: 141; Khalafalla 2004: 97). At the same time, Sudan's established political parties agreed to support the DUP candidate in Khartoum's Ṣaḥāfa constituency, where Ḥasan al-Turābī had chosen to run for a seat in Parliament and effectively prevented Ḥasan al-Turābī from obtaining a seat (Prunier 1989: 375).

By 1985, al-Numayrī's policies had deeply transformed Sudanese society and had led to the at least partial disintegration of established bonds and loyalties. The development of modern mass media, rapid urbanisation, the influx of hundreds of thousands of migrants into Sudan's major cities, especially greater Khartoum, as well as the emigration of more than a million Sudanese (in the region of 1.1 to 1.6 million) as workers to Saudi Arabia and the Gulf seriously challenged the established social order (el-Affendi 1991: 132). Greater Khartoum had grown from approximately 245,000 inhabitants in 1955 to 438,000 inhabitants in 1964 to about 1,343,000 in 1983, while the urban population grew from 11.1 per cent of the total population in 1971 to 26.5 per cent in 1980 (el-Affendi 1991: 133; Woodward 1990: 189). By 2004, greater Khartoum had possibly grown to 7to 8 million inhabitants (Fluehr-Lobban 2012: 1; see also Simone 1994), mostly migrants from Sudan's peripheric regions, including the south. As the Sudanese state was increasingly unable to provide basic services, the religious movements, in particular the Islamic Movement and its party, the NIF, started to provide basic securities. The Islamic Movement was successful in these endeavours, as its members had gained influence over the new Islamic banks that had been established in the mid-1970s, and that had started to supply small- and middle-scale merchants and businessmen as well as farmers with money, people who otherwise were unable to obtain credit. Of particular importance was the Faiṣal Islamic Bank of Sudan (FIBS), launched in 1978 by Muḥammad b. Faiṣal, a son of King Faiṣal of Saudi Arabia. This bank was owned to the tune of 60 per cent by businessmen from Saudi Arabia and the Gulf, while 40 per cent was controlled by Sudanese businessmen, only a minority of them being members of the Islamic Movement. However, the ikhwān were able to manage the new banking system: 'The significance of the Islamic financial institutions was that they opened up avenues of economic mobility for many who would otherwise have been at most high civil servants' (el-Affendi 1991: 117).

In many ways, the new banking system allowed the evolution of a new class of businessmen. In more general terms, the new system revolutionised access to credit, and the ikhwān were in a strategic position to utilise this revolution (el-Affendi 1991: 116). By 1982, FIBS had outstripped all other banks in terms of growth and profitability (Woodward 1990: 183). Due to the fact that the Islamic Movement was well placed in Arabia and the Gulf (due to their influence among the *mughtaribūn* and old networks between ikhwān and Salafi-oriented scholars in Saudi Arabia), the ikhwān were also able to play a paramount role in the emerging Islamic banking sector in the Sudan from 1978 (Sidahmed 1997: 208). The Islamic banking sector had free access to hard currency and such access was exempt from exchange control regulations: the *mughtaribūn* could thus use Islamic banks to transfer their remittances outside state control and invest freely (Sidahmed 1997: 209). These funds were often used in *mughtaribūn*-ikhwān business ventures and gave rise to a Salafi-oriented modern business class (Sidahmed 1997: 210): by the early 1980s, the Islamic Movement owned about 500 companies (Gallab 2008: 92). Thus, from 1977 there was a process of transformation of the Islamic Movement which has been characterised as 'the transformation of the Islamic Movement into an invisible corporation' (Gallab 2008: 79). Different groups and persons,

> were transferred and promoted back and forth from the party to the private institutions, from government to the public sector and from private and public sector to government. In this way, these groups developed and shared knowledge, accumulated wealth, and developed new tastes . . . [W]ithin the different phases of ascendancy to wealth, status and power, these groups and individuals worked together within the expanding Islamic economy and its banking system. (Gallab 2008: 79)

After the 1986 elections, a new government was formed by al-Ṣādiq al-Mahdī, yet failed to overcome the structural political crisis of the Sudan and collapsed in 1988. The NIF joined the new coalition government in 1988 and Ḥasan al-Turābī was appointed Minister of Justice and Attorney General of the Sudan. These positions enabled him to resume his 1979–83 political and administrative policy, and to push a series of Islamic laws to replace the 1983 'September' laws that had been suspended after al-Numayrī's fall in 1985 (el-Affendi 1991: 188). The NIF's insistence on the implementation of a codified system of Islamic law eventually led to the downfall of the coalition government in 1989 and to a third coup by the army under the leadership of

General ᶜUmar Ḥasan Aḥmad al-Bashīr on 30 June 1989: Ḥasan al-Turābī's concern to implement a codified system of Islamic law had turned out to be the major obstacle for peace with the Sudan People Liberation Army (SPLA) that fought for a secular Sudan and southern autonomy and that was not willing to accept *sharīᶜa* as the exclusive system of law for the Sudan. As a result of the coup, peace negotiations with the south were stopped by the new Revolutionary Command Council (RCC).

The 1989 coup was planned in detail by Ḥasan al-Turābī and his group and executed by fifteen junior officers, and was the introductory step of Ḥasan al-Turābī's project to rule Sudan himself (Gallab 2008: 78). Although imprisoned for a short period of time, Ḥasan al-Turābī and the NIF emerged quickly as the major supporter of the military regime and Ḥasan al-Turābī became the *éminence grise* of Sudan politics after 1990, although he initially acted only as a government emissary, in particular to Saudi Arabia. De facto, the Sudanese Army shared power with Ḥasan al-Turābī and the NIF until 1999, most probably due to the fact that the military lacked other civilian allies in the Sudan (Burr and Collins 2010: 131). The initial power group was the RCC led by ᶜUmar al-Bashīr, while the *éminence grise* was Ḥasan al-Turābī and the *tanẓīm sirrī*, the 'secret organization' (Gallab 2008: 80), of which ᶜUmar al-Bashīr was not a member.[35] In 1991, Ḥasan al-Turābī also established the Popular Arab Islamic Conference (PIAC) (al-muᵓtamar al-ᶜarabī al-shaᶜbī al-Islāmī) and became its secretary general. The PIAC was conceived as a coalition of revolutionary and non-governmental Islamic groups and organisations and as a counter-weight to the conservative and government-controlled Organization of the Islamic Conference (OIC) (Burr and Collins 2010: 60; see also de Waal 1994 and de Waal and Abdel Salam 2004). Until 1992, the NIF succeeded in taking control of both the RCC and a new security apparatus, the *amn al-ᶜāmm al-thawra* and in occupying a significant number of high-ranking positions in the army and the new Popular Defence Forces (*quwwāt al-difāᶜ al-shaᶜbī*). In 1993, the RCC was dissolved (Ahmed 2007: 192) and, in 1995, the National Congress (*al-muᵓtamar al-waṭanī*) took over as the supreme political body.

At the same time, the revolutionary regime expropriated the properties of al-Ṣādiq al-Mahdī and interdicted the Mirghāniyya, thus implementing a policy of marginalisation of the established political and religious movements in the Sudan. In order to compensate this policy, which was directed against the Anṣār and the Khatmiyya, and to broaden the social basis of the revolution, Ḥasan al-Turābī inaugurated a new policy toward Sufism that differentiated between blameworthy Sufi practices and 'false' Sufis on the one hand and 'true' Sufis in line with the revolution on the other. For these 'true' Sufis, the regime started to use the term '*ahl al-dhikr*' ('those who remember God'), invoking a verse of the Qurʾān that asks believers to 'remember God with much remembrance' (*udhkurū Allāha dhikran kathīran*) (Qurʾān 33: 41; Seesemann 2006b: 34; see also Mahmoud 1997: 162ff). In 1993, this policy led to a first 'conference of remembrance and those who remember God' (*al-muʾtamar al-dhikr wa-l-dhākirīn*) in Khartoum that united delegates from African countries such as Egypt, Libya, Nigeria and Senegal, declaring their loyalty towards the regime. In 1995, ᶜAlī ᶜUthmān Muḥammad Ṭāhā, the Minister of Social Planning, set up a sub-section of the ministry, the *majlis al-qawmī li-l-dhikr wa-l-dhākirīn* that was assigned the task of linking the regime with Sudan's Sufi orders and coordinating their activities (Seesemann 2006b: 35). ᶜAlī ᶜUthmān Muḥammad Ṭāhā (b. 1947) was Ḥasan al-Turābī's 'right hand man' in the NIF. Like al-Turābī, he had studied law at the University of Khartoum since 1966, had become President of KUSU in 1969 and was central to the implementation of *sharīᶜa* laws from 1979. ᶜAlī ᶜUthmān Muḥammad Ṭāhā also was a schoolmate of ᶜUmar Ḥasan al-Bashīr, and was seen as the architect-in-chief of the 1989 coup (Gallab 2008: 2). He represented a younger generation of the Islamic Movement in 1989. After 1992, he set up a number of revolutionary mass organisations such as the People's Police (*al-shurṭa al-shaᶜbiyya*) and the Comprehensive Mission (*al-daᶜwa al-shāmila*) which targeted 'detrimental customs and traditions' (*al-ᶜādāt wa-l-taqālīd al-ḍārra*), such as the *zār* spirit possession ritual, the production and consumption of millet beer, lengthy funeral ceremonies and the practice of 'wailing' (*bikāʾ*), visiting the tombs of saints and female genital mutilation (Seesemann 2006b: 28). He was appointed Minister of Social Planning in 1993 and Minister of Foreign Affairs in 1995.[36]

After the coup, Ḥasan al-Turābī and ᶜUmar al-Bashīr started to purge the judiciary of non-NIF members and new special courts were established that implemented the new Islamic jurisdiction (Burr and Collins 2010: 19–20). The 'September' *ḥudūd* regulations that had been suspended in

1985, were enforced again, civil judges who protested against these measures were imprisoned on 31 July 1989 and fifty-seven high-ranking civil judges were permanently dismissed from office on 21 August 1989. They were replaced by judges known for their NIF sympathies (Köndgen 1993: 239). Equally, middle and lower officer ranks in the army were purged and non-commissioned officers were replaced by NIF sympathisers. In 1989, nearly 40 per cent of the officer corps were dismissed (Warburg 2003: 210) and in 1990, in the region of 20,000 functionaries of the state, judges and professors as well as army officers were replaced by members or sympathisers of the Islamic Movement (Köndgen 1993: 239). A consequence of the take-over of power of the NIF in 1989 was a generational turn-over in Sudanese politics: the 60–70-year-olds were replaced by 30–40-year-olds, often coming from a provincial background. The new ruling elites were less Westernised than their predecessors, who had ruled Sudan since 1954 (O'Fahey 1997: 59).

The coup was quickly re-labelled a revolution for 'national salvation' (*al-inqādh al-waṭanī*) and its task was to implement an Islamic 'civilizing project' (*mashrū*ᶜ *al-ḥaḍarī*),[37] understood as a new Islamic social order, by pushing for the 'Islamization of knowledge'[38] and by introducing a comprehensive codified system of Islamic law. However, since the enactment of the new penal code based on the *sharīᶜa* on 22 March 1991, it has been implemented rather leniently (compared to the application of the September laws in 1984/5): there has been almost no stoning, amputation or crucifixion, but widespread flogging, mostly for alcohol consumption. This lenient application of the *sharīᶜa* penal laws was intended to show the 'merciful' nature of Islam by limiting *ḥudūd* punishments (Sidahmed 1997: 220). After 1991, *sharīᶜa* became less a method to implement a social model and a specific agenda, but a symbol that enhanced the regime's Islamic legitimacy and served to draw a boundary between Sudan and its opponents. It showed the regime's authenticity and independence. *Sharīᶜa* was thus a central part of the *mashrū*ᶜ *al-ḥaḍarī*, like Islamic economics, Islamisation of the media and education, imposition of the *ḥijāb* (but not the *niqāb*) for women and a new ministry of social planning that was in charge of the implementation of the Islamisation programme (Sidahmed 1997: 222). A major feature of the *mashrū*ᶜ *al-ḥaḍarī* (or *mashrū*ᶜ *al-islāmī*) was the mobilisation of Muslim women, a programme formulated in Ḥasan al-Turābī's text *al-marʾa fī l-taᶜalīm al-Islām* ('Woman in the Teachings of Islam') (published 1973), where Ḥasan al-Turābī advocated the freedom of women, for instance to conduct business and to take part in politics (Seesemann 2005a: 9–10).

In order to enforce the *mashrū*ᶜ *al-ḥaḍarī*, a 'totalitarian system' (*niẓām shāmilī*) was established (Gallab 2008: 94). This was resented by parts of the 'corporation' who preferred a military ruler to Ḥasan al-Turābī's ideological programme (Gallab 2008: 94/95). Opponents of the regime of the Islamic Movement criticised the *mashrū*ᶜ *al-ḥaḍarī* as a 'grandiose name' that was but 'a cover for a totalitarian regime that needed ideological and intellectual legitimacy' (el-Tinay 2005: 20). The most notorious feature of the *niẓām shāmilī* were the 'ghost houses' where the regime tortured hundreds of opponents (Gallab 2008: 113). The regime also controlled the media, purged the higher and middle ranks of the state apparatus and replaced them by loyal party members. The 'corporation' also tightened control over the state apparatus and used party members as an auxiliary arm of the security apparatus, using the coercive powers of the state to eliminate other seats of power. The result was an authoritarian regime that ruled more and more over the lives of the citizens. The Ministry of Social Planning, led by ᶜAlī ᶜUthmān Muḥammad Ṭāhā, was the central institution for overseeing the *mashrū*ᶜ *al-ḥaḍarī* and monitoring the internal affairs of the entire regime (Gallab 2008: 119).

In 1996, elections for the National Assembly took place, and Ḥasan al-Turābī was elected President of the National Assembly and subsequently also Speaker of Parliament, while ᶜUmar al-Bashīr was elected president of the Sudan. In 1999, Ḥasan al-Turābī was deposed, however, in the context of a power struggle with General ᶜUmar al-Bashīr and those senior officers within the Sudanese Army who did not support Ḥasan al-Turābī's project of Islamisation of the Sudan. On 12 December 1999, the Sudanese Army surrounded the legislative building, dismissed al-Turābī as Speaker of Parliament and dissolved the Assembly (Gallab 2008: 129). A state of emergency was proclaimed and the PIAC was shut down on 10 February 2000. Nine ministers loyal to Ḥasan al-Turābī were fired, while others, led by ᶜAlī ᶜUthmān Muḥammad Ṭāhā, went over to al-Bashīr and abandoned Ḥasan al-Turābī (Burr and Collins 2010: 273). ᶜAlī ᶜUthmān Muḥammad Ṭaha represented the younger generation in the Islamic Movement that had been incorporated into the system and allowed to rise in the 'corporation' after 1985 and that had slowly replaced the older generation (Gallab 2008: 109). Ḥasan al-Turābī was the last representative of the older generation to be replaced in 1999. By spring 2000, al-Bashīr had disarmed Ḥasan al-Turābī. Ironically enough, Ḥasan al-Turābī's old foes within the Islamic Movement, who had rejected 'coalition' (*iʾtilāf*), now started to support al-Bashīr and were rewarded with positions in the government: the ḥizb al-ikhwān al-muslimīn got the Ministry of Religious Affairs, while the al-Hadiyya/*markaz*-branch of the anṣār al-sunna al-muḥammadiyya got the Ministry of Education (E. Ahmed 2007: 206, 2015: 172). In order to mobilise ideological support, ᶜUmar al-Bashīr thus turned to the 'educationalist' core group of the ikhwān, that is, 'the enemy of its enemy' (Ahmed 2007: 199). Since then, the ikhwān and the al-Hadiyya branch of the anṣār al-sunna al-muḥammadiyya supported the regime of ᶜUmar al-Bashīr against Ḥasan al-Turābī and his network, while Ḥasan al-Turābī, having lost institutional protection, became the 'favorite whipping boy for everyone from Sufis to Salafis'(Salomon 2009a: 149).

The critique from within the Islamic Movement against Ḥasan al-Turābī started in 1995 with the publication of ᶜAbd al-Wahhāb el-Affendī's book *al-thaura wa-l-iṣlāḥ al-siyāsī fi-l-Sūdān* (The Revolution and Political Reform in the Sudan), in which the author claimed that the revolution had betrayed itself and appealed to Ḥasan al-Turābī to bring the revolution back on course. This text triggered a lively internal debate in newspapers and magazines (O'Fahey 1997: 62). In December 1998 a memorandum of ten leading members of the Islamic Movement and members of the Consultative Council (for the new constitution) protested against Ḥasan al-Turābī's preponderant powers and thus unveiled divisions within the leading elite. Sayyid al-Khaṭīb, Ghāzī Ṣalaḥ al-Dīn al-ᶜAṭabānī, Aḥmad ᶜAlī al-Imām, Aḥmad Torin, Bakrī Ḥasan Ṣāliḥ, Ibrāhīm Aḥmad ᶜUmar, Bahāʾ al-Dīn Ḥanafī, Mutrif Ṣidīq, Nafī ᶜAlī Nafī and ᶜUthmān Khālid Mudāwī (Gallab 2008: 129) criticised the achievements of the first ten years of the revolution and proposed reforms that would have stripped Ḥasan al-Turābī of his powers. The conflict between General ᶜUmar al-Bashīr and Ḥasan al-Turābī also led to a split within the NIF. In May 2000 supporters of al-Bashīr led by Ḥasan al-Turābī's old protégé ᶜAlī ᶜUthmān Muḥammad Ṭāhā took over control of the National Congress Party (founded by Ḥasan al-Turābī in 1998), while Ḥasan al-Turābī and a minority of the NIF set up the Popular National Congress in October 2000. Despite a number of prison terms in 2001–3, 2004, 2009, 2010 and 2011, Ḥasan al-Turābī continued to be active in politics and built alliances with forces from Sudan's peripheral regions, in particular Darfur.[39] He was quickly accused of supporting the dissident Justice and Equality Movement (JEM) (ḥarakat al-ᶜadl wa-l-musāwa) in Darfur, led by a friend of Ḥasan al-Turābī, Dr Khalīl Ibrāhīm. This movement had started a rebellion against the central government in 1999, fired by the publication, in 2000, of the *kitāb al-aswad* on Darfur's historical and ongoing marginalisation, a document that targeted the al-Bashīr administration for its corrupt politics.[40]

Ḥasan al-Turābī's fall came at a time when it had become clear that he was about to directly attack ᶜUmar al-Bashīr's leading role in the government of the Sudan and to develop a plan for his effective removal from power. Ḥasan al-Turābī started manoeuvring in 1998, although a political gap between him and ᶜUmar al-Bashīr had already started to develop in 1996, when Ḥasan al-Turābī's radical allies, in particular, parts of the Bin Lādin family, which had been residing in Khartoum since 1991, threatened to become a dangerous liability for the stability of the military regime. In 1996, the Sudanese Government asked Usāma b. Lādin to leave the Sudan. Still, the USA kept Sudan under surveillance and decided to bomb the al-Shifāᵓ factory for medical supplies in 1998, adding to the pressure on the al-Bashīr regime to dissociate itself from Ḥasan al-Turābī (Burr and Collins 2010: 69ff). In addition to slow rehabilitation of its international standing, the regime hoped to improve its economic standing by first exports of oil in 1999, and thus to develop a policy of development independent of Saudi Arabia and the Gulf, in particular, Qaṭar, from where Ḥasan al-Turābī drew major support. The demise of Ḥasan al-Turābī also led to the demise of the *mashrūᶜ al-ḥaḍarī*. This movement became increasingly unpopular among Sudan's rising middle-class groups because of its moralistic programme and policies of supervision and patrolling of the public sphere by special security forces as well as the Public Defence Forces. This practice was stopped in 2000 (Fluehr-Lobban 2012: 187–207) and secured the al-Bashīr regime the support of the urban middle-class groups.

As a result of the 1999 coup against Ḥasan al-Turābī, a younger generation of *tarbiya*-minded Muslims came to power and ᶜUmar Ḥasan al-Bashīr now became the strong man of the regime. 'Confronted with the looming threat of Islamism or al-Turabism as an enforced religion' (Gallab 2008: 139, 149), many Muslims beyond the Islamic Movement reaffirmed their religious identity in opposition to the Islamic Movement's concepts of religion. The enforcement of a particular interpretation of religion mobilised opposition on the part of those who were excluded by the Islamist vision of religion: 'Thus, religion as a private activity presented a serious challenge to state-imposed religiosity and became a source of empowerment for those who stood in defiance of the regime' (Gallab 2008: 149) or in defiance of Ḥasan al-Turābī within the army. These dynamics led to an increase of participation in Sufi activities and *mawlid* celebrations, not only those organised by the Anṣār or the Khatmiyya, but also those of other Sufi groups (Gallab 2008: 140).

Central to Ḥasan al-Turābī's ideological position was his stress of *tajdīd* (reform) with respect to *fiqh* and, consequently, his claim to *irshād* (guidance). According to Ḥasan al-Turābī, 'the Muslim community had fallen into the abyss of dogma and blind imitation' (el-Affendi 1991: 171). Ḥasan al-Turābī's programme of reform consequently addressed the issue of the religious and political role of Muslim women most clearly and demanded their religious and political liberation (el-Affendi 1991: 174), a demand that had already been made in his 1973 text *al-marʾa fī t-taᶜalīm al-Islām* that was influenced by his wife Wisāl al-Mahdī who also became a leading figure in the NIF (Seesemann 2005a: 15). In a famous interview with al-ᶜArabiyya on 10 April 2006, Ḥasan al-Turābī stressed his emancipatory positions by declaring, among other things, that women, having converted to Islam, could remain married to their non-Muslim husbands. Equally, women could act as *imām* under certain circumstances. In addition, he defended the citizens' rights to a private sphere and condemned efforts to supervise this private sphere and control the consumption of alcohol by Muslims. An important argument in the discussion over the duty of 'commanding right and forbidding wrong' was that Muslims were obliged to respect 'privacy', that is, the sanctity of the home: one should not seek to expose people or spy on them, an injunction that is based on the Qurʾān (49: 12; 2: 189 and 24:27) and Prophetic traditions (Cook 2000: 44, 80f). As a result of his highly controversial statements, which have to be seen, however, in a history of independent reasoning, Ḥasan al-Turābī was accused of heresy in a *fatwā* entitled *al-qawl al-fasl fi l-radd ᶜalā man kharāj ᶜan al-aṣl* ('The statement of dismissal in response to him who deviated from the foundation') by the Islamic Jurisprudence Council of Sudan and he was asked to either repent or face the *ḥadd* punishment for heresy (Fluehr-Lobban 2012: 297). Ḥasan al-Turābī had been accused of apostasy for the first time in 1995/6 by members of the 'educationalist' wing of the Islamic movement, in particular Jaᶜfar Shaykh Idrīs, in a reaction to his call for dialogue between the Abrahamitic religions, his idea that 'rising in arms' against other Muslims should be seen as true apostasy and his statement that Salman Rushdie would not have been sentenced for apostasy if he had been tried in the Sudan (Ibrahim 1999: 217).

Ḥasan al-Turābī's thinking was characterised by his opposition to established religious authorities, Sufis, Mahdists and *ᶜulamā'*, who he regarded as incapable of addressing the challenges of modernity as represented by Sudan's 'effendiyya' class (Ibrahim 1999: 196). Sufis were seen as being too withdrawn from the state to tap its potential in a world where the state had become indispensable to religion. Mahdists were seen as being plagued by their millenaristic beliefs and their willingness to wait for the 'guided one', while Muslims, according to Ḥasan al-Turābī, could not afford to wait any longer. The *ᶜulamā'* were seen as intruders into the affairs of the state, as self-appointed keepers of the faith who should never have existed at all (Ibrahim 1999: 196–207). Ḥasan al-Turābī, by contrast, proposed to merge tradition and modernity, and to establish a third path between modernity and tradition, beyond Sufis and the Mahdiyya. In this concept, Islam was seen as a way to 'humanize' modernity (Ibrahim 1999: 196). At the same time, Ḥasan al-Turābī criticised the claims of the effendi-class, that is, the modern educated elite, consisting of bureaucrats and graduates, to represent modernity: they had been colonised and become secular in their thinking. As a consequence, they had become unable to interrogate modernity as Muslims (Ibrahim 1999: 197, 206 and 213).

Due to the fact that his father, ᶜAbdallāh Dafᶜallah al-Turābī (1889–1990), had been a *qāḍī* in the British colonial administration from 1924 onwards, Ḥasan al-Turābī had the chance to witness first hand the colonial separation of politics and Islamic law (that was reduced, in any case, to Islamic personal law). In the colonial judicial system, the *qāḍī* had been the 'primitive other' of the modern judge (Ibrahim 1999: 200), a differentiation that continued after independence until Ḥasan al-Turābī had the chance to change this set-up after 1990 by building a new system of law courts, making the established system of jurisdiction redundant. The state was at the centre of Ḥasan al-Turābī's political thinking, yet, due to the fact that the state and religion had been separate in the history of Islam after the time of the 'venerable forefathers' and even more so in modernity, the state had become 'inattentative' to religion (*ghāfila min al-dīn*). The task of reform was thus to gain control over the state and to transform the state in a way that it would 'atone to religion' (*tatūb ilā l-dīn*) (Ibrahim 1999: 204). One aspect of such a strategy would be to create a united judiciary, a demand that had already been made in 1968, and to end the separation between *qāḍī* courts and civil courts, a policy that was implemented in 1989.

Closely connected to Ḥasan al-Turābī's ideas about the state was the concept of *ibtilāʾ* (trial, visitation), that is, experiencing life as a perpetual challenge by God to test a Muslim's faith. According to Ḥasan al-Turābī, modernity was the *ibtilāʾ* of present times for Muslims (Ibrahim 1999: 202). Ḥasan al-Turābī also stressed the need to differentiate between *al-dīn al-ḥaqq* (true religion) and *al-dīn al-kasb* (acquired traditional religion). In many ways, Ḥasan al-Turābī must be seen as an innovative and provocative thinker, who has often been portrayed as a power-hungry politician and opportunist. However, such a perspective omits the fact that many of Ḥasan al-Turābī's ideas, such as those on the role of Muslim women, were formulated early in his career and that he consistently stuck to his basic concepts. Second, it has to be taken into account that Ḥasan al-Turābī's political strategy was informed primarily by his efforts to broaden the social basis for his movement of reform and that he was willing to swallow bitter pills in order to achieve this goal. The fact that he was able to score a remarkable result in the 1986 democratic elections and to acquire a power-sharing role in the revolution after 1990 proved him right, even though he eventually failed to realise his programme of reform due to the fact that the leading ranks of the Sudanese Army were not willing to be phased out of power.

The history of the Sudan since independence shows that the Salafi-oriented movement was divided into at least two groups. On the one hand there was the 'ideological' *tarbiya*-oriented line, which essentially intended to form a small intellectual elite, rejected coalitions of convenience or strategy with other Muslim groups and insisted on the purity of the doctrine. On the other hand, there was a pragmatic *siyāsa*-oriented line that wanted to broaden the social basis of the Islamic Movement, was willing to enter strategic coalitions and was willing to sideline ideological arguments for the sake of the greater cause. Ḥasan al-Turābī consistently followed a pragmatic line, which led to accusations of opportunism.[41] Due to his undisputable successes, such as the formation of the ICF in the 1960s and the victory of the NIF in the elections of 1986, he was, however, repeatedly able to silence or marginalise his internal opponents among the 'ideologists'.

Throughout his life, Ḥasan al-Turābī pursued three major goals: the establishment of an Islamic constitution and a codified system of Islamic law, the emancipation of Muslim women and the expansion of the social basis of the Islamic Movement in its different forms, that is, ICF and NIF. In the 1980s, and especially in the 1990s, he seemed to be about to achieve these goals due to the fact that he had been able to win major parts of the new urban middle-class groups, the students, the *mughtaribūn*, the *jallāba* and the Fallāta, as well as parts of the army, the judiciary and the bureaucratic echelons of the state, yet these new social groups were not willing to follow him on the path towards a strict Islamic moral order and thus remained inactive when ᶜUmar al-Bashīr started to move against Ḥasan al-Turābī in 1999. The al-Bashīr regime promised to stop interference in private affairs and to respect the economic interests of the middle-class groups. In exchange, these social groups were willing to support the military regime and to drop an overzealous Ḥasan al-Turābī and his *mashrūᶜ al-ḥaḍarī*.

Ethiopia

While in Sudan Muslims constituted an undisputed but fragmented majority (that became even greater after the independence of Southern Sudan in 2011), Ethiopia was characterised by the fact that its Muslim population was not only highly fragmented but also marginalised in political terms, although Muslims constitute a strong minority within Ethiopia's total population. At the same time, Ethiopia's Islamic legacy is the oldest in Africa, going back to the early seventh century, while the advent of Islam in the Sudan occurred in the sixteenth century only (see Hussein Ahmed 2006; Loimeier 2013;

Moten 1993). The representation of Ethiopia as a Christian island surrounded by Islam is thus misleading, even if Ethiopia is surrounded by mostly Muslim societies: first, Muslims have been living in the 'Christian' highlands for a long period of time, possibly since the seventh century, that is, almost as long as Christians. These Muslims were not outsiders but belonged to the ethnic groups of the highlands. As traders (*jabarti*), Muslims formed an important link to Ethiopia's neighbouring markets.[42] Second, Muslims in the lowlands have been integrated in multiple relations of exchange with highland populations, in particular, trade (see Triulzi 1981). Third, Ethiopian (Muslim) history shows that Muslims were not automatically united by the fact that they were Muslims – with the historical exception of the *jihād* by Imām Aḥmad b. Ibrāhīm al-Ghāzī (in Christian traditions Aḥmad 'Grañ'), one reason why this episode has become so important for Ethiopian history, both Christian and Muslim. However, in major parts of Ethiopian history, the different Bija groups, the Tigre, the different groups of the (Muslim) Oromo, the Somali and ᶜAfar, the Hadiya or the Bānū Shangul have been disunited and have been characterised by their different linguistic, ethnic and cultural traditions and historical legacies. In many respects, Muslims in Ethiopia have thus been a 'double periphery' (Triulzi 1981: 181), with respect to both the dominant Christian highland populations and the Muslim populations and empires of the larger region, that is, northeast Africa and the Arabian Peninsula. At the same time, Muslims (and Christians) were marked by a history of entanglements through trade and shrine visits, as well as the emergence in the nineteenth century of a number of Sufi-oriented movements of reform.[43] Even before the emergence of Sufi orders as major religious movements in nineteenth-century Ethiopia, Muslim religiosity in Ethiopia was informed by the cult of saints and their tombs, and shrine visits, such as the shrine pilgrimage to the *Dirre* ('open field') of Shaykh Ḥusayn in Gololcha district in northern Bale (Østebø 2008a: 77).

In the mid-nineteenth century, Sufi orders started to expand to different parts of Ethiopia, led by scholars such as Muḥammad Shāfī b. ᶜAskarī Muḥammad (1743–1806) for the Qādiriyya, al-Ḥājj Bushra Ay Muḥammad (d. 1863) for the Sammāniyya (Hussein Ahmed 2001: 89) or Talḥa b. Jaᶜfar b. Yūsuf (Hussein Ahmed 1989: 17ff). These scholars can be regarded as a group of religious scholars who represented a first tradition of Sufi-oriented reform in Ethiopia, characterised by its struggle against local religious traditions, against 'lax' Muslims and compromising rulers, against the mixing of Islam with pre-Islamic cults, and active resistance to Ethiopian imperial expansion under emperors Yohannes IV (r. 1868–89) and Menilek II (r. 1889–1913), which led to the forceful integration into the Ethiopian empire of numerous Muslim polities in Wällo, Shäwa and Wälläga in the second half of the nineteenth century. Yet again, the Sufi-oriented movements of reform were never united, but split by their affiliation with different Sufi orders as well as their local focus in Wällo or in the Gibe region, where Jimma became a major centre of Islam (see Guluma Gemeda 1993, 2008).

After the incorporation into the Ethiopian Empire in the late nineteenth century of vast territories in the east, south and west that had considerable Muslim populations, Islam was more or less tolerated by Emperors Menilek II, Lij Iyasu (r. 1913–16)[44] and Haile Selassie (r. 1916–74). The treatment of Muslims as 'second class' citizens in Imperial Ethiopia backfired when Italy invaded Ethiopia in 1935 and gained support among the marginalised Muslim populations, in particular the Somali and the Oromo (Loimeier 2013: 193f). Under Italian administration, Islam experienced a boom, Amhara dominance was broken, land was granted to the tenant farmers and tribute obligations were abolished. From 1936 to 1941, fifty new mosques were built and sixteen old ones were restored. Arabic was accepted as an official language and the pilgrimage to Mecca was supported: in 1933, only eleven Ethiopians had gone on pilgrimage, while in 1936 the number rose to in the region of 1,600 to 1,900, and in 1939 to 3,585; in 1942, the number dropped to 57 again (Hussein Ahmed 2006: 9; Østebø 2008a: 131). Also, Italy recognised *qāḍī* courts. This situation changed again in 1941, when Haile Selassie resumed power and Muslims were regarded as collaborators and systematically excluded from high-level government and army positions (Desplat and Østebø 2013: 7). Still, Muslim jurisdiction in the form of *qāḍī* courts was accepted without being recognised officially. In 1944, the Muhammedan Courts Act recognised Islamic personal law (Abbink 2007: 70). Also, a *sharī^{c}a* court of appeal was established in Addis Ababa in 1944. However, Muslim jurisdiction was never formally accepted as part of the Ethiopian legal system, even if Muslims were assured that Muslim courts could function informally (Markakis 2011: 117). In 1958, Haile Selassie commissioned the translation of the Qurʾān into Amhariña, saying: 'The country is a public, religion is a private matter' (Abbink 2007: 70). At the same time, the monarchy observed Muslim activities attentively. In 1966, for instance, an association of several hundred Muslims united in the Salamawi Mahaber at the Anwār mosque in Addis Ababa's Mercato area was asked to stop their meetings, and in 1967, the appearance of a Muslim Students' Association at the University of Addis Ababa triggered a ban on all student religious associations (Markakis 2006: 222).

From the 1940s, Ethiopia had to deal with a number of secessionist and regionalist movements that were informed by the fact that Muslims played a major role. These movements were triggered by – among other things – the suppression by the central government of everything non-Amharic, a tradition that was continued implicitly by the military regime of Mengistu Haile Mariam (r. 1974–91). In the 1940s, Muslims in Harar supported the idea of a greater Somalia, and in July 1960, the Eritrean Liberation Front (ELF) started a rebellion against Ethiopia that led to Eritrea's independence in 1993 (Marcus 2002: 174).[45] Another object of Ethiopian preoccupations was the (Somali) Ogaden Liberation Front, that had become active militarily in June 1963 and that was led by a Muslim scholar, Ṭāhir Maqtal, a movement crushed in March 1964. In the 1970s, Somali nationalist aspirations were represented by – among others – the Western Somali Liberation Front (WSLF) that managed to liberate major parts of the Ogaden region in 1977 and cooperated in President Siad Barre's invasion of Ethiopia in 1977. When Ethiopia, with Cuban and Soviet support, defeated the Somali invasion in March 1978, the WSLF collapsed and had to withdraw to Somalia (Marcus 2002: 197f). Last but not least the Bale region saw a first Oromo rebellion from 1963 to 1970 led by Waqo Gutu (Erlich 2010: 152). The Bale rebellion caused a lot of insecurity and state repression, in particular against pilgrims and shrine pilgrims and wandering mystics (Østebø 2013a: 54).[46]

In 1974, the situation changed completely: a devastating drought and famine uncovered the monarchy's basic inability to deal with the crisis and implement reforms. In June 1974, Haile Selassie's government was deposed by the army and Haile Selassie himself was dethroned on 12 September 1974. The revolution led to the emergence of a new (military) regime, led by the Derg (committee), established on 28 June 1974 and led first by

General Aman Mikael Andom (r. until late 1974), and subsequently by Major Mengistu Haile Mariam (r. 1974–91). In the period of transition from 1974 and the consolidation of the dictatorial rule of the Derg in 1977, so far muted voices had the chance to express their expectations. Muslims used this chance: on 20 April 1974, there was a first mass demonstration of Muslims in Addis Ababa who raised thirteen demands regarding the position of Muslims in Ethiopia (Hussein Ahmed 2006: 10). Three of these demands were granted on 23 December 1974: the new regime declared equality of all religions, recognised the *ᶜīd al-fiṭr*, the *ᶜīd al-aḍḥa* and the *mawlid al-nabī* as national holidays (Erlich 1977: 15), and agreed to change the official way of referring to Muslims in Ethiopia who were not labelled any more as 'Muslims living in Ethiopia' but as 'Ethiopian Muslims' (Østebø 2008a: 194). In 1976, the Ethiopian Supreme Council for Islamic Affairs (ESCIA) was established (but was registered de jure only in 1991). Also, new mosques and *madāris* were permitted to be built, although this triggered Christian protest (Hussein Ahmed 2006: 12f). This tolerant policy toward religion, and especially Islam, changed in 1977 into a policy with an anti-religious character (Abbink 2007: 70): the Derg ended the privileged status of the Orthodox Church,[47] nationalised all Church and waqf properties, eliminated all state subventions and put religious activities under surveillance. Both pilgrimage and the import of texts were seriously restricted (Desplat and Østebø 2013: 7). Also, the building of mosques was stopped, although old ones were not demolished or closed. There was a marked decline in shrine pilgrimages and religion was officially shunned or even repressed. Equally, the nascent Salafi-oriented movement of reform was checked and made no progress, due to state repression, and went underground. The Derg period saw a massive growth of secular education, the demise of established religious and political authorities and propaganda by a regime denying the existence of God (Østebø 2008a: 223). The Derg considered religion as a private matter, and public manifestations of religion were shunned or outright prohibited: the Derg was the time 'when Muslims started to eat Christian meat' (Østebø 2013a: 52), and after 1991 the youth were 'dissociated from the past, frustrated about the present and bewildered about the future' (Østebø 2013a: 53). In many ways the Derg had the same agenda as the Salafis who also criticised established religious authorities and traditions, and thus prepared the way for the growth of Salafi-oriented reform after the collapse of the Derg in 1991 (Østebø 2008a: 226).

The victory of the Tigray People's Liberation Front (TPLF) and its allies, such as the Eritrean People's Liberation Front (EPLF), over the regime of Mengistu Haile Maryam in 1991 changed this situation. In May 1991 Ethiopia was transformed into a federal state where regional autonomies and even secession (Eritrea in 1993) was possible.[48] The change of regime in 1991 came to constitute a real watershed: religious freedom was finally granted and the new government under the leadership of Meles Zenawi (1955–2012) (r. 1991-2012)[49] and the Ethiopian People's Revolutionary Democratic Front (EPRDF) actively encouraged Muslims to participate in national and regional politics. Since 1991, Islam has been equal to Christianity in the face of the law and the constitution (and religious freedom was enshrined in the 1995 constitution). The year 1991 also brought the lifting of the ban on religious activities, freedom of the press, a boom in mosque and *madrasa* building, as well as a significant rise in the number of pilgrims: in 1993, in the region of 4,000 pilgrims from Ethiopia were able to perform the pilgrimage (Hussein Ahmed 1998: 104). In 1992, the Ethiopian Supreme Council for Islamic Affairs' (ESCIA, or, for short, *majlis*) was restructured (Østebø 2008a: 229), and al-Ḥājj Muḥammad Aḥmad Saᶜīd became its chairperson (Hussein Ahmed 1998: 99).

As a result of this liberalisation, numerous Christian and Islamic NGOs were established: in 2000, there were thirteen Muslim NGOs in Ethiopia, while none had existed in 1980 (Abbink 2007: 73). Since 1992, a number of new Muslim associations were founded in Addis Ababa, such as the Ethiopian Muslim Youth Association led by Sayyid Aḥmad Muṣṭafa and Muḥammad ᶜUthman, and the Islamic Daᶜwa and Knowledge Association led by Ṭāhir ᶜAbd al-Qādir from Bale. The Ethiopian Muslim Youth Association got financial support from Saudi Arabia and was affiliated with the World Association of Muslim Youth (WAMY) (Østebø 2008a: 232, 2008b: 421). Last but not least, there was the Awaliyah School and Mission Centre that has received support from International Islamic Relief since 1993. The centre for Salafi-minded Muslims in Addis Ababa was the Ayr Tena quarter (Østebø 2008b: 421). In 1994 a new radical Salafi-minded group emerged, al-takfīr wa-l-hijra, founded by Muḥammad Amīn, who had come back from Sudan in 1992. The group grew to considerable strength in Gondar from 1994 to 1997, and also spread to Addis Ababa in 1994, where it acquired a foothold in the Terro quarter. Due to the fact that al-takfīr wa-l-hijra pronounced the *takfīr* not only against other Muslims but even against other Salafis, it became increasingly isolated after Muḥammad Amīn's death in 2004 (Østebø 2008b: 423, 2010: 23ff). In addition to the emergence of new Muslim associations, there was a boom in other Islamic activities from 1991, often centred in the Anwār mosque in Addis Ababa. The number of Ethiopian pilgrims to Mecca continued to grow, and so did the number of new mosques (Hussein Ahmed 2006: 16). At the same time, Salafi-minded groups found a social basis among the unemployed urban youth. As a result, clashes between these radical groups and followers of Sufi traditions, as well as Christians, have become more frequent since 1991 (Abbink 2007: 74). Particularly conspicuous in Muslim–Christian relations in Ethiopia were the events in Jimma in 2006 and 2011, where Muslims, possibly affiliated with al-takfīr wa-l-hijra, clashed with Christians (Østebø 2010: 23, 32):[50] On 1 October 2006, nine Muslims and two Christians were killed and two churches set ablaze in Dembi, about 70 km northwest of Jimma, when Christians accused Muslims of interfering in (Orthodox) Meskal (Holy Cross) festivities, while Muslims accused Christians of desecrating the Qurʾān. On 3 March 2011, one Christian was killed in Asendabo, about 50 km northeast of Jimma. He was accused of desecrating the Qurʾān. In the 2011 riots, almost sixty church buildings were destroyed. This time, the targets for destruction were a broad range of Ethiopian evangelical churches and not the Ethiopian Orthodox Church, including thirty-eight church buildings of the Ethiopian Kale Hiwot Church, twelve buildings of the Mekane Yesus Church, six buildings of the Seventh Day Adventist Church, two Muluwongel buildings and one Jesus Only building.[51]

After 1991, there was also an increase in the number of texts in Arabic and Amhariña, as well as translations of texts from English into Amhariña, often financed by private Muslim publishing houses such as the Najashi Publishing House or organisations such as the Ethiopian Muslim Youth Organization (Hussein Ahmed 1998: 90). From 1992 (to 1995), the first Islamic magazine, *Bilāl* was published. This magazine and the University of Addis Ababa became the major strongholds of the 'intellectualist' group of

Salafis in Ethiopia that has remained, however, rather marginal, due to its urban and 'university campus' elitism (Østebø 2008b: 425ff). In the first editions of the magazine, one issue of debate was the wish of Muslims to build a mosque in Axum, a city that was regarded by Ethiopian Orthodox Christians as a holy city of Christianity. While this claim was rejected by the EOC, Muslims argued: 'Mecca is Arab, Axum is Ethiopian, a town of both Christians and Muslims' (Hussein Ahmed 1998: 98). Other articles claimed that Muslims formed 65 per cent of the Ethiopian population (Carmichael 1996: 177). Since 1991, Ethiopia has indeed known a 'numbers game', like Nigeria, Kenya and Tanzania, regarding the true number of Muslims and Christians: the census of 1994 announced that there were 50.6 per cent Orthodox Christians, 32.8 per cent Muslims and 10.1 per cent Protestants, while the 2007 census resulted in 43.5 per cent Orthodox Christians, 33.9 per cent Muslims and 18.6 per cent Protestants (Desplat and Østebø 2013: 5). These census data have been rejected by Muslims due to the fact that they show a significant growth of evangelical churches in some 'Muslim' parts of Ethiopia: the 1994 census, for instance, claimed that only 45 per cent of the population of the Oromia Regional State were Muslims, but 42 per cent Orthodox Christians and 9 per cent Protestant (Fiquet 2006: 54), while other estimates had assumed 55–60 per cent Muslims (Zitelmann 1994: 45) or even more. Some of the results of the 2007 census were indeed quite surprising, attesting, for instance, to the growth of evangelical churches in Ethiopia: for Gambella regional state, the 2007 census indicated a majority of 70 per cent Protestants, a minority of 16 per cent Ethiopian Orthodox Church (EOC), 5 per cent Muslims and 3 per cent Catholics (Markakis 2011: 346)

In 1992/3, *Bilāl* published a number of articles on Muslims in Ethiopia. One theme was the history of Islam from the first *hijra* and stressed that due to the protection Muslims received in Ethiopia at that time, Ethiopia had become a *dār al-ḥiyād*, a land of asylum, where Muslims were protected by the state.[52] As a consequence, Ethiopian Muslims should be proud that their country was the first country outside Arabia to have known Islam. Subsequently, the articles switched to a second theme, namely, that Ethiopia's rulers had turned away from Islam and oppressed Muslims up to contemporary times (Carmichael 1996: 176). These articles reflected two different 'Muslim' perspectives on Ethiopian history: for many Muslims, in and beyond Ethiopia, Ethiopia was a *dār al-ḥiyād*, where Muslims from Mecca were granted asylum in 615, in the context of the first hijra (*al-hijra al-ūlā*), by a benevolent Christian king, the *al-Najāshī Ashāma* (al-Najāshī al-Asham b. Ella Gabaz also known as 'Abjar') (Cuoq 1981: 32). His example showed that it was possible for Muslims to live under Christian rule. The largely legendary *Najāshī Ashāma* episode was also regarded as the starting point for the development of an indigenous Ethiopian Muslim community, the *Jabarti*. The *Najāshī Ashāma* legend was complemented, however, by a second legend, namely, that the *Najāshī Ashāma* converted to Islam in 628, an act that transformed his kingdom into an Islamic polity. Ethiopia's first Muslim ruler was soon deposed by his Christian followers, however, who re-imposed Christianity as the 'official' religion of the empire. Due to this development, Ethiopia ceased to be a *dār al-ḥiyād* and Muslims had the task of liberating Ethiopia by way of a *jihād* as in the times of Aḥmad 'Grañ' (Erlich 2010: 3).[53] The *al-Najāshī* theme has been used by Ethiopian Muslims most particularly to renegotiate their 'foreignness' in Ethiopia and 'to make national reconstruction on an inclusive basis attainable' (Dereje Feyissa 2013: 31). That means that Ethiopia should be seen not only as a 'chosen nation' by Orthodox Christians, but also as the land of the first *hijra* and the first country where Islam got recognition by a head of state (Dereje Feyissa 2013: 31): the message is that Ethiopian Muslims are not 'foreigners' but Ethiopians with the same rights as Christians.

After 1991, Ethiopian Muslims moved from an initial 'thanksgiving mood' towards the ruling party to the assertion of their rights (Dereje Feyissa 2013: 33). The debates, however, caused numerous splits among Muslims regarding doctrinal issues or their relationship with the Ethiopian state. In 1995, personal conflicts within the ESCIA escalated and led to a serious clash with security forces in the Anwār mosque as well as on the campus of the university in Addis Ababa on 21 February 1995. In these riots, 9 worshippers were killed and 129 wounded (Abbink 1998: 118; Hussein Ahmed 2006: 17; Østebø 2008b: 433).[54] Subsequently, a number of Muslims were imprisoned, the ESCIA was dissolved and a new leadership was elected (Desplat 2010: 244). The Anwār mosque riots had been preceded by a large demonstration of Muslims in Addis Ababa on 25 November 1994 for more rights for Muslims (Abbink 1998: 122). ESCIA leadership suffered from a lack of popular legitimacy as it was seen as an instrument of the ruling party. In particular, the general secretary, Elias Redwan, was believed to be professionally inept (Dereje Feyissa 2013: 34). In 2004, all Salafi-oriented scholars in the ESCIA were replaced by loyalist scholars (Østebø 2010: 40). In 2009, another new leader of the ESCIA was elected, the chairperson now being Aḥmadin ᶜAbdallāh Qallo (formerly Oromia *majlis*). The post of deputy was taken by Muḥammad Ibrāhīm (formerly Harar *majlis*) and the new secretary general was Muḥammad Sirāj (formerly Amhara *majlis*), but the new leaders were again suspected of being selected by the ruling party (Dereje Feyissa 2013: 35).[55] As a result of government efforts to control the ESCIA, mosques acquired increasing importance as platforms for the articulation of independent opinion, although the government tried to gain control over them by requiring them to register officially, and to submit information in respect of their funding and outside donors. Also, Addis Ababa's central mosque, al-Anwār, was brought under governmental control and two *imāms* of the Bānī Nūr mosque in Addis Ababa were suspended from their positions in 2009 (Østebø 2013b: 243).

Since 1991, the Ethiopian Government has thus developed its own Islam policy, for instance by accepting Muslims in the government as ministers and administrators, by trying to instrumentalise the ESCIA or by cooperation with the rich Ethiopian-Saudi businessman al-Amoudi (Erlich 2010: 158): Muḥammad Ḥusayn al-Amoudi, a businessman of mixed Saudi-Ethiopian extraction and the biggest private investor in Ethiopia was born in Dessie in historical Wällo in 1946 and grew up in nearby Woldiya. While his mother was Ethiopian, his father was a Saudi citizen of Hadhrami origin. He emigrated to Saudi Arabia in 1965. According to Forbes, he was the sixty-third richest man in the world in 2014, and owned a fortune of more than 15 billion US dollars. He built his fortune in construction and real estate before investing in oil refineries and is regarded today as the most important foreign investor in Ethiopia. Al-Amoudi has invested in Ethiopia since the mid-1980s, where he holds a major share in Ethiopia's gold-mining activities. One of his companies, MIDROC Ethiopia, is Ethiopia's sole licensed gold exporter, and he is also active in many other business fields, such as agriculture, in particular in Gambela and Beni Shangul-Gumuz kilils. He also owns

70 per cent of National Oil Ethiopia and is presently building Ethiopia's first steel plant in Tossa (Amhara Regional Zone). The al-Amoudi-owned Saudi Star Agricultural Development Company plans to develop in the region of 500,000 hectares of land for sugar cane, edible oil and grain production. Al-Amoudi has also contributed considerably to Ethiopia's 'Renaissance Dam' project on the Blue Nile. At the same time, he has invested heavily in philanthropic and social welfare projects beyond religious affiliation, supports both Muslim and Christian charity projects in Ethiopia and has been a major donor to the William J. Clinton Foundation.[56]

As a symbol of Ethiopia's new Islam policy, al-Najashi Mosque & Centre in Negash/Tigray was recognised as an official Ethiopian historical site (Erlich 2010: 179). Crucial to the strategy of building 'government Islam' (Østebø 2013b: 241) was the aḥbāsh movement led by ᶜAbdallāh b. Muḥammad b. Yūsuf al-Ḥarārī (1910–2008). This scholar from Harar had left Ethiopia in 1948 and eventually settled in Beirut where he became the spiritual guide of the jamᶜiyyat al-mashāriᶜ al-khayriyya al-islāmiyya, the Association of Islamic Charitable Projects founded in the 1930s (Desplat 2013: 171). From the 1930s onwards, the jamᶜiyyat al-mashāriᶜ al-khayriyya al-islāmiyya spread worldwide, known as the aḥbāsh-movement, due to the fact that ᶜAbdallāh b. Muḥammad hailed from Ethiopia (in Arabic: *al-ḥabasha*). The aḥbāsh movement was not only marked by its Sufi orientation, but also by its advocacy of modern (religious) education that stressed *tawḥīd*, as propagated by its own newspaper, *manār al-hūdā* (since 1992). Due to its attacks on 'Wahhabism', ᶜAbdallāh b. Muḥammad was accused by Saudi Arabia of creating *fitna* in 1992, and of allying with non-Muslims in 1994. He was also accused of having fought the early Salafi movement in Harar in alliance with Haile Selassie in the 1940s (Desplat 2013: 173). In 2008, Muḥammad b. ᶜAbdallāh al-Ḥarārī was invited to visit Ethiopia by Meles Zenawi, but he died in September 2008, before he could make the journey (Erlich 2010: 178). In order to counter-balance 'Wahhabi' influence, the Ethiopian Government invited fifteen Lebanese *ᶜulamāʾ* of the aḥbāsh movement to come to Ethiopia in order to boost 'moderate' Islam. This delegation was quickly denounced as an 'import' (and the Lebanese were attacked as 'late-comers' to Islam when compared with Ethiopia's legacy of Islam) (Dereje Feyissa 2013: 39). The visit of the aḥbāsh delegation led by the vice-president of the association, Dr Samīr

Qāḍī, to Ethiopia in 2011 took the form of a lecture campaign throughout the country, in university campuses and military camps. More than 18,000 people attended the lectures, which attacked 'Wahhabis' but also stressed the central role of the ESCIA (Østebø 2013b: 246). During a workshop at the Ghion Hotel in Addis Ababa, for instance, Dr Samīr Qāḍī said:

> They (the Wahhabis) claim that anyone that celebrates the birth of the Prophet is doing an act similar to an idol worshipper . . . They claim that anyone that calls upon Muhammad or Jesus or Moses in the absence after their death . . . is a blasphemer and has to be killed. They claim that anyone who visits the grave of a pious person seeking blessings by God has to be killed. . . . In brief, they literally stated that anyone . . . who doesn't hold the same system of belief that they hold is a non-believer that has to be killed. (quoted in Østebø 2013b: 245)

As a result, the aḥbāsh movement came to be seen as a tool of the ESCIA. In 2012, some aḥbāsh members were in fact appointed members of the ESCIA (Marchal and Sheikh 2013: 215), while critical voices such as the journal *Muslimoch Goday* (Muslim affairs) were harassed. Muslims in particular resented that Christians dared to proclaim a *takfīr* against Muslims they did not like, such as the 'Wahhabis' (in Amhariña *Wahhabiyoch* or *ya tawhid gewoch*) (Østebø 2013b: 246; Zerihun Woldeselassie 2013: 156).[57] At the same time, moderate Muslims in Ethiopia have argued that 'Wahhabis' have infiltrated Ethiopia from outside (Hussein Ahmed 1998: 108), trying to manipulate peaceful Ethiopian Muslims, and stirring hatred against Ethiopian Christians (Desplat and Østebø 2013: 8). Such a perspective means that even Muslims in Ethiopia cultivate the image of Ethiopia as an 'island', while bad influences come from outside (Abbink 2007: 77). Due to the fact that the aḥbāsh movement was hijacked by the Ethiopian Government, Ethiopia has seen a series of anti-aḥbāsh demonstrations in recent years that led to several government crackdowns on the leaders of these demonstrations who were imprisoned and charged with 'terrorism' (communication Terje Østebø, 19 December 2014).

The years 1995/6 became watershed years for Ethiopia's Islam policy when, due to terrorist attacks in Ethiopia, the Ethiopian Government decided on a policy of containment in respect of Salafi activities (Østebø 2013b: 242).

The new policy was initiated in 1995, when Egyptian terrorists tried to assassinate President Mubarak of Egypt in Addis Ababa on 25 June 1995. Also, the Somalia-based al-ittiḥād al-islāmī organised several attacks in Ethiopia from 1995 to 1997, including an attack on Ghion Hotel in Addis Ababa on 18 January 1995, which claimed the lives of nine people (Woldeselase Woldemichael 2010: 132). Since 1995, Ethiopian politics have been dominated by security considerations and the development of Muslim activities has been observed through the 'national security lens' (Dereje Feyissa 2013: 27). As a result, many Islamic associations and NGOs were closed down and tight control was imposed. Of particular concern was the development in Oromia and Somali regional states, where a number of (mostly secular) militant movements (re-)emerged (see Hansen 2013b; ICG 2013c; Markakis 2011; Woldeselase Woldemichael 2010).

After 1991, Salafis offered a 'perspective for a future' (Østebø 2013a: 55): public prayers were possible and Salafism became the dominant religious orientation in regions such as Bale or Jimma. The late emergence of Salafi-oriented reform can be explained by several factors: isolation and restrictive politics under Haile Selassie, repression under the Derg, the marginality of social groups in Ethiopia that would have espoused Salafi ideas, in particular students, traders, functionaries, *ᶜulamāᵓ* and a small urban bourgeoisie, as well as the highly fragmented character of Muslim populations in Ethiopia.[58] Due to this fragmentation, the establishment of Salafi-oriented movements of reform varied from region to region. Apart from Addis Ababa, the Siltē region and Jimma as well as the Woldiya–Desē–Bati triangle, Harar[59] and Bale were key regions for the development of Salafi-oriented reform.

The start of Salafi-oriented reform in Harar was probably linked with the scholar Ibrāhīm 'Shāsh' Ḥasan,[60] who went on pilgrimage to Saudi Arabia in 1935 and came back in 1936. In Saudi Arabia, he met another scholar from Harar, al-Ḥājj Yūsuf ᶜAbd al-Raḥmān (b. 1916) who had arrived in Saudi Arabia in 1928 and who influenced Ibrāhīm 'Shāsh' Ḥasan (Desplat 2010: 203). After his return to Harar, Ibrāhīm 'Shāsh' Ḥasan was appointed teacher in Harar's first modern Islamic school, the gē madräsa, and started to attack local practices of saint veneration (Desplat 2013: 171). The gē madräsa had been established in 1933 by Harari traders united in the jamᶜiyyat al-khayriyya al-islāmiyya under the leadership of al-Ḥājj ᶜUmar Muḥammad ᶜAbd al-Raḥmān (Østebø 2008a: 133), an endeavour that had been supported by the Ethiopian state (Desplat 2010: 201). The school also became known as the jamᶜiyya madrasa. In 1939, al-Ḥājj Yūsuf ᶜAbd al-Raḥmān returned to Ethiopia and opened an Islamic bookshop in Addis Ababa. In 1941, he returned to Harar and started to advocate Harar's independence from Ethiopia and to cooperate with the jamᶜiyyat al-khayriyya al-islāmiyya. He built a group of followers who were united in the jāmiᶜa al-waṭaniyya al-islāmiyya, which had a distinct Salafi character. He cooperated with Ibrāhīm 'Shāsh' Ḥasan at the gē madräsa that became a major base for Harar's Salafis in the early 1940s (Desplat 2010: 204).[61] This development worried the local traders and merchants who were united in the jamᶜiyyat al-khayriyya al-islāmiyya, as well as locally established scholars, in particular Shaykh ᶜAbdallāh b. Muḥammad, an itinerant scholar from Harar who had studied in Wällo and Jimma and who had lived in Addis Ababa during the time of the Italian occupation. He now returned to Harar and started to attack Ibrāhīm 'Shāsh' Ḥasan (Deplat 2010: 205). The major bone of contention was the question of God's attributes, and a dispute grew up over the interpretation of certain verses in the Qurᵓān, in particular those that were interpreted rather literally by 'Wahhabis', such as Qurᵓān 7: 54, 10: 3, 20: 5, 25: 59, 32: 4 and 57: 4, although such an interpretation implied an anthropomorphic concept of God. In 1941, ᶜAbdallāh b. Muḥammad called for a boycott of the gē madräsa, which was effectively put under government control in 1942. In 1942, Ibrāhīm 'Shāsh' Ḥasan was imprisoned by the Ethiopian authorities. Together with fifteen followers he was deported to Gondar and left from there to go to Saudi Arabia (Desplat 2010: 203).

In 1947 a second conflict developed in Harar over the question of Harar's political orientation. This story became known as the 'plot of the kulub' (club) (Erlich 2007: 145). Haile Selassie had planned to win Somali support for re-unification of the Ogaden and Hawd regions with Ethiopia,[62] and had consequently accepted the establishment of a branch of the Somali Youth Club (SYC) in Harar in 1947 (Erlich 2007: 144).[63] The Somali nationalists, however, opted for Somali independence and a greater Somalia rather than for union with Ethiopia, but wanted Harar to become the Somali capital city. The SYC call for a greater Somalia was initially rejected by a majority of Hararis who supported Harar's independence on its own terms (Desplat

2010: 207). After some time, however, the SYC was able to garner increasing support, mostly due to the repressive government policies in the region, which were a counter-reaction to the fact that a majority of Hararis had collaborated with the Italians from 1936 to 1941. In late 1947, the SYC bureau in Harar and the jāmiᶜa al-waṭaniyya al-islāmiyya formed a union and sent thirteen delegates to Mogadishu to meet a UN mission in January 1948. The UN mission in Mogadishu rejected the 'kulub' idea of a greater Somalia, however, stating that Harar was Ethiopian. The 'kulub' initiative was answered by the Ethiopian authorities with the imprisonment of more than 700 Hararis on 10 January 1948, 81 of whom were deported to other parts of Ethiopia (Desplat 2010: 208). Although the 'kulub' movement was nationalistic and not linked with the Salafi-oriented movement of reform (Østebø 2008a: 186), it radiated into Arsi and Bale in the late 1940s and also found support at the *Dirre* Shaykh Ḥusayn shrine (Østebø 2008a: 188).

The Harari delegation to Mogadishu did not return to Harar immediately after the failure of its mission but travelled to Saudi Arabia in March 1948, and then to Egypt, where they met Ḥasan al-Bannā. After being granted amnesty by Haile Selassie, the 'kulub' delegates returned to Harar in January 1949, but their movement subsequently collapsed. While Ibrāhīm 'Shāsh' Ḥasan found a path of accommodation with the Ethiopian authorities, ᶜAbdallāh b. Muḥammad left Ethiopia in 1948.[64] Ibrāhīm 'Shāsh' Ḥasan later became a member of the Ethiopian Parliament (Markakis 2006: 196). In 1976, he left Ethiopia and went to Saudi Arabia, but returned to Ethiopia in 2004. Having started out as a leading representative of Harar's Salafi-oriented movement of reform in the 1930s and 1940s, he became a 'moderniser' who strove to support Harar's efforts to consolidate its own cultural legacy and identity (Desplat 2010: 213). Due to his influence, a majority of Hararis accepted modern Islamic education under Ethiopian (secular) auspices (Desplat 2010: 213).

As in other parts of Ethiopia, the critique of practices of saint veneration has been a major concern of the Salafi-oriented movement of reform in Harar. Due to the fact that Hararis regard their city as the 'city of saints', Salafis found it particularly hard to attack such practices. In the late twentieth century, the critique of saint cults in Harar was affected by three major developments: the return of students from Saudi Arabia, the influence of

Harari migrant workers in the Gulf region and the influence of the growing Harari diaspora in Western countries. These forces generated 'trans-national pressure' (Desplat 2002: 152) on local practices. The case of Harar shows, however, that the local middle-class was willing to defend saint veneration against the attacks of the 'foreign' Wahhabis, even though some middle-class members started to distance themselves from these cults (Desplat 2010: 164): Hararis were proud of their own Islamic legacy and despised Wahhabis as 'outsiders' or as 'Oromo' (Desplat 2013: 168–70). However, the veneration of saints was no longer defended for religious reasons but rather for political and cultural ones: saints were regarded as being central to identity formation in Harar (Desplat 2010: 179).

The Islamisation of Bale started in the late eighteenth century and followed patterns similar to those in Gibe and Wällo (Østebø 2008a: 87). The development of larger settlements was also a relatively late phenomenon. Goba in Bale was founded in 1893 only (Østebø 2008a: 138), and early towns were often dominated by Christian Amhara settlers and elites. Salafi ideas of reform were introduced into Bale by traders in the 1960s, as well as by Oromo Muslims returning from studies in Saudi Arabia (Østebø 2013a: 53). From Bale, only a few Muslims went on pilgrimage, however. More important was the link to Harar, especially to al-Ḥājj Yūsuf ᶜAbd al-Raḥmān and Ibrāhīm 'Shāsh' Ḥasan. From Harar, Salafi ideas spread to Bale in the 1950s (Østebø 2008a: 133). Traders, in particular, supported the establishment of Salafi ideas, as expressed, for instance, in the construction of the first mosque in Robe in 1959 (Østebø 2008a: 141). This mosque became the core of the first Salafi-oriented social group, distinguished by its rejection of local religious practices such as drumming during the *dhikr*. The leading scholar was Muḥammad Ḥājj Muṣṭafā from Dire Dawa, an Azhar graduate who became *qāḍī* of Bale in 1963. He remained in office until 1969, when he went to Addis Ababa and taught at the Anwār mosque (Østebø 2008a: 141). In 1963/4 Salafi-oriented Muslims established a *jamāᶜa* in al-Nūr mosque that became the first organisational structure of a non-esoteric interpretation of Islam in Robe (Østebø 2008a: 142). This movement was characterised by its rejection of shrine visits and prayers at graveyards and tombs, but it was not yet seen as a Salafi movement and it kept a low profile. By the late 1960s, the group had only 24 members (Østebø 2008a: 144). This was soon to change due to the revolution of 1974 and due to Saudi efforts to boost the Salafi movement internationally: in 1961 the Islamic University of Medina had been founded and in 1962 the rābiṭat al-ᶜālam al-islāmī followed suit. In the 1970s, Saudi Arabia started to finance *daᶜwa* and NGOs and established grants for students, also attracting students from Ethiopia (Østebø 2008a: 146) – a policy that has been appropriately labelled 'riyālpolitik' (Gause 1990: 112).

An important event for the development of Salafi-oriented reform was the 'journey of the eighty' that took place in 1962: eighty students from Hararge, Arsi and Jimma, who met by coincidence in Ethiopia on their way to Saudi Arabia, eventually travelled together and stayed in Saudi Arabia, first to study Arabic for a period of three years, and then to continue higher studies at the Islamic University in Medina or at Umm al-Qurā in Mecca (Østebø 2008a: 147). Most of these students returned to Ethiopia individually, most before 1974, some only after 1991. Some were paid salaries through the Royal Saudi Arabia Embassy in Addis Ababa (even in the time of the Derg), established *madāris* and eventually surfaced after 1991 (Østebø 2008a: 148). One of the scholars to return from Saudi Arabia in the late 1960s was Abūbakar Muḥammad who hailed from a small village near Robe (see Østebø 2009b: 436ff). Abūbakar Muḥammad was educated at the *Dirre* Shaykh Ḥusayn shrine in Bale, and then moved on to Harar and Dire Dawa before departing to Saudi Arabia in 1962. He returned to Bale in 1969 and held a famous sermon in Robe's Nūr mosque in 1971, in which he openly attacked local Islamic practices. This sermon triggered a bitter dispute between local Salafis and established scholars until the Ethiopian Government decided to intervene in 1972 and to urge local parties to end their dispute. However, instead of reaching a consensus, government intervention granted the local Salafi movement official recognition and thus stimulated further growth of the local Salafi-oriented movement of reform (Østebø 2009b: 348).

In 1976, two University of Medina graduates, Kadir Hamid and ᶜAbd al-Raḥmān Adam, who had returned from Saudi Arabia in 1972 and 1971 respectively, established a 'Salafiyya *madrasa*' in al-Nūr mosque in Robe, supported by local Salafi-minded traders (Østebø 2008a: 199). In 1980, the Salafiyya *madrasa* was allowed to move to new and larger buildings comprising eight classrooms, a mosque and a teahouse, all financed by Muslims in

Robe. However, the new school also had to teach the government syllabus apart from its own Islamic studies syllabus. Still, student numbers grew considerably from about 100 in 1976 to 1,480 in 1991 (850 boys and 630 girls) (Østebø 2008a: 200). This school formed the basis for a second generation of Salafi-oriented Muslims in Robe and beyond. In 1983, the school was confiscated by the Derg (Østebø 2008a: 213), and staff and students had to move to yet another area and start again from scratch.

In Bale, the first generation of Salafi-oriented merchants and scholars thus saw the rise of a second generation of more radical Salafis who became known as ahl al-sunna in the 1990s (Østebø 2008a: 233). In fact, the Salafi movement of reform was a loosely knit movement rather than an organisation and could count on charismatic *dāᶜis* such as Aḥmad ᶜUthmān 'Zagiro' (the 'short one'), who arrived in Robe in about 1988 (Østebø 2008a: 234, 2009b: 350). Also important were Oromo refugees (in Somali *Qawetti*), mostly lowlanders, who started to come back from Somalia in 1991 due to the civil war there (Østebø 2008a: 236). The ahl al-sunna were even more critical of Oromo cultural practices than the older generation of Salafi-oriented reformers. At the same time, they criticised Western influence, videos, Western fashion and Western youth culture (Østebø 2013a: 55). However, their harsh teachings and behaviour led to conflict with the older generation of Salafis in al-Nūr mosque when they wanted to push harder for reform. Following the assassination of a Salafi elder in al-Nūr mosque in 1993, many of the younger generation dissociated themselves from the ahl al-sunna (Østebø 2013a: 60). The youth in Robe, Bale, moved from initial support for Salafi-oriented Islam towards Oromo nationalism and interest in Western consumer and leisure culture (Østebø 2013a: 47).[65] As a consequence of the 1993 incident, state authorities reacted, and five ahl al-sunna members were imprisoned. Many others left for Saudi Arabia or the Gulf and the movement suffered considerably. Efforts to revive the movement in 1997 by a returnee from Saudi Arabia misfired and led to even stronger repression (Østebø 2013a: 61).

When looking back at the origins of the Salafi movement in the 1960s, it is possible to say that apart from students, traders were the major social support group, while *ᶜulamā᾽* were conspicuously absent. There was thus initially no conflict between Salafi-oriented Muslims and established religious authorities. Unlike the merchants of the 1960s, the ahl al-sunna of the 1990s did not rely on independent sources of revenue. Their attacks against shrine visits and shrine sacrifices (*wareega*) threatened the economic basis of established scholars and shrine guardians, however, and thus triggered disputes between ahl al-sunna and guardians of established traditions (Østebø 2008a: 166). Attacks on shrine visits and other local practices were also seen as attacks against the Muslim identity of local populations, and were thus rejected in local contexts. This explains why the ahl al-sunna of the 1990s found it very hard to get a grounding: their ideas were seen as 'foreign' (Østebø 2008a: 172). In addition, there was resistance among women, who defended established ritual practices, as well as among elders and supporters of the shrines, in particular the *Dirre* Shaykh Ḥusayn, who attacked the ahl al-sunna as being pro-Saudi and lax Muslims (Østebø 2008a: 255).

The ahl al-sunna soon also developed a number of specific traits when compared with the older generation of Salafi reformers who were characterised by their focus on education and quietest piety: first, the ahl al-sunna stressed public piety and moral uprightness and were willing to enforce public piety and morals by acts of vigilantilism based on the principle of 'commanding right and forbidding wrong'. Second, some radical Salafi-oriented groups practised 'isolationism', cutting off relations with Christians and mainstream Muslims, and pronouncing the *takfir* against fellow Muslims, even fellow Salafis (Østebø 2008a: 241, 2008b: 431).[66] Third, they were very strict regarding observance of the ritual, in particular fasting and praying, and stressed the importance of personal piety as expressed, for instance, in additional prayers, such as *witr* prayers; fourth, they adopted a specific dress and body language code: men shortened trousers and grew beards (but no moustaches), while women donned the *niqāb*; fifth, they condemned Oromo cultural and religious traditions such as the practice of *bikāʾ* as shirk and *bidʿa* and dissociated themselves from their own Oromo identity; sixth, they developed a growing distance towards Saudi Arabia, and its scholarly establishment, which was criticised as being a pro-US corrupt monarchy; and, finally, they provoked communal disputes by entering mosques with their shoes on (Østebø 2008a: 246), and they rejected ritual practices such as *mawlid* celebrations, mortuary rituals and shrine visits (Østebø 2008a: 238). In this way, the Salafi-oriented movement of reform in Bale was marked by features of symbolic distanciation and social separation.

In a defensive counter-reaction, the Salafi critique of local practices has led to a revivication of local practices such as saint veneration (Zerihun Woldeselassie 2013: 140). This was particularly visible among the Muslim Gurage, in particular, the Siltē: they started to defend established practices – as part of their own Islamic traditions – against attacks from outside. Islam was indeed an important part of their identity in the context of the conquest of their region by Menilek in the late nineteenth century. The Siltē managed to get their own administrative zone within the Southern Regional State (Debub) after a referendum in 2001, and thus split from the major Gurage administrative zone. Curiously enough, reformist critique of local practices such as saint veneration was supported by the modernist administration that also agitated against obsolete 'traditional practices'. 'Ethnicity rather than religion remains people's primary public identity' (Zerihun Wolde Selassie 2013: 156). This has so far also prevented Islam from becoming a national identifier and has blocked Salafi-oriented claims to hegemony.

The case of Ethiopia shows that the most important 'identifiers' in contemporary Ethiopia are still ethnic affiliation and language and not religion, as manifest, for instance, in the new regional states that were organised along ethnic and linguistic lines. This has come to mean that a person is not primarily Muslim or Christian, but (Muslim or Christian) Oromo, Amhara or Gurage (Abbink 1998: 121). As a result, the different Salafi-oriented groups are closely linked with their respective ethnic backgrounds (such as Oromo or Somali), and there has so far been no supra-ethnic Salafi-oriented movement of reform (Desplat and Østebø 2013: 14). Even the Muslim Oromo were unable to unite, and to this day Salafis are usually perceived as outsiders fighting against venerable local practices. The fact that these local practices are of major significance for the identity of ethnic groups is of central importance in a state where ethnic (and linguistic) identity has become the main criteria for the allocation of resources such as land and administrative institutions.

Somalia

Like sub-Saharan West Africa and the Sudan, Somalia can look back on a history of Sufi-oriented movements of reform in the guise of two major movements of *jihād* in the mid-nineteenth century and early twentieth, namely the community of Baardhere in central Somalia and the movement of reform inspired by the 'Sayyid' Muḥammad ᶜAbdille Ḥasan in northern Somalia. Among other things, this movement was directed against established religious traditions as represented by the Qādiriyya Sufi order. At the same time, the Qādiriyya produced a movement of reform that rejected the purist demands of Muḥammad ᶜAbdille Ḥasan. This movement was led by Uways b. Muḥammad al Bārawī and was based in southern Somalia (Loimeier 2013: 199ff; Reese 1999: 169ff). Although the movement of Muḥammad ᶜAbdille Ḥasan, which was linked with the Aḥmadiyya Sufi order, criticised things such as 'ecstatic ritual' and the use of *qāt* during religious practices, this critique still came from a Sufi-oriented tradition of reform. The tradition of reform represented by the Aḥmadiyya and the Qādiriyya informed the history of Somalia in the twentieth century to a large extent. Indeed, Sufi scholars were prominent in Somalia not only in the pre-colonial period, but also in colonial times: among the thirteen founders of the Somali Youth League (SYL) (in 1947) were four prominent Sufi scholars, namely ᶜAbd al-Qādir Shaykh Sakawadin, Aweys Dhere, al-Ḥājj Muḥammad Ḥusayn and Sayyid Dīn Hirsi Nūr (Marchal and Sheikh 2013: 220). At the same time, the success of Salafi-oriented movements of reform in Somalia was real, but limited in the face of the lasting influence of Sufism (Marchal 2009: 382).

While the development of Sufi-oriented traditions of reform can be traced back to the mid-nineteenth century, Salafi-oriented movements of reform are of a much more recent date in Somalia, and essentially go back to a small number of charismatic scholars who started to spread a Salafi-oriented *daᶜwa* in Mogadishu's mosques after their return from Saudi Arabia or Egypt. The year 1950 saw the establishment of the Somali Islamic League led by Sharīf Maḥamad ᶜAbd al-Raḥmān and Sharīf al-ᶜAydarūs (Abdurahman Moallim Abdullahi 2011: 103, henceforth AMA). Sharīf Maḥamad ᶜAbd al-Raḥmān (1904–94) from Luuq studied in Egypt in the 1920s, returned to Somalia in the 1930s and became a leading member of the SYL in the 1940s (AMA 2011: 104). He argued that Islam should be the basic source of legislation and supported the foundation of an Islamic university (a plan that was approved in 1971) (AMA 2011: 105).[67] In the north, Aḥmad Shaykh Muse (d. 1980) played a similar role. He established an organisation named ḥizb Allāh in 1956, a group that was affiliated with the Muslim Brotherhood (AMA 2011: 108). At the same time, the Somali Youth League (SYL) pushed educational reforms and in 1950 appealed for Egyptian support to build (Islamic) education. Egypt granted twenty-five scholarships and sent six Azhar teachers to Somalia to establish an Azhar school, the Institute of Islamic Studies, in 1953 (AMA 2011: 97). By 1958, fifteen schools had been opened and in the region of 1,200 students enrolled. Further scholarships were granted. From 1957 (until 1969), the SYL published a journal called *al-Waḥda* (AMA 2011: 99). In Somaliland, the Burᶜo Islamic Institute was opened in 1959 and became part of the al-Azhar schools after 1960 (AMA 2011: 100). By 1971, there were thirty-five 'Egyptian' schools in Somalia.

Other scholars who were involved in the formation of a Salafi-oriented movement of reform were Maḥamad Nūr Aḥmad Garyare who returned from Saudi Arabia in 1965, and Nūr ᶜAlī ᶜOlow, another Saudi-trained scholar, who started to teach in Gaalkayo in 1967 (Marchal and Sheikh 2013: 221).[68] Both scholars were supported by other Somali returnees from Saudi Arabia and the Gulf (Afyare Abdi Elmi 2010: 56, henceforth AAE). After the independence and union of (formerly Italian) Somalia and (formerly British) Somaliland in 1960, a Salafi-oriented movement of reform continued to grow in Somalia's urban centres, in particular Mogadishu in the south and Hargeysa in the north. In 1967, the munādamat (*sic*)[69] al-nahḍa al-islāmiyya (short 'al-nahḍa') was founded as the first Salafi-oriented association by ᶜAbd al-Qani (ᶜAbd al-Ghanī) Shaykh Aḥmad (president)[70] and Maḥamad Aḥmad Nūr Garyare (vice-president), both members of the Muslim Brotherhood (AMA 2011: 144–6). Although al-nahḍa was conceived as a vanguard organisation and membership was restricted, al-nahḍa included Sufi-oriented scholars. And, like most other Salafi-oriented movements of reform, al-nahḍa was set up as a modern treasurer-association (AMA 2011: 150).

Independence, the efforts to build a secular Somali nation state by General Maḥamad Siyad Barre (1910–95) (r. 1969–91) and the collapse and subsequent political fragmentation of Somalia in 1988 also triggered the emergence of an array of *jihād*-minded groups that have tried, since the early 1990s, to gain hegemony of interpretation. The civil war in Somalia (starting in 1988) created conditions that favoured the growth of militant and activist groups. In this sense, it can be said that the civil war has distorted the history of both Somalia (independent since 1 July 1960) and Somaliland (independent since 26 June 1960, and again since May 1991): wars indeed 'provide a poor environment for debating the validity of religious views or their re-interpretation' (Marchal 2009: 382).

Of major importance for the doctrinal formation of the Salafi-oriented movement of reform in Somalia was Maḥamad Maᶜallim Ḥasan (d. 2001), a Qādirī-educated scholar who turned Salafi in Egypt. He was born in 1934 near Buur Hakaba, attended qurᵓānic school, went to Harar in 1942, became a teacher at the central mosque in Hargeysa in 1952, went to al-Azhar in 1957 and graduated in 1968. In 1969, Muḥammad Muᶜallim Ḥasan came back from Egypt and started to spread his *daᶜwa*, based on his *tafsīr* that was inspired by Sayyid Quṭb's *tafsīr 'fi-ẓilāl al-Qurᵓān'*, in the Maqaamka Shaykh Abdulqadir mosque in Mogadishu, a major centre of the Qādiriyya (AAE 2010: 57). He also joined al-nahḍa and became the pivotal person in al-nahḍa's *daᶜwa* programme (AMA 2011: 152).[71] In 1969, according to other sources in 1968 (Marchal and Sheikh 2013: 222), some of Muḥammad Muᶜallim Ḥasan's students established ahl al-islām (colloquially 'Ahal' or 'Ahli'). Being affiliated with the Qādiriyya and linked with the 'Jabarti' mosque in Mogadishu these students represented Somali resistance against processes of Westernisation in Somalia rather than Salafi reform. Through Maḥamad Maᶜallim Ḥasan, however, the group turned Salafi. The leadership of Ahal fell to ᶜAbd al-Qādir Shaykh Maḥamūd Faraḥ (AMA 2011: 157), a scholar originally linked with the Qādiriyya (Marchal and Sheikh 2013: 222).

In 1969, Maḥamed Ḥājj Du'aale Shaykh founded the waḥdat al-shabāb al-islāmiyya (for short, al-waḥda) in Hargeysa (Renders 2007: 54). Although this group initially had a strong basis among Sufi-oriented Muslims, it soon turned towards the Egyptian ikhwān al-muslimūn and was equally influenced by the teachings of Sayyid Quṭb and Abū l-Āᶜlā Maudūdī (AAE 2010: 57; Marchal 2004: 119). It also turned against Westernisation and the upheaval of the times and supported modern Islamic education. Like al-nahḍa, it was a treasurer-organisation, with its centre in Hargeysa. In the 1970s, al-waḥda spread to other parts of the north. In the 1970s, al-waḥda was led by ᶜAbd al-Qādir Ḥājj Jaamaᶜ, who was imprisoned, like many other al-waḥda members, in 1978 (AMA 2011: 169).

After the take-over of power by General Maḥamad Siyad Barre in 1969, a period of politics of transformation started. In 1969/70, all political and religious organisations were banned and became dormant. Ahal strategy at that time was to infiltrate state institutions, in particular the army (AMA 2011: 159). In 1972, the Siyad Barre government introduced the Latin script for the Somali language, based on the Afmaxaa dialect of the 'pastoralist' clans (Isaaq, Darood, Dir and Hawiye), and organised national alphabetisation campaigns in 1973 and 1974.[72] In 1974, legal reforms, in particular a reform of Somalia's family law, followed (Bradbury 2008: 37). In 1975, a new family law improved the legal position of women in Somalia. It limited, for instance, polygamic options, set eighteen as the minimum age for marriage and liberated women in respect of the choice of their husbands (Touati 1997: 168). These reforms were rejected by Somalia's religious scholars as being anti-Islamic.

After a short honeymoon after the coup, a period of mistrust between regime and religious scholars followed and led to outright repression in 1975 over the issue of family law (AMA 2011: 179). Muslim scholars such as Muḥammad Muᶜallim Ḥasan and Muḥammad Nūr Aḥmad Garyare protested against these reforms and were imprisoned in 1975 in the context of widespread demonstrations in Mogadishu. Others fled into neighbouring countries, mainly Saudi Arabia. Ten scholars were executed by the Barre regime that turned out to be increasingly brutal in its dealings with the opposition (Lewis 2008: 47) and that courted the Qādiriyya and Aḥmadiyya Sufi orders in order to contain the emerging Salafi-oriented groups (Marchal and Sheikh 2015: 144). By August 1975 government institutions had been purged of sixty high-ranking Muslim personalities. Many of them were imprisoned; others fled and began to regroup in Sudan or Saudi Arabia (AMA 2011: 190). After an aborted military coup on 9 April 1978, a second wave of repression followed and strengthened the opposition, both clans and religious groups (AMA 2011: 208). The regime also established a dense network of spies within Somalia (Touati 1997: 227). In the context of these developments, ᶜAbd al-Qādir Shaykh Maḥamad Faraḥ, the leader of Ahal, fled to Saudi Arabia and founded a new organisation, al-takfīr wa-l-hijra. Many Ahal members at that time decided to follow him and joined al-takfīr wa-l-hijra (Marchal and Sheikh 2013: 223), while others remained moderate and established al-jamāᶜa al-islāmiyya, led by Maḥamad ᶜIsā (Ciise), in 1979 (AMA 2011: 160). Still other Ahal members decided to remain neutral and founded al-iṣlāḥ. The history of Ahal thus shows that internal divisions over questions of leadership, strategy and clan loyalties were a pervading feature of the development of Salafi-oriented movements of reform in Somalia (Marchal and Sheikh 2013: 223).

Three months after the Somali defeat by Ethiopia in the Ogaden War, on 11 July 1978, al-iṣlāḥ (also: ḥarakat al-iṣlāḥ) was established in al-Riyādh by exiled members of Ahal and al-nahḍa, who elected Maḥamad Nūr ᶜAlī Ibrāhīm Garyare[73] as its first president (AMA 2011: 192; Marchal 2004: 119). Al-iṣlāḥ emerged from a predominant al-nahḍa background (AMA 2011: 199). Up to 1989 its name in English was Iṣlāḥ Islamic Society. In 1990, al-iṣlāḥ changed its name to al-ḥaraka al-islāmiyya fi-sumāl (The Islamic Movement in Somalia) (AMA 2011: 252), but the popular name remained al-iṣlāḥ. The leaders of al-iṣlāḥ studied mostly in Somalia and Saudi Arabia, in particular at the Islamic University of Medina, and some in Sudan (AMA 2011: 203). Up to 2013 it had the following chairmen: Maḥamad Aḥmad Nūr Garyare (1978–90), Dr Maḥamad ᶜAlī Ibrāhīm (1990–99),[74] Prof. ᶜAlī Abukar Aḥmad ᶜAlī Dhere (1999–2008)[75] and Dr ᶜAlī Baasha ᶜUmar Roraaye (2008–13)[76] (AMA 2011: 194; Marchal and Sheikh 2013: 223).

Al-iṣlāḥ's organisation was federal, it had a chairman and a *majlis al-shūra*, as well as zonal congresses: it was a treasurer-organisation (AMA 2011: 214–15). After its foundation it started its *daᶜwa* among the Somali diaspora and among Somali pilgrims to Saudi Arabia (AMA 2011: 221). The foundation of al-iṣlāḥ was resented by both al-takfīr wa-l-hijra and 'Ahal' members, who regarded al-iṣlāḥ as a competing organisation, especially when al-iṣlāḥ refused to merge with the jamāᶜa al-islāmiyya in 1983 (AMA 2011: 226). In the 1980s, al-iṣlāḥ worked mostly underground, but still found support in the educated elite and administration, as well as among students and in the army, especially after 1987, when the grip of the regime relaxed (AMA 2011: 237). In 1987, al-iṣlāḥ became a member of the International Muslim Brotherhood organisation. This allowed al-iṣlāḥ to gain followers in the Somali diaspora (AMA 2011: 239). The real break-through came after the collapse of the regime in 1990 and 1991. This collapse also brought about the liberation of many political prisoners. Especially in Somaliland, al-iṣlāḥ, in coalition with al-waḥda, focused on humanitarian work (AMA 2011:

241) and eventually developed into Somalia's biggest and most influential Salafi-oriented movement of reform in the 1990s. As an Islamic charitable organisation, it cultivated a strong focus on humanitarian and educational work, as well as a strategy of gradual peaceful expansion (for details of its programme, see AMA 2011: 211ff).[77] Since 1992, al-iṣlāḥ has worked in particular in the field of education, and established Mogadishu University (opened in 2007), today Somalia's biggest university (AMA 2011: 294). Al-iṣlāḥ has also acquired a dominant role in the Formal Private Education Network in Somalia (FPENS), an Islamic NGO that had more than 100 schools and more than 120,000 students in Mogadishu and other cities in Somalia in the early 2000s (see Rabasa 2009: 32; ICG 2005: 13). Al-iṣlāḥ's educational activities were financed by the Islamic Development Bank and the World Assembly of Muslim Youth (WAMY) (AAE 2010: 114). In general terms, al-iṣlāḥ found support among small- and middle-rank traders and also won over followers of al-ittiḥād al-islāmī who did not want to follow the strategy of armed struggle (Marchal 2004: 126–7). Al-iṣlāḥ criticised the *jihād*-minded strategy of al-ittiḥād (AMA 2011: 266). The organisation also opposed Somalia's warlords and stayed neutral in the civil war after 1991.

In 1983, most members of al-jamāᶜa al-islāmiyya and some members of the mostly northern-based al-waḥda group decided to merge and form a competing organisation, al-ittiḥād al-islāmī, which in the 1990s became Somalia's most influential Salafi-oriented movement, propagating armed struggle as a means to fight against Somalia's enemies, in particular Ethiopia (AAE 2010: 58). The majority of al-waḥda in the north remained independent, however, and it became the major Salafi-oriented group in independent Somaliland, where it came to play a role similar to al-iṣlāḥ in the south. After the merger with al-jamāᶜa al-islāmiyya in 1983, al-waḥda thus continued to exist as a parallel structure, but its 'southern' branch disappeared in 1999, when its members in the south joined other organisations, such as tajammuᶜ or al-iṣlāḥ or, finally, a new organisation that emerged from al-ittiḥād al-islāmī and that became known as iᶜtiṣām al-kitāb wa-l-sunna (for short, 'al-iᶜtiṣām') (AMA 2011: 169–70). Equally, while a majority of the jamāᶜat al-islāmiyya had merged with a minority of al-waḥda to become al-ittiḥād al-islāmī, the remaining minority of the jamāᶜat al-islāmiyya followed Maḥamad Maᶜallim

Ḥasan who, after his release from prison in 1982, set up a new organisation, al-ikhwān al-muslimūn, which perceived itself as being the 'true' Muslim Brotherhood organisation in Somalia (AMA 2011: 229).[78] In 2001, the ikhwān al-muslimūn group became al-tajammu^{c} al-islāmī (or short, 'tajammu^{c}'). In 2008, tajammu^{c} merged with al-i^{c}tiṣām and chose the name jamā^{c}at al-wifāq al-islāmiyya (AAE 2010: 58). These splits and mergers attest not only to the importance of 'Islamic' labels but also to a history of political fragmentation, religious dispute and social competition among the Salafi-oriented groups in Somalia that mirrors the fragmented structure of Somali society and the ever-changing composition of clan alliances: 'No organization in Somalia can escape the clan trap' (Hansen 2013a: 7). Even al-iṣlāḥ, which turned out to be probably the most successful Salafi-oriented group in Somalia in the 1990s and early 2000s, split into two groups simply called 'new blood' (*dam al-jadīd*) and 'old guard' in 2005/6. This was due to the rise of the Islamic Courts Union (ICU) (al-ittiḥād al-maḥākim al-islāmiyya) (AAE 2010: 58) and the issue of participation in it. A majority of al-iṣlāḥ refused to join the ICU (AMA 2011: 313).

It is thus possible to identify the emergence of three trends of Salafi-oriented reform in Somalia in the late 1960s: al-nahḍa and Ahal in southern and central Somalia, and al-waḥda in northern Somalia. After 1969, these early movements went either underground or into exile, and gave birth in the late 1970s to three 'successor' movements: al-iṣlāḥ, which built mostly on former al-nahḍa members, al-takfīr wa-l-hijra, and al-jamā^{c}a al-islāmiyya, which won many al-waḥda followers. Other al-waḥda members remained committed to the al-waḥda programme and either joined al-ittiḥād al-islāmī in 1983, when the bulk of al-waḥda united with al-jamā^{c}a al-islāmiyya to form al-ittiḥād al-islāmī, or continued to remain independent until the early 2000s, when the remaining al-waḥda members became followers of either al-i^{c}tisām or al-tajammu^{c} al-islāmī. Al-tajammu^{c} al-islāmī again managed to recruit many followers of al-ittiḥād al-islāmī, which had ceased to exist in the late 1990s.

From the mid-1970s, the Barre regime was characterised by increasingly authoritarian rule based on Maḥamad Siyad Barre's Marehan-Ogaden-Dulbahante (MOD) clan alliance and terror against oppositional groups. In 1983, in another crack-down on the Islamic opposition, hundreds of Muslims fled the country or were imprisoned, such as Ḥasan Dahir Aweys, one of the future leaders of the Islamic Courts movement. In 1989, another round of repression hit even moderate Muslim scholars, such as Ibrāhīm Muḥammad Shaqane, Sharīf Sharafow and ᶜAbd al-Rashīd ᶜAlī Sufi, who were imprisoned after a demonstration in Mogadishu had been brutally repressed by army and police forces (AAE 2010: 59). In 1988, these political developments started to escalate in several parts of Somalia: after a peace agreement with Ethiopia on 3 April 1988, the oppositional Somali National Movement (SNM) had to leave its Ethiopian exile and tried to gain control of northern Somalia, occupying Hargeysa, Berbera and Burᶜo in May 1988 (Gascon 1990: 47). In a counter-move, the Barre regime intervened militarily, causing the death of tens of thousands and laying the foundations for the secession of the north as Somaliland in May 1991 (Bradbury 2008: 46; Höhne 2015; Kapteijns 2013; Krech 1996: 38ff). In the south, clan disputes over grazing rights and access to water led to the escalation of a conflict between Barre's own Marehan sub-clan and competing Ogaden herders. When Siyad Barre ordered the army to support the local Marehan in this conflict[79], his clan-based alliance disintegrated[80] and left him isolated against increasing active opposition from all other clans (Little 2003: 43–4). The resulting civil war quickly led to the collapse of Siyad Barre's regime. On 27 January 1991 he evacuated Mogadishu, and two warlords, ᶜAlī Mahdi Muḥammad (b. 1939), a Hawiye-Abgal, and Muḥammad Farah Ḥasan ᶜAidīd (1936–96),[81] a Hawiye-Habr Gedir by clan affiliation, started to fight for power. In the context of this civil war and the resulting famine, in the region of 300,000 people were killed in Somalia, while about two million people were displaced and fled either to safe territories within Somalia or to refugee camps in neighbouring Kenya (Höhne 2011b: 64f; Kapteijns 2013).

The 1989 wave of repression also convinced a number of Salafi-oriented activists to change their course and resort to a strategy of armed opposition against the regime. In particular al-ittiḥād al-islāmī prepared for *jihād* and in 1991 actually started an armed struggle against Muḥammad Faraḥ Ḥasan ᶜAidid in the region of Kismayo. Al-ittiḥād was not in a position, however, to hold out against the vastly superior forces of Muḥammad Faraḥ Ḥasan ᶜAidid and was militarily defeated in 1991 (AAE 2010: 59). In reaction to this defeat, al-ittiḥād decided to relocate to smaller cities, in particular port towns such as Brawa, Merca and Bosaso. Due to the managerial qualities of al-ittiḥād members, the organisation had some success, but al-ittiḥād claims to political power in these port cities were quickly countered by the warlords (Marchal 2004: 127). While al-ittiḥād forces were quickly defeated in Kismayo by Muḥammad Faraḥ Ḥasan ᶜAidid's forces, and while al-ittiḥād was unable to find acceptance in Brawa, they held out in Merca until 1993, but left in order to evade confrontation with US troops (Marchal 2004: 130).

Al-ittiḥād al-islāmī was able to control the harbour of Bosaso for a short period of time and to establish a degree of security under the leadership of ᶜAlī Warsame and Ḥasan Dahir Aweys. But in June 1992, al-ittiḥād was also forced to evacuate this region by ᶜAbdallāh Yūsuf Aḥmad's Somali Salvation Democratic Front (SSDF) that claimed hegemonic control over Puntland.[82] The positive impression al-ittiḥād had created in Bosaso helped the movement, after a short stint in Warsangeli territory, to build a third basis[83] in the Gedo region (Luuq and Buulo Haawa) in 1992. Here, they established some sort of stability and launched the struggle against Ethiopia, which was regarded as an occupier of Somali lands in the Ogaden region.[84] In 1992, al-ittiḥād organised a series of attacks on Ethiopian territory, including Addis Ababa, triggering Ethiopia's military counter-attack against its base in the Gedo region in August 1996 and January 1997. The 1992 attacks were engineered by al-ittihad's 'Ethiopian' branch, al-ittiḥād ee Somalia galbeed (al-ittiḥād of Western Somalia), which sought the unification of the Ethiopian Ogaden region with Somalia (Østebø 2015b: 10).[85] In the direct confrontation with the Ethiopian Army, al-ittiḥād was defeated decisively in 1997 (AAE 2010: 60; Marchal 2004: 128). After 1997, al-ittiḥād merged into new religious and political structures and became a major factor in the Islamic Courts movement.

Although al-ittiḥād al-islāmī had been able to gain some popularity due to its struggle against both Ethiopia and the US and although it had been able to deliver security, stability and justice, the organisation suffered internal splits due to both its strategic decisions and the problem of clan solidarities that usually proved to be stronger than Islam.[86] As a result of these internal dynamics of discussion and dispute, an al-ittiḥād majority decided to abandon the strategy of armed struggle in 1997. The leader of al-ittiḥād, ᶜAlī Warsame (since 1993 the successor to ᶜAbd al-Azīz Faraḥ who had been killed in Bosaso in 1992), stepped down and returned to Burᶜo to lead al-waḥda. As a result of its defeat and the strategic decision to abandon armed struggle, al-ittiḥād split into several fractions: al-waḥda in Puntland and Somaliland, al-ittiḥād in the Ogaden and the Gedo region, and al-iᶜtiṣām in the Hawiye-controlled coastal regions (Marchal 2009: 384). In addition, there was the Ras Kamboni group led by Ḥasan ᶜAbdallāh Hirsi Turki (AAE 2010: 61)[87] and, last but not least, those al-ittiḥād fighters who followed Ḥasan Dahir Aweys to Mogadishu, where he set up the Ifka Halane court in 1998.

Ḥasan Dahir Aweys (b. about 1937), a Hawiye-Habr Gedir by clan affiliation, was a colonel in the Somali Army and was seriously wounded in 1977 in the war against Ethiopia. Due to his Salafi orientation, he was jailed several times by the Barre regime after 1979. In 1991, he was sent to negotiate with al-ittiḥād in Kismayo by General ᶜAidīd. In Kismayo, Aweys changed sides, became 'Shaykh' Ḥasan Dahir Aweys and joined al-ittiḥād (Höhne 2009: 4). In 1997, he was seriously wounded in the confrontation with Ethiopia and subsequently supported (for the time being) a new strategy that did not rely on military strength but endorsed the idea of Islamic courts, which should be built from the ground up and evolve slowly (Marchal 2009: 384). According to Somali opinion, Ḥasan Dahir Aweys 'speaks his mind, is courageous and a very accessible man, but not a scholar of Islam' (Marchal 2009: 401). When the Islamic Courts movement was crushed by the Ethiopian Army in 2006, Ḥasan Dahir Aweys was granted asylum in Eritrea and joined the new Islamic opposition movement to the Transitional Federal Government (TFG), the Alliance for the Re-Liberation of Somalia (ARS) that was formed in 2007, but split into two factions in 2008. While Sharīf Shaykh Aḥmad led the 'moderate' ARS-Djibouti group that joined the TFG in 2008, Ḥasan Dahir Aweys chaired the ARS-Asmara that refused cooperation with the TFG. When the Ethiopian Army left Somalia in 2009, Ḥasan Dahir Aweys returned to Somalia on 23 April 2009 and assumed leadership of another radical group, ḥizb al-islam. Ḥizb al-islam had been founded in February 2009 by Ḥasan al-Mahdi and integrated most followers of the ARS-Asmara group (Stuke 2011: 103f). In December 2010, ḥizb al-islam joined al-shabāb (AAE 2010: 61; Höhne 2014b: 14; Hansen 2013a: 80f, 108).

Al-ittiḥād's strategic move away from armed struggle can be explained by a number of factors. First, a majority of surviving al-ittiḥād members realised that the use of arms against opponents who were Muslims had created doctrinal problems. In particular, scholars affiliated with al-iṣlāḥ criticised al-ittiḥād for its armed struggle. Second, all efforts by al-ittiḥād to gain a territorial base had failed militarily and al-ittiḥād had lost a large number of members and leaders. This showed that al-ittiḥād was not in a position to hold territory militarily. Third, when al-ittiḥād gained control over a region, local clans became increasingly nervous regarding security issues and issues of jurisdiction: although one of the most prominent al-ittiḥād leaders, Ḥasan Dahir Aweys, claimed that al-ittiḥād was above clan loyalties ('no clan but Islam', Menkhaus 2004: 58) and rejected the idea that clans should have political control over 'their region' ('land was not owned by clans'), al-ittiḥād politics (and legal rulings) were repeatedly interpreted as following clan loyalties and neglecting or even violating the interests of local clans (AAE 2010: 79; Menkhaus 2004: 60–1).

The failure of al-ittiḥād's strategy in 1996/7 strengthened the peaceful approach of al-iṣlāḥ. Also, al-iṣlāḥ managed to transcend clan divisions and thus prepared the way for Islamic courts. It also worked consistently for reconciliation and consequently became highly influential in the 2000 ᶜArta conference in Djibouti (AMA 2011: 283). The history of al-ittiḥād disputes with local clans in Mogadishu, Bosaso and Gedo, on the other hand, shows how, under the extraordinary conditions of the civil war in Somalia, local and clan interests prevailed over doctrinal considerations, and eventually contributed to the political failure of a fairly successful Salafi movement of reform such as al-ittiḥād. At the same time, the military failures of al-ittiḥād showed that the competing 'generational project' of al-iṣlāḥ, namely, to work for a peaceful transformation of Somalia towards Salafi-oriented concepts of society (Menkhaus 2004: 65), was perceived as being more promising than the concept of *jihād*.

If we regard the 1960s, the 1970s and the early 1980s as the time when Salafi-oriented concepts of reform germinated, the late 1980s and the 1990s can be regarded as the time when Salafi-oriented organisations solidified and tried to implement concrete social and religious policies, for instance in the guise of Islamic courts. This was the time when a series of social actors in Somalia tried to overcome chaos by introducing and implementing a new model of social, religious and political organisation. Salafi-oriented groups acquired increasing popularity at this time because they were seen as a force that could be able to overcome the legacy of warlordism. It needs to be stressed, however, that Islamic courts and their law-enforcing Islamic militias were successful only as long as they were financed by Somali businessmen and traders, who had a keen interest in ending arbitrariness and habits of over-taxation by warlords, and cultivating a degree of stability and reliability (Little 2003: 154; Marchal and Sheikh 2015: 150ff). These courts were not the result of strategic efforts by al-ittiḥād or al-iṣlāḥ or other Salafi-oriented groups, but of local initiatives, mostly by traders and businessmen, and therefore they represented local Islamic traditions. Although groups such as al-ittiḥād tried to infiltrate and take over the courts, they were often unable to do so, or were quickly contained, or even ousted, as in Merca in June 2000 (Marchal 2004: 136). Islamic courts collapsed (or were forced to become more moderate) as soon as traders and businessmen withdrew their support because they gained the impression that Salafi-oriented groups were misusing their influence (Marchal 2004: 136).

The first Islamic court was organised in 1991 in Mogadishu by Sharīf Sharafow, Ibrāhīm Suley and Muḥammad Muᶜallim Ḥasan and his majmūᶜ al-ᶜulamāᵓ, but this court quickly came to an end when it started to prosecute and punish criminals, and when the warlords started to perceive the activities of the court as a threat to their own authority (AAE 2010: 63). A second court was started in Luuq in the Gedo region in 1992 by Muḥammad A. Nūr and worked under the protection of al-ittiḥād. In 1997, this court was dissolved, however, in the context of the invasion of the Ethiopian Army and related actions by Somali National Front militias. The Ḥasan Dahir Aweys court in Merka lasted from February to December 1992, but could not stop the military take-over by General ᶜAidīd. By contrast, the court established by Ḥasan ᶜAbdallāh Hirsi Turki in Ras Kamboni in 1992 survived (Marchal 2009: 385). In 1994, a fifth court was established in the Medina quarter of northern Mogadishu under the guidance of ᶜAlī Muḥammad Rage alias ᶜAlī 'Dhere' (Hawiye-Abgal by clan affiliation, d. 2014), supported by local businessmen and elders and protected by the warlord ᶜAli Mahdi (Marchal 2004: 133ff; Höhne 2009: 4, 2011a: 125f). This court managed to stabilise a notoriously unstable northern Mogadishu and created the saying 'if you want peace, establish an Islamic court' (AAE 2010: 65; on the different Islamic courts, see Marchal 2009: 384ff). Also, people were impressed by the fact that the militias of the Islamic courts, 'whatever past they had, stopped chewing qaat and harassing civilians' (Marchal 2013: 346).

In 1994, courts were created in northern Mogadishu, in 1996 in Hiran (Beledweyne) and the Bay (Baidoa) regions, and in 1998 in southern and western Mogadishu, among them the Ifka Halane court of Ḥasan Dahir Aweys. From there, the Courts Movement spread to the Lower Shebelle region, where a series of courts was established after 1998. In 1998, the ᶜAlī Dhere court in northern Mogadishu was dissolved when ᶜAlī 'Dhere' was increasingly perceived as being too power-hungry by local elders and businessmen, and chaos returned to northern Mogadishu (AAE 2010: 66; Marchal 2004: 134). At the same time, two new courts were established by Ḥasan Dahir Aweys in southern Mogadishu and Merca, and this initiative led to the establishment of a Sharīᶜa Implementation Council in 2000, and to the establishment of the Islamic Courts Union (al-ittiḥād al-maḥākim al-islāmiyya) with ᶜAlī 'Dhere' as chairman and Ḥasan Dahir Aweys as his deputy (Hansen 2013a: 34; Rabasa 2009: 56; Stuke 2011: 65).

In 2000, the Islamic courts joined the Transitional National Government (TNG) in the context of the ᶜArta conference in Djibouti, and most leaders of the courts became members of the transitional parliament, even if radical Islamists criticised this strategy (Marchal 2009: 386). The fact that approximately 25 per cent of all members of the new transitional parliament were affiliated with or sympathised with al-islāḥ points to the strength this Salafi-oriented organisation had gained in Somalia by 2000 (Marchal 2013: 351). Immediately after its establishment, the TNG was opposed, however, by an alliance of warlords from southern and central Somalia, led by Puntland's president, ᶜAbdallāh Yūsuf Aḥmad (supported by Ethiopia), and thus quickly turned out to be a political failure (communication Markus Höhne, 26 February 2015). In 2004, the Transitional Federal Government (TFG) was set up as a successor to the defunct Transitional National Government (TNG). The major result of the ᶜArta conference was the acceptance of a system of power sharing following the '4.5' formula: while the Darood, Digil/Digil-Mirifle (or Rahanweyn), Dir and Hawiye clan collective received one full share each in government and administration, the weaker clans and ethnic minorities were allocated half a share, the '0.5' share (AMA 2011: 19).

This formula discriminated not only against non-Somali ethnic groups in southern Somalia, such as the Boni, which are often subsumed under the term jareer ('hard haired'),[88] but also against the mixed populations of the southern coastal cities of Merca, Brawa and Kismayo, as well as the Swahili-speaking Bajuni fisher populations on the southern Somali coast.

The Islamic Courts Union was complemented in 2004 by a second umbrella council of Islamic courts led by Sharīf Shaykh Aḥmad (b. 1964), comprising about ten courts (Rabasa 2009: 56). Sharīf Shaykh Aḥmad was a Hawiye-Abgal by clan affiliation and a Sufi scholar affiliated with the Qādiriyya. He had studied geography in the Sudan and Arabic in Libya and had come back to Somalia in 1998 (Rabasa 2009: 56). In 2000, Sharīf Shaykh Aḥmad became leader of the reorganised ahl al-sunna wa-l-jamāᶜa group in Mogadishu. His 'Sii Sii' court was supported by the Benaadir Company business group, which managed the Eel Maᵓaan port north of Mogadishu, and was also linked with the majmūᶜ al-ᶜulamāᵓ (Marchal 2009: 388). The Islamic courts were thus supported by both Sufi- and Salafi-oriented groups and all groups competed over questions of leadership.

After 11 September 2001, the situation changed again, when local militias and warlords started to hunt down 'Islamists' in cooperation with Ethiopia and the USA in the newly proclaimed 'war on terror'. As a result, some Salafi-oriented groups rethought their strategy and resumed the armed struggle, this time consciously attacking Muslims, in particular warlords who were seen as collaborating with Ethiopia or the USA. At the same time, Ethiopia, the USA and their local allies abducted and assassinated Somali 'terror suspects'. This low-intensity warfare and outside interference, as well as the assassination of a number of religious scholars from 2002 to 2005, considerably increased the popularity of *jihād*-minded groups (Höhne 2009: 8, 2011a: 131). In late 2005, a coalition of Salafi-oriented groups, including tajammuᶜ, the dam al-jadīd faction of al-iṣlāḥ, a faction of al-iᶜtiṣām and a new group, the ḥarakat al-shabāb al-mujāhidīn (for short 'al-shabāb'), joined forces, and on 18 February 2006 started to fight a coalition of fourteen warlords in Mogadishu (AAE 2010: 62; Hansen 2013a: 32ff). By May 2006, they had gained control over all of Mogadishu and quickly expanded into the rural regions, gaining control over most of southern and central Somalia. In June 2006, the two court unions united to form the Supreme

Islamic Court of Somalia that consisted of a *shūra* of ninety-seven members, representing about thirty courts in action (Woodward 2013: 86). Of these ninety-seven members, al-shabāb commanded the loyalty of nine members (Hansen 2013a: 36). Despite this process of unification, internal differences remained, for instance over strategic issues or clan alliances, and led to the disintegration of the Supreme Council after the Ethiopian invasion on 27 December 2006 (Rabasa 2009: 59–60; Stuke 2011: 72). The rapid expansion of the Islamic Courts movement under chairman Sharīf Shaykh Aḥmad and his deputy, Ḥasan Dahir Aweys had threatened the seat of Somalia's TFG in Baidoa[89] and, as a result, the Ethiopian Army with the support of the USA again intervened in December 2006 and quickly defeated the Islamic Courts movement, occupying Mogadishu in the process. As a result of the Ethiopian intervention, the Islamic courts were dissolved and insecurity returned to Ethiopian and TFG-controlled territories, in particular Mogadishu, until the Ethiopian Army evacuated Somalia in 2009.

While Somalia's TFG tried to consolidate its position, al-shabāb regrouped its forces, started a protracted guerrilla struggle against the Ethiopian Army and its allies in Mogadishu and built a number of bases (and courts) in southern Somalia. The establishment of al-shabāb is shrouded in a number of tales of origin (see Hansen 2013a: 19ff; Höhne 2011a: 131ff; Marchal and Sheikh 2015: 154ff): according to one tale, al-shabāb was established in 1998 as a militia of the Islamic courts in Mogadishu by Ḥasan Dahir Aweys; other sources mention al-shabāb as a youth organisation of the Islamic courts in Mogadishu in 2005 or stress the role of informal networks of 'been-tos', that is, young Somalis who had been to training camps in Pakistan or Afghanistan. One such youth, ᶜAden Hashi ᶜAyro, a Hawiye-Habr Gedir[90] by clan affiliation, was the military leader of al-shabāb from 2005 until 1 May 2008, when he was killed in action and replaced by Aḥmad ᶜAbdi Godane also known as Mukhtār Abū Zubayr (1969–2014) from Hargeysa, an Isaaq by clan affiliation.[91] Still other sources stress the biographical link of al-shabāb with members of al-ittiḥād in the 1990s and al-waḥda in the 1980s (Stuke 2011: 74; Hansen 2013a: 15ff). Most probably, Ḥasan Dahir Aweys took over military training and organisation of the courts' militias in a training camp in Mogadishu in 2004, where the muᶜaskar Muḥammad (army of Muḥammad) was formed, and later renamed jamāᶜat al-shabāb (Marchal

2009: 388). In charge of everday activities in this camp was Ḥasan Dahir Aweys' young deputy, ᶜAden Hashi ᶜAyro, who became the first field leader of al-shabāb and who commanded the Ifka Halane court militia from 2005 (ICG 2005: 11). He came from an al-iᶜtiṣām background and, like a number of other Somalis, had been in Afghanistan (Marchal 2009: 388). The second in command was Mukhtār Roobow, also known as 'Abū Manṣūr' (b. 1971 in the Bay region), a Rahanweyn by clan affiliation, who had studied Islamic law at the University of Khartoum in the 1990s, had then joined al-ittiḥād al-islāmī and worked for the al-ḥaramayn foundation until 2002 (Marchal 2009: 389; until 2004 according to Fergusson 2013: 122). The problem of identifying the proper date of origin of al-shabāb points to a characteristic feature of Somali Islamic trajectories: they are in continual flux (see Hansen 2013a; Marchal 2009; Rabasa 2009; Stuke 2011).

Since the creation of the African Union Mission for Somalia (AMISOM) in 2007 by Uganda and Burundi, and the Kenyan military intervention in southern Somalia supported by Ethiopia in 2011, al-shabāb has been on the defensive: in November 2012, Kenyan armed forces captured Kismayo (Höhne 2014b: 27). When al-shabāb was pushed out from major parts of southern and central Somalia in 2012, a new centre of al-shabāb activities emerged in the Golis mountains between Somaliland and Puntland (Fergusson 2013: 425; Hansen 2013a: 122ff; Höhne 2014a: 358ff, 2015: 119ff).[92] In 2012, al-shabāb adopted a new strategy, abandoning large-scale territorial moves in favour of using suicide attacks to assassinate prominent members of the TFG/SFG and representatives of Somali civil society trying to disrupt Somalia's recovery (Bryden 2014: 2).

Recent al-shabāb defeats were due to a number of internal disputes. These disputes were linked, for instance, with the fact that the al-shabāb coalition consisted of at least four major sub-groups in 2009, each of which followed its own agenda.[93] Two of these sub-groups, namely the 'Ras Kamboni Brigade' led by Ḥasan ᶜAbdallāh Hirsi Turki, and the ḥizb al-islām[94] led by Ḥasan Dahir Aweys split (for different reasons) from the al-shabāb coalition in 2010 and 2013 or were decimated in the context of internal purges. Two other fractions have been in open dispute since at least 2013, namely the group led by Aḥmad ᶜAbdi Godane and the group of Rahanweyn fighters led by Mukhtār Roobow. The conflict between the Godane and the

Roobow groups probably started in 2008, when Roobow prevailed over Godane regarding the re-opening of the Aden Adde International Airport, while Godane accused Roobow of being too closely linked with Rahanweyn clan interests (Hansen 2013a: 78). This conflict over authority intensified in September 2010 when a military offensive against AMISOM troops and the Somali TFG, planned by Aḥmad ᶜAbdi Godane, misfired, causing major losses for al-shabāb (Höhne 2011a: 152f). Shortly before this offensive, two Kenyan scholars of Salafi orientation and Somali extraction, Maḥamad ᶜAbdi Umul and Maḥamūd Shaykh Maḥamūd Shiblī, had condemned al-shabāb by comparing the group to the early Kharijites. Their sermons spread widely in Somalia and contributed to the doctrinal isolation of al-shabāb (Marchal and Sheikh 2015: 161).

As a consequence of al-shabāb's defeat, the amniyāt al-shabāb units that had been in charge of al-shabāb's internal security and were commanded by Aḥmad ᶜAbdi Godane were dissolved, although Godane was confirmed as supreme commander and also kept informal control over the amniyāt units.[95] The final break between the Roobow and the Godane groups occurred between 19 and 22 June 2013 in Brawa, when the Godane group was able to remove followers of Roobow and Aweys from supreme command positions. In this conflict, several leading al-shabāb and ḥizb al-islam members were killed, including an old companion of Aḥmad ᶜAbdi Godane, Ibrāhīm Ḥājj Jamāᶜ ᶜAlī Meeᵓaad also known as 'Ibrāhīm al-Afghānī' (an Isaaq by clan affiliation like Godane). Ḥasan Dahir Aweys fled into SFG-controlled territory and was arrested there (ICG 2014b: 9-12; Höhne 2014b: 33; Bryden 2014: 5). Mukhtār Roobow, by contrast, led a majority of the Rahanweyn fighters into the Bay- and Bakol region, that is, Rahanweyn homeland (Hassan M. Abukar 2013). As a result, the remainder of al-shabāb true to Aḥmad ᶜAbdi Godane lost a major part of its fighting force and had to evacuate considerable territory hitherto under al-shabāb control. On 4 October 2014, the last al-shabāb-controlled town, Brawa, was abandoned by al-shabāb and taken over by AMISOM troops. Since then, al-shabāb has undergone a process of unravelling into a plethora of small groups that have either withdrawn into the southern Somalian bush or surrendered to SFG authorities. Due to the fact that the remainder of al-shabāb was no longer able to hold territory, it focused instead on guerrilla and suicide attacks (*New York Times International*

Weekly, 14 November 2014), a strategy that can be viewed as the most radical form of spatial segregation and re-location: to paradise.

Despite the civil war, the Somali economy has performed surprisingly well since the late 1990s and has even become an interesting market for foreign investors such as Turkey since the late 2000s.[96] Apart from income through the export of cattle to the tune of approximately 100 million US dollars annually, Somalia profits from remittances by the Somali diaspora amounting to 500 million to one billion US dollars annually (Stuke 2011: 34; Menkhaus 2004: 54). Remittances, in particular, have helped to boost (urban) investment and give traders and businessmen decisive power, as the 'bazaar' is increasingly able (and willing) to finance its own militias. As a result, 'businessmen have emerged as a major political force in the urban centres' (Menkhaus 2004: 38). The new power of the 'bazaar' was signalled by the refusal of Mogadishu's businessmen in 1999 to pay 'taxes' to militia leaders and 'instead bought the militiamen away from the warlords and sub-contracted the management of the militia to *sharīᶜa* courts' (Menkhaus 2004: 44). As a result of economic recovery since the late 1990s, Somali traders and businessmen have managed to establish efficient networks of trade and finance, including Somalia's largest banking and telecommunications network, al-barakāt. As a result, Somali business interests have been able and willing to invest money in reliable protective and administrative structures, and Salafi-oriented groups have been able to respond to such aspirations (Marchal 2013: 332).

The fact that Somali businessmen and traders were increasingly leaning towards Salafi-oriented concepts of society meant a significant loss of influence of Sufi-oriented movements, even if some Sufi-oriented traders or elders sympathised with some of the political (not religious) aims of Salafi-oriented groups such as the political unity of Somalia (Renders n.d.). A major Sufi-oriented organisation that was supported and financed by traders and businessmen was the ahl al-sunna wa-l-jamāᶜa group that recruited its members mostly among the followers of the Qādiriyya (Marchal and Sheikh 2013: 224). This group had been established in 1992 by General Muḥammad Faraḥ Ḥasan ᶜAidīd and had some support in southern Somalia (Marchal 2004: 124). In 1994, ᶜAlī Mahdī set up his own ahl al-sunna wa-l-jamāᶜa group that acquired an important role in the Islamic Courts movement in northern

Mogadishu (Marchal and Sheikh 2013: 225ff). The ^{c}Aidīd branch of the ahl al-sunna wa-l-jamā^{c}a reorganised itself in 1996 and gained support in southern and central Somalia. Both ahl al-sunna wa-l-jamā^{c}a groups were supported by businessmen and clan elders as well as the Somali diaspora (Marchal and Sheikh 2013: 226). In 2008, ahl al-sunna wa-jamā^{c}a reorganised itself with Ethiopian support in reaction to al-shabāb policies to eradicate Sufism in its territories. In 2008, apart from a Catholic church in Kismayo, al-shabāb destroyed the tombs of eighteen well-known Sufi *shuyūkh* in Kismayo, and in the Banādir and lower Shebelle regions (Marchal and Sheikh 2013: 238), including the tomb of Uways al-Barawī in Biyoley (Fergusson 2013: 90). The destruction of tombs and pilgrimage places contributed to the break between Sufi-oriented groups and al-shabāb. Ahl al-sunna wa-l-jamā^{c}a scholars accused al-shabāb of *fitna* and and *bid^{c}a*, and the population supported the ahl al-sunna wa-l-jamā^{c}a group against al-shabāb's austerity policies (Marchal and Sheikh 2013: 228). An opposition movement against al-shabāb thus formed, led by ahl al-sunna wa-l-jamā^{c}a scholars, uniting a number of clans, in particular the Dir, Darood-Marehan, Hawiye-Habr Gedir and others (Marchal and Sheikh 2013: 228). In December 2009, ahl al-sunna wa-l-jamā^{c}a elected a *shūra* of forty-three members in the context of a conference in Aabudwaaq. ^{c}Umar Shaykh ^{c}Abd al-Qādir was elected chairperson, and the diaspora gave him strong support, although local disputes led to the subsequent fragmentation of the ahl al-sunna wa-l-jamā^{c}a movement: 'Clearly clan competition mattered' (Marchal and Sheikh 2013: 230). By 2014, three ahl al-sunna wa-l-jamā^{c}a branches had emerged in the Galgaduud, Gedo and Banadir regions (Höhne 2014b: 21), which were united in their support for Somalia's SFG.[97] In general terms, however, Sufism as a social movement has been in decline in central and southern Somalia, as well as in Somaliland, since the early 1990s, while Salafi-oriented groups of reform have grown in terms of social influence (communication Markus Höhne, 26 February 2015).

Boko Haram, al-shabāb and Northern Mali in Comparison

In our analysis of Salafi-oriented movements of reform we have examined three local contexts where Muslims have chosen to follow a path of extremely militant action: northern Mali, north-eastern Nigeria and Somalia. It is now time to look at these contexts in a comparative perspective and to see whether there are patterns of agency. Due to their will to fight (even against other Muslims, including Salafi-oriented scholars), and due to their extremely weak doctrinal basis, I have defined groups such as Boko Haram and al-shabāb as *jihād*-minded. A first analytical problem when comparing Boko Haram and al-shabāb, as well as the different religio-political groups in northern Mali, is the fact that both Boko Haram and al-shabāb are religio-political movements, while northern Mali constitutes a geographical frame of reference where a series of militant groups operate. Only some of these militant groups have a distinct religious agenda. This analytical problem points to the fact that *jihād*-minded groups mirror vastly different local contexts and should not be studied from one particular angle only.

When comparing Boko Haram, al-shabāb and the different religio-political movements in northern Mali, we see that they all emerged in the 2000s[98] and that they managed to gain territorial control over parts of their respective countries, a fact that reflects their quest for spatial segregation. Regions under control of *jihād*-minded groups are characterised by the fact that they are geographically remote and often difficult to access. Such *Grenzwildnisse* (borderland wildernesses)[99] have historically (and currently) escaped tight government control and governments have often been unable (or unwilling) to provide security for local populations. Due to this fact, oppositional movements have had the chance to act as alternative sources of authority and security. Also, all *jihād*-minded groups have spread into neighbouring countries: in the case of al-shabāb to northern and coastal Kenya; in the case of Boko Haram into Cameroon and Niger (ICG 2013b: 41); in the case of the different groups in northern Mali into Algeria, Niger, Mauretania and Burkina Faso. However, their modes of expansion differ: the region of Diffa in Niger constituted a safe haven for Boko Haram until 2014 (communication Abdoulaye Sounaye, 31 October 2014); al-shabāb, in contrast, has exported war into Kenya and has found support in Kenya among a minority of marginalised coastal Muslims as well as ethnic Somali; in northern Mali, the different religio-political 'rebel' groups have found refuge in Algeria, Niger, Mauretania and Burkina Faso and have been instrumentalised (mostly by Algeria) for national politial interests.

It is equally important to stress that contemporary *jihād*-minded groups had precursors in the eighteenth and nineteenth centuries: in the context of rebellions against established (Muslim) rulers in vast parts of sub-Saharan Africa, *jihād*-minded movements of reform emerged that managed to found emirates and caliphates legitimised on the basis of Islam (Loimeier 2013: 108ff). All of these *jihād*-minded movements of reform were led by religious scholars (*ᶜulamāᵓ*) who were linked with a Sufi order. They thus represent a tradition of militant Sufism that has been largely neglected in Western academic analyses, although these movements of reform continue to inform Muslim politics in sub-Saharan Africa to this day. In contrast to their historical predecessors, contemporary *jihād*-minded groups have adopted anti-esoteric positions and have developed a record of destroying the tombs of Muslim saints, and even mosques, in northern Mali, in north-eastern Nigeria and in Somalia. In this context, we have to ask which specific historical context has informed such acts of destruction: have all tombs of saints been destroyed or only some (and which ones)? Are there historical predecessors such as Somalia where the followers of Sayyid Muḥammad ᶜAbdille Ḥasan fought the competing Sufi order of the Qādiriyya in southern Somalia in the early twentieth century, and killed their major leader, Uways al-Barawī, in 1909? Or were contemporary anti-iconic acts an expression of radical Salafi opposition to saint veneration only?

In contrast to the historical movements of *jihād* led by *ᶜulamāᵓ* affiliated with a Sufi order, contemporary leaders of *jihād* were not *ᶜulamāᵓ*, but militant activists with a comparatively limited knowledge of texts, essentially the Qurᵓān (and a rather narrow reading of the Qurᵓān), the Sunna of the Prophet (and *ḥadīth* literature). As such, the quest for doctrinal distinction (and doctrinal debates) has been relatively weak among contemporary *jihād*-minded groups. Contemporary *jihād*-minded groups stress the paramount role of the Prophet as a model for the organisation of both religious and everyday life, and activists have adopted a 'prophetic' habitus, such as long hair, a full beard (but a trimmed moustache) and they usually reject the practice of *isbāl*, and thus demonstrate their quest for symbolic distanciation. In matters of symbolic distanciation and the 'proper' Prophetic habitus, contemporary *jihād*-minded groups usually followed the teachings and *fatāwa* of Muḥammad Nāṣir al-Dīn al-Albānī and other Salafi thinkers, who were often characterised by their opposition to the Saudi royal family as well as the Saudi religious establishment.

In contrast to their historical predecessors, contemporary *jihād*-minded groups are also characterised by their liberal recourse to *takfīr*, that is, their willingness to attack other Muslims who reject their own position or who cooperate with an 'un-Islamic' government, referring to them as 'unbelievers'. The accusation of unbelief has often been directed at dissidents within *jihād*-minded groups or at religious scholars who are close to *jihād*-minded groups, if they do not share their ultra-militant strategies. Boko Haram, as well as al-shabāb and some of the Malian groups, have in fact assassinated religious scholars who turned against such movements. 'Moderate' Salafi-oriented scholars have thus come to see *jihād*-minded groups as a threat, not only to their own claims to hegemony of interpretation, but also to their educational and charitable activities as well as their long-term programmes of social reform. As a consequence of internal disputes over questions of authority, as well as different modes of accommodation with local contexts, contemporary *jihād*-minded groups have split into a plethora of groups with different religious and political orientations: there has been no unity among religio-political movements in northern Mali and neither Boko Haram nor al-shabāb represent monolithic organisations. Boko Haram and al-shabāb, as well as the 'rebel' groups in northern Mali, all emerged from 'mother' movements characterised by internal disputes.

Another important observation is that the local context engenders *jihād*: in the case of northern Mali, it was the structural weakness of the Malian state (and its army) together with the destabilising impact of the destruction of Muᶜammar al-Qadhdhāfī's regime in Libya by France, Great Britain, Qaṭar and the USA; in the case of north-eastern Nigeria, it was Nigerian Government repression and arbitrary rule, as well as Nigeria's inability to develop this region economically;[100] in the case of Somalia, it was the Somalian civil war since 1988: without the civil war (and the repeated Ethiopian military interventions), al-shabāb would most probably not have been born. In this context we may ask why Mali and not Niger (that even has a common frontier with Libya), why northeastern Nigeria and not northwestern Nigeria, why Somalia and not Somaliland. Here, more research would be highly welcome. Still, some basic assumptions can be made: Niger, for instance, has managed much better than Mali to integrate its Saharan populations (both Tuareg and 'Toubou') since independence, despite the 1991–8 and 2007–9 rebellions (see Klute and Lecocq in print; ICG 2013b);[101] in northwestern Nigeria, local political elites have managed much better than those in the northeast to win national resources for their region. In addition, both Sufi- and Salafi-oriented religio-political alliances in the Hausa regions of central northern and northwestern Nigeria (that is, Kano, Kasina, Sokoto, Zamfara and Bauchi states, as well as northern Kaduna) have been able to create social stability to a much larger extent than such alliances in the northeast (or in the Middle Belt region), and to integrate religious movements into regional political structures; Somaliland has managed to create broad consensus regarding the peaceful resolution of conflicts in the context of its own national development.

The *jihād*-minded groups in northern Mali, north-eastern Nigeria and Somalia can all look back on a long history of internal conflict and splits. The internal development of these *jihād*-minded groups has been informed by three major dynamics, namely:

1. disputes over strategy and strategic goals
2. disputes over questions of authority
3. disputes over questions of accommodation with local populations.

As a consequence of these disputes, *jihād*-minded groups have not been able to develop a common long-term agenda. Equally, disputes over the issues mentioned above have led to internal conflict and factional friction. This is best illustrated by the development of al-shabāb in Somalia, which has seen many internal conflicts since its foundation.

A central question regarding the development of *jihād*-minded groups is the question of why such groups have found support in local populations despite the fact that they represent extremely narrow doctrinal positions that are rejected by a majority of Muslims due to their literalist limitations and despite the fact that such groups often establish a regime of terror and extreme justice. An understanding of the social background of such groups will enable us to diagnose the phenomenon properly and to develop a therapy that will eventually help to prevent the emergence of ultra-radicalisms. Which social forces have supported the *jihād*-minded groups in northern Mali, in Somalia and in north-eastern Nigeria?

1. All of these groups were youth movements (exception: the religio-political movements in northern Mali); in its foundational period, Boko Haram rebelled against the authority of elder scholars, while al-shabāb rejected the authority of the last remaining senior leader (Ḥasan Dahir Aweys) in its 2013 purge.
2. All *jihād*-minded groups have gained support, at least for limited periods of time, among populations that have been marginalised in multiple ways (such as political, economic, social and ethnic) by promising a better allocation of ressources and an end to discrimination and marginalisation: in northern Mali, the different Tuareg and Arab populations; in north-eastern Nigeria the marginalised farmers and pastoralists of the most underdeveloped federal state (Bornu) within the federation of Nigeria; in Somalia, the Rahanweyn clan federation as well as some of the smaller ethnic groups of southern Somalia that were excluded from national politics by the '4.5' formula of 2000, and finally the Darood-Ogaden sub-clan that sought to gain access to a port (Kismayo) on the Indian Ocean by entering into an alliance with al-shabāb (ICG 2014b: 13).
3. *Jihād*-minded groups have also been able to gain support among local populations due to the fact that such groups were able to provide (limited) security and a new order based on a rigid interpretation of the *sharīᶜa*. A classical example was Somalia, where since 1991 Islamic courts have managed repeatedly to provide stability and security for limited periods of time and in geographically restricted areas. On a larger scale, the Rahanweyn clan federation suffered most from a lack of security in the civil war that began in 1988: while the large pastoral (and Afmaxaa-speaking) clans of the Dir, Hawiye and Darood were able to defend their own interests with their own militias, the sedentary and/or agro-pastoral (and Afmaay-speaking) Rahanweyn (Digil and Digil-Mirifle) have been raided time and again by different warlords.[102] As a consequence, many Rahanweyn joined al-shabāb in 2006, hoping that al-shabāb (that was not linked with any specific clan) would provide security (Hansen 2013a: 5; Ferguson 2013: 66, 76). Equally, other Rahanweyn supported the TNG of Somalia and the Ethiopian Army for similar reasons, until the Ethiopian Army and the TFG proved unable to provide either security or stability in 2007. As a consequence, numerous Rahanweyn soldiers and

army units within the Somali Army changed sides and joined al-shabāb or withdrew to the Rahanweyn home region in the Bay and Bakol provinces where they established militias for self-defence (Hansen 2013a: 58).

4. In both northeastern Nigeria and in Somalia, or better, in the Muslim areas of northern and coastal Kenya, *jihād*-minded groups profited from local solidarities by fighting Nigerian/Kenyan Christian 'settlers' who had encroached on local lands since the 1980s and threatened to assume control over local resources, not only land, but also jobs.

Last but not least, it must be remembered that *jihād*-minded groups pass through several stages of development: in their first stage, they are still fairly well integrated in existing social, political and religious structures and form part of Salafi-oriented movements of reform. In the germinal stage of their development, they thus share Salafi-oriented patterns of doctrinal distinction, symbolic distantiation and social separation. Efforts by *jihād*-minded groups to form spatially segregated communities signal their transition to a second stage in their development, namely the onset of *jihād* (often triggered by state repression) and their quest to gain control over territory, a *dār al-Islām*. Such efforts may lead to the establishment of an 'emirate' that usually lasts for a limited period of time only. The collapse of such efforts at state-building lead to a third stage of development, the 'wounded-animal' stage, characterised by guerrilla warfare and terror. Due to the fact that the trajectory of *jihād*-minded groups usually spans several years, sometimes even decades, time is a crucial factor for the transformation of *jihād*-minded groups: after years of moving, hiding and fighting, many of those who have survived *jihād* are exhausted and increasingly willing to consider exit-options and re-integration into the more moderate Salafi-oriented mainstream. However, such a path towards peace is always shaped by local conditions. Our comparison between different *jihād*-minded groups shows that the local context is the ultimate frame of reference that informs the dynamics and the course of *jihād*-minded movements. The analysis of al-shabāb, Boko Haram and the different religio-political groups in northern Mali also shows that these groups have not been able, despite favourable conditions (that is, neglect, marginalisation, injustice, civil war and so forth) to gain popular support and territorial control over an extended period of time, except in limited territories and limited population groups.

Conclusion

Chad, Sudan, Ethiopia and Somalia are exceptional cases in many respects. Sudan was 'blocked' in its development as an Islamic state by its efforts to keep control over the south, which forced it to compromise. In Chad, the Salafi-oriented movement of reform has so far not managed to develop beyond a very rudimentary stage of popularisation among students and traders, and the functionaries of NGOs who are kept under very tight government supervision. Ethiopia's Muslims are divided by multiple historical, linguistic, ethnic, social and regional legacies and have never managed to unite under one umbrella, while Somalia has been torn by a civil war since 1988. Such conditions are not found in any other state in sub-Saharan Africa. The cases of Chad, Sudan, Ethiopia and Somalia show that the emergence and success of Salafi-oriented movements of reform is intrinsically linked with local contexts: in Chad and in Ethiopia, Salafi-oriented movements have so far failed to gain a larger audience or following; in Ethiopia, Salafis are often regarded as outsiders who criticise established and respected local traditions that are of major importance for the formulation of legacies of identity in the construction of contemporary Ethiopian nationalism. In Somalia, Salafi-oriented movements of reform were able to present a convincing even if harsh programme for local stability, and thus able to gain local followers. Here, outside intervention has not only radicalised Salafi-oriented movements of reform but also prevented the emergence of a Salafi-oriented political system and supported instead the emergence of a merchant-based model of moderate reform and social order. In Sudan, a Salafi-oriented movement of reform has been successful, and even gained control of the state from 1989 to 1999. It marginalised established religious movements and, for a time at least, gained considerable popular support, in particular among the middle-class groups. Yet ultimate success failed to materialise, due to the fact that Sudan's most important political player, the army, was not willing to be sidelined in a new Islamic system. Equally, the urban middle-class groups (and Sudan's 'fat cats') were not willing to support a rigid system of Islam morals and intervention in private affairs. Sudan's middle-class groups were quite happy with 'Salafism light', which fought local traditions that had come to be regarded as obsolete in modern contexts, but they were not willing to support an Islamic state that infringed considerably on personal freedom. When looking at Sudan, it is also remarkable that a Salafi-oriented movement of reform was able not only to conquer bits of territory, but also to take control of a whole state, at least from 1989 to 1999. Such a success has been denied, so far, to Salafi-oriented movements of reform in Somalia, in particular radical groups such as al-shabāb, despite the large-scale destabilisation of Somalia since 1988. In this, the trajectory of al-shabāb in Somalia is comparable to the trajectory of Boko Haram in northeastern Nigeria, as well as some of the religio-political groups in northern Mali.

Notes

1. The French colonial administration differentiated between the 'Tchad utile', the 'useful Chad', south and southwest of the Chari River, populated by mostly 'heathen' ('kirdi') populations such as the Sara before 1900, and the largely Sahelian and desert-like regions north and northeast of the Chari, inhabited by Muslim pastoral groups such as the Teda, Daza and Kréda ('Toubou') of the Tibesti and Borku regions, the Zaghawa of Ennedi, the sedentary Muslim populations of Wadai, Guéra, Bagirmi and Kanem, and the various Arab and FulBe tribal groups in the Kanem, Bahr al-Ghazal, Guéra and Salamat regions (see Arditi 2003; Bouquet 1982).
2. When talking about Sudan here, I am referring to northern Sudan only, not Sudan as it was before the secession of the South in 2011.
3. By contrast to other Sahelian countries such as Senegal, Mali and Niger, Chad's national census of 1993 showed that only 53.8 per cent of the population were Muslim (north and northeast of the Chari 97.3 per cent), while 35.3 per cent were Christian (south and southwest of the Chari 71.9 per cent) (Roné 2000: 408). Pockets of Muslims existed south and southwest of the Chari, while pockets of Christians existed north and northeast of the Chari.
4. In the context of recurring droughts in the 1970s and 1980s, Chadian pastoralists, mostly Arab and FulBe groups, pushed south into the Guéra and Bagirmi regions as well as into Sara territory, triggering numerous small-scale conflicts over access to water and pasture, as well as rights of passage. Such conflicts have also been a significant feature of war in neighbouring Sudan, in particular in Darfur and Kordofan (see Zeltner 1988; Bouquet 1982).
5. In the twentieth century, the Tijāniyya, in particular, the Niass branch, spread quickly in central Chad, expecially along the major trade routes and in Wadai (see Seesemann 2005b).

6. A number of followers of Aḥmad Khullamallāh were also among the founders of the Front de Libération Nationale du Tchad (FROLINAT) in 1966. FROLINAT attracted a number of al-Azhar graduates (Bouquet 1982: 122ff). On the development of the FROLINAT, see Buijtenhuijs (1978, 1987); on the role of Aḥmad Khullamallāh in Chad's political development, see Roné (2000: 126ff).
7. Since 1990, Idriss Déby has been able to hold on to the reins of power in Chad, supported by the fact that Chad became an oil-producing country in 2003 and was thus able to invest considerable amounts of money in military training and equipment and to build an army that intervened militarily in Darfur, Sudan from 2003, in northern Mali in 2013, in the Central African Republic in 2013, as well as Cameroon and Nigeria in 2015.
8. For a divergent interpretation, see Roné (2000: 270ff). Roné disputes Buijtenhuijs' interpretation of the secular (and Marxist) character of the FROLINAT. After comparing all arguments, I follow Buijtenhuijs' analysis.
9. These numbers make Chad one of the least developed countries worldwide in terms of children's enrolment in schools and confirm Chad's place at the very bottom of global developmental criteria. The failure to build a comprehensive government school system enhances the role of private schools, both Christian and Muslim, financed and maintained by a plethora of NGOs.
10. Déby's rise to power in 1990 started a period of close cooperation with Sudan and Ḥasan al-Turābī's Islamic Movement. Seventy students from Chad, for instance, got grants for studies at Khartoum's Islamic Institute (Roné 2000: 277). Déby's alliance with Ḥasan al-Turābī may also explain the fact that Chad was willing to lend support in the early 2000s to the dissident (and Zaghāwa-based) Justice and Equality Movement in Darfur, led by Dr Khalīl Ibrāhīm who was seen as an ally of Ḥasan al-Turābī.
11. See Seesemann (2005b: 336ff) for one case of a local conflict among Muslims over a doctrinal issue, namely the question of whether 'God sits on his throne', that is, the problem of literal or metaphorical interpretation of the Qurʾān, and the hidden agenda behind this conflict, namely the struggle for local hegemony between the Salafi-oriented movement of reform in Abéché, the anṣār al-sunna and the local Tijāniyya, as represented by the Sulṭān, Muḥammad Ibrāhīm. This conflict, which started in 1986, was eventually decided in favour of the religious estabishment in Abéché and the deposition of the *imām* of the Am-Siégo mosque, a member of the local anṣār al-sunna, in 1995 (Seesemann 2005b: 341).

12. Kaag has observed that Islamic charities have become less visible as organisations in many African countries since 9/11: they tend to present themselves as general humanitarian organisations and to advertise their 'Islamic' activities as side activities (Kaag 2014: 87).
13. The dissolution of Salafi-oriented associations (as well as the imprisonment of a number of Salafi-oriented *imāms*) in 1996 was possibly due to the fact that Salafi-oriented associations had attacked representatives of the Tijāniyya, that is, a major ally of Déby, in Sarh, southern Chad in 1994 (Roné 2000: 278).
14. The Majdhūbiyya was founded by Muḥammad al-Majdhūb al-Sughayyir (1796–1833) and established its centre in al-Dāmir, north of Khartoum (see Hofheinz 1996).
15. Muḥammad Aḥmed himself had been a member of the Sammāniyya Sufi order until he eventually split with his teacher. The Sammāniyya was introduced in the Sudan by Aḥmad al-Bashīr al-Ṭayyib (1739–1825) in 1774 and gained a following in the Jazīra region.
16. In addition, the movement of the Mahdi allied with Sudan's smaller Sufi orders, in particular the Majdhūbiyya, against Egyptian rule and the Khatmiyya.
17. Bakht al-Rawḍa College was opened in September 1934 and grew from 30 students in 1934 to 85 in 1939 and 161 in 1941. After World War II, its growth continued to 522 students in 1952. Also it expanded from teacher training to include an elementary school, and intermediate school and classes for Sudanese staff. As a model school Bakht al-Rawḍa opened its doors to students from other British colonies, in particular northern Nigeria (Daly 1991: 111).
18. In 1956, 130 Sudanese were studying in Britain, but 4,500 in Egypt (2,500 at al-Azhar) (Daly 1991: 337).
19. The dominance of the Anṣār and the Khatmiyya should not hide the fact that there is a number of smaller Sufi orders in contemporary Sudan such as the different branches of the Qādiriyya, the Sammāniyya and the Majdhūbiyya as well as the Burhāniyya and the Tijāniyya, which have shown remarkable resilience in a number of regions, even if they have not been able to gain influence on a national scale comparable to the Anṣār or the Khatmiyya (see Seesemann 2006b: 23ff; al-Karsani 1985; Karrar 1992).
20. In chronological sequence, Sudan was ruled by the following Heads of State: Ismāᶜīl al-Azharī (1902–69) (r. 1954 to July 1956), ᶜAbdallāh Khalīl (1888–1970) (r. July 1956 to November 1958), Ibrāhīm ᶜAbbūd (1900–83) (r. November 1958 to November 1964), Sirr al-Khatm al-Khalīfa (1919–2006) (r. November 1964 to June 1965), Muḥammad Aḥmad Maḥjūb (1908–76)

(r. June 1965 to July 1966), al-Ṣādiq al-Mahdī (b. 1935) (r. July 1966 to May 1967), Muḥammad Aḥmad Maḥjūb (r. May 1967 to May 1969), Ja^{c}far al-Numayrī (1930–2009) (r. May 1969 to April 1985), ^{c}Abd al-Raḥmān Siwār al-Dhahab (b. 1930) (r. April 1985 to May 1986), al-Ṣādiq al-Mahdī (several cabinets, May 1986 to June 1989), ^{c}Umar Ḥasan al-Bashīr (b. 1944) (r. since June 1989). It should be noted here that all Heads of State with one exception (Siwār al-Dhahab from al-Ubayyiḍ in Kordofan) were rooted in families representing the riverain elites, the *awlād al-baḥr*.

21. After being expelled from Sudan by the British authorities due to his 'anti-colonial activities', ^{c}Abd al-Raḥmān Abū Ḥajar was appointed president of the al-amr bi-l-ma^{c}rūf wa-l-nahy ^{c}an al-munkar organisation in Jidda by King ^{c}Abd al-^{c}Azīz (Salomon 2009: 146).
22. A major bone of contention was the fact that Muḥammad Ḥāshim al-Hadiyya was prepared to cooperate with Ḥasan al-Turābī and the NIF, a political move that was facilitated by Ḥasan al-Turābī's long time protégé and minister of social planning, ^{c}Alī ^{c}Uthmān Muḥammad Ṭāhā (Salomon 2009: 149, footnote 14).
23. Confusingly enough, the term '*ikhwān*' is used in the Sudan as an umbrella term for both a broad array of Salafi-minded Muslims and a much smaller group of followers of the 'educationalist' and 'ideological' faction within the Islamic Movement that was itself divided into a pro-Egyptian faction and a pro-independence faction.
24. For a discussion of Sudanese emic perceptions of the term 'Salafiyya', see Salomon (2009: 147, footnote 10).
25. Muḥammad Ṣālih ^{c}Umar (1934–70) graduated from the Faculty of Law at the University of Khartoum in 1959 and got a master's degree from the School of Oriental and African Studies in London in 1961. While still in primary school, he joined the ikhwān and became minister of animal resources in Sirr al-Khatm al-Khalīfa's transitional cabinet in 1964. From 1965 to 1969, he represented the ICF in Parliament, and then joined al-Hādī al-Mahdī in his opposition against the al-Numayrī regime and was responsible for the smuggling of guns from Ethiopia to Sudan. Muḥammad Ṣālih ^{c}Umar was killed on 27 March 1970 on Aba Island together with approximately 12,000 Anṣār and other ikhwān (Collins 2008: 98).
26. Ja^{c}far Shaykh Idrīs (b. 1931 in Port Sudan) was affiliated with the anṣār al-sunna group and later became an ardent critic of Ḥasan al-Turābī (see below). Ja^{c}far Shaykh Idrīs followed the typical career of a Muslim *^{c}ālim*, but went

to the British colonial elementary and secondary schools before studying at the University of Khartoum, where in 1970 he received a PhD in philosophy for his thesis on the 'concept of causality in Islam'. Ja[c]far Shaykh Idrīs held numerous consultative and teaching posts at Sudanese, US American and Saudi Arabian institutions and eventually moved to Saudi Arabia, where he became a professor of Islamic studies at the Imām Muḥammad b. Sa[c]ūd University in al-Riyādh (see Wolf 1993: 210; 'Islamevents' webpage: www.islamevents.com).

27. In the 1970s, the Islamic movement also started to spread into smaller urban centres such as Shendi, although the Salafis were not able to win significant support in the population. In Shendi, for instance, followers of the Islamic movement constituted between 3 and 6 per cent of the population in 2014 (Osman Mohamed Osman Ali 2014: 19).
28. For the changing role of women in contemporary Sudan, see Hale (1996) and Nageeb (2004).
29. Mālik Babikir Badrī (b. 1932) has become widely known as a Sudanese psychologist. He did his BA at the American University in Beirut in 1956, to be followed by his master's in 1958. He then studied in England, where he received a PhD at the University of Leicester in 1961. He was appointed reader in psychology at the Omdurman Islamic University in Sudan in 1967 and was appointed full professor of psychology at the Imām Muḥammad b. Sa[c]ūd University in al-Riyādh in 1971. In 1977, he became dean of the Faculty of Education at the University of Khartoum, and then left Sudan again in 1981 to take up a position as professor of psychology at the Imām Muḥammad b. Sa[c]ūd University in al-Riyādh. In 1985, he was re-appointed professor of psychology at the University of Khartoum (until 1992). At the same time, he served at the International African University in Khartoum and founded the Faculties of Education and Islamic Studies at this university. In 1994, he again left Sudan for Malaysia, where he was appointed professor of psychology at the International Islamic University of Malaysia (see the Arabpsynet homepage www.arabpsynet.com).
30. The African Islamic Centre (al-markaz al-islāmī al-ifrīqī bi-l-Kharṭūm) was founded in 1966 and opened in 1967 in Umm Durmān, but was closed again in 1969 after the coup. It was re-opened in 1977 in South Khartoum. Its diplomas opened entry to an Islamic University, in particular, the Islamic University of Umm Durmān. It specialised in the training of African students, mostly from East Africa, and became the International University of Africa

(Jāmi^{c}a Ifrīqiyya ^{c}Alamiyya) in 1992 (Grandin 1993: 114ff). Its first director was Dr ^{c}Abd al-Rahīm ^{c}Alī Ibrāhīm, a NIF member (Burr and Collins 2010: 87). The Islamic University of Umm Durmān was founded in 1912 as the Ma^{c}had al-Islāmī (of Umm Durmān), became a Faculty of *Sharī^{c}a* in 1963 and the Islamic University of Umm Durmān in 1965. It was closed in 1970, but reopened in 1977 (Hodgkin 1998: 220; Ch. Ahmed 2015: 146).

31. From August 1984 to March 1985, 106 Sudanese citizens lost limbs in the context of ḥudūd punishments (Mahmoud 1997: 184).
32. On Maḥmūd Muḥammad Ṭāhā (1909 or 1911–75), see Oevermann (1993).
33. On the organisation, programme and structure of the NIF, see Khalafalla (2004: 109ff).
34. A total of 28 seats (out of 236) were 'geographical' and 23 (out of 28) were 'graduate constituency' seats. The 'graduate constituencies' were established in 1953 in order to allow the educated classes to exert greater influence in politics than their numerical strength allowed (Warburg 2003: 181). The fact that the NIF was able to win 23 out of 28 'graduate constituencies' shows how strong the NIF and the Islamic Movement had become at this time among the 'educated' middle-class groups.
35. The core group around Ḥasan al-Turābī was characterised by its corporate identity manifested in a specific dress code and habitus, namely, *libs al-shāl wa-isti^{c}māl al-jawal* ('wearing the shawl and using the mobile phone') (Gallab 2008: 148).
36. In 1998, ^{c}Alī ^{c}Uthmān Muḥammad Ṭāhā became vice president, deputy vice president in 2005 and again first vice president in 2011. In the conflict between Ḥasan al-Turābī and ^{c}Umar al-Bashīr he sided with ^{c}Umar al-Bashīr. As vice president he became chief negotiator in the peace talks with the south and was regarded as al-Bashīr's 'right hand man' (Fluehr-Lobban 2012: 83). On 6 December 2013 ^{c}Alī ^{c}Uthmān Muḥammad Ṭāhā retired and was replaced by an officer of the Sudanese Army.
37. See Salomon (2009: 148) for a discussion of these terms.
38. For details of this project, see Salomon (2013: 820–51).
39. For details of more recent political developments in the Sudan and the disputes within the ruling party, the NCP, see ICG (2012a). An important new trend was the emergence in the early 1990s of a new generation of *jihād*-minded activists. They not only started to attack Christian churches, such as the Anglican Cathedral in Khartoum on 21 April 2012, but also attacked Sudan's Sufi orders, as, for instance, Muslims in Khartoum celebrating the

mawlid al-nabī on 31 December 2012 (see E. Ahmed 2015: 166ff). Last but not least, *jihād*-minded activists have started to describe Salafi-oriented thinkers such as Ḥasan al-Turābī and even al-Ṣādiq al-Mahdī as 'heretics' due to their controversial statements on issues such as women's rights (ICG 2012a: 15).

40. Khalīl Ibrāhīm was killed on 25 January 2011 by an airstrike. The leadership of JEM passed to his brother Jibrīl Ibrāhīm on 25 January 2012. In the 2000s, the war in Darfur in many respects assumed the character of a proxy war between the competing factions of the Islamic Movement in Khartoum, in which the Justice and Equality Movement led by Dr Khalīl Ibrāhīm was seen as an ally of Ḥasan al-Turābī (Seesemann 2006b: 51).
41. Both Sudanese and Western sources repeatedly 'indulged in a ritual of al-Turābī-bashing' (Ibrahim 1999: 217) and reduced his politics to pure tactics (see, for instance, Prunier 1989: 379), thereby neglecting the larger historical context in which Ḥasan al-Turābī's tactics evolved. Ḥasan al-Turābī expressed his larger political goals in a lecture in Khartoum in February 2015, when he addressed a large audience in Khartoum, including President ʿUmar al-Bashīr. Among other things, he stressed the need for Muslim unity, dialogue between the different factions of the Islamic Movement and reconciliation with the regime, 'wanting to be assured regarding the future of the country before leaving his life' (Osman Mirghani, 2015, 'The Mystery that is Hassan al-Turabi', <http://www.aawsat.net/2015/article 55341422> (last accessed 25 August 2015)). Ḥasan al-Turābī passed away on 5 March 2016.
42. However, Christians and Muslims were divided, among other things, by 'dietary boundaries', that is, a double restriction of commensality regarding food and drink: Muslims and Christians do not eat meat slaughtered by the respective other and Muslims should not drink alcohol, while Christians should not chew Qat (Fiquet 2006: 41).
43. On the development of Sufi orders in Ethiopia, see Desplat (2010), Desplat and Østebø (2013), Guluma (1993, 2008), Hussein Ahmed (2001), Kapteijns (2000), Kifleyesus (1995), Østebø (2008a), Trimingham (1952) and Triulzi (1981).
44. Lij Iyasu was accused of having converted to Islam and was deposed for his lenient policy towards Muslims (see Sohier 2011).
45. For Eritrea, see Miran (2005) and Østebø (2010).
46. In the 1990s, ʿAbd al-Karīm Ibrāhīm Jarra Abba Gada led the Islamic Front for the Liberation of Oromia (IFLO) otherwise known as the Islamic Oromo

Liberation Front (IOLF) into a new rebellion, while the 1960s rebel leader Waqo Gutu sat in the constituent transitional assembly in 1991 before returning into the bush (Markakis 2011: 285).

47. The Orthodox Church had the status of a state church until 1974 and was thus identified with the monarchy. This had become particularly clear when Emperor Haile Selassie declared the Ethiopian Church autocephalous, that is, independent from the Coptic Patriarchate in Alexandria (Erlich 2010: 94).
48. Ethiopia was restructured as a federal republic with eleven 'national regional states' (in Amhariña: *kilil*), organised according to ethnic and linguistic criteria, namely, Tigray, Amhara, Benishangul-Gumuz, Oromia, Gambella, the 'Southern People's Region' (Debub), Somali and Afar, as well as the city states of Addis Ababa, Harar and Dire Dawa that were regarded as multi-ethnic and thus distinct from the larger national regional states. Each *kilil* was based on a hierarchy of administrational 'zones', districts (*woreda*) and communities (*kebele*), which may again reflect ethnic and linguistic particularities.
49. Meles Zenawi's successor was Hailemaryam Desalegn (b. 1965) from the Southern Regional State, a Walaytta by ethnic affiliation, who studied at the universities of Addis Ababa and Tampere (Finnland). Hailemaryam Desalegn was the first Ethiopian head of state who was a member of an Ethiopian Evangelical Church, the Apostolic Church of Ethiopia.
50. In 2009, Ethiopian security forces arrested more than 1,500 followers of al-takfīr wa-l-hijra in the Jimma region who had for some time refused to hold Ethiopian identity cards and to pay tax and who had publicly announced this position in 2009 (Østebø 2010: 32).
51. For earlier riots between Muslims and Christians in Harar and in Kamisē, see Hussein Ahmed (2006: 17).
52. This position is based on the *ḥadīth*, '*utruku al-ḥabasha* . . .' ('leave the Ethiopians in peace, as long as they do not attack', recorded in Abū Daʾūd, kitāb al-sunan, II: 133, Cuoq 1981: 37).
53. By contrast, there is a belief among Muslims that Ethiopia is the ultimate enemy of Islam: this is a reference to General Abrāha's alleged effort to destroy the Kaᶜba in 570, an event alluded to in the Qurʾān (sūra 105, al-fīl, the Elephant, verses 1–5) and based on a *ḥadīth* related by a son of the conqueror of Egypt, ᶜAbdallāh b. ᶜAmr b. al-ᶜĀṣ (Abu Daʾūd, kitāb al-sunan, Vol. II: 133) that one day 'a lean-legged from among the Ethiopians will destroy the Kaᶜba' (Erlich 2010: 129). These tales have become household tales in Ethiopia and have been quoted in various contexts: when President Meles Zenawi, for

instance, commanded Ethiopia's invasion of Somalia in 2006 he was depicted in Muslim propaganda as the 'new Abrāha' (Erlich 2007: 7).

54. Sayyid Aḥmad Muṣṭafa managed to flee to Saudi Arabia in 1995 (Østebø 2008b: 433).
55. In 2004, all Salaf-minded members had been excluded from ESCIA's executive council (Østebø 2008b: 433).
56. For al-Amoudi, see a series of Internet entries, such as wikipedia.org.wiki (accessed 15 July 2015).
57. Salafis usually refer to themselves as ahl al-tawḥīd or ahl al-sunna. In Oromifa, Salafis call themselves 'nama tawḥīd', a 'person of tawḥīd' or 'warra tawḥīd', 'people of tawḥīd' (Østebø 2008a: 18).
58. This fragmented character is mirrored in the fact that most supporters of the Ethiopian *tablīgh* movement are traders of Gurage extraction (Østebø 2008b: 426f, 436). The *tablīgh* movement in Ethiopia is associated with the Gurage ethnic group and its traders' diaspora.
59. On Harar, see Desplat (2010). Harar, the *madīnat al-awliyāʾ* (the city of saints), which is also regarded as Islam's fourth holiest city, the *rābiʿ al-ḥaramayn* (Desplat 2010: 15), became Ethiopian in 1887. One of the first actions of the Ethiopian administration was to demolish the central mosque and to build a Christian cathedral (Desplat 2002: 146).
60. The term 'Shāsh' refers to a headscarf worn by married Somali women and, by extension, a piece of black or blue gauze, sometimes silk, imported from India (Luling 2002: 68).
61. In 1961, al-Ḥājj Yūsuf ʿAbd al-Raḥmān was one of the scholars who were commissioned to participate in the translation of the Qurʾān into Amhariña in 1961 (communication Terje Østebø, 19 December 2014), a project that was concluded in 1969. Another scholar who took part in the translation of the Qurʾān into Amhariña was Sayyid Muḥammad Ṣādiq ʿAbd al-Mālik (1889–1969) from Tahuladare in Wällo. He had participated in the struggle against the Italians as a 'patriot' and worked from 1950 in the Ministry of the Interior as a translator for Arabic texts (Hussein Ahmed 1998: 100).
62. Communication Terje Østebø, 19 December 2014. The Ogaden and Hawd regions, which had been claimed by Ethiopia before the Italian invasion of Ethiopia in 1935, were annexed to Somaliland by Great Britain in 1941 and formed the southern extension of Isaaq pastures in British Somaliland. While the Ogaden was returned to Ethiopia in 1948, the Hawd was re-united with Ethiopia in 1955 only.

63. The Somali Youth Club was established in 1943, and was renamed Somali Youth League (SYL) in 1947. This movement claimed the political union of all Somali territories in the Horn under the slogan in Somali, *kulub hanolatto*, 'long live the Club'), and thus became known as the 'kulub' movement. Due to the fact that Britain, which at that time occupied and administered almost all Somali territories except for the French Afar and Issa colony of Djibouti, planned to create a greater Somalia, including the Italian and British Somali territories, the Hawd and the Ogaden, this call for Somali unity was not unrealistic.
64. For details of ᶜAbdallāh b. Muḥammad's career and disputes with Saudi scholars, see Desplat (2010: 215ff).
65. Similar developments, in particular the move towards Western consumer and lifestyle models, were observed among young Muslims in Jimma (see Mains 2007).
66. This observation extends to some rural regions such as Wällo, where women in *niqāb* can be seen today. New mosques have been built, inter-religious marriages have decreased in number, mixed burial rites have declined and followers of 'Wahhabism' shun Muslim friends and Christians: social interaction has become selective (Abbink 2007: 75). The sharing of cults by Christians and Muslims and the joint veneration of saints has been a widespread feature in Ethiopia, as, for instance, in the cult of Gebre Menfes Qiddus at Mount Zeqwala (Desplat 2005: 486–7).
67. After 1991, Sharīf Maḥamad ᶜAbd al-Raḥmān moved to Brawa, and then to Mombasa and finally to Cairo (AMA 2011: 105).
68. Nūr ᶜAlī ᶜOlow (1918–95) graduated from al-Azhar in 1963, established a small Salafi-oriented association, jamᶜiyyat iḥyāᵓ al-sunna al-muḥammadiyya in 1967, and became director of religious affairs in 1969. He was imprisoned in 1969/70 and again from 1973 to 1976 (AMA 2011: 146, 193).
69. The term '*munādama*' actually means 'drinking companionship'. The term '*munāẓẓama*' (organisation) would thus be more fitting to render AMA's translation of this group as Organization of the Islamic Renaissance.
70. Shaykh ᶜAbd al-Qani (1935–2007) was born in the Bakool region, and went to a Qurᵓānic school there. He then moved to Egypt and studied at al-Azhar from 1951, graduating in 1957. After his return to Somalia, he became a lecturer at the Somali University Institute and obtained a position in the Ministry of Justice and Religious Affairs. He was imprisoned in 1973 and emigrated to Kuwait in 1982 (AMA 2011: 148).

71. Maḥamad Maᶜallim Ḥasan was employed by the Ministry of Justice and Religious Affairs, but was dismissed from his position in 1975. He was imprisoned from 1976 to 1982, and from 1984 to 1988 (AMA 2011: 152–3).
72. This reform affected most importantly the Digil and the Rahanwayn clans (also known as Digil-Mirifle), that is, Somalia's Afmaay-speaking southern clan federations, which became increasingly marginalised in the twentieth century due to the fact that the Digil and Rahanwayn were not pastoralists like the Dir, Darood, Isaaq and Hawiye, but farmers and agro-pastoralists, cultivating the fertile valleys and flood-plains of the Juba and Shebelle rivers. The Afmaay dialects are southern Somali dialects that are not easily understood by speakers of Afmaxaa (see Besteman and Cassanelli 2003 [1996]; Höhne and Luling 2010; Luling 2002).
73. Maḥamad Nūr Aḥmad Garyare (b. 1935) graduated from the Islamic University of Medina in 1965. After the 1969 coup, he was appointed Director of Islamic Affairs, but was demoted in 1972 and sent to Camp Halane, a military camp designed to re-educate civil servants along the lines of Somali socialism. In 1976, he managed to flee from Somalia and went to Saudi Arabia. There he got a job at the Dār al-Iftāᵓ but stopped working for this agency in 1985. In 1990, he migrated to Toronto in Canada for security reasons (AMA 2011: 176ff).
74. Dr Maḥamad ᶜAlī Ibrāhīm, *amīr* of al-iṣlāḥ 1989–99, acquired a PhD in *ḥadīth* studies in 1994 at the University of Medina. In 2006 he was expelled from al-iṣlāḥ due to his active joining of the Islamic Courts movement, thus defying the non-partisan and non-violence policies of al-iṣlāḥ (AMA 2011: 308).
75. Prof. ᶜAlī Abukar Aḥmad ᶜAlī Dhere acquired a PhD in Islamic Studies at the Islamic University of Medina in 1984. He later became President of Mogadishu University (Marchal and Sheikh 2013: 223).
76. Dr ᶜAlī Baasha ᶜUmar, *amīr* of al-iṣlāḥ from 2008 to 2013, had become a medical doctor in 1976 (AMA 2011: 309).
77. Since 1974, when Somalia joined the Arab League, Islamic charitable organisations increased their activities in Somalia, a development that acquired speed in the 1980s and led to the emergence of close ties between Saudi Arabia and a number of emirates on the Gulf, as well as a growing group of Somali businessmen, who were instrumental in building and financing the Islamic Courts movement in the 1990s (Marchal 2013: 334).
78. In 1991, Maḥamad Maᶜallim Ḥasan founded the majmūᶜ al-ᶜulamāᵓ with the aim of creating a Supreme Islamic Council, an Islamic umbrella organisation

(AMA 2011: 267). However, the majmū[c] failed quickly due to clan divisions. It was the first group to establish an Islamic court in 1991 (AMA 2011: 268).

79. In 1988, more than 50 per cent of the officers in the Somali army were Marehan (Krech 1996: 20).
80. After the peace agreement with Ethiopia, officers of Ogadeni descent were not regarded as 'reliable' any more, while officers of (northern) Dulbahante clan origin refused to command action in the north against the SNM (Krech 1996: 38).
81. In Somali transliteration, the name of Muḥammad Farah Ḥasan [c]Aidīd would be rendered as Maxamad Farax Xasan Caidiid. In order to keep the text readable, I have stuck to the Arabic transliteration of Somali names.
82. [c]Abdallāh Yūsuf Ahmad (1934–2012), a Darood-Harti-Mijerteen by clan affiliation and a colonel in the Somali Army, had managed to flee to Ethiopia in 1978 where he founded the Somali Salvation Democratic Front (SSDF) in 1981. He was imprisoned in Ethiopia from 1986 to 1991 and resumed leadership of the SSDF in 1991 (Krech 1996: 235). In 2004, he became the president of Somalia's Transitional Federal Government (TFG) and in 2006 he accepted Ethiopian support against the Islamic Courts movement. He retired as President of the TFG in December 2008. Puntland was set up as a distinctive administrative unit on 1 August 1998 and was controlled by the Darood-Harti-Majerteen dominated Somali Salvation Democratic Front led by [c]Abdallāh Yūsuf (Höhne 2014b: 23). His successors as presidents of Puntland were [c]Abd al-Raḥmān Farole (2004–14) and [c]Abdiwali [c]Alī Gaas, who defeated [c]Abd al-Raḥmān Farole in elections in 2014 (see ICG 2013a; Höhne 2015).
83. A smaller group under Ḥasan [c]Abdallāh Hirsi Turki, the 'Ras Kamboni Brigade', moved back south and established a base in the Kismayo region in 1992 (ICG 2005: 7).
84. A major factor for the success of al-ittiḥād in Luuq was that al-ittiḥād supported local Marehan clan elders against Marehan guests (*galti*) from the south and from Mogadishu, who were former members of the Siyad Barre regime (Menkhaus 2004: 59).
85. On Ethiopia's policies in respect of Somalia, see Østebø (2015b).
86. Höhne remarks 'that the convergence between descent groups and territory grew stronger all over Somalia in the course of the civil war' (Höhne 2015: 23).
87. In early 2009, the Ras Kamboni brigade under Ḥasan [c]Abdallāh Hirsi Turki (1942–2015, a Darood-Ogadeni by clan affiliation), which had been founded

in 1992 as a militia of the Ogaden subclan in the Juba valley, formed an alliance with al-shabāb. Due to old age and diabetes, Ḥasan ^{c}Abdallāh Hirsi Turki lost power, however, to his son-in-law, Aḥmad Muḥammad Islām also known as Aḥmad Madobe, who rejected al-shabāb domination. In the subsequent confrontation in late 2009, al-shabāb defeated Aḥmad Madobe and took control of Kismayo. The surviving followers of Aḥmad Madobe allied with Kenyan troops in 2010 (Höhne 2014b: 28), while a minority faction joined al-shabāb. Since 2011, Aḥmad Madobe has been able to regain control over parts of southern Somalia ('Jubaland') with Kenyan (and Ethiopian) support, in particular the port city of Kismayo, and was elected president of Jubaland in 2013, which claimed autonomy within Somalia on the model of Puntland (communication Anna Bruzzone, 8 July 2015). Somaliland, Puntland, Galgadood, Jubaland and the SFG-controlled region around Mogadishu have come to form a 'cordon sanitaire' on Ethiopia's eastern borders that has served to contain al-shabāb. Ḥasan ^{c}Abdallāh Hirsi Turki died on 28 May 2015. At that time he had surrendered to Somalian authorities.

88. For the *jareer* and the history of Somalia's 'Bantu' populations in the Juba valley, see Besteman (1999).
89. The first president of Somalia's TFG, ^{c}Abdallāh Yūsuf Aḥmad, former leader of the SSDF in Puntland, resided in Baidoa until 2006 and then moved with the Ethiopian Army to Mogadishu in 2006. In 2009, Sharīf Shaykh Aḥmad was elected second president of Somalia's TFG. He remained in office until 2012 and was followed by Ḥasan Shaykh Maḥamūd, a member of the dam al-jadīd faction of al-iṣlāḥ, who became the first president of the Somali Federal Government (SFG) (Höhne 2014b: 15).
90. Despite the stress on 'clans' and 'sub-clans', the basic social unit in Somali society is the *reer* that can be described as an extended family or a group that forms one distinct economic cell, defined, for instance, by the use of the same pastures (Zitelmann 2011: 39ff). While murder may lead to counter-action on clan and sub-clan levels, such conflicts are solved within the *reer* by the payment of *diya* ('blood money', in Somali: *mag*), often in the form of camels (usually 100 camels per man). In order to identify, for instance, ^{c}Aden Hashi ^{c}Ayro's social status within the clan system, it would be necessary to reproduce the complete line of descent, in his case Hawiye-Habr Gedir-^{c}Ayr-Absiye-Kulmiya (*reer Hirole*).
91. Before he became a member of al-shabāb, Aḥmad ^{c}Abdi Godane worked for the Somali finance network al-Barakaat. He was killed in an American airstrike

on 1 September 2014 (*The Guardian*, UK, 6 September 2014). His successor as supreme commander of al-shabāb was Aḥmad ᶜUmar 'Abū ᶜUbaydah', who was born in the Ethiopian Ogaden region and who had been living in Kismayo for a long time.

92. This region is part of the territory of the Warsangeli, a Darood sub-clan that plays a marginal role in both Somaliland and Puntland. As a result of the attempt by the Majerteen (Darood) in Puntland to control the natural resources in the Warsangeli region, armed conflict erupted from which al-shabāb benefited (Höhne 2014a: 358ff, 2015: 119ff).
93. Another issue of internal conflict was the role of the foreign fighters within al-shabāb, most prominently, Abū Manṣūr al-'Amrikī', who was killed by al-shabāb's *amniyāt* in 2014 (communication Markus Höhne, 26 February 2015).
94. Ḥasan Dahir Aweys' ḥizb al-islām competed with the Ras Kamboni brigade and al-shabāb in 2009 and 2010 over control of the port town of Kismayo, as well as other regions in central Somalia. Ḥizb al-islām was eventually defeated and forced to join al-shabāb in late 2010. In this context, Ḥasan Dahir Aweys was also forced to submit to the authority of (the much younger) Aḥmad ᶜAbdi Godane (Höhne 2011a: 143).
95. On al-shabāb's internal structure, see Höhne (2011a: 148f); on al-shabab's international links and the role of its foreign fighters, see Steinberg (2013) and Steinberg and Weber (2015).
96. Turkish activities in Somalia peaked on 25 January 2015, when President Erdoğan opened Mogadishu's biggest hospital (Digfer), which was built by Turkey, in the context of a state visit. The focus on Saudi Arabia, the Gulf and Egypt as poles of orientation for Salafi-oriented movements of reform has obscured the rise of Turkey as a major player in sub-Saharan Africa, in particular in Sudan, Ethiopia, Somalia, Kenya and Tanzania. In 2014/15 alone, Turkey provided 1,000 scholarships for students from sub-Saharan Africa. And Africa received one-third of Turkey's development assistance in 2012. Turkish trade with Africa has grown from about 750 million in 2000 to approximately 23.4 billion US dollars in 2014. Since 2008 Turkey has been a non-regional member of the African Development Bank and has been declared a 'strategic partner of the continent' by the African Union. Turkey's African policy is based on a first action plan of 1998 that was complemented by a trade strategy in 2003. The year 2005 was declared 'Year of Africa' in Turkey and in 2008 Turkey accommodated the first Turkey-Africa summit in Istanbul with forty-

nine African guest nations (a second summit took place in Malabo, Equatorial Guinea, in 2014) (see Republic of Turkey, 2015, Ministry of Foreign Affairs, www.mfa.gov.tr/turkey-africa-relations.en.mfa, accessed 22 March 2015).

97. In 2013, al-iṣlāḥ had followed suit and joined the SFG (Höhne 2014b: 29). Since 2009, the TFG and the SFG have thus gained increasing support in major parts of Somalia (except Somaliland) (Höhne 2014b: 42).

98. From an external perspective this suggests that the development of *jihād*-minded movements was linked with the terrorist attacks of 11 September 2001. But our analysis of Boko Haram, al-shabāb and the religio-political movements in northern Mali has shown that their development was intrinsically linked with the dynamics of specific local contexts.

99. The term '*Grenzwildnisse*' has been employed in the analysis of Trypanosomiasis in sub-Saharan Africa to denote areas that have historically divided larger regions due to their inaccessible and inhospitable nature. In historical times (that is, well into the colonial period), such wildernesses have been scarcely populated and have often been a refuge for bandits and rebels. It must be stressed, however, that '*Grenzwildnisse*' do not automatically form a refuge for the lawless: they are often created in the context of political and economic crises.

100. In 2012, northeastern Nigeria, in particular Bornu and Yobe federal states, had the highest poverty indices in Nigeria (75 per cent of the population being 'relatively poor' and 51.5 per cent 'hardly able to feed itself') and the highest rate of unemployment in Nigeria (39 per cent for Yobe and 27 per cent for Bornu), in contrast to Lagos, where unemployment stood at 8 per cent of the workforce (Mustapha 2014b: 173).

101. Tuareg leaders were even integrated in Nigerien governments. Major trans-Saharan trade routes pass through Mali and Algeria rather than through Niger; also, refugees from Libya were allowed to enter Niger in 2011 but were disarmed (ICG 2013b: 35; communication Abdoulaye Sounaye, 31 October 2014). Many Tuareg leaders have stopped seeing independence of the Tuareg region in Niger as a viable option for the near future (ICG 2013b: 30). Last but not least, Niger's security forces are better trained and equipped than Mali's army, due to French strategic interests in Niger's uranium, that is, the Areva mine near Arlit in the northern Aïr mountains (ICG 2013b). For an extensive discussion of Niger's stability in the context of the Boko Haram crisis, see Pérouse de Montclos (2014: 26–7).

102. The Rahanweyn founded the Hizbia Dighil Mirifle (later Hizbia Dastur

Mustaqil al-Sumal) as a first political organisation in 1947 and were supported up to 1960 by the Italian colonial power as a counter force to the major pastoral clans that supported the Somali Youth League (SYL). After Somalia's independence, the Rahanweyn were increasingly marginalised and their demand for a census rejected, possibly due to the assumption that such a census would have established the Rahanweyn (and not the Darood) as Somalia's biggest clan. After the start of the civil war in 1988, the comparatively fertile Rahanweyn territory, that is, the provinces of Bay and Bakool between the rivers Juba and Shebelle, was raided and devastated by the different warlords and their respective militias. Drought and famine from 1991 to 1993 cost about 500,000 lives among the Rahanweyn. Humanitarian aid for the Rahanweyn was siphoned off by other clans and their militias. After the Ethiopian intervention in 1996, the Rahanweyn sided with Ethiopia and established the Rahanweyn Resistance Army, which in 2004 tried to establish an autonomous state in Rahanweyn territory along the model of Puntland and Somaliland (Prunier 2010: 35ff; Zitelmann 2011: 51f).

6

REFORM IN CONTEXT IV: TANGANYIKA/TANZANIA (AND KENYA)

Introduction

This chapter is organised along the same lines as the chapters on Senegal/Mali and Nigeria/Niger: following a presentation of the historical context of the development of Islamic reform, I focus on the trajectory of Sufi-oriented reform, before delving into the evolution of Salafi-oriented reform. Like Senegal, Mali, Niger, Chad and Ethiopia, post-colonial Tanganiyka (Tanzania, after the union with Zanzibar in 1964) established state control over Islamic activities after independence. This policy misfired, however, and was challenged in the early 1980s by oppositional Islamic associations. At the same time, these associations had to come to terms with the growth of evangelical churches. The confrontation between Muslim associations and Pentecostal churches has informed (mainland) Tanzania's public sphere to a considerable extent since the 1980s, comparable only to the situation in northern Nigeria, although conflict in Tanzania has so far been mostly non-violent. Finally, I will compare the development of Salafi-oriented reform in (mainland) Tanzania with Kenya, where Muslims had to respond to similar colonial and post-colonial challenges.

In contrast to West Africa, Islam expanded into the East African interior fairly late, essentially in the nineteenth century in the context of the commercial expansion of the Sultanate of Zanzibar. This spread of Islam continued under colonial rule. Muslim scholars acquired considerable influence in societies that had come into contact with Islam only recently. The influence of religious scholars, in particular those of the Sufi orders, in Swahili society became manifest in the context of the so-called 'Arab uprising' of 1888–9, and in the Maji-Maji rebellion of 1905. In the context of these movements of resistance against German colonial rule, the trader and scholar networks of the Sufi orders, in particular the Qādiriyya that had won great influence among traders, served to link the rebel groups. After the repression of the Maji-Maji rising, a wave of conversion to Islam started in the areas affected by it, stimulated by the religious scholars of the Sufi orders and their networks. After Maji-Maji, the *mawlid ᶜAbd al-Qādir* celebrations quickly spread, for instance, and African socio-religious rituals were replaced by the *dhikr* of the Qādiriyya. *Dhikr* groups of the Qādiriyya also organised other aspects of social life, such as burials, and thus catered for the social and religious needs of African Muslims 'outside the tribal environment' (Iliffe 1969: 198). In this way, the Qādiriyya acted not only as a religious, but also as a social and a political movement, and acquired paramount importance for the movement of conversion among 'hinterland' Muslims in what was to become Tanganyika in the twentieth century (see Becker 2008).

The movement of conversion to Islam also led to a rapid change in the religious set-up of Tanganyika's population, which was accelerated in the context of the massive disruptions during World War I. While 3 per cent of the population were Muslim in 1914, this figure had risen to 25 per cent by 1924. Nimtz sees one reason for this movement of conversion to Islam as the wish of many to bring back order after the disruptions of Maji-Maji and World War I (Nimtz 1980: 14–15). However, the expansion of Islam in Tanganyika was connected not only with the fact that many people converted to Islam as a form of resistance against colonial rule, but may also be explained by the fact that Islam had been known as a religion through the mediation of Swahili traders in the hinterland (*bara*) areas for some time before the colonial period (see Iliffe 1969, 1979). In addition, the German colonial administration relied on local cadres, the so-called *akidas*, *jumbes* and *liwalis*, mostly Swahili-speaking Muslims. Swahili culture, as well as Islam and the Swahili language, thus retained the nimbus of a superior culture and, as a consequence, the Tanganyikan interior was not only increasingly

Islamised but also adopted Kiswahili as a language of communication. In addition, the German colonial administration followed a policy of cooperation with (Kiswahili-speaking) Muslims and, to the chagrin of a number of missionaries, heeded the advice of Carl Heinrich Becker, a German orientalist, who had declared in 1908/9, after an extensive study of Islam in East Africa, that 'Islam did not constitute a threat to the colonial government and should rather be treated as an ally' (Becker 1932: 172–85).

Still, the colonial period was a time of hardship and crisis for Tanganyika's Muslims. Referring to the 1930s, Reusch stresses, for instance, that the 'house of Islam' was seemingly about to crumble in East Africa: the caliphate had come to an end, movements of the emancipation of Muslim women had started to spread and a Salafi-oriented movement of reform propagated new ideas. In addition, Muslims were subject to increasing Western influence that would, in their eyes, bring about atheism and unbelief:

> The cinema has entered the cities and is visited by both men and women. The sewing machine is invading the harems. Journals and books are in the hands of girls and young women, telephone and telegraph make men and women familiar with events in the world outside. (Reusch 1931: 335; my translation)

In the course of their integration into the new political structures of Tanganyika, which had become a British Trust territory after World War I, the Muslim populations of the coastal areas suffered from the interference of the colonial administration in Muslim affairs, in particular the bureaucratisation of Islamic jurisdiction. In the British colonial period, Muslims also became disadvantaged in terms of education, as the development of modern education remained largely confined to mission schools. In 1933 schools were maintained by twenty-one missionary organisations. Under Governor Cameron (1925–31), the British had decided to 'promote education by working in partnership with Christian missions' (Njozi 2003: 15). Thus, an indigenous Christian elite was groomed that came to replace the Muslim functionaries of the German administration. Mission schools were shunned by many Muslims who saw in them vehicles to promote conversion to Christianity. As a result, new African elites emerged in the 1920s, which were almost exclusively Christian, often Catholic. In 1955, colonial statistics showed that Muslims had become disadvantaged in the sphere of education, not only with respect to the number of primary schools, but also with respect to rural middle schools, secondary schools and teacher-training centres, as well as medical and technical schools (Mbogoni 2004: 107–8). About two-thirds of all schools (as well as half of all hospitals) were in missionary hands at the time of independence. The 'Christian/Catholic' domination of Tanganyika remained a central issue in Muslim–Christian disputes in Tanganyika and since 1964 in Tanzania, and led to the cultivation of corresponding perceptions, in particular that of the marginalisation of Muslims by Christians. Such interpretations of Muslim–Christian relations in Tanganyika/Tanzania[1] may be surprising, as the number of Muslims had grown considerably since the late nineteenth century. However, this growth was not translated into corresponding political and economic strength.

Tanganyikan and Tanzanian post-independence history may be divided into a number of distinctive periods with respect to the development of state–religion relations. A first period was the time from independence in 1961 to the Arusha Declaration in 1967,[2] when President Julius Nyerere (r. 1961–85) tried to consolidate power and to remove established (Muslim and non-Muslim) elites from positions of power. The period from the Arusha Declaration in 1967 to the end of Nyerere's administration in 1985 may be characterised as the *ujamaa* (community) period of Tanzanian politics. This period was marked, in religious terms, by the disenchantment of the churches, in particular the Catholic Church, with *ujamaa* politics, and the development of a new Muslim bureaucratic elite that supported *ujamaa*. A third period from 1985 to the present day has been characterised by the development of a multi-party system and a liberal market economy.

In the context of President Nyerere's *ujamaa* policies, a group of loyalist Muslim functionaries emerged, often linked to the Qādiriyya, who supported state-informed policies of reform and tried to translate them into an 'Islamic code'. In the 1970s, scholars such as ᶜAbdallāh Chaurembo and Adam Nasibu formed a group of Tanzanian *islamologues fonctionnariés*, organised in a party-linked association, the Baraza Kuu la Waislamu Tanzania (BAKWATA) (Supreme Council for Tanzanian Muslims). These 'BAKWATA shaykhs' marginalised the most outspoken representatives of the earlier tradition of reform, such as Ḥasan b. ᶜAmeir who was the most respected scholar of the Qādiriyya and *muftī* of Tanzania until 1968. But despite their closeness to the ruling party, the Tanzanian *islamologues fonctionnariés* largely failed to develop a convincing programme of reform for a majority of Tanzania's Muslims. The failure of Muslim functionaries to fight for Muslim interests led to the development of oppositional Muslim organisations of both Sufi and Salafi orientation in the early 1980s. Although often in dispute over matters of ritual, Muslim oppositional associations agreed in their complaints regarding the marginalisation of Muslims in Tanzania and the growing influence of Christians. In the eyes of many Muslims, Tanzania had become a Christian country, while Muslims had been pushed to the wall. Muslims maintain today that since Nyerere's times there has been a 'Christian (master) plan' (*mfumo Kristo*) to gain control over the Tanzanian state (van de Bruinhorst 2007: 103). By attacking Christians, Muslims want to force the state to redress this imbalance.[3]

Sufi-oriented Reform

Like Senegal and northern Nigeria, coastal East Africa has a tradition of Sufi-oriented reformers that dates back to the nineteenth century. Among the different Sufi orders, the Qādiriyya became the major religious force in both German East Africa and British Tanganyika, and was able to defend this role in colonial as well as post-colonial times (see Nimtz 1980; Iliffe 1979). In fact, the Qādiriyya turned out to be the most influential Muslim movement in almost all parts of Tanganyika in colonial times. The *ṭarīqa* became particularly famous for its *dhikr*, to the extent that local leaders of the Qādiriyya in some cases managed to convince the British administration to ban the religious activities of other Sufi orders, in order to 'maintain peace', as happened in Ruvu in 1933 with respect to the ᶜAskariyya (Nimtz 1980: 84). A prominent branch of the Qādiriyya in Tanganyika was the branch led by Yaḥyā b. ᶜAbdallāh also known as 'Shaykh Ramiya' (d. 1931/2), a manumitted slave from Manyema (eastern Congo), of Amīr b. Sulaimān al-Lamkī, a trader and local representative (*liwali*) of the Sultan of Zanzibar in Bagamoyo. Shaykh Ramiya became a student of Abū Bakr b. Ṭāhā al-Jabrī al-Bārawī, who taught in Bagamoyo in the 1880s, and ᶜAbdallāh b. ᶜAlawī Jamal al-Layl. In about 1900, Shaykh Ramiya established his own *madrasa* in Bagamoyo and became the leader of a new network of students, who were of remarkably diverse origins, while older branches of the Qādiriyya in Bagamoyo, such as that of Uways b. Muḥammad al-Barawī (1847–1909), were often linked with established families that had close links to Zanzibar. In 1905, Shaykh Ramiya was introduced (or re-introduced) into the Qādiriyya by an enigmatic Middle Eastern scholar of this *ṭarīqa*, Muḥammad b. Ḥusayn al-Lughānī. This initiation possibly did not take place in Bagamoyo, as Nimtz has claimed, but in Zanzibar, at least according to Shaykh Ramiya's grandson, ᶜAbdallāh Muḥammad Jembe, and would be another proof of Shaykh Ramiya's efforts to dissociate himself from Bagamoyo's scholarly establishment (Nimtz 1980: 118; Bromber 2001: 3).

Shaykh Ramiya became particularly famous for his magico-therapeutic practices and the celebration of the *mawlid al-nabī*, which became a distinctive feature of his branch of the Qādiriyya: while most branches cultivated different forms of the *dhikr*, Shaykh Ramiya chose the celebration of *mawlid al-nabī* as the central feature of his movement. We may suspect that Shaykh Ramiya used these ritual differentiations as a symbol to enhance the uniqueness of his movement. This assumption is supported by the fact that he sought an *ijāza* from an outsider to the East African networks of the Qādiriyya, Muḥammad b. Ḥusayn al-Lughānī: Shaykh Ramiya's activities could consequently be interpreted as an effort to establish his own and independent (and non-Zanzibar-oriented) branch of the Qādiriyya, that was, by contrast, open for the new Muslims from the *bara* regions, whose affiliation with him was a major factor for the success of his movement as a mass movement of the Qādiriyya in Tanganyika.

In 1911, Shaykh Ramiya was nominated *imām* of the Bagamoyo Friday mosque, and in 1916 the new British administration recognised him as *qāḍī* of Bagamoyo. After his death in 1931, his son, Muḥammad Ramiya (d. 1985), followed him as leader of the Qādiriyya in Bagamoyo. In 1938, Muḥammad Ramiya started a dispute with Zanzibar's established scholars when he claimed that the Prophet had not been an 'Arab', but a mixture of all races, a claim that was rejected by one of East Africa's leading religious scholars, ᶜUmar b. Aḥmad b. Sumayṭ (Bromber 2001: 6). However, this dispute does not seem to have damaged Muḥammad Ramiya's reputation as a scholar. Rather, his claim echoed Shaykh Ramiya's legacy to open the Qādiriyya for the new (and comparatively uneducated) Muslims from the *bara* regions, who came from all kinds of different places, while at the same time rejecting notions of Arabness that were highly esteemed by the scholarly establishment in Zanzibar.

In the colonial period, the Bagamoyo-oriented Qādiriyya supported the establishment and development of Tanganyika's first African political association, the Tanganyika African Association (TAA) (see Said 1998: 170) and, later, the Tanganyika African National Union (TANU), and Muḥammad Ramiya was the first African to be elected into the city council of Bagamoyo in 1948. After the establishment of TANU, the Qādiriyya continued to play a major role within this party, as well as within the movement for independence. After independence, the Qādirī scholars of Bagamoyo continued to support President Nyerere, even after the dissolution of the East African Muslim Welfare Society (EAMWS) and the foundation of BAKWATA (see below): Muḥammad Ramiya was one of the few prominent religious scholars in Tanzania who supported the establishment of BAKWATA. After his death in 1985, the leadership of the Qādiriyya in Bagamoyo was taken over by ᶜAbdallāh b. Muḥammad Jembe, a grandson of Shaykh Ramiya, who had studied with ᶜAlī Ḥemedi al-Buḥrī al-Hināwī (Bromber 2001: 9; Ahmed 2008: 129; Constantin 1988b: 138ff).

However, support for TANU politics and BAKWATA was not confined to the Ramiya family in Bagamoyo. ᶜAlī Ḥimid ('Ḥemedi') al-Buḥrī al-Hināwī (1891–1957), a religious scholar of Omani origin represented another loyalist family that came to support TANU, Nyerere and, later, BAKWATA. He was born in Tanga and studied with scholars in Tanga and Zanzibar, including Aḥmad b. Sumayṭ. He also went to Mombasa to study for a short period of time with al-Amīn b. ᶜAlī al-Mazrūᶜī. He was appointed *qāḍī* of Tanga in 1920 and served in this position until it was dissolved in 1936. Over time, he became one of the most respected religious scholars and legal experts in Tanganyika. ᶜAlī Ḥemedi al-Buḥrī had numerous students. Many of them later became leaders of BAKWATA, such as his own nephew Ḥemedi b. Juma al-Buḥrī (d. 2002) who was appointed the first 'Grand Shaykh' of BAKWATA in 1975, and his son Muḥammad b. ᶜAlī al-Buḥrī (1927–95). Muḥammad b. ᶜAlī al-Buḥrī was one of the first prominent religious scholars to study law at the University of Dar es Salaam. He was linked with the oppositional Muslim Students Association of the University of Dar es Salaam (MSAUD) as well as with other critical voices such as Dr Malik (see below) of the Kinondoni Secondary School, and ᶜAbbās Muṣṭafa of the al-ḥaramayn-Foundation. At the same time, he was elected the first Secretary General of BAKWATA in 1968 and held this office until he was forced to retire in 1982 (see Chande 1998: 98ff.; Gilsaa 2012: 200ff).

While the Ramiya and the Buḥrī families came to represent a (mostly) loyalist perspective in Tanganyikan and Tanzanian politics, another prominent scholar of the Qādiriyya represented a more ambivalent position. This was Ḥasan b. ᶜAmeir al-Shirāzī, who also bridged pre-independence and post-independence times (for his biography, see Loimeier 2009; Dar es Salaam University Muslims' Trusteeship 2004; Tajo n.d.; Ziddy 2001, 2003a and 2003b). Ḥasan b. ᶜAmeir from Makunduchi (Zanzibar) was born in 1880 and died on 8 October 1979. He went through the usual stages of Islamic education and studied with a number of well-known Muslim scholars in Zanzibar. From 1907, he attended the first Zanzibari Government school and was trained as a teacher for Kiswahili. Subsequently, he worked as a government teacher in a number of schools in Zanzibar. After some time, he left government school teaching and worked in the 1920s and 1930s as a clerk in the office of the Chief Qāḍī of Zanzibar. In reaction to the increasing activities of Christian missions in Tanganyika, he left Zanzibar in 1940 and started his own *daᶜwa* activities on the mainland and in other territories in East and Central Africa. He also visited the holy places in Saudi Arabia, ᶜIraq, Lebanon, Palestine and Egypt, as well as Baghdad, where he visited the tomb of ᶜAbd al-Qādir al-Jīlānī in 1944. After his return to Tanganyika in 1945, he joined the EAMWS and from 1950 supported the struggle of the TAA for independence. In 1954, he became a prominent founding member of TANU and issued membership cards for TANU in the context of his visits to mosques and *madāris* in Tanganyika (Said 1998: 295).

Ḥasan b. ᶜAmeir not only rallied widespread Muslim support for TANU, as most *ṭarīqa* leaders followed him in this policy, but also developed a close personal link with Julius Nyerere, the future president of Tanganyika, in the struggle for Tanganyika's independence. In the 1950s, he rose to the position of *muftī* of Tanganiyka, a position he was to keep until 1968. Ḥasan b. ᶜAmeir can thus be regarded as a major figure in Tanganyika's religio-political development, especially in respect of the struggle for independence. In the

1960s, Ḥasan b. ᶜAmeir continued to be the most prominent Muslim scholar in mainland Tanganyika, both as the *muftī* of Tanganyika and on account of his prominent role within the EAMWS. After 1964, the relations between the state and the EAMWS soured, however, on a number of issues such as the question as to whether the EAMWS should become a Tanganyikan national organisation or remain a supra-national East African organisation. As Ḥasan b. ᶜAmeir supported the latter model and was not prepared to legitimise the socialist (and seemingly anti-religious) turn of the Nyerere administration after the Arusha Declaration of 1967, he was increasingly marginalised within the Tanganyikan branch of the EAMWS and was finally deported to Zanzibar in 1968, where he died in 1979.

On account of his role in Tanganyikan and Tanzanian politics as well as religious life, Ḥasan b. ᶜAmeir continues to be discussed in controversial terms by Muslims in Tanzania. At the same time, he has become an icon of Muslim memories: while some maintain that Ḥasan b. ᶜAmeir was a non-political character and interested in teaching and *daᶜwa* rather than in politics, and that he supported TANU and Nyerere, with whom he cultivated personal ties, as a way of promoting Islamic education, other Muslims contend that he played a prominent role in the EAMWS to its very end, that he spoke out against the TANU faction within EAMWS in order to conserve its unity and that he was deported to Zanzibar due to his opposition to the TANU faction that finally took control of the EAMWS and established BAKWATA. Still other sources claim that Ḥasan b. ᶜAmeir ceased to take part in politics after independence and concentrated on religious issues: he became a problem for Nyerere due to the fact that he couldn't be convinced to cooperate with the government in political terms. In the 1980s, Tanzania's younger generation of Salafi-oriented activists started to oppose the older generation of state-paid 'BAKWATA Muslims' by making reference to Ḥasan b. ᶜAmeir. Even though Ḥasan b. ᶜAmeir was known to have been affiliated with the Qādiriyya, that is, a *ṭarīqa* that was attacked by Salafi-minded Muslim activists as representing 'BAKWATA (that is, government) Islam', his legacy could be presented as an example of Tanzanian anti-Muslim policies because he was victimised by both Nyerere and a generation of post-independence 'BAKWATA' Muslim functionaries. The trans-generational link between contemporary reformers in Tanzania and a major figure of Islamic reform of the 1950s and 1960s thus has a distinctive trans-traditional character. In this context, we should, however, consider the fact that Ḥasan b. ^{c}Ameir's fate was not singular: rather, a considerable number of religious scholars were treated badly by the Nyerere administration in the 1960s.

The policy of marginalising established religious scholars, as in the case of the Badawī family and the case of Nūr al-Dīn Ḥusayn (see below), seems to have had the aim of eliminating potentially competing centres of authority, such as the old (and respected) scholars, but also the old guard of politicians within TANU. In the course of the 1960s, these established authorities were replaced by new, technocratic elites that were prepared to support the modernising programme of TANU, and that were dependent – in their position as religious scholars – on the government. These contradictory positions essentially reflect pro- and anti-government or pro- and anti-BAKWATA positions among Tanganyika's Muslims, as different groups have been trying to claim Ḥasan b. ^{c}Ameir's legacy as their own in order to justify their critique of specific actions by the government. Ḥasan b. ^{c}Ameir has thus become an icon of reference that has been instrumentalised for specific reasons, and consequently interpreted in different ways by different groups.

While the Qādiriyya has been at the forefront of the political development of both Tanganiyka and Tanzania, the Shādhiliyya-Yashruṭiyya has been almost as influential, although this *ṭarīqa* was not as widespread in Tanganyika as the Qādiriyya; Dar es Salaam and the coastal areas south of Dar es Salaam were the major regions of Shādhilī influence. However, the Shādhiliyya-Yashruṭiyya spread widely in the Comoros, in Madagascar, in northern Mozambique, in Kenya and in Uganda (see Ahmed 2008: 45ff.). Historically, the Shādhiliyya-Yashruṭiyya was rooted in the Comoros and spread to Tanganyika in the early twentieth century, especially to the Kilwa region. The major *dā^{c}iya* of the Shādhiliyya-Yashruṭiyya in the Comoros, but also in Madagascar and Mozambique, was Aḥmad b. Muḥammad al-Ma^{c}rūf (1853–1905), a *sayyid* of the Bin Sālim family from the Comoros, who was initiated into the Yashruṭiyya branch of the Shādhiliyya by ^{c}Abdallāh b. Sa^{c}īd al-Darwīsh. ^{c}Abdallāh b. Sa^{c}īd al-Darwīsh was a Comorian scholar who had established direct contact with the founder of the Yashruṭiyya, ^{c}Alī Nūr al-Dīn al-Yashrūṭī (1793–1899). This Tunisian scholar had founded this branch of the Shādhiliyya in ^{c}Akka, Palestine, although the centre was shifted to Beirut after 1948. After the death of Aḥmad b. Muḥammad al-Maᶜrūf on 27 Jumada II 1323, the annual commemoration of his death on 27 Jumādā II (Swa. *saba ishirini*) became the most important religious ritual of the Shādhiliyya-Yashruṭiyya and the *ṭarīqa* has become known as *saba ishirini* in East Africa (Ahmed 2008: 76ff.).

After the demise of Aḥmad b. Muḥammad al-Maᶜrūf, the cultivation of the networks of the Shādhiliyya-Yashruṭiyya in East Africa was linked with one of the closest disciples of Aḥmad b. Muḥammad al-Maᶜrūf, Ḥusayn b. Maḥmūd al-Ghassānī (d. 1971), an ᶜUmani from Kilwa, whose *zāwiya* in Kilwa (established 1919) became the major centre of the Shādhiliyya-Yashruṭiyya in Tanganyika. From Kilwa, the *ṭarīqa* spread into Kenya, Uganda and northern Mozambique. Ḥusayn b. Maḥmūd al-Ghassānī's work was continued by his son Nūr al-Dīn Ḥusayn (1924/5–2007) (see Ahmed 2008: 66ff). Nūr al-Dīn Ḥusayn became the undisputed leader of the Shādhiliyya-Yashruṭiyya in post-colonial Tanzania. He studied with local teachers in Tanzania and at al-Azhar in Cairo before settling in Lindi in southern Tanzania in the early 1950s. In Lindi, he started a *madrasa* and worked in different fields, for instance as secretary for a mangrove wood company, before starting his own business as a trader of dried fish. In 1965, he was put under arrest for allegedly plotting against Nyerere, and spent eight months in prison in Mtwara. After his release from prison he settled in Tanga, resumed his trading and teaching activities and established a new *madrasa* in Korogwe, near Tanga. In 1980 he moved to Dar es Salaam and established another *zāwiya* and *madrasa* in the Kariakoo area. In 1992, he set up Hajj Trust, a private company that specialised in the organisation of the *ḥajj* for Tanzanian (mainland) pilgrims, although this task technically remained a prerogative of BAKWATA until 1995. Through the Ḥajj Trust, Nūr al-Dīn Ḥusayn became a household name in virtually every large town in Tanzania. He has become one of the most respected religious scholars in contemporary Tanzania, partly due to the fact that he was seen to be independent from BAKWATA. In addition, Nūr al-Dīn Ḥusayn gained national importance as the leader of the Baraza Kuu la Jumuiya na Taasisi ya Kiislamu ('Baraza Kuu') (the Supreme Council of Muslim Associations and Institutions in Tanzania), established in 1992 in order to counter the influence of BAKWATA (communication Sören Gilsaa, 21 April 2005; for Nūr al-Dīn Ḥusayn's biography, see Ahmed 2006, 2008).

In the context of the political and economic liberalisation of the 1980s and 1990s, leaders of both the Qādiriyya and the Shādhiliyya established NGOs of their own. While Nūr al-Dīn Ḥusayn established the Hajj Trust, Muḥammad ᶜAbd al-Raḥmān Dedes, a mainland leader of the Qādiriyya from Zanzibar, became one of the leaders of the Katiba ya jumuiya zawiyatul Qadiriyya Tanzania (Constitution of Qādirī Associations of Tanzania), a Qādirī NGO founded by Muḥammad Nassor and Muḥammad ᶜAbd al-Raḥmān Dedes in 1990 in Arusha. Muḥammad Nassor, as well as his *khalīfa*, Muḥammad ᶜAbd al-Raḥmān Dedes, were regarded by the Tanzanian Government as scholars who were needed in order to convince the followers of the Qādiriyya to support the social programmes of the government. Today, the Nassor-Dedes branch of the Qādiriyya is recognised as a *jumuiya*, an association with the status of an NGO and is entitled as such to construct mosques and schools, as well as to develop its own education and social-development programmes. As a consequence, the Qādiriyya has been able to consolidate its status as an 'official *ṭarīqa*' of Tanzania.

In the 1930s to the 1950s, Muslims affiliated with Sufi orders thus came to constitute the vanguard of Tanganyika's struggle for independence and acquired considerable weight in pre-independence politics. It is misleading, however, to assume that Sufi orders in Tanzania formed a homogeneous block. Rather, the disputes between scholars of the Qādiriyya and the Shādhiliyya in the late 1960s and the 1970s, which led to the foundation of BAKWATA, show that the Sufi orders were split into a number of networks, some who supported the state and others, such as Nūr al-Dīn Ḥusayn, who opposed it or tried to keep their distance. Nūr al-Dīn Ḥusayn's example shows that an independent and at times critical position with respect to the state in Tanzania was not a privilege of Salafi-oriented activist groups, but was also cultivated by scholars who represented the esoteric episteme. Tanganyika's path towards independence was characterised by the fact that Muslims were prominent in the struggle for independence and that Tanganyika's first Muslim political associations, such as the Muslim Association of Tanganyika (MAT) (jamᶜiyyat al-islāmiyya fi-tanganyika) and the EAMWS supported this struggle (Gilsaa 2012: 128ff). Muslim politicians such as Bibi Titi Muhammad (1926–2000), a famous ngoma singer and first president of TANU's women's organisation, or Tewa Said Tewa, one of the seventeen founders of TANU in 1954, featured prominently in TANU as well as in the EAMWS (see Said 1998). Membership in MAT, the first African-controlled Muslim association in Tanganyika, was identical with the TAA (and later TANU), and prominent MAT leaders such as Ḥasan b. ᶜAmeir and ᶜAbdallāh Chaurembo in Dar es Salaam, ᶜAbd al-Muḥsin Kitumba in Ujiji, Mzee b. Fereji in Tabora or Muḥammad b. Yaḥyā in Bagomoyo were strong supporters of TANU and Nyerere. They saw their support for TANU as a way to redress the imbalance in education produced by the British administration (Nimtz 1980: 88). However, some Muslims, such as Ramadhani Mashado Plantaan, the editor and owner of the TANU Party paper *Zuhra*, or Yaḥya Ḥusayn, resented Nyerere's rise within TANU and in 1957 they established the All Muslims National Union of Tanganyika (AMNUT), led by Yaḥya Ḥusayn (Gilsaa 2912: 147). AMNUT failed to mobilise support among Muslims, as most leaders of the Sufi orders continued to follow Ḥasan b. ᶜAmeir and supported TANU. In 1959, AMNUT opposed the rapid transition to independence by arguing that Tanganyika should wait until Muslims had achieved greater educational progress. Nyerere rejected this position by responding that if people waited for the British to improve the situation, they would have to wait for a long time. By 1961, AMNUT was moribund and was dissolved in 1964 (Nimtz 1980: 90).

BAKWATA Islam

While Muslims played a prominent role in the struggle for independence, the relationship between Muslims and the state changed completely after independence in 1961, when Nyerere gradually adopted 'Christian' positions with respect to national development. The first national government had eleven Christian and four Muslim ministers, which contributed to Muslim dissatisfaction and led to protests within TANU. Many Muslim party members supported ᶜAbdallāh Fundikira, the leader of the EAMWS, who opposed Nyerere in the run-up to the 1962 presidential elections. According to TANU Party sources, 'the Muslims backed Fundikira very strongly and it was not clear for several days that Nyerere would be in' (Ludwig 1999: 53). In a reaction to the increasing influence of representatives of the churches, Ḥasan b. ᶜAmeir urged Muslims to become more active with respect to education 'so that they could share power with the Christians in governing the country' (Said 1998: 295). Even before Muslims were able to develop a new strategy, the government used a dispute among Muslims to expel a well-known scholar, Ḥusayn Badawī, and his brother: in January 1963, in the context of a *mawlid* celebration in Dar es Salaam, Ḥusayn Badawī and his brother had criticised ᶜAbdallāh Chaurembo because he appealed to Muslims to be grateful to the government (Said 1998: 267). ᶜAbdallāh Chaurembo was a leader of the Shādhiliyya in Dar es Salaam who had studied with Ḥasan b. ᶜAmeir until 1961, but then broke with him. In the 1960s, he became the chairperson of the *mawlid* committee, as well as a member of the TANU central committee, a Nyerere and TANU supporter. The expulsion of the Badawī brothers from Dar es Salaam hit one of most respected scholarly families in East Africa and can be viewed as a deliberate political move against the scholarly establishment.

The Badawī family originated from Lamu in Kenya and not only represented Lamu's scholarly establishment, but was also linked, by marriage ties, with Ḥabīb Ṣāliḥ Jamal al-Layl, a representative of the ᶜAlawī elite in East Africa: Aḥmad al-Badawī (1898–1939) had married a daughter of Ḥabīb Ṣāliḥ (1844–1935); Aḥmad al-Badawī's son, ᶜAlī b. Aḥmad al-Badawī (1907–89), was a student of al-Amīn b. ᶜAlī al-Mazrūᶜī and a teacher at the Muslim Academy in Zanzibar until 1964. In 1948 (Mwakimako 2010: 124ff) he was Chief Qāḍī of Kenya, as the successor of al-Amīn b. ᶜAlī al-Mazrūᶜī in that position and the predecessor of Muḥammad b. Qāsim al-Mazrūᶜī. The latter held the position of Chief Qāḍī of Kenya until 1968, when ᶜAbdallāh Ṣāliḥ al-Farsy was nominated Chief Qāḍī. Ḥusayn Badawī's expulsion to Kenya, the original home of the Badawī family, effectively started a movement of de-Islamisation of the government and administration that became conspicuously public on 1 March 1963 when Nyerere dissolved the TANU Elders' Council that was dominated by Muslims. In January 1964, Nyerere used the opportunity of a mutiny by the Tanganyika Rifles to arrest prominent Muslims such as Bilali Rehani Waikela, who had started to criticise his government.

Muslims thus encountered increasing problems in the sphere of politics. In a first reaction, a pan-territorial congress of all Muslim organisations in Tanganyika was convened in 1962 and brought together organisations such as the EAMWS, the MAT, the jamāᶜat al-islāmiyya, the Muslim Education

Union and other groups, which were supposed to unite, 'from Kigoma to Dar es Salaam, from Lindi to Arusha', in a new national Islamic organisation, the Jumuiya al-Dawa al-Islamiyya that was registered on 26 August 1963. The congress elected Tewa Said Tewa as president and decided to support the establishment of an Islamic university in Jang'ombe, Dar es Salaam. During a state visit to Egypt in April 1964, Tewa Said Tewa was able to sign an agreement that provided funds for such a university. However, the project was shelved when Tewa Said Tewa was removed from the government in a cabinet reshuffle in the context of the union agreement with Zanzibar in late April 1964 (that actually increased the number of Muslims in the cabinet to ten, while fourteen ministers were Christian). Only in 2004 was an Islamic university eventually established in Morogoro. At the same time, Bibi Titi Muhammad, the leader of the Tanzanian Women's Union (UWT) (Umoja wa Wanawake wa Tanzania) was also sidelined: in 1965, she lost her seat in her constituency and when she protested against the Arusha Declaration in February 1967, she was quickly accused of collaborating with Nyerere's opponents and enemies. This applied especially to Oscar Kambona, TANU's organising secretary, who was increasingly seen by Nyerere as a competitor, although Kambona had actually saved Nyerere in the context of the 1964 army mutiny. In 1969, Bibi Titi Muhammad was accused of having taken part in a plot to remove Nyerere from power. After a trial in 1970/1, she was condemned to a life sentence, although she was released from prison in 1972. She was only rehabilitated in 1984. Apart from Nyerere, Bibi Titi Muhammad had been one of the few TANU politicians known throughout the country in 1961, at the time of independence. Like most leading TANU women of the 1950s and early 1960s in the UWT, she was Muslim (for her biography, see Geiger 1997).

The next victim of Nyerere's policy of marginalising old elites was the East Africa Muslim Welfare Society (EAMWS) that had been founded by the Aga Khan in 1937, but was only formally established as the EAMWS in 1945. In 1961, the centre of the EAMWS was moved, under the leadership of ᶜAbdallāh Fundikira, a leading TANU member and an opponent of Nyerere, from Mombasa to Dar es Salaam. As a consequence of Tanganyika's turn to 'African socialism' after the Arusha Declaration of 1967, the EAMWS, which had propagated the unity of East Africa's Muslim populations, became obsolete as a supranational organisation in the context of emerging nationalisms in East Africa and the different paths of development propagated by Tanzania, Uganda and Kenya. The dissolution of the EAMWS was triggered, however, by internal rivalries that had started as a local dispute in Bukoba in 1965 over a question of ritual with respect to the Friday prayers. One group of Muslims in Bukoba, supported by the Indian Muslim community, claimed that Friday (*jum*^{c}*a*) communal prayers, consisting of two *raka*^{c}*āt*, had to be joined with *ẓuhr* prayers, consisting of four *raka*^{c}*āt*. Their opponents, led by a Muslim teacher from Bukoba, Adam Nasibu, insisted that Friday *jum*^{c}*a* prayers replaced the normal routine of *ẓuhr* prayers and that the number of *raka*^{c}*āt* was only two. Due to this issue, the 'jum^{c}a-dhuhuri' group split off and established the Tanzania Muslim Education Union (TMEU), while Adam Nasibu remained in command of the Bukoba branch of the EAMWS (see Chande 1998: 135ff).

The Bukoba dispute led to the disintegration of the organisation in 1967/8, when a dissident group led by Adam Nasibu organised an internal coup and pledged support for TANU politics of nationalisation, as well as the 1967 Arusha Declaration (Azimio la Arusha), by proclaiming that 'socialism was compatible with Islam' (Said 1998: 285). In this strategy, Adam Nasibu was supported by local opponents of the EAMWS in Dar es Salaam, in particular ^{c}Abdallāh Chaurembo, who claimed that the EAMWS was too 'Indian', anti-Arusha and thus 'anti-Tanzanian'. At the same time, members of the old EAMWS elite, such as Tewa Said Tewa and Bibi Titi Muhammad, lost their influence within TANU. There was thus nobody within TANU to defend the EAMWS against the dissident group led by Adam Nasibu. In the context of a meeting of the EAMWS in Bukoba in June 1968, the Nasibu branch finally split away from the EAMWS, a decision rapidly followed by nine other regional branches. The disintegration of the EAMWS was demonstrated symbolically in June 1968, when, for the first time since independence, two separate *mawlid* celebrations were held in Dar es Salaam, one on the Mnazi Mmoja grounds led by ^{c}Abdallāh Chaurembo, the other in Ilala led by Ḥasan b. ^{c}Ameir (Gilsaa 2012: 168). The final break came in the context of a conference in Iringa in December 1968, when Abeid Amani Karume, Tanzania's Vice-President from Zanzibar, opened the meeting with wild attacks against the EAMWS and accused the organisation of 'colluding with foreigners' (Chande 1998: 138). Abeid Amani Karume supported the dissolution of the EAMWS as a way of fighting Indian influence in Tanganyikan institutions, as he had done in Zanzibar, and so he supported the EAMWS dissidents against Ḥasan b. ᶜAmeir and the 'Indians'.

As a consequence of the dissolution of the EAMWS at the end of the Iringa meeting, a new organisation, BAKWATA, was established. Saleh Masasi, a TANU Central Committee member, was appointed national chairman, ᶜAbdallāh Chaurembo deputy chairman and Adam Nasibu acting secretary general (Gilsaa 2012: 170). BAKWATA thus came to function as a 'Muslim wing' of TANU, which in 1977 was renamed Chama Cha Mapinduzi (CCM) (Party of the Revolution). Muslims became increasingly dissatisfied with BAKWATA, not least because BAKWATA was responsible for issuing documents, permits and marriage certificates among Muslims and was thus difficult to ignore. Equally, the *Shaykh Mkuu* (grand shaykh) of BAKWATA, Ḥemedi b. Juma al-Buḥrī al-Hināwī, and other leading BAKWATA officials repeatedly defended government policies (see Chande 1998: 142). In 1971, for instance, BAKWATA decided to hold (communal) *jumᶜa* prayers in Kiswahili instead of Arabic. Most Muslims would agree that while the *khuṭba*, the Friday sermon, may be delivered in the vernacular language, the language of the (Friday) prayers as such should be Arabic. By starting to conduct prayers in Kiswahili, BAKWATA broke with this consensus. BAKWATA was consequently seen as a government institution that failed to promote Muslim positions and to unite Tanzania's Muslims. In the 1970s, BAKWATA was one of the few religious groups that supported Nyerere's *ujamaa* policies.

To Nyerere's chagrin, the churches had started to criticise some expressions of *ujamaa*, in particular the resettlement of villages. As Nyerere needed the churches' support for his policies, and as this support was not forthcoming as quickly as he wished, church–state relations became rather volatile in the 1970s. Nyerere 'complained that the Catholic Church had failed to give him the support he needed'. According to him, 'the churches had seen (in the colonial period) the existing social, political and economic system as being fixed and unchangeable and had helped to preach resignation' (quoted in Ludwig 1999: 105). Nyerere criticised the 'silence of the churches' in the post-colonial situation, and attacked them for being 'shaped by hierarchical thinking and structures'. Yet, times had changed, and churches ought to adapt to the new situation (Ludwig 1999: 105f). Also, Nyerere saw the problem of Muslim–Christian inequalites in education and appealed to the churches to open their schools for Muslims. As the churches were not willing to meet these demands, Nyerere understood the nationalisation of the mission schools in 1970 as a major step in the implementation of *ujamaa* politics. Eventually, the churches had to accept the nationalisation of their schools on the basis of a bill passed on 15 March 1970, a move that was intended 'to neutralize the religious influence of the schools' (Ludwig 1999: 134).

The nationalisation of mission schools was implemented, however, without consulting the churches. The 'churches expressed their astonishment' with respect to the subsequent procedures, even if they did not oppose nationalisation, in particular when Nyerere declared that church and mission grounds (not school buildings) would remain church property. By 1974, Nyerere seems to have been thoroughly frustrated by the churches, in particular the Catholic Church, due to their critique of *ujamaa* politics. The question thus arises why Muslims today perceive this part of post-independent history as being disadvantageous to them. Why were Muslims not able to use their privileged position in the 1970s to exercise influence in spheres of life such as education? This is surprising in light of the fact that the Nyerere Government nationalised the mission schools, thus depriving the churches of a major means of socio-religious influence. A possible answer to this question may be that BAKWATA was unable to translate its privileged political position into a long-term strategy for the development of Muslim education, and relied on its privileged access to power and political representation within the regime. BAKWATA acted in essentially political terms and saw its role as representing the government with respect to political development, instead of representing Muslim aspirations: BAKWATA continued to perform as a government institution and to enjoy its political privileges, without using the historical opportunity to redress the structural imbalance between Muslims and Christians.

BAKWATA's controversial role became manifest in the 'seminary dispute' of 1981/2, which led to the emergence of an important Muslim oppositional movement, WARSHA (see Chande 1998: 144ff.; Gilsaa 2012: 201ff). WARSHA (Swa. *workshop*) had started out in 1975 as a working group within BAKWATA that had been asked to set up an Islamic studies syllabus for BAKWATA's Kindondoni secondary school, as well as a number of other BAKWATA-led primary schools. This initiative was directed by a Pakistani teacher, Dr Muḥammad Ḥusayn Malik,[4] who taught at Kindondoni Secondary School and who was closely linked with the Muslim Student's Association of the University of Dar es Salaam (MSAUD) (Gilsaa 2012: 177). In 1981, BAKWATA got permission to convert three of its four private secondary schools into 'seminaries', that is, schools that would offer a combined secular and religious syllabus along the model of Christian secondary schools. This decision was a success for BAKWATA's secretary general, Muḥammad b. ᶜAlī al-Buḥrī, who had been criticised within and beyond BAKWATA for his rather meagre achievements as secretary general of BAKWATA. However, the transformation of the Kindondoni Secondary School into a Muslim 'seminary' was greeted by Christian critique. As a result, President Nyerere, who did not want Kinondoni to become a centre of Muslim activism, asked Vice-President Aboud Jumbe to look into this question and to persuade Muḥammad b. ᶜAlī al-Buḥrī to revise the status of the Kinondoni School. Muḥammad b. ᶜAlī al-Buḥrī resisted this pressure, however, and in 1982 he was forced to resign from his position as Secretary General of BAKWATA. He was followed by Adam Nasibu (Gilsaa 2012: 214, 220; Chande 1998). The BAKWATA seminaries were re-transformed into regular secondary schools: BAKWATA once again demonstrated that it was a government institution controlled by the ruling party and did not represent independent Muslim interests. The Kinondoni affair was not only a watershed with respect to the relations between state, BAKWATA and 'free' Muslims, but also the starting point for WARSHA to become a Muslim oppositional association that subsequently inspired the foundation of a number of Muslim activist associations outside BAKWATA. Further BAKWATA scandals and personal rivalries within BAKWATA contributed to this development. Most important were allegations of mismanagement of funds by BAKWATA functionaries and irregularities regarding the selection of pilgrims and the organisation of the pilgrimage. These scandals added to the rise of independent Muslim associations in the mid- and late 1980s (Chande 1998: 149ff; Gilsaa 2012: 210). Muslim scholars who were active in politics in the 1950s and early 1960s, and who often supported the struggle for independence, thus either became loyal supporters of Nyerere's *ujamaa* politics in the 1960s and 1970s or withdrew from politics, only to re-emerge as major players and critics of *ujamaa* politics in the 1980s. Their biographies attest to the efforts of the Nyerere era to impose hegemonic control over Muslim affairs at this time, as well as to the efforts of Muslims to navigate these pressures and to gain as much freedom as possible under adverse conditions (see Gilsaa 2012: 11–12, 501–2).

New Muslim Organisations

While the Sufi orders followed political strategies to defend their social position in Tanganyika in the colonial and post-colonial periods, other Muslims cultivated different 'paths of accommodation' with modernity, and developed programmes of reform that adopted a Salafi inspiration. The most paradigmatic representatives of this Salafi-oriented movement of reform in East Africa were al-Amīn b. ^{c}Alī al-Mazrū^{c}ī (1891–1947) and, after him, ^{c}Abdallāh Ṣāliḥ al-Farsy (1912–82). Although they both did not become active in Tanganyika, but emerged as major leaders of a Salafi-oriented agenda in Zanzibar and Kenya, they taught numerous students from mainland Tanganyika. Salafi-oriented reformers such as al-Amīn b. ^{c}Alī al-Mazrū^{c}ī and ^{c}Abdallāh Ṣāliḥ al-Farsy rejected the locally established Sufi-oriented traditions of religious practice, particularly the *dhikr* or specific forms of the *mawlid*,[5] and advocated new and modern approaches to Islamic education. Al-Amīn b. ^{c}Alī al-Mazrū^{c}ī also founded the first Salafi-oriented newspapers in East Africa, *al-Saheefa* and *al-Iṣlāḥ* (in 1930 and 1932 respectively). He commented on the development of Islamic reformist thought, and criticised mission education as well as other features of colonial modernity. Neither al-Amīn b. ^{c}Alī al-Mazrū^{c}ī nor ^{c}Abdallāh Ṣāliḥ al-Farsy became active in the struggle for independence of Zanzibar, Tanganyika or Kenya. Rather, they cooperated with the colonial and post-colonial administrations of Zanzibar and Kenya: al-Amīn b. ^{c}Alī al-Mazrū^{c}ī was Chief Qāḍī of Kenya from 1937[6] and ^{c}Abdallāh Ṣāliḥ al-Farsy worked as a teacher and supervisor for religious classes in the service of the British administration in Zanzibar from 1934. Thus, both al-Amīn b. ^{c}Alī al-Mazrū^{c}ī and ^{c}Abdallāh Ṣāliḥ al-Farsy adopted the accommodating positions typical of Sufi orders in Senegal and northern Nigeria, where Sufi scholars were willing to work with the colonial powers for various reasons. In contrast, Tanganyika's independence movement, led by Julius Nyerere, was supported by religious scholars affiliated with Sufi orders. As in northern Nigeria (and unlike in Senegal), the genesis of a Salafi-oriented programme of reform in East Africa was not linked with the struggle for independence of Tanganyika or Zanzibar.

After Tanganyika's independence and in the wake of Nyerere's *ujamaa* policies, some disciples and students of al-Amīn b. ᶜAlī al-Mazrūᶜī and ᶜAbdallāh Ṣāliḥ al-Farsy started to develop more radical positions with respect to Sufism and the post-colonial state. This intermediary generation of Salafi-oriented reformers was characterised by staunch, albeit individualistic and unorganised opposition to the post-colonial state. Among them, scholars such as Saidi Musa[7] and the first returnees from Saudi Arabia such as Sālim ᶜAbd al-Mālik b. Rajab b. Sima[8] or Yūsuf Rajab Mnenge[9] also cultivated new regional orientations towards Sudan, Saudi Arabia and Iran (Gilsaa 2012: 255, 2015: 41f). However, their attitudes failed to hold sway over local populations for the time being. Only in the 1980s did a new generation of Salafi-oriented Muslim reformers gain larger audiences in the context of the collapse of the *ujamaa* system. By intensifying their critique of the post-colonial state and by adopting increasingly militant forms of action that included new forms of public preaching (*mihadhara*), often inspired by Pentecostal forms of preaching, they gained greater influence over local populations than earlier Salafi-oriented reformers.

An important feature of this new generation of Muslim reformers was that they established activist organisations, such as Uamsho (Reawakening) or the Shura ya Maimamu and others that were independent of BAKWATA. Also, they redirected their attacks away from Sufi scholars toward the state and the Christian churches operating in the region. These Salafi-oriented associations have become known in East Africa under the umbrella term 'anṣār al-sunna', although they do not exist as a single, united and registered organisation or association. Rather, different anṣār al-sunna groups have come together under the Jamaat wa Ansar Sunnah Tanzania (JASUTA) that has come to form a third major Muslim umbrella organisation in Tanzania, apart from BAKWATA and the 'Baraza Kuu'. JASUTA is present, today, in all of Tanzania's thirty regions and, under different labels such as anṣār al-sunna, Islamic Foundation or anṣār al-sunna youth centre, runs hundreds of dispensaries, orphanages, nursery schools and primary schools, several secondary schools and a teacher-training college in Tanga. Despite the common label, anṣār al-sunna groups have remained divided over a number of religious and political issues, such as the question of whether it is permissible to pray in a non-'anṣārī' mosque, to attend Sufi-oriented celebrations such as the *mawlid al-nabī*, or to take part in elections. As a result, JASUTA does not mean much; more important are individual anṣār al-sunna groups such as the anṣār al-sunna youth in Tanga (Gilsaa 2012: 252ff, 387ff).

The establishment of new Muslim organisations in Tanzania in the 1980s must be seen in the context of the crisis of *ujamaa* politics and the opening of Tanzania, in 1986, to the International Monetary Fund (IMF) and World Bank demands for economic liberalisation. This led, in the 1990s, to the introduction of a multi-party system, in which, however, the CCM still dominated. Economic superstructures have been a major defining factor in the development of state–religion dialectics during Tanzania's post-independence history. The importance of economic structures was of paramount importance in the 1967–85 period, when *ujamaa*-policies (and economics) dominated Tanzania's development and defined religious dynamics. The same is true of the period of economic and political liberalisation since 1985, which has favoured better educated Christians in disproportionate ways. Liberalisation led to a multiplication of choices in the arenas of religion and politics. As a result, Muslim activist groups, with the backing of international donor organisations from the Near East, were able to build new schools and to improve their chances to gain public acceptance.[10] As a consequence, new and independent Muslim organisations emerged that were defined by their efforts to develop modern Islamic education and to oppose state-informed concepts of 'true Islam' as presented by BAKWATA. The proliferation of new organisations gained momentum when Muslims realised that their far-reaching aspirations with respect to an official 'rectification' of existing conditions would not be realised under Ali Hassan Mwinyi, a Muslim politician from Zanzibar, who became President of Tanzania in 1985. In 1987, Ali Hassan Mwinyi declared, in a public speech in Dar es Salaam: 'The government of our nation has no official creed and the same is true for our party: it has no religion' ('Serikali ya taifa letu haina dini yake rasmi. Na chama chetu vivyo hivyo hakina dini') (quoted in Lacunza Balda 1989: 288).

Among the new Muslim organisations that were established in the 1980s, a large number were critical of BAKWATA. Apart from some influential Muslim voices, such as Saidi Musa, who did not build an organisational basis of their own, there are some important associations such as the Baraza Kuu (established in 1992) led by Nūr al-Dīn Ḥusayn – who acquired a considerable national reputation on account of his independent views – as well as numerous non-*ṭarīqa*-oriented and mostly oppositional activist Muslim groups and Islamic NGOs (see Gilsaa 2012: 308ff). Today, Tanzania is swamped by Islamic organisations, associations and NGOs, a few with a nationwide network of branches, some represented in a few regions only, such as Tabora, Morogoro, Tanga, Ujiji, Dodoma, Bukoba or Dar es Salaam, and others remaining confined to a single school and/or mosque. These associations attest to the efforts of Tanzania's Muslims to navigate national politics. At the same time, the development of most of these associations has been characterised by histories of fragmentation caused by personal rivalries and disputes over strategy. The most important among these associations are:

- The National Association for the Promotion of the Kuran in Tanzania (Baraza la Uendelezaji Kuran Tanzania) (BALUKTA), which was founded in 1987 as a branch of BAKWATA by Yaḥyā Ḥusayn[11] (chairman, d. 2011) and Qassim Juma (secretary general, d. 1993), a scholar affiliated with the Qādiriyya (see Chande 1998: 157–60). While Yaḥyā Ḥusayn was Tanzania's representative in the rābiṭat al-ᶜālam al-islāmī in the 1960s, as well as Secretary General of the EAMWS and a prominent member of BAKWATA (Gilsaa 2012: 247), Qassim Juma was a prominent member of BAKWATA and WARSHA, yet became a vociferous critic of BAKWATA and a well-known *mihadhara* preacher in the 1980s and early 1990s (Gilsaa 2012: 335f, 343). BALUKTA was possibly founded as a protest against the embezzlement of BAKWATA funds by Adam Nasibu, the Secretary General of BAKWATA in the mid-1980s (Gilsaa 2012: 238). Both Yaḥyā Ḥusayn and Qassim Juma leaders were accused of being involved in the 1993 'pork butchery riots' in Dar es Salaam (see below). Although Qassim Juma had not been in the country at the time of the riots, he was imprisoned after his return to Tanzania and died shortly after his release from prison. BALUKTA was dissolved as an organisation in June 1993 (Gilsaa 2012: 343).

- The Baraza la Misikiti Tanzania (BAMITA) (Council of Mosques in Tanzania) was another Muslim umbrella organisation set up in 1981 by the Vice-President of Tanzania, Aboud Jumbe, to coordinate the activities of mosques. This association was regarded as having the potential to replace BAKWATA, but although it was provided with funds by Saudi Arabia, the organisation quickly disintegrated. Accusations of mismanagement of funds and fraud led to a quick loss of support (see Gilsaa 2012: 211; Chande 1998: 277).
- The Baraza Kuu la Jumuiya na Taasisi ya Kiislamu (Baraza Kuu) (Supreme Council of Muslim Associations and Institutions in Tanzania), was established in 1992 as a Muslim umbrella organisation to counter the influence of BAKWATA at a time when efforts to reform BAKWATA from within had failed. The Baraza Kuu was led by Nūr al-Dīn Ḥusayn. Other prominent Muslim scholars such as Muḥammad b. ᶜAlī al-Buḥrī, Yaḥyā Ḥusayn and Qassim Juma initially joined this organisation. Its headquarters were moved into the premises of the Tanzania Islamic Centre (TIC) on Morogoro Road in Magomeni, Dar es Salaam.[12] The Barazu Kuu brought together Muslim scholars, activists and intellectuals who were members of other organisations, such as UWAMDI, WARSHA, the IPC and al-Mallid, and even members of some anṣār al-sunna groups, as well as numerous *imāms*. It thus became a truly national organisation, yet lacked the organisational structure of BAKWATA and the state's funding, and thus quickly encountered administrative and managerial problems. Only in 1995, for instance, was a National Executive Committee elected. These elections confirmed the old guard of Muslim scholars in power, while the young as represented by the different anṣār al-sunna groups, the Islamic Propagation Centre (IPC) and MSAUD were either marginalised or boycotted the electoral process. Personal rivalries and power struggles thus led to the failure of the Baraza Kuu; it 'became a big name with nothing in it' (Gilsaa 2012: 370). Although the Baraza Kuu failed to replace BAKWATA, it continued as a Muslim umbrella organisation and was there 'as a potential structure' (Gilsaa 2012: 375). The failure of the 'Baraza Kuu' stimulated the emergence of the Shura ya Maimamu.

- The Shura ya Maimamu (council of *imāms*) is another Islamic umbrella organisation that has strong activist tendencies. The Shura ya Maimamu was established in Dar es Salaam in 1997 or 1998 as an informal network of mosques and *imāms* and other mosque officials. It was set up when it became clear that the Baraza Kuu would not work. So far, the Shura ya Maimamu has remained an independent non-registered umbrella association that has no 'bureaucratic contact' (Gilsaa 2012: 397) with the state or the government, but is based on individual commitment. The first chairperson (*amīr*) of the Shura ya Maimamu was Juma Mbukuzi, who was followed by Musa Yusuf Kundecha. Other leading scholars have been Ally Bassaleh (secretary general) and Issa Ponda Issa (also secretary general), all involved in other Muslim associations such as the Baraza Kuu, UWAMDI (see below), WARSHA, the IPC, the TIC, al-Mallid, TAMPRO (see below) or MSAUD, a fact that demonstrates the entanglement of Tanzania's Muslim activist scene. In 1992, together with Juma Mbukuzi, Issa Ponda Issa had established a Muslim Rights Committee that was a forerunner of the Shura ya Maimamu (Gilsaa 2012: 333). All prominent Shura ya Maimamu members were also well-known *imāms*: Juma Mbukuzi was *imām* of the Mujāhidīn mosque in Mburahati, Issa Ponda Issa was *imām* of the Kibangu mosque in Ubungo, Ally Bassaleh was *imām* of the Idrīs mosque in Kariakoo and Yusuf Kundecha was *imām* of the TIC mosque in Magomeni (see Gilsaa 2012: 395ff).
- The Consultative Assembly of Dar es Salaam Imams is an organisation of the *imāms* of the capital city, led until 2001 by Juma Mbukuzi, who was removed from his position, however, when he chose to support the government (and BAKWATA) in the context of the Dibagula dispute (see below) (Gilsaa 2012: 395ff).
- The Jumuiya ya Uamsho (Society of revivication, awakening) is the most important of the different anṣār al-sunna groups united in the Jamaat wa Ansar Sunnah Tanzania (JASUTA) (see Gilsaa 2012: 387ff). The Jumuiya ya Uamsho on the mainland is separate from the Jumuiya ya Uamsho in Zanzibar, although both groups cooperate closely.
- The Umoja wa Vijana wa Kiislamu Tanzania (UVIKITA), the Tanzanian Muslim Youth Union, is a group established in 1975/6 of University of Medina graduates who then joined WARSHA and that was finally

registered as an independent activist group, the anṣār al-sunna youth, in 1988 (Chande 1998: 217ff; Gilsaa 2012: 208, 264ff).

- The anṣār al-sunna youth (also Anṣār Muslim Youth) (AMY) started out in the late 1970s as part of UVIKITA (see van de Bruinhorst 2007: 96) and was finally registered as the Anṣār Muslim Youth in 1988. Since 1992, the Director (*mudīr*) of AMY has been Sālim ᶜAbd al-Raḥīm Barahiyan, who also teaches at the AMY Centre and its mosque in Tanga. Tanga is AMY's major centre (on AMY, see van de Bruinhorst 2007: 96ff). AMY has many followers among students who have returned from Saudi Arabia and who follow Salafi dress and body codes such as shortened trousers, clipped beards and walking sticks for men, and the *niqāb* for women. Sālim ᶜAbd al-Raḥīm Barahiyan was born into an Arab family in Tanga, studied in Tanga and at the Muslim Academy in Zanzibar, and then continued his studies in Riyadh (Saudi Arabia) in the 1980s and was subsequently employed at the Tanzanian Embassy in Saudi Arabia. In the early 1990s, he studied briefly in Islamabad (Pakistan) and then returned to Tanga to assume the leadership of AMY (see Ahmed 2008: 298; van de Bruinhorst 2007: 113; Gilsaa 2012: 265f).
- The Union of Muslim Preachers of Equivalent Religions (Umoja wa Wahubiri wa Kiislamu wa Mlingano wa Dini) (UWAMDI) was established by Musa Husayn, a scholar born in Ujiji in 1918, who was closely affiliated with the South African *dāᶜiya* Aḥmad Deedat, as well as Saidi Musa. As Tanzania's first 'Muslim Bible Preachers' association, UWAMDI possibly emerged as a reaction to Aḥmadiyya activities in the Ujiji and Kigoma region in 1934, but most probably, however, in reaction to Christian missionary activities in this region. The association was established in the mid-1980s and based at the kwa Mtoro mosque in Dar es Salaam (Lacunza Balda 1993: 229; Ahmed 2008: 348; Gilsaa 2012: 282ff). Since 1990, UWAMDI has published the newspaper *Mizani*. In the 1990s, one of the most outspoken UWAMDI preachers was a former priest, Ngariba Mussa Fundi, a student of Musa Husayn, who died in the early 2000s. In the late 1980s, the pro-Iranian leanings of leading members and sympathisers of UWAMDI such as Saidi Musa led to a split in the organisation and to the emergence of al-Mallid (see Loimeier 2007b; Ahmed 2008: 332).

- Al-Mallid (al-markaz al-islāmī li-tanbīh al-ghāfilīn ᶜan al-dīn; Kituo cha kuwazindua walio ghafilika katika Dini; 'Islamic centre for the awakening of those who have become negligent in religion') was established in 1992 by al-Ḥājj Ndallamah Saᶜīd Suleman, together with others. It rejected the pro-Iranian stance of UWAMDI. Al-Mallid also cultivated positions that were closer to 'Wahhābī' interpretations of Islam. At the same time, it laid greater emphasis on *daᶜwa* among Muslims, rather than the struggle against Christian missions, although it also came to form part of the 'Muslim Bible Preachers' movement (see Ahmed 2008: 331ff; Gilsaa 2012: 289ff).
- The Warsha ya Waandishi wa Kiislam (WARSHA) (Workshop of the Commission of Islamic Authors) (see above) started out in 1975 as a BAKWATA workshop at the Kinondoni Secondary School in Dar es Salaam. Its aim was to develop an Islamic syllabus and it was joined by a number of young Muslims, mostly affiliated with UVIKITA, who wanted to support the independent scholars in the workshop against government scholars. In 1982, WARSHA became an independent organisation of Muslim intellectuals, scholars and teachers based in the Masjid Qubah complex, consisting of a mosque, a secondary school and a conference centre, established in 1983/4 (Gilsaa 2012: 230). Today, WARSHA maintains a number of schools, such as the Masjid Qubah & Islamic Center in Dar es Salaam, and is developing new forms of Islamic education (see Chande 1998: 147).
- An offshoot of WARSHA, and in many ways the 'new WARSHA', was the Islamic Propagation Centre (IPC), established in 1985 by WARSHA members Burhani Mtengwa and Muḥammad Qassim, together with Qassim Juma (Gilsaa 2012: 235, 246f). Other prominent members were Dr Hamza Njozi, since 2005 the first Vice-Chancellor of the Muslim University of Morogoro (MUM), and Issa Ponda Issa. Its major centre was in Ubungo, Dar es Salaam, but the IPC was also present in other towns such as Tanga. The IPC concentrated on Islamic *daᶜwa*, educational work and the publication of school books, and cooperated closely with other activist groups, such as the Shura ya Maimamu, the Baraza Kuu or the Tanzania Muslim Professionals Organization (TAMPRO). In 1991, the IPC launched the newspaper *an-Nuur* (van de Bruinhorst 2007: 99).

- The Muslim Students' Association at the University of Dar es Salaam (MSAUD), or Jumuiya ya Wanafunzi wa Kiislamu, was established in 1970 and gained influence in the 1990s, due to its educational activities. MSAUD also became the 'mother organization' for Muslim activists in a number of Muslim associations, not only anṣār al-sunna groups. MSAUD members produce the most influential Muslim paper in Tanganyika, *an-Nuur* (see Chande 1998: 161; Gilsaa 2012: 196).
- The Taasisi na Jumuiya za Kiislamu Tanzania (The Council of Muslim Associations of Tanzania), was led by Ally Bassalleh and Issa Ponda Issa, the secretary (katibu) of this association. Issa Ponda Issa (b. 1958) was also affiliated with the Shura ya Maimamu and in 2001 he established his own association, al-Huda, which publishes the journal *al-Huda* (Gilsaa 2012: 398). In the 1990s, he became one of the most prominent *mihadhara* speakers in Tanzania. In recent years, he has gained notoriety due to his fiery sermons and his alleged involvement in anti-Christian activities, including an acid attack against two British volunteer teachers in Zanzibar in August 2013.[13] Although his implication in this and other incidents could not be substantiated, he has been attacked by an unsympathetic national and Western press as a 'Muslim cleric inciting religious hatred'.[14] ᶜAlī ('Ally') Saᶜīd Bassalleh (b. 1946) was born and educated in Zanzibar and has become one of the best known *mhadhiri* preachers in Tanzania. He attended secondary school and the Zanzibar Teacher Training College and taught at both primary and secondary schools in Zanzibar and mainland Tanzania. In 1974, he moved to Dar es Salaam where he became involved in conflicts with the Aḥmadiyya over the way in which the Aḥmadiyya used the Bible in their disputes with Christian churches (Ahmed 2008: 379). This period can be regarded as seminal for the formation of Tanzania's 'Muslim Bible Preachers' movement. In November 2001, Ally Bassalleh was imprisoned for declaring that 'Jesus was not God' (Yesu si Mungu) in the context of an ongoing conflict between activist Muslims and Pentecostal churches. He has written extensively for *an-Nuur*, *al-Huda* and *Nasaha*, Tanzanias's most important Islamic newspapers. In recent years, almost no issue of *an-Nuur* appeared without an article by or about Ally Basalleh. In addition, he was close to the Umoja wa wahubiri wa kiislamu na mlingano wa dini (UWAMDI).

- The Tanzanian Muslim Professionals' Organization (TAMPRO) was established in 1997 and became a basis for educated Muslims who have come to serve and work in charities, schools, hospitals and mosques. TAMPRO started the journal *Nasaha* and is close to the IPC and the MSAUD. Its headquarters are in Ilala, Dar es Salaam. The organisation has branches in most regions of Tanzania (Gilsaa 2012: 385).

This list of Muslim associations shows that Tanzania's public sphere continued to be informed by intra-Muslim rivalries and disputes even after the demise of *ujamaa* politics in the early 1980s. Apart from disputes over ritual issues and the timing of Islamic festival days (see van de Bruinhorst 2007: 131ff), a recurring feature of intra-Muslim disputes were attacks against BAKWATA that, in a reader's letter to *an-Nuur*, was said to 'cause the humiliation of Islam' (Bakwata hii ni kuudhalilisha Uislamu) due to its collaboration with the government or its alleged support for the 'sell-out of Tanzania to foreigners in a free-for-all policy' (*an-Nuur*, 18 July 2003). Muslims close to BAKWATA were consequently called 'Bakwata Muslims' by the anṣār al-sunna groups and were accused of hypocrisy (*unafiki*). At the same time, Muslims have tended to accuse BAKWATA of creating *fitna* among Muslims, as Muslim claims have been repeatedly torpedoed by BAKWATA functionaries, as in the case of the al-Furqaan school. In that case, as in many others, BAKWATA was accused of contributing to disputes among Muslims, instead of working for Muslim unity ('Baada ya al-Furqaan waislamu kaeni chonjo': Muslims continue to quarrel, *an-Nuur*, 13 August 2004). At the same time, the public visibility of radical and activist Muslim groups, often summarily called 'anṣār al-sunna', has increased considerably in recent decades, not only in Dar es Salaam, Tanga, Kigoma, Bukoba and Mwanza, but also in small towns such as Bagamoyo, Ujiji, Tabora and Morogoro. In 1988 in Ujiji, for instance, anṣār al-sunna groups introduced a new form of the Islamic funeral that was characterised by a quick procedure and the omission of locally established rites and festivities. Also, anṣār al-sunna groups established a new mosque in Ujiji in the 1980s, where women were allocated a place for prayer. This triggered a curious response from a Qādirī-scholar, Muḥammad Naṣṣor, who claimed in a pamphlet that women were not allowed to pray in mosques (Lacunza Balda 1989: 281).[15] Religious dynamics in post-independence

Tanzania thus implied conflict among Muslims, as activist groups were hesitant to accept the *irshād* (guidance) of established authorities for the sake of unity among Muslims and tried to establish their own ideas of 'true Islam'.

Yesu Hakusulubiwa – Jesus Was Not Crucified

While the development of intra-Muslim relations in post-independence Tanzania was characterised on the one hand by the struggle over hegemony of interpretation between BAKWATA and a plethora of oppositional associations, another important field of confrontation was that between Islam and Christianity that began in the 1980s. This confrontation was driven to some extent by the growth of Pentecostal churches and the efforts of Muslim associations such as the Union of Muslim Preachers of Equivalent Religions (Umoja wa Wahubiri wa Kiislamu wa Mlingano wa Dini) (UWAMDI) to respond to this new challenge. The disputes between Muslim activists and Pentecostal churches started in 1981. In this year, the South African Muslim *dāʿiya* Aḥmad Deedat (1918–2005)[16] visited Tanzania and the University of Dar es Salaam. He was invited by MSAUD in order to support Muslim struggles against an increasingly visible and audible Christian presence on the Dar es Salaam University campus. What made the Pentecostal churches particularly dangerous in the eyes of Aḥmad Deedat and Muslim reformers in Tanzania was the fact that they introduced new forms of addressing audiences and new forms of presenting their faith, which became immediately popular and attractive. The new type of public preaching became known as *mihadhara* preaching and implied not only aggressive preaching to large audiences outside churches (or mosques), but also reference to the Qurʾān (or the Bible, in the case of Muslim *mihadhara* meetings), in order to prove the essential falsehood of the respective other religion. Public conversion to Christianity (or Islam) was another widespread feature of *mihadhara* meetings (on the development of *mihadhara* preaching in Tanzania and Aḥmad Deedat's first visit to Tanzania, see Njozi 2000: 10ff).[17]

Pentecostal activities included not only mass sermons and church services for thousands, but also faith healing and spirit exorcism, the experience of rebirth as an integral part of Pentecostal services and the manifestation of the presence of God in tongue-talking. People could get advice in respect of their everyday problems and were taught the power of the holy scriptures, mediated by the Holy Spirit, to heal and to gain (material) wealth ('the gospel of prosperity'), the importance of personal faith, prayer and intercession, in both individual and communal terms, in order to achieve change, as well as the assurance of security in the community of the faithful (Maxwell 2005: 20; see also Dilger 2007). However, the gospel of awakening, or *uamsho* in Swahili,[18] was also attractive to poor urban Muslims, especially Muslim women, often widows or single women.[19] In particular, the exorcism of spirits (*wapepo* and *jinni*), the healing of ailments by laying hands on the sick and the invocation of the 'healing' name of Jesus were popular features of Pentecostal activities and were copied by Muslim activists, in particular those united in the 'Muslim Bible Preachers' movement. Muslim activists advertised prophetic medicine and started to practise spirit exorcism through the ritual recitation of the Qur'ān (Kiswahili: *kusoma Koran, uganga wa kitabu*), although such activities were criticised as *bida*ᶜ. At the same time, Muslim activists have not (yet) adopted other forms of Pentecostal activities, such as the integration of music into sermons and the practice of talking in tongues.

In reaction to the preaching activities of the Pentecostal churches and their success among Muslims, Muslim scholars, in particular those organised in the Muslim Bible Preachers movement, adopted not only a series of Pentecostal rituals and ideas, but also the strategies for dealing with Pentecostal churches developed by Aḥmad Deedat in South Africa in the late 1950s. Of particular importance for Deedat was the confrontation with the German evangelical preacher Reinhard Bonnke and his 'Christ for all Nations' (CFAN) organisation.[20] The adoption of Pentecostal strategies in public preaching was of particular importance for the Muslim Bible Preachers movement. The Muslim Bible Preachers have deliberately abandoned using Arabic terms for their preaching activities, such as *dā*ᶜ*iya* or *wā*ᶜ*iẓ*, and call themselves *wahubiri* (sing. *mhubiri*), like the preachers of Pentecostal churches. At their preaching meetings they make polemical comparisons between the Bible and the Qur'ān, in an attempt to persuade Christians that they interpret specific Bible texts wrongly, often referring to the character of Christ, and substantiating their allegations by quoting respective verses from the Qur'ān.[21] Due to these new preaching strategies, the relationship between Muslims and Christians in Tanzania deteriorated, in particular due to the fact that in 1984

Muslim Bible Preachers started to hold their *mihadhara* sermons outside mosques in public spaces (Njozi 2000: 11–80).[22]

Although the Tanzanian Government prohibited public preaching in 1992, as violent conflicts between Muslims and Christians had erupted again and again, *mihadhara* meetings continued to be organised outside churches and mosques.[23] They were often announced in the Muslim newspapers, such as the announcement that there would be a *mihadhara* in the Mskiti Answaar Sunna in Kinondoni in Dar es Salaam on 4 September 2004, organised by the Jumuiya ya Maendeleo ya Wanawake wa Kiislamu ya Salafiyya, with a number of unspecified *wahubiri* from Dar es Salaam (DSM). The Muslim weekly *an-Nuur* also published invitations to *mihadhara* rallies, such as in late July 2004, when it was announced that Nassor Bachu from Zanzibar would give a lecture in Moshi as part of an East African anṣār al-sunna rally organised by the Markaz Ansar of Moshi. Apart from Nassor Bachu, other *wahubiri* were Jabiri Katura (Mwanza), Nassoro Khamisi (Mombasa), Ahmad Musala (Nairobi), Salīm Barahiyan (Tanga), Abdallah A. Mushi (DSM), Ally Zubeir (Tanga), Yahya Khamisi (Arusha), Muhammad Awadhi (Dodoma), Abu Hamza (Mombasa), Juma Poli (DSM) and Yusufu Abdul (Mombasa).

Christians tended to object to preaching with inter-religious references by arguing that 'religious lectures will cause war' (mihadhara ya dini itazua vita) (Njozi 2000: 81), although radical Christian groups also practised this kind of public preaching. Consequently, a series of conflicts evolved from *mihadhara* meetings: in April 1993, Muslims attacked three butcheries in the Magomeni and Manzese districts of Dar es Salaam that had allegedly sold pork to Muslims. In the aftermath of these riots, thirty-eight Muslims were imprisoned. Yaḥyā Ḥusayn, the leader of BALUKTA, who publicly declared that he had been the driving force behind that action, and Qassim Juma, who was not even in the country at the time of the riots, were subsequently imprisoned and taken to court (Gilsaa 2012: 338ff). In another incident, the 'Mwembechai killings' on 13 February 1998, four Muslims were killed by Field Force units outside the Mwembechai mosque in Dar es Salaam, a major centre of Muslim opposition, after a priest had denounced activities in the mosque; he had told the police that Muslims had insulted Jesus Christ in a *mihadhara* sermon. The Mwembechai killings took place in the context of rising religious tension: in January 1998, President Benjamin

Mkapa, in office since 1995, declared war 'on people who go about distributing cassettes, booklets, and convening meetings, where they insulted and ridiculed other religions' (Njozi 2000: 31; Gilsaa 2012: 413). Today, the 1998 Mwembechai incident has become a historical marker for radical Muslim groups; memories of Mwembechai are revived and re-enacted every year. Thus, Muslim groups and organisations used the *ᶜīd al-fiṭr* celebrations in January 1999 to raise complaints about the treatment of Muslims by the Government of Tanzania and about the way in which Muslims were treated in the Mwembechai incident. In 2001, anṣār al-sunna groups tried to transform the *yawm al-ᶜArafat* celebrations into demonstrations of Muslim unity and to use the Mwembechai killings as a historical marker (Waislam kusimama Jangwani jumapili: 'Muslims will stand upright in Jangwani on Sunday', *an-Nuur*, 2 March 2001). By 'standing upright in Jangwani', the anṣār al-sunna were translating a central feature of the *ḥajj*, namely 'standing' (*wuqūf*) at ᶜArafat (on 9 Dhū l-Ḥijja), into a platform of political protest and thus linking a major religious ritual with local politics.

The increasing tensions resulting from disputes between Muslim and Christian Bible preachers became visible in an incident on 16 March 2000, when Hamisi Rajab Dibagula, a Muslim from Morogoro, was arrested for stating that 'Jesus was not the son of God', that 'anybody who says that Jesus was a son of God was an unbeliever' and that 'Jesus had not been crucified' (Njoji 2003: 22f). In the subsequent court case (*The Republic of Tanzania* v. *H. R. Dibagula*, 2001), Dibagula was found guilty by the Morogoro District Court and was sentenced to a prison term of 18 months on 31 July 2001. The Dibagula case subsequently became a major cause of Muslim mobilisation throughout Tanzania, even though the verdict against Dibagula was reviewed by the Tanzania High Court in August 2001: as a result of the High Court ruling, Dibagula was released, although the High Court confirmed that 'slandering religion' had correctly been identified as a criminal offence by the Morogoro District Court. The statement 'Jesus is not God' has since become a major bone of contention, as Muslim *wahadhiri* have quoted it deliberately in order to incite Christian reactions. In June 2007, a public debate raged throughout Tanzania after a leading Pentecostal *mhubiri*, Godwin Dihigo, claimed in an article in *Msema Kweli* (No. 510, 10 June 2007) that even the Prophet Muhammad had accepted that Jesus Christ had been tortured on the cross, had died and had been resurrected from the dead (kuteswa, kufa na kufufuka). This statement was immediately disputed by Ally Bassalleh in a number of Muslim weekly papers such as *an-Nuur* and *Nasaha*. He based his counter-argument on the Qurʾān, *sūra* 4, al-nisāʾ, verse 157:

> wa-qaulihim, inna qatalnā al-masīḥa ᶜIsā, ibn Maryam rasūl Allāhi, wa-mā qatalūhu wa-mā salabūhu, wa-lākin šubbiha lahum (and they – *namely the Jews* – said: we have killed Jesus Christ, the son of Mary, the messenger of God, but they killed him not, nor crucified him, but so it was made to appear to them. (Yusuf Ali translation of the Qurʾān; emphasis added)[24]

The qurʾānic evidence was complemented by quotes from the Bible such as the second book of Samuel 2:1–2 or Luke 22: 41–2 and Mark 14:35 ('And he went on, threw himself on the ground and prayed that this hour would pass by him') that confirmed, according to Ally Basalleh, that Jesus could not be the son of God (but was the son of Mary) and 'had not been crucified' ('*Yesu hakusulubiwa*'): the alleged crucification of the Prophet Jesus was an infamous Christian allegation that could not be substantiated by the Bible. The arguments used by Ally Bassalleh and other Muslim Bible Preachers do not really reveal, however, how far the quotations from the Bible, and especially from the Old Testament, can substantiate the claim that Christ had not been crucified. We should remember here that an apologetic argument is usually intended to convince not one's opponent but one's own supporters.[25] The Tanzanian Muslim Bible Preachers movement should thus be seen as a direct response to the increasing activities of Pentecostal churches in Tanzania, as well as forming part of a larger Muslim struggle against Pentecostal churches. In this struggle, information is exchanged and discussed on a global scale.

What are the implications of the dispute with Pentecostal churches for Muslims in Tanzania? First, the attitudes of Muslim activists in the context of this dispute have to be seen as a new positioning within Tanzanian society. According to their own view, the Muslim Bible Preachers have 'finally' started to struggle against the aggressive Pentecostal churches, especially in the form of public *mihadhara* meetings, often linked with public conversions (to Islam). They have also challenged the Pentecostal churches by referring to the Holy Scriptures, which has led to debates in the media in which both parties (mis)quote each other. The Muslim Bible Preachers have shown that

Muslims are capable of fighting against the Pentecostal churches, despite their seemingly uninterrupted rise and growth. In their polemics against these churches, Muslim Bible Preachers have stressed the necessity of Muslim unity and overcoming dispute (*fitna*) among Muslims, which has handicapped Muslim participation in national politics since independence. With this argumentation, the Muslim Bible Preachers established themselves as an influential social and religious group in Tanzania since the 1980s, and to discredit competing Muslim groups and organisations, in particular loyalist Muslim state-informed organisations such as BAKWATA, as 'ineffective', 'corrupt' and 'inefficient'. The activities of the Muslim Bible Preachers should thus not only be seen as a struggle against the Pentecostal churches, and thus as an aspect of Muslim–Christian disputes, but also as an aspect of Muslim internal disputes and competition.

The seemingly obvious, namely the religious conflict between Christians and Muslims, thus turns out to be yet another facet of a kaleidoscope of religious positions and politics. For an analysis of Muslim movements of reform, it is thus necessary to examine not only the characteristic markers of reform and their respective connotation and weight, but also the function and *Sinnbesetzung* (significance and meaning) of these markers in a specific historical context. Parallels and phenotypical similarities in the appearance and orientation of religious movements of reform, interesting as they may be, are not proof of real structural similarities. Only an encompassing analysis of the historical context will enable us to say whether specific movements of reform are equivalent in structural terms and whether Muslim reformers may indeed be labelled Pentecostal Muslims. Even if the encounter with Pentecostal churches has inspired Muslim reformers to take a specific course, a Muslim movement of reform is always an attempt to provide convincing answers to historical challenges within Islam.

Muslim–Christian Disputes and the Tanzanian State

The confrontation between Muslim associations and Pentecostal churches was not the only issue in Muslim–Christian disputes from the 1980s. Rather, a number of issues have emerged that have been central to the public discourse of the Muslim opposition. These issues were activated whenever a specific context allowed for citation. Areas of confrontation, even if only symbolic, were manifold, such as a dispute over the shifting of graves because of plans to construct new buildings in Ilala, Dar es Salaam, in 2003. In their opposition to these plans, the anṣār al-sunna referred to a *fatwā* by Ḥasan b. ᶜAmeir against the shifting of graves (Asikanyage mtu kufukua kaburi, *an-Nuur*, 15 August 2003). News about police storming a mosque near Mwanza (*an-Nuur*, 6 September 2002) or about Christians 'slandering' (kukashifu) Islam (*an-Nuur*, 21 March 2003) was typical of reports that appeared almost weekly in Muslim papers. Muslim–Christian disputes, Muslim-state disputes and intra-Muslim disputes have changing local or national dimensions and may change their character quickly (see Gilsaa 2012: 422ff).

Muslim anxieties concerning Christian domination were confirmed when Professor Kigoma Malima (1938–95) became the first Muslim minister of education in 1987, and publicly declared that Muslims had been disadvantaged by the Tanzanian system of education in the past, so that they should now enjoy preferential treatment in the process of selection for secondary school education. This declaration incensed Christian groups that, in the context of a meeting in 1989 of the Christian Council of Tanzania (CCT) in Dodoma, claimed that Muslims in the government were preparing Tanzania for a *jihād*. The dispute over issues of education acquired a new dimension in February 1992, when the government decided to hand back property like hospitals and schools, which had been nationalised in 1972, to their former owners, mostly Christian churches. Muslims immediately complained that missions and churches would benefit most from this decision. Twelve years later, in 2004, Ally Bassalleh, the leader of the Taasisi na jumuiya za Kiislam Tanzania, commented that, despite a 1992 parliamentary inquiry as well as a report by the Catholic Church and a respective memorandum of understanding that had acknowledged structural imbalances in politics and education between Muslims and Christians, nothing had changed: Muslims were still marginalised, as they had been since 1961, and the number of Muslims in schools was still small in comparison to their proportion of Tanzania's population. Thus, only 20 per cent of secondary school pupils in Dar es Salaam were Muslim, while their proportion of Dar es Salaam's population was 80 per cent (*an-Nuur*, 6 August 2004). In his litany of complaints, Ally Bassalleh proceeded to recite historical cases of discrimination against Muslims, such as the dissolution of the EAMWS in 1968, until he arrived at the most recent case of 'government marginalization of Muslims', namely the case of the al-Furqaan school (*an-Nuur*, 6 August 2004). The temporary closure of the al-Furqaan Islamic Primary School in Buguruni/Ilala, Dar es Salaam, in summer 2004, as well as the closure of the school's bank accounts at the Akiba Commercial Bank in July 2004, at the request of the Bank of Tanzania, fuelled Muslim anxieties, as this school was regarded as a showcase school, the best Muslim school in Dar es Salaam, to which 'even Christian parents' sent their children (Wazazi Wakristo waitaka al-Furqaan). In a series of articles in *an-Nuur* (23 July 2004, 6 August 2004) and *Nasaha* (5 August 2004), the state was accused of engineering the closure of the al-Furqaan-school.

The statistical strength of the different religious groups was another topic of dispute: while Muslims maintain that they constitute the majority of the population, outnumbering Christians by three to two (Said 1998: 276), Christians maintain that they constitute the majority, making reference to the 1967 census that suggested that Christians made up 32 per cent of the population, while Muslims were estimated at 30 per cent and African cults at 37 per cent, that is, more or less the same ratio as in the 1957 census (32 per cent Muslims, 31 per cent Christians). The census data gave rise to a debate about the respective strength of each group and this debate continued to disturb public discourses. Kettani, for instance, claimed that the proportion of Muslims in Tanzania in 1978 was 55 per cent (approximately 10.2 million in a population of about 18.57 million) (Kettani 1982), while Christian voices such as Reverend Curthwell Omari claimed that by the mid-1980s Christians constituted 44 per cent of the population, while Muslims made up 32 per cent and adherents of African cults 22 per cent (Omari 1984: 373ff.). Abdin Chande's discussion of numbers and statistics, based on a critical analysis of the different sources, supports the impression that Muslims are Tanzania's largest religious group, even if estimations range wildly from 34 per cent (Cuoq 1975, based on the 1957 census) to 60 per cent (*Africa Confidential*, No. 26, p. 24, 27 November 1985), while Christians form the second largest group, even if they are more visible (Chande 1998: 7).[26]

The imbalance between Muslims and Christians is not just something that has been felt or polemically debated, but is a concrete fact that is confirmed by some key figures: a survey of the names of students admitted to the University of Dar es Salaam in the academic year 2003/4 shows that out of 2,420 students admitted (24 per cent being women), only 12 per cent (or 304) were Muslims. The same applies to the enrolment of Muslims in other educational institutions (see Chande 1998: 196ff). At the same time, church buildings have been proliferating in Dar es Salaam: while the 1995 city map of Dar es Salaam registered a total of 303 places of worship, with a majority of mosques at 187 mosques, against 112 churches and 4 Hindu temples, this situation had changed completely by the late 2000s: when driving through Dar es Salaam, not only the centre and Kariakoo but, more importantly, the different Ilala districts, as well as Kigamboni, Temeke, Tandika, Kinondoni, Mwenge or the new districts on the major roads leading to Bagamoyo and Morogoro, there were not only more church buildings than mosques in evidence, but these were of a surprising size, especially the Pentecostal churches.

The establishment of *qāḍī* courts has been another issue in Muslim–Christian relations in recent years. Like Zanzibar, Tanganyika had a plural legal system in both the German and the British colonial periods, and had a system of *qāḍī* courts in the coastal areas. Islamic personal (family) law was recognised as part of Tanganyikan 'native law' in colonial times. While this plural legal tradition continued into the post-colonial period, *qāḍī* courts were abolished in 1951, together with the abolishment of the native courts. After independence, the Judicature and Application of Laws Ordinance (JALO) of 1963 ruled that Tanganyika would have only one tier of jurisdiction. Yet, courts were not to be precluded from applying Islamic law. As a consequence, Tanganyikan mainland courts and judges continued to apply Islamic (personal) law where Muslims were concerned (Makaramba 2010: 278). This meant in practice that mainland courts and judges who were not specifically trained in Islamic law, nevertheless applied it in matters of marriage, divorce, guardianship, inheritance or *waqf*, wherever Muslims were concerned. This was a fertile ground for discontent among Muslims who considered it inappropriate that (mostly) 'Christian' judges and magistrates should administer Islamic (personal) law. It made no difference that in such cases the courts called on Muslim scholars to give an expert opinion. The fact that these legal scholars were usually members of BAKWATA only increased Muslim discontent, as BAKWATA was widely rejected by Muslims in Tanzania as an institution representing government interests. As a consequence, Muslims started to call for the re-institution of *qāḍī* courts. In 1984, the Union of Muslim Youth took up the demand for *qāḍī* courts, and their call was heeded by BAKWATA in 1987. The call for *qāḍī* courts peaked in 1998 when a respective bill was tabled (and rejected) in the Tanzanian Parliament (Makaramba 2010: 283). In 2005, however, the ruling party declared in its election programme that the institution of *qāḍī* courts would be one of the aims of a future CCM government.

The call for *qāḍī* courts has stirred up a lot of unrest in mainland Tanzania, but opposition to the re-institution of *qāḍī* courts came not only from Christians, but also from a number of Muslim groups and individuals. Some Muslims saw *qāḍī* courts as a BAKWATA idea, and were afraid that they would not be independent from the government. The re-institution of *qāḍī* courts was attacked as a political propaganda strategy by the ruling party and was rejected because it would be extremely costly to finance (see Kopwe 2014: 220ff.). There was also the problem that Muslims in Tanzania followed not one but several different schools of law. In addition, there was no institution to train judges in Islamic law, and the respective course at the University of Dar es Salaam was elective only. The idea of *qāḍī* courts was even rejected by anṣār al-sunna voices who objected that they would be limited to Islamic personal law. Also, *qāḍī* courts would only form another field of employment for BAKWATA members (Mfumbusa 2014: 250). Some Muslims maintained that the existing system served quite well, so that there was no real need to create *qāḍī* courts. Last but not least, Muslim women argued that *sharīᶜa* personal law would disadvantage Muslim women in the area of inheritance (Ndaluka 2012: 89). The issue of *qāḍī* courts thus came to play a prominent role in Tanzanian public discourses and has become an important theme of Muslim–Christian disputes since the 1990s: Muslims complain, for instance, that they have to respect the Christian Sunday and other Christian holidays, while Christians are hesitant to accept similar symbolic demands by Muslims, such as the re-institution of *qāḍī* courts.

Another major bone of contention in Muslim–Christian disputes is the role of Muslims in the national struggle for independence. Muslim authors such as Muhammad Said claim that the role of Muslims in this struggle was deliberately de-emphasised by Christians, while the role of Christians is consistently over-emphasised. Tanzania's history after independence is consequently seen as a history of increasing marginalisation of Muslims in many respects. Instances such as the 1964 dissolution of AMNUT and the failure to build an Islamic university in Dar es Salaam, the 1968 dissolution of the EAMWS and its replacement by BAKWATA, the constant under-representation of Muslims in government, administration and education and, not least, the intervention by the union government to prevent Zanzibar from joining the Organization of the Islamic Conference (OIC) in 1993, are a constant reminder of these policies of marginalisation. In 1970, the Tanzanian Parliament had twenty-three Muslim members, while eighty were Christians (fifty-six Catholic), and five of 'traditional religion'. In 1993, there were only eight Muslim district commissioners, as compared to 113 Christians. Muslims often fail to realise, however, that Christians may argue that Muslims are at least formally 'over-represented' in a number of institutions, due to the strong position of ('Muslim') Zanzibar in union institutions. This applies, for instance, to the parliament, even if the CCM members from Zanzibar are not seen as 'proper' Muslims by Salafi-oriented Muslims. Thus, the present parliament of Tanzania has 50 members from Zanzibar (approximately 20 per cent), while 182 represent the mainland. Yet, the mainland accounts for 97 per cent of the population of the union, and Zanzibar for only 3 per cent. Also, the mainland has 21 administrative regions while Zanzibar has five, as well as a House of Representatives of its own, in contrast to the mainland that does not have a comparable institution. In addition, 'Muslim' Zanzibar gets 4.5 per cent of all foreign aid. This allocation exceeds Zanzibar's 3 per cent share of the Tanzanian population by 50 per cent. Radical Muslims are seen by Christians as a threat to Tanzania's security and are portrayed as such in public, especially since the embassy bombing in Dar es Salaam in 1998.

From the late 1980s, attacking the government and its branches, such as BAKWATA, and accusing them of protecting 'the Christians' while suppressing Muslims has been a favourite strategy of the anṣār al-sunna. This theme has appeared constantly in Muslim papers like *an-Nuur* in articles with titles like 'There is constant war against Islam and Muslims' (Vita kamili dhidi ya Uislamu na Waislamu) (*an-Nuur*, 13 August 2004). These perceptions of marginalisation have been linked with discourses of othering: Muslims feel that somebody has to be blamed for historical failures. When looking at the long-term development of Muslims, Christians and the state in German East Africa, Tanganyika and Tanzania, Muslims' perceptions of marginalisation should not be accepted at face value. Muslims had a privileged role in the German colonial period, and in the Tanganyikan independence movement. Also, it cannot be said that the British administration followed a conscious policy of discrimination against Muslims. However, the German as well as the British administrations supported the activities of the Christian churches and missions, and in the 1950s and 1960s mission-educated Tanganyikans acquired paramount importance as administrative cadres. At the same time Muslims largely failed to develop modern systems of education that would have produced a comparable number of Muslims with a modern education.

When Tanganyika became independent, in 1961, Muslims were still in an advantageous political position but lacked Western-educated elites who would have been able to translate this prominent political role into structural advantages. And even when Muslims had a second chance, in the 1970s, to translate a politically favourable context into structural advantages, they were unable to do so. As a consequence, the class of the educated, those who were able to administer a modern state, hospitals, schools, companies and so forth became even more Christian in the 1980s and 1990s, to the chagrin of many Muslims, who increasingly came to see the time since independence as a time of chances missed. In order to explain their failure, Muslims recur to scenarios of intrigue and, at least sometimes, they are right, as a number of post-independence events do reveal patterns of intrigue and marginalisation of Muslims. However, despite Muslim litanies of complaint, it would be wrong to assume that every Muslim failure in Tanzania is due to Christian intrigues. Some Muslims have thus started to challenge established interpretations of Muslim failures. These Muslims have stopped waiting for state intervention and have started to implement their own ideas, for instance by setting up modern Islamic schools, often in the face of resistance by BAKWATA-oriented scholars.

A major explanation for the multiple conflicts among Muslims in Tanzania is thus not only Muslim opposition to the state, but also Muslim opposition to established Muslim cadres in the government: the state is seen as being controlled not only by Christians, but also by corrupt Muslim functionaries who collide with Christians. Since the 1980s, Muslims have recognised that responsibility for failure lies not only with the state or with those involved in Christian intrigues, but that it is also due to the inactivity of two generations of Muslim functionaries, with the result that disputes among Muslims are probably as acid today as polemics between Muslims and Christians. Conflicts among Muslims in Tanzania strikingly resemble a conflict between generations. In this conflict, young and radical Muslims make legitimatory references to old and conservative scholars who can point to similar experiences of marginalisation in the early years of the Nyerere administration. Ḥasan b. ᶜAmeir, for instance, despite his *ṭarīqa* affiliation, is seen today as a representative of a decent form of political Islam that is not corrupt and is independent of government concepts of development.

The history of Tanzania, and in particular of Muslim–state relations, thus shows that religion (Islam) has been used and understood as a function of politics. Islam and Islamic codes and symbols have been instrumentalised to attack and delegitimise political decisions. In the context of strategies of legitimisation and delegitimisation of politics, religion has become a tool, a platform to present political demands. This political use of religion is confirmed by Muslim representations of Islam as well as non-Muslim ones as a political code, a 'theology of liberation' or, its flipside, an ideology condoning terror. Each of these essentialist representations of Islam as either a positive or negative force in politics has triggered apologetic reactions that seek to defend the construction of 'political Islam'. Apologetic constructions of religion have entrenched the notion of Islam as being primarily a political ideology. Such an essentialist reduction of Islam must be viewed, however, as an orientalist trap that ultimately leads Muslims to confirm Western notions of political Islam in a self-defeating dialectic, even if it is presented in more sympathetic terms. A political reading of Islam not only denies the non-political dimensions of religion, but also turns religion into a factor in a political equation that may be manipulated and instrumentalised at random.

. . . and Kenya?

As in Tanganyika, the development of Islam in Kenya was confined for centuries to the immediate coastal belt (*pwani*). Muslims spread up-country (*bara*) only in the mid-nineteenth century. As a result, Islam is strongest today in Kenya in the coastal region and the north-eastern frontier regions bordering Somalia. In contrast to Tanganyika, Islam has not gained substantial support in the *bara* regions of up-country Kenya and has remained the religion of a minority in urban centres such as Nairobi,[27] Nakuru and Limuru. Islam spread into up-country Kenya along the major trade routes, but not into the areas beyond them (Wandera 2013: 28). While colonial and post-colonial language politics have diluted ethnic distinctions in Tanzania, Kenya's Muslim population has been marked by distinct racial, ethnic, linguistic and religious fragmentation: apart from the Arab and Indian Muslims who settled on the East African coast from at least the fourteenth century, there are numerous indigenous Muslim groups. These include not only the Swahili-speaking populations on the coast, in particular the Digo, Duruma and other Mijikenda groups, but also the Pokomo, Taita, Rendille and Oromo (Borana), as well as Muslim minorities among the Luo, the Kamba and the Kikuyu (Mwakimako 2007b: 17). Even on the coast, where the historical legacies of Islam were strongest, Muslims did not form a uniform population but were divided into numerous ethnic groups that disputed Arab claims to political supremacy (see Ndzovu 2014: 20ff).[28] In recent decades, Kenya has seen a significant growth of its Somali population, due not only to natural increase,[29] but also to the immigration of at least 500,000 Somali refugees in the context of the civil war in Somalia (Ndzovu 2014: 9). As a consequence of this ethnic fragmentation, racial, ethnic and religious divisions (into a series of Sunni and Shīʿī groups, Salafi-oriented reformers and the followers of Sufi orders) have informed modes of participation in local and national politics as well as the internal dynamics of Muslim community development.

In contrast to Tanzania, Muslims form a minority of Kenya's total population today. While Muslims would maintain that up to 45 per cent of Kenya's population was Muslim, official census data in both the colonial and post-colonial period show a Muslim population of 6–11 per cent. Due to the influx of refugees from Somalia since the 1990s, a more realistic estimate would put the number of Muslims today at 20 per cent to 25 per cent of Kenya's population, the majority living in the Coast and North Eastern Provinces. Like countries such as Nigeria, Ethiopia and Tanzania, where Muslims do not form a clear majority of the population, Kenya has seen 'wars over statistics' that mirror Muslim perceptions of marginalisation and/or non-integration, as well as both Muslim and Christian claims to power based on what is claimed to be demographic evidence.[30] An interesting case in this context was Ayubi and Moyhuddin's estimate that Kenya had a Muslim population of 5,750,000 (or 25 per cent of the population) according to the census of 1989 (see Ayubi and Mohyuddin 1994: 144ff). A footnote points to respective statistical data in a text by Kettani (1982). In this text, Kettani advanced a number of approximately 4,750,000 Muslims in Kenya in 1979 (in a population of about 15,800,000 Kenyans). The endnote that supposedly substantiated this claim reads: 'Muslim percentages for Kenya, Tanzania, Rwanda and Burundi have been obtained from official censuses'. Kettani's text does not specify, however, which specific censuses were meant (Kettani 1982: 119). According to the 2009 national census, Kenya had a population of about 38.6 million, approximately 4.3 million being Muslims (ICG 2012f: 5), that is, 11 per cent of the population. These census results have been rejected by many Muslim organisations.

Muslim perceptions of being marginal in Kenya started in 1963, when coastal Muslim aspirations to regional autonomy in the context of the Mwambao movement were cast aside and Zanzibar resigned its historical rights to the coastal strip in Kenya in exchange for Kenya's acceptance of *qāḍī* courts in the coastal regions (see Salim 1973: 233ff). Due to the fact that Muslims in Kenya (in contrast to Tanganyika) were not in the forefront of Kenya's struggle for independence, but instead acquired notoriety for their autonomist aspirations (in the Coast Province) and for irredentist desires in the predominantly Somali settled regions (North Eastern Province), Muslims have come to be seen as foreigners and as being disloyal by a majority of Christian Kenyans. In many respects, Muslims in Kenya form a double periphery: as Muslims within Kenya and as Muslims within the larger *ummah* of Muslims (Kresse 2009: 578). In historical terms, Kenya's Muslims were disadvantaged in comparison to Christians due to their lack of Western education.[31] In addition, economic and political power has been in the hands of up-country Christians since independence. The coast was left to stagnate after independence: only the harbour of Mombasa and coastal tourism were important and were kept under control to serve up-country interests. Today Mombasa is a city with a non-Muslim majority (Cruise O'Brien 1995: 204). Increasing up-country migration into the coastal areas, in particular Mombasa and the major tourist resorts, has even started to challenge the numerical predominance of Muslims in these regions and has increased Muslim perceptions of being pushed to the wall (Oded 2000: 142). Increasing tensions between up-country settlers and coastal populations surfaced in a number of ethnic clashes in Mombasa from August to November 1997 (Kresse 2009: 583). In these clashes, hundreds of non-coastal Kenyans were killed or forced to move back to up-country Kenya (Parkin 2000: 102).

The fact that not a single Kenyan president since independence has been Muslim (Jomo Kenyatta 1963–78, Daniel arap Moi 1978–2002, Mwai Kibaki 2002–13 and Uhuru Kenyatta since 2013), and that Muslims have been under-represented in government, parliament, ministries and administration, has added to the feeling of estrangement of Kenya's Muslims. Jomo Kenyatta was seen by Muslims as neutral: religion did not play a central role in politics in his time and Kenyatta was cautious not to show any predisposition toward a particular religion (Ndzovu 2014: 54). Moi's rule meant not only a shift from a Kikuyu to a Kalenjin ethnic bias, but also a shift to a more authoritarian government and a bias in favour of evangelical churches. Daniel arap Moi presented himself increasingly as a devout Christian (Ndzovu 2014: 56), incurring critique not only from Muslims but also from the Catholic, Anglican and Presbyterian churches. In a speech in 1992, he even accused Muslims of having been slave owners (Mazrui 1993: 88). He made several public statements depicting Muslims as slave traders and being responsible for the slave trade (Mwakimako 2007a: 293). Such accusations were part of strategies intended to demonise Muslims as slave owners or slave traders and as separatists. At the same time, Moi was sympathetic to individual Muslims, such as Maḥmūd Muḥammad, a Somali army officer who had foiled a coup attempt against Moi in 1982. Yet, Moi's personal sympathies did not translate into a more generally favourable position towards Islam: the ultimate rationale of Moi's presidency was the maintenance of power (Ndzovu 2014: 74).

President Kibaki's administration was characterised by increasing opposition to Muslims as expressed in a series of anti-Muslim legislative reforms. First Muslim anti-government demonstrations started in early 2002 in the context of a new regulation requiring Muslims to produce extra documentary evidence of citizenship when applying for identity cards or passports. This regulation was specifically targeted at the Somali population: Somali Kenyans were required to carry additional forms of identification to prove that they were Kenyan citizens. The screening of Somalis was stopped only in August 2002 in the context of the impending elections of that year (Ndzovu 2014: 74). The Kibaki era also saw increasing disputes between Muslims and Christians over issues such as constitutional reform and the role of *qāḍī* courts, as well as the intensification of ethnic conflict, especially in the context of national elections.

At the same time, Kenya's governments, and in particular that of Jomo Kenyatta, have tried to include Muslims symbolically in Kenyan politics, for instance by sending representatives to attend *mawlid* celebrations in Lamu and by meeting with Muslim dignitaries.[32] Muslim perceptions of marginalisation and Christian perceptions of Muslim disloyalty have gained further currency, however, in the context of increasingly militant Muslim activism since the 1990s. There have been acts of 'Islamic' terrorism such as the embassy bombings in Nairobi and Dar es Salaam on 7 August 1998,[33] or the missile attack against an Israeli charter plane with 261 passengers on 28 November 2002. On the same day, there was an attack on Paradise Hotel near Mombasa, which had an Israeli clientele, resulting in thirteen people dead. In recent years, terrorist attacks have multiplied in Kenya and have targeted institutions linked with Israeli investment, tourist hotels, Christian churches and up-country settler enclaves in the periphery of tourist installations.[34] An al-shabāb attack on the Westgate shopping mall in Nairobi on 21 September 2013 was allegedly supported by radical Kenyan Muslims. In the context of such terrorist attacks, public voices against Islam have multiplied, and Muslims have become a target of Kenyan, US and Israeli security and intelligence agencies. Kenya has allowed the FBI, the CIA and Mossad to operate in Kenya, and Mombasa's Kilindini Harbour has become a base for NATO activities (Seesemann 2007: 159). In the aftermath of the embassy bombing on 7 August 1998 (referred to in Kenya colloquially as '8/7') as well as the terrorist attacks of 11 September 2001 (in the USA '9/11'), Islamic NGOs such as al-ḥaramayn, the International Islamic Relief Organization, the 'Ibrāhīm b. ᶜAbd al-ᶜAzīz Foundation' and the rābiṭat al-islām were closed (Ahmed 2008: 196; Scharrer 2013: 66), although they had played an important role in the development of Islamic education in Kenya. The publication of the Suppression of Terrorism Bill on 30 April 2003 was perceived as another instance of unfair treatment, as Muslims felt that they were targeted by this law (Mwakimako 2007b: 43). Muslim–Christian tensions in Kenya were further aggravated by Maurice Cardinal Otunga's remark in the context of an African Episcopal Conference in Nairobi in 1993 that Christians should actively combat Islam 'since Muslims were attempting to turn Africa into an Islamic continent and destroy Christianity' (quoted in Oded 2000: 107). As further provocation, evangelical preachers such as the American Edward Andrews Stagl attached posters to mosques saying that the Prophet was an adulterer (Quinn and Quinn 2003: 119).

As in Zanzibar and Tanganyika, Islam in Kenya was characterised by the coexistence of a number of Islamic orientations: apart from a Sunni-Shāfiᶜī majority, there were a number of Shīᶜī groups such as the Khoja and the Bohora Ismāᶜīlis, as well as the followers of the Twelver Shīᶜa (Ithnāᶜshara) group. In addition, Kenya has known a tradition of Sufi-oriented reform since the nineteenth century, mostly linked with the Qādiriyya and the ᶜAlawiyya groups on the coast. In the twentieth century, the ribāṭ al-riyāḍa of Ḥabīb Ṣāliḥ in Lamu became the most important centre of ᶜAlawī teaching traditions in Kenya (see el-Zein 1974). At the same time, Kenya was part of the East African Salafi-oriented movement of reform under its charismatic founder, al-Amīn b. ᶜAlī al-Mazrūᶜī (based in Mombasa). His legacy was continued by his son, Muḥammad b. Qāsim al-Mazrūᶜī,[35] as well as by ᶜAbdallāh Ṣāliḥ al-Farsy and Muḥammad b. ᶜAbdallāh b. Muḥammad al-Ghazzālī (d. 1960), the first director of the Mombasa Institute of Muslim Education (MIOME),[36] and a leading figure in the Mwambao movement (Kresse 2007a: 187). ᶜAbdallāh Ṣāliḥ al-Farsy taught at the Shibu, Nūr and Mūsa mosques in Mombasa for three days in the week and had hundreds of students, while his sermons were widely listened to in Kenya (Bakari 1989: 4). Al-Farsy trained a whole generation of students who continued this legacy of reform. His impact was intensified by the return of students who had been in Umm Durmān (Sudan), Medina, al-Riyādh, Cairo and Benghazi where they had become part of a global network of Salafi-oriented activists (Bakari 1989: 6).

In the 1980s, this new generation of Salafi-oriented thinkers and scholars took over from ᶜAbdallāh Ṣāliḥ al-Farsy. Prominent representatives of this new generation of reformers were Ḥārith Ṣāliḥ al-Maᶜawī, who had studied in Umm Durmān, Naṣṣor Khamīs, ᶜAlī Shee and Aḥmad Msallam (see Desplat 2001; Kresse 2007a: 94ff; Bakari 1989). ᶜAlī Shee studied with

Ḥārith Ṣāliḥ in Kisingitini, before going on to study Islamic law in Umm Durmān. He graduated in the mid-1970s, and then returned to Kenya and worked for the Supreme Council of Kenya Muslims (SUPKEM). He was then appointed *qāḍī* of Garissa by ᶜAbdallāh Ṣāliḥ al-Farsy, but was soon transferred to Malindi, and then Mombasa under the direct control of the new Chief Qāḍī Naṣṣor al-Nahdī. His fiery sermons against all kinds of *bidᶜa* attracted much attention. ᶜAlī Shee became a leading figure in Kenya's anṣār al-sunna movement. In 1987, he was suspended as *qāḍī* in Mombasa due to his radical positions and was subsequently hired by the National Union of Kenya Muslims (NUKEM) to advise on an Islamic studies syllabus for a teacher-training institute.

Aḥmad Muḥammad Msallam studied with ᶜAbdallāh Ṣāliḥ al-Farsy and also went to Umm Durmān, where Ḥārith Ṣāliḥ was his mentor, and where he studied Arabic literature and language. After his return to Kenya, he became a teacher at different *madāris*, first in Kilifi, and then in Namanya. He translated texts into Kiswahili and eventually became a translator for the Saudi Arabia Embassy in Nairobi. At the same time, he started to give sermons in mosques in Nairobi, Mombasa and Lamu, attacked the Shīᶜa and became the major opponent of ᶜAbdillāhi Nāṣir. Naṣṣor Khamīs, a Digo from the southern coast, had studied *fiqh* in Medina and returned to Kenya in 1982, an heir to ᶜAbdallāh Ṣāliḥ al-Farsy. In the 1980s, he started to build the madrasa al-munāwwara al-islāmiyya in Mombasa, a school that already had in the region of 1,000 students in 1989.

A major opponent of Salafi-oriented scholars was ᶜAbdillāhi Nāṣir (b. 1932 in Mombasa). He had studied at colonial schools, and then with Muḥammad b. ᶜAbdallāh b. Muḥammad al-Ghazzālī at the MIOME. He was taught by Sayyid ᶜUmar ᶜAbdallāh in Zanzibar, as well as Muḥammad b. Qāsim al-Mazrūᶜī in Mombasa. ᶜAbdillāhi Nāṣir attended Dole school in Zanzibar in the 1950s and used the chance to study with Sayyid ᶜUmar ᶜAbdallāh at the Muslim Academy (Kresse 2006: 219f, 2007a: 102). After his studies in Zanzibar, he returned to Mombasa and became a leading figure in the Coast People's Party (CPP) that represented the Mwambao movement and advocated political autonomy for the coastal region (Salim 1973: 233ff). When these aspirations misfired in 1963, ᶜAbdillāhi Nāṣir worked as a teacher at the MIOME, but then became an editor at the Oxford University

Press in Nairobi. At the same time, he started to give lectures at the Nairobi *jum*ᶜ*a* mosque. In 1977, he left the Oxford University Press and established his own publishing house, Shungaya Publishers, which went bankrupt in 1985. ᶜAbdillāhi Nāṣir then joined WAMY in Nairobi and continued to give sermons at the Nairobi *jum*ᶜ*a* mosque, but changed camp again in 1987 to become a follower of the IthnaᶜSharа Shīᶜī group (Bakari 1989; Desplat 2001: 109; Kresse 2006: 218; Ahmed 2008: 397ff).

Since the 1980s, due to Salafi critique of established religious practices, Kenya has witnessed a decline of Sufi-related activities, such as *mawlid* celebrations, and a corresponding growth of Salafi-oriented groups. In his 2007 study of 103 mosques and mosque communities in Kenya, Mwakimako establishes that 43 per cent of all interviewees never attend a *mawlid* (Mwakimako 2007b: 20). *Mawlid* rejection was strongest on the coast and in the North Eastern Province, but negligible in the Western, Nyanza, Central and Rift Valley Provinces. At the same time, mosque building exploded from the 1980s to the early 2000s, but has decreased again since then (Mwakimako 2007b: 25). Internal conflicts within mosque communities were mostly connected with disputes over *fiqh* and *ᶜaqīda* and less with questions of leadership. Mosque conflicts were most serious in the Eastern and Central Provinces and in Nairobi, and almost unknown in the North Eastern and Nyanza provinces (Mwakimako 2007b: 35).

In order to coordinate Muslim activities in Kenya, a first Muslim umbrella organisation (NUKEM) was founded in Mombasa in 1968, headed by two Muslim assistant ministers, Muḥammad Jahazi and Muḥammad Salīm Balala. In the 1970s, NUKEM's influence was superseded by SUPKEM (founded in 1973). SUPKEM was linked with KANU, and was supported by the government as Kenya's official umbrella body for Muslim affairs. It was recognised in 1979 as the only organisation to represent Muslims in Kenya and to maintain links with Islamic organisations outside Kenya (Oded 2000: 24). Due to this fact, SUPKEM was denounced as a 'government agent'. According to Mwakimako's sample, SUPKEM is nevertheless the strongest Muslim umbrella organisation in Kenya. Second is the Council of Imams and Preachers of Islam in Kenya (CIPK) (founded 1997 in Mombasa), chaired by ᶜAlī Shee (and since 2008 by Muḥammad Dor), which has acquired a reputation of being critical of the government (Seesemann 2007: 160;

Ndzovu 2014: 100–2). Since the 1980s, Kenya has seen a proliferation of Islamic associations and competition between them over questions of authority, distribution of funds and issues of doctrine. Among these associations are the Nairobi-based Young Muslims Association (YMA) (established in 1964), which has become the Kenyan branch of the World Association of Muslim Youth (WAMY), the Kenya Muslim Youth Alliance (KMYA) (established in 2003), the Anṣār Muslim Youth, the Muslim Students Association of the University of Nairobi (MSAUN), the Muslim Education Welfare Association (MEWA) (established in 1986), the majlis ᶜulamāᵓ (or National Council of Muslim Scholars of Kenya) (established in 2005),[37] the Kenya Council of Imams and ᶜUlamāᵓ (KCIU), the Kenya Assembly of ᶜUlamāᵓ in Islam (KAULI) and al-waḥda, an association formed by *madrasa* teachers (Mwakimako 2007b: 44; Scharrer 2013: 65). In addition, there are numerous local Muslim associations, such as the Kisumu Muslim Association led by Shaaban Wegulo Yusuf (Ahmed 2008: 216ff; Mwakimako 2007b: 80; Scharrer 2013: 74–5).[38] Fifty per cent of all *imāms* were affiliated with al-waḥda, 27 per cent with CIPK and 8 per cent with the majlis ᶜulamāᵓ. In the Coast Province, 58 per cent of all *imāms* were linked with the CIPK (Mwakimako 2007b: 44). The fragmented character of Islam in Kenya is mirrored in the training of *imāms*: while most *imāms* in the North Eastern Province are trained in the Sudan and in Somalia, Somalia is paramount for Nairobi. Saudi Arabia is the leading destination for Western and Nyanza Provinces, while Saudi Arabia, Pakistan and Zanzibar are prominent for the Coast Province (Mwakimako 2007b: 39). Many Salafi-oriented groups, such as the 'Muslim Bible Preachers' (Wahubiri wa Kiislamu), also have links with Tanzania.

The 2000s brought about a further fragmentation of Kenya's Muslims and radicalisation of activist groups. This development was aggravated in 2011 when Kenya decided to intervene directly in Somali politics and sent the Kenyan Army into southern Somalia to support the Transitional Federal Government against al-shabāb attacks. Since then, violence and police repression have escalated in the North Eastern and Coast Provinces, as well as in Nairobi (see ICG 2012f; ICG 2014a). A major representative of the new generation of militant and activist Muslims in Kenya was ᶜAbbūd Rogo (1968–2012) from Siyu (Lamu archipelago) who was assassinated on 27

August 2012.[39] The escalation of the conflict in Somalia, and the Kenyan military intervention in Somalia, led to the emergence of al-shabāb groups in Kenya, supported by militant Kenyan Muslim activists. A spectacular manifestation of violence (after the attack on the Westgate shopping mall in Nairobi in 2013) was an al-shabāb attack on the village of Mpeketoni near Lamu on 15 June 2014, which caused the death of forty-eight people (ICG 2014a: 5). Mpeketoni was targeted by al-shabāb (and its Kenyan supporters) because Mpeketoni had been founded in the context of Kenyatta's efforts in the 1960s to resettle landless Kikuyu from up-country Kenya in the less densely populated coastal areas. In the context of such resettlement programmes, (Christian) settlers had moved to the Muslim coastal region (ICG 2014a: 5, 14).

The constitutional change in 1992 and the introduction of a multi-party system added to the proliferation of political parties and corresponding disputes among Muslims over questions of political orientation. Multi-party politics gave Muslims a significant role as voters, however, and thus triggered competition for the 'Muslim vote'.[40] Thus, the National Muslim Leaders Forum (NAMLEF) (see Ndzovu 2014: 102–5) supported the Orange Democratic Movement (ODM) of Raila Odinga in 2007, while the United Congregation of Imams in Nakuru supported Mwai Kibaki and his National Rainbow Coalition (NARC). Partisan competition and disputes among Muslims created frustration, in particular among the youth. In the context of political liberalisation, Muslim activists in Mombasa, such as ᶜUmar Mwinyi and ᶜAbd al-Raḥmān Mirimo Wandati, founded the Islamic Party of Kenya (IPK) in December 1991, which became the strongest political force in Mombasa in 1992. The IPK essentially fought for civil rights with reference to Islamic principles, and was not 'sectarian' (Mwakimako 2007b: 51). Rather, it expressed Muslim protest against marginalisation in politics and economics and constitutional and legal matters (Oded 1996: 407–8). Although the IPK had a secular constitution, it was refused registration on account of its name.[41]

In 1992, Khālid Balala (b. 1958), a Kenyan citizen of Yemeni descent born in Mombasa, rose to a leading position in the IPK. He had studied in local *madāris*, and then travelled to Saudi Arabia at the age of seventeen to perform the *ḥajj*. He stayed in Saudi Arabia to continue his studies at the

University of Medina, making a living by selling books (Oded 2000: 149). He then visited a number of Asian and European countries, studying business administration in Britain, and Islamic studies as well as comparative religion in India. After his return to Mombasa in 1990, he tried to make a living as a book seller and started to give sermons in Mombasa's Mwembe Tayari market, attracting growing public attention due to his eloquence and his critique of the Moi government. In 1992, he joined the IPK and quickly became the major IPK leader. The fact that the IPK was not registered as a party in 1992 led to an escalation of conflict in 1992 and 1993. This conflict was aggravated by the fact that Kenyan police and security forces, in particular the General Service Unit, acted with great brutality against Muslim protesters (Scharrer 2013: 63). In May 1992, riots in Mombasa occurred due to the arrest of seven Muslim scholars linked with the IPK. In this context, Kenyan police broke into mosques and shot several people (Oded 1996: 406).

The initial success of the IPK in Mombasa was also a protest against Sharīf Nāṣir, an assistant minister in Daniel arap Moi's cabinet and KANU chairperson for Mombasa. He had become highly unpopular due to his arrogant and pompous manner (Oded 1996: 410). The elections in December 1992 resulted in a KANU defeat in Mombasa: only one out of four seats was won by KANU, the other three were won by IPK-supported opposition parties (Oded 1996: 410). The Daniel arap Moi regime reacted with further police repression in Mombasa. Khālid Balala was imprisoned several times, the first time in June 1992. In June 1994, Khālid Balala was excluded from the IPK due to internal conflicts over his increasing radicalism. He subsequently formed the Islamic Salvation Front. In 1994, he left Kenya for Europe (Oded 1996: 413), but returned to Kenya in 1997. He has since been rather isolated (Quinn and Quinn 2003: 123; Scharrer 2013: 63). At the same time, that is, the 1990s, the regime took recourse to 'stick or carrot' policies. Applications for the pilgrimage were granted liberally and quickly, government officials took part in Muslim public festivities and Muslims were appointed to fill government positions (Oded 1996: 412).

Typical of Kenya's Islam policies and respective Muslim preoccupations was the development of Kenya's *qāḍī* courts and the debate over the role of *sharīʿa* jurisdiction: in 1963, *qāḍī* courts were accepted in the independence constitution (section 66), and granted Muslims living in the former

Protectorate region (that is, the coastal strip) the right to solve personal status issues according to Islamic law (Salim 1973: 244; Seesemann 2007: 163). The Qāḍī Courts Act of 1967 extended this right to all Muslims in Kenya and recognised their role in the Kenyan constitution and judicial system (Mwakimako 2007b: 70). The Qāḍī Courts Act of 1967 also created the position of a Chief Qāḍī to be appointed by the president. The Chief Qāḍī was empowered to appoint regional *qāḍīs* who had to be approved by the president. In 1996, Kenya had fifteen regional *qāḍīs* (Oded 2000: 41). Due to their central role, the position of *qāḍī* has become a focus of Muslim internal disputes.

In 1968, ᶜAbdallāh Ṣāliḥ al-Farsy from Zanzibar was appointed Chief Qāḍī of Kenya. His major opponents were the mostly Lamu-based members of the ᶜAlawī network of scholars, most prominently ᶜAlī Badawī Jamal al-Layl and ᶜAbd al-Raḥmān Aḥmad Badawī Jamal al-Layl alias 'Sharīf Khitāmī', who portrayed ᶜAbdallāh Ṣāliḥ al-Farsy as a 'foreigner who created *fitna*'. ᶜAbdallāh Ṣāliḥ al-Farsy resigned in 1981 and was followed by Naṣṣor al-Nahdī (who remained in office until 2002).[42] Naṣṣor al-Nahdī did not command the respect of his predecessor and was attacked by oppositional Muslim scholars as a 'government stooge' (Oded 2000: 50). The authority of the Chief Qāḍī declined, and disputes over the sighting of the moon increased. In 1994, this conflict escalated when the *imām* of the Nairobi *jumᶜa* mosque, ᶜAlī Muḥammad Shee, refused to accept the date set by the Chief Qāḍī for the *ᶜīd al-fiṭr* and set his own date, claiming that he had received information from the North Eastern Province that the new moon had been sighted. He accused the Chief Qāḍī of failing to respect the opinion of Somali Muslims in Kenya by ignoring such information (Scharrer 2013: 62).

In 1995, SUPKEM invited an assembly of ninety religious scholars to resolve this dispute. The assembly elected a majlis ᶜulamāᵓ,[43] consisting of fifteen members who were asked to study the problems involved and to give their advice. The first chairman of the majlis ᶜulamāᵓ was Ḥārith Ṣāliḥ, his deputy was ᶜAlī Shee and the secretary was Aḥmad Muḥammad Msallam: the majlis ᶜulamāᵓ was thus dominated by Salafi-oriented scholars opposed to al-Nahdī (Oded 2000: 50). The majlis ᶜulamāᵓ was authorised to give *fatāwā* and to consult directly with the Kenyan Government. This development was resented, however, on the coast, where established Muslims scholars feared a weakening of al-Nahdī's authority and opposed the increasing power of Salafi-oriented scholars. As a result, the majlis ᶜulamāᵓ was unable to overcome the problems, which led to calls for Naṣṣor al-Nahdī's resignation from office, a demand that was supported by the *qāḍī* of Nairobi, Ḥammad Muḥammad Kassim. In 2002 he succeeded al-Nahdī as Kenya's Chief Qāḍī (Oded 2000: 51). The matter of the sighting of the moon was eventually referred back to SUPKEM and has remained unresolved to this day.

In the 2000s, the debate over the role of the *qāḍī* courts resurfaced: in 2002, the draft version of the new constitution was published by the Constitution of Kenya Review Commission (CKRC) and sparked a debate on the position of *sharīᶜa* courts that was characterised by Christian efforts to eliminate *sharīᶜa* jurisdiction completely from the constitution. Sections 199 and 200 of the draft version proposed an extension of the *qāḍī* court system to include matters of civil and commercial law, and also provided for the creation of a three-layered system of *qāḍī* courts (district, regional and national), as well as a Supreme Court of Appeal. Although it was clear that *sharīᶜa* jurisdiction would apply to Muslims only, and although Muslims would still have the right to ignore the *qāḍī* courts and go to civil courts, even in matters of personal law, these proposals triggered Christian attacks that were answered in kind by Muslims (Seesemann 2007: 165). Due to Christian protests, *qāḍī* courts were practically reduced to their 1967 status in the revised draft constitution, but Christian lobbies went ahead and demanded that *qāḍī* courts should be completely eliminated from the new constitution and threatened to reject it if *qāḍī* courts were retained. The Kenyan Government and the CKRC tried to solve this dilemma by proposing to set up 'religious courts' for Muslims, Hindus and Christians, but the referendum on the 'Wako draft'[44] of the new constitution, held on 21 November 2005, brought about the defeat of the government proposal that was rejected by 58 per cent of the vote. As a result, Kenya's independence constitution remained in force and nothing changed with respect to the position of *qāḍī* courts (Seesemann 2007: 167; Mraja 2011). The draft constitution was rejected by majorities in all provinces except Central Province (Halkano Abdi Wario 2014: 162). In August 2010 another referendum eventually accepted a new constitution by 66.9 per cent of the vote. The new constitution left the status of *qāḍī* courts unchanged and thus confirmed their role as part of the constitution since 1967 (Halkano Abdi Wario 2014: 175).

Although Muslims in East Africa live in the same geographical region and have been informed by similar historical experiences, in particular the influence of the Sultanate of Zanzibar and British colonialism, the examples of Tanganiyka/Tanzania and Kenya show that the local context was again decisive for the different trajectories of Muslim communities in these two countries. Major differences are due to the fact that Muslims possibly form the largest religious group in Tanzania and a minority only in Kenya. Muslims have also been represented in government in Tanzania to a much larger extent than in Kenya, despite litanies of complaint. However, they have not achieved unity in either political or religious terms and have become fragmented into a multitude of competing associations in both Tanzania and Kenya. Even confrontation with Pentecostal churches has not led to greater unity. The development of both Sufi- and Salafi-oriented movements of reform in Tanzania and Kenya shows that particularistic interests prevail over larger yet abstract goals, such as the unity of the *ummah*, and that the divide-and-rule policies of national governments have been successful in preventing the emergence of a united 'Islamic' opposition led, possibly, by a Salafi-oriented movement of reform. It may even be said that Kenya's Muslims, who have been marginalised in Kenyan politics since independence, have continued to marginalise themselves due to their inability to achieve unity in the face of internal disputes that continue to enhance processes of social, ethnic and political fragmentation. The next chapter will compare Tanganiyka/Tanzania and Kenya with Zanzibar, a country where, as in Senegal, Mali or Niger, Muslims form the undisputed majority of the population. Due to the fact that Zanzibar's revolution in 1964 virtually eliminated the establishment of religious scholars, we will address the question of what happens when the *ᶜulamāᵓ* are gone. The next chapter also takes a look at the Comoros, where another revolution, in 1975, targeted religious scholars, in particular those linked with local traditions of Islam. As a result, Salafi-minded reformers had a chance to grow roots in the Comoros when the country's revolutionary period came to an abrupt end in 1978.

Notes

1. While Tanganyika retained its name after independence in 1961, the merger with Zanzibar in April 1964 led to the new name 'Tanzania'. As Zanzibar is discussed in another chapter, however, the term 'Tanzania' refers here just to the 'Tanganyikan' part of Tanzania.
2. The Arusha Declaration of 1967 (Azimio la Arusha) started a programme of *Ujamaa* (community) development policies that have been labelled 'African socialism'.
3. In 1987, Muslim groups in Zanzibar claimed that Tanzania was dominated by Catholics. Presidents Julius Nyerere (1961–85) and Benjamin Mkapa (1995–2005) were Catholic, but Ali Hassan Mwinyi (1985–95) from Zanzibar and Mrisho Kikwete from Bagamoyo (2005–15) were Muslims. John Pombe Joseph Magufuli, Tanzania's president since October 2015, is a Christian (from Chato Disrict, northwestern Tanzania).
4. Muḥammad Ḥusayn Malik arrived in Tanzania in 1964 and taught at a number of secondary schools in Dar es Salaam. He introduced Tanzanians to the ideas of Abū l-Āᶜla Maudūdī and was a key figure in the East Africa branch of the Islamic Foundation (Chesworth 2006: 176ff). The fact that Dr Malik played an important role in WARSHA has been used to emphasise the importance of foreign influence on WARSHA. In fact, WARSHA was always 'more than just Malik' (Gilsaa 2012: 208). After the 'seminaries dispute', Dr Malik was expatriated from Tanzania. He was appointed a students' chaplain at the University of Nairobi and taught religious studies. In Kenya, he was linked with the YMA (the Kenyan WAMY branch) in Nairobi (Chesworth 2006: 176ff).
5. On disputes over the issue of the *dhikr*, see above. Similar disputes have focused on the *mawlid al-nabī* that has come to be celebrated in many parts of East Africa in different forms, from the 'sober' and solemn recitation in Arabic of the *Mawlid Barzanji* to ecstatic forms of the maulidi ya Kiswahili, which was celebrated not only on the actual date of the Prophet's birthday (twelfth Rabīᶜ al-Auwal) but also in the context of various social occasions. As a consequence, *mawlid* celebrations were attacked by Muslim reformers and by the British colonial administration in Zanzibar as 'un-Islamic' and a feature of 'conspicuous consumption' that should be stopped. Disputes over *mawlid* celebrations in East Africa started in the late nineteenth century, and have continued to this day. On the fight against *mawlid* in Zanzibar, see Loimeier (2006a, 2006b).
6. In some of his writings, al-Amīn b. ᶜAlī al-Mazrūᶜī may have criticised specific

forms of social change in East Africa in the 1930s and 1940s, which he condemned as aspects of colonialism, but this was a form of general cultural critique and not a politically motivated struggle for Kenya's independence. The Muslim population of Kenya's coastal Sayyidiyya province did not join in the Kenyan struggle for independence and sought to achieve autonomy of the coastal region under British protection.

7. Saidi Musa (b. 1943) was born in Simbom near Ugweno, a village in Northern Pare. In 1962, he moved to Zanzibar, where he became a student of ᶜAbdallāh Ṣāliḥ al-Farsy until 1967, when al-Farsy left Zanzibar. In 1968, Saidi Musa left Zanzibar as well and settled in Kariakoo, Dar es Salaam, where he worked, from 1968 to 1992, as an employee of the Tanzania Shoe Factory. At the same time, he started his *daᶜwa* activities, published numerous writings, allegedly more than 200, and became an outspoken representative of activist reformist Muslim groups in Tanzania. In the late 1970s, he started to support the Iranian revolution. Although his home in Ugweno was registered as the Shaykh Saidi Musa Islamic Development Center (SSMIDC), his permanent residence was his house in Dar es Salaam. Every Friday, he gave a sermon in the Manyema mosque (in Mafia Street, an old mosque established in 1912) or the Qiblatayn mosque (in Zigua/Mahiwa Streets). Although Saidi Musa was very active in *daᶜwa* and influenced a number of activist Muslims in Tanzania in the 1970s and 1980s, he never became the leader or organiser of a proper organisation (see Loimeier 2009).
8. Rajab b. Sima studied at the University of Medina from 1972 to 1982 and established a first anṣār al-sunna group in Singida after his return from Saudi Arabia.
9. Yūsuf Rajab Mnenge studied at the University of Medina from 1978 and started an anṣār al-sunna group in Kigoma after his return from Saudi Arabia.
10. The most important of these charitable associations was al-ḥaramayn, established in Dar es Salaam in the early 1970s and directed by a Sudanese scholar, ᶜAbbās Muṣṭafa. Through al-ḥaramayn, BAKWATA got a number of scholarships for students from Tanzania to study in Saudi Arabia (Gilsaa 2012: 193). These 'Medina graduates' were supposed to build a group of Saudi-trained state functionaries, yet many of the returnees came to form the nucleus of the different anṣār al-sunna groups in the early 1980s. Since 1985, other Middle Eastern charities followed, in particular the Africa Muslim Agency (AMA) (registered in 1987), WAMY and the Sudan-based munaẓẓamat al-daᶜwa al-islāmiyya (the Islamic call society) (registered in 1987). Both AMA and the munaẓẓamat al-daᶜwa al-islāmiyya provided grants for studies abroad, mostly in Sudan.

11. Yaḥyā Ḥusayn was born in Dar es Salaam into a family of religious scholars. He grew up in Dar es Salaam's Kariakoo quarter, studied with scholars in Dar es Salaam and also attended courses at Zanzibar's Muslim Academy in the early 1950s. Subsequently, he went to Egypt (al-Azhar) for further studies and visited Jordan and Malaysia. After his return to Tanganyika, he founded AMNUT and criticised Nyerere well into the 1960s, yet joined BAKWATA in the late 1960s. In this period of time, he became famous for his expertise in ^{c}ilm al-falak (tafsiri ya nyota) and acquired considerable wealth as an astrologer. Gilsaa characterises Yaḥyā Ḥusayn as 'colourful': 'in the 1960s . . . one of Nyerere's strongest political challengers and Secretary General of the EAMWS . . . (he) who would join BAKWATA after having opposed its formation, form BALUKTA as part of BAKWATA, but during this decade finally break with BAKWATA and begin to build a new political base outside CCM, perhaps having foreseen the one-party-state's end a few years later. Rather than two faces, Sheikh Yahya Hussein appears to have had a range of hats and masks, partly as a cleric and a Koran citer, partly as a famous astrologer, partly as an ethnic leader, and always as a "politician" and/or "businessman"' (Gilsaa 2012: 247; for Yaḥyā Ḥusayn's biography see also Said 2015).
12. The Tanzania Islamic Centre (TIC) was originally the Magomeni Muslim Association and was linked with the Badawī mosque in Magomeni and the Tanganyika Islamic Centre of the 1960s.
13. See www.bbc.com/news/world-africa23629334, last accessed on 20 February 2016.
14. In October 2012, Issa Ponda Issa was allegedly involved in an incident in Dar es Salaam when Muslim protesters torched five churches in response to rumours that a Christian boy had urinated on the Qur$^{\circ}$ān. Such incidents show how quickly rumours may escalate into riots and how tense the atmosphere regarding Muslim–Christian relations has become. The analysis of such events is often fogged, however, by the narrow 'war-on-terror' view of the media and other observers, who suspect Tanzanian involvement in al-Qā^{c}ida activities. This mode of representing Muslim–Christian conflict in Tanzania started with the embassy bombing in Dar es Salaam in August 1998, when a Zanzibar-born Tanzanian, Khalfān Khamīs Muḥammad, became known as the country's first al-Qā^{c}ida activist (see <http://www.bagamoyo.com>; <http://www.africajournalismtheworld.com> and <http://www.historycommons.org> (all last accessed on 9 January 2014)). Reports on such events are seldom based on objective research, and must be treated with due care.

15. This dispute was discussed in an article in *Zanzibar Leo*, on 17 March 2003, entitled 'Sheikh Muhammad Nassor al-Qadiry atakumbukwa kwa Ucha Mungu na mchango mkubwa katika dini ya Kiislamu'.
16. On Aḥmad Deedat, see Sadouni (1998: 149ff, 2011), Vahed (2009) and Westerlund (2003: 263ff). Aḥmad Deedat's organisation, the Islamic Propagation Centre in Durban was established in 1957. Aḥmad Deedat became famous in sub-Saharan Africa for his public disputes with the US TV evangelist Jimmy Swaggart (see Westerlund 2003: 267). Aḥmad Deedat developed his style and strategy of preaching in the confrontation with South African Pentecostal churches, in particular Reinhard Bonnke's Christ for all Nations (CFAN) movement.
17. The first Pentecostal community was established in Mbeya in 1959, but Pentecostal churches expanded rapidly from the early 1980s. By the late 1990s, they had about one million members in Tanzania, a growth that startled not only Muslims but also the Catholic Church. On the development of Pentecostal churches in Tanzania, see Ludwig (1996: 222f, 1999: 183, 186ff). According to Maxwell, by 2005 Pentecostal communities had grown to more than 250 million members worldwide, and several dozens of millions in sub-Saharan Africa (Maxwell 2005: 5). Pentecostal churches are probably 'the largest self-organized movement of the urban poor on the planet' today (Maxwell 2006: 389).
18. Uamsho is also the name of a Muslim activist movement in Tanzania. Muslim activists, in particular those belonging to the 'Muslim Bible Preacher' movement, stress the importance of personal 'reversion' to Islam and integrate personal experiences of reversion, of being 'born again' as a Muslim, as a feature of their *mihadhara* meetings.
19. My own observation in Tanzania, in 2007. Pentecostal services in Dar es Salaam are characterised by the presence of Muslim women and the fact that some of them convert during services. See also Ndaluka (2012).
20. In the 1980s, Bonnke's CfaN movement mobilised major support in the context of a series of 'crusades' in many African countries and triggered numerous confrontations with Muslims due to its aggressive public preaching. Reinhard Bonnke (b. 1940), a German evangelist who trained as a preacher from 1959 to 1961 at the Bible College of Wales in Swansea, went to Lesotho in 1967 for the Apostolic Faith Mission and was then active in South Africa for some time. In South Africa, Bonnke built a new organisation based in Johannesburg with the support of US evangelists such as Kenneth Copeland from Texas. This organisation, Christ for all Nations (CfaN), carried out a first mission crusade in

Botswana in 1975 with the slogan 'Africa shall be saved'. In subsequent years, his crusades led Bonnke to South Africa, Zaire, Zambia, Zimbabwe and Kenya, and then Tanzania, Nigeria (1990) and Sierra Leone (Gifford 1987: 64). In the early 1990s Bonnke's organisation had 129 permanent staff, 19 trucks and a tent that could accommodate in the region of 34,000 people but that soon became too small for his growing audiences. As a consequence, Bonnke moved into football stadiums (see Loimeier 1992). Since 1986, his organisation has been located in Seckbach near Frankfurt.

21. See Ahmed (2008: 152–73) for a Muslim Bible Preachers document that sets out in detail the arguments used in an exemplary dispute between Muslim Bible Preachers and Christians.
22. According to Ally Bassalleh, the emissaries of the Aḥmadiyya had already developed counter-strategies against Christian missionary activities in the 1950s (communication Chanfi Ahmed, 25 September 2007).
23. On Muslim–Christian relations in Tanzania in general, see Ndaluka (2012). His work shows that Muslim–Christian relations are often harmonious as far as everyday relations and eye-to-eye contacts are concerned. This is substantiated, for instance, by the fact that inter-religious marriages occur and are regarded as normal by both Muslims and Christians (Ndaluka 2012: 59). Violent clashes, such as the Mwembechai riots, are regarded as exceptional (Ndaluka 2012: 232). Most participants in his enquiry saw Tanzania as a secular state, and religion was portrayed as being a purely personal matter (Ndaluka 2012: 232).
24. To this day, the meaning of the last part of this verse (. . . but so it was made to appear to them) has not been clarified by Muslim scholars (Khoury 2004: 180).
25. In their campaign, the Muslim Bible Preachers got support from other East African countries, in particular Kenya, but also South Africa and even the USA. Both *an-Nuur* and *al-Huda* published articles by US Muslims against Pentecostal positions (my own observation, Tanzania, 2007).
26. Due to the fact that 'religion' was not included in Tanzanian censuses after 1967, there is no reliable information on this issue today. As a consequence, estimates range from 30 to 45 per cent Muslim, 30 to 63 per cent Christians to 20 to 30 per cent followers of African religions.
27. On the development of Islam in Nairobi, see Kubai (1992: 31ff).
28. While Arabs were represented by the Coast Arab Association (CAA), established in 1921, non-Arab Muslims were represented in the Afro-Asian Association (AAA), established in 1927. The rivalries between different Muslim groups on the coast were a major obstacle in the struggle for political autonomy of the

coastal region by the Mwambao ('coast') movement of the early 1960s (see Brennan 2015; Ndzovu 2014: 20ff).

29. The Kenyan Somali population grew to approximately 2.4 million in 2009 (ICG 2012e).
30. See Ayubi and Mohyuddin (1994), Cruise O'Brien (1995), Kettani (1982, 1985), Mazrui (1993), Mwakimako (2007a, 2007b), Ndzovu (2014), Oded (1996, 2000), Quinn and Quinn (2003) and Scharrer (2013).
31. Since the 1980s, Muslims have tried hard to overcome this bias and were supported by Islamic NGOs from Saudi Arabia, Kuwait and other Arab countries. In 1980, the Leicester-based Islamic Foundation founded the Kisauni Islamic Institute (Ma^{c}had Kisauni al-Islāmī) near Mombasa, which was complemented by the Islamic College of Kisauni in 1995 and the Kisauni Islamic University in 2002 (Ahmed 2008: 197ff).
32. In 1971, the Kenyan Government recognised *^{c}īd al-fiṭr* as a national holiday (Oded 2000: 34). In 1983, President Moi granted Muslims the right of immediate burial (Oded 2000: 36).
33. In this terrorist attack 258 people, mostly Kenyans, died, while approximately 5,000 were wounded. After the embassy bombing, five Islamic NGOs were banned: Mercy International, al-ḥaramayn, Help African People, the International Islamic Relief Organization and the Ibrāhīm b. ^{c}Abd al-^{c}Azīz Foundation (Ndzovu 2014: 82).
34. These attacks have been linked with the Kenyan military intervention in Somalia that started in October 2011 (Code name 'Operation Linda Nchi'). This intervention led to an expansion of al-shabāb activities on Kenyan territory, supported by Kenyan Muslims affiliated with al-shabāb. Major targets of attack since 2011 have been bars, tourist installations, churches and police posts, as well as Kenya Defence Force installations and Kenyan Christians (see the documentation at <http://en.wikipedia.org/wiki/2011-14_terrorist_attacks_in_Kenya> (last accessed 22 February 2016)). On 22 November 2014, al-shabāb attacked a bus in north-eastern Kenya, killing 28 (Christian) passengers, on 2 December 2014, al-shabāb hit a quarry near Mandera in north-eastern Kenya, killing 36 (Christian) workers and on 3 April 2015 an al-shabāb commando massacred 148 (Christian) students in the context of an attack against Garissa University College.
35. Muḥammad b. Qāsim al-Mazrū^{c}ī (1912–82) was Chief Qāḍī of Kenya from 1963 to 1968 (after being acting Chief Qāḍī since 1948, when he took over from ^{c}Alī b. Aḥmad al-Badawī). His students became leading figures in the Salafi-oriented movement of reform in Kenya (Kresse 2007a: 94; Mwakimako

2010: 128ff). The text Hukuma za sharia by Muḥammad b. Qāsim al-Mazrūᶜī has become a key text for Salafi-oriented Muslims in East Africa. In this text, he lists a series of issues that are reprehensible from a Salafi point of view and that recur in numerous Salafi-oriented texts in other parts of Africa, such as the practice of *tawassul*, prayers at the tombs of Sufi saints or a number of practices associated with 'khitma', that is, the practices of mourning, such as hiring other persons to mourn, as well as shrine pilgrimage (Kresse 2003: 294).

36. The Mombasa Institute of Muslim Education was the result of a merger between Muḥammad al-Ghazzālī's madrasat al-Ghazzālī (est. 1933) and the Arab School (est. 1913) in 1936. In 1951, this school was renamed 'MIOME' (Hoffmann 2013: 100). In 1964, MIOME became a government polytechnic (Cruise O'Brien 1995: 206).
37. The majlis ᶜulamāᵓ was established in the context of a nationwide meeting of 300 Muslim scholars in Nairobi in 2005, presided over by the Chief Qāḍī, Ḥammad Muḥammad Kassim (Ahmed 2008: 248). The first president of the majlis ᶜulamāᵓ was Khalfān Khamīs Ismāᶜīl (b. 1965 in Homa Bay, a Luhya). Khalfān Khamīs Ismāᶜīl attended a government school and a *madrasa* in Sio, and then continued his *ṭalab al-ᶜilm* by studying at the ribāṭ al-riyādha in Lamu in 1980. In 1983, he moved to the Kisauni Institute in Mombasa, where he came under increasing Salafi influence. In 1986, he was sent with a Saudi grant to Karachi, Pakistan. In 1993, he returned to Kenya, moved to Homa Bay in the late 1990s, and then to Kisumu in 2002 (Ahmed 2008: 248ff).
38. Shaaban Wegulo Yusuf (b. 1972 in Sio near Busia) stemmed from a Muslim family of Luo extraction. After completing basic *madrasa* training, he continued his *ṭalab al-ᶜilm* by moving to Mombasa, and then to Mambrui, where he attended the madrasat al-nūr of Muḥammad Sharīf Saᶜīd al-Biẓ, a Sufi-oriented scholar from Lamu. He returned to Mombasa in 1984, where he studied at the madrasat al-falāḥ of ᶜAbd al-Raḥmān al-Malabārī and came under Salafi influence. In 1988, he moved to the Maᶜhad Kisauni al-Islāmī, and then became a teacher at the madrasat al-fatḥ in Mombasa in 1991, but left for Saudi Arabia in 1992 to study at the Islamic University of Medina. In 1997, he returned to Kenya, where he became the chief administrator of the Kenya branch of the al-muntadā al-islāmī foundation in Kisumu. In 1998 he became the secretary general of this foundation in Nairobi, but left for Mombasa in the same year to teach at the madrasat al-munāwwara al-islāmiyya. In 2004, he moved back to Nairobi, and then continued to Nakuru (Ahmed 2008: 216ff).
39. ᶜAbbūd Rogo attended both government and Islamic schools, and went through

a number of business activities in his youth before moving to Mombasa in 1989, where he became an ardent supporter of the IPK and Khālid Balala (see below). Although he has been linked with the 1998 embassy bombing and the Kikambala hotel attack in 2002, these accusations could never be substantiated and ᶜAbbūd Rogo had to be released from detention in 2005. In 2007, he become famous for his increasingly radical sermons at Mombasa's Mūsa mosque, declaring, for example, that working for the Kenyan Government was forbidden (*ḥarām*). ᶜAbbūd Rogo's assassination in 2012 was the fifth case of murder involving Muslim activists in Kenya in that year. For a discussion of possible links with al-shabāb, see Hansen (2013a: 126ff). ᶜAbbūd Rogo's successor, Ibrāhīm Rogo, was assassinated on 3 October 2013. On 3 June 2014, another prominent (and radical) religious scholar, Abubakar Shariff Ahmad 'Makaburi' (b. 1961), who had been based at Mombasa's Mūsa mosque, was assassinated in front of a court house in Mombasa, probably in the context of Kenya's counter-terrorism operations that have turned increasingly nasty in recent years (see <http://www.thedailybeast.com/.../death-squads-in-kenya-s-shadow-war-on-shabaab-sympathizers.html > (last accessed 22 February 2016)).

40. The introduction of the multi-party system in 1992 also led to an increased representation of Muslims in politics: in the coalition government of 2008, 13 out of 44 cabinet positions were filled by Muslims, while there were 33 Muslim members of parliament (out of a total number of 222) (Scharrer 2013: 67). In 1987 7 out of 170 members of parliament were Muslim, and 24 in 1992 (Quinn and Quinn 2003: 114).
41. The IPK operated until recently and signed its statements as statements of the 'unregistered IPK' (Mwakimako 2007b: 51).
42. Naṣṣor al-Nahdī was followed by Ḥammad Muḥammad Kassim (2003–10), a son of Muḥammad b. Qāsim al-Mazrūᶜī. He was replaced in 2011 by Aḥmad Muḥdhar from Malindi, who had previously been Qāḍī of Nairobi. Ḥammad Muḥammad Kassim had been Qāḍī of Lamu since 1992 (see Abdulkadir Hashim 2009: 137).
43. This majlis ᶜulamāᵓ was not identical with the majlis ᶜulamāᵓ (that is, the National Council of Muslim Scholars in Kenya) mentioned above.
44. After Attorney General Amos Wako who was responsible for the revised version of the 2002 draft that was the subject of a referendum in 2005 (Halkano Abdi Wario 2014: 162).

7

REFORM IN CONTEXT V: ZANZIBAR (AND THE COMOROS)

Zanzibar under Colonial Rule and the Revolution of 1964

Like Senegal, Mali, northern Nigeria, Niger, Chad, Sudan, Ethiopia, Somalia, Kenya and Tanganyika, Zanzibar[1] saw the development of several distinct traditions of reform in the nineteenth and twentieth centuries, but in 1964 it experienced a revolution that led to the almost complete collapse of existing Islamic scholarship. As a result, Islamic learning had to restart from scratch in the 1970s, and was characterised by the emergence of a state-controlled elite of Saudi- and Sudan-trained Muslim functionaries, as well as an activist Islamic opposition to the government of the Chama Cha Mapinduzi (CCM) (Party of the Revolution).[2] Due to the importance of the revolution for the reconfiguration of Islamic learning and the development of Islamic reform in Zanzibar, I will discuss the revolution and its impact in some detail.

Zanzibar's history was characterised in the nineteenth century by the expansion of the Sultanate of Zanzibar and its politics of economic and political transformation (see Loimeier 2009). Led by the Bū Saᶜīdī family, the Sultanate of Oman gained control over most coastal settlements in the 1820s and 1830s. In his policy of expansion, Sultan Saᶜīd b. Sulṭān (r. 1806–56) was supported by local allies, such as Lamu, which had managed to defeat a coalition of Mombasa and Pate forces in 1812 (Fuglesang 1994: 47). In 1822, the Omani fleet conquered Brawa and Pate, in 1823 Pemba and in 1824 the rest of the Lamu archipelago. Finally, Mombasa, which had been ruled by the Mazrūʿī family since 1730, was forced to accept Omani overrule in 1837. With her fleet of originally 70–80 warships, the Sultanate was able not only to effectively protect her trading connections in the Indian Ocean but also to exert effective control over the East African coast north of Mozambique. As a consequence, Oman was not forced to occupy the coastal strip and to maintain costly fortresses and bases there: the Sultanate was capable of cutting off the seaborne communication and trade of any coastal settlement at any time (Bennett 1978: 44). Although Zanzibar's development as the paramount political and economical centre on the East African coast had started under Sultan Saʿīd b. Sulṭān, and was reinforced by the shift of Oman's seat of government from Muscat to Zanzibar in 1840, the emergence of Zanzibar as an African trading empire took place only after the division of the Omani empire into two halves: before he died in 1856, Sultan Saʿīd b. Sulṭān split his empire between his sons Mājid and Thwaynī, who now effectively ruled two separate states, the Sultanates of Zanzibar and Oman-Muscat. Zanzibar thus became an 'African' empire ruled by Omani elites (Bennett 1978: 63).

While Zanzibar's economy had been booming since the 1820s, its decline started in the 1870s, when the Sultanate was forced to stop the overseas slave trade under British pressure in 1873 (see Gilbert 2004: 60ff). In 1872 a devastating hurricane destroyed the Zanzibari commercial navy and a great part of the clove production on the island of Unguja and, finally, Zanzibari companies had to fight against the competition of European trading companies in addition to political intervention by the European powers. As a result, the Sultan lost control over Zanzibar's possessions and markets, to the Germans on the Mrima coast, and to the British on the northern coast. Zanzibar suffered a further set-back when Mombasa, after the construction of the Uganda railway, became the new and major harbour in British East Africa in the early twentieth century (Martin 2007 [1978]: 44). Zanzibar did not have a real chance to assert her claims to the mainland after Britain and Germany came to a mutual agreement in 1888 concerning the division of the territories of the Sultanate (Pouwels 1987: 164). When Zanzibar finally became a British Protectorate on 7 November 1890, Zanzibar's last remainders of independence were cut down to size as well. However, British politicians did not seem to have any clear idea as to what kind of rule they wanted to establish in Zanzibar (Flint 1965: 641).

The Foreign Office, responsible for Zanzibar's administration until 1913, initially relied on governing through the existing administrative structures. This was common practice in other British dominions such as India, or, later, northern Nigeria, where 'indirect rule' came to be the administrative norm. However, from the very beginning, the British interfered in internal affairs: on 1 August 1890, Sultan ᶜAlī b. Saᶜīd (r. 1890–3) was forced to sign another anti-slavery decree that prohibited all sales or exchanges of slaves. He closed down the slave markets and granted slaves the right to purchase their freedom. But total abolition of slavery was rejected by the Sultan (Pouwels 1987: 164ff). The arrival of Sir Gerald Portal in 1891 as the first Consul General produced other radical changes in Zanzibar's political set-up, as Portal was committed to the idea of establishing direct control over Zanzibar's internal affairs. To him, 'Arab' administration was 'an embodiment of all the worst and most barbaric characteristics of primitive Arab despotism' (Flint 1965: 642). Only two months after his arrival, Portal undertook what Flint called a 'coup d'état' by seizing control of the Sultan's finances and administration and by appointing Europeans, removable only with British consent, to take control of the treasury, army, police, customs, post office and public works. The Sultan lost control over the public revenue and was eventually granted a 'civil list' fixed at 250,000 rupees per annum for personal expenses and his court (Flint 1965: 643). Although the Sultan and the court were shocked by these measures, and although even Lord Salisbury urged Portal to take caution, the British continued to undermine the Sultan's sovereignty, not only under Portal's administration but also under that of his successor, Rennell Rodd. Rodd also used the opportunity of Sultan ᶜAlī b. Saᶜīd's death in 1893 to intensify the British grip on Zanzibar's administration by enforcing the succession of Ḥamad b. Thwaynī (r. 1893–6) (Flint 1965: 644; Pouwels 1987: 164; Bissell 1999).

As a consequence of these policies, the Sultan started to support the anti-British party at the court and replaced Muḥammad b. Sayf as Muftī of Zanzibar by Hilāl b. ᶜAmūr, who was known for his critical views of the British. In addition, the Sultan started to build a private bodyguard that reached a force of approximately 1,000 men in October 1895. He was forced, however, to disband these troops in December 1895, when the British Consul General Hardinge brought in naval forces (Martin 2007 [1978]: 41). When

Sultan Ḥamad b. Thwaynī died on 25 August 1896, Khālid b. Barghash, who had been pushed aside as successor to the throne by the British in 1893, seized the opportunity to take control over the Palace and proclaimed himself the new Sultan (see Flint 1965: 646; Martin 2007 [1978]: 41). The British naval forces off Zanzibar's coast reacted quickly, and on 27 August 1896, shelled the Sultan's Palace, forcing Khālid b. Barghash to flee into the German consulate, thus ending the 'shortest war on record' according to the Guinness Book of Records (Martin 2007 [1978]: 41–2). The new Sultan selected by the British, Ḥamad b. Muḥammad (r. 1896–1902), was an admirer of European ways of life, and sent his son and successor, Sultan ᶜAlī b. Ḥamūd (r. 1902–11), to Harrow School in Britain. In order to ensure his son's succession he made further concessions to the British: 'From this time forward, the Sultan's sovereignty was to be no more than a legal fiction' (Flint 1965: 646). In 1911, Sultan ᶜAlī b. Ḥamūd was convinced by the Foreign Office to abdicate, and henceforth led a life of luxury in Europe. His successor, Khalīfa b. Ḥārub (1911–60) was an admirer of British rule.

In 1913, Zanzibar was transferred from the auspices of the Foreign Office to the administration of the Colonial Office. A new position of British Resident was created, not subordinate to the administration of British India in Bombay any more, but to the Governor of the British East Africa Protectorate. Due to the Sultan's protests over this administrative reorientation, the Colonial Office created new institutions of Protectorate Government that were designed to stress Zanzibar's formal autonomy. The new Protectorate Government consisted of the Protectorate Council, presided over by the Sultan, and the Resident as vice-president. Other members were the chief secretary, the treasurer, the attorney general and initially two, later three, representatives of the different categories of Zanzibar's population, Arabs, Indians and (later) Africans (Flint 1965: 656). In a further series of administrative reforms after 1925, the Governor of Kenya lost his position as High Commissioner for Zanzibar. Also, the Protectorate Council was abolished and replaced by an Executive Council and a Legislative Council (LegCo), in 1926.

Although colonial Zanzibar has often been portrayed as a peaceful tropical island paradise that was eventually shocked by one of the most violent revolutions of the twentieth century, historical realities were different: in late 1923 and early 1924, skirmishes between Shiḥiri Arabs and Hindus had broken the colonial peace, while another riot between Somalis and Sūri Omanis at Malindi (Zanzibar) was recorded on 15 March 1925. 'Manga'[3] were at the root of another set of disturbances, starting in Pemba in 1928 that were directed against Indian shopkeepers. In 1936, 'Manga riots' took place in Zanzibar Town. Disturbances such as these worried the British colonial administration and showed that Zanzibar's peace was superficial (Sheriff 2001: 310ff). The riots of the 1920s and 1930s were largely motivated by economic matters, however, and mobilisation for politics, beyond the lobbying activities of the different associations, started only in the late 1940s. Political agitation became visible in the form of a strike by the harbour workers from March to June 1946, the establishment of a first labour union, the Labour Association, in October 1946, a shop closure protest on 12 December 1947 and a general strike in 1948 in Zanzibar Town that lasted from 20 August to 11 September (Clayton 1976: 31ff; Sheriff and Ferguson 1991: 203).

The time of politics, 'zama za siasa', started definitively with the foundation of the Zanzibar National Party (ZNP) in 1955, under ᶜAli Muḥsin al-Barwānī. The formation of the ZNP triggered the establishment of a plethora of other parties, twenty-three in total ('Babu' 1991: 224), but only one group – the Afro-Shirazi Union (ASU) that was renamed Afro-Shirazi Party (ASP) in 1959 – acquired political importance (Clayton 1981: 39). The 1950s were ridden by quarrels concerning questions such as who could legitimately claim to be an indigenous Zanzibari. Strategies of exclusion were directed against almost every group in Zanzibar, leading to riots in 1961, and affected the course of the 1964 revolution. Questions of race also influenced the process of politics after 1956/7, as political movements tried to discredit their opponents by calling them foreign. Thus, in 1957 the ZNP tried to discredit Abeid Amani Karume, the ASP leader, by accusing him of not being an authentic Zanzibari and taking him to court on account of this accusation. Karume won the court case, however ('Babu' 1991: 226). The ASP, by contrast, was not known for an anti-colonial stance but rather for its anti-Arab polemics that were directed particularly against 'criminal' Manga and Shiḥiris from Oman and Yemen (Glassman 2000: 407). At the same time, the ASP sought to foster solidarity with the African immigrants from the 'mainland'.

While political mobilisation acquired increasing momentum from the mid-1950s, the question as to when Zanzibar would regain its independence became a paramount issue of political debates in the early 1960s, and eventually led to a split within both political blocks, ZNP and ASP. In political terms, the ZNP, representing the island's elites, supported Zanzibari nationalism and immediate independence. The party was originally backed by Arab landlords and shop owners, but advocated a non-racialist nationalistic programme and thus won support in the Indian community, as well as among Shirazi groups in Pemba. At the same time, the ZNP became known for its polemics against immigrants from the mainland (Glassman 2000: 407). In 1960, an ideological dispute developed in the ZNP, when ZNP youth voiced dissident ideas with respect to the question of Arab privileges in Zanzibar and what should be done about them. A minority group led by ᶜAbd al-Raḥmān Muḥammad 'Babu' even supported the overthrow of the Sultan and the distribution of land to African farmers, while a majority was against such radical policies (Burgess 2005: 218ff). In 1963, this radical group split from the ZNP and established a new party, Umma, led by 'Babu'.

The second major political party, the ASP, was founded at a meeting held on 1 February 1957. Its founders included Abeid Amani Karume, Abdallah Kassim Hanga and Ibrahim Saadalla from the 'African Association', as well as Thabit Kombo, Ameir Tajo 'Mdogo' and Othman Sharif from the Shirazi Association (Mapuri 1996: 20; Clayton 1981: 41). After the first elections in 1957, the ASP and mainlander organisations joined up in Unguja, although not in Pemba, where ASP members, like the ZNP, supported early independence and opposed the increasing influence of 'mainlanders' within the ASP. In Unguja, by contrast, the ASP, supported by a majority of the 'Hadimu fringe'[4] in Unguja and African immigrant populations (Bakari 2001: 60), rejected immediate independence under the slogan '*Uhuru zuia*' (stop independence), arguing that the country was not yet prepared: should Zanzibar become independent too early, 'the Arabs would take over and reinstitute slavery' ('Babu' 1991: 231). Due to its anti-Arab polemics, the ASP appeared to be even more racialist than the ZNP (Bakari 2001: 60). However, the decision of the ASP to reject immediate independence brought about an internal split: in October 1959, Ameir Tajo, who led the Shirazi Association Unguja, was excluded from the ASP on account of allegations of financial mismanagement (Bakari 2001: 57). In December 1959, together with Muhammad

Shamte and a number of other political activists from Pemba, he founded a new party, the Zanzibar and Pemba People's Party (ZPPP). The ZPPP soon entered into an alliance with the ZNP, strengthening its national orientation ('Babu' 1991: 232).

With the formation of parties, the political process acquired additional steam. In 1956, the Legislative Council had been expanded to twenty-five members (twelve unofficial) and in 1957 six of the twelve unofficial members were elected in Zanzibar's first elections (Lodhi 1986: 412). These elections were not based on the criteria of racial and communal affiliation that had defined membership in the LegCo so far, but were universal elections, although only men older than twenty-five with an annual minimum income of £75 were entitled to vote. In January 1961, another round of elections was held, and as the voting age had been lowered to twenty-one years, 94,310 people were now entitled to vote. The ASP scored an absolute majority of votes, but due to the British majority voting system it only got ten seats (eight in Unguja and two in Pemba). The ZNP, by contrast, won nine seats, while the ZPPP won three seats in Pemba, but split into two factions after the elections (Mapuri 1996: 32). Thus, each political block now held eleven seats in the Parliament. Due to the stalemate in the January 1961 elections, a new round of elections was held in early June 1961. The failure of the ASP to win a decisive majority of seats in the January 1961 elections and the resulting frustration eventually triggered fighting between ZNP and ASP supporters in Zanzibar's streets on 1 June 1961. The riots started in Zanzibar Town, where seventeen people were killed, and then spread to the rural areas, where 'Manga' were the major victims. A figure of 64 of the 68 dead and many of the 381 injured were Arabs (Ayani 1977 [1970]: 86; Glassman 2011). These riots possibly showed radical ASP (and ZNP Youth League) members that it would be possible to overthrow a ZNP government after independence when British troops would no longer protect the regime of the Sultan (Bowles 1991: 104).

In July 1963, fresh elections brought another victory for the ZNP-ZPPP coalition: the ZNP won twelve seats (six in Zanzibar and six in Pemba), the ZPPP six seats (all Pemba), while the ASP gained thirteen seats (eleven in Zanzibar and two in Pemba). The ZNP and the ZPPP again formed a coalition government that led Zanzibar to self-government on 24 June 1963,

Muhammad Shamte being the first Prime Minister. The LegCo became the first National Assembly, and on 10 December 1963, Zanzibar regained her independence as a Sultanate (Martin 1978: 57). However, the Sultanate had undergone a serious crisis after the demise of Sultan Khalīfa b. Ḥārub, who had been in office for almost 50 years, and the death of his son and successor, Sultan ᶜAbdallāh b. Khalīfa, in 1963, for the throne had passed to Sultan Jamshīd b. ᶜAbdallāh, who was not only very young but also highly unpopular and regarded as a 'playboy'. Pre-independence and pre-revolutionary Zanzibar was thus characterised by disputes and deep divisions between the supporters of two major political blocks represented by the ZNP and the ASP.

The first government of independent Zanzibar was seen by both the ASP and British observers as a government that represented the interests of the 'Arab' establishment (PRO DO 185/68). Even though this assessment was misleading, it nevertheless expressed the political realities after independence, which meant the exclusion from power of a large group of 'mainland' Africans, as well as the majority of the Hadimu fringe. After independence, tensions continued, and even increased when the new government started to implement a number of decisions that confirmed African anxieties. Thus, all men of mainland origin were dismissed from the police force with the argument that the government was no longer able to finance their salaries due to a crisis in clove exports and consequent budgetary problems. At the same time, the government was neither able nor willing to finance their repatriation. As a consequence, disgruntled ex-policemen, organised by John Okello, were increasingly prepared to revolt against the government (Clayton 1981: 53).

The revolution as such took place in the morning of 12 January 1964, one month after independence, and was led by John Okello and his followers in the police force, supported by disgruntled youths from the Ng'ambo areas. The revolutionaries did not encounter much resistance and had occupied all major strategic positions by noon (see Clayton 1981; Petterson 2002; Mrina and Mattoke 1980; Wimmelbücker 2001; Loimeier 2006e). On the same day, Okello proclaimed himself minister of defence, while Abeid Amani Karume was declared president. Kassim Hanga, who, together with Seif Bakari, had organised the ASP Youth League, was nominated vice-president and 'Babu' was nominated minister of external affairs, although all three, Karume,

'Babu' and Hanga, were in Dar es Salaam, and came back to Zanzibar only on the next day. The former ruling parties, ZNP and ZPPP, were proscribed and replaced by a Committee of 14 (Clayton 1981: 79). The revolution assumed a more organised character with the gradual take-over of power on 14 January and the following days by ASPYL and Umma cadres. From 16 January they formed the Revolutionary Council (RC), in which only Okello and Mfarinyaki represented the group of original revolutionaries. Anarchic killings went on for some time in the rural areas, however, and other acts of 'revolutionary violence' and abuse of power were still rampant. At the same time, control over the revolution passed into Zanzibari hands. In Raha Leo, the new revolutionary centre of Zanzibar, Karume, 'Babu', Hanga and the other revolutionaries formed a revolutionary leadership that on 24 January proclaimed the first revolutionary government of Zanzibar. By 24 January, it was clear that Okello and his group had lost their influence over the government and the RC. Okello was deported to mainland Tanganyika on 20 February 1964 (Clayton 1981: 93).

In the RC, led by Abeid Amani Karume, the radical group under the leadership of 'Babu' now became increasingly influential. Zanzibar was renamed the 'People's Republic of Zanzibar and Pemba' and a policy of nationalisation started that was to change the social set-up of Zanzibar considerably. After Okello had been excluded from power, competition for control of the revolution continued, concentrated on a struggle between the 'moderates', the 'radicals' and the 'Karume group'. On 26 April, the internal struggle for power more or less came to an end, when Karume agreed to form a union with Tanganyika. In the context of the formation of a union government with Tanganyika, Karume was able to marginalise the major remaining threat to his power, as many radical members of his government such as Hanga, 'Babu' and Moyo were nominated to fill union government posts in Dar es Salaam. As a consequence, Zanzibar's development became increasingly dominated by Karume and his supporters (Clayton 1981: 114ff).

The revolution of 12 January 1964 put an end to more than 130 years of Omani rule in Zanzibar, and the new revolutionary regime that had come to power changed Zanzibar's social structure, political set-up and economic development in fundamental ways. Under the slogan 'Mapinduzi daima' (revolution forever) the revolutionaries became a new elite united by a strong sense of power. Karume's rule may be characterised as a constant effort to marginalise possible competitors and to monopolise access to power. The consolidation of the revolution was expressed in a series of decisions by the new government, as well as by the implementation of socialist programmes, such as land distribution, housing, state management of import and export trade, state marketing of the clove harvest and mass education (Burgess 1999: 40). In cultural terms, English was replaced by Kiswahili as the national language on 20 January 1964. On 5 March 1964, rickshaws were prohibited as a symbol of 'feudal exploitation'. On 7 July 1964, the government took over control of all schools. Zanzibar's symbolic centre of power shifted from Stone Town and the sea front to Ng'ambo, in particular to Raha Leo, where Radio Zanzibar, the new People's Court and a recreation park were created. Shops that had printed books and newspapers in Arabic were closed and periodicals such as *al-Falaq* and *The ᶜAdal Inṣāf* were stopped. The judicial system was changed as well: in 1966, *qāḍī* courts were abolished by the Courts Decree, as were the *mudīr* courts. The prerogatives of the courts were newly defined, although *qāḍīs* retained jurisdiction in civil matters with only minor changes (Hanak 1994: 70; Abdulkadir Hashim 2005: 37). On 1 January 1970, Revolutionary Courts replaced the legal system that had existed since colonial times (Martin 1978: 64). Yet, in 1985, the Kadhis' Courts Act re-established *qāḍī* courts, although jurisdiction remained confined to personal status, until the Written Laws Act of 2003 again expanded the *qāḍīs'* jurisdiction to all aspects of civil law (Abdulkadir Hashim 2005: 37–8).

As a result of the revolution and its aftermath, Zanzibar's demographic structure changed decisively, due not so much to the fact that thousands of Zanzibaris were killed in the first days and weeks of the revolution,[5] as to the fact that many who were branded as 'non-Zanzibaris' were either deported or forced to emigrate, or fled the islands as refugees in the years to come (Bakari 2001: 79). Harassment and arbitrary imprisonment of Arab, Comorian and Indian citizens continued into the 1970s (Clayton 1981: 124). After 1964, the emerging one-party state extended its powers of intervention in the lives of citizens by developing institutions such as an army, a security apparatus and a youth league with sub-organisations such as the Young Pioneers and the Green Guards. Citizenship in Zanzibar became synonymous with revolutionary notions of discipline, sacrifice, vigilance and volunteerism, while notions of leisure and consumption were condemned (Burgess 2002b: 290). The revolution consequently touched upon all kinds of popular culture, and Karume tended to meddle with details of everyday life. He banned make-up, shorts, mini-skirts, long hair, tight-fitting clothes and wigs, and prescribed instead school uniforms (Martin 2007 [1978]: 67). Taarab music was prohibited and taarab clubs were closed, accused of being 'Arab'. All public and private meetings had to be registered and approved by the Ministry of Interior. This applied not only to religious activities such as *dhikr* and *mawlid* meetings or the celebration of the Mwaka Kogwa (New Year) festival in Makunduchi, but also to marriage ceremonies and *ngomas*. In 1972, Karume was about to start a campaign against moral decay, and especially alcoholism, when he was killed in an aborted coup on 7 April 1972.

While colonial times, at least until 1954, were characterised in Zanzibar by harmonious cooperation between the British administration and the local elites in many fields such as education, legislation or 'popular culture' (see Loimeier 2006a), the *zama za siasa* after 1954 and the revolution of 1964, in particular, brought about a total change in the relationship between rulers and *ᶜulamāʾ*. The *ᶜulamāʾ* were seen by the revolutionaries as being part of a political and religious establishment that had to be crushed. At the same time, the new socialist government of Abeid Amani Karume that came to power in 1964 continued to follow established approaches towards 'popular culture' and a number of religious practices in a policy that acquired a rather moralistic undertone. The major difference between colonial times and present-day Zanzibar was that the British administration had cooperated closely with the local elite as well as the scholarly establishment, when fighting, for instance, popular religious practices such as *zikri ya dufu*, while Zanzibar's revolutionary government after 1964 more or less rejected such cooperation. Karume's campaigns against popular culture and 'religious superstition' were thus enforced without the support of the scholarly establishment, which was seen by Karume as a lingering threat to his position of power. Karume once even remarked with respect to the influence of the ᶜAlawī families: 'When I hold a speech and they address the public as well, whom do you think will people follow?' He thus admitted the popularity of the ᶜAlawī scholars (communication Ahmad Maulid, 17 August 2002).

The 1964 revolution meant a real break in Zanzibar's development and

Karume initiated an anti-religious policy that was influenced by the 'comrades', the left wing of the revolution, led by the Umma party. Ali Sultan Issa, the minister of education (MoE) from December 1964 to 1968, was an Umma member and a close associate of 'Babu'. As minister of education, he was responsible for a series of anti-religious policies. Under his administration, numerous teachers and administrators were sacked and many of them subsequently left the country. Equally, religious teaching at government schools was abolished in 1965 and the Muslim Academy closed, while government Qur᾽ānic school teachers were sacked on 1 April 1967.[6] The teaching of Islamic studies (such as religion and Qur᾽ān) was stopped with the argument that the government 'was not responsible for the religion of the population' (Ziddy 2001: 61). In the context of a visit to Egypt together with Nyerere in 1967, Karume also stopped the grants for all students who had been sent to Egypt for studies and training since 1958 (Ziddy 2001: 61). Ali Sultan Issa, in particular, is said to have humiliated scholars and forced religious scholars such as ᶜAbdallāh Ṣāliḥ al-Farsy or Sayyid ᶜUmar ᶜAbdallāh into exile. In their place, the Karume administration appointed local scholars who were willing to condone revolutionary policies. In mosques, schools and law courts, religious scholars were replaced by religious functionaries nominated by the revolutionary government, but often not accepted by the population. The new scholars, often rural qur᾽ānic school teachers, did not have the reputation of scholars such as ᶜUmar b. Sumayṭ. Thus, Muhammad Latif, a Qādirī scholar, said, as quoted by Purpura: 'Zanzibar lost the last of the great men of Islamic learning, the men who should have become the mentors of today' (Purpura 1997: 136). Even ᶜAbdallāh Ṣāliḥ al-Farsy, who had sympathised with the revolution insofar as the revolution had put an end to 'inequality', finally fled and some of those who stayed 'mysteriously died before their time', such as Sulaymān al-ᶜAlawī (d. 1970), Aḥmad Ḥāmid Manṣab (d. 1977) and Juma Abd al-Wadud (d. 1978/9) (Purpura 1997: 136). Karume's and Ali Sultan Issa's policies in respect of Islamic education thus amounted to policies of self-mutilation, imposed to enforce not only a consistent policy of Zanzibarisation, but also to bring about a complete shift in education, in which religion was replaced by a new discipline called *siasa* (politics). However, Ali Sultan Issa's radical and often arbitrary measures came to an end in 1968, when he was replaced as MoE by Hassan Nassor

Moyo (in office until 1977). In his time, Islamic education in government schools was restarted.

Subsequent to the consolidation of the revolution, Abeid Amani Karume and his successors (Jumbe 1972–84, Mwinyi 1984/5, Abdul Wakil 1985–90, Amour 1990–2000 and Amani Abeid Karume 2000–10) were able to use their power in order to eternalise their own interpretation of history in schools, in the public representation of the revolution and in the cult of the revolution.[7] This was made easier by the fact that a large majority of Zanzibar's religious scholars were forced into exile from 1964 to 1968 or emigrated voluntarily. In the aftermath of the revolution, established traditions of Islamic learning thus collapsed almost completely. This collapse produced an intellectual vacuum. The revolutionary regime eventually based its efforts to rebuild Islamic education on a number of expatriate Muslim teachers from Egypt and Sudan, as well as some Zanzibari graduates from Islamic universities in Egypt, Sudan and Saudi Arabia who became loyalist functionaries of the regime after their return from Khartoum or Medina. All of these groups, that is, qur°ānic school teachers, Muslim expatriates and graduates from Medina and Khartoum, profited from the collapse of the old order and consequently supported the regime in its efforts to build a new system of Islamic education that was no longer defined by the religious scholars themselves but by the plans of a socialist and secular government apparatus. In addition, the new teachers and Muslim functionaries supported CCM government efforts to build and sustain an Islamic façade that could be presented to Arab donors, if need arose.

The Qādiriyya and the ᶜAlawiyya

With regard to the analysis of Sufi-oriented movements of reform in Zanzibar, the major focus of interest to date has been the scholars of the ᶜAlawiyya. This is possibly due to the fact that the texts of ᶜAlawī scholars have been more accessible, but also to the fact that the scholars of the ᶜAlawiyya, despite being a small intellectual elite, have been important for the development of reforms in the sphere of Islamic education. By contrast, the scholars of the Qādiriyya have so far attracted little attention, possibly due to the fact that these scholars have been more active in the sphere of ritual than in education.

The historical development of the Sultanate of Zanzibar in the nineteenth century, as well as the processes of social and economic change, were marked in general terms by large-scale movements of migration from the East African interior to the coast, and the development of a plantation economy based on slave labour. The migrants from the hinterland were not only looking for work but also sought personal freedom from 'hinterland' customs and obligations. However, on the coast and on the islands, migrants from the interior, like the slaves on the plantations, were refused integration into local '*Shirazi*' society, since local elites were hesitant to accept these *Washenzi* (barbarians) as members of their communities. The migrants consequently started to create their own 'Swahili' (coastal) Muslim associations, organisations, dancing clubs, mosques and unions. For the time being, *Shirazi* elites continued to control institutions such as mosques, Qurʾānic schools and religious foundations. Yet, in the second half of the nineteenth century, these elites experienced increasing pressure in the social and religious spheres when scholars from Hadramawt, Brawa and the Comoros started to question their position in mosques and schools (see Glassman 1995; Bang 2003).

The new religious scholars from Hadramawt and the Benadir coast started to compete with local scholars for influence and social positions, and cultivated support among other marginalised groups, in particular migrants from the interior, since they suffered from similar strategies of exclusion (Glassman 1995: 138). Zanzibar was a comparatively new centre of Islamic learning, which only emerged in the 1860s. Reform-oriented scholars linked with the ʿAlawiyya and the Qādiriyya had no difficulty settling down in Zanzibar from the mid-nineteenth century, as no scholarly establishment blocked their activities (Freitag 1999: 178; Pouwels 1987: 76; Bang 2003: 93). Sufi-oriented reformers introduced rituals that had hitherto been unknown on the East African coast or that had been confined to exclusivist circles: the *dhikr*, the *mawlid* (swa. maulidi) of the Prophet, the *ziyāra* to the tombs of saints. By the mid-1880s, some Qādirī versions of the *dhikr* such as the *zikri ya dufu*, a *dhikr* implying the use of *dufu* drums, and the *zikri ya kukohoa*, a *dhikr* implying rhythmic inhaling and exhaling, had become a popular form of worship on the coast, especially among slaves. And although many Shirazi patricians at first rejected the new rituals, they sooner or later ceased their opposition and started to support them in order to maintain their influence over the 'plebeians' (Glassman 1995: 140-2). The adoption of these rituals by converts acquired such momentum that even some of the new Qādirī scholars started to criticise them: they were not willing to accept all forms of localisation of Islamic rituals. On the basis of the new rituals, new concepts of religion and community were propagated. These were no longer characterised by competition (*mashindano*) and exclusion, but by integration and communal ritual, such as the *dhikr* of the Qādiriyya. Thus, Sufi scholars became focal points of social reorganisation and challenged existing social and religious institutions that had been characterised by their exclusivity (Bang 2003: 131).

The development of the Qādiriyya in nineteenth- and twentieth-century Zanzibar was marked by the emergence of three major branches of this *ṭarīqa*, established and led by a number of leading scholars, all from Brawa, namely, Ḥusayn b. ᶜAbdallāh al-Mūᶜīnī (Mwinyi), who came to Zanzibar in about 1875, then ᶜAbd al-ᶜAzīz b. ᶜAbd al-Ghānī al-Amawī and finally Uways b. Muḥammad al-Bārawī (see Loimeier 2009). Among them, one scholar acquired particular importance, namely Uways b. Muḥammad al-Bārawī (1847–1909).[8] After having studied the Qurᵓān and *tafsīr*, he followed the advice of his teachers, Muḥammad Taynī al-Shāshī and Muḥammad Jenay al-Baḥlūl, who also introduced him to some Sufi teachings, and went to Baghdad where he was initiated into the Qādiriyya by his teacher Muṣṭafā b. al-Sayyid Salmān al-Jīlānī. In 1873, he went on pilgrimage and after several more years of studies he returned in 1880 via the Ḥijāz, Yemen and the Benadir coastal towns, arriving in Brawa in 1883. During this journey, he visited the tomb of ᶜAbd al-Raḥmān b. Aḥmad al-Zaylaᶜī (Lewis 2001: 230; Reese 2008: 111–12), a Qādirī scholar and saint in Qulunqul in the Ogaden region, who had died in 1882. After his visit to the saint's tomb, he claimed to have received a 'symbolic' *ijāza* from this highly venerated Sufi scholar (Samatar 1992: 52). Due to his scholarship and his direct connections with the centre of the Qādiriyya in Baghdad, he claimed after his return home to be entitled to a leading role in the local scholarly establishment. This claim was rejected in Brawa (see Martin 1976: 161–2; Samatar 1992: 53), but found some support in Zanzibar and on the Mrima coast opposite Zanzibar. From 1883 to 1900, he undertook numerous journeys, among others to Zanzibar, possibly following an invitation by Sultan Barghash. He entertained excellent relations with a number of Sultans of Zanzibar, in particular Barghash,

Khalīfa b. Saᶜīd and ᶜAbd al-Ḥamīd b. Thwaynī b. Saᶜīd. He also founded a new branch of the Qādiriyya in Zanzibar that propagated a new form of the *dhikr*, the *zikri ya kukohoa* (Bang 2003: 94). This new form of the *dhikr* was soon attacked as a *bidᶜa* by other Qādirīs, in particular ᶜAbd al-ᶜAzīz b. ᶜAbd al-Ghānī al-Amawī (1838–96) (for his biography, see Hoffman 2006; Bang 2003: 94).

ᶜAbd al-ᶜAzīz b. ᶜAbd al-Ghānī al-Amawī was born in Brawa where his family occupied the position of *khaṭīb* and performed other legal services such as marriages. Even before he came to Zanzibar as a young man, al-Amawī underwent extensive studies under scholars such as Abū Bakr al-Miḥḍār, who was also the teacher of ᶜAbd al-Raḥmān b. Aḥmad al-Zaylaᶜī. In addition, he studied under ᶜAlī b. ᶜAbd al-Raḥmān, as well as one Aḥmad al-Maghribī who introduced him to Sufism (O'Fahey forthcoming: 15). In 1849, he left Brawa and settled in Mombasa, but in 1854, at the age of sixteen, he was appointed *qāḍī* of Kilwa by Sultan Saᶜīd b. Sulṭān. In 1860, he went to Zanzibar, where he studied under Muḥyī al-Dīn al-Qaḥṭānī (*c.* 1790–1869), a respected scholar of the Qādiriyya (Bang 2003: 94). He served as *qāḍī* to Sultan Barghash and was followed in this position by his son Burhān b. ᶜAbd al-Ghānī al-Amawī, who acted as *qāḍī* in Zanzibar from 1891 to 1932. Together with his teacher Muḥyī al-Dīn al-Qaḥṭānī from Brawa, who had been the first major representative of the Qādiriyya in Zanzibar and who had come to Zanzibar in 1859, he published a treatise in defence of Sufism, in particular with regard to the use of musical instruments such as '*dufu*' drums in the *dhikr* (O'Fahey forthcoming). Like al-Bārawī, ᶜAbd al-ᶜAzīz b. ᶜAbd al-Ghānī al-Amawī established a new branch of the Qādiriyya, the Nūraniyya, in Zanzibar. His popularity, and the popularity of the ritual practices of the Nūraniyya, that were based on the *zikri ya dufu*, were later described as being of a 'highly visible nature' (Pouwels 1987: 196–7).

Most local scholars, as well as some scholars of the Qādiriyya in Zanzibar, criticised the new practices of the *dhikr* introduced by Uways b. Muḥammad al-Bārawī, while others continued to support the new *dhikr* although the new practices had a markedly ecstatic character. ᶜAbd al-ᶜAzīz b. ᶜAbd al-Ghanī al-Amawī probably felt threatened in his own position as a paramount scholar of the Qādiriyya by the rapid spread of this new *zikri* movement led by Uways b. Muḥammad al-Bārawī, his 'Brawan foe' (communication ᶜAbd al-Wahhāb ᶜAlawī ᶜAbd al-Wahhāb Jamal al-Layl, 21 February 2003). The growing strength of the Uways branch of the Qādiriyya, which propagated this new *dhikr*, was seemingly linked to a corresponding growth of al-Bārawī's influence at the court of the Sultans of Zanzibar, and al-Bārawī was consequently able to eclipse, or at least balance, the influence of the Amawī branch, which had previously been favoured by the Sultans (Pouwels 1987: 143). In order to fight the growing influence of the Uways branch, ᶜAbd al-ᶜAzīz b. ᶜAbd al-Ghanī al-Amawī thus turned against it and against new practices of the *dhikr*. Al-Amawī particularly criticised the rhythmic movement of bodies and new techniques of breathing in this new form of the *dhikr* that he described as 'coughing' (*kukohoa*). In a polemical poem, al-Amawī claimed that the *zikri ya kukohoa* resembled African spirit possession cults such as Ngoma, Lelemama or Pepo, and he posed the polemical question as to where this 'worship through coughing' had been invented ('wapi ilikozuliwa ibada ya kukohowa'; see al-Farsy 1972: 14–5 for the whole poem).

Yet, although ᶜAbd al-ᶜAzīz b. ᶜAbd al-Ghanī al-Amawī attacked the *zikri ya kukohoa* as a *bidᶜa* and as a form of mixing 'African' customs with Islam, in the 1860s, as we have seen above, he had himself introduced another form of the *dhikr*, the *zikri ya dufu*, that had also been attacked by the established scholars of that time as an un-Islamic innovation. In the 1890s the Amawī branch of the Qādiriyya criticised the *zikri ya kukohoa* of Uways b. Muḥammad al-Bārawī as an un-Islamic innovation, yet the *zikri ya kukohoa* was nothing new to al-Bārawī, who had witnessed this form of the *dhikr* when he was studying in Baghdad, where it was part of an old Qādirī tradition. Thus, whereas the Amawī branch saw the *zikri ya kukohoa* in the context of their competition with other scholars of the Qādiriyya, accusing them of turning the *dhikr* into an 'African' form of ritual, this *dhikr* was perceived by scholars of the Uways branch as absolutely normal, and even a more authentic Qādirī, since it was practised in the very centre of the Qādiriyya, in Baghdad.

The attacks on the *zikri ya kukohoa* as an un-Islamic innovation can thus be seen as a function of local religious disputes that activated well-known strategies of legitimisation and delegitimisation. The critique of specific Sufi teachings and rituals has often been connected with dialectics of competition among religious scholars over questions of authority in local contexts of dispute, even if the discursive elements that are activated for the legitimisation of specific religious positions are quoted from greater, translocal discursive traditions or frames of reference. These traditions and respective strategies of argumentation have a residual character and can be activated in comparable constellations of dispute at any time, should the need arise. In the 1940s, ᶜAbdallāh Ṣāliḥ al-Farsy thus used al-Amawī's polemics against the *zikri ya kukohoa* of Uways b. Muḥammad al-Bārawī in his own struggle against the *zikri ya kukohoa* practices of Maḥmūd b. Kombo from Makunduchi, Zanzibar (d. 1968), who was linked through ᶜUmar Qullatayn with the Uways branch of the Qādiriyya, by quoting the poem al-Amawī had composed to attack the *zikri ya kukohoa* of Uways b. Muḥammad al-Bārawī in the 1890s. ᶜAbdallāh Ṣāliḥ al-Farsy was thus able to point out in a very scholarly and clever way to the Qādiris of his time (the 1940s) that even well-known and respected Qādirī scholars of those days (the 1890s), such as ᶜAbd al-ᶜAzīz b. ᶜAbd al-Ghanī al-Amawī, had criticised these rituals (al-Farsy 1972: 14–15).

In his polemic against the *zikri ya kukohoa*, ᶜAbdallāh Ṣāliḥ al-Farsy never mentioned, however, that al-Amawī had written the above-mentioned treatise in defence of the *zikri ya dufu*, although this practice could be attacked as a *bidᶜa* just as easily as the practice of the *zikri ya kukohoa*. Although ᶜAbdallāh Ṣāliḥ al-Farsy's reference to al-Amawī's poem was thus taken out of its original temporal context, it was set within a similar context of confrontation, and in each case of conflict, legitimatory links were cultivated: to Baghdad, in the case of Uways b. Muḥammad al-Bārawī's against al-Amawī in the 1890s; to an earlier tradition of Islamic learning that was represented as being more authentic Qādirī than contemporary practices, in the case of ᶜAbdallāh Ṣāliḥ al-Farsy against Maḥmūd b. Kombo, in the 1940s. The dispute between al-Amawī and al-Bārawī thus had not only a trans-local dimension beyond Uways b. Muḥammad al-Bārawī's legitimising reference to Baghdad, namely that of a dispute within the same tradition of reform, the Qādiriyya, in the same period of time, namely, the 1890s, but also a trans-traditional notion in a historical perspective when their dispute was quoted, in the 1940s, by ᶜAbdallāh Ṣāliḥ al-Farsy in the context of his own struggle against Maḥmūd b. Kombo. The *zikri* dispute between the two sheikhs of the Qādiriyya, ᶜAbd al-ᶜAzīz b. ᶜAbd al-Ghanī al-Amawī and Uways b. Muḥammad al-Bārawī (and later, ᶜAbdallāh Ṣāliḥ al-Farsy) thus points to the importance of trans-tradition(al), trans-historical, trans-generational and trans-local legitimising references.

The students and followers of Uways b. Muḥammad al-Bārawī were able to maintain their social position in East Africa after his death and to become part of the local establishment of scholars. Patterns of legitimisation and delegitimisation thus seem to persist as tenaciously as alleged 'un-Islamic innovations': strategies of legitimisation often imply a legitimatory reference to a major centre of Islamic learning, preferably outside Africa, while strategies of delegitimisation often tend to denounce specific religious practices as African survivals. These disputes also show, however, that the presentation of a specific ritual as orthodox or unorthodox, Islamic or un-Islamic, African or Arab, in the respective texts and discourses of a specific era may not only be deceptive with regard to legitimatory considerations, but should also be seen as being rooted in contexts of dispute and the negotiation of claims to leadership and hegemony of interpretation ('Deutungshegemonie'). As a consequence, the interpretation of the issues at stake, as well as the legitimatory references, may change at any time, if the context changes.

Scholarly disputes did not impede the development of the Qādiriyya as a major Sufi order in East Africa or Zanzibar. Under the leadership of the three founding fathers mentioned above, the Qādiriyya in Zanzibar developed into a number of different, yet interrelated, branches in the twentieth century. This fragmentation into several branches and numerous family networks came to mean that the Qādiriyya never constituted a homogeneous religio-political movement in Zanzibar. Rather, different branches and family networks, even single scholars, were prepared to cooperate with different political forces, or to abstain from politics, as has been shown in the life and legacy of Ḥasan b. ᶜAmeir. The fragmentation of the Qādiriyya also meant, however, that it was not seen as a political threat by Abeid Amani Karume and the revolutionary government in Zanzibar. As a consequence, it suffered much less in the revolution than, for instance, the ᶜAlawiyya, which was perceived by Karume as a corporate group with a corporate identity.

From the 1860s, scholars affiliated with the ᶜAlawiyya, a religious group that recruited its followers among families of sharīfian descent in the Hadramawt region of southern Arabia, came to represent a second Sufi-oriented tradition of reform on the East African coast. As a result of its historical importance, the ᶜAlawiyya has been studied and documented extensively, for instance in ᶜAbdallāh Ṣāliḥ al-Farsy's biographical account of East African scholars and in the work of Bang, Hoffman, Martin, Pouwels and Reese. Despite its *ṭarīqa*-like appearance, the ᶜAlawiyya can be seen as a union of scholars of Hadrami origin, united by their ancestry as *sayyids*, descendants of the Prophet or, even better, as a 'family order' (Freitag 2003: 91). The ᶜAlawī families in Hadramawt, Zanzibar, Lamu, Mombasa and the Comoros indeed formed family networks that were in constant contact. These families influenced Islamic scholarship in Zanzibar from the late nineteenth century to 1964 and formed a large network of relationships. During this period, almost every learned Zanzibari studied in a *madrasa* with a scholar from these families. Their influence was so pervasive that the Kenyan religious scholar, ᶜAbdilāhi Nāṣir, compared the ᶜAlawī tradition of education with the British college system and added that students educated within the ᶜAlawī tradition of Islamic learning wore the 'same college tie' ('college tie moja') (quoted in Kresse 2007b: 239).

ᶜAlawī families also cultivated a number of rituals that linked them epistemically to Sufi orders, such as the recitation of a *rātib*, a litany of prayers, in particular, the *rātib* al-Ḥaddād (Bang 2014: 148ff), or the celebration of the *mawlid al-nabī*, but the genealogical link to the Prophet was more important than Sufi teachings, even if many ᶜAlawī shaykhs claimed, like the Shādhiliyya, a spiritual link to the Maghribinian Sufi saint Shuᶜayb Abū Madyan. However, the most important ᶜAlawī communal ritual was the veneration of the Prophet, as emphasised in the celebration of the *mawlid* (Bang 2003: 18ff, 148ff). A major difference between ᶜAlawī traditions of learning and earlier traditions was that ᶜAlawī scholars opened up education, broadened the spectrum of the canon of texts, started to translate texts into Kiswahili and stressed disciplines such as *fiqh* that had been less prominent on the East African coast before the 1860s. ᶜAlawiyya scholars also adopted a critical position towards the religious establishment on the East African coast, as well as towards the Qādiriyya. The efforts of ᶜAlawī scholars in the sphere of education led to the foundation of new schools. By abandoning exclusivist forms of Islamic education, the scholars of the ᶜAlawiyya thus went one step further than the scholars of the Qādiriyya who, with their communal *dhikr*, had contributed to the opening of Islamic ritual to all Muslims. As a result of the endeavours of ᶜAlawī scholars to open up education and to develop new schools, Zanzibar's major Arabic language newspaper, *al-Falaq*, eventually came to call Zanzibar 'the *qibla*' (point of orientation) for education in East Africa (*al-Falaq*, 20 May 1939).

Due to the absence of established traditions of learning in Zanzibar, ᶜAlawī scholars found it easy to start new schools. They introduced new concepts of Islamic learning that were directly linked with the prestigious centres of scholarship in the Hadramawt and Hijaz and were thus independent of local traditions of learning in other parts of the East African coast (Pouwels 1987: 139). And even though scholarship remained elitist in some families, at least until the early twentieth century, ᶜAlawī scholars started to translate texts into Kiswahili and entered into intense competition among themselves as well as with the scholars of the Qādiriyya who had opened the ritual to *wageni* (foreigners) and *watumwa* (slaves). ᶜAlawī scholars introduced many texts unknown so far in East Africa and expanded the canon of Islamic learning. In addition to the study of the Qur'ān, which, like *ᶜilm al-falak*, was already established on the East African coast, they introduced new texts in *fiqh* and its branches, as well as *ᶜaqīda*, *tawḥīd*, *ḥadīth*, *naḥw* and *taṣawwuf* (Pouwels 1987: 149).

The two most important representatives of the first generation of the ᶜAlawiyya reform movement in Zanzibar were ᶜAbdallāh Bā Kathīr (see Bang 2003: 97ff) and Aḥmad b. Sumayṭ (al-Farsy 1972: 53ff; Bang 2003). Aḥmad b. Sumayṭ (1861–1925) was born in Itsandraa on the island of Ngazidja in the Comoros. He studied under his father and other local scholars in Itsandraa. After completing his basic religious education, he became, like his father, a trader and captain of a dhow. He visited the Hadramawt in 1880/1 for the first time, continued his religious education and was initiated into the teachings of the ᶜAlawiyya (Bang 2003: 64ff). In 1883, after his return from Hadramawt to East Africa, Aḥmad b. Sumayṭ was appointed by Sultan Barghash of Zanzibar, despite his youthful age, to the office of a *qāḍī* (al-Farsy 1972: 53–4). Seemingly, Aḥmad b. Sumayṭ did not feel quite at ease as a *qāḍī*. As he did not dare to publicly break with the Sultan, he abandoned his position in 1886 and returned to Itsandraa (al-Farsy 1972: 58; Bang 2003: 77). From Itsandraa he undertook a journey to Istanbul in 1886, where he was received by the Ottoman Sultan, ᶜAbd al-Ḥamīd, and was put under the tutelage of Faḍl b. ᶜAlawī b. Sahl alias 'Faḍl Pasha' (1824–1900), an adviser of the Ottoman Sultan from Hadramawt. Faḍl Pasha was instrumental in shaping the Sultan's pan-Islam policy in a way similar to that of Jamāl al-Dīn al-Afghānī, who was staying in Istanbul at the same time. Faḍl Pasha had been instrumental in supporting pro-Ottoman movements in India and the Yemen. Aḥmad b. Sumayṭ, however, left Istanbul again in late 1886 or early 1887 and went to Cairo where he taught at al-Azhar without meeting Muḥammad ᶜAbduh, although he later started to correspond with him. From Cairo, Aḥmad b. Sumayṭ continued his journey to Mecca and Medina and then to India and Java, where he visited a number of Hadrami diaspora communities before finally returning to Itsandraa. After the death of Sultan Barghash, who had him declared a 'persona non grata' after his unauthorised departure from Zanzibar in 1885 (Bang 2003: 77), he returned to Zanzibar in 1888 and was again appointed *qāḍī* by the new Sultan, Sayyid Khalīfa (al-Farsy 1972: 58). In the early twentieth century, he became involved, however, in a major dispute-cum-power-struggle in Zanzibar.

This dispute was triggered by an attack on the Qādiriyya, formulated in a *fatwā* against the *dhikr* of the Qādiriyya and practices connected with it such as dancing societies (ngoma) (Bang 2003: 123). In 1903/4, Burhān b. ᶜAbd al-ᶜAzīz al-Amawī (d. 1935), the Chief Qāḍī of Zanzibar at that time (who retired only in 1932), a leading scholar of the Qādiriyya and one of the advisers of Sultan ᶜAlī b. Ḥamūd (r. 1902–11), managed to get Aḥmad b. Sumayṭ dismissed as *qāḍī* of Zanzibar Town and his responsibilities restricted to the rural (*shamba*) areas (Pouwels 1987: 180). As a result of this intrigue, Aḥmad b. Sumayṭ seems to have been willing to cooperate with the British against Sultan ᶜAlī b. Ḥamūd and his ally, Burhan b. ᶜAbd al-ᶜAzīz al-Amawī, when the British decided, in the context of the 1908 jurisdictional reforms in Zanzibar, to take the right to decide appeal cases away from the Sultan. Sultan ᶜAlī b. Ḥamūd, in contrast to his predecessors, was not knowledgeable in *fiqh* and had even been educated in Britain. In the course of the 1908 legal reforms, which further weakened the position of the Sultan, Aḥmad b. Sumayṭ was restored to his position as 'town' *qāḍī* in 1908 and was acknowledged as *muftī* in the context of the reorganisation of the jurisdiction (Pouwels 1987: 176; Bang 2003: 123). In this position,

Aḥmad b. Sumayṭ was able to overrule any other legal decision, thus eclipsing the legal authority of both the Sultan and his Chief Qāḍī, Burhān b. ᶜAbd al-ᶜAzīz al-Amawī. This case shows that although some members of the ᶜAlawī network of families were respected scholars, they were not necessarily allies of the Sultans of Zanzibar. Rather, some scholars of the Qādiriyya, both from the Amawī and the Uways branches, seem at times to have had more influence at the court than ᶜAlawī scholars. Indeed, disputes between scholarly families were an important feature of life on many levels and may explain some otherwise astonishing alliances across religious affiliations. Aḥmad b. Sumayṭ's case also shows that conflict in Zanzibar was not so much defined by brotherhood (or religious) affiliation, as by family politics (Bang 2003: 119).

In his function as *qāḍī*, Aḥmad b. Sumayṭ criticised some traditions of teaching on the East African coast, as has already been mentioned. In contrast to the widespread veneration of saints, he propagated veneration of the Prophet, and in the case of existing magico-religious practices he stressed the importance of religious teachings. He started to communicate his ideas of reform to his disciples in private classes in his house. Besides, he taught at Barza mosque in Ukutani in Zanzibar's old city. It should be noted, however, that although scholars such as Aḥmad b. Sumayṭ introduced new texts, they did not introduce 'subjects' that were not part of the established canon of Islamic sciences. Their achievement was confined to the cultivation of some aspects of the Islamic canon of sciences that had hitherto been neglected, and to the formalisation of teaching (Bang 2003: 150ff).

Apart from Aḥmad b. Sumayṭ, ᶜAbdallāh b. Muḥammad b. Sālim b. Aḥmad b. ᶜAlī Bā Kathīr al-Kindī (1860–1925) must be mentioned as a second major representative of the early ᶜAlawī tradition of reform in Zanzibar (al-Farsy 1972: 21ff). He was descended from a poor Hadrami family that had migrated from Tarīm to Lamu in the late eighteenth century (Kagabo 1991: 64; al-Farsy 1972: 21ff). On the Swahili coast, ᶜAbdallāh Bā Kathīr introduced the custom of holding public classes (*darsas*) on questions of religion during the month of Ramadan. His efforts at reform were concentrated particularly on the establishment of a new model of Islamic learning. But whereas many of the trader-scholar families who had migrated from Hadramawt could claim sharīfian descent, ᶜAbdallāh Bā Kathīr came from non-sharīfian origins (Ho 2005: 230). He had, however, a number of prominent students, such as Muḥammad ᶜUmar al-Khaṭīb (1876–1957). In contrast to Aḥmad b. Sumayṭ, ᶜAbdallāh Bā Kathīr shunned government contact (Bang 2003: 116). ᶜAbdallāh Bā Kathīr left East Africa for the first time in 1887 and travelled to Mecca where he studied at the feet of famous scholars (Pouwels 1987: 155). As recommended by one of his Meccan teachers, ᶜUmar b. Abī Bakr Abū Junayd, he undertook a journey to Java in order to teach there. After his return to East Africa in about 1890, he settled in Zanzibar in the Kajificheni district (Bang 2003: 147). Later on he built a house in Ukutani on a piece of land belonging to the al-Ḥusaynī family. After 1892 he started to teach in this house. In 1909, when it became too small, it was expanded, by adding an antechamber that became the Madrasat Bā Kathīr, where he continued to teach until his death in 1925, together with Aḥmad b. Sumayṭ.

In the 1930s, 1940s and 1950s, a new generation of Sufi-oriented reformers, such as ᶜUmar b. Sumayṭ (d. 1976) and Sayyid ᶜUmar ᶜAbdallāh (d. 1988), modified the now established modes of reform. Some of these scholars contributed to the struggle for independence of their respective countries. Like their predecessors, they stressed the importance of Islamic education. A good example of their activities was the establishment of the Muslim Academy in Zanzibar in 1951 and its subsequent administration by ᶜUmar ᶜAbdallāh, a well-known religious scholar affiliated with both the ᶜAlawiyya and the Qādiriyya (see Loimeier 2009). The Muslim Academy represented a different approach to Islamic education in so far as it was no longer marked by teacher/master forms of learning in the *madrasa*, but by institution-oriented learning in a new type of school, the *maᶜhad* (institute). As was the case with the Senegalese *écoles franco-arabes*, these new forms of learning adopted Western European concepts of education, even when combined with traditional Islamic disciplines. It is important to note, however, that the establishment of a new type of Islamic school, such as the Muslim Academy in Zanzibar was still linked with religious scholars who identified with the ᶜAlawiyya and the esoteric episteme (communication Abdulkader Hashim, 10 September 2008).

However, ᶜAlawī scholars never monopolised reforms in Islamic education. They were supported by a group of scholars of mostly Comorian origin who were well represented in the lower and medium echelons of the colonial administration (communication Othman Miraji Othman, 10 May 2002). Most notable were the scholars of the 'Manṣab' (al-Ḥusaynī) family, a family of Comorian royal origin that has so far been neglected in research, possibly due to the great attention paid to the Sumayṭ and Bā Kathīr families, or due to the fact that the Manṣab family did not quite fit into sharīfian ᶜAlawī traditions and could even be regarded as forming a link with a later, Salafi-oriented tradition of reform. The genealogical chain of the Manṣab family in Zanzibar stretches from Aḥmad b. ᶜAlī Manṣab al-Ḥusaynī (1863–1927) through Ḥāmid b. Aḥmad (1901–65), to Aḥmad b. Ḥāmid Manṣab (1928–77). Like his younger brother, Muḥammad b. Ḥāmid Manṣab, who died in 2003, Aḥmad b. ᶜAlī Manṣab al-Ḥusaynī became attached to Salafī ideas of reform (communication Maalim Idris, 30 July 2003 and Yunus Sameja, 22 August 2002). It is interesting to note that the scholars of the (Comorian) Manṣab family and their students cultivated contacts with ᶜAbdallāh Bā Kathīr (who was not a Sayyid, like Aḥmad b. Sumayṭ, and who shunned government service) and his school in Ukutani. At the same time, there was little interaction with Aḥmad b. Sumayṭ, who served as *qāḍī* for the Sultans of Zanzibar, and his students. However, a considerable number of scholars and students in the Bā Kathīr, Manṣab and Sumayṭ 'networks' became government school teachers, *qāḍīs* and bureaucrats.

Aḥmad b. ᶜAlī Manṣab's son, Ḥāmid (b. Aḥmad) Manṣab al-Ḥusaynī (1901–65), was a student of ᶜAbdallāh Bā Kathīr and became a teacher of ᶜAbdallāh Ṣāliḥ al-Farsy, the founder of Zanzibar's Salafi-oriented tradition of reform. From 1919, he taught the Ramadan class at Barza mosque and he also acted as *imām* of the Forodhani mosque until his death on 25 December 1965, during a class in Gofu mosque. In 1921, he became a government teacher and was speaker of the Government School Teachers' Association (al-Farsy 1972: 39; Maalim Idris, 30 July 2003 and 26 July 2007). His own son, Aḥmad b. Ḥāmid (b. Aḥmad) Manṣab al-Ḥusaynī (1928–77), was educated at the Government Secondary School. He was *khaṭīb* and *imām* of the *jumᶜa* mosque in Forodhani for nine years and seems to have turned 'salafī' at some point in his life. He taught at the Muslim Academy from 1960, and again, after the revolution, from about 1970, and became deputy director of the Muslim Academy.

The biographies of Aḥmad b. Sumayṭ, ᶜAbdallāh Bā Kathīr and Sayyid Manṣab show not only how deeply their families and those of their students were interrelated in both scholarly and personal terms (see Bang 2003: 101), but also how these networks extended from Istanbul via Cairo and the Ḥijāz to Cape Town in South Africa, and from the central African trading centres on the Congo across the Indian Ocean to India and Indonesia. The networks of the ᶜAlawī families thus represent a significant 'enlargement of scale' on the East African coast from the late nineteenth century onwards (Bang 2003: 129). The spread of knowledge, news and ideas mediated by these scholarly networks did not pose a problem due to the technological innovations of these times, such as the steam ship, the telegraph and the printing press. In Mecca, in the Hadramawt, in Zanzibar and in Cairo, pilgrims, travelling scholars and students from different regions formed networks of information, correspondence and scholarly relations that were so densely woven that they even surpassed those of the colonial empires of the time (Reese 2004: 244ff).

ᶜAbdallāh Ṣāliḥ al-Farsy and the Development of Salafi-oriented Reform in Zanzibar

From the 1930s, East Africa saw the emergence of a Salafi-oriented tradition of reform that tried to translate multiple modernities, including non-Muslim modernities, into (local) Muslim contexts, while adopting associationist modes of organisation and expression and fighting against the esoteric episteme.[9] The emergence of this new orientation of reform was linked with the names of al-Amīn b. ᶜAlī al-Mazrūᶜī and ᶜAbdallāh Ṣāliḥ al-Farsy. Al-Amīn b. ᶜAlī al-Mazrūᶜī, the major inspirer of Salafi-oriented reform in East Africa and teacher of many subsequent reformist scholars, was also the first scholar to start a distinct anti-*bidᶜa* discourse in East Africa, which was directed against Sufi practices. In addition, he stressed the importance of modern (not only Islamic) education and of female education, and wrote texts in the vernacular, Kiswahili. Like Abubakar Gumi in Nigeria, al-Amīn b. ᶜAlī al-Mazrūᶜī fought a hard struggle against the Indian Aḥmadiyya movement that started to propagate its own concept of a modern Islamic society in East Africa in the 1930s. Through its translation of the Qurᵓān into Kiswahili, the Aḥmadiyya was able to gain public attention. The struggle against the Aḥmadiyya became a major motivation for another, proper, translation of the Qurʾān, an effort started by al-Amīn b. ʿAlī al-Mazrūʿī and finished by ʿAbdallāh Ṣāliḥ al-Farsy in 1969 (see Lacunza Balada 1997).

The biography and career of an East African reformer such as ʿAbdallāh Ṣāliḥ al-Farsy (1912–82)[10] shows, however, how difficult it is to present a clear picture of Islamic reform, particularly due to the biographical dimension of the development of reformist ideas and positions. ʿAbdallāh Ṣāliḥ al-Farsy was born in the Malindi-Jongeani district of Zanzibar on 12 February 1912. He belonged to a large family of traders, scholars, medical doctors and employees of the Bū Saʿīdī rulers and, later, the British administration. In 1922, at the age of ten, ʿAbdallāh Ṣāliḥ al-Farsy started to study at Barza mosque and eventually studied at the feet of almost every eminent religious scholar in Zanzibar, including ʿAbdallāh Bā Kathīr and ʿUmar b. Sumayṭ (1896–1976). Through these scholars, ʿAbdallāh Ṣāliḥ al-Farsy was initiated into the circles of the ʿAlawī scholars in Zanzibar, taught in their *madāris* and rose to become *imām* and *khaṭīb* in some of their most respected mosques.

In 1925, ʿAbdallāh Ṣāliḥ al-Farsy also started primary school and finished his primary school education at Zanzibar's Government Central School in 1930 (Rajab 2001; Musa 1986: 25). From primary school, al-Farsy went to the Zanzibar Teacher Training College (TTC), where he finished in 1932 (Rajab 2001; Musa 1986: 25). His first appointment as a teacher started on 24 January 1933 and he continued to work both as a teacher and in other functions in the Department of Education (DeptoE) until 22 March 1960 (al-Farsy 1972: 45). In 1941, he was promoted to teacher grade II on the salary scale and, in 1947, due to his good performance as a teacher, he was appointed Inspector of Religious Teaching in Zanzibar and Pemba, a position that had become important due to the integration of the Qurʾānic schools into the government school system in 1940. He remained in this position until 1952. From 1950, his position was that of a Religious Supervisory Teacher of Koran schools in the Protectorate. In 1952 and 1953, ʿAbdallāh Ṣāliḥ al-Farsy went on a number of journeys to Tanganyika where he acted as adviser for religious teaching and was able to win first disciples on the mainland (Musa 1986: 43–55). From 1954 to 1956, he took part in a teacher refresher course and taught Arabic at the Government Secondary School (GSS) and at the TTC (Rajab 2001; Bakari 1989: 3). From the late 1930s, ʿAbdallāh Ṣāliḥ al-Farsy also assumed a number of religious functions.

Thus, he led the morning prayers at Gofu mosque from 1938 to 1966 and took over prayers from Ḥāmid b. Aḥmad Manṣab al-Ḥusaynī (1901–65) at Forodhani Friday mosque. He taught *tafsīr* at Barza and some other mosques. In addition, he took over *witr* and *tarāwīḥ* prayers at Gofu mosque from Muḥammad b. ᶜUmar al-Khaṭīb from 1933 to 1939. He then became the *muqri*ᵓ of the Qurᵓān at Gofu, where he also led *fajr* prayers until 1966, when he was replaced by his sister's son, Ṣāliḥ b. Salīm b. Zagar al-Farsy (Rajab 2001; al-Farsy 1972: 38–9).

ᶜAbdallāh Ṣāliḥ al-Farsy worked closely with and for the British administration not only as a teacher and supervisor of religious instruction, but also in other functions: in 1950, he was appointed member of a board directed by ᶜUmar b. Sumayṭ, the Chief Qāḍī, to consider and give advice on the syllabus and the standards of the Government Arabic Language Examination. The British also asked ᶜAbdallāh Ṣāliḥ al-Farsy to help with respect to the problem of Arabic teaching and Arab teacher training that continued to bother the Protectorate administration, and sent him to Somaliland in 1955. From 7 January 1960 to 19 February 1960, al-Farsy also travelled to Nyasaland to give advice to Muslim communities on matters of Islamic education (ZNA AB 86/136), and later in the same year he was sent to London to attend courses at the Institute of Education, after the return of Saᶜīd Hilāl Bualy, who had been employed as a Swahili teacher at SOAS (ZNA BA 5/9). On 9 August 1954 (9 Dhū l-Ḥijja), al-Farsy participated in the first *yaum al-ᶜarafat* celebrations in Zanzibar, a practice started by the *milād al-nabī* association in Mnazi Mmoja and presided over by the Chief Qāḍī, ᶜUmar b. Sumayṭ and the President of the Arab Association. During this occasion, he gave a sermon on the 'social and public life of scholars' and led the *ẓuhr* prayers afterwards (Mwongozi, 13 August 1954). In 1963, al-Farsy was again present, in his function as *qāḍī*, during the official *mawlid al-nabī* celebrations. These celebrations shocked an Egyptian teacher, an al-Azhar and Dar al-ᶜUlūm graduate who had come to Zanzibar for a teaching appointment, as being most 'un-Islamic' in character (Schacht 1965: 122).

Al-Farsy was not only visibly present on the stages of colonial representation as a representative of the scholarly establishment, but also started to publish texts with the support of the colonial administration, such as a text on the history of East African Muslim scholars (*Tarehe ya Imam Shafi na*

Wanazanoni wakubwa wa Afrika ya Mashariki) in August 1944. This book was republished in an extended version in 1972, under the title *Baadhi ya wanavyuoni wa kishafi wa mashariki ya Afrika*. Despite the omission of some scholars, this text can still be regarded as a fairly comprehensive overview of East Africa's established traditions of learning since the late nineteenth century. In 1951, ᶜAbdallāh Ṣāliḥ al-Farsy started to publish a first translation of some *sūras* of the Qur'ān. He also wrote numerous other texts, mostly in Kiswahili, in the course of his career as a scholar (see a fairly complete list in Musa 1986: 74–5). These texts show that he was not only interested in Islamic history, but also wrote about prophetic tradition, local custom and, in particular, a large number of *ᶜaqīda* texts. He was concerned with the struggle against the Aḥmadiyya movement, known as the 'Makadiani' movement in East Africa, and he wrote the biographies of some *ṣaḥāba* and members of the family of the Prophet, as well as poetry (*mashairi*). In addition, ᶜAbdallāh Ṣāliḥ al-Farsy published articles in journals and periodicals, in particular, *Mwongozi* and *al-Falaq*, religious articles (*tafsīr* and *maamrisho*, advice) with respect to topics such as prayer or *ḥadīth*, such as 'tafsiri ya Koran' in 1957, and, in 1963, a series titled 'Sala na Maamrisho yake'. Finally, he was active as a radio commentator from the early 1950s and gave regular talks on religious issues, as documented in 1956 in Zanzibar's official weekly gazette, *Maarifa*. He also contributed, in Kiswahili, to *Sauti ya Unguja*, Zanzibar's Kiswahili radio station, where he had a programme on 'mawaidha' (religious advice) every Thursday from 11.15am to 11.30am.

In the 1940s, his outspoken and sometimes rather critical positions with respect to some aspects of Islamic popular ritual started to trouble religious scholars affiliated with the Sufi orders, especially the Qādiriyya. According to one of his students, he criticised specific aspects of the *mawlid* celebrations, burial rites and visits to the graves of the deceased, as well as Sufi practices such as the *dhikr* (see Musa 1986). The struggle against the practice of the *dhikr*, in particular those forms of the *dhikr* that were known in Zanzibar as *zikri ya dufu* and *zikri ya kukohoa*, led to a conflict, in 1949, with Maḥmūd b. Kombo in Makunduchi and the first religious rally in Zanzibar. This affair was recorded by the colonial administration (ZNA AB 70/7) and demonstrated not only the extent to which the colonial administration was prepared to interfere in religious issues, and willing to fight popular culture, but also that the colonial administration and local elites formed an alliance, dominated by the Omani elite in political terms and the ᶜAlawī scholars in religious terms. These elites probably saw the Makunduchi affair triggered by ᶜAbdallāh Ṣāliḥ al-Farsy as a welcome opportunity to teach the *washamba* Muslims of Zanzibar a lesson (see Loimeier 2006a).

In January 1960, ᶜAbdallāh Ṣāliḥ al-Farsy's career as government school teacher came to an end when he applied for the job of a Shāfiᶜī Qāḍī in Unguja. He was to become deputy to Saᶜīd b. ᶜAbdallāh al-ᶜAzrī who had followed ᶜUmar b. Sumayṭ as Chief Qāḍī after the latter's retirement in 1959/60 (ZNA AB 86/136). Al-Farsy's nomination as Deputy (not Chief) Qāḍī in 1960 was possible because four other candidates had rejected this position as long as ᶜUmar b. Sumayṭ was still alive (communication Yunus Sameja and Saidi Musa, 22 August 2002). ᶜUmar b. Sumayṭ allegedly encouraged al-Farsy to apply for the position. When ᶜUmar b. Sumayṭ retired in 1959/60, the Sulṭān had asked him who could replace him, and he proposed ᶜAbdallāh Ṣāliḥ al-Farsy. As a result, the Sulṭān wrote a letter and asked ᶜAbdallāh Ṣāliḥ al-Farsy to accept the position (communication Saidi Musa, 19 August 2004). Al-Farsy accepted and was appointed 'Deputy Qāḍī' on 18 March 1960, as approved by Sulṭān Khalīfa b. Ḥārub on 19 March 1960. He was to be in charge of the urban and rural districts of Unguja (ZNA AB 86/136) and continued to act as (Deputy) Qāḍī until 13 July 1967. At the same time, he continued to teach Arabic at the TTC (Rajab 2001) and the GSS, and until 1967, he still taught his class at Mskiti Barza (Musa 1986: 59).

In contrast to many other scholars in Zanzibar, ᶜAbdallāh Ṣāliḥ al-Farsy's career was not interrupted by the revolution. It has often been asked why he stayed in Zanzibar after the revolution, and continued his work in the Department of Education as a teacher at Mskiti Barza, and as a *qāḍī*, since he had been closely connected to all major pillars of the pre-revolutionary regime. According to some of his students who witnessed this time in ᶜAbdallāh Ṣāliḥ al-Farsy's life, there was a rumour in the first days of the revolution that al-Farsy had been imprisoned, although he had continued to teach in the *madāris* and to conduct *maghrib* and *ᶜishāʾ* prayers. These rumours were supported by the fact that people could no longer hear his voice on the radio. When he gave a sermon on the radio on the eve of 1 Ramadan 1383

(15 January 1964) and announced that 'by command of the President' (*wa amri ya rais*), fasting would start from the next morning (16 January 1964), people were surprised and went to his house to congratulate him (communication Saidi Musa, 19 August 2004).

A major explanation for ᶜAbdallāh Ṣāliḥ al-Farsy's continued career in revolutionary Zanzibar may have been the fact that he had taught numerous students, in secular institutions, in Qurᵓānic schools or in his evening classes at Mskiti Barza. As members of the revolutionary government, these students recognised his neutrality as a teacher and as a citizen. Also, ᶜAbdallāh Ṣāliḥ al-Farsy may have been part of the Arabophone elite, as were a number of leading revolutionaries, but he was not a member of the ᶜAlawī scholarly establishment and even criticised its members at times, especially in respect of their ideas of intellectual and racial superiority. Equally, he was Omani, yet not part of the ruling family or linked with the prominent families of plantation owners and politicians. Karume and the ASP could thus easily sympathise with him. The revolutionary government respected him, for the time being, as a scholar, and appreciated the fact that he had not discriminated against 'colour' (*ubagozi*) before the revolution (communication Yunus Sameja, 22 August 2002 and Othman Miraji Othman, 10 May 2002; Musa 1986: 59; Bakari 1989).

ᶜAbdallāh Ṣāliḥ al-Farsy thus stayed in Zanzibar and continued his activities as a religious scholar. As his teachers were either dead or had emigrated, he had a chance to rise in scholarly rank, but the revolutionary regime preferred to have a *mshamba* (rural) scholar, Fatawi Issa, as Chief Qāḍī. As a consequence, al-Farsy survived the revolution as Deputy Qāḍī and became known as *khadi ndugu* (comrade *qāḍī*) (Glassman 2000: 422). In July 1967, however, ᶜAbdallāh Ṣāliḥ al-Farsy left Zanzibar, a decision that may have been triggered by a nocturnal visit by Aboud Jumbe and a summons to the office of the minister of education, Ali Sultan Issa, in 1967, when Ali Sultan Issa summarily dismissed all four members of the al-Farsy family, including ᶜAbdallāh Ṣāliḥ al-Farsy, from government service (communication Othman Miraji Othman, 10 May 2002 and Abdul Sheriff, 12 August 2002). The revolution in Zanzibar had indeed caused upheavals in national institutions as well as in everyday life and such an atmosphere was hardly conducive to intellectual pursuits and scholarly activities.

In the end, ᶜAbdallāh Ṣāliḥ al-Farsy left Zanzibar on 13 July 1967 and went to Dar es Salaam. He tried to find new work there, but failed, possibly due to the fact that the position of Chief Qāḍī in Tanzania was about to be filled by ᶜAlī b. Muḥammad al-Buḥrī from Tanga, who was well connected with the ruling party, TANU and who was about to replace Ḥasan b. ᶜAmeir as the leading religious authority. As a result, al-Farsy went to Kenya at the invitation of Muḥammad b. Qāsim al-Mazrūᶜī, the Chief Qāḍī. Shaykh Qāsim also gave ᶜAbdallāh Ṣāliḥ al-Farsy his address in Mecca, and following an invitation from Saudi Arabia, al-Farsy went to Mecca, where he performed his first *ḥajj* in March 1968. In Mecca, he came into contact with the rābiṭat al-ᶜālam al-islāmī and was invited to become the *mudīr* of Umm al-Qurā University, where he had applied for a position but received no reply. ᶜAbdallāh Ṣāliḥ al-Farsy subsequently applied for the position of the editor of the gazette of the rābiṭa and worked briefly for the rābiṭa in Medina, although he was never appointed editor. Finally, he received a telex offering him the position of Chief Qāḍī of Kenya, as successor to Muḥammad b. Qāsim al-Mazrūᶜī (Musa 1986: 60). Muḥammad b. Qāsim had recommended al-Farsy for the position of Chief Qāḍī, when he retired from this position in 1967, and again proposed him to President Kenyatta as his successor in 1968, 'as there was no other scholar of comparable qualifications around' (communication ᶜAbdillāhi Nāṣir, 10 July 2008).

ᶜAbdallāh Ṣāliḥ al-Farsy thus returned to Mombasa and never visited Zanzibar again. In Mombasa, al-Farsy became a protégé of his old friend, fellow student and Chief Qāḍī of Kenya, Muḥammad b. Qāsim al-Mazrūᶜī, who had been his host in the 1930s when ᶜAbdallāh Ṣāliḥ al-Farsy had studied with his father in Mombasa. Al-Farsy was granted Kenyan citizenship and Mombasa became his new home (Bakari 1989). From 29 May 1968 to 3 September 1981 he was Chief Qāḍī of Kenya (al-Farsy 1972: 45). He started with a series of inauguration parties in Nairobi, Mombasa and Malindi (Musa 1986: 65-6). In addition to his work as Chief Qāḍī, he taught in three mosques in Mombasa and managed to rapidly form a circle of disciples and followers, who listened to his teachings and preaching, especially in the month of Ramadan. In Mombasa, ᶜAbdallāh Ṣāliḥ al-Farsy also managed to complete the translation of the Qurʾān that he had started in Zanzibar. His translation did not find undivided support, however: in particular the scholars connected with the Qādiriyya, as well as those connected with the ᶜAlawiyya tradition of learning and their spiritual centre in Lamu, the ribāṭ al-riyāḍa, under the leadership of the sons, grandsons and nephews of Ḥabīb Ṣāliḥ, refused to acknowledge ᶜAbdallāh Ṣāliḥ al-Farsy's translation (Lacunza Balda 1997: 113; 1993a: 234). Al-Farsy had not consulted them or sought their approval, although he seems to have sent his work to some scholars before publishing it and they seem to have commented on his text and suggested some changes (communication Muḥammad Bakari, 20 February 2003).

ᶜAbdallāh Ṣāliḥ al-Farsy's translation of the Qurʾān was not only rejected by the Lamu-based ᶜAlawiyya tradition of learning, but also puzzled many of his Salafi-oriented followers, who wondered why, in his translation of the Qurʾān, he rejected a literalist interpretation of a number of *ayāt* of the Qurʾān known for their anthropomorphic connotation such as Qurʾān 7: 54 (*'inna rabbakum allāhu alladhi khalaqa al-samāwāt wa-l-arḍ fi sitta ayāmin thummā istawā ᶜalā l-ᶜarsh'*: 'your Lord is God, who created the Heavens and the earth in six days and (then) ascended His throne'), as well as in 10: 3 (Yūnis); 20: 5 (Ṭāʾhā); 25: 59 (al-furqān); 32: 4 (al-sajdah) and 57: 4 (al-ḥadīd). In each of these *ayāt*, the verb '*istawā*' (form VIII of the verb '*sawiya*', that is, 'to sit down') could be translated either in a literal sense as God actually sitting down on his throne (as in the verb '*istaqarra*'), or in a metaphorical (*taʾwīl*) sense as God 'settling down, establishing himself in order to rule', as a metaphorical expression of God's almightiness. ᶜAbdallāh Ṣāliḥ al-Farsy translated *aya* 7: 54 as '*Hakika Mola wenu ni Mwenyezi Mungu, aliyeziumba mbingu na ardhi kwa siku sita, kisha akatawala juu ya arshi Yake*', employing the verb '*kutawala*' (to reign, rule, govern) and thus translating the verse as 'then (after having created the Heavens and the earth) he reigned on his throne'. ᶜAbdallāh Ṣāliḥ al-Farsy repeated this translation in verses 10: 3; 25: 59 and 32: 4 as '*kisha akatawala juu ya arshi yake*', except in 20: 5, where he translated '*aliyetawala juu ya kiti chake*' ('then he ruled on/from his chair') and 57: 4, where he rendered the verse as '*kisha akakaa katika Enzi (yake)*' ('then he settled down and started to reside in his dominion') (see al-Farsy 1969: 205), thus remaining true to the established consensus, which interpreted these verses in a metaphorical way (communication ᶜAbd al-Wahhāb ᶜAlawī ᶜAbd al-Wahhāb Jamal al-Layl, 2 March 2003 and Yunus Sameja, 27 February 2003).[11]

ᶜAbdallāh Ṣāliḥ al-Farsy's rejection of a literal translation of these verses and his insistence on a metaphoric interpretation was interpreted by neither his followers nor his opponents in Kenya as a purely (but well-founded) doctrinal choice, but was regarded as indicating his rejection of a major 'Wahhābī' tenet of faith. It implied a rejection of Saudi politics, a political turn expressed in a religious code, motivated by ᶜAbdallāh Ṣāliḥ al-Farsy's alleged (and somehow enigmatic) late-life opposition to Saudi politics and 'Wahhābī' Islam: his followers (and his opponents) were unable to see a doctrinal argument as a doctrinal argument. This should be taken as a warning of the danger of over-interpretation by reading politics into doctrinal discussions.

The Lamu-oriented scholarly establishment, which was chiefly linked to the ᶜAlawiyya, refused to accept his claim to spiritual guidance based on both his position as Chief Qāḍī and his *tafsīr*, and responded with a text entitled *Fimbo ya Musa* by Aḥmad al-Badawī. This text rejected al-Farsy's doctrinal positions, although al-Farsy had insisted on the allegoric interpretation of Qurʾān 7: 54 and a number of other *āyāt* (Lacunza Balda 1989: 235–7; Loimeier 2005b), which troubled Saudi scholars to such an extent that they have since tried to reformulate his translation (communication Masoud Ahmad Shani, 20 March 2003). His translation also formed the background to numerous polemics in Kenya, where *ᶜulamāʾ* refused to acknowledge his translation (Bakari 1989). Despite being the new Chief Qāḍī, and even though he taught *tafsīr* and *ḥadīth* in many mosques and *madāris* in Mombasa, ᶜAbdallāh Ṣāliḥ al-Farsy thus continued to be regarded as an outsider in Kenya (Saidi Musa, 19 August 2004). He had been introduced to Kenya by the Mazrūᶜī family and was confronted with opposition from Lamu, probably due to an old conflict between Lamu and Mombasa, and the influence of the Mazrūᶜī family in Mombasa, but more prominently due to the fact that Lamu represented the most prominent centre of Islamic learning in mid-twentieth century Kenya and resented the nomination of an outsider to the position of Chief Qāḍī (communication Abdulkader Hashim, 29 July 2004).

In Kenya, al-Farsy also continued to fight against all kinds of *bidaᶜ*, such as *hitima*, the recitation of the Qurʾān at the tomb of a deceased person as part of the mourning ceremonies (khitima pia ni uzushi), as well as the celebration of the *mawlid*, or at least specific forms of the *mawlid*, in particular the *mawlid al-Ḥabshī* that had come to replace the *mawlid Barzanjī* (Lacunza Balda 1989: 247) and was cultivated in Lamu. Al-Farsy also criticised the blind imitation (*taqlīd*) of established wisdom in Islamic law as well as the veneration of saints in Islam (Salim 1985: 118; Musa 1986: 65–6) and introduced his students to the teachings of Muslim thinkers such as Ibn Taimiyya and Muḥammad b. ᶜAbd al-Wahhāb, or contemporary Muslim intellectuals such as Sayyid Quṭb and Abū l-Āᶜla Maudūdī (Bakari 1989: 7).

Due to his increasingly radical positions, ᶜAbdallāh Ṣāliḥ al-Farsy's life and career have been divided by his contemporaries into two periods, namely a 'moderate' period before leaving Zanzibar in 1967, and a 'radical' period after moving to Kenya to become Kenya's Chief Qāḍī. Many observers have described al-Farsy's time in Kenya as controversial and ambiguous; he was presented as somebody who often reacted to diverse (and contradicting) challenges; as somebody in a stage of transition, a torn man, who adopted different positions at different times. According to some, ᶜAbdallāh Ṣāliḥ al-Farsy was a 'relentless orthodox', 'who emphasized purism with respect to anachronistic ritual and religious observance' (communication Muḥammad Bakari, 21 February 2003). He was also seemingly radicalised by recent reformist thought. Some of his views were contested by local *ᶜulamāᵓ* and were debated during evening seminars or whenever the opportunity presented itself (Bakari 1989). In Kenya, he was said to have 'become a sworn enemy of all those he considered innovators. The veneration of saints became one of the great anathemas in his eyes. To his opponents in Kenya he remained a foreigner who had come to sow mischief among Kenyan Muslims', whereas for his followers he became an uncompromising representative of 'orthodox' Islam (Bakari 1989). At the same time, he was regarded as a 'moderate' during his time in Zanzibar. In Zanzibar he allegedly did not talk openly about his Salafi ideas as there were many scholars in Zanzibar who were higher in rank and who would have criticised him. He became more outspoken only after 1964 and, in particular, after 1967, when his old teachers were either dead or had emigrated. His connection with al-Amīn b. ᶜAlī al-Mazrūᶜī did not yet inform his positions while in Zanzibar. According to Bakari (1989), his 'controversial streak' became evident in Kenya only, but remained dormant in his Zanzibari times. As *qāḍī* in Zanzibar, he was not known for partisanship or any other sectarian views and in the last months of his life, which were spent in Oman, al-Farsy seems to have 'reconverted' to moderate 'Zanzibari' positions (communication Yunus Sameja, 25 and 27 February 2003).

It is indeed possible that ᶜAbdallāh Ṣāliḥ al-Farsy's intellectual approach changed while he was in Kenya. However, in order to achieve a more balanced view of his life and legacy, some additional elements should be added. The different views of ᶜAbdallāh Ṣāliḥ al-Farsy represent different historical approaches to his biography. Salafi-oriented Muslims have cultivated a view of him that is different from that of followers of the Qādiriyya and the ᶜAlawiyya, who have preferred to condemn his work under the impression of his 'Kenyan' period. The different representations of ᶜAbdallāh Ṣāliḥ al-Farsy's legacy can thus be seen as constructions that describe his ideas, life, work and legacy from a specific bias. Salafi-oriented Muslims tend to omit or de-emphasise his role as a government scholar in colonial times, while his opponents tend to emphasise his 'radical' ideas for Islamic reform in Kenya.

When looking at ᶜAbdallāh Ṣāliḥ al-Farsy's life and legacy in context, however, it is first of all obvious that he always worked closely with the governments of his time, whether post-independence Kenyan, revolutionary Zanzibari or colonial British. At the same time, he was rather outspoken in Zanzibar as far as some Islamic popular practices were concerned and even had to be defended in his radical stances by ᶜUmar b. Sumayṭ against the attacks of Sufi scholars. The assumption that al-Farsy was moderate up to 1967 and did not become known for outspoken reformist positions while in Zanzibar (Bakari 1989) thus needs to be revised. The division of his life into a moderate Zanzibari and a radical Kenyan phase omits, for instance, that he fought against specific features of popular religious culture while in Zanzibar. However, al-Farsy seems to have confined his struggle against *bidaᶜ* in Zanzibar to his campaign against specific forms of the *dhikr*. He was not known, for instance, as being an opponent of *mawlid* ceremonies in Zanzibar. Rather the opposite: as an inspector of religious teaching he actually supervised the teaching of *mawlid* in Zanzibar government schools. In Kenya, al-Farsy continued to take part in *mawlid* celebrations that were, as a rule, recitations of the *mawlid barzanjī*, and he led *mawlid* prayers in Mombasa (communication Muhdhar al-Khitami, 21 February 2003). Even in Kenya, he did not fight against the *mawlid* as such. Rather, he rejected a specific ᶜAlawī tradition of performing the *mawlid*, namely, the Lamu-based *mawlid al-Ḥabshī* that was a form of the *maulidi ya dufu*, a *mawlid* implying the use of '*dufu*' drums. But again, by speaking out against the *maulidi ya dufu*, he did not start something new, but followed the position of the previous Chief Qāḍī of Kenya, Muḥammad b. Qāsim al-Mazrūᶜī (communication Ḥammad Muḥammad Kassim al-Mazrūᶜī, 22 May 2007). Consequently, his attacks against specific forms of the *mawlid* should be seen as being part of a campaign against his opponents in Kenya, rather than a campaign informed by a general critique of all kinds of *bidaᶜ*.

His life thus evolved in a way that cannot really be divided into contradictory stages. ᶜAbdallāh Ṣāliḥ al-Farsy's struggle against the *dhikr* of the Qādiriyya in Zanzibar in the 1940s, for instance, shows that had already adopted radical positions in Zanzibar, yet he refused to completely adopt 'Wahhābī' positions while in Kenya. The difference was that in Kenya he was fighting against the scholarly establishment as a powerful outsider from a highly visible position, namely that of the Chief Qāḍī, while in Zanzibar he fought together with other representatives of the Muslim elite as an accepted insider, but from a subordinate position. Thus, instead of describing him as a torn person it may be better to say that he was not quite as radical in Kenya as his opponents claimed, while he was not as moderate in Zanzibar as his followers claimed. From such a perspective, ᶜAbdallāh Ṣāliḥ al-Farsy's life and career are not as ambivalent as has been suggested. Essentially, he was a government scholar, a teacher, a *qāḍī*, and a prolific writer and educator all his life. He fought against specific popular practices, both in Kenya and in Zanzibar. In the end, ᶜAbdallāh Ṣāliḥ al-Farsy must be seen as a controversial figure due to the divergent interpretations of his life by different religious and political groups.

The Rise of the '*Watu Wa Bidaa*'

After having successfully marginalised or forced into emigration the existing networks of scholars, in particular the influential ᶜAlawī scholars, President Karume was willing to tolerate some form of Islamic education and some forms of religious activity, as long as they took place under state control. In 1967, the same year in which ᶜAbdallāh Ṣāliḥ al-Farsy left Zanzibar for Kenya, the Karume government allowed the grandson of a well-known scholar, ᶜAbdallāh b. Abī Bakr Bā Kathīr alias 'Muᶜallim' Bā Kathīr, who had returned from his studies at the Islamic University in Medina, to take over the Qurᵓānic class in his father's and grandfather's house in Ukutani, as well as the school linked to that house, the Madrasat Bā Kathīr. And, in 1969, some teachers of the defunct Muslim Academy, which had been closed by the revolutionary government in 1965, started to discuss the possibility of reopening the Muslim Academy under a new name, Chuo Cha Kiislamu (Islamic School). This development eventually got Karume's personal support, in March 1972, only two weeks before he was assassinated on 7 April 1972 (Loimeier 2009: 442).

When the revolutionary government eventually restarted religious education, in 1972, under Karume's successor, Abeid Jumbe (r. 1972–84), it did so by importing scholars from Egypt and the Sudan, as well as by promoting some non-descript and obliging *Washamba* (peasant) scholars (see al-Farsy 1972: 65).[12] Formal positions in schools (religious education), in particular, the Chuo Cha Kiislamu,[13] administration (such as the *waqf* commission) and (*qāḍī*) courts were consequently filled with government scholars and Muslim functionaries who depended on their government positions and were willing to legitimise government decisions, even highly unpopular ones such as the institution of the office of the *muftī*. Despite the reopening of the Muslim Academy in 1972 as Chuo cha Kiislamu (CCK), the revolutionary regime was still committed to a socialist discourse and did not accept a revival of the old ᶜAlawī networks of scholars, a policy that was continued by Aboud Jumbe's successors, Ali Hassan Mwinyi (1984–5), Idrissa Abdul Wakil (1985–90), Salmin Amour (1990–2000) and Amani Abeid Karume (2000–10) who closed down the CCK again in 2007. From 1976, Zanzibari students were also sent to universities in Saudi Arabia (mostly the Islamic University of Medina, established in 1961), a few to the Imām Muḥammad b. Saᶜūd Islamic University (established in 1974) and some to the Umm al-Qurā University in Mecca that has become an 'Islamic model university' (Hefner and Zaman 2007: 253). Students were equally sent to the universities of Khartoum and Omdurman in Sudan and to al-Azhar in Egypt, and to Malaysia, Kuwait, Iraq, Libya and Turkey, where they could study at universities that were organised along the lines of the Islamic University of Medina. As the number of graduates from the Islamic University of Medina in leading administrative positions is very high in comparison to the number of those trained in other Muslim countries, this group of Muslim reformers is subsumed here under the label 'Medina graduates'.[14]

In 2004, there were about twenty graduates from Medina in high or intermediate government posts in Zanzibar (communication Sulaima Fadhil Soraga, 20 February 2004). These graduates complement another influential group in Zanzibar's administration, the 'Makunduchi' group, representing the 'Hadimu fringe' of southern Unguja, which has consistently supported the CCM since the revolution. In many cases, 'Makunduchi' origin and University of Medina-type education are identical. Graduates from the Islamic University of Medina and related universities have taken over not only the Chuo Cha Kiislamu but also the majority of positions in the spheres of jurisdiction (the office of the Chief Qāḍī and the District Qāḍīs, the Waqf and Trust Commission and the office of the *muftī*), in formal government education (secondary and primary schools), in Zanzibar University and the State University of Zanzibar (SUZA) or the College of Education that was established in 1998 in Chukwani, as well as in some *madāris* such as the madrasat al-nūr. As a result, 'Medina graduates' have dominated not only government schools such as the Chuo Cha Kiislamu but also many mosques and some important Qur᾿ānic schools in Zanzibar. A new generation of Muslim scholars has thus filled the vacuum created by the exodus of Hadrami and Comorian scholarly families, and the marginalisation of the ᶜAlawī tradition of learning. The new scholars and the traditions of teaching they represent are no longer defined by charismatic teacher personalities but by institutional affiliation. In addition, the new scholars are often dependent on the state: they are state-employed *ᶜulamā᾿*, Muslim functionaries, who work within the confines of state bureaucracies and legitimise the policies of the state.

While the institutions, organisations and associations mentioned above essentially represented 'government (official) Islam' and were controlled by Muslim functionaries, disciples and students of ᶜAbdallāh Ṣāliḥ al-Farsy came to form a first generation of Salafi-oriented activists. These activists started to fight openly against state-paid Muslim functionaries and have influenced the Islamic public sphere in Zanzibar in much more spectacular ways than earlier generations of reformers, for instance by intensifying critique of the post-colonial state and by adopting militant forms of action. An important feature of this new generation of Muslim activists is that they have established organisations, such as Uamsho, which form part of a larger East African agglomeration of anṣār al-sunna groups. Equally, they have redirected their attention, although not totally, from attacks against Sufi scholars to polemics against the state. This younger generation of Salafi-oriented Muslims has also often studied abroad and acquired an 'authorization' (*ijāza*) empowered by distance and secular criteria such as a diploma (Purpura 1997: 132). The new Salafi-oriented scholars and activists, in contrast to the former scholars, do not stress the importance of descent for their teaching but qualification through skills (Purpura 1997: 135). Also, they doubt the authority of the old scholars and maintain that a Muslim is obliged to acquire as much knowledge as possible (Purpura 1997: 370). One of Allyson Purpura's interlocutors, Bwana Umar, expressed this change as it emerged in Zanzibar in the 1980s, by saying:

> We never questioned our shaykhs. We accepted everything they said as true and right . . . we used to kiss their hands . . . even in the streets they would hold out their hand to passing children for them to kiss. But you don't see that today. Now the youth ask their shaykhs things, they question their teachings: what aya? Where does it say that? They challenge them, they want to know more. (quoted in Purpura 1997: 131–2)

Rashid Salim, another of Allyson Purpura's interlocutors, who was trained in Saudi Arabia, characterised the emergence of these new scholars in similar terms:

> Suddenly these new shaykhs started popping up, this one and that one, each promoting himself. Now, these shaykhs try to show that they have such great knowledge of Islam when in fact they don't; they try and get people to follow them . . . In the past, there were shaykhs who were truly recognized for their great knowledge of Islam. But today, these new shaykhs use piles of words in their lectures, opposing the things that the great shaykhs practiced in the past and that are recognized in Islam. They say 'maulidi is not permitted, to pray for the dead is not permitted'. They say this but they have no knowledge, no ancestry, no grace, but still they oppose these practices, now that the great ones are dead. They oppose all these activities and confuse

> Muslims; but in Islam all Muslims should be united. Now, they bring tension and conflict and they are using Islam for political aims to oppose the union. (quoted in Purpura 1997: 357)

Since the early 1980s, Salafi-oriented activist Muslims have become increasingly influential due to their outspoken opposition to government policies, in particular when the CCM stopped enforcing rigid Karume decrees on public morality that had prohibited, for instance, make-up, shorts, mini-skirts, long hair and tight-fitting clothes, in order to boost tourism and economic liberalisation. A new Salafi-oriented movement of reform thus developed in Zanzibar and became active in *da^{c}wa*, the construction of mosques and the mobilisation of Muslim women, as expressed in the spread of the *ḥijāb* or even the *niqāb*. The move toward the *niqāb*, which started in the 1980s, became even more marked in the 1990s and early 2000s.[15] Since the early 1980s, Muslim activist groups such as Uamsho have also adopted Abeid Amani Karume's struggle against religious superstitions by attacking all kinds of local traditions as un-Islamic innovations, *bida^{c}*. Since this time, Muslim activists have been fighting a war of symbols against a number of religious traditions, including conspicuous spending on festivities such as the *^{c}īd* festivals or *mawlid* celebrations. Other traditions rejected by Muslim activist groups include a large array of local socio-religious practices, such as *uganga* (healing with plants),[16] *kupunga pepo* (ghost exorcism), *kuoandisha mashetani* (devil exorcism), *kuchuchia kichwani* (ghost talking, *uchawi*), *falaki*/*ilm za nyota* (astrology), *ilm za basit al-hurufi* (numerology), *kupiga ramli* (sand oracle), *kuzingua uchawi* (white magic), *kisomo* (ritual reading of the Qur$^{\circ}$ān), *kombe* (the drinking of ink with which 'magical' Qur$^{\circ}$ānic verses have been written on wooden slates) and faith in amulets (*hirizi, hijāb*). Muslim activist groups have also protested against time-consuming and conspicuous festivities, such as those connected with funeral rites, in particular extensive commemoration of the deceased, and they have attacked the respectful kissing of the hands of religious scholars. Muslim activists have thus tried to propagate their interpretation of Islam in opposition to local Swahili cultural influences and the corruption of the 'West'. Due to their polemics against 'un-Islamic innovations', the politics of economic liberalisation, mass tourism and popular religious practices that were summarily denounced as *bida^{c}*, Muslim activists came to be known rather ironically as 'watu wa bidaa', 'the innovation people'. In Zanzibar they were also labelled *wenye msimamo mkali* (people having a 'hot' position), or *watu wa siasa kali* (people of 'hot' politics), whereas they prefer to call themselves in Arabic anṣār al-sunna (helpers of the sunna), or in Kiswahili *waislamu wapya* (new Muslims) or *wenye hamasa ya dini* (religious enthusiasts) (Purpura 1997: 351).[17]

However, the anṣār al-sunna or *watu wa bidaa* do not form an organisation of any kind and have consequently not been registered in any form. As in Tanzania, the term 'anṣār al-sunna' should thus be understood as an umbrella term for many different activist Muslim organisations, such as the Muslim National Conference (Baraza Kuu) or the Warsha ya Waandishi wa Kiislamu (Workshop of the Commission of Islamic Authors) (established in 1982), based on the mainland, or groups like Uamsho and others in both Zanzibar and mainland Tanzania that constitute formal bodies (see Loimeier 2007b: 137ff). The anṣār al-sunna or *watu wa bidaa* represent a spectrum of different Salafi-minded groups and personalities that propagate different approaches in terms of doctrinal orientation, strategy and activist positioning. However, these groups and persons are united by their rejection of both 'popular' and 'government (official) Islam', Sufi orders, and 'atheist' CCM rule.

Since the early 1980s, a number of anṣār al-sunna groups have been formed, the most important being the Jumuiya ya Uamsho (The Society of [Islamic] Awareness, also Jumuiya ya Uamsho na Mihadhara ya Kiislamu) (JUMIKI), which was registered as an Islamic NGO in 2002. In the 1990s and 2000s, Uamsho was led by Nassor Bachoo (also spelled Nassoro Bachoo or Nassor Pachu), Ally Bassalleh and Saloum Msabbah (on Msabbah, see Bakari 2001: 268), as well as Farid Hadi Ahmad 'al-ᶜArab', the 'Amiri Mkuu', and Azzan Khalid Hamdan, the Deputy Amir. Farid Hadi Ahmad was an army officer in Qaṭar before returning to Zanzibar, where he became *imām* of the Chukwani College of Education mosque (*an-Nuur*, 6 September 2002 and 3 September 2004). The Jumuiya ya Uamsho must be regarded as an umbrella organisation: while some members were affiliated with the anṣār al-sunna movement, others were not. The same applies to another organisation that is often said to be part of the anṣār al-sunna movement, the Jumuiya ya Maimamu, the Union of Imāms (jamᶜīyat majlis al-āʾima bi-Zinjibār) (*an-Nuur*, 6 September 2002). In 2002, the Jumuiya ya Maimamu was led by Said Mwinyi, Nassor Majid and Farid Hadi Ahmad (*an-Nuur*, 9 August 2002).

The most outstanding representative of the *watu wa bidaa* in the 1980s and early 1990s, at least for a short time, was Khamisi Jaᶜfar of Michenzani (Purpura 1997: 144). He was born in about 1950 in Kikwajuni. His grandfather was of Indian origin. He attended Qurᵓānic school and a *madrasa* and also studied under his grandfather, who had been a student of ᶜAbdallāh Ṣāliḥ al-Farsy. Other teachers were ᶜAlī Rashad and the Sudanese and Egyptian teachers who had come to Zanzibar in the early 1970s. In the early 1990s, Khamisi Jaᶜfar taught at three *madāris* in Zanzibar town. He also held female classes and had a shop (Purpura 1997: 145, 360). In the early 1990s, Khamisi Jaᶜfar no longer featured among Zanzibar's anṣār al-sunna leaders. According to local scholars, he is virtually unknown today and the Raha Leo mosque, which Purpura claims to have been his centre, is linked with the name of Nassor Bachu (communication Issa Ziddy, 4 May 2005).

Since the early 1980s, the different *watu wa bidaa* groups influenced discussions in the public sphere in Zanzibar in a more decisive way than reformers in Kenya, although the latter could count on ᶜAbdallāh Ṣāliḥ al-Farsy's support. So far, the *watu wa bidaa* have recruited most of their followers in Zanzibar among the young and unemployed. Their success was linked to the economic stagnation in Zanzibar that resulted from the economic policies of the revolution and the liberalisation of the economy that began in 1986 (Purpura 1997: 44). After a formative period in the late 1960s and 1970s, the *watu wa bidaa* in Zanzibar were able to present themselves as an outspoken voice of religious opposition to the regime of the CCM in Zanzibar. Recently, the *watu wa bidaa* have even been perceived as threatening the Civic United Front (CUF)'s role as the only legitimate political opposition, due to CUF's willingness to negotiate an agreement (*muafaka*) with the CCM (communication Mohamed Ahmed Saleh, 3 April 2005).

As has been mentioned above, the key person for the development of contemporary Salafi-oriented reform in Zanzibar was ᶜAbdallāh Ṣāliḥ al-Farsy, who taught one of the first radical Muslim scholars of the 1960s, Rashīd b. Ḥāmid 'al-Ḥaḍramī Mmakonde'. Rashīd b. Ḥāmid also was a student of Sālim b. Saᶜīd b. Sayf al-Shuhaybī and continued his work in the Jamīᶜat al-Islāmiyya (al-Farsy 1972: 40). Historically, Zanzibar's Salafi-oriented movement of reform was rooted in the Kikwajuni district, an area of Ng'ambo close to Stone Town, and home to the Manṣab family. To this day, representatives of the anṣār al-sunna are based primarily in Kikwajuni, which has two major mosques: while 'lower Kikwajuni' (Kikwajuni Chini) has maintained its ᶜAlawī orientation, 'upper Kikwajuni' (Kikwajuni Juu) is known for its oppositional leanings, under the leadership of Nassor Bachu (communication Jabir Haydar Jabir al-Farsy, 2 March 2003 and Issa Ziddy, 23 July 2002).

The group around Nassor Bachu started to form in the late 1970s under the influence of teachers from the Sudan, namely Muḥammad Ṣāliḥ, Shaykh Badawī and Shaykh ᶜAbd al-Qādir, as well as an Egyptian teacher, ᶜAbd al-Wārith Saᶜīd, all based at the Muslim Academy, and, finally Saidi Njugu, *imām* of a Kikwajuni mosque and an active member of the ZNP who was known for his exegetic talent. He had taught, at least for a short time, at the Muslim Academy in the early 1960s, but was dismissed in 1964 because he mixed politics with his teaching (Purpura 1997: 354–5; communication Issa Ziddy, 2 May 2005). After his dismissal, he continued to teach at his mosque and seems to have become a major source of inspiration for the leaders of the anṣār al-sunna movement, Nassor Bachu and Khamisi Jaᶜfar in Kikwajuni and Michenzani in the 1970s and 1980s. ᶜAbd al-Wārith Saᶜīd was one of the scholars who restarted activities at the Muslim Academy in the early 1970s, before handing over to Musa Makungu (communication Issa Ziddy, 2 May 2005). ᶜAbd al-Wārith Saᶜīd, Saidi Njugu and their colleagues also started the discussion about the sighting of the moon that has continued to trouble Zanzibar. In the 1970s, this group gathered for *ᶜīd* prayers on the grounds of the Egyptian consulate near the High Court building in Shangani, until the government asked the Egyptian consulate to stop these activities. Subsequently, the Sudanese *shaykhs* were expelled from Zanzibar, first to mainland Tanzania, and then to Sudan. Nassor Bachu and his group took over in 1978 and formed the core of a new generation of Salafi-oriented Muslim activists in Zanzibar (communication Issa Ziddy, 2 May 2005).

In the early 1990s, Nassor Bachu (d. 13 February 2013) replaced Khamisi Jaᶜfar as leader of the anṣār al-sunna movement in Zanzibar and as founder of Uamsho. His father or grandfather, Musa Bachu, was a religious scholar in Donge (Purpura 1997: 145; Ameir 2006: 356), while his father or uncle,

Ḥusayn Bachu, was imprisoned in the Mtoni detention camp after the 1964 revolution in Zanzibar (see al-Barwani: 1996). Nassor Bachu himself studied under ᶜAbdallāh Ṣāliḥ al-Farsy (Purpura: 1997: 145). In 2003, Nassor Bachu was the *imām* of the Kikwajuni Juu mosque in Zanzibar and his group was in control of the Raha Leo *jumᶜa*-mosque. He published a text on the disputes over the sighting of the moon (*Ufafunuzi wa mgogoro wa kuandama kwa mezi*, 1998, n.p.; see van de Bruinhorst, 2007), in which he refers to the work of al-Farsy and the Yūsuf ᶜAlī translation of the Qur'ān, as well as the *tafsīr* works of Ibn Kathīr, the Jalālayn, Abū Daud and al-Nasafī. In the 1980s and 1990s, the group around Nassor Bachu included activists such as Shaykh Kondo, possibly Khamisi Jaᶜfar, then Saloum Msabbah, 'Ustādh' Jamal, Farid Hadi Ahmad, Azzan Khalid Hamdan and Ally Basalleh (see Loimeier 2007b), although the latter went to the mainland.

Nassor Bachu was not only the most outspoken Muslim opponent of the CCM regime in Zanzibar, especially Salmin Amour's administration, but in the 1980s he also started to attack *mawlid* celebrations. Despite the polemics of the *watu wa bidaa*, this ritual has retained its popularity. *Mawlid* celebrations have taken on numerous forms in Zanzibar and have come to be celebrated not only in the 'proper' context of the Prophet's birthday, but also on many different occasions throughout the year, such as parents' day, school festivals or marriage ceremonies. *Mawlid* has also become an integral part of Islamic education and every major *madrasa* and school celebrates its own *mawlid* (communication Masoud Ahmad Shani, 16 July 2002). Eventually, the *watu wa bidaa* realised that their approach would not yield results. Since about 1999/2000, Nassor Bachu and the majority of the *watu wa bidaa* groups have adopted a more conciliatory approach and reduced their critique of *mawlid* (Bakari 2001: 90; communication Husayn ᶜAlī Husayn, 7 August 2002 and Farid Himid, 9 March 2001).

While the anṣār al-sunna have largely stopped attacking *mawlid* traditions, they have identified other objects of wrath for which the government has been made responsible. Thus, the *watu wa bidaa* have tried to build common ground for a generally acceptable Muslim opposition to government policies (communication Abdul Sheriff, 26 July 2002). At the same time, the anṣār al-sunna try to evade accusations of creating *fitna* (strife, chaos) among Muslims (*Maarifa*, No. 8, 2002; communication Mwalimu Mmanga and Husayn ᶜAlī Husayn, both 30 July 2002). Equally, Nassor Bachu has accepted that women are not obliged to wear the *niqāb* (communication Issa Ziddy, 20 March 2003). On the other hand, Nassor Bachu and the majority of anṣār al-sunna have started to focus on the alleged decay of morals, prostitution, tourism and drugs, or the increasing presence of Christians in Zanzibar (see Loimeier 2011). In addition, the anṣār al-sunna have attacked the Zanzibar International Film Festival (ZIFF) and the *Mwaka Kogwa* (New Year Festival) in Makunduchi. Both ZIFF and the *Mwaka Kogwa* are seen as manifestations of the corruption of Zanzibar's Muslim society by tourism.[18] In reaction to this change of strategy, a small group under the leadership of Ustādh Jamal has split off, maintaining the more radical positions of the anṣār al-sunna, and established yet another radical Muslim group. The development towards more moderate positions may thus be reversed in the future, not least due to the fact that Nassor Bachu's health deteriorated after 2000, culminating in his death on 13 February 2013. In recent years, Farid Hadi Ahmed has been the major spokesman of Zanzibar's anṣār al-sunna groups. The leading role of Farid Hadi Ahmed became manifest in 2010, when Zanzibar's long-time opposition party, the CUF, formed a coalition government with the CCM under President Ali Muhammad Shein (CCM).[19]

The Political Agenda of Salafi-oriented Activism in Zanzibar

From their very beginning, the anṣār al-sunna formed a Muslim activist opposition against Zanzibar's socialist CCM government and corrupt administration. This was particularly so in the mid-1980s, when the CCM under President Ali Hassan Mwinyi (r. 1984/5) and his successors stopped enforcing rigid Karume decrees on public morality in order to boost tourism and economic liberalisation. In 1988, a statement by Sofia Kawawa, the chairwoman of the Association of Tanzanian Women (Umoja wa Wanawake wa Tanzania), triggered the first religious riots in post-revolutionary Zanzibar. Sofia Kawawa had urged the CCM to abrogate the Islamic Marriage Act as it discriminated against women, a demand that has resurfaced regularly since that time (see *The Guardian* [Tanzania] and *an-Nuur* documentation of the Divorcee Protection Act of 1984 in July and August 2003; Loimeier 2007b: 137ff). Sofia Kawawa's statement may have been linked with BAKWATA demands of 1987 to reinstate Islamic courts in Tanzania, which had been abolished in 1971 in the context of the unification of Tanzanian laws and the integration of *sharīᶜa* personal law into Tanzanian civil law. Her statement triggered riots in Zanzibar in May 1988, led by Nassor Bachu as well as Saleh Juma of Forodhani mosque and Ali Hemed Jadir of Mchangani mosque (Lacunza Balda 1989: 328; Purpura 1997: 379). When Ali Hassan Mwinyi, who had become President of Tanzania in 1985, reacted in defence of Sofia Kawawa, he was attacked in *Sauti ya Zanzibar Huru* (no. 1, p. 5, 1989) for giving Christians too much consideration:

> The leaders of the Zanzibari government dare to join forces with the great enemy of Islam and to persecute the Shaykhs. Today, Christian preachers are left free to preach and spread Christianity in Zanzibar while the Shaykhs of Islam are squeezed to make them restless. Where do these things come from? How is it that Christians have no obstacles? (quoted in Lacunza Balda 1989: 304–5)

In 1989, Muslim activism continued in the form of *bismillahi al-rahmani al-rahim* stickers that claimed religious hegemony over the realm of politics. In 1992, a third incident occurred when Shaykh Kondo entered the stage as a major figure. Riots occurred near Forodhani mosque, directed against a family-planning programme and against plans to increase tourism (Purpura 1997: 379). In the early 2000s, the conflict between the government and Muslim activists escalated. In 2001, an explosive device caused some damage in a well-known Zanzibar brothel and night-bar, the New Happy Lodge in Shangani, and was seen as a protest by activist Muslims against prostitution and the public consumption of beer (communication Othman Saidi Khamis, 4 August 2002). The New Happy Lodge was closed down in 2006, yet similar venues close to mosques, such as the Sunrise Bar in Baghani, Mercury's in Malindi or the Starehe Club in Shangani, were allowed to continue business.[20] The most serious disturbances occurred in March 2004, when the Uamsho group was accused of being responsible for five (according to other sources: seven) incidents that were interpreted by the government as 'Islamist terrorist' attacks. Thus, a grenade was thrown into Mercury's, a bar on the seafront close to the Malindi Friday mosque, at a point of time when a delegation from the British High Commission was apparently sitting at the bar. The grenade did not explode, however, as the pin had not been pulled. Also, a number of electric transformers were blown up, an explosive device went off in the garden of the *muftī*'s house without causing major damage and a disused car of the commissioner of police was set on fire (communication Ulrike Haffner, 1 April 2004; Arngeir Langas, 17 July 2004; Sulaima Fadhil Soraga, 21 April 2004). The 2004 bombings were thus rather unspectacular affairs. Yet, they pointed to central themes of Muslim critique. A spokesperson from the *muftī*'s office even claimed that the CCM government deliberately used these events in the context of the USA-inspired 'war against terror' to convey credibility to an Islamist terrorist threat in Zanzibar and as a strategy to delegitimise the political opposition, in particular the Civic United Front (CUF) as a party with an 'Islamist' orientation (communication Sulaima Fadhil Soraga, 20 April 2004). At the same time, the CCM government accused the 'radical Islamic opposition' of opposing local politics, thus trying to hit two birds with one stone.

The efforts of the government to establish a state-controlled religious sector, to control public religion and to present at least some state policies as Islamic in order to pre-empt religious opposition and to gain credibility for investors from the Gulf, opened an epistemic trap, a crisis of legitimacy that could be exploited by a religious opposition. The efforts of the state to exert hegemonic power over all aspects of everyday life, including religion, and the instrumentalisation of Muslim functionaries for these ends encouraged the development in the late 1970s of Muslim activist movements, such as the different anṣār al-sunna groups that tried to escape state control and to criticise the revolutionary government in terms of its own religio-political rhethoric. In the 1980s and 1990s, the attacks of Salafi-oriented activists were directed chiefly at aspects of popular religion such as *mawlid* celebrations, and thus, implicitly, against the legacy of Zanzibar's religious establishment that supported such practices, as well as against the socialist government of the CCM that continued to condone these (and other) forms of popular religion. Salafi-oriented activists in Zanzibar thus had both a political and a religious agenda. Yet these agendas were not equally present in the public discourse of Salafi-oriented activists at all times. Rather, foci of attention and polemics oscillated and can be read as a function of local politics and public debates.

The anṣār al-sunna multiplied their attacks on 'official Islam' in the late 1990s. From the early 2000s, Salafi-oriented activists focused their critique on the *muftī*, Harith b. Khelef Khamis al-Ghaythi (d. 2010),[21] and the office of the *muftī* (created by decree in September 2001). In the eyes of the anṣār al-sunna, the office of the *muftī* was created in order to legitimise the un-Islamic decisions of the government and to provide the government with an aura of religious legitimacy. At the same time, the anṣār al-sunna accused the government of using the office of the *muftī* to exert pressure on Muslims and to 'control' Muslims (communication Sulaima Fadhil Soraga, 22 May 2007). The office of the *muftī* issued (or refused to issue) permits for religious activities, such as sermons, rallies or *mawlid* celebrations: to criticise the *muftī* has thus come to mean to attack the legitimacy of the CCM government: 'For their sins, the cadres of the CCM will be firewood for hell' was a claim in the Muslim media (*an-Nuur*, 3 September 2004, 'Makada wa CCM kuni za Jahannam').

An article entitled 'Uislam Unguja watiwa kitanzi' ('Islam in Unguja commits suicide') in *an-Nuur* (6 September 2002) claimed that the office of the *muftī* had been created in order to fight Muslims, and that since its very beginnings, the *muftī*'s office had permitted 'illegal' things. For example, a *fatwā* had been issued in a bi-weekly radio programme (masuali ya dini) that allowed the taking of interest and spending this money on the construction of roads or the buying of medicine. It also claimed that Christians were free to do whatever they wanted, while Muslims were restricted. The *muftī* even suppressed Muslims: Christians were treated differently, as there was no corresponding institution (to the office of the *muftī*) in charge of 'Christian affairs'. The *muftī* was accused of following the commands of Adam Mwakanjuki, the president's adviser on religious affairs who was in charge of the *waqf* commission, the *muftī* and the *maḥkama* (court, judiciary). The creation of the office of the *muftī* was against both the Zanzibar and Union constitutions: the *muftī* simply did what the government commanded him to do (*an-Nuur*, 28 February 2003). In fact, the *muftī* was used by the enemies of Islam. Instead of fighting against Muslims, the government should punish prostitution and the consumption of alcohol, as another article in *an-Nuur* (28 February 2003) claimed (SMZ iwacharaze bakora wazinifu: 'SMZ (Serikali ya Mapinduzi ya Zanzibar) (the Revolutionary Government of Zanzibar) (my translation) should beat those who practise prostitution). Finally, the *muftī* was accused of implementing government policies with respect to highly visible Muslim rituals such as the declaration of the start of the holy month of Ramadan as well as the fixing of the days of *ᶜīd.*

Since the 2000s, disputes over the sighting of the moon have become a regular feature of Zanzibar's religious discussions. Muslim activists use the sighting of the moon to protest against the government's instrumentalisation of Islam. While the *muftī* insists that local sightings of the moon should be used for fixing the dates of religious holidays, the anṣār al-sunna support the 'universal' Saudi timing for the different *ᶜīds* (communication Ahmed Mgeni, 22 March 2003; Purpura 1997: 221). The disputes between Muslim activists and the *muftī* are very clear with respect to the sighting of the moon and the corresponding fixing of Islamic holidays, in particular *ᶜīd al-fiṭr* in Ramadan and *ᶜīd al-ḥajj* (also *ᶜīd al-aḍḥā* or *ᶜīd al-kabīr*) in the month of pilgrimage, Dhū l-Ḥijja. In the context of these debates, the *muftī* has been accused by the Muslim opposition of being a government stooge and of interfering in religious affairs that have nothing to do with a socialist and secular government but should be managed by the Muslims themselves. The anṣār al-sunna demand that Muslims in Zanzibar, like those in Kenya and on the Tanzanian mainland, should follow 'universal Mecca-time' with respect to the sighting of the moon, not only because Saudi Arabia is the *qibla*, the pole of orientation for all Muslims, but also because Saudi Arabia is in the same time zone as Zanzibar. The *muftī*, by contrast, insists on the independence of religious scholars in Zanzibar and their autonomy of agency, so that the local sighting of the moon is valid (communication Harith al-Ghaythi, 2. September 2002). The issue of the sighting of the moon has thus come to symbolise controversial religious and political positions in Zanzibar.

First debates over the sighting of the moon started in the mid-1970s, but reached a climax in 2001 when security forces imprisoned twenty leading members of the activist Jumuiya ya Uamsho for 'praying too early' (see van de Bruinhorst 2007: 187ff). In concrete terms, they had started Ramadan one day before the official announcement by the *muftī.* In 2003, there was a further escalation when the anṣār al-sunna celebrated the *ᶜīd al-ḥajj* on 11 February, whereas the *muftī* fixed the next day as a public holiday and said that anybody who did not heed his command 'would commit a big mistake' ('atakayekwenda kinyume cha agizo hilo atakuwa anatenda kosa kubwa', quoted in van de Bruinhorst 2007: 187ff). When Muslim activists protested against this decision of the *muftī* in the context of an (illegal) public rally, a *mihadhara*, the government called upon Tanzanian field force units (riot police). These security troops from the mainland patrolled throughout Zanzibar in full combat gear and intimidated the population, using tear gas. Even some *baraza* (men's meeting places) in Jaws' Corner, a well-known centre of the political opposition, were vandalised. The Muslim opposition protested against these brutalities and organised a second rally on the following Friday on the Malindi ground close to Darajani Market. It was again dissolved, however, by Tanzanian field force units with tear gas (*Dira*, 14 February 2003).

The degree of violence used against the protesters shocked the public and led to broad publicity and reports in the media. In an article about the religious policy of the government in *Dira*, entitled 'Ni dini, kipigo na utawala bora?',[22] Muhammad Ghassany argued with respect to the incidents in Zanzibar in the context of the *ᶜīd* celebrations 'that to pray or not to pray (on a specific day), to fast or not to fast (on a specific day), were becoming questions of politics decided by the Mufti Bill',[23] instead of being decided by Muslims:

> Muslims in Zanzibar have different opinions about the day of praying and Muslims have so far been free to do so. Now, the government wants to impose one regulation only, and this in the context of the enactment of the Mufti bill (sheria ya Mufti) that has been discussed since 2002. Through the Mufti bill, freedom of religion will disappear, something that will contravene the 1984 constitution of Zanzibar. Therefore, to pray or not to pray, to fast or not to fast are becoming questions of politics instead of being issues decided by the people themselves. People just want to continue to practise their faith, they should be free to do so, why should they be beaten? As many people do not understand religion, this dispute will raise many dangers: thus, people may become atheist (lā-dīnī) through this quarreling about religion. Or, people who already have a better understanding of Islam may become 'protestant' and there will be 'protestant Islam' (Uprotestanti wa Kiislamu). (*Dira*, 21 February 2003)

In another article in *an-Nuur* the government was accused of being the source of all evil in Zanzibar (Acheni kutafuta mchawi serikali ndio chanzo cha mgogoro: 'Don't look for the sorcerer, the government is the source of trouble'): although the *muftī* had fixed 12 February 2003 as the date for *ᶜīd al-ḥajj*, the *muftī*'s announcement could not be accepted as the office of *muftī* had been created only recently. The 1977 (union) constitution had explicity provided for freedom of religion and the freedom to choose the right day for *ᶜīd* celebrations, which were national holidays in Zanzibar. The announcement of the *muftī* and the behaviour of the police raised the question of whether Zanzibar really was a Muslim country: why did the government give power to representatives of one group only as represented by the *muftī*? There should either be no *muftī* or a *muftī* for every group. The creation of the office of the *muftī* was an infringement of the constitution that granted freedom of religion. Thus, the union government should intervene and force the Zanzibar Government to abolish the office of the *muftī* (*an-Nuur*, 28 February 2003).

As a consequence of these protests, the *muftī* was eventually forced to allow further rallies by Muslim activist groups (*an-Nuur*, 28 February 2003). In October 2003, shortly before the start of Ramadan, the *muftī* accepted that followers of the Islamic opposition could start to fast on another day, but decreed that they must perform their *ᶜīd* prayers inside their own mosques (communication Issa Ziddy, 28 October 2003). Rallies in Malindi were prohibited, however, and anṣār al-sunna rallies were shifted to the Lumumba Secondary School sports grounds in Saateni (that is, they were removed from the old city centre and the market area). The controversial question of the correct sighting of the moon and the fixing of Islamic holidays remained unsolved and continued to bother Zanzibar's population in 2004, 2005 and 2006. Further clashes between the Islamic opposition and security forces occurred on 5 March 2004 due to a new dispute over the correct date for the next *ᶜīd al-ḥajj*, and one anṣār al-sunna group, the Jumuiya ya Uamsho, was subsequently prohibited and its leadership imprisoned. Only in 2007, for the first time in years, did the onset of the month of Ramadan not lead to disputes over the sighting of the moon and the beginning of fasting. It seems that the population had become tired of never-ending debates over this issue and the fact that the annual disputes had brought no result (communication Maalim Idris, 10 September 2007).

Apart from the sighting of the moon for Ramadan, there were other conflicts between the *muftī* and the anṣār al-sunna, such as discussions regarding the dates of the *Mwaka Kogwa* (Swa.: 'washing the year', that is, the celebration of the new year) in Makunduchi, where the established calendar, the Persian *Nauruziyya* solar calendar, collided with the Western (Gregorian) calendar and the Muslim lunar calendar. In order to improve the chances of marketing this event for tourism in Zanzibar, the *muftī*, speaking for the government in 2002, proposed to fix the date for this event on a date of the Western calendar in the major tourist month of July, while the anṣār al-sunna advocated sticking to the local, Makunduchi (*Nauruziyya*, that is, pre-Islamic) calculation of times, which rotated the festival. Thereby, the anṣār al-sunna acknowledged the authority of the council of elders of Makunduchi, which had until then been attacked for preserving an 'un-Islamic festival' such as the *Mwaka Kogwa*. In an earlier article in *an-Nuur* on 26 July 2001 ('Epikeni ushirikina wa Mwaka Kogwa': 'Let's Distance Ourselves from the Superstitions of the Mwaka Kogwa'), the *Mwaka Kogwa* celebration held on 22 July 2001 had even been characterised by Naṣṣor Bachu as a form of *shirk* (ushirikina, idolatry) that 'went back to Namrudh'. According to him, there were only two Muslim holidays: *ᶜīd al-fiṭr* and *ᶜīd al-adhḥa*. Indeed, the *Mwaka Kogwa* 'knew no law': mwaka hamna sheria (communication Mohamed Ahmed Saleh, 2 April 2005).

The public discourse of the anṣār al-sunna, as presented in their public sermons and in a number of papers such as *an-Nuur*, *Dira*, *Maarifa* or *Nasaha*, was not confined, however, to polemics against popular religion, politics and/or the role of the *muftī*. From the late 1990s, it also focused on a number of additional issues, such as the nefarious effects of tourism, beauty contests and other forms of alleged moral decay in Zanzibari society that were more or less tolerated by the government. Articles in *an-Nuur*, but also in *Maarifa* and *Dira*, attacked the sale and advertising of alcohol, the spread of public bars, prostitution, drug trafficking, tourism, beauty contests (disguised as '*kanga* parties'), homosexuality or free sex on the beaches (see Loimeier 2011), as well as the increasing presence of Christians in Zanzibar. In 1992, the first graffiti appeared: '*Ondosha Utalii! Weka Uislamu*' ('Get rid of tourism, commit to Islam') (Purpura 1997: 379)[24] and in 1994, protest against the increasing presence of churches in Zanzibar was manifested in attacks on some churches, in particular Saint Mark's, which was burned down on 22 September 1994 (Niwagila 1999: 172).

An important theme of oppositional Muslim discourses was the increasing Christian influence in Zanzibar and the way in which the government manipulated Muslim–Christian relations. In an article in *an-Nuur* on 9 August 2002 entitled 'Makanisa madanguro kulipuliwa Zanzibar', Muslim leaders were quoted as having said that there was a plan 'that churches and hotels would burn' and that Muslims would then be accused of being responsible for these incidents. Thus, the government would have a reason to imprison Muslims. Frequently, as reported in *Maarifa* on 16 March 2002, private schools were accused of spreading Christian culture (Skuli binafsi zinafundisha mila za kinasara). Also, the Catholic Church was accused of bringing Zanzibar under its control by infiltrating the revolutionary government (*an-Nuur*, 27 August 2004) (Wakatoliki waponia kuingia ndani ya SMZ). Accusing the government of protecting Christians while suppressing Muslims has been a favourite strategy of the anṣār al-sunna for some time, and the alleged growth of Christian influence has been discussed in a number of articles in *an-Nuur*. Drugs, alcohol and homosexuality are themes that have been discussed in the context of tourism, possibly as an effort to discredit the liberal tourism policies of the revolutionary government.

While criticising Amani Abeid Karume's administration, the religious and political discourse of the anṣār al-sunna has often alluded to the regime of Zanzibar's first revolutionary president, Abeid Amani Karume (1964–72), despite the fact that he had smashed Zanzibar's religious establishment. His regime has nevertheless been praised for its policy of 'moral correctness' that prohibited the public sale of alcohol, prostitution and other kinds of what was judged to be immoral behaviour, such as shorts or hot pants, the Afro-look or indecent behaviour on the beaches. In fact, Karume was 'not content with telling people where they were to live [such as the Michenzani flats in *Ng'ambo*, that is, on the 'other side' of the creek that up to the 1950s divided the old town of Zanzibar from its numerous suburbs], he also decreed how they were to live', and offenders were tried in the People's Court (Martin 2007 [1978]: 67). One reference to Karume's politics has acquired particular quality, namely, his proclamation that the Arusha Declaration and TANU's Policy on Socialism and Self Reliance 1967 may be acceptable for the mainland, but not for Zanzibar, that it would and should 'stop at Chumbe'. Chumbe, a small island off the Unguja coast that marks entry into Zanzibar's territorial waters when approaching through the 'southern pass' from Dar es Salaam, was portrayed as the symbolic limit to mainland influences. As Chumbe was a military area and thus 'off limits' for civilian use, until the island became a privately managed national reserve, the reference to Chumbe was highly symbolical and expressed Zanzibar's distinctness and legacy of independence as stressed by Abeid Amani Karume after the unification of Zanzibar and Tanganyika in 1964.

The Chumbe argument was taken up in an article in *an-Nuur* on 25 July 2003, already quoted above, entitled '*Udhamini wa kampuni ya bia marufuku kuingia Zanzibar*' ('Advertising for Beer is Illegal in Zanzibar'). The author argued that the Zanzibar Government should not only declare advertisements for beer illegal in Zanzibar, but follow this line also with respect to things such as drugs, prostitution and fashion competitions: thus, beauty contests should stop at Chumbe as well (*mashindano ya urembo nayo mwisho Chumbe*). Even if legal on the mainland, the island of Chumbe should mark a boundary. The reference to Chumbe thus expresses the wishes of the anṣār al-sunna to keep Zanzibar apart from a mainland that is seen as being increasingly influenced by Christians. At the same time, Zanzibar was portrayed as a last resort for Muslims in East Africa. The reference to Abeid Amani Karume's policy of moral rigidity and political independence was also an implicit critique of Amani Abeid Karume, who followed his father as president of Zanzibar in 2000. His administration was portrayed by the anṣār al-sunna as a government tolerating moral decay, Christian influence and the demise of Islam, and as being a sell-out to the mainland, international finance and tourism.

Most recently, the reference to Chumbe has been complemented or even replaced by another geographical point of reference, namely the hamlet of Mkwajuni, in northern Unguja, about 5 km south-east of Mkokotoni (or 35 km north of Zanzibar Town), in the very heart of the island. This seemingly unimportant place is an important junction on the main road that commands access to the tourist resorts in the north, in particular Nungwi, as well as to those in the north-east, in particular Matemwe and Mnemba Island. These centres of tourism have come to symbolise today the most obnoxious manifestations of tourism in Zanzibar, namely prostitution and drugs. The 'geography of evil' has changed in recent years: while bad things stopped at Chumbe, at least in Abeid Amani Karume's times, they now touch the very heart of Zanzibar and can be felt throughout Zanzibar. In the eyes of the Islamic opposition, the religious elite as represented by the *muftī*, is intrinsically linked with this kind of development, because it failed to oppose the spread of tourism, as one of the articles in *an-Nuur* (Mufti akwama kwa changudoa) has stressed. Interestingly, the authors of this article comment on another development, again linked with Mkwajuni: while women in Zanzibar have always played netball, in Mkwajuni they have now started to play football, another obvious sign of moral decay (*an-Nuur*, 5 August 2004). For the first time in the history of religious discourse in Zanzibar, radical Muslims have thus started to attack football as a form of evil popular culture. However, this kind of critique has not yet gained widespread currency in Zanzibar, and the popularity of football, not only among men but also among women, may in the end frustrate Muslim moralist discourses.

. . . and the Comoros?

The Comoros[25] compare well with Zanzibar in many different respects and have historically been closely linked with Zanzibar not only in terms of trade, social development, language and culture, but also in terms of traditions of scholarship: since the mid-nineteenth century, the ᶜAlawiyya, the Qādiriyya and the Shādhiliyya have represented important Sufi-oriented traditions of reform in the Comoros.[26] Under the influence of the Bū Saᶜīdī Sultanate in Zanzibar, scholars from the Comoros, such as the Manṣab, Jamal al-Layl and Sumayṭ families,[27] settled in Zanzibar and contributed to the growth of Islamic learning in Zanzibar. Comorian scholars migrated to Zanzibar in order to escape the political instability and endless feuding among the petty sultanates of the Comoros, while Zanzibar provided stable conditions under the Bū Saᶜīdī Sultanate (Bang 2014: 54). In the colonial period, Comorians formed a numerically important diasporic group in Zanzibar and numerous Comorians studied with scholars such as Burhan Mkelle, Sayyid ᶜUmar b. Sumayṭ or Sayyid ᶜUmar ᶜAbdallāh who had a Comorian background.[28] After the revolution of 1964, many Comorians were forced to leave Zanzibar: they were not only regarded as foreigners but also as scholars linked with the pre-revolutionary scholarly establishment. Both ᶜUmar b. Sumayṭ[29] and Sayyid ᶜUmar ᶜAbdallāh subsequently moved to the Comoros.

Sayyid ᶜUmar ᶜAbdallāh (1918–88) (for his biography, see Loimeier

2009) can be regarded as a scholar who mirrored the upheavals of his time in paradigmatic ways, bridging colonial times and revolutions, as well as two post-revolutionary regimes: first in Zanzibar, and then in the Comoros. Having studied with local scholars in Zanzibar, including Sayyid ᶜUmar b. Sumayṭ and Abū l-Ḥasan b. Aḥmad Jamal al-Layl, Sayyid ᶜUmar ᶜAbdallāh was affiliated not only with the Qādiriyya and the ᶜAlawī network of scholars, but also with the Shādhiliyya. From 1928, he attended government schools, was sent to Makerere University Kampala in Uganda and became a teacher at the Dole Rural Middle School in Zanzibar in 1943. Later, he taught at the Beit al-Ras Teacher Training College. In 1948, he did a refresher course in Makerere and in 1951 he was awarded a Zanzibar Government Scholarship for a three-year degree course in Islamic studies, comparative law and Arabic at SOAS. In June 1954, his training at SOAS ended and he was appointed the new principal of the Muslim Academy, as successor to Muḥammad Muḥammad al-Dahhān, whose contract ended in September 1954. In 1961, his career in Zanzibar was interrupted again, as he got a Commonwealth scholarship grant to read for a B.Phil. at Oriel College, Oxford, for the period October 1961 to October 1963. For this degree (equivalent to a master's degree), he undertook research in Nigeria, Syria and in the Hadramawt. In June 1963, he graduated in Oxford (Bakari 2003: 3) and in September 1963, he finally returned to Zanzibar to work again as principal of the Muslim Academy until 1964 (Muhammad 1992: 13). After the revolution, the Muslim Academy continued to exist for some time and Sayyid ᶜUmar ᶜAbdallāh's salary was paid to him until June 1964. In the same year, he was imprisoned for a period of two months but was personally released by President Karume because he had been the teacher of many revolutionaries. After his release, Sayyid ᶜUmar ᶜAbdallāh continued to teach in Zanzibar, although he was imprisoned again for a period of four months in 1968. He was again liberated by Karume, but subsequently left Zanzibar for the Comoros in late 1968 (Bakari 2003: 7).

After his arrival in the Comoros, Sayyid ᶜUmar ᶜAbdallāh was hired by the French colonial administration as a teacher of English at the French Lycée in Moroni. Although he spoke Kingazidja fluently, he was required to learn French before he could take up this position. The French colonial administration granted him a fellowship to study French in Paris. He accepted and subsequently lived in the Quartier Latin for one year. After his return to Moroni, he was appointed as a teacher and also taught at his own mosque and *madrasa*. In the Comoros, he continued to take part in the *mawlid barzanjī* celebrations, while criticising the tradition of the *grand mariage*.[30] After the independence of the Comoros in 1975, he was appointed ambassador plenipotentiary for the Comoros for Islamic affairs (Ahmed 1999: 121, 137). He served in this function until 1978. Despite having defended the esoteric episteme all his life, he eventually agreed in 1978 to work as a *dāᶜiya* for the rābiṭat al-ᶜālam al-islāmī. He was recruited for the rābiṭa by ᶜAbdallāh ᶜUmar Naṣīf (b. 1939), scion of a family of rich traders and notables in Jiddah, who was elected general secretary of the rābiṭa in 1983 (Schulze 1990: 242ff), and who had been trained in England at the University of Leeds. Sayyid ᶜUmar ᶜAbdallāh had met him while in London (communication Muhammad Bakari, 11 September 2004). As a *dāᶜiya* of the rābiṭa, he taught in Kenya, especially in the month of Ramadan, and repeatedly met ᶜAbdallāh Ṣāliḥ al-Farsy, from whom he was 'worlds apart' but with whom he had a relationship in which 'they respected each other and did not see each other as opponents' (communication Muhammad Bakari, 21 February 2002). Sayyid ᶜUmar ᶜAbdallāh attracted large crowds of followers to the mosques where he taught and preached. In his sermons, which were recorded for the sake of the women at home, he remained critical of a literalist interpretation of the Qurᵓān. In his late years, he was increasingly drawn into Sufi-Wahhābī disputes, often started by University of Medina graduates who taught in the new *madāris* that had been set up by the rābiṭa (Bakari 2003: 6). After 1968, he travelled widely in Africa, Europe and America, invited by local Muslim organisations, transcending local, racial, national and ethnic boundaries, preaching a message of tolerance to his audience (Bakari 2003: 5). Sayyid ᶜUmar ᶜAbdallāh died in the Comoros on 6 March 1988 (17 Rajab 1408) due to diabetes (Bakari 2003: 9, 2006: 363–88).

Although scholars such as Sayyid ᶜUmar b. Sumayṭ and Sayyid ᶜUmar ᶜAbdallāh brought reformist ideas from Zanzibar to the Comoros in the late 1960s, first 'ripples of reform' (Bang 2014) occurred much earlier: first, notions of reform most probably reached the Comoros in the late nineteenth century through the family networks of the Comorian scholars who had settled in Zanzibar and who communicated with both the Hadramawt and

Egypt (see Bang 2003; Loimeier 2009). Second, Comorian scholars such as Aḥmad Qamar al-Dīn and Aḥmad Mfoihaya who had been abroad either for studies or for the pilgrimage, or both, also introduced concepts of reform in the Comoros. In 1933, Aḥmad Mfoihaya (1880–93) (for his biography, see Mohamed 2008: 128ff) established the first modern *madrasa* of the Comoros in Mbeni, Ngazidja. Inspired by Egyptian initiatives of educational reform, this *madrasa* was named madrasat al-azhar. The madrasat al-azhar became the centre for the formation of a new generation of Comorian religious scholars who were committed to a reformist agenda in Islamic education, while still being linked with the esoteric episteme: both Aḥmad Mfoihaya and his son, Muḥammad 'Azhar', were linked with the Qādiriyya (Mohamed 2008: 41).

In 1956, madrasat al-azhar graduates established a first activist association in Mbeni, al-anṣār. Anṣār members not only built new mosques and qur'ānic schools, but also started to supervise attendance of *jumᶜa* prayers and 'proper' Islamic ritual in Mbeni (Mohamed 2008: 40f). Anṣār activists attacked the *grand mariage* and propagated the *dhikr* (of the Qādiriyya) and celebration of the *mawlid al-nabī*. Due to political disputes, the anṣār disintegrated in the early 1960s, but re-emerged in 1975 in the guise of a new activist association, the jamᶜiyyat al-taḍāmun al-islāmiyya (JTI), again led by Muḥammad 'Azhar' and still linked with the Qādiriyya (Mohamed 2008: 42). The group now also advocated the education of women. In 1976, the JTI founded a markaz al-islāmiya in Mbeni that formed a new generation of scholars in the Comoros such as ᶜAbd al-Ḥakīm Muḥammad Shākir (b. 1967).[31] Due to its anti-'communist' orientation, markaz and JTI were prohibited by the ᶜAlī Soilih administration in 1976, but re-emerged in late 1978 as a charitable association. The time from 1978 to 1990 was characterised by a *baisse d'activités* (Mohamed 2008: 45) due to the fact that many *markaz* students went to Saudi Arabia to study at the Islamic University of Medina, or to Sudan. At the same time, the JTI was able to garner financial support from Libya and to build a new school that was opened in 1986. In 1991, this school became the 'Collège de la Solidarité Islamique', the first Islamic private school of the Comoros (Mohamed 2008: 45). The *collège* also became a home for the *markaz* students who started to come back from Saudi Arabia in 1990 and to introduce Salafi concepts of reform. In 1996, the *collège* became the Lycée de la Solidarité Islamique (Mohamed 2008: 64f).[32] The history of the madrasat al-azhar and the markaz al-islāmiyya and their students in Mbeni are a paradigmatic case showing the evolution of a tradition of reform that was originally linked with the esoteric episteme, yet eventually turned Salafi, in three generations of scholars. The case of Mbeni also shows, however, that the emergence of a Salafi-oriented tradition of reform must not necessarily mean complete rupture with an earlier, Sufi-oriented tradition of reform: family links have prevented outright conflict in Mbeni so far, and have to be seen as a major integrative force.

Ritual and *jum^ca* prayers, in particular, were a major issue of dispute (and reform) in Mbeni and Ngazidja, while in Mayotte dispute over questions of the ritual and, thus, doctrinal distinction and symbolic distantiation were also central to religious conflict: in 1951, Shaykh Ibrāhīm, a member of Mayotte's religious establishment who had been abroad for studies, started to challenge local scholars on the issue of the *jumᶜa* prayer on Fridays: according to local customs, *jumᶜa* prayers had six *rakaᶜāt*, two for *jumᶜa* prayers and four for the obligatory *ẓuhr* prayers. Shaykh Ibrāhīm, however, insisted on two *rakaᶜāt* only for *jumᶜa* prayers, arguing that *jumᶜa* prayers superseded *ẓuhr* prayers and did not supplement them (Lambek 1993: 181). Despite this critique of established ritual practice, Shaykh Ibrāhīm's ideas spread slowly and only became a matter of broader debates in Mayotte in 1985.

More important than religious disputes for the political development of the Comoros were the politial debates triggered by the shift of the capital from Dzaoudzi (Maoré/Mayotte) to Moroni (Ngazidja) in 1962, a move that started a movement for secession on Mayotte and decisively influenced the development of political parties in the Comoros in the 1960s and 1970s. Up to 1968, political groups in the Comoros were divided into a 'white' and a 'green' party, which represented communal divisions rather than distinct political programmes. In 1968, the 'green' party became the Rassemblement Démocratique du Peuple Comorien (RDPC) led by Sayyid Muḥammad Cheikh, while the 'white' party became the Union Démocratique des Comores (UDC) led by Sayyid Ibrāhīm. These parties were characterised by the fact that they united a number of divergent factions and frequently formed coalitions of convenience. In the elections of June 1971, the UDC won, but ousted Sayyid Ibrāhīm from power in June 1972. In the aftermath of this intrigue, RDPC and UDC members merged to form Udzima under the leadership of Aḥmad ᶜAbdallāh (1919–89) (from Ndzawani), who also became the new Président du Conseil du Gouvernement,[33] while dissident groups of both parties formed Umma under the leadership of ᶜAlī Soilih (1937–78) (from Ngazidja). In another round of elections in December 1972, Udzima defeated Umma. While Udzima advocated a policy of modernisation, represented a 'Comorian' agenda and was supported by most notables and the Grand Qāḍī, Sayyid Muḥammad ᶜAbd al-Raḥmān (1912–90), Umma stood for an Arabo-socialist orientation and was supported by the 'learned' and 'cosmopolitan' religious scholars such as Muḥammad Sharīf b. Aḥmad Jamal al-Layl and Ṭāhir Mawlāna Jamal al-Layl, who had studied in Arab countries (Ahmed 1999: 132). In a referendum in 1974, a majority of the population of the Comoros (with the exception of Mayotte) voted for independence from France in 1978, yet, when it became clear that Mayotte would remain a French *territoire d'outre mer* (TOM), Aḥmad ᶜAbdallāh unilaterally declared the Comoros's independence on 6 July 1975.

The fact that religious scholars participated in political debates in the 1960s and 1970s led to the division of religious scholars into two factions: those supporting Udzima and those supporting Umma. This division extended to the field of religious ritual that saw the emergence of '*mawlid*-Udzima' and '*mawlid*-Umma' celebrations. Equally, mosque communties were divided and communities were polarised (Ahmed 1999: 142). Furthermore, there was a split between local notables and village scholars on the one hand, and religious scholars who represented a somewhat broader and transnational orientation on the other. These scholars not only saw themselves as being superior to local scholars, in moral terms as well as in terms of Islamic knowledge, but they also condemned local religious practices as superstition and *bidaᶜ*. As a result of infighting and disputes, the established religious scholars lost their credibility as a moral institution in Comorian society, a development that seriously damaged their reputation in the context of the revolution of 1975 and beyond (Ahmed 1999: 143). Prior to 1975, religious scholarship in the Comoros was characterised by its hierarchical nature: the Grand Qāḍī formed the top of this hierarchy, followed by the district *qāḍīs* and *imāms*, often *masharifu*, that is, the descendants of the Prophet Muḥammad of Hadrami extraction, and then the qurᵓānic school teachers (*fundis*), the scholars and representatives of the Sufi orders, the *walimu*. At the bottom of the hierarchy were the *waganga*, the local healers.

On 3 August 1975, the first post-independence government of the Comoros under President Aḥmad ᶜAbdallāh was overthrown by ᶜAlī Soilih. On 6 July 1976, after an initial process of political consolidation, he started a programme of social reforms that resembled the reforms in revolutionary Zanzibar (and South Yemen) and that have been called a 'toilette sociale', a 'nettoyage des mentalités et des traditions' (Vérin and Vérin 1999: 108): French was replaced by Shikomoro and the national archives were burned in order to symbolise the 'new start'. Land was nationalised and the estates of the big landowners and expatriate companies were taken over by the state.[34] The new order was policed by youth brigades, the Commandos Moissi, trained and supported by approximately 200 Tanzanian police officers and advisers, another parallel to post-revolutionary Zanzibar.[35] Due to the fact that France froze all financial support for the regime, Algerian and Tunisian teachers came to replace French teachers. The revolutionary government of ᶜAlī Soilih also received support from Egypt, Irak and the Sudan. In order to save resources, in the region of 3,500 (out of about 5,000) public employees were dismissed (but reinstated in 1978) (Djabir 1993: 55f, 87).

ᶜAlī Soilih wanted to change Comorian society as quickly as possible and proceeded radically in order to achieve his aims. Being a socialist (and an atheist), ᶜAlī Soilih, the *mongozi* (guide) of the nation, who had also not gone through the *grand mariage* (Mattoir 2004: 71), was indifferent towards religion. He saw economic development, politics and education as the paramount features of his programme of reform, yet his politics damaged the three major social, religious and political pillars of Comorian society: village notables, religious scholars and local political leaders. They were accused of blocking progress and replaced by village committees (*ikayo sha mdji*) (Ahmed 1999: 164). *Qāḍīs* and local scholars were replaced by such committees, with a national Islamic Committee (jamᶜiyya al-islāmiyya) that assumed jurisdiction and authority over the village committees (Ahmed 1999: 164). The new institutions were dominated by the young, the *mashababi*, as well as men (*walezi*) who had already gone through the *grand mariage* but respected the revolution (Mattoir 2004: 10). The old elites were removed from power. In reality, however, local issues were decided by the President of the Republic and were communicated to village committees across the islands by radio, the most important medium of communication at that time (Ahmed 1999: 165). On 23 April 1977, a new 'loi fondamentale' declared the Comoros a 'république démocratique laique et sociale'. This 'loi fondamentale' also initiated a struggle against 'superstitions' and religious authorities.

Major targets of ᶜAlī Soilih's revolution were superstition and *bidaᶜ* as well as magico-religious practices, burial ceremonies, the *dhikr* and *mawlid* of the Sufi orders and time-consuming supererogatory prayers, such as the *waẓīfa* of the Sufi orders. In the larger context of the 'Comorization' of the Comoros, the new regime introduced the singing of the national anthem in mosques before prayers were allowed to start (Barraux 2009: 247). The Arabic *khuṭba* was replaced by a *khuṭba* in Comorian (Ahmed 1999: 167). In 1977, the *khuṭba* was even replaced by political speeches (Barraux 2009: 247). Religious authorities, in particular, qurᵓānic school teachers (*fundis*), teachers (*walimu*) and scholars of the Sufi orders (*shuyūkh*), as well as ritual healers (*waganga*), were ridiculed and accused of 'holding unacceptable power over the population' (Blanchy 1998: 183). Equally, the ᶜAlī Soilih administration encouraged women to abandon the *ḥijāb* (Barraux 2009: 247; Vérin and Vérin 1999: 108). Burial and mourning ceremonies, as well as the festivals of the Sufi orders, were prohibited in 1976 due to their social and economic costs. A major goal of the prohibition of social and religious rituals was to curb the consumption of (imported) rice and to boost local production of food.[36] The prohibition of costly burial rites turned out to be particularly successful, as these practices were not resumed after 1978 (Ahmed 1999: 171). In addition, the ᶜAlī Soilih administration banned *uganga* practices and forced *waganga* underground (Ahmed 1999: 173). The *grand mariage* was also attacked and prohibited (on 6 April 1976) as a major symbol of the old order, a move that again hit the local scholars and notables who were in charge of its organisation.

In 1978, ᶜAlī Soilih was deposed by French and South African mercenaries under the command of Bob Denard, who brought Aḥmad ᶜAbdallāh back to power on 13 May 1978.[37] On 24 May 1978, the Comoros became the Islamic Republic of the Comoros that continued to strengthen its ties with the Arab world, in particular, Saudi Arabia and Kuwait. In 1993, the Comoros became a member state of the Arab League.[38] Under the new

President Aḥmad ᶜAbdallāh (r. 1978–89) the Comoros saw a period of re-Islamisation that can be viewed as a reaction to the politics of 'de-Islamization' or 'de-sacralization' of the ᶜAlī Soilih administration (Ahmed 1999: 181; Mattoir 2004: 114). Religion became the basis for the legitimisation of political power and all spheres of life were gradually Islamised. Most particularly, the *grand mariage* was re-introduced. Arabic was declared the second official language in addition to French. President Aḥmad ᶜAbdallāh even acted as *imām* and led Friday prayers personally. He also created the office of the Grand Muftī and appointed the former Grand Qāḍī, Muḥammad ᶜAbd al-Raḥmān, to this position.[39]

In the 1980s and 1990s, government in the Comoros became characterised by nepotism, corruption and chronic theft of state funds. Financial resources were syphoned off by the political elite (Walker 2007: 597) that fought for privileged access to resources.[40] In 1990, Saᶜīd Muḥammed Djohar (b. 1918 in Majunga, Madagascar) followed President Aḥmad ᶜAbdallāh, who had been assassinated by Bob Denard's mercenaries in 1989, but had to be evacuated to Réunion by French troops following another coup attempt by Bob Denard in September 1995. From 1996, the Comoros were led by Muḥammed Taki ᶜAbd al-Karīm (1936–98), succeeded by Interim President Tāj al-Dīn b. Saᶜīd Massunde in 1998. As a result of chronic crisis, the infractructure of the Comoros (roads, schools, hospitals and so forth) collapsed and villages started to establish their own administration in the 1990s. At the same time, the Comoros disintegrated politically: in 1997, both Mwali and Ndzawani declared their independence, but were forced by French troops to abandon their secessionist plans. In April 1999, Colonel Assumani (al-Thamānī) Azali (from Ngazidja) seized power in the eighteenth coup or attempted coup in the short history of the Comoros since attaining independence in 1975. In 2002, Assumani Azali was voted into power in democratic elections and introduced far-reaching constitutional reforms that transformed the Union of the Comoros into a loose federation, including a system of rotational presidency.[41]

After religious scholars had been weakened as the major moral institution of the Comoros for a number of reasons in the 1960s and 1970s, the 1990s saw the social and political rise of a generation of young graduates who had been to universities in Saudi Arabia, Sudan, Egypt and Kuwait. First graduates from the Comoros had gone to Saudi Arabia in the early 1970s and since 1978, the number of Comorian students in Arab countries multiplied considerably. This development was stimulated by the opening of Comorian embassies in Cairo and in the Gulf. From 1975, an increasing number of Comorian students also went to Egypt to study at al-Azhar University, where they established the Ligue des étudiants de la République fédérale et islamique des Comores au Caire in 1975 (Ahmed 2002a: 237). In 1986, about 200 Comorian students were studying at the Islamic University of Medina, about 100 in Kuwait and in the region of 40 at al-Azhar in Cairo. In 1990, the number of Comorian students in Saudi Arabia had risen to about 600. At the same time, the number of students in Egypt rose to more than 1,600 in 1999. In 2005, about 1,200 Comorian students were based at Egyptian universities (in the region of 800 at al-Azhar), while in the region of 300 were studing in Syria, about 500 in Tunisia and Morocco and about 500 in the Sudan (Ahmed 2005: 62). While Comorian students in the countries of the Maghrib remained committed to a Francophone system of education, students in Libya, Egypt, Saudi Arabia and the Gulf became 'Arabisants' and started to fight the 'école française' after their return to the Comoros. The collapse of the national (Francophone) educational system of the Comoros in the 1990s gave private Arab/Islamic schools a chance to develop into a second tier of education and provided jobs for the 'Arabisants' (Ahmed 2002a: 238). After 1990, graduates opened their own village qurʾānic schools or worked at one of the new Islamic colleges (*maᶜāhid*) that were built in the 1980s, as well as at government secondary schools. In 2005, the Comoros had six *maᶜāhid*: three in Ngazidja, two in Ndzawani and one in Mwali. Often, the teachers' salaries were paid by Saudi Arabia or the rābiṭa. Since the 1990s, al-ḥaramain and the Africa Muslim Agency became increasingly important donor organisations (Ahmed 2005: 63).

In social terms, these graduates often represented marginal groups in the Comoros, because they were not taught in the schools of the established religious scholars and did not belong to well-respected families of Hadrami origin. As a consequence, they came to represent a Salafi-oriented movement of reform that opposed the Comoros's religious establishment, both village scholars (*fundis*) and Hadrami *masharifu* (Ahmed 1999: 202). The paramount role of the *masharifu* was criticised by the Salafi-oriented reformers as a form of 'sharifocracy' due to the fact that 'masharifu' still occupied a disproportionate number of public religious positions and had an elevated role in society as *imāms*, *qāḍīs*, qurʾānic school teachers and negotiators in local disputes (Mohamed 2008: 147). The Salafi-oriented reformers also criticised the 'French' government schools and local practices such as the *grand mariage*, which was accused of pushing Comorians into debt. The graduates organised their *daᶜwa* in the villages during the school holidays and attacked local practices and local scholars. In their critique of local practices they came close to ᶜAlī Soilih's discourse of reform (Ahmed 1999: 213, 2002a).

In 1990, graduates who had come back from studies abroad established the Front National pour la Justice (FNP) in 1990, which became the Comoros's first 'fundamentalist party' in the 1990s (Ahmed 2005: 49). In the 1990s, the FNJ was led by three charismatic persons: Aḥmad ᶜAbdallāh Muḥammad Sambi, who had studied at the Islamic University of Medina and at the University of Qom in Iran, where he had come to assume a politically radical and pro-Iranian position, without turning Shīᶜī; Aḥmad Rashīd, who had studied in Kuwait, in Medina and in the Sudan; and Ṣādiq Mbapandza, who had also studied in Medina. Aḥmad Rashīd and Ṣādiq Mbapandza formed a radical wing of the FNJ, while Aḥmad ᶜAbdallāh Muḥammad Sambi was more pragmatic (Ahmed 1999: 222). In 1990, the FNJ took part in the presidential elections in the Comoros for the first time and supported Muḥammad Taki ᶜAbd al-Karīm. He was credible in Islamic terms, due to the fact that he had been in prison under ᶜAlī Soilih, but he lost against Saᶜīd Muḥammad Djohar (Jaffar), a half-brother of ᶜAlī Soilih, who was supported by France. In the 1993 parliamentary elections, the FNJ garnered 15 per cent of the votes. The FNJ supported Muḥammad Taki ᶜAbd al-Karīm again in the 1996 presidential elections. This time he won, with 64 per cent of the votes. The elections in 2006 were won by Aḥmad ᶜAbdallāh Muḥammad Sambi from Ndzawani, who represented a pragmatic Salafi-oriented tradition of reform.

Conclusion

In the past few years, a broad spectrum of both Sufi- and Salafi-oriented brokers of Islam has emerged in Zanzibar, comprising government scholars, such as the *qāḍīs*, the Muslim functionaries and teachers of 'Islamics' at the Chuo

Cha Kiislamu and other government schools, and religious scholars, such as ᶜAbdallāh b. Abī Bakr 'Muᶜallim' Bā Kathīr, who, until his death in 2000, was the *imām* of the Madrasat al-Nūr and who cooperated closely with the government. The efforts of the state to exert hegemonic power over all aspects of everyday life, including religion, and the instrumentalisation of Muslim functionaries for these ends have encouraged the development of oppositional groups that try to escape and to oppose state control and who have attacked existing religious, social and political structures. Both Muslim functionaries and 'Medina graduates', as well as the different *watu wa bidaa* groups, are characterised by the fact that their leading representatives were trained in countries such as Saudi Arabia, Egypt and Sudan, in particular at the Islamic University of Medina, the Omdurman Islamic University and al-Azhar, and are often far removed from older, Sufi-oriented traditions of reform.

In recent decades, politics and public discourses in many North African, West Asian and sub-Saharan African Muslim societies have been informed by religious issues, and Muslim religious scholars have gained considerable acceptance as moral authorities. Authoritarian, secular and socialist regimes have come under attack from a pious opposition and Salafi-oriented movements have accused such regimes of violating Islamic norms or Islamic morality. The state's reactions to this kind of religious critique are (often, but not always) presented in an Islamic (doctrinal) disguise, confirming the eminent role of religion in contemporary politics. Both the state and the pious opposition have tried to instrumentalise religion and notions of piety in order to de-legitimise the respective other. Due to these religio-political dynamics, politicians and religious scholars have become prisoners of their own moralistic discourses. Escape from this piety trap is difficult as long as both the state and religious scholars accept the dialectics of a religious argumentation and the norms of Islamic morality as defined by those Muslim religious scholars, politicians and intellectuals who seek hegemony of interpretation (*Deutungshoheit*) in the public sphere and who have established criteria for 'proper Islamic' morals and piety.

Looking at the *longue durée* of the struggle against popular culture, popular religious practices, beauty contests or *kanga* parties, it can be said that the British colonial government, the religious establishment of colonial times, the Karume administration and the *watu wa bidaa* have been united in their endeavours to eradicate a broad spectrum of seemingly immoral, wasteful or un-Islamic features of everyday life. This struggle is not only an old and recurring one, but also one that may be impossible to win. Despite the popularity of their critique of the CCM government, the *watu wa bidaa* have so far failed to make any deep impact on Zanzibari society and to translate their agenda into religious and political realities. This may be due to the fact that the revolutionary government of Zanzibar, while trying to control public religion, for instance through the office of the *muftī*, has refused to adopt Islamic legitimatory discourses and politics, and has thus escaped the piety trap: the legitimatory basis of the CCM administration is not Islam, but socialism. Zanzibar's government scholars and Muslim functionaries have not been willing to accept the argumentation of the religious opposition and have staunchly defended Zanzibar's socialist character and the legacy of the revolution. In addition, the distinct political (anti-government) character of the moral discourse of the anṣār al-sunna is often perceived by a majority of Zanzibar's population as a blatant instrumentalisation of religion for political ends. In addition, Salafi-oriented activists have failed to develop a convincing social agenda. While controlling some mosques and, at times, influencing public debates, the *watu wa bidaa* have not gained a foothold in state-controlled institutions, such as the Waqf Commission, or institutions of Islamic learning. The efforts of the *watu wa bidaa* to establish their own realm within Islamic education have not yet reached a tangible stage. Like in mainland Tanzania and in Kenya, the agenda of Salafi-oriented groups has largely remained confined to the political sphere, the mobilisation of the youth and public moral discourses. By contrast, Salafi-oriented movements of reform in other African countries, such as Senegal or Nigeria, have developed a much broader programme that includes not only the mobilisation of women and youth, as well as a political agenda, but also the development of competitive educational and social programmes.

This analysis does not apply to the Comoros: here, the socialist period was very short (1975–8) and subsequent administrations have clearly identified Islam as their most important legitimatory basis. As a result, the Comorian governments of the 1980s and 1990s have walked into a piety trap. Due to the shrinking credibility of established religious scholars, the young Comorian graduates managed to acquire increasing social and political influence in the 1990s and contributed to the rise to power of at least two Comorian presidents, Muḥammad Taki and 'Ayatollah' Aḥmad ᶜAbdallāh Sambi. Despite the fact that Salafi-oriented reformers do not have a social basis among middle-class groups, which are virtually non-existent in the Comoros, Salafi-oriented reformers have nevertheless become a major factor in Comorian politics and society, because they have come to be regarded as being morally credible, and not involved in corruption.

The failure of Salafi-oriented activists to become a popular mass movement in Zanzibar may also be due to the fact that over time moralistic discourses and polemics create a certain degree of exhaustion among those who have to listen to them. In 2007, before the start of the month of Ramadan, the *watu wa bidaa* refrained for the first time in years from entering into a dispute over the official sighting of the moon. This was most probably due to the fact that recurring disputes had not led to a solution of the issue, and that the Muslim population of Zanzibar had reached a certain degree of 'compassion fatigue' regarding this theme (communication Maalim Idris, 10 September 2007). At the same time, the *watu wa bidaa* started to focus on a new theme, namely conspicuous spending in the context of the celebration of the *ᶜīd al-fiṭr* at the beginning of the month of Shawwāl. Thus, as in the 1980s and 1990s, popular practices again became the target of the *watu wa bidaa*, while political critique became secondary (for the time being). This has led to a further loss of popularity of the *watu wa bidaa*, as I was able to observe in 2009, when *watu wa bidaa* discourses completely failed to gain a public audience: the majority of Zanzibaris are unwilling to abandon cherished socio-religious practices that are seen as Islamic and as grounded in an old and respected tradition of Islamic learning. Finally, the majority of Zanzibaris dispute the legitimacy of Salafi-oriented activists and their claim to speak for all Muslims. Salafi-oriented activists are generally seen as an 'import' from Saudi Arabia, as people who do not represent sound local Islamic traditions. While local traditions of Islamic learning have been compared in the past to an ocean (*baḥr*) of learning, Salafi traditions are perceived as shallow and as representing foreign and narrow textbook standards of Islam. Thus, even in their absence, local Islamic traditions are still respected in Zanzibar, while Salafi-minded activists have been unable to fill the intellectual and educational void created by the elimination of Zanzibar's religious establishment in 1964.

This may change, however, in view of the way that the *watu wa bidaa* have adopted a number of political positions that have up to now been represented by Zanzibar's long-time opposition party, the CUF. In 2011 and 2012, Uamsho publicly rejected the new draft union constitution, including its harsh rules regarding opposition to union regulations, and called for Zanzibar's independence in order to protect Muslims in Zanzibar against encroaching Christianity and Western influences coming from the mainland. As a result, Uamsho gatherings were stopped by the CCM-CUF coalition government under President Ali Muhammad Shein in April 2012. As Uamsho continued to hold rallies, clashes with security forces followed and several leading Uamsho members were imprisoned. When Farid Hadi Ahmed went missing for four days in October 2012, a new series of riots caused upheaval, attesting to the capacity of Uamsho to mobilise its followers. Since then, the situation in Zanzibar has remained tense, as evidenced by an acid attack in November 2012 against Fadhil Sulaiman Soraga, the secretary to the *muftī*'s office (katibu wa mufti wa Zanzibar), who was accused of rampant corruption in office; the murders of two catholic priests, Ambrose Mkenda and Evarist Mushi in December 2012 and February 2013; and two further acid attacks against two British volunteer teachers in August 2013 (Bergmann 2013). Although both national and international media have accused Uamsho of being the masterforce behind these events and of being linked with both al-Qāᶜida and al-Shabāb, Uamsho has so far denied any involvement (see Howden 2014). Yet, these recent events clearly point to an escalation and a strategic shift in violence: while earlier attacks targeted buildings such as churches and government structures, political violence has now started to target people, in particular corrupt state functionaries, church representatives and tourists, who are accused of violating local dress and behavourial codes.

Notes

1. Zanzibar is an umbrella term for an archipelago of two large islands (Unguja and Pemba) and a great number of smaller islands such as Uzi and Tumbatu. Colloquially, 'Zanzibar' is used to refer to either the island of Unguja or Zanzibar Town. In political terms, Zanzibar has formed one of the two autonomous and constitutive parts of the Federation of Tanzania since 1964 (the other being the

'mainland', formerly the Republic of Tanganyika). Historically, the Sultanate of Zanzibar became a British Protectorate in 1890 and re-acquired independence on 10 December 1963. The revolution of 12 January 1964 led to a complete re-orientation of Zanzibar. On 26 April 1964, Zanzibar united with Tanganyika.

2. Before 1977, the party of the revolution was called the Afro Shirazi Party (ASP). In 1977, the ASP merged with the mainland Tanganyika Africa National Union to form the federal Tanzanian Chama Cha Mapinduzi (CCM).
3. The term 'Manga' denoted poor Omanis who had settled in Zanzibar. The term is derived from the Arabic word '*naqa*ᶜ*a*', meaning 'to soak', and denotes somebody soaked (*manqū*ᶜ) in (sea) water (Glassman 2011: 195).
4. The 'Hadimu fringe' denotes a belt of rather poor soils outside Unguja's clove and palm tree plantations in the centre of the island, which was mostly owned by rich Arabs and Indians. The 'Hadimu fringe' had become the refuge of marginalised 'Wahadimu' farmers who had been pushed from the fertile central and western parts of Unguja in the nineteenth century, in the context of the formation of huge clove, and later coconut, plantations. Major support for the revolution in 1964 came from the Hadimu fringe, in particular Makunduchi, and the eastern and southern regions of Unguja still provide support for the revolutionary government today.
5. Numbers regarding the numbers of people killed in the revolution range from 3,000 to 11,000 dead (Clayton 1981: 81) in a population of approximately 340,000 in 1964.
6. The statistical record of staff in the Ministry of Education (MoE), in both schools and administration, from 1963 (last data recorded before the revolution) to 1974 (when data became available again) is quite revealing: in early 1964, the MoE had 827 teachers (including 52 walimu) and an administrative staff of 35 (as well as technical staff who are not considered here), that is, a total staff of 862 people. In 1964, all British staff (20) as well as 282 local teachers left Zanzibar ('ran away' in the respective pamphlets produced by the Afro Shirazi Party), that is, the total number of staff was reduced to approximately 540. Before 1972, another 200 teachers and staff were sacked, mostly in the context of the purges of Ali Sultan Issa in 1967, reducing the staff of the MoE to a mere 340 in 1974, that is, approximately 40 per cent of the 1963 workforce (Loimeier 2009: 494f).
7. See Burgess (1999, 2002a, 2002b) for details of the revolutionary cult. The legacy of the revolution has been kept alive in multiple ways to this day by the CCM, for instance in the instrumentalisation of public festivals and celebrations, especially in the field of sports, in the media, in the continued existence of

revolutionary structures such as Zanzibar's security apparatus and the Zanzibari secret service, as well as in the marginalisation of oppositional forces, especially the Civic United Front (CUF).

8. On this scholar, see Cassanelli (1973), Lewis (2001: 227ff), Martin (1976) Reese (1999, 2008) and Samatar (1992).
9. A first Salafi-oriented organisation was established in Zanzibar in 1910, namely, the ḥizb al-iṣlāḥ as led by Nāṣir b. Sulaimān al-Lamkī and Nāṣir b. Sālim al-Ruwāḥī (Hoffman 2007: 23). For the time being, the endeavours of the Muslim reformers remained confined, however, to a small intelligentsia that discussed questions of proper education and the role of the Arabic language rather than the anti-colonial struggle. The first Islamic group with an associationist character in Zanzibar was the jamᶜiyyat al-islāmiyya, established by Sālim b. Saᶜīd b. Sayf al-Shuhaybī in 1922 (Loimeier 2009: 195, 111), which assumed a distinct Salafi character due to the influence of al-Shuhaybī's main student, Rashīd b. Ḥamīd al-Ḥaḍramī (d. 1963) in the 1950s. Yet, this association did not acquire a following beyond the circles of a few scholars: the time for Salafi-oriented associations was to come in the 1970s only (see also Bang 2014: 184ff.; al-Farsy 1972: 40).
10. For his biography, see Bakari (1989), Bang (2003), Bilal Muslim Mission of Tanzania (1999), Kresse (2007a), Lacunza Balda (1997), Loimeier (2009), Rajab (2001), Seesemann (2006a) and the biographical text by his student Saidi Musa (Maisha ya al-Imam Sheikh Abdulla Saleh Farsy katika ulimwengu wa Kiislamu, 1986). His personal file (ZNA AB 86/136) must also be mentioned. In addition, a little booklet by ᶜAbdallāh Ṣāliḥ al-Farsy entitled *bid-a (sehemu ya pili)* contains a short account of ᶜAbdallāh Ṣāliḥ al-Farsy's life by Saidi Musa, authorised by ᶜAbdallāh Ṣāliḥ al-Farsy.
11. A similar observation may be made with respect to the *tafsīr* of Abubakar Gumi (Gumi 1979) in northern Nigeria. He translates *ṣūra* 7: 54 as: *Lalle ne Ubagajinku Allah ne, wanda ya halitta sammai da kasa a cikin kwanaki shida, saᵓannan kuma ya daidaita a kan alᵓarshi.* The key word here is the verb '*daidaita*', which means in Hausa 'to arrange symmetrically', 'to adapt to' or 'to bring into line', as in '*ya daidaita masar da sauran kasashan dunya*' ('he brought Egypt into line with other countries'). Gumi thus sticks to the allegoric interpretation of the verse as well, even if he never stressed or clarified this issue. In any case, he did not insist on a literal translation, although he had undoubtedly been Saudi Arabia's closest ally in Nigeria, and was even a founding member of the rābiṭat al-ᶜālam al-islāmī. A number of his students and followers adopted a much clearer position with respect to these problematic verses by sticking to literalistic interpretations (see

Loimeier 1997a; communication Andra Brigaglia 28 February 2005 and Sanusi Lamido Sanusi, 16 June 2005).

12. Many '*Washamba*' scholars (such as the first Chief Qāḍī after the revolution, Fatawi Issa, who died in 1987) came from Makunduchi and other parts of the so-called Hadimu fringe of the island of Unguja, that is, the eastern and southern sections of the island.
13. The Chuo Cha Kiislamu was established in 1972 as a loyalist replacement for the Muslim Academy, Zanzibar's first modern Islamic college that had been closed by the revolutionary government in 1965. After the revolution, even private and/or *waqf*-funded schools such as the madrasat al-nūr, Zanzibar's biggest *madrasa*, were taken over by obliging scholars such as ᶜAbdallāh b. Abī Bakr 'Muᶜallim' Bā Kathīr, who, until his death in 2000, was the *imām* of the madrasat al-nūr and who cooperated closely with the government.
14. Zanzibar Muslim students were often close to Salafī ideas of reform but did not necessarily sympathise with the Saudi religious establishment. Many African Muslims who studied in Saudi Arabia did not become 'Wahhābī' but were appalled by many aspects of life in Saudi Arabia, such as racism toward Africans and the hypocrisy of Saudi lifestyles (communication Masoud Ahmad Shani, 31 August 2002).
15. As a matter of fact, the number of women donning the full veil, the *niqāb*, has been consistently growing over the past few years. This growth may point to a corresponding increase in strength of the radical wing of the anṣār al-sunna. However, the movement towards the full veil should not be over-interpreted as women have also adopted the *niqāb* for non-religious reasons (Herrera 2000: 32).
16. Nisula has stressed that *uganga* has never been separate from the cosmos of Islamic sciences: rather, *uganga* ceremonies that address Muslim spirits have remained widespread and these ceremonies are characterised by recitation of the Qurᵓān or of *qaṣāᵓid*, or by the performance of *dhikr*. A *dhikr* may thus be an essential part of *uganga* ceremonies (Nisula 1999: 107) and although pious men publicly condemn such superstitions they do not object if their wives attend such ceremonies (Nisula 1999: 163). During research trips to Zanzibar in 2004 and 2007, I was able to witness *uganga* ceremonies involving recitation of the Qurᵓān (*kisomo*) by young Muslim scholars who had been trained at the Chuo Cha Kiislamu and clearly belonged to the spectrum of the *watu wa bidaa*. This can be seen as an effort by *watu wa bidaa* groups to acquire more social integration and increase popular support. This signals change since the mid-1990s, when Allyson Purpura could still claim that *watu wa bidaa* rejected the practice of *uganga* (Purpura 1997: 33).

17. For details of the development of the anṣār al-sunna and their educational background, see Loimeier (2009). Like the term '*watu wa bidaa*', the label 'anṣār al-sunna' should be seen as an umbrella term for a number of activist groups characterised by their oppositional stances towards the government. Muslim functionaries and the different *watu wa bidaa* groups are characterised by the fact that their leading representatives studied in countries such as Saudi Arabia (the Islamic University of Medina), Egypt (al-Azhar) and Sudan (Omdurman Islamic University) and are often far removed from Sufi-oriented traditions of reform.
18. My own observations, and reports in *an-Nuur* and *Maarifa*; Ahmed (2002a: 147ff, 2002b: 194ff); Larsen (2004); Loimeier (2006d); Purpura (1997: 221, 279–80); communication Jabir Haydar Jabir al-Farsy, 2 August 2003.
19. Ali Muhammad Shein (from Pemba) was confirmed in office in March 2016. The results of the presidential elections in October 2016 had been cancelled by Zanzibar's Election Commission due to fraud allegations. The re-run in March 2016 was boycotted by the Opposition.
20. The Government of Zanzibar has been reluctant to close bars. Such an act would not only establish a case for a policy of closures, but also go against an important achievement of the revolution: in the first hours and days of the revolution, a number of exclusive bars and clubs such as the British Staff Club (today the Africa House Hotel), the British Yacht Club (since 1964, the Starehe Club) and the club of the elitist Arab Association (today the Chavda Hotel) were stormed by the revolutionaries and opened to the public.
21. Before being appointed *muftī* of Zanzibar, Harith b. Khelef Khamis al-Ghaythi was BAKWATA's regional secretary in Iringa. In 2011, Saleh Omar Kaabi from Pemba was appointed successor to Harith al-Ghaythi. At the same time, Khamis Haji was appointed successor to ᶜAlī Khatib Mranzi as Chief Qāḍī.
22. 'Is this religion: beating up and good governance?' This is a reference to beating up Muslims who oppose government policies while claiming to stick to the rules of 'good governance' (utawala bora).
23. The Mufti Bill regulated the position of the *muftī* but, from 2002, it led to riots as Muslims objected to the political instrumentalisation of the office of the *muftī* by the government of Zanzibar.
24. The number of tourists in Zanzibar has grown from approximately 6,100 in 1977, about 82,700 in 1991 to about 120,000 in 1994, in the region of 170,000 in 1997 and about 350,000 in 2003 (Purpura 1997: 473; communication Othman Saidi Khamis, 4 August 2002).
25. The Comoros consist of four major islands, Ngazidja (Grande Comore),

Ndzawani (Anjouan), Mwali (Mohéli) and Maoré (Mayotte). Mayotte came under French control in 1841, while the other islands were occupied by France in 1885 and 1886. From 1912 to 1946, the Comoros were administered as part of Madagascar. In 1974, Mayotte voted against independence; in 2011 it became a French Overseas Department and thus part of the European Union (EU). In the nineteenth century, Ngazidja, Ndzawani and Mwali were governed by a series of small Sultanates (seven on Ngazidja, one each on Ndzawani and Mwali). From the mid-1960s until today, the islands' population (including Mayotte) has grown from about 200,000 people to in the region of 950,000. In 1995, in the region of 130,000 Comorians were living in France.

26. On these traditions of reform, see Ahmed (1999, 2002a), Bang (2003, 2014) and Mohamed (2008).
27. See Bang (2003) and Loimeier (2009).
28. Such a Comorian scholar was Ṭāhir Mawlāna Jamal al-Layl, who grew up in Zanzibar, and then studied at al-Azhar and finally settled in the Comoros, where he became 'le ᶜālim le plus en vue de l'archipel' (Ahmed 2002a: 236). A relative, Muḥammad Sharīf b. Aḥmad Jamal al-Layl (1935–2006) studied in Zanzibar and in the Sudan, and then returned to the Comoros in 1964. He became Président of the rābiṭat al-khayriyya al-islāmiyya in 1991 and Président of the Conseil des ᶜUlamāᵓ of the Comoros in 1997, an institution that replaced the office of the *muftī* (Ahmed 1999: 132f; Mohamed 2008: 145). Another cosmopolitan Comorian scholar was Aḥmad Qamar al-Dīn (1895–1974) who travelled to Mauritius in 1925, where he studied with two scholars from Saudi Arabia, Ḥammad b. Abī Bakr Ṣādiq al-Madanī and ᶜAbdallāh Rashīd al-Nawwāb. After his return to the Comoros in 1926, he taught *tafsīr* in Mbeni (Mohamed 2008: 61, 2010). Sayyid Muḥammad ᶜAbd al-Raḥmān (1912-1991), the Grand Qāḍī of the Comoros from 1964 to 1975 studied in Zanzibar from 1928 to 1939. He was the Grand Muftī of the Comoros from 1978 to 1991.
29. ᶜUmar b. Aḥmad b. Sumayṭ (1886–1976) was born in Ngazidja and lived in both the Comoros and Zanzibar. After the death of his father, he left Zanzibar and returned to the Comoros only to discover that his business there had been ruined (Bang 2003: 194). He left the Comoros for Madagascar and settled in Diego Suarez, where he seems to have founded a school. After another stop-over in the Comoros, he returned to Zanzibar in 1936/7 at the invitation of Sulṭān Khalīfa b. Ḥārub, to fill the position of district *qāḍī* in Mkokotoni. In Zanzibar, he became a teacher of ᶜAbdallāh Ṣāliḥ al-Farsy. In 1937, he was appointed *qāḍī* of Pemba, and then *qāḍī* of Unguja in 1938, when Ṭāhir b. ᶜAbd al-ᶜAzīz

al-Amawī died. He then became the Shāfiʿī Chief Qāḍī of Zanzibar from 1942 to 1959. After the revolution in 1964, he left Zanzibar on 25 April 1965 for Shiḥr in the Hadramaut, where he witnessed a second socialist revolution in 1967, and finally went back to the Comoros in 1967, where he was appointed Grand Muftī. He died in 1976 and was buried in Itsandraa (Rajab 2001; Bang 2003: 196; al-Farsy 1972: 35; communication Maalim Idris, 25 May 2004).

30. The Comorian *petit mariage* (*ndola ntiti*) is a marriage of free choice between partners of different social backgrounds that leads to a *petite famille* and a *petite maison*. The *grand mariage* (*ndola nku*), by contrast, is a marriage within the same social milieu and symbolically leads to the establishment of a *grande famille* and a *grande maison*. In concrete terms, a *grand mariage* means an intricate and costly system of gift exchanges between the bride's and the groom's families, as well as the village community involved, in the form of food, the distribution of gifts and monetary donations. In exchange, the village community helps to cultivate the fields and to build the house. The *grand mariage* symbolises the transition from the status of a 'child' (*mnamdji*) to the status of a fully grown adult person, entitled to speak publicly (Mohamed 2008: 107) and initiation into the ranks of the *wadrwazima* ('the senior people') and the *wadrwababu* ('the father people'). The prestige of a person is directly related to the size of the *grand mariage* (Ahmed 1999: 69f).
31. ʿAbd al-Ḥakīm Muḥammad Shākir was a grandson of Aḥmad Mfoihaya and started his education at the 'markaz' in Mbeni. In 1977 he continued his studies at the madrasat al-falāḥ in Moroni, moving to the maʿhad al-islāmiyya in Moroni in 1980. In 1984, he went to the Sudan and in 1989 to Medina, where he graduated in 2004 with a PhD in Islamic Law. After his return to the Comoros in 2004, he became the director of the Département Islamique of the University of the Comoros (Mohamed 2008: 161).
32. Other markaz graduates established new Qurʾānic schools after their return from studies abroad, such as the madrasat al-arqām al-islāmiyya in Mbeni (established in 1993 by Ibrāhīm ʿAbd al-Rashīd) (Mohamed 2008: 50).
33. As such, he became successor to Sayyid Ibrāhīm (1911–75, in office from 1970 to 1972), who had followed the Comoros's first Président du Conseil, Sayyid Muḥammad Cheikh (1904–70, from Ngazidja; in office from 1961). Sayyid Muḥammad Cheikh had been the Comoro's first deputy in the French Parliament from 1946 to 1961. Sayyid Ibrāhīm followed him in this position from 1961 to 1970.
34. In 1938 two French companies, the Société agricole de la Grande Comore and

the Société Comores-Bambao d'Anjouan, owned 46 per cent of Ngazidja, 22 per cent of Mwali, 37 per cent of Ndzawani and 15 per cent of Maoré, usually the best land for the cultivation of ylang-ylang, vanilla, cloves and cocopalms (for copra) (Vérin and Vérin 1999: 19). Indigenous farmers were pushed into marginal lands or forced to work as squatters on the French plantations or to migrate to Madagascar.

35. In late 1977, Tanzania stopped its support for the ᶜAlī Soilih regime and brought its officers and advisers back to Tanzania. Tanzanian security forces had acquired a reputation of brutality and had increasingly become the target of attacks (Barraux 2009: 246; Mattoir: 2004: 71).
36. In 1974, the import of rice alone was equal to the value of all Comorian exports (Mattoir 2004: 94).
37. This coup d'état was financed and organised from their exile in France by Aḥmad ᶜAbdallāh and his old foe from Ndzawani, Muḥammad Aḥmed (d. 1984), both big landowners in the Comoros, together with a wealthy Indian trader, Khalfan (Barraux 2009: 248; Mattoir 2004: 122). The ᶜAlī Soilih regime had been weakened greatly in financial terms in 1977 due to the fact that it had to shoulder the repatriation of 16,000 Comorians from Madagascar who had become victims of a communal pogrom in Majunga in December 1976. In this pogrom, 1,300 Comorians were killed (Djabir 1993: 20; Barraux 2009: 243).
38. In recent years, Qaṭar has become inreasingly important for the Comoros. The Comoros have also cultivated contacts with Iran, in particular under President Muḥammad Sambi, who studied in the Sudan, in Saudi Arabia and in Iran, and who was nick-named 'Ayatollah' due to his liking for the attire of an Iranian mullah.
39. Sayyid Muḥammad ᶜAbd al-Raḥmān had been deposed in 1975 as Grand Qāḍī by ᶜAlī Soilih. He justified the assassination of ᶜAlī Soilih on 28 May 1978 by Bob Denard's mercenaries arguing that ᶜAlī Soilih had apostasised and had to be regarded as a *murtadd* (Ahmed 1999: 151).
40. In the early 1990s, 91 per cent of the Comoro's annual budget went into salaries for the state's bureaucracy (Djabir 1993: 12). 'Venal bureaucrats' and functionaries destroyed the legitimacy of the state and contributed considerably to the popularity of Salafi-oriented reformers (Djabir 1993: 101).
41. President Aḥmad ᶜAbdallāh Muḥammad Sambi (2006–11) came from Ndzawani, while President Ikiliu Dhoinine (in office since 2011) is from Mwali.

8

CONCLUSION: THE MEANING OF ISLAMIC REFORM

Patterns and Peculiarities of Islamic Reform in Sub-Saharan Africa

Processes of reform do not come out of the blue, but look back on a long history of traditions of reform. Equally, processes of reform are not uniform, but are characterised by their fragmented nature and internal ambiguities, expressed in competing centres and traditions of learning. Muslim reform movements thus represent a broad spectrum of groups that have attempted to translate specific interpretations of a 'great tradition' (Redfield 1956: 41) into multiple local contexts. This process implies a constant process of translation, negotiation, contestation and re-interpretation of the canon in different geographic, social, political and religious contexts. Reform movements thus develop distinct positions with respect to their environment and with respect to other contemporary reform movements, as well as earlier traditions of reform. They have synchronic and diachronic dimensions that require careful examination: each tradition of reform has a distinctive context, distinctive markers of reform and distinctive positions with respect to other traditions of reform.

Salafi-oriented movements of reform in Africa are equally not a recent phenomenon, as we have seen in the preceding chapters. Rather, they can look back on several generations of reformist endeavours that were based on even older Sufi-oriented traditions of reform. The countries discussed here have developed two chains of reform, namely, Sufi- and Salafi-oriented movements of reform, each of which over time came to adopt features of the respective other tradition. It is important to stress that Sufi-oriented movements of reform preceded Salafi-oriented movements of reform in each of the countries discussed here: in Senegal, Mali and northern Nigeria, we have Sufi movements of reform since the late eighteenth century and early nineteenth, in Sudan since the early nineteenth century, in Ethiopia, Somalia and East Africa since the mid-nineteenth century and in Chad since the late nineteenth century. These Sufi-oriented movements of reform were not uniform and have not remained frozen in a particular mode of Sufi reform, but have developed their own dynamics in the course of several generations of reform. To some extent, the first generation of Salafi-minded reformers was inspired by Sufi reformers. At the same time, Salafi-oriented movements of reform have so far not been able to achieve hegemony of interpretation with respect to issues of reform in their respective countries and societies, despite their success in some regions and among some social strata: rather, they have had to compete with Sufi movements, which have sometimes represented a more vibrant approach to reform. The competition between different families of reform has led to an opening of the market offering religious and social options in the different countries.

The distinct character of each movement of reform has been informed by the dynamics of the local context. As a result, each national and regional case is different, despite the fact that there are obvious entanglements, through the pilgrimage and through trade, but also through students who studied in Arab countries in the twentieth century, and through the influence of Saudi-financed NGOs and trans-national Muslim organisations, such as the rābiṭat al-ᶜālam al-islāmī. Beyond these entanglements, however, there have been marked differences in the development of both Sufi- and Salafi-oriented movements of reform, for instance with respect to the historical take-off of such movements: early Salafi-oriented thinkers, intellectuals, scholars, students and traders became visible in East Africa in the 1930s, in Sudan, in Chad and in Mali in the 1940s, in Senegal and northern Nigeria in the 1950s, in parts of Ethiopia and in Somalia in the 1960s and in the 1970s; a second generation of Salafi-oriented reform movements, characterised by larger organisations and a broader popular basis among middle-class groups (beyond traders, functionaries and students) materialised two or three decades later: in Sudan in the 1960s, in Zanzibar, Tanzania, Kenya, Somalia, northern Nigeria, Mali and Senegal in the 1970s, in Niger, Ethiopia and in the Comoros in the 1990s, and in Chad to date not at all. The second generation of Salafi-oriented intellectuals and activists often had to come to terms with the fact that many representatives of the older generation were not willing to hand over leadership to their students. As a result, the historical period of the second generation saw first organisational splits and disputes over leadership. These internal conflicts still rage today, and have contributed to the fragmentation of Salafi-oriented movements of reform such as *siyāsa*- and *tarbiya*-oriented groups.

In this context, we have to ask the question as to why the historical take-off of Salafi-oriented movements of reform actually took place at different times in different places: what were the major differences in the local contexts that could explain the different take-offs and the different orientations of seemingly similar Muslim movements of reform in sub-Saharan countries? First, it is important to stress different historical legacies: none of the countries we have discussed have comparable social or political structures or historical experiences. In Senegal, processes of social and political disruption started early and led to the mobilisation of Muslims in the 1850s in the context of the collapse of local principalities. The crisis of Senegalese society was answered, however, by the efforts of two Sufi orders, the Murīdiyya and the Tijāniyya, which, in alliance with the colonial power, were able to organise large-scale economic and social reforms, to compensate the effects of World War I (such as mass recruitment and taxes) and to act as stabilising forces. In the 1920s, first modern religious associations were established in the urban centres, but these associations remained under the control of religious leaders affiliated with the Tijāniyya. Only in the 1950s did the UCM develop as a Salafi-oriented movement of reform that adopted a more encompassing programme of change. The UCM attacked the collaboration of the marabouts with the colonial power and advocated early independence. The development of the UCM thus coincided with Senegal's struggle for independence in the 1950s.

In northern Nigeria, the British established a system of indirect rule in the early 1900s and granted the Sultan of Sokoto and the emirs of Kano,

Zaria or Katsina a fair amount of autonomy in the administration of the north. Ahmad Bello's policies of reform in the early 1950s led to the first moments of social instability, yet these policies of reform were propagated as being Islamic and were engineered by Muslim politicians. Mismanagement of military administrations, the erosion of regional autonomy and the effects of the oil boom, however, led to a deep social and political crisis in the 1970s, so that Salafi-minded Muslims found an audience for their ideas of reform that included protest against the social and political elites of the north as well as 'obsolete' local customs. Northern Nigeria's Salafi-oriented movement of reform thus developed so late that it did not coincide with Nigeria's struggle for independence. The same was true for Niger, where a Salafi-oriented movement of reform developed in the late 1980s, and thus played no role in Niger's struggle for independence, in contrast to Mali, where the Salafi-oriented movement of reform was a major factor in Mali's independence movement in the 1940s and 1950s. As Sufi orders were historically weaker in Niger and Mali, in comparison to Senegal, the take-off of Salafi-oriented movements of reform at different times in Niger and Mali requires another explanation: one factor to explain the temporal disjuncture between Mali and Niger is different political regimes and different state policies with respect to Salafi-oriented movements of reform, another is the central role of reform-minded traders in Mali, Ivory Coast and Guinea, as well as a longer tradition of Islamic learning and education in Mali by comparison to Niger.

East Africa is characterised historically by the fragmentation of coastal societies. The history of the East African coast may be seen as a history of competing trading centres that never achieved political unity and that were marked in the nineteenth century by social contradictions between new (Omani) elites, increasingly marginalised local elites and a growing number of migrants and slaves from the African interior, who sought a legitimate position in Swahili society. With the exception of Somalia and Somaliland, Muslim societies on the East African coast (as well as in Niger, in Chad and in Ethiopia) cannot point to a legacy of *jihād* as in Senegal, Mali or northern Nigeria. The social problems of the nineteenth century continued to bother coastal societies in the colonial period, yet, in contrast to northern Nigeria, there were no over-arching political authorities (emirs): the Sultan of Zanzibar had lost most of his power and territorial basis. Also, there were no influential religious movements and powerful Sufi orders, as in Senegal, which could have generated unity. The Qādiriyya in East Africa was highly fragmented. In such a context, an Islamic movement of reform had the chance to develop early. This happened so early that it did not coincide with the struggle for independence: Ḥasan b. ᶜAmeir (d. 1979), a key figure in the struggle for independence in Tanganyika, belonged to a Sufi order, the Qādiriyya. By contrast, Al-Amīn b. ᶜAlī al-Mazrūᶜī and ᶜAbdallāh Ṣāliḥ al-Farsy, the founding fathers of Salafi-oriented reform in East Africa, worked for the British colonial administration and did not turn into scions of anti-colonial struggle.

While the development of Salafi-oriented reform in Somalia has been informed to a major extent by the civil war since the late 1980s, and thus has to be considered as an exceptional case, the late development of Salafi-oriented reform in Ethiopia in the 1990s is mostly due to repressive state policies under both Emperor Haile Selassie (until 1974) and the Derg (until 1991), as well as the extreme regional and ethnic fragmentation of Ethiopia's Muslim populations. This fragmentation has handicapped the development of a united Salafi-oriented movement of reform to this day. In Sudan, by contrast, we encounter a local context where Salafi-oriented ideas of reform developed fairly early, in the 1940s, yet were contained by the overwhelming social, religious and political power of the Mahdiyya and the Khatmiyya, as well as many smaller Sufi orders. Only Ḥasan al-Turābī's strategy of opening the Islamic Movement to other social forces enabled the Islamic Movement to acquire a greater political role from the 1960s and to take power in 1989.

The examples of Senegal and Mali, northern Nigeria and Niger, Chad, Sudan, Ethiopia, Somalia and the East African countries show that the emergence, the speed and the mode of development of specific types of reform, and the time for the historical take-off of different programmes of change were influenced to a considerable extent by the local context. The unique social and political conditions, specific historical legacies and economic situation of each region defined the specific dynamics of each social and religious development. Movements of reform had to find a position with respect to existing social and political forces in their particular context, and thereby established specific dialectics of religious dispute. Due to the importance of the local context, Salafi-oriented movements of reform have cultivated different positions with respect to their relationship with the state; these are situated between extreme *siyāsa*-oriented pragmatism and extreme *tarbiya*-oriented pietism: in Senegal, Mali and Niger, Salafi-oriented movements of reform, such as the UCM and the JIR, have developed a culture of accommodation; in northern Nigeria, the 'Yan Izala have mostly supported state governments and established authority; in Kenya, Tanzania and Zanzibar, as well as in Ethiopia, Salafi-minded groups have been highly critical of the respective governments; in Sudan, the Islamic Movement even managed to take over power, at least for a limited period, from 1989 to 1999, while other groups have remained aloof. The same is true of Sufi-oriented movements of reform that have not always been loyalist: Sufi opposition to state politics has been virulent several times in Senegal, in Mali and in Sudan.

It is thus possible to speak of several generations or stages of Salafi-oriented reform in all of the countries that have been discussed here: each of these movements of reform has seen stages of development that we may describe as the genesis and formative period, followed by a stage of increasing popularisation and cooperation with colonial and postcolonial administrations. In the 1980s there was a turn in the development of Salafi-oriented movements and a new generation of activists has come forward. This most recent generation of activist Muslims in northern Nigeria, in Sudan, in Mali, in Niger, in Chad, in Ethiopia, in Zanzibar, in the Comoros and in Senegal is connected with northern sources of inspiration such as the Iranian revolution, the Egyptian ikhwān al-muslimūn or radical Salafi-oriented organisations of the recent past such as the jamāᶜāt al-islāmiyya. Members of these movements have often studied at al-Azhar, at the Islamic University of Medina in Saudi Arabia, in Pakistan or Sudan, and have received funds from these countries. Recent activist groups struggle against the state, sometimes even in modes of *jihād*, whereas earlier traditions of reform were often prepared to cooperate to a certain extent with the state.

The emergence of the most recent generation of Muslim activists in sub-Saharan Africa is connected with the specific dynamics of political development in these countries and, in particular, with the weakness of the state and its failure to implement a policy of development that would generate hopes of integration and material security. Many of the countries have experienced authoritarian government by diverse military regimes, as in Nigeria, Chad and Sudan, while in Tanganyika, Zanzibar, the Comoros and Kenya, as well as Senegal, Mali and Niger, political structures have been dominated by the respective ruling party. In every case this has provided a good basis for religious opposition. The failure of the state to implement policies of development and to provide for education and social security has encouraged the development of religious movements that point to the shortcomings of secular regimes. As a result, we have seen the emergence of a series of *jihād*-minded movements, such as al-shabāb in Somalia, some anṣār al-sunna groups in Zanzibar, Kenya and Tanzania, some ahl al-sunna groups in Ethiopia and Boko Haram in northern Nigeria. These movements are characterised by attacks against Christians, in particular Pentecostal churches, and critique of fellow Muslims, who are accused of being too compromising, too accommodating and too 'superficial' in religious matters. However, there is not a single country where *jihād*-minded movements have managed to gain broad support among the Muslim population. Even in Somalia, where the local context has been highly favourable to radical groups, moderate Salafi-oriented groups have prevailed. In all countries, Muslim majorities have developed 'compassion fatigue' after decades of doctrinal dispute, and it is possible to observe the emergence of Muslim milieus that dispute Salafi efforts to enforce public piety. This development is particularly clear in Senegal, but also in Zanzibar, in the Sudan and in northern Nigeria. In some states, in particular Senegal and Niger, but also in Tanzania and Zanzibar, and in Ethiopia, governments have managed to establish a national consensus regarding the peaceful nature of religious disputes and to postulate the secular state as a protector of all religions. Mali, northern Nigeria and Sudan have failed in such efforts. Not a single state, however, has really fallen into an Islamic piety trap, although some northern Nigerian states in the 2000s, Niger in the 1990s, Mali in the 1980s, Sudan in the late 1970s and early 1980s and the Comoros in the 1980s and 1990s have come quite close. Somalia again constitutes an exception due to its particular history since the late 1980s.

The Social Basis of Islamic Reform

In general terms, it has to be stressed that movements of reform work on three different levels of 'selfing', 'othering' and 'boundary making'. Doctrinal argumentation is central to establishing doctrinal distinction, for instance with respect to Sufi practices and Sufi movements. Symbols serve to establish symbolic distantiation from the 'impure' other. Specific codes of social behaviour help to create social separation from a polluting environment; and the goal of some radical Salafi-oriented movements of reform is spatial segregation in different guises and stages of escalation, such as Salafi mosques, separate communities or Salafi-controlled territories where Islam rules supreme.

When looking at societal support for Salafi-oriented movements of reform, it is possible to say that all such movements started out as movements of students, traders and functionaries (mostly teachers), often emerging from a Sufi background, but rebelling against established authorities. Equally, all Salafi-oriented movements of reform began as urban movements and mostly remain confined to urban contexts to this day. Exceptions are northern Nigeria and Ethiopia. Urban centres, small and large, have become foci of reform and urban populations form the major basis for Muslim reformist agendas. Thus, Salafi-oriented movements of reform have won support among teachers, doctors, engineers and employees, but also traders and entrepreneurs, the small but growing group of comparatively well-educated people who aspire to wealth and status or are threatened by social marginalisation. The members of these middle-class groups are characterised by the fact that they refuse to accept established religious authorities, often Sufi scholars. At the same time, they are looking for new social, economic and religious orientations that are compatible with modern life and their interpretation of modern life. They consequently support reformers who preach against the numerous forms of alleged *bidaᶜ* as well as against costly and time-intensive religious practices, such as marriage and naming ceremonies, or funeral rites. Equally, all Salafi-oriented movements of reform have attracted youth. In particular, they have proposed a new role for women, for instance by opening mosques for women, an issue that has repeatedly created disputes. In addition, Salafi-oriented movements of reform have advocated the active participation of women in public life and politics, and this has contributed to an increasing visibility of Muslim women in religious and political contexts. However, very few Salafi-oriented movements of reform have become real mass movements and have gone beyond the student-trader-functionary clientele into the realm of other middle-class groups: the 'Yan Izala must be mentioned here, but also the Islamic Movement in the Sudan and, to a certain extent, the Islamic Court movement in Somalia, the jamāᶜt ᶜibād al-raḥmān in Senegal and the ahl al-sunna in Mali.

At the same time, Salafi-oriented movements of reform have stimulated the rejuvenation of Sufi movements and have contributed to the emergence of modern forms of Sufi-oriented reform that have developed in a dialectic interaction with other reformist trends: even if Sufi movements oppose modernity or reform, they develop and support, consciously or not, programmes of reform that are modern in structural terms, due to the fact that Sufi-oriented movements of reform usually adopt Salafi-oriented patterns with respect, for instance, to modern Islamic education, school organisation, school structure, didactics, pedagogy and curriculum development. Programmes of reform may look different in ideological or doctrinal terms, yet they are often similar in structural terms.

Processes of reform are also characterised by the link between the religious and the social, although these fields are stressed in different ways in different movements of reform. Salafi-oriented movements of reform have supported the development of Muslim leisure organisations, such as sports clubs, and have thus gained considerable support among the youth (Loimeier 2000c: 101ff). In addition, they have discovered and cultivated public spaces: Islam has left the mosques and qurʾānic schools and has gone public in different modes: *mihadhara* and *waʿẓ*-preaching, public *tafsīr* outside mosques, in stadiums and other public places. Debates on religion are no longer confined to scholars; new media (such as radio, TV and Internet) are used actively, and we also observe the emergence of loudspeaker wars. Movements of reform are often (but not always)[1] educational movements. Yet, Salafi-oriented movements of reform (and later Sufi-oriented movements) have stressed the paramount importance not only of Islamic religious education, but also of modern education, and again, not only education for men but also for women. Salafi-minded reformers have also stressed the importance of the vernacular languages as the means of communication and religious discourse, and support the translation of the holy texts into Kiswahili, Wolof or Hausa. In Senegal, Mali, Nigeria, Niger, Ethiopia, Somalia and East Africa there has been an increasing number of texts written in languages other than Arabic. The number of modern Islamic schools has exploded in sub-Saharan Africa in the last fifty years and the number of Muslims who are able to read and write not only Arabic but also African languages, as well as English or French, has grown tremendously (see Loimeier 2005b). The movement towards mass education in Africa has had considerable repercussions on Islamic culture, as it has made possible new approaches to texts and translations of texts, both sacred and profane. Alphabetisation campaigns have contributed to the translation of vast numbers of Arabic religious texts into African languages (as well as English and French),[2] a process that has led in recent decades to the increasing marginalisation of Arabic as a language of religious learning. In the context of increasing alphabetisation in African languages, Arabic has lost its status as the major language for the production of texts, as alphabetisation today usually implies alphabetisation in African languages. Texts in African languages are bought by an increasing numbers of readers, while Arabic remains the language of a scholarly elite. Religious scholars who aspire to mass readership and corresponding commercial success have thus stopped writing in Arabic and have switched to the respective local and national languages. The East African reformer, ᶜAbdallāh Ṣāliḥ al-Farsy (1912–82), argued in this context that 'Islam does not want colonialism in religion, Arabic is not at all necessary' ('*Uislamu hautaki istimaari wa dini, si lazima lugha ya Kiarabu*') (quoted in Lacunza Balda 1993: 233), while Gerard C. van de Bruinhorst remarks that only 30 per cent of the 700 titles he was able to collect in about thirty local bookshops in ten East African urban centres were still written in Arabic, while approximately 50 per cent were written in Kiswahili and 20 per cent in English (van de Bruinhorst 2001: 6). Similar observations can be made in respect of Senegal, Ethiopia and northern Nigeria where an increasing number of Islamic texts are published in either French or English, or national languages of communication such as Wolof, Amhariña or Hausa (see Loimeier 1997a, 2001).

The processes of change that characterised modernity in the twentieth century also had to be digested in legal terms. A famous early example for such a process of 'digestion' was Muḥammad ᶜAbduh's 'Transvaal' *fatwā*, which answered, among other things, the question of whether a Muslim was allowed to eat meat slaughtered by a Christian. His response was that Muslims in a minority position, as in South Africa, could consume such meat. His argument was based on *ijtihād*, or his own interpretation of a qurʾānic ruling ('And the food of those who have been given the Book is lawful for you') ('*wa-taᶜāmu alladhina utūwa al-kitāba ḥillun lakum*') (Qurʾān 5: 5). This *fatwā* not only challenged established scholarly consensus, but also went back to the Qurʾān to 'reach a ruling that authorized a new Islamic practice, a practice that takes into account the special needs of Muslims in the present context' (Haj 2009: 148). This was one of the first attempts to deal with the conflict between modernity and Muslim legal traditions. It reflects Muḥammad ᶜAbduh's efforts to create a legal framework that would enable Muslims to function more successfully in a changed world (Haj 2009: 146). It foreshadows the emergence of *sharīᶜa* debates in the colonial period, and even more so in the post-colonial period. In almost all Muslim societies in sub-Saharan Africa in the post-colonial period, there was a flood of *fatāwā* production and *sharīᶜa* debates. Often, such debates were confined to issues of personal law, as in Senegal and in Tanzania, but sometimes reformers demanded the implementation of Islamic penal law or 'complete *sharīᶜa*' as in northern Nigeria and in the Sudan.

Last but not least, the development of movements of reform is linked with disputes over symbols (veils, shortened trousers and beards) and rituals (*qabḍ* and *sadl*). The campaign against established features of religious ritual had an important social and economic dimension, as Salafi-oriented movements of reform rejected costly and time-consuming practices. As a result, Salafi-oriented critique has been accepted by many Muslims as a welcome and religiously legitimate avenue of argumentation for the rejection of established religious and social obligations, customs and practices. Legitimatory references to reformist discourses on the *bidaᶜ* are made even by Muslims who are not affiliated with Salafi-oriented movements of reform, but who reject the ritual practices and symbols of past times as obsolete and who wish to redefine social and religious life in the modern context. It is possible to characterise the process of distantiation from Sufi practices as the passage from a social, practised, communal, contextualised type of Islam to an individualistic 'worldly Islam' that lays less emphasis on communal practices and that tries to reformulate religiosity in individualistic terms. The passage from Sufism to anti-Sufism, at least in urban centres, thus brings about a reorientation from communal religiosity towards a more individualistic mode of religiosity (Roy 2002: 146). The stress on individual religiosity may be seen as forming part and parcel of a larger process of reorientation that frees the individual from the established bonds of religious authority, while stressing individual (and subjective) judgement in a context of increasing disenchantment of the world. In his major doctrinal work, *Afin que tu deviennes musulman* (1957), Cheikh Touré thus attacked local customs such as saint veneration, time-consuming burial rites and faith in amulets as un-Islamic innovations (*bida*^{c}) and maintained: 'The true saints are those who really believe in God, who live an honest life, who do not exploit other believers and who obey the laws of God while shunning the forbidden.' This is the ^{c}*aqīda* (doctrine) of Muslim reformers that stresses the direct relationship between God and individual believers (Touré 1957: 41–2).

On account of these far-reaching repercussions of Salafi-oriented movements of reform, it is possible to say that, following the initial period of conversion to Islam, a second process of Islamisation of Muslim societies started in sub-Saharan Africa in the twentieth century characterised by social and cultural transformations within bigger processes of change. If we accept such a longue durée perspective of Islamic reform in Africa, and look at processes of reform from a phenomenological, as well as a chronological, perspective, we may talk about a new dimension of Muslim reform in Africa, and come to the conclusion that these movements of social and religious protest represent a dimension of reform that could be described as having a 'Protestant' quality, or better, in French, 'une qualite protestantisante'.[3] Indeed, these movements of reform have some, if not all, of the structural features that were characteristic of European Protestantism in the fifteenth and sixteenth centuries (see Loimeier 2005a). However, the anti-esoteric discourse of the most recent Muslim movements of reform has not been very consistent, and a number of them have been prepared to discard their anti-Sufi positions in favour of strategic positions intended to promote Muslim unity and support the struggle against oppressive (un-Islamic) governments. Thus, Zanzibar's anṣār al-sunna cultivated a distinctive anti-Sufi and anti-bida^{c} discourse in the 1980s and early 1990s. Since the mid-1990s, however, they have more or less abandoned this discourse for the sake of Muslim unity. The same is true of the 'Yan Izala movement in northern Nigeria, and the jamā^{c}at ^{c}ibād al-raḥmān in Senegal, even if individual members of these organisations privately express their aversion to the veneration of saints (Villalon 1995: 219–20).

At the same time, recent Salafi-oriented groups have cultivated a moralistic discourse that condemns imperialism as well as Zionism, Christian mission as well as freemasonry, drug abuse, prostitution and other features of moral decay that, in their eyes, corrupt Muslim society. This discourse is not only directed against 'the West' but also against the political elites of (Muslim) countries that are often accused of blindly following policies of Westernisation. Recent Salafi-oriented groups often view local Muslim society as *jāhil* and consequently threaten 'deviant' Muslims with *takfīr*. This idea goes back to the Egyptian thinker, Sayyid Quṭb, and his treatise *ma^cālim fi-l-ṭarīq*, and it has become a major source of inspiration for many recent Muslim reformist organisations.

The increasing prominence of Salafi-oriented movements of reform in sub-Saharan Africa should not hide the fact, however, that Sufi-oriented movements of reform continue to persist and to coexist with Salafi-oriented movements of reform. Salafi-oriented movements of reform have thus not brought about an increasing homogeneity of African Muslim societies, nor do they form a united front: their poles of orientation in the northern Muslim world (Morocco, Algeria, Libya, Egypt, Saudi Arabia, Iran, Kuwait, Iran and Pakistan, more recently also Turkey) are characterised by strong political and religious antagonisms as well as a long tradition of internal rivalry. In addition, northern Salafi-oriented movements of reform should also be seen as an array of different expressions and historical experiences of reform, ranging from the accommodating and intellectualist Salafiyya movement inspired by Muḥammad ^cAbduh and later Muḥammad Rashīd Riḍā, to the populist mass organisation of the ikhwān al-muslimūn and to a plethora of politically radical networks, often inspired by Muslim intellectuals such as Sayyid Quṭb and Abū l-Ā^clā Maudūdī. Their writings have gained considerable influence in recent decades, as they are mostly in English and are easily understandable to large numbers of non-Arab (and Arabic-speaking) Muslims in Africa and India. Due to these vast differences in programmes, styles, orientation, financial backing and claims to spiritual superiority in the Muslim north, Salafi-oriented movements of reform in sub-Saharan Africa have been able to profit from these rivalries and to juggle northern influences in their own national and local strategies of development and political orientation.

Conclusion

The biographies of reformers such as Cheikh Touré in Senegal, Abubakar Gumi in northern Nigeria, Ḥasan al-Turābī in the Sudan and al-Amīn b. ᶜAlī al-Mazrūᶜī or ᶜAbdallāh Ṣāliḥ al-Farsy in East Africa reflect the peculiarities of the local context in the development of their discourse on reform. Their biographies also show that the founding fathers of Salafi-oriented reformist thought in Senegal and Mali, in northern Nigeria and Niger, in Chad, in Sudan, in Ethiopia, in Somalia and in East Africa not only influenced later generations of Salafi-oriented reformers, but also drew inspiration from earlier, Sufi-inspired movements of reform. And although the biographies of Cheikh Touré, Abubakar Gumi, Ḥasan al-Turābī, al-Amīn b. ᶜAlī al-Mazrūᶜī and ᶜAbdallāh Ṣāliḥ al-Farsy represent an anti-esoteric turn in the development of Islamic reformist thought in Africa, the religious, ideological and political convictions of these founding fathers of twentieth-century Islamic reform in Africa show that their positions were constantly subject to change. Muslim movements of reform may thus be seen as expressions of processes of change linked to historical transformations of longue durée. As a consequence, they cannot be regarded as a sudden change of paradigm. A longue durée perspective can help to reveal the peculiarities of Islamic reformist movements in Africa and will show that, as a Nigerian saying goes, 'no condition is permanent'.

A general resumé of our observations with respect to the development of Muslim movements of reform thus leads to the almost tautological affirmation that in sub-Saharan Africa we have a long history of movements of reform or rather, a history of a number of waves of reform. These waves of reform seem to change their direction again and again: Sufi or anti-Sufi, mass-movement and popular orientation, or political bias. In structural terms, the character of Salafi-oriented movements of reform is, however, remarkably similar: Salafi-minded reformers tend to argue in anti-esoteric terms, while they advocate modern Islamic education and the implementation of a moralistic system of Islamic norms. At the same time, they complain about structurally similar issues, such as the superstitious beliefs of the populations, their ignorance and their indulgence in wasteful popular festivities.

From wave to wave of reform, only little seems to have changed in the character of Muslim societies, but this impression results from a short-term historical view of Muslim society. Over a longer period, the nineteenth and twentieth centuries, for instance, we see fundamental changes in the character of Muslim society in Africa that are connected with the gradual intensification and the cumulative impact of reformist endeavours and achievements. The analysis of these movements of reform forces us to the conclusion that this history of reform is complex and ambiguous. Thus, it is necessary to differentiate between regions that have a long tradition of Islamisation, such as northern Nigeria, northern Senegal and the East African coast, and areas that, at least in parts, have been Islamised only recently, such as Burkina Faso, Ghana, major parts of Chad and parts of Ethiopia, as well as mainland Tanzania and up-country Kenya. Second, it is necessary to differentiate between regions that have a long tradition of Sufism, such as Senegal, and regions such as Mali where Sufi orders played a smaller role in the development of Muslim society.

At the same time, we can observe different speeds in the development of Salafi-oriented movements of reform. Countries with a long tradition of reform, such as Zanzibar, where Salafi-oriented ideas of reform have gone through several stages of development, are distinct from other countries, such as Ethiopia, where Salafi-oriented reform is an isolated or a recent or weak phenomenon. It is important to see that there is no such thing as a unified, homogenous Salafi-oriented movement of reform. Rather, there is a large spectrum of different expressions of reform (and we must not forget that ideas of reform are not confined to reformist groups proper, but may be found among Sufi orders as well). Finally, it is essential to pay attention to government policies with respect to Muslim reformist movements and to Islam in general. Some colonial and post-colonial administrations were willing to support specific forms of Muslim reform and even to use different Muslim reformist movements for their own politics of reform. But there have also been governments that were prepared to merely tolerate Muslim reformist movements or that tried to marginalise any form of Muslim reform. These different positions of the state have influenced, and continue to influence, the strategies and the development of Muslim reformist movements, as well as the biographies of Muslim reformers.

Inevitably, these conditions change with time. Still, there are a number of constant traits and structural similarities that can be said to characterise Muslim reformist movements in Africa. Thus, most contemporary Muslim reformist movements try to find and cultivate a proper place for Muslims in present-day African societies that would give Muslims the chance to lead a life according to the prescriptions of the faith in a world characterised by rapid change. The responses of Muslim reformist movements to change and Westernisation are manifold and necessarily ambiguous. Yet, they seem to point to a new understanding of Islam and society, as well as the faith. This new understanding and interpretation of society and religion stresses the position of the individual and his or her right to interpret the sources of the faith, independently and in an autonomous way, as well as his or her right to define or redefine social space, gender relations and time, and to reject established institutions, mediators and authorities.

Notes

1. While education has been a major theme for most Salafi-oriented movements of reform, recent radical and activist movements seem to see education as being secondary to more political aspirations.
2. Translations of Arabic religious texts into English are often produced nowadays in India and, to a lesser extent, in Pakistan and Malaysia.
3. I prefer to use the French term 'protestantisant' as it expresses, better than the term 'protestant', the look-alike nature of religious phenomena in different religious contexts (see also Loimeier 2003).

BIBLIOGRAPHY

Anonymous (2012), 'The Popular Discourses of Salafi Radicalism and Salafi Counter-Radicalism in Nigeria: A Case Study of Boko Haram', *Journal of Religion in Africa*, 42: 2, 118–44.

Abbink, Jan (1998), 'An Historical-Anthropological Approach to Islam in Ethiopia: Issues of Identity and Politics', *Journal of African Cultural Studies*, 11: 2, 109–24.

—— (1999), 'Ethiopian Islam and the Challenge of Diversity', *ISIM Newsletter*, 4, 24.

—— (2007), 'Transformations of Islam and Communal Relations in Wallo, Ethiopia', in Réné Otayek and Benjamin Soares (eds), *Islam and Muslim Politics in Africa*, New York, pp. 65–84.

Abdoulaye Galilou (2007), *L'Islam béninois à la croisée des chemins: Histoire, politique et développement*, Cologne.

Abdulkadir Hashim (2005), 'Servants of the Sharīᶜa: Qāḍīs and the Politics of Accommodation in East Africa', *Sudanic Africa*, 16, 27–52.

—— (2009), 'Scholars of the Circles: Training of Qāḍīs and Transmission of Islamic Scholarship along the East African Coast from the mid-19th Century to the 21st Century', *Journal for Islamic Studies*, 29, 104–38.

—— (2010), 'Coping with Conflicts: Colonial Policy towards Muslim Personal Law in Kenya and Post-Colonial Court Practice', in Shamil Jeppie, Ebrahim Moosa and Richard Roberts (eds), *Muslim Family Law in Sub-Saharan Africa: Colonial Legacies and Post-Colonial Challenges*, Amsterdam, pp. 221–46.

Abdurahman Moallim Abdullahi (AMA) (2011), *The Islamic Movement in Somalia: A Historical Evolution with a Case Study of the Islah Movement (1950–2000)*, PhD Thesis, McGill University, Montreal.

Adam, Sani Yakubu (2013–2014), 'Note on the Succession to the Kano Emirate, 2014', *Annual Review of Islam in Africa*, 12: 1, 2013-2014, 80–4.

Adama, Hamadou (1999), 'L'enseignement privé islamique dans le Nord-Cameroun', *Islam et Sociétés au Sud du Sahara*, 13, 7–40.

—— (2004), *L'Islam au Cameroun: Entre tradition et modernité*, Paris.

—— (2007), 'Islamic Associations in Cameroon: Between the Umma and the State', in Benjamin Soares and Réné Otayek (eds), *Islam and Muslim Politics in Africa*, New York, pp. 227–42.

—— (2009), 'Pèlerinage musulmane et stratégies d'accumulation au Cameroun', in Jean-Louis Triaud and Leonardo Villalon (eds), *Afrique Contemporaine*, 231, pp. 121–38.

—— (2013), 'Communication islamique, medias et opinion publique au Cameroun: Enjeux et perspectives', *Islam et Sociétés au Sud du Sahara (nouvelle série)*, 3, 55–72.

Adamu, Abdalla Uba (2012), 'Insurgency in Nigeria: The Northern Nigerian Experience', unpublished conference paper.

Adesoji, Abimbola (2010), 'The Boko Haram Uprising and Islamic Revival in Nigeria', *Africa Spectrum*, 45: 2, 95–108.

—— (2011), 'Between Maitatsine and Boko Haram: Islamic Fundamentalism and the Response of the Nigerian State', *Africa Today*, 57: 4, 98–119.

El-Affendi, Abdelwahab (1991), *Turabi's Revolution: Islam and Power in Sudan*, London.

Afyare Abdi Elmi (AAE) (2010), *Understanding the Somalia Conflagration: Identity, Political Islam and Peacebuilding*, London.

Ahmed, Abdallah Chanfi (Ch. Ahmed) (1999), *Islam et politique aux Comores*, Paris.

—— (2002a), *Ngoma et mission islamique (daᶜwa) aux Comores et en Afrique orientale. Une approche anthropologique*, Paris.

—— (2002b), 'Rites de mort aux Comores et chez les Swahili. Entre islam savant et culture locale', *Afrique-Arabie*, 72: 2, 187–202.

—— (2005), 'Tariqa, État et enseignement islamique aux Comores: Réseaux d'hier et d'aujourd'hui', in Muriel Gomez-Perez (ed.), *L'Islam politique au sud du Sahara: Identités, discours et enjeux*, Paris, pp. 49–68.

—— (2006), 'Networks of the Shādhiliyya-Yashrūtiyya Sufi Order in East Africa', in Roman Loimeier and Rüdiger Seesemann (eds), *The Global Worlds of the*

Swahili: Interfaces of Islam, Identity, and Space in the 19th and 20th-Century East Africa, Hamburg, 325–50.

—— (2008), *Les conversions à l'Islam fondamentaliste: Le cas de la Tanzanie et du Kenya*, Paris.

—— (2015), *West African ʿulamāʾ and Salafism in Mecca and Medina: Jawāb al-Ifrīqī – The Response of the African*, Leiden.

Ahmed, Einas (E. Ahmed) (2007), 'Political Islam in Sudan: Islamists and the Challenge of State Power (1989–2004)', in Réné Otayek and Benjamin Soares (eds), *Islam and Muslim Politics in Africa*, New York, pp. 189–210.

—— (2015), 'Militant Salafism in Sudan', *Islamic Africa*, 6, 164–84.

Ameir, Amina Issa (2006). 'The Legacy of Qādirī Scholars in Zanzibar', in Roman Loimeier and Rüdiger Seesemann (eds), *The Global Worlds of the Swahili: Interfaces of Islam, Identity and Space in 19th and 20th Century East Africa*, Berlin, pp. 343–62.

Amiji, H. M. (1982), 'Islam and Socio-Economic Development: Case Study of a Muslim Minority in Tanzania', *Journal of the Institute of Muslim Minority Affairs*, IV, Nos 1–2, 175–87.

Amoretti, Biancamaria Scarcia (ed.) (2001), *Islam in East Africa: New Sources*, Rome.

Amselle, Jean-Loup (1985), 'Le Wahhabisme à Bamako (1945–1985)', *Canadian Journal of African Studies*, 19: 2, 345–57.

Arditi, Claude (2003), 'Les violences ordinaires ont une histoire: le cas du Tchad', *Politique Africaine*, 91, 51–67.

Asad, Talal (1986), 'The Idea of an Anthropology of Islam', *CCAS Occasional Papers*, Georgetown.

—— (2015), 'Do Muslims Belong to the West? An Interview with Talal Asad (by Hasan Azad)', <www.jadiliyya.com/page/index/20768/do-muslims-belong-to-the-west> (last accessed 13 April 2015).

Assmann, Jan (2000), *Das kulturelle Gedächtnis. Schrift, Erinnerung und politische Identität in frühen Hochkulturen*, München.

Audrain, Xavier (2004), 'Du 'Ndiggël' avorté au Parti de la Vérité. Évolution du rapport religion/politique à travers le parcours de Cheikh Modou Kara (1999–2004)', *Politique Africaine*, 96, 99–118.

Augis, Erin (2003), *Dakar's Sunnite Women: the Politics of Person*, PhD Thesis, University of Chicago.

—— (2005), 'Dakar's Sunnite Women: The Politics of Person', in Muriel Gomez-Perez (ed.), *L'islam politique au sud du Sahara: Identités, discours et enjeux*, Paris, pp. 309–26.

—— (2009a), 'Jambar or Jumbax-out? How Sunnite Women Negotiate Power and Belief in Orthodox Islamic Femininity', in Mamadou Diouf and Mara Leichtman (eds), *New Perspectives on Islam in Senegal: Conversion, Migration, Wealth, Power and Femininity*, New York, 211–36.

—— (2009b), 'Les jeunes femmes Sunnites et la libéralisation économique à Dakar', *Afrique contemporaine*, 231: 3, 79–98.

—— (2013), 'Dakar's Sunnite Women: The Dialectic of Submission and Defiance in a Globalizing City', in M. Diouf (ed.), *Tolerance, Democracy, and Sufis in Senegal*, New York, pp. 73–99.

Ayani, Samuel G. (1977 [1970]), *A History of Zanzibar. A Study in Constitutional Development 1934–1964*, Nairobi.

Ayubi, Shaheen and Sakina Mohyuddin (1994), 'Muslims in Kenya: An Overview', *Journal Institute of Muslim Minority Affairs*, XV, 144–56.

Azumah, John (2014), 'Boko Haram: A Cocktail of Romanticized Jihadist Legacy, Factionalism and Disillusionment', unpublished conference paper.

Babou, Cheikh (2007), *Fighting the Greater Jihad: Amadu Bamba and the Founding of the Muridiyya of Senegal, 1853–1913*, Athens.

—— (2013a), 'The Senegalese "Social Contract" Revisited: The Muridiyya Muslim Order and State Politics in Postcolonial Senegal', in M. Diouf (ed.), *Tolerance, Democracy, and Sufis in Senegal*, New York, pp. 125–46.

—— (2013b), 'Entre Dieu et César. Abdoulaye Wade, la Mouridiyya et le pouvoir', in M. C. Diop (ed.), *Le Sénégal sous Abdoulaye Wade: Le Sopi à l'épreuve du pouvoir*, Paris, pp. 297–318.

'Babu', Abdulrahman Muhammad (1991), 'The 1964 Revolution: Lumpen or Vanguard?' in Abdul Sheriff and Ed Ferguson (eds), *Zanzibar under Colonial Rule*, London, 220–49.

Bakari, Mohammed Ali (2001), *The Democratization Process in Zanzibar: A Retarded Transition*, Hamburg.

Bakari, Muḥammad (1989), The New ᶜUlamāᵓ in Kenya, unpublished conference paper.

—— (2003), 'Sheikh Abdallah Salih al-Farsy: An Appreciation', unpublished conference paper.

—— (2006), 'Sayyid Omar Abdallah (1918–1988): The Forgotten Muslim Humanist and Public Intellectual', in Roman Loimeier and Rüdiger Seesemann (eds), *The Global Worlds of the Swahili:Interfaces of Islam, Identity and Space in 19th and 20th Century East Africa*, Hamburg, pp. 363–88.

—— and Saad Yahya (eds) (1995), *Islam in Kenya*, Nairobi.

Bala, Salisu (2013–2014), 'Salafi Targets for "Boko Haram": The Murder of Shaykh Muhammad Auwal Adam "Albani" Zaria (d. 2014)', *Annual Review of Islam in Africa*, 12: 1, 31–8.

Bang, Anne K. (2003), *Sufis and Scholars of the Sea: Family Networks in East Africa, 1860–1925*, London.

—— (2014), *Ripples of Reform: Islamic Sufi Networks in the Western Indian Ocean (c. 1880–1940)*, Leiden.

Bangstad, Sindre (2007), *Global Flows, Local Appropriations: Facets of Secularization and Re-Islamization among Contemporary Cape Muslims*, Amsterdam.

Bari, Sarki Bello (1997), *Taurarin Kadiriyya: Littafi na farko (1)*, Kano.

Barraux, Roland (2009), *Du corail au volcan: L'histoire des îles Comores*, Moroni.

Bauer, Thomas (2011), *Die Kultur der Ambiguität: Eine andere Geschichte des Islams*, Berlin.

Baumann, Gerd (1996), *Contesting Culture: Discourses of Identity in Multi-Ethnic London*, Cambridge.

—— (2005), 'Grammars of Identity/Alterity: A Structural Approach', in Gerd Baumann and Andre Gingrich (eds), *Grammars of Identity/Alterity: A Structural Approach*, London, pp. 18–52.

Bayat, Asef (2007), *Making Islam Democratic: Social Movements and the Post-Islamist Turn*, Stanford.

—— (2013), *Life as Politics: How Ordinary People Change the Middle East*, Stanford.

Beck, Kurt (1993), 'Islamischer Fundamentalismus und die Wege der Ausbreitung der nilo-sudanischen Hochkultur', unpublished conference paper.

Becker, Carl-Heinrich (1932), 'Ist der Islam eine Gefahr für unsere Kolonien?' in C. H. Becker, *Islamstudien Vol. II*, Leipzig, pp. 156–86.

Becker, Felicitas (2008), *Becoming Muslim in Mainland Tanzania, 1890–2000*, Oxford.

Behrman, Lucy (1970), *Muslim Brotherhoods and Politics in Senegal*, Cambridge, MA.

Ben Amara, Ramzi (2011), *The Izala Movement in Nigeria: Its Split, Relationship to Sufis and Perception of Sharia Re-Implementation*, PhD Thesis, University of Bayreuth, Germany.

—— (2014), 'We Introduced Sharīᶜa: The Izala Movement in Nigeria as Initiator of Sharīᶜa-Reimplementation in the North of the Country: Some Reflections', in John A. Chesworth and Franz Kogelmann (eds), *Sharīᶜa in Africa Today: Reactions and Responses*, Leiden, pp. 125–48.

Bennett, N. R. (1978), *A History of the Arab State of Zanzibar*, London.

Benthall, Jonathan (2007), 'Islamic Charities in Southern Mali Today', *Islam et sociétés au sud du Sahara (nouvelle série)*, 1, 165–74.

—— and Jérome Bellion-Jourdan (2003), *The Charitable Crescent. Politics of Aid in the Muslim World*, New York.

Bergmann, Danja (2013), *Aufruhr im Paradies: Religiöse Spannungen auf Sansibar*, Berlin.

Besteman, Catherine (1999), *Unreveling Somalia: Race, Violence, and the Legacy of Slavery*, Philadelphia.

—— and Lee Cassanelli (eds) (2003 [1996]), *The Struggle for Land in Southern Somalia: The War Behind the War*, London.

Bilal Muslim Mission of Tanzania (1999), *Swali la Sjeikh Abdullah Saleh al-Farsy wa Zanzibar na Jibu la Imam Muhammad Husain Kashiful Ghitaa wa Najaf*, Dar es Salaam.

Bissell, William Cunningham (1999), *City of Stone, Space of Contestation: Urban Conservation and the Colonial Past in Zanzibar*, 3 vols, PhD Thesis, University of Chicago.

Blanchy, Sophie (1998), 'Pouvoir religieux aux Comores', in Françoise Le Guennec-Coppens and David Parkin (eds), *Autorité et pouvoir chez les Swahili*, Paris, pp. 181–202.

Bochinger, Christoph (2003), 'Religionsvergleiche in religionswissenschaftlicher und theologischer Perspektive', in H. Kaelble and J. Schriewer (eds), *Vergleich und Transfer*, Frankfurt, pp. 251–81.

Bodian, Mamadou and Leonardo Villalon (2015), 'Islam et réforme éducative au Sénégal: tensions et négociations vers un modèle hybride', in Abdourahmane Seck, Mayke Kaag and Cheikh Gueye (eds), *État, Sociétés et Islam au Sénégal: Un aire de nouveau temps?*, Paris, pp. 73–94.

Bokhari, Yusra, Nasim Chowdhury and Robert Lacey (2014), 'A Good Day to Bury a Bad Charity: Charting the Rise and Fall of the Al-Haramayn Islamic Foundation', in Robert Lacey and Jonathan Benthall (eds), *Gulf Charities and Islamic Philanthropy in the 'Age of Terror' and Beyond*, Berlin, pp. 199–230.

Bouquet, Christian (1982), *Tchad: genèse d'un conflit*, Paris.

Bourdieu, Pierre (1970), *Zur Soziologie der symbolischen Formen*, Frankfurt.

—— (1982), *Die feinen Unterschiede*, Frankfurt.

Bourgeot, François (2013), 'Des Touaregs en rebellion', in Patrick Gonin, Nathalie Kotlok and Marc-Antoine Pérouse de Montclos (eds), *La tragédie malienne*, Paris, pp. 113–30.

Bowen, John (1993), *Muslims through Discourse: Religion and Ritual in Gayo Society*, Princeton.

Bowles, B. D. (1991), 'The Struggle for Independence, 1946–1963', in Abdul Sheriff and Ed Ferguson (eds), *Zanzibar under Colonial Rule*, London, pp. 79–106.

Bradbury, Mark (2008), *Becoming Somaliland*, Oxford.

Braukämper, Ulrich (2004), *Islamic History and Culture in Southern Ethiopia*, Münster, Germany.

Brégand, Denise (2007), 'Muslim Reformists and the State in Benin', in Benjamin F. Soares and Réné Otayek (eds), *Islam and Muslim Politics in Africa*, New York, pp. 121–36.

—— (2009), 'Du soufisme au réformisme: la trajectoire de Mohamed Habib, Imam à Cotonou', *Politique Africaine*, 116, 121–42.

Brennan, James R. (2015), 'A History of Sauti ya Mvita (Voice of Mombasa): Radio, Public Culture and Islam in Coastal Kenya, 1947–1966', in Rosalind Hackett and Benjamin Soares (eds), *New Media and Religious Transformations in Africa*, Bloomington, pp. 19–38.

Brenner, Louis (1984), *West African Sufi: The Religious Heritage and Spiritual Search of Cerno Bokar Saalif Taal*, London.

—— (1988), 'Concepts of Tariqa in West Africa: The Case of the Qadiriya', in D. B. Cruise O'Brien and Christian Coulon (eds), *Charisma and Brotherhood in African Islam*, Oxford, pp. 33–52.

—— (1993a), 'Constructing Muslim Identities in Mali', in Louis Brenner (ed.), *Muslim Identity and Social Change in Sub-Saharan Africa*, London, pp. 59–78.

—— (1993b), 'La culture arabo-islamique au Mali', in René Otayek (ed.), *Le radicalisme islamique au sud du Sahara*, Paris, pp. 161–96.

—— (2001), *Controlling Knowledge: Religion, Power and Schooling in a West African Muslim Society*, Bloomington.

Brigaglia, Andrea (2004), *Testo, tradizione e conflitto esegetico: Gli ᶜulamāᵓ contemporanei e gli sviluppi dell'esegesi coranica nella società nord-nigeriana (Kano e Kaduna: 1960–2002)*, PhD Thesis, Università degli studi di Napoli 'L'orientale', Naples.

—— (2005), 'Two Published Hausa Translations of the Qurᵓān and their Doctrinal Background', *Journal of Religion in Africa*, 35: 4, 424–49.

—— (2007), 'The Radio Kaduna *Tafsīr* (1978–1992) and the Construction of Public Images of Muslim Scholars in the Nigerian Media', *Journal for Islamic Studies*, 27, 173–210.

—— (2009), 'Learning, Gnosis and Exegesis: Public *Tafsīr* and Sufi Revival in the

City of Kano (Northern Nigeria), 1950–1970', *Die Welt des Islams*, 49: 3–4, 334–66.

—— (2012), 'A Contribution to the History of the Wahhabi Da[c]wa in West Africa: The Career and the Murder of Shaykh Ja[c]far Mahmoud Adam (Daura, ca. 1961/1962–Kano 2007)', *Islamic Africa*, 3: 1, 1–23.

—— (2013–2014a), 'Note on Shaykh Dahiru Bauchi and the July 2014 Kaduna Bombing', *Annual Review of Islam in Africa*, 12: 1, 39–42.

—— (2013–2014b), 'Abubakar Shekau: The "Boko Haram" Leader Who Never Came "Back from the Dead"', *Annual Review of Islam in Africa*, 12: 1, 43–8.

—— (2015), 'The Volatility of Salafi Political Theology, the War on Terror and the Genesis of Boko Haram', *Diritto e questioni publiche*, 15/2, 174–201.

Bromber, Katrin (2001), Die Qādiriyya in Bagamoyo im Spannungsfeld zwischen Bildung und Politik, unpublished conference paper.

Brossier, Marie (2004), 'Les débats sur le droit de la famille au Sénégal: Une mise en question des fondements de l'autorité légitime', *Politique Africaine*, 96, 78–98.

Browers, Michelle and Charles Kurzman (eds) (2004), *An Islamic Reformation*, Lanham.

Bryden, Matt (2014), *The Reinvention of al-Shabaab: A Strategy of Choice or Necessity*, Center for Strategic International Studies, Washington, DC.

Buckley, David T. (2013), *Benevolent Secularism: The Emergence and Evolution of the Religious Politics of Democracy in Ireland, Senegal and the Philippines*, PhD Thesis, Georgetown University, Washington, DC.

Buggenhagen, Beth (2012), *Muslim Families in Global Senegal: Money Takes Care of Shame*, Bloomington.

Buijtenhuijs, Robert 1978), *Le Frolinat et les revoltes populaires du Tchad 1965–76*, Den Haag.

—— (1987), *Le Frolinat et les guerres civiles du Tchad*, Paris.

—— (1992), 'Le FROLINAT: mouvement islamique ou mouvement de musulmans', in Jean-Pierre Magnant (ed.), *L'Islam au Tchad*, Talence, pp. 127–38.

Bunza, Mukhtar Umar (2004), 'Muslims and the Modern State in Nigeria: A Study of the Impact of Foreign Religious Literature, 1980s–1990s', *Islam et Sociétés au Sud du Sahara*, 17–18, 49–66.

—— (2005), 'The Iranian Model of Political Islamic Movement in Nigeria', in Muriel Gomez-Perez (ed.), *L'Islam politique au sud du Sahara: Identités, discours et enjeux*, Paris, pp. 227–42.

Burgess, Thomas Gary (1999), 'Remembering Youth: Generation in Revolutionary Zanzibar', *Africa Today*, 46: 2, 29–52.

—— (2002a), *Youth and the Revolution: Mobility and Discipline in Zanzibar, 1950–1980*, PhD Thesis, Indiana University, Bloomington.

—— (2002b), 'Cinema, Bell Bottoms, and Miniskirts: Struggles over Youth and Citizenship in Revolutionary Zanzibar', *The International Journal of African Historical Studies*, 35: 2–3, 287–314.

—— (2005), 'An Imagined Generation: Umma Youth in Nationalist Zanzibar', in Gregory H. Maddox and James L. Giblin (eds), *In Search of a Nation. Histories of Authority and Dissidence in Tanzania*, Oxford, 216–49.

Burr, J. Millard and Robert O. Collins (2010), *Sudan in Turmoil: Hasan al-Turabi and the Islamist State*, Princeton.

Cantone, Cléo (2005), 'Radicalisme au féminin? Les filles voilées et l'appropriation de l'espace dans les mosques à Dakar', in Muriel Gomez-Perez (ed.), *L'islam politique au sud du Sahara: Identités, discours et enjeux*, Paris, pp. 119–30.

—— (2012), *Making and Remaking of Mosques in Senegal*, Leiden.

Carmichael, Tim (1996), 'Contemporary Ethiopian Discourses on Islamic History: The Politics of Historical Representation', *Islam et Sociétés au Sud du Sahara*, 10, 169–86.

Cassanelli, L. V. (1973), *The Benadir Past: Essays in Southern Somaali History*, Madison.

Chande, Abdin N. (1998), *Islam, Ulamaa and Community Development in Tanzania: A Case Study of Religious Currents in East Africa*, San Francisco.

Charlick, Robert B. (2007), 'Niger: Islamist Identity and the Politics of Globalization', in William Miles (ed.), *Political Islam in West Africa: State–Society Relations Transformed*, London, pp. 19– 42.

Chesworth, John (2006), 'Fundamentalism and Outreach Strategies in East Africa: Christian Evangelism and Muslim Da^{c}wa', in Benjamin F. Soares (ed.), *Muslim–Christian Encounters in Africa*, Leiden, pp. 159–86.

Chih, Rachida (2013), 'What is a Sufi Order? Revisiting the Concept through a Case Study of the Khalwatiyya in Contemporary Egypt', in Julia Day Howell and Martin van Bruinessen (eds), *Sufism and the Modern in Islam*, London, pp. 21–38.

Christelow, Allan (1987), 'Three Islamic Voices in Contemporary Nigeria', in William R. Roff (ed.), *Islam and the Political Economy of Meaning*, London, pp. 226–53.

Cissé, Issa (1998), 'Les médersas au Burklina, l'aide arabe et l'enseignement arabo-islamique', in Ousmane Kane and Jean-Louis Triaud (eds), *Islam et Islamismes au sud du Sahara*, Paris, pp. 101–16.

Cissé, Seydou (1992), *L'enseignement islamique en Afrique Noire*, Paris.

Clayton, Anthony (1976), 'The 1948 Zanzibar General Strike', *The Scandinavian Institute of African Studies Research Report 32,* Uppsala.

—— (1981), *The Zanzibar Revolution and its Aftermath*, London.

Collins, Robert O. (2008), *A History of the Modern Sudan*, Cambridge.

Comolli, Virginia (2015). *Boko Haram: Nigeria's Islamist Insurgency*, London.

Constantin, François (1983), *Les communautés musulmanes d'Afrique orientale*, Pau.

—— (1987), *Les voies de l'islam en Afrique orientale*, Paris.

—— (1988a), 'Charisma and the Crisis of Power in East Africa', in D. B. Cruise O'Brien and Christian Coulon (eds), *Charisma and Brotherhood in African Islam*, Oxford, pp. 67–90.

—— (1988b), 'Bagamoyo 1987: Retour aux sources de la branche est-africaine de la Qadiriyya', *Islam et sociétés au sud du Sahara*, 2, pp. 138–50.

—— (1995), 'The Attempts to Create Muslim National Organizations in Tanzania, Uganda and Kenya', in H. Hansen and M. Twaddle (eds), *Religion and Politics in East Africa*, London, pp. 19–31.

Cook, Michael (2000), *Commanding Right and Forbidding Wrong in Islamic Thought*, Cambridge.

Cooper, Barbara M. (2006), *Evangelical Christians in the Muslim Sahel*, Bloomington.

Coulon, Christian (1981), *Le Marabout et le prince*, Paris.

Coulibaly, Abdou Latif (1993a), 'Les itinéraires politiques de l'Islam au Nord-Nigeria', in J.-F. Bayart (ed.), *Religion et Modernité Politique en Afrique Noire*, Paris, pp. 19–63.

—— (1993b), 'Les nouveaux oulémas et le renouveau islamique au Nord-Nigeria', in Réné Otayek (ed.), *Le radicalisme islamique au sud du Sahara*, Paris, pp. 123–50.

—— (1999), *Le Sénégal à l'épreuve de la démocratie: Enquête sur 50 ans de lutte et de complots au sein de l'élite socialiste*, Paris.

—— (2003), *Wade, un opposant au pouvoir: L'alternance piegée?* Dakar.

Crecelius, Daniel (1978), 'Nonideological Responses of the Egyptian Ulama to Modernization', in Nikki R. Keddie (ed.), *Scholars, Saints and Sufis. Muslim Religious Institutions in the Middle East since 1500*, Berkeley, pp. 167–209.

Cruise O'Brien, Donal B. (1971), *The Murides of Senegal, The Political and Economic Organization of an Islamic Brotherhood*, Oxford.

—— (1992), 'Le contrât social sénégalais à l'épreuve', *Politique Africaine*, 45, 9–20.

—— (1995), 'Coping with the Christians. The Muslim Predicament in Kenya', in B. Hansen and M. Twaddle (eds), *Religion & Politics in East Africa*, London, pp. 200–22.

—— (1996), 'A Lost Generation? Youth Identity and State Decay in West Africa', in Richard Werbner and Terence Ranger (eds), *Postcolonial Identities in Africa*, London, pp. 55–74.

—— (2003), *Symbolic Confrontations: Muslims Imagining the State in Africa*, London.

Cuoq, Joseph (1975). *Les musulmans en Afrique*, Paris.

—— (1981), *L'Islam en Ethiopie des origines au XVe siècle*, Paris.

Dahou, Tarik and Vincent Foucher (2004), 'Le Sénégal, entre changement politique et révolution passive', *Politique Africaine*, 96, 5–21.

Daly, M. W. (1991), *Imperial Sudan: The Anglo-Egyptian Condominium 1934–56*, Cambridge.

dan Fodio, ʿUthmān (n.d.), *Iḥyāʾ al-sunna wa-ikhmād al-bidʿa*, Beirut.

Danfulani, Umar H. D. (2005), *The Sharia Issue and Christian–Muslim Relations in Contemporary Nigeria*, Stockholm.

D'Aoust, Sophie (2012), *L'effectivité du droit à l'éducation au Sénégal: Les cas des enfants talibés dans les écoles coraniques*, Paris.

Dar es Salaam University Muslims' Trusteeship (2004), *Tusikubali Kubaguliwa Kielimu: Nasaha za Sheikh Hasan bin Ameir (1880–1979)*, Dar es Salaam.

Dereje Feyissa (2013), 'Muslims Struggling for Recognition in Contemporary Ethiopia', in Patrick Desplat and Terje Østebø (eds), *Muslim Ethiopia: The Christian Legacy, Identity Politics and Islamic Reformism*, New York, pp. 25–46.

Desplat, Patrick (2001). *Islamische Gelehrte zwischen Text und Praxis: Wandlungsprozesse im Islam am Beispiel von Kenia/Ostafrika*, Master's Thesis, Johannes Gutenberg University of Mainz, Germany.

—— (2002), 'Muslime in Äthiopien: Die Heiligenverehrung in Harar in Auseinandersetzung mit islamischen Reformströmungen', *Afrika Spectrum*, 37: 2, 141–58.

—— (2005), 'The Articulation of Religious Identities and their Boundaries in Ethiopia: Labelling Difference and Processes of Contextualization in Islam', *Journal of Religion in Africa*, 33: 4, 482–505.

—— (2010), *Heilige Stadt – Stadt der Heiligen: Ambivalenzen und Kontroversen islamischer Heiligkeit in Harar, Äthiopien*, Cologne.

—— (2013), 'Against Wahhabism? Islamic Reform, Ambivalence and Sentiments of Loss in Harar', in Patrick Desplat and Terje Østebø (eds), *Muslim Ethiopia: The Christian Legacy, Identity Politics and Islamic Reformism*, New York, 163–86.

—— and Terje Østebø (2013), *Muslim Ethiopia: The Christian Legacy, Identity Politics and Islamic Reformism*, New York.

Dia, Mamadou (1985), *Mémoires d'un militant du tiers-monde*, Cahors.

Diagne, Pathé (2013), 'Abdoulaye Wade ou la fin du cycle senghorien', in M. C. Diop (ed.), *Le Sénégal sous Abdoulaye Wade: Le Sopi à l'épreuve du pouvoir*, Paris, pp. 97–118.

Diaw, Aminata, Momar-Coumba Diop and Mamadou Diouf (2000), 'Le baobab a été déraciné: L'alternance du Sénégal', *Politique Africaine*, 78, 157–79.

Dilger, Hansjörg (2007), 'Healing the Wounds of Modernity: Salvation, Community and Care in a Neo-Pentecostal Church in Dar es Salaam, Tanzania', *Journal of Religion in Africa*, 37: 1, 59–83.

Dione, Maurice Soudieck (2013), 'De la réception-réappropriation du concept de la laïcité au Sénégal, ou la spécificité d'une laïcité de collaboration entre le politique et le religieux', in Gilles Holder and Moussa Sow (eds), *L'Afrique des Laïcités: Etat, Religion et Pouvoirs au Sud du Sahara*, Paris, pp. 111–24.

Diop, Momar-Coumba (ed.) (2013a), *Le Sénégal sous Abdoulaye Wade: Le Sopi à l'épreuve du pouvoir*, Paris.

—— (2013b), 'Introduction: État, pouvoirs et société: Essai sur les trajéctoires du Sénégal contemporain', in M. C. Diop (ed.), *Le Sénégal sous Abdoulaye Wade: Le Sopi à l'épreuve du pouvoir*, Paris, pp. 41–96.

Diouf, Mamadou (ed.) (2013a), *Tolerance, Democracy, and Sufis in Senegal*, New York.

—— (2013b), 'Introduction', in M. Diouf (ed.), *Tolerance, Democracy, and Sufis in Senegal*, New York, pp. 1–35.

—— and Mara Leichtman (eds) (2009), *New Perspectives on Islam in Senegal: Conversion, Migration, Wealth, Power and Femininity*, New York.

Djabir, Abdou (1993), *Les Comores: un état en construction*, Paris.

Doutoum, Mohamat Adoum (1992), 'L'Islam au Ouaddaï avant et après la colonisation', in Jean-Pierre Magnant (ed.), *L'Islam au Tchad*, Talence, pp. 67–92.

Eickelman, Dale (1997), 'Print, Islam, and the Prospects for Civic Pluralism: New Religious Writings and their Audiences', *Journal of Islamic Studies*, 8:1, 43–62.

—— (1998), 'Inside the Islamic Reformation', *The Wilson Quarterly*, 22: 1, 80–9.

—— and James Piscatori (1996), *Muslim Politics*, Princeton.

—— and Jon W. Anderson (2003), *New Media in the Muslim World: The Emerging Public Sphere*, Bloomington.

Erlich, Haggai (1977), 'Ethiopia and Islam in Postrevolutionary Perspective', *Ethiopianist Notes*, 1: 1, 9–16.

—— (2007), *Saudi Arabia and Ethiopia: Islam, Christianity and Politics Entwined*, London.

—— (2010), *Islam and Christianity in the Horn of Africa*, Boulder.

Evers-Rosander, Eva (2003), 'Mam Diarra Bousso – the Mourid Mother of Porokhane, Senegal', *Jenda: A Journal of Culture and African Women Studies*, 4.

Fall, Mar (1993), 'Les arabisants au Sénégal: contre-elite ou courtiers?', in René Otayek (ed.), *Le radicalisme islamique au sud du Sahara*, Paris, pp. 197–212.

Falola, Toyin (1998), *Violence in Nigeria: The Crisis of Religious Politics and Secular Ideologies*, Rochester.

Farschid, Olaf (2014), 'Salafismus als politische Ideologie', in Behnam T. Said and Hazim Fouad (eds), *Salafismus: Auf der Suche nach dem wahren Islam*, Freiburg, pp. 160–92.

al-Farsy, Shaykh ᶜAbdallāh Ṣāliḥ (1969), *Kurani Takatifu*, Nairobi.

—— (1972 [1944]), *Baadhi ya wanavyuoni wa kishafi wa mashariki ya Afrika*, Mombasa.

—— (1982), *Bid-a II*, Mombasa.

Faulkner, Mark R. J. (2006), *Overtly Muslim, Covertly Boni: Competing Calls of Religious Allegiance on the Kenyan Coast*, Leiden.

Feichtinger, Walter and Gerald Heinzl (eds) (2011), *Somalia: Optionen – Chancen – Stolpersteine*, Wien.

Ferchl, Dieter (1991), *Ṣaḥīḥ al-Buḫārī: Nachrichten von Taten und Aussprüchen des Propheten Muhammad*, Stuttgart.

Fergusson, James (2013), *The World's Most Dangerous Place: Inside the Outlaw State of Somalia*, London.

Ficquet, Éloi (2006), 'Flesh Soaked in Faith: Meat as a Marker of the Boundary between Christians and Muslims in Ethiopia', in Benjamin F. Soares (ed.), *Muslim–Christian Encounters in Africa*, Leiden, pp. 39–56.

Fietze, Beate (2009), *Historische Generationen: Über einen sozialen Mechanismus kulturellen Wandels und kollektiver Kreativität*, Bielefeld.

Filali-Ansary, Abdou (2003), *Réformer l'Islam? Une introduction aux débats contemporains*, Paris.

Fischer Weltalmanach (2014), Frankfurt.

Flint, J. E. (1965), 'Zanzibar 1890–1950', in Vincent Harlow, E. M. Chilver and Alison Smith (eds), *History of East Africa, Vol. II*, Oxford, pp. 641–71.

Fluehr-Lobban, Carloyn (2012), *Shariᶜa and Islamism in Sudan: Conflict, Law and Social Transformation*, London.

Förster, Till (2005), 'Globalisierung aus einer Handlungsperspektive: Versuch einer ethnologischen Klärung', in R. Loimeier, D. Neubert and C. Weissköppel (eds), *Globalisierung im lokalen Kontext. Perspektiven und Konzepte von Handeln in Afrika*, Hamburg, pp. 31–62.

Fourchard, Laurent, André Mary and René Otayek (2005), *Entreprises religieuses transnationales en Afrique de l'Ouest*, Paris.

Freitag, Ulrike (1999), 'Hadhramaut: A Religious Centre for the Indian Ocean in the Late 19th Century and Early 20th Centuries?' *Studia Islamica*, 165–83.

—— (2003), *Indian Ocean Migrants and State Formation in Hadhramaut*, Leiden.

Fuchs, Simon Wolfgang (2013), 'Do Excellent Surgeons Make Miserable Exegetes? Negotiating the Sunni Tradition in the Jihādī Camps', *Die Welt des Islams*, 53: 2, 192–237.

Fuglesang, Minou (1994), *Veils and Videos. Female Youth Culture on the Kenyan Coast*, Stockholm.

Gallab, Abdullahi A. (2008), *The First Islamic Republic: Development and Disintegration of Islamism in the Sudan*, Aldershot.

Gardinier, David E. (1989), 'The Ma^c^had al-^c^Ilmi of Muhammad Awuda Oulech at Abéché (Chad)', *Islam et Sociétés au Sud du Sahara*, 3, 159–85.

Gascon, Alain (1990), 'La Somalie éclatée: crise de régime ou crise d'identité nationale?' *Islam et sociétés au sud du Sahara*, 4, 47–56.

Gause, Gregory (1990), *Saudi–Yemeni Relations: Domestic Structures and Foreign Influence*, New York.

Gauvain, Richard (2013), *Salafi Ritual Puritiy: In the Presence of God*, London.

Geiger, Susan (1997), *TANU Women: Gender and Culture in the Making of Tanganyikan Nationalism, 1955–1965*, Oxford.

Gellar, Sheldon (2005), *Democracy in Senegal. Tocquevillian Analytics in Africa*, New York.

—— (2013), 'The Rise of Citizen Movements and the Consolidation of Democracy under the Abdoulaye Wade Regime (2000–2012)', in M. C. Diop (ed.), *Le Sénégal sous Abdoulaye Wade: Le Sopi à l'épreuve du pouvoir*, Paris, pp. 119–52.

Gervasoni, Olivia and Cheikh Gueye (2005), 'La confrérie Muride au centre de la vie politique sénégalaise: le "Sopi" inaugure un nouveau paradigme?', in Muriel Gomez-Perez (ed.), *L'islam politique au sud du Sahara: Identités, discours et enjeux*, Paris, pp. 621–40.

Gharaibeh, Mohammed (2014), 'Zur Glaubenslehre des Salafismus', in Behnam T. Said and Hazim Fouad (eds), *Salafismus: Auf der Suche nach dem wahren Islam*, Freiburg, pp. 106–31.

Gifford, Paul (1987), '"Africa Shall be Saved": An Appraisal of Reinhard Bonnke's Pan-African Crusade', *Journal of Religion in Africa*, 17: 1, 63–92.

Gilbert, Eric (2004), *Dhows and the Colonial Economy of Zanzibar, 1860–1970*, Oxford.

Gilsaa, Sören (2012), *Muslim Politics in Tanzania*, Kopenhagen.
—— (2015), 'Salafism(s) in Tanzania: Theological Roots and Political Subtext of the Ansār Sunna', *Islamic Africa*, 6, 30–59.
Glassman, Jonathon (1995), *Feasts and Riots. Revelry, Rebellion and Popular Consciousness on the Swahili Coast, 1856–1888*, Portsmouth.
—— (2000), 'Sorting out the Tribes: The Creation of Racial Identities in Colonial Zanzibar's Newspaper Wars', *Journal of African History*, 41, 395–428.
—— (2011), *War of Words, War of Stones: Racial Thought and Violence in Colonial Zanzibar*, Bloomington.
Glew, Robert S. (1996), 'Islamic Associations in Niger', *Islam et sociétés au sud du Sahara*, 10, 187–206.
—— (1998), 'Islamic Culture and Muslim Identity in Zinder, Niger: A Historical Perspective', *Islam et sociétés au sud du Sahara*, 12, 129–48.
—— (2001), 'A Discourse Centred Approach toward Understanding Muslim Identities in Zinder', *Islam et Sociétés au Sud du Sahara*, 14: 5, 99–122.
Gomez-Perez, Muriel (1991), 'Associations islamiques à Dakar', *Islam et sociétés au sud du Sahara*, 5, 5–20.
—— (1994), 'L'Islamisme à Dakar: d'un contrôle social total à une culture du pouvoir?', *Afrika Spectrum*, 29: 1, 79–98.
—— (1997), *Une histoire des associations islamiques sénégalaises (Saint-Louis, Dakar, Thiès): itinéraires, stratégies et prises de parole (1930–1993)*, Thèse pour le Doctorat (Nouveau Régime), Université de Paris VII.
—— (2005), 'Généalogies de l'islam réformiste au Sénégal des années 1950 à nos jours: figures, savoirs et réseaux', in Laurent Fourchard, André Mary and René Otayek (eds), *Entreprises religieuses transnationales en Afrique de l'Ouest*, Paris, pp. 193–220.
—— and Selly Ba (2015), 'Les prédicatrices au Séneégal: de la visibilité à la légitimité religieuse et sociale (des années 1980 à nos jours)', in Abdourahmane Seck, Mayke Kaag and Cheikh Gueye (eds), *État, Sociétés et Islam au Sénégal: Un aire de nouveau temps?* Paris, pp. 175–204.
Gonin, Patrick, Nathalie Kotlok and Marc-Antoine Pérouse de Montclos (eds) (2013), *La tragédie malienne*, Paris.
Graham, William A. (1993), 'Traditionalism in Islam: An Essay in Interpretation', *Journal of Interdisciplinary History*, 23: 3, 493–522.
Grandin, Nicole (1993), 'Al-Merkaz al-islami al-ifriqi bi'l Khartoum: La République du Soudan et la propagation de l'islam en Afrique Noire (1977–1991)', in René Otayek (ed.), *Le radicalisme islamique au sud du Sahara*, Paris, pp. 97–122.

Gray, Christopher (1988), 'The Rise of the Niassene Tijaniyya, 1875 to the Present', *Islam et Sociétés au Sud du Sahara,* 2, 34–60.

Grégoire, Emanuel (1991), 'Accumulation marchande et propagation de l'islam en milieu urbain: le cas de Maradi', *Islam et sociétés au sud du Sahara,* 5, 43–56.

—— (1993), 'Islam and Identity of Merchants in Maradi (Niger)', in Louis Brenner (ed.), *Muslim Identity and Social Change in Sub-Saharan Africa,* London, pp. 106–15.

Greven, Thomas (2013), 'Tuareg-Rebellion: Islamismus und Staatskrise in Mali', *Prokla 170,* 43: 1, 89–96.

Griffel, Frank (2015), 'What Do We Mean by "Salafi"? Connecting Muḥammad [c]Abduh with Egypt's Nūr Party in Islam's Contemporary Intellectual History', *Die Welt des Islams,* 55: 2, pp. 186–220.

Gueye, Cheikh (2002), *Touba, la capitale des Murides: L'organisation de l'espace dans une ville religieuse, Touba (Senegal),* Dakar.

Guluma, Gemeda (1993), 'The Islamization of the Gibe Region, Southwestern Ethiopia from c. 1830s to the Early Twentieth Century', *Journal of Ethiopian Studies,* 26: 2, 63–79.

—— (2008), Religion and Politics in the Gibe Region: The Establishment of the Tijaniyya Order in Jimma, Southwestern Ethiopia, unpublished conference paper.

Gumi, A. M. (1976 [1972]), *Al-[c]aqīda aṣ-ṣaḥīḥa bi-muwāfaqat ash-sharī[c]a,* Ankara.

—— (1979), *Tarjamar Ma'anonin Alkurani Maigirma,* Beirut.

—— and Ismaila A. Tsiga (1992), *Where I Stand,* Ibadan.

Haenni, Patrick (2005), *L'islam de marché: L'autre révolution conservatrice,* Paris.

Haj, Samira (2009), *Reconfiguring Islamic Tradition: Reform, Rationality and Modernity,* Stanford.

Hale, Sondra (1996), *Gender Politics in Sudan: Islamism, Socialism and the State,* Boulder.

Halkano Abdi Wario (2014), 'Debates on Kadhi's Courts and Christian–Muslim Relations in Isiolo Town: Thematic Issues and Emergent Trends', in John A. Chesworth and Franz Kogelmann (eds), *Sharī[c]a in Africa Today: Reactions and Responses,* Leiden, pp. 149–76.

Hamdi, Mohamed Elhachmi (1998), *The Making of an Islamic Political Leader: Conversations with Ḥasan al-Turābī,* London.

Hanak, Irmi (1994), *Gericht – Sprache – Macht. Überlegungen zur Realisierung von Dominanzverhältnissen in und durch sprachliche Kommunikation am Beispiel des Familiengerichts in Zanzibar,* Wien.

Hanretta, Sean (2009), *Islam and Social Change in French West Africa: History of an Emancipatory Community*, Cambridge.

Hansen, Stig Jarle (2013a), *Al-Shabaab in Somalia: The History and Ideology of a Militant Islamist Group 2005–2012*, London.

—— (2013b), 'Transborder Islamic Activism in the Horn of Africa, the Case of Tadamun – the Ethiopian Muslim Brotherhood?', in Patrick Desplat and Terje Østebø (eds), *Muslim Ethiopia: The Christian Legacy, Identity Politics and Islamic Reformism*, New York, 201–14.

Hansen, William W. and Umma Aliyu Musa (2013), 'Fanon, the Wretched and Boko Haram', *Journal of Asian and African Studies*, 48: 3, 281–96.

Hardy, Ferdaous and Jeanne Semin (2009), 'Islam au Sénégal et initiatives féminines: Une économie morale du pèlerinage à La Mecque', *Afrique contemporaine*, 231: 3, 139–56.

Harnischfeger, Johannes (2006), *Demokratisierung und Islamisches Recht: Der Scharia-Konflikt in Nigeria*, Frankfurt.

—— (2012), 'Rivalität unter Eliten: Der Boko Haram Aufstand in Nigeria', *Leviathan*, 40: 4, 491–516.

Haruna, Mohammed and Abdullahi Salisu (1991), 'The Kano Soccer Craze and Club Formation among Hausa Youth in Kano, Nigeria', *Kano Studies, Special Issue*, 113–24.

Hassan M. Abukar (2013), 'Somalia: The Godane Coup and the Unraveling of al-Shabaab', *African Arguments*, 2 July.

Hassane, Souley (2005), 'Les nouvelles élites islamiques du Niger et du Nigeria du Nord: itinéraires et prédications fondatrices', in Laurant Fourchard, André Mary and Réné Otayek (eds), *Entreprises religieuses transnationales en Afrique de l'Ouest*, Paris, pp. 373–94.

—— (2007), 'Le Nigeria, entre la sharia et la démocratie', in Jean-Louis Triaud (ed.), *Islam, sociétés et politique en Afrique subsaharienne. Les exemples du Sénégal, du Niger et du Nigeria*, Paris, pp. 75–96.

—— (2009), 'Société civile islamique et nouveaux espaces publics au Niger: Esquisse sur l'Islam postmoderne et les pratiques religieuses globales en Afrique', in Gilles Holder (ed.), *L'Islam, nouvel espace public en Afrique*, Paris, pp. 101–26.

Havard, Jean-François (2004), 'De la victoire du « Sopi » à la tentation du « Nopi »? « Gouvernement de l'Alternance » et liberté d'expression des médias au Sénégal', *Politique Africaine*, 96, 22–38.

Haykel, Bernard (2003), *Revival and Reform in Islam: the Legacy of Muhammad al-Shawkani*, Cambridge.

—— (2009), 'On the Nature of Salafi Thought and Action', in Roel Meijer (ed.), *Global Salafism: Islam's New Religious Movement*, London, pp. 33–57.

Hefner, Robert W. and Muhammad Qasim Zaman (eds) (2007), *Schooling Islam: The Culture and Politics of Modern Muslim Education*, Princeton.

Hegghammer, Thomas (2009), 'Jihadi-Salafis or Revolutionaries? On Religion and Politics in the Study of Militant Islamism', in Roel Meijer (ed.), *Global Salafism: Islam's New Religious Movement*, London, pp. 244–66.

Herrera, Linda (2000), 'Downveiling: Shifting Socio-Religious Practices in Egypt', *ISIM Newsletter*, 6, 1 and 32.

Higazi, Adam (2007), 'Violence urbaine et politique à Jos (Nigeria): de la période coloniale aux élections de 2007', *Politique Africaine*, 106, 69–91.

—— (2013), 'Les origines et la transformation de l'insurrection de Boko Haram dans le Nord du Nigeria', *Politique Africaine*, 130, 137–64.

Hill, Joseph (2011), 'Languages of Islam: Hybrid Genres of Taalibe Baay Oratory in Senegal', unpublished conference paper.

—— (2013), 'Sovereign Islam in a Secular State: Hidden Knowledge and Sufi Governance among "Taalibe Baay"', in M. Diouf (ed.), *Tolerance, Democracy, and Sufis in Senegal*, New York, pp. 99–124.

Hiskett, Mervyn (1980), 'The "Community of Grace" and its Opponents, the "Rejecters": A Debate about Theology and Mysticism in Muslim West Africa with Special Reference to its Hausa Expression', *African Language Studies*, 17, 99–140.

—— (1987), 'The Maitatsine Riots in Kano, 1980: An Assessment', *Journal of Religion in Africa*, 17: 3, 209–23.

Ho, Engseng (2005), *The Graves of Tarim: Genealogy and Mobility across the Indian Ocean*, Berkeley.

Höchner, Hannah (2012), 'Koranfestes Kanonenfutter', *taz*, 27 February.

—— (2015a), 'Traditional Qur'anic Students (almajirai) in Nigeria: Fair Game for Unfair Accusations?', in Marc-Antoine Pérouse de Montclos (ed.), *Boko Haram: Islamism, Politics, Security and the State in Nigeria*, Los Angeles, pp. 71–96.

—— (2015b), 'Porridge, Piety and Patience: Young Qur'anic Students' Experiences of Poverty in Kano, Nigeria', *Africa*, 85: 2, 269–88.

Hock, Carsten (1999), *Fliegen die Seelen der Heiligen? Muslimische Reform und staatliche Autorität in der Republik Mali seit 1960*, Berlin.

Hock, Klaus (1992), 'How Religious are Religious Riots?: A Case Study from Bauchi State, Nigeria', *Afrika Spectrum*, 27: 1, 43–58.

—— (1996), *Der Islam-Komplex: Zur christlichen Wahrnehmung des Islams und der christlich-muslimischen Beziehungen in Nordnigeria während der Militärherrschaft Babangidas*, Hamburg.

Hodgkin, Elisabeth (1998), 'Islamism and Islamic Research in Africa', in Ousmane Kane and Jean-Louis Triaud (eds), *Islam et Islamismes au sud du Sahara*, Paris, pp. 197–262.

Hodgson, Marshall G. S. (1960), 'Une comparaison entre Islam et Christianisme en tant que structures de la vie religieuse', *Diogène*, 32, 60–89.

Hoffman, Valerie (2006), 'In his (Arab) Majesty's Service: The Career of a Somali Scholar and Diplomat in Nineteenth-Century Zanzibar', in Roman Loimeier and Rüdiger Seesemann (eds), *The Global Worlds of the Swahili: Interfaces of Islam, Identity and Space in 19th and 20th Century East Africa*, Hamburg, 251–72.

—— (2007), 'Ibadi Muslims in Oman and Zanzibar: The Impact of Local Context on a Translocal Tradition', unpublished conference paper.

Hoffmann, Liese (2013), *Politics and Memories of the Arab School in Colonial Kenya*, Master's Thesis, Humboldt University, Berlin.

Hofheinz, Albrecht (1996), *Internalising Islam. Shaykh Muḥammad Majdhūb – Scriptural Islam and Local Context in the Early 19th Century Sudan*, 2 vols, PhD Thesis, University of Bergen, Germany.

Höhne, Markus (2009), 'Counterterrorism in Somalia, or: How External Interferences Helped to Produce Militant Islamism', unpublished conference paper.

—— (2011a), 'Al-Shabaab in Somalia: Von einer Terrorzelle zu einem regierungsähnlichen Akteur', in Walter Feichtinger and Gerald Hainzl (eds), *Somalia: Optionen, Chancen, Stolpersteine*, Wien, pp. 121–57.

—— (2011b), 'Die somalische Diaspora: Rollen und Chancen in (Bürger-)Krieg und Wiederaufbau', in Feichtinger, Walter and Gerald Heinzl (eds), *Somalia: Optionen – Chancen – Stolpersteine*, Wien, pp. 57–82.

—— (2014a), 'Resource Conflict and Militant Islamism in the Golis Mountains in Northern Somalia (2006–2013)', *Review of African Political Economy*, 41: 141, 358–73.

—— (2014b), 'Alternatives for Conflict Transformation in Somalia: A Snapshot and Analysis of Key Political Actor's Views and Strategies', *ACTS Report for the Life & Peace Institute*, Uppsala.

—— (2015), *Between Somaliland and Puntland: Marginalization, Militarization and Conflicting Political Visions*. London.

—— and Virginia Luling (eds) (2010), *Milk and Peace, Drought and War: Somali Culture, Society and Politics*, London.

Holder, Gilles (ed.) (2009a), *L'islam, nouvel espace public en Afrique*, Paris.

—— (2009b), '« Maouloud » 2006, de Bamako à Tombouctou: Entre résislamisation de la nation et laïcité de l'État: la construction d'un espace public religieux au Mali', in Gilles Holder (ed.), *L'Islam, nouvel espace public en Afrique*, Paris, pp. 237–90.

—— (2012), 'Chérif Ousmane Madani Haidara et l'association islamique Ançar Dine: Un réformisme malien populaire en quête d'autonomie', *Cahiers d'Études Africaines*, 52: 2, 206–7, and 3, 389–425.

—— (2013a), 'Un pays musulman en quête d'État-nation', in Patrick Gonin, Nathalie Kotlok and Marc-Antoine Pérouse de Montclos (eds), *La tragédie malienne*, Paris, pp. 131–58.

—— (2013b), 'Les Ançars de la République: la bay'a au prisme de la laïcité malienne', in Gilles Holder and Moussa Sow (eds), *L'Afrique des Laïcités: État, Religion et Pouvoirs au Sud du Sahara*, Paris, pp. 277–90.

Howden, Daniel (2014), 'Trouble in Paradise as Radical Islam Grows in Zanzibar', <www.independent.co.uk/news/world/africa/trouble-in-paradise-as-radical-Islam-grows-in-Zanzibar> (last accessed 7 January 2014).

Howell, Julia Day and Martin van Bruinessen (eds) (2013), 'Introduction: Sufism and the "Modern" in Islam', in Julia Day Howell and Martin van Bruinessen (eds), *Sufism and the 'Modern' in Islam*, London, pp. 3–18.

Human Rights Watch (HRW) (2004), 'Political Sharia? Human Rights and Islamic Law in Northern Nigeria', <www.hrw.org/report/2004/09/21/political-sharia/human-rights-and-Islamic-law-in-Northern-Nigeria> (last accessed 5 July 2012).

—— (2012), 'Spiraling Violence: Boko Haram Attacks and Security Force Abuses in Nigeria', <www.hrw.org/report/2012/20/11/spiraling-violence/boko-haram-attacks-and-security-force-abuses-in-Nigeria> (last accessed 5 July 2012).

Hunwick, John O. (1995), *Arabic Literature of Africa, Vol. 2: The Writings of the Central Sudanic Africa*, Leiden.

Hussein Ahmed (1988), 'Introducing an Arabic Hagiography from Wallo', in Bayene Tadesse (ed.), *Proceedings of the 8th International Conference of Ethiopian Studies*, Addis Ababa, pp. 185–97.

—— (1989), 'The Life and Career of Shaykh Talha b. Ja^{c}far (c. 1853–1936)', *Journal of Ethiopian Studies*, 22, 13–30.

—— (1993), 'Trends and Issues in the History of Islam in Ethiopia', in Muhammad Nur Alkali (ed.), *Islam in Africa*, Ibadan, pp. 205–20.

—— (1998), 'Islamic Literature and Religious Revival in Ethiopia (1991–1994)', *Islam et Sociétés au Sud du Sahara*, 12, 89–108.

—— (2001), *Islam in Nineteenth Century Wallo, Ethiopia: Revival, Reform and Reaction*, Leiden.

—— (2006), 'Coexistence and/or Confrontation? Towards a Reappraisal of Christian–Muslim Encounter in Contemporary Ethiopia', *Journal of Religion in Africa*, 36: 1, 4–22.

Hütte, Moritz, Guido Steinberg and Annette Weber (2015), 'Boko Haram: Gefahr für Nigeria und seine nördlichen Nachbarn', in Guido Steinberg and Annette Weber (eds), *Jihadismus in Afrika: Lokale Ursachen, regionale Ausbreitung, internationale Verbindungen*, Berlin, pp. 91–106.

Ibrahim, Abdullahi Ali (1999), 'A Theology of Modernity: Hasan al-Turabi and Islamic Renewal in Sudan', *Africa Today*, 46: 3–4, 195–222.

Ibrahim, Jibrin (1991), 'Religion and Political Turbulence in Nigeria', *Journal of Modern African Studies*, 29, 115–36.

Idrissa, Abdourahmane (2005), 'Modèle islamique et modèle occidental: le conflit des élites au Niger', in Muriel Gomez-Perez (ed.), *L'Islam politique au Sud du Sahara*, Paris, pp. 347–74.

Ihle, Annette Haber (2003), *It's All about Morals: Islam and Social Mobility among Young and Committed Muslims in Tamale, Northern Ghana*, PhD Thesis, University of Copenhagen, Denmark.

Iliffe, J. (1969), *Tanganyika under German Rule 1905–12*, Cambridge.

—— (1979), *A Modern History of Tanganyika*, Cambridge.

International Crisis Group (ICG) (2005), *Somalia's Islamists*, Africa Report 100 (12 December).

—— (2012a), *Sudan: Major Reform or More War?* Africa Report 194 (29 November).

—— (2012b), *Mali: The Need for Determined and Coordinated International Action*, Africa Briefing 90 (24 September).

—— (2012c), *Mali: Avoiding Escalation*, Africa Report 189 (18 July).

—— (2012d). *Somalia: An Opportunity That Should not be Missed*, Africa Briefing 87 (22 February).

—— (2012e), *The Kenyan Military Intervention in Somalia*, Africa Report 184 (15 Febaruary).

—— (2012f), *Kenyan Somali Islamist Radicalisation*, Africa Briefing 85 (25 January).

—— (2013a), *Somalia: Puntland's Punted Polls*, Africa Briefing 97 (19 December).

—— (2013b), *Niger: Another Weak Link in the Sahel?* Africa Report 208 (19 September).

—— (2013c), *Ethiopia: Prospects for Peace in Ogaden*, Africa Report 207 (6 August).

—— (2013d), *Mali: Security, Dialogue and Meaningful Reform*, Africa Report 201 (11 April).

—— (2014a), *Kenya: al-Shabaab – Closer to Home*, Africa Briefing 102 (25 September).

—— (2014b), *Somalia: al-Shabaab: It Will be a Long War*, Africa Briefing 99 (26 June).

—— (2014c), *Curbing Violence in Nigeria II: The Boko Haram Insurgency*, Africa Report 216 (3 April).

—— (2014d), *Mali: Reform or Relapse?* Africa Report 210 (10 January).

Isa, Kabiru Haruna and Sani Yakubu Adam (2013–14), 'The Shia and its Factions in Nigeria: The Case-Study of Kano, 1980–2011', *Annual Review of Islam in Africa*, 12: 1, 61–8.

Jamā^{c}at Izālat al-Bid^{c}a wa-Iqāmat al-Sunna (1978), *Tsarin Ka'idojin Kungiyar Jama'atu Izalatil Bid^{c}ah wa Ikamatis Sunna*, Jos, Nigeria.

Janson, Marloes (2009), 'Searching for God: Young Gambians' Conversion to the Tabligh Jama^{c}at', in Mamadou Diouf and Mara Leichtman (eds), *New Perspectives on Islam in Senegal: Conversion, Migration, Wealth, Power and Femininity*, New York, pp. 139–68.

Johnson, G. (1991), *Naissance du Sénégal contemporain: Aux origines de la vie politiques modernes (1900–1920)*, Paris.

Kaag, Mayke (2007), 'Aid, Umma, and Politics: Transnational Islamic NGOs in Chad', in Benjamin Soares and Réné Otayek (eds), *Islam and Muslim Politics in Africa*, New York, pp. 85–102.

—— (2014), 'Gulf Charities in Africa', in Robert Lacey and Jonathan Benthall (eds), *Gulf Charities and Islamic Philanthropy in the 'Age of Terror' and Beyond*, Berlin, pp. 79–94.

Kaba, Lansiné (1974), *The Wahhabiyya. Islamic Reform and Politics in French West Africa*, Evanston.

—— (2004), *Cheikh Mouhammad Chérif et son temps ou Islam et société à Kankan en Guinée 1874–1955*, Paris.

Kabara, Shehu Usman (1981), *Shakhsiyyat al-Sheikh Muhammad al-Nasir Kabara wa–adabuhu*, Master's Thesis, University of Khartoum, Sudan.

Kagabo, José (1991), 'Réseaux d'ulama swahili et liens de parenté', in F. Le Guennec-Coppens and P. Caplan (eds), *Les Swahili entre Afrique et Arabie*, Paris, pp. 59–75.

Kane, Momar (2005), 'Figures islamiques: El-Hadj Cheikh Touré, je me souviens . . .', <www.etudiantmusulman.com/Pages/figures%20islamiquesem.htm> (last accessed 14 July 2006).

Kane, Moustapha (1997), 'La vie et l'ouvre d'al-Hajj Mahmoud Ba Diowol (1905–1978): Du pâtre au patron de la "Révolution al-Falah"', in David Robinson and Jean-Louis Triaud (eds), *Le temps des marabouts: Itinéraires et stratégies islamiques en Afrique occidentale française v. 1880–1960*, Paris, pp. 431–65.

Kane, Ousmane (1989), 'La confrérie « Tijaniyya Ibrahimiyya » de Kano et ses liens avec la zawiya mère de Kaolack', *Islam et Sociétés au Sud du Sahara,* 3, 27–40.

—— (1990), 'Les mouvements religieux et le champ politique au Nigeria septentrional: le cas du réformisme musulman à Kano', *Islam et sociétés au sud du Sahara,* 4, 7–24.

—— (1998), 'Le réformisme musulman au Nigeria du Nord', in Ousmane Kane and Jean-Louis Triaud (eds), *Islam et Islamismes au sud du Sahara*, Paris, pp. 117–36.

—— (2003), *Muslim Modernity in Postcolonial Nigeria: A Study of the Society for the Removal of Innovation and Reinstatement of Tradition*, Leiden.

—— (2006), 'Political Islam in Nigeria', in Michael Bröning and Holger Weiss (eds), *Politischer Islam in Westafrika: Eine Bestandsaufnahme*, Hamburg, pp. 153–78.

—— and Jean-Louis Triaud (eds) (1998), *Islam et Islamismes au Sud du Sahara,* Paris.

—— and Leonardo Villalon (1995), 'Entre confrérisme, réformisme et islamisme: les Moustarshidin du Senegal. Analyse et traduction commentée du discours électoral de Moustapha Sy et reponse de Abdou Aziz Sy junior', *Islam et sociétés au sud du Sahara*, 9, 119–202.

Kaplan, Steven (1992), *The Beta Israel (Falasha) in Ethiopia: From Earliest Times to the Twentieth Century,* New York.

Kapteijns, Lidwien (2000), 'Ethiopia and the Horn of Africa', in Nehemia Levtzion and Randall L. Pouwels (eds), *The History of Islam in Africa*, Athens, pp. 227–50.

—— (2013), *Clan Cleansing in Somalia: The Ruinous Legacy of 1991*, Philadelphia.

Karrar, Ali Salih (1992), *The Sufi-Brotherhoods in the Sudan*, London.

al-Karsani, Awad al-Sid (1985), *The Tijaniyya Order in the Western Sudan: A Case Study of Three Centers, Al-Fasher, An-Nahud and Khursi*, PhD Thesis, University of Khartoum, Sudan.

—— (1993), 'Beyond Sufism: The Case of Millenial Islam in Sudan', in Louis Brenner (ed.), *Muslim Identity and Social Change in sub-Saharan Africa*, London, pp. 135–53.

Kettani, Ali (1982), 'Muslim East Africa: An Overview', *Journal Institute of Muslim Minority Affairs*, IV: 2, 104–19.

—— (1985), 'Muslims in Tanzania: A Rejoinder', *Journal Institute of Muslim Minority Affairs*, VI: 1, 219.

Khalafalla, Khalid Yousif (2004), *Political Islam in Sudan: Political Opportunities and Mobilizing Structures*, Phd Thesis, University of Bonn, Bonn.

Khayar, Issa H. (1976), *Le refus de l'école: contributions à l'étude des problèmes de l'éducation chez les Musulmans du Ouaddaï (Tchad)*, Paris.

Khoury, Adel Theodor (2004), *Der Koran: Arabisch–Deutsch*, Gütersloh.

Kifleyesus, Abebe (1995), 'Sufism and the Rural and Urban Reality of Argobba Mysticism', *Islam et sociétés au sud du Sahara*, 9, 27–48.

King, Ethel (2006), 'Burka, Hidschab, Nonnenschleier: Über Mode und Kleiderordnungen', *Le Monde Diplomatique*, March.

Klute, Georg (1995), 'Hostilités et alliances: Archéologie de la dissidence des Touaregs au Mali', *Cahiers d'Études Africaines*, 137, XXXV: 1, 55–71.

—— (2013a), *Tuareg-Aufstand in der Wüste: Ein Beitrag zur Anthropolgie der Gewalt und des Krieges*, Cologne.

—— (2013b), 'Post-Gaddafi Repercussions, Global Islam or Local Logics?', in Lucy Koechlin and Till Förster (eds), *Mali: Impressions of the Current Crisis*, Basel Papers on Political Transformations, 5, pp. 7–13.

—— and Baz Lecocq (in print), 'Tuareg Separatism in Mali and Niger', in Wolfgang Zeller and Jordi Tomás (eds), *Secessionism in Africa*, London.

Kobo, Ousman Murzik (2012), *Unveiling Modernity in Twentieth Century West African Islamic Reforms*, Leiden.

—— (2015), 'Shifting Trajectories of Salafi/Ahl al-Sunna Reformism in Ghana', *Islamic Africa*, 6, 60–81.

Koch, Julia (2014), *Sunni Vohras in Gujarat und in den ehemaligen Homelands Südafrikas: Migrationsprozesse und religiöse Praktiken einer indo-muslimischen Kaste*, PhD Thesis, University of Münster, Germany.

Kogelmann, Franz (1994), *Die Islamisten Ägyptens in der Regierungszeit von Anwar as-Sādāt (1970–1981)*, Berlin.

—— (2006), 'The Sharīᶜa Factor in Nigeria's 2003 Elections', in Benjamin F. Soares (ed.), *Muslim–Christian Encounters in Africa*, Leiden, pp. 256–74.

Köndgen, Olaf (1993), 'Die Kodifikation des islamischen Strafrechts im Sudan', in Sigrid Faath and Hanspeter Mattes (eds), *Wuquf 7-8: Sudan*, Hamburg, pp. 223–55.

Kone-Dao, Maimouna (2005), 'Implantation et influence du wahhabisme au Burkina Faso de 1963 à 2002', in Muriel Gomez-Perez (ed.), *L'islam politique au sud du Sahara: Identités, discours et enjeux*. Paris, pp. 449–60.

Kopwe, William Andrew (2014), 'Demand for the Re-Introduction of Kadhi's Courts on the Tanzanian Mainland: A Religious, Social and Political Analysis', in John A. Chesworth and Franz Kogelmann (eds), *Sharīᶜa in Africa Today: Reactions and Responses*, Leiden, pp. 215–40.

Kouanda, Assimi (1998), 'Les conflits au sein de la communauté musulmane du Burkina', in Ousmane Kane and Jean-Louis Triaud (eds), *Islam et Islamismes au sud du Sahara*, Paris, pp. 83–100

Kraus, Werner (2000), 'Imaginierte und reale Netzwerke in Südostasien', in Roman Loimeier (ed.), *Die islamische Welt als Netzwerk: Möglichkeiten und Grenzen des Nertzwerkansatzes im islamischen Kontext*, Würzburg, pp. 289–310.

Krech, Hans (1996), *Der Bürgerkrieg in Somalia (1988–1996)*, Berlin.

Kresse, Kai (2003), 'Swahili Enlightenment? East African Reformist Discourse at the Turning Point: The Exemple of Shaykh Muhammad Kasim Mazrui', *Journal of Religion in Africa*, 33: 3, 279–309.

—— (2006), 'Debating *maulidi*: Ambiguities and Transformations of Muslim Identity along the Kenyan Swahili Coast', in Roman Loimeier and Rüdiger Seesemann (eds), *The Global Worlds of the Swahili: Interfaces of Islam, Identity and Space in 19th and 20th Century East Africa*, Berlin, pp. 209–28.

—— (2007a), *Philosophising in Mombasa: Knowledge, Islam and Intellectual practice on the Swahili Coast*, Edinburgh.

—— (2007b), 'The Uses of History: Rhetorics of Muslim Unity and Difference on the Kenyan Swahili Coast', in Edward Simpson and Kai Kresse (eds), *Struggling with History: Islam and Cosmopolitanism in the Western Indian Ocean*, London, pp. 223–60.

—— (2009), 'Muslim Politics in Postcolonial Kenya: Negotiating Knowledge on the Double Periphery', *Journal of the Royal Anthropological Institute* (N.S.), 576–94.

Kubai, Anne (1992), 'The Early Muslim Communities of Nairobi (Kenya)', *Islam et sociétés au sud du Sahara*, 6, 33–46.

Kukah, Matthew (2012), 'Nigeria: A Nation of Strong Believers', in *Economic Confidential*, <http://economicconfidential.net/new/features/893> (last accessed 29 May 2012).

Lacey, Robert and Jonathan Benthall (eds) (2014), *Gulf Charities and Islamic Philanthropy in the 'Age of Terror' and Beyond*, Berlin.

Lacher, Wolfram and Guido Steinberg (2015), 'Transnationaler Jihadismus, lokal verwurzelt: AQIM und MUJAO in der Sahara', in Guido Steinberg and Annette Weber (eds), *Jihadismus in Afrika: Lokale Ursachen, regionale Ausbreitung, internationale Verbindungen*, Berlin, pp. 73–89.

Lacroix, Stéphane (2009), 'Between Revolution and Apolitism: Nasir al-Din al-Albani and his Impact on the Shaping of Contemporary Salafism', in Roel Meijer (ed.), *Global Salafism: Islam's New Religious Movement*, London, pp. 58–80.

Lacunza Balda, Justo (1989), *An Investigation into Some Concepts and Ideas Found in Swahili Islamic Writings*, PhD Thesis, SOAS, London.

—— (1993), 'The Role of Kiswahili in East African Islam', in Louis Brenner (ed.), *Muslim Identity and Social Change in Sub-Saharan Africa*, London, pp. 226–38.

—— (1997), 'Translations of the Qur°ān into Swahili, and Contemporary Islamic Revival in East Africa', in David Westerlund (ed.), *African Islam and Islam in Africa*, London, pp. 95–126.

Ladiba, Gondeu (2011), *L'emergence des organisations islamiques au Tchad: enjeux, acteurs et territoires*, Paris.

—— (2013), 'Les organisations islamiques au Tchad', *Islam et Sociétés au Sud du Sahara (nouvelle série)*, 3, 19–54.

Laible, Johanna (2005), *Hasan al-Turabi: Aufstieg und Niedergang des politischen Islam im Sudan im späten 20. Jahrhundert*, BA Thesis, University of Bayreuth, Germany.

Lambek, Michael (1993), *Knowledge and Practice in Mayotte: Local Discourses of Islam, Sorcery and Spirit Possession*, Toronto.

Lamont, Michèle and Virág Molnár (2002), 'The Study of Boundaries in the Social Sciences', *Annual Sociological Review*, 28, 167–95.

Larkin, Brian (2008), *Signal and Noise: Media, Infrastructure, and Urban Culture in Nigeria*, Durham, NC.

—— (2015), 'Binary Islam: Media and Religious Movements in Nigeria', in Rosalind Hackett and Benjamin Soares (eds), *New Media and Religious Transformations in Africa*, Bloomington, pp. 63–81.

Larsen, Kjersti (2004), 'Change, Continuity and Contestation: The Politics of Modern Identities in Zanzibar', in Pat Caplan and Farouk Topan (eds), *Swahili Modernities: Culture, Politics and Identity on the East Coast of Africa*, London, pp. 121–44.

Last, Murray (1967), *The Sokoto Caliphate*, London.

—— (1979), 'Some Economic Aspects of Conversion in Hausaland', in Nehemia Levtzion (ed.), *Conversion to Islam*, New York, pp. 236–46.

—— (2000), 'La charia dans le Nord-Nigeria', *Politique Africaine*, 79, 141–52.

—— (2009), 'The Pattern of Dissent: Boko Haram in Nigeria, 2009', *Annual Review of Islam in Africa*, 10, 7–11.

—— (2011), 'Who and What Are Boko Haram?', *Royal African Society*, 14 July, <www.royalafricansociety.org/component/con tent/article/937.html> (last accessed 29 May 2012).

—— (2014), 'From Dissent to Dissidence: The Genesis and Development of Reformist Islamic Groups in Northern Nigeria', in Abdul Raufu Mustapha (ed.), *Sects and Social Disorder: Muslim Identities and Conflict in Northern Nigeria*, Woodbridge, Suffolk, pp. 18–53.

Launay, Robert (1992), *Beyond the Stream. Islam and Society in a West African Town*, Long Grove, IL.

—— and Benjamin F. Soares (1999), 'The Formation of an "Islamic Sphere" in French Colonial West Africa', *Economy and Society*, 28: 4, 497–519.

Lauzière, Henri (2010), 'The Construction of *Salafiyya*: Reconsidering Salafism from the Perspective of Conceptual History', *International Journal of Middle Eastern Studies*, 42, 369–89.

—— (2016a), 'What We Mean Versus What They Meant by "Salafi": A Reply to Frank Griffel', *Die Welt des Islams*, S6:1, 89–96.

—— (2016b), *The Making of Salafism: Islamic Reform in the Twentieth Century*, New York.

LeBlanc, Marie Nathalie (2005). 'Hadj et changements identitaires: les jeunes musulmans d'Abidjan et de Bouaké, en Côte d'Ivoire, dans les années 1990', in Muriel Gomez-Perez (ed.), *L'islam politique au sud du Sahara. Identités, discours et enjeux*, Paris, pp. 131–58.

—— (2009), 'Foi, prosélytisme et citoyenneté culturelle: le rôle sociopolitique des jeunes arabistants en Côte d'Ivoire au tournant du XXI siècle', in Gilles Holder (ed.), *L'Islam, nouvel espace public en Afrique*, Paris, pp. 173–96.

—— (2005), 'Hadj et changements identitaires: les jeunes musulmans d'Abidjan et de Bouaké, en Côte d'Ivoire, dans les années 1990', in Muriel Gomez-Perez (ed.), *L'islam politique au sud du Sahara. Identités, discours et enjeux*, Paris, pp. 131–58.

—— (2013), 'The Local Face of Jihadism in Northern Mali', <https://www.ctc.usma.edu/posts/the-local-face-of-jihadism> (last accessed 15 July 2015).

Lecker, Michael (1995), *Muslims, Jews and Pagans: Studies on Early Islamic Medina*, Leiden.

Legros, Olivier (2004), 'Les tendances du jeu politique à Yeumbeul (banlieue est de Dakar) depuis l'alternance', *Politique Africaine*, 96, 59–77.

Lewis, Ioan (2001), 'Saints in North East African Islam', in B. S. Amoretti (ed.), *Islam in East Africa. New Sources*, Rome, pp. 227–40.

—— (2008), *Understanding Somalia and Somaliland: Culture, History, Society*, New York.

Little, Peter D. (2003), *Somalia: Economy without a State*, Oxford.

Lô, Magatte (1985), *L'heure du choix*, Paris.

Lodhi, Abdulaziz Y. (1986), 'The Arabs in Zanzibar: From Sultanate to Peoples' Republic', *Journal of the Institute of Muslim Minority Affairs*, VII: 2, 404–18.

Lofchie, Michael (2015), 'The Political Economy of the African Middle Class', in Mthuli Ncube and Charles Leyeka Lufumpa (eds), *The Emerging Middle Class in Africa*, London, pp. 34–59.

Loimeier, Roman (1992), 'Die Dynamik religiöser Unruhen in Nordnigeria', *Afrika Spectrum*, 27: 1, 59–80.

—— (1994a), 'Religiös–Ökonomische Netzwerke in Senegal: Das Beispiel der muridischen Expansion in Dakar', *Afrika Spectrum*, 1994: 1, 99–112.

—— (1994b), 'Cheikh Tourè: du réformisme à l'islamisme, un musulman sénégalais dans le siècle', *Islam et Sociétés au Sud du Sahara*, 8, 55–66.

—— (1997a), *Islamic Reform and Political Change in Northern Nigeria*, Evanston.

—— (1997b), 'Die radikale islamische Opposition in Nordnigeria', *Afrika Spectrum*. 32: 1, 5–23.

—— (2000a), 'Cheikh Tidiane Sy und die Dāʾirat al-Mustarshidīn wa-l-Mustarshidāt', in R. Loimeier (ed.), *Die Islamische Welt als Netzwerk: Möglichkeiten und Grenzen des Netzwerkansatzes im islamischen Kontext*, Würzburg, pp. 445–60.

—— (2000b), 'L'Islam ne se vend plus: The Islamic Reform Movement and the State in Senegal', *Journal of Religion in Africa*, 30: 2, 168–90.

—— (2000c), 'Ist Fußball unislamisch? Zur Tiefenstruktur des Banalen', in R. Loimeier (ed.), *Die Islamische Welt als Netzwerk: Möglichkeiten und Grenzen des Netzwerkansatzes im islamischen Kontext*, Würzburg, pp. 101–20.

—— (2001), *Säkularer Staat und islamische Gesellschaft. Die Beziehungen zwischen Staat, Sufi-Bruderschaften und islamischer Reformbewegung in Senegal im 20. Jahrhundert*, Hamburg.

—— (2002), 'Je veux étudier sans mendier: The Campaign against the Qur'anic Schools in Senegal', in H. Weiss (ed.), *Social Welfare in Muslim Societies in Africa*, Uppsala, pp. 118–37.

—— (2003), 'Patterns and Peculiarities of Islamic Reform in Africa', *Journal of Religion in Africa*, 33: 3, 237–62.

—— (2005a), 'Is There Something Like "Protestant Islam"?', *Die Welt des Islams*, 45: 2, 216–54.

—— (2005b), 'Translating the Qur'ān in Sub-Saharan Africa: Dynamics and Disputes', *Journal of Religion in Africa*, 35: 4, 403–23.

—— (2005c), 'Playing with Affiliations: Muslim in Northern Nigeria in the 20th Century', in André Mary and Réné Otayek (eds), *Réseaux transnationaux et nouveaux acteurs religieux en Afrique de l'Ouest*, Paris, pp. 349–71.

—— (2006a), 'Fighting Popular Culture: The Ulama and the State in Zanzibar', in R. Loimeier and R. Seesemann (eds), *The Global Worlds of the Swahili: Interfaces of Islam, Identity, and Space in the 19th and 20th-Century East Africa*, Hamburg, pp. 113–32.

—— (2006b), 'Sufis and Politics in Sub-Saharan Africa', in *Princeton Papers, Interdisciplinary Journal of Middle Eastern Studies, Vol. XV, Sufism and Politics: The Power of Spirituality*, Princeton, pp. 59–101.

—— (2006c), 'Translocal Networks of Saints and the Negotiation of Religious Disputes in Local Contexts', *Archives de Sciences Sociales des Religions* (ASSR, Paris), 135, 17–32.

—— (2006d), 'Der dhikr: Zum sozialen Kontext eines religiösen Rituals', *Der Islam*, 83, 180–6.

—— (2006e), 'Memories of Revolution: Zur Deutungsgeschichte einer Revolution (Sansibar 1964)', *Afrika Spectrum*, 41: 2, 175–97.

—— (2007a), 'Nigeria: The Quest for a Viable Religious Option', in William Miles (ed.), *Political Islam in West Africa. State–Society Relations Transformed*, Boulder, pp. 43–72.

—— (2007b), 'Perceptions of Marginalization: Muslims in Contemporary Tanzania', in Réné Otayek and Benjamin Soares (eds), *Islam and Muslim Politics in Africa*, London, pp. 137–56.

—— (2009), *Between Social Skills and Marketable Skills: The Politics of Islamic Education in 20th Century Zanzibar*, Leiden.

—— (2010), 'Traditions of Reform, Reformers of Tradition: Case Studies from Senegal and Zanzibar/Tanzania', in Zulfiqar Hirji (ed.), *Diversity and Pluralism in Islam: Historical and Contemporary Discourses among Muslims*, London, pp. 135–62.

—— (2011), 'Zanzibar's Geography of Evil: The Moral Discourse of the Anṣār al-Sunna in Contemporary Zanzibar', *Journal of Islamic Studies*, 31, 4–28.

—— (2012), 'Boko Haram: The Development of a Militant Religious Movement in Nigeria', *Afrika Spectrum*, 47: 2–3, 137–56.

—— (2013), *Muslim Societies in Africa: A Historical Anthropology*, Bloomington.

—— and Anke Bosaller (1995), 'Radical Muslim Women and Male Politics in

Nigeria', in M. Reh and G. Ludwar-Ene (eds), *Gender and Identity in Africa*, Hamburg, pp. 61–70.

—— and Rüdiger Seesemann (eds) (2006), *The Global Worlds of the Swahili: Interfaces of Islam, Identity, and Space in the 19th and 20th-Century East Africa*, Hamburg.

Lubeck, Paul (1985), 'Islamic Protest under Semi-Industrial Capitalism: Yan Tatsine Explained', *Africa*, 55: 4, 369–89.

Luckmann, Thomas (1991), *Die unsichtbare Religion*, Frankfurt.

Ludwig, Frieder (1996), 'After Ujamaa: Is Religious Rivalism a Threat to Tanzania's Stability', in D. Westerlund (ed.), *Questioning the Secular State: The Worldwide Resurgence of Religion in Politics*, London, pp. 216–36.

—— (1999), *Church and State in Tanzania: Aspects of a Changing Relationship, 1961–94*, Leiden.

Lufumpa, Charles Leyeka, Maurice Mubila and Mohammed Safouane Ben Aïssa (2015), 'The Dynamics of the Middle Class in Africa', in Mthuli Ncube and Charles Leyeka Lufumpa (eds), *The Emerging Middle Class in Africa*, London, pp. 9–33.

Luling, Virginia (2002), *Somali Sultanate: The Geledi City-State over 150 Years*, London.

Magassa, Hamidou (2006), 'Islam und Demokratie in Westafrika: Der Fall Mali', in Michael Bröning and Holger Weiss (eds), *Politischer Islam in Westafrika: Eine Bestandsaufnahme*. Berlin, pp. 115–52.

Magnant, Jean-Pierre (ed.) (1992), *L'Islam au Tchad*, Talence.

Mahida, Ebrahim Mahomed (1993), *History of Muslims in South Africa: A Chronology*, Durban.

Mahmood, Saba (2005), *Politics of Piety: The Islamic Revival and the Feminist Subject*, Princeton.

Mahmoud, Muhammad (1996), 'The Discourse of the Ikhwan of Sudan and Secularism', in David Westerlund (ed.), *Questioning the Secular State: The Worldwide Resurgence of Religion in Politics*, London, pp. 167–82.

—— (1997), 'Sufism and Islamism in the Sudan', in David Westerlund and Eva Evers Rosander (eds), *African Islam and Islam in Africa*, London, pp. 162–92.

Mahmud, Saidu Sakah (2004), 'Islamism in West Africa: Nigeria', *African Studies Review*, 47, 83–96.

Mains, Daniel (2007), 'Neoliberal Times: Progress, Boredom, and Shame among Young Men in Urban Ethiopia', *American Anthropologist*, 34: 4, 659–73.

Makaramba, Robert V. (2010), 'The Secular State and the State of Islamic Law in Tanzania', in Jeppie, Shamil, Ebrahim Moosa and Richard Roberts (eds), *Muslim Family Law in Sub-Saharan Africa: Colonial Legacies and Post-Colonial Challenges*, Amsterdam, pp. 273–304.

Mannheimer, Karl (1984), 'Das Problem der Generation', in K. Mannheimer, *Wissenssoziologie: Auswahl aus dem Werk*, Berlin, pp. 509–65.

Mapuri, Omar (1996), *Zanzibar: The 1964 Revolution: Achievements and Prospects*, Dar es Salaam.

Marchal, Roland (2004), 'Islamic Political Dynamics in the Somali Civil War: Before and after September 11', in Alex de Waal (ed.), *Islamism and its Enemies in the Horn of Africa*, Bloomington, 114–45.

—— (2009), 'A Tentative Assessment of the Somali Harakat al-Shabab', *Journal of Eastern African Studies*, 3: 3, 381–404.

—— (2013), 'Islamic Political Dynamics in the Somali Civil War', in Pade Badru and Brigid Maa Sackey (eds), *Islam in Africa South of the Sahara*, Plymouth, pp. 331–53.

—— and Zakaria M. Sheikh (2013). 'Ahlu Sunna wa l-Jama^{c}a in Somalia', in Patrick Desplat and Terje Østebø (eds), *Muslim Ethiopia: The Christian Legacy, Identity Politics and Islamic Reformism*, New York, pp. 215–40.

—— and Zakaria M. Sheikh (2015), 'Salafism in Somalia: Coping with Coercion, Civil War and its Own Contradictions', *Islamic Africa*, 6, 135–63.

Marcus, Harold G. (2002), *A History of Ethiopia*, Berkeley.

Markakis, John (2006), *Ethiopia: Anatomy of a Traditional Polity*, Oxford and Addis Ababa, Ethiopia.

—— (2011), *Ethiopia: The Last Two Frontiers*, Woodbridge, Suffolk.

Martin, B. G. (1976), *Muslim Brotherhoods in 19th Century Africa*, Cambridge.

Martin, Esmond Bradley (2007 [1978]), *Zanzibar – Tradition and Revolution*, London.

Martinez-Gros, Gabriel and Lucette Valensi (2004), *L'Islam en Dissidence: Génèse d'un affrontement*, Paris.

Masquelier, Adeline (2001), *Prayer has Spoiled Everything: Possession, Power and Identity in an Islamic Town of Niger*, Durham, NC.

—— (2007), 'Negotiating Futures: Islam, Youth and the State in Niger', in Benjamin F. Soares and Réné Otayek (eds), *Islam and Muslim Politics in Africa*, New York, pp. 243–62.

—— (2009), *Women and Islamic Revival in a West African Town*, Bloomington.

Masud, Muhammad Khalid (ed.) (2000), *Travellers in Faith: Studies of the Tablighi Jamā^{c}at as a Transnational Islamic Movement for Faith Renewal*, Leiden.

Mattes, Hans-Peter (1986), *Die innere und äußere islamische Mission Libyens*, Mainz.
Mättig, Thomas (n.d.), *Das Gespenst Boko Haram: Nigeria nach dem Anschlag auf die UN–Zentrale*, Berlin.
Mattoir, Nakidine (2004), *Les Comores de 1975 à 1990: Une histoire politique mouvementée*, Paris.
Maxwell, David (2005), 'The Durawell of Faith: Pentecostal Spirituality in Neo-Liberal Zimbabwe', *Journal of Religion in Africa*, 35: 1, 4–32.
Mazrui, Ali A. (1993), 'The Black Intifadah? Religion and Rage at the Kenya Coast', *Journal of Asian and African Affairs*, 4: 2, 87–93.
Mbogoni, Lawrence E. Y. (2004), *The Cross versus the Crescent: Religion and Politics in Tanzania from the 1880s to the 1990s*, Dar es Salaam.
Meijer, Roel (ed.) (2009), *Global Salafism: Islam's New Religious Movement*, London.
Menkhaus, Ken (2004), *Somalia: State Collapse and the Threat of Terrorism*, London.
Merad, ᶜAlī (1967), *Le réformisme musulman en Algérie de 1925 à 1940*, Paris.
—— (n.d.). *Iṣlāḥ*, entry in *Encyclopaedia of Islam*, second edition, Leiden.
Meunier, Olivier (1997), *Dynamique de l'enseignement islamique au Niger: le cas de la ville de Maradi*, Paris.
Mfumbusa, Bernardin (2014), '"Chaos Will Never Have a Chance": Sharia Debates and Tolerance in a Provincial Tanzanian Town', in John A. Chesworth and Franz Kogelmann (eds), *Sharīᶜa in Africa Today: Reactions and Responses*, Leiden, pp. 241–58.
Miran, Jonathan (2005), 'A Historical Overview of Islam in Eritrea', *Die Welt des Islams*, 45: 2, 177–215.
Miran, Marie (1998), 'Le wahhabisme à Abidjan: dynamisme urbain d'un islam réformiste en Côte d'Ivoire contemporaine (1960–1996)', *Islam et Sociétés au Sud du Sahara*, 12, 5–74.
—— (2005), 'D'Abidjan à Porto Novo: associations islamiques et culture religieuse réformiste sur la Côte de Guinée', in Laurant Fourchard, André Mary and Réné Otayek (eds), *Entreprises religieuses transnationales en Afrique de l'Ouest*, Paris, pp. 43–72.
—— (2006a), *Islam, histoire et modernité en Côte d'Ivoire*, Paris.
—— (2006b), 'The Political Economy of Civil Islam in Côte d'Ivoire', in Michael Bröning and Holger Weiss (eds), *Politischer Islam in Westafrika: Eine Bestandsaufnahme*, Berlin, pp. 81–114.
Mitchell, Richard P. (1993 [1969]), *The Society of the Muslim Brothers*, London.
Mohamed, Toibibou Ali (2008), *La transmission de l'Islam aux Comores (1933–2000): Le cas de la ville de Mbéni (Grand-Comore)*, Paris.

—— (2010), *Ahmad Qamardine (1895–1974): Un intellectuel Comorien et ses réseaux*, PhD Thesis, Paris Diderot University – Paris 7, France.

Mohammed, Kyari (2015), 'The Message and Methods of Boko Haram', in Marc-Antoine Pérouse de Montclos (ed.), *Boko Haram: Islamism, Politics, Security and the State in Nigeria*, Los Angeles, pp. 3–32.

Mommersteeg, Geert (2012), *In the City of the Marabouts: Islamic Culture in West Africa*, Long Grove, IL.

Moosa, Ebrahim (2000), 'Worlds Apart: The Tablīghī Jamāᶜat in South Africa under Apartheid, 1963–1993', in Muhammad Khalid Masud (ed., *Travellers in Faith: Studies of the Tablighi Jamāᶜat as a Transnational Islamic Movement for Faith Renewal*, Leiden, pp. 206–21.

Morier-Genoud, Eric (2002), 'L'islam au Mocambique après l'indépendance', in Dominique Darbon (ed.), *L'Afrique Politique: Islams d'Afrique: entre le local et le global*, Paris, pp. 123–46.

Moten, Rashid (1993), 'Islam in Ethiopia: An Analytical Survey', in Muhammad Nur Alkali (ed.), *Islam in Africa*, Ibadan, pp. 221–31.

Mouiche, Ibrahim (2005), 'Islam, mondialisation et crise identitaire dans le royaume Bamoum, Cameroun', *Africa*, 75: 3, 378–420.

Mraja, Mohamed Sulaiman (2011), 'Sheikh al-Amin Mazrui (1891–1947) and the Dilemma of Islamic Law in the Kenyan Legal System in the 21st Century', *Journal of Islamic Studies*, 31, 60–74.

Mrina, B. F. and Mattoke, W. T. (1980), *Mapambano ya Ukombozi Zanzibar*, Dar es-Salaam.

Muhammad, Yusuf Abdulrahman (1992), *Memoirs of the Late al-Marhum al Seyyid Omar bin Abdulla Ali-Sheikh*, Zanzibar (mimeograph).

Musa, Saidi (1986), *Maisha ya al-Imam Sheikh Abdulla Saleh Farsy katika ulimwengu wa kiislamu*, Dar es Salaam.

Mustapha, Abdul Raufu (ed.) (2014a), *Sects and Social Disorder: Muslim Identities and Conflict in Northern Nigeria*, Woodbridge, Suffolk.

—— (2014b), 'Introduction: Interpreting Islam: Sufis, Salafists, Shi'ites and Islamists in Northern Nigeria', in Abdul Raufu Mustapha (ed.), *Sects and Social Disorder: Muslim Identities and Conflict in Northern Nigeria*, Woodbridge, Suffolk, pp. 1–17.

—— (2014c), 'Understanding Boko Haram', in Abdul Raufu Mustapha (ed.), *Sects and Social Disorder: Muslim Identities and Conflict in Northern Nigeria*, Woodbridge, Suffolk, pp. 147–98.

—— and Mukhtar U. Bunza (2014), 'Contemporary Islamic Sects and Groups in Northern Nigeria', in Abdul Raufu Mustapha (ed.), *Sects and Social Disorder:*

Muslim Identities and Conflict in Northern Nigeria, Woodbridge, Suffolk, pp. 54–97.

Mwakimako, Hassan (2006), 'The *ᶜUlamāʾ* and the Colonial State in the Protectorate of Kenya: The Appointment of *shaykh al-islām sharīf* ᶜAbd al-Raḥmān b. Aḥmad Saggaf (1844–1922) and Chief Kadhi Sh. Muḥammad b. ᶜUmar Bakore (c. 1932)', in Roman Loimeier and Rüdiger Seesemann (eds), *The Global Worlds of the Swahili: Interfaces of Islam, Identity and Space in 19th and 20th Century East Africa*, Berlin, pp. 289–316.

—— (2007a), 'Christian–Muslim Relations in Kenya: A Catalogue of Events and Meanings', *Islam and Christian–Muslims Relations*, 18: 2, 287–307.

—— (2007b), *Mosques in Kenya: Muslim Opinions on Religion, Politics and Development*, Berlin.

—— (2010), 'Conflicts and Tensions in the Appointment of Chief Kadhi in Colonial Kenya, 1898–1960s', in Shamil Jeppie, Ebrahim Moosa and Richard Roberts (eds), *Muslim Family Law in Sub-Saharan Africa: Colonial Legacies and Post-Colonial Challenges*, Amsterdam, pp. 109–34.

Nageeb, Salma Ahmad (2004), *New Spaces and Old Frontiers: Women, Social Space and Islamization in Sudan*, Lanham.

Ncube, Mthuli and Charles Leyeka Lufumpa (eds) (2015), *The Emerging Middle Class in Africa*, London.

Ndaluka, Thomas Joseph (2012), *Religious Discourse, Social Cohesion and Conflict: Muslim–Christian Relations in Tanzania*, Berlin.

Ndiaye, Alfred Inis (2013), 'L'action collective protestataire (1996–2004)', in M. C. Diop (ed.), *Le Sénégal sous Abdoulaye Wade: Le Sopi à l'épreuve du pouvoir*, Paris, pp. 461–76.

Ndzovu, Hassan J. (2014), *Muslims in Kenyan Politics: Political Involvement, Marginalization and Minority Status*, Evanston.

Niehaus, Inga (2008), *Muslime Südafrikas im Spannungsfeld zwischen politischer Beteiligung und Ausgrenzung: Partizipation einer religiösen Minderheit im Demokratisierungsprozeß*, Münster.

Nietzen, R. W. (1990), 'The "Community of Helpers of the Sunna": Islamic Reform among the Songhay of Gao (Mali)', *Africa*, 60: 3, 399–424.

—— and Barbro Bankson (1995), 'Women of the Jama'a Ansar al-Sunna: Female Participation in a West African Islamic Reform Movement', *Canadian Journal of African Studies*, 29: 3, 403–28.

Nimtz, August (1980), *Islam and Politics in East Africa: The Sufi Order in Tanzania*, Minneapolis.

Nisula, Tapio (1999), *Everyday Spirits and Medical Interventions: Ethnographic and Historical Notes on Therapeutic Conventions in Zanzibar Town*, Saarijärvi, Finland.

Niwagila, Wilson B. (1999), 'Nationalismus und Fundamentalismus in Tansania', in Dieter Becker (ed.), *Globaler Kampf der Kulturen: Analysen und Orientierungen*, Stuttgart, pp. 157–74.

Njozi, Hamza (2000), *Mwembechai Killings and the Political Future of Tanzania*, Ottawa.

—— (2003), *Muslims and the State in Tanzania*, Dar es Salaam.

Nyamnjoh, Francis (2005), 'Disquettes and Thiofs in Dakar', *Africa*, 75: 3, 295–324.

O'Brien, Susan (2007), 'La charia contestée: Démocratie, débat et diversité musulmane dans les 'États charia' du Nigeria', *Politique Africaine*, 106, 46–68.

Oded, Arye (1996), 'Islamic Extremism in Kenya: The Rise and Fall of Sheikh Khalid Balala', *Journal of Religion in Africa*, 26: 4, 406–15.

—— (2000), *Islam and Politics in Kenya*, Boulder.

Oevermann, Annette (1993), *Die 'Republikanischen Brüder' im Sudan: Eine islamische Reformbewegung im Zwanzigsten Jahrhundert*, Frankfurt.

O'Fahey, Sean Rex (1990), *Enigmatic Saint: Ahmad ibn Idris and the Idrisi Tradition*, Evanston.

—— (1993), 'Islamic Hegemonies in the Sudan: Sufism, Mahdism and Islamism', in Louis Brenner (ed.), *Muslim Identity and Social Change in Sub-Saharan Africa*, London, pp. 21–35.

—— (1997), '"Defining the Community": The National Islamic Front, its Opponents and the Sharia Issue', *Islam et sociétés au sud du Sahara*, 11, 55–66.

—— (forthcoming), *Arabic Literature of Africa, Vol. IIIb: The Writings of East Africa*, Leiden.

Olivier de Sardan, Jean-Pierre (2013), 'Evitons un Munich sahélien', in Lucy Koechlin and Till Förster (eds), *Mali: Impressions of the Current Crisis*, Basel Papers on Political Transformations, 5, pp. 15–21.

Omari, Cuthbert K. (1984), 'Christian–Muslim Relations in Tanzania: The Socio-Political Dimension', *Journal of the Institute of Muslim Minority Affairs*, 5: 2, 373–90.

Ortner, Shery B. (2006), *Anthropology and Social Theory: Culture, Power and the Acting Subject*, Durham, NC.

Osella, Filippo and Benjamin F. Soares (eds) (2010), *Islam, Politics, Anthropology*, Oxford.

Osman Mohamed Osman Ali (2014), 'Sharīᶜa and Reality: A Domain of Contest among Sunni Muslims in the District of Shendi, Northern Sudan', in John A.

Chesworth and Franz Kogelmann (eds), *Sharīᶜa in Africa Today: Reactions and Responses*, Leiden, pp. 13–40.

Østebø, Terje (2008a), *Localising Salafism: Religious Change among Oromo Muslims in Bale, Ethiopia*, Stockholm.

—— (2008b), 'The Question of Becoming: Islamic Reform Movements in Contemporary Ethiopia', *Journal of Religion in Africa*, 38: 4, 416–46.

—— (2009a), 'Une économie salafie de la prière dans la région du Balé en Éthiopie', *Afrique contemporaine*, 231: 3, 45–60.

—— (2009b), 'Growth and Fragmentation: The Salafi Movement in Bale, Ethiopia', in Roel Meijer (ed.), *Global Salafism: Islam's New Religious Movement*, London, pp. 342–63.

—— (2010), 'Islamism in the Horn of Africa: Assessing Ideology, Actors and Objectives', *International Law and Policy Institute*, Oslo, Report 2.

—— (2013a), 'Being Young, Being Muslim in Bale', in Patrick Desplat and Terje Østebø (eds), *Muslim Ethiopia: The Christian Legacy, Identity Politics and Islamic Reformism*, New York, pp. 47–70.

—— (2013b), 'Postscript', in Patrick Desplat and Terje Østebø (eds), *Muslim Ethiopia: The Christian Legacy, Identity Politics and Islamic Reformism*, New York, pp. 241–58.

—— (2015a), 'African Salafism: Religious Purity and the Politicization of Purity', *Islamic Africa*, 6, 1–29.

—— (2015b), '*Realpolitik* and Religious Fault-lines: Religion and Ethiopia's Foreign Policy', in Fanta Chweru, Kjetil Tronvoll and Goitom Gebreluel (eds), *Ethiopia: Foreign Policy and the Rise of a Regional Hegemon*, London, pp. 1–22 (draft version).

Osterhammel, Jürgen (2001), *Geschichtswissenschaft jenseits des Nationalstaats: Studien zu Beziehungsgeschichte und Zivilisationsvergleich*, Göttingen.

Ostien, Philip (2006), 'An Opportunity Missed by Nigeria's Christians: The 1976–78 Sharīᶜa Debate Revisited', in Benjamin F. Soares (ed.), *Muslim–Christian Encounters in Africa*, Leiden, pp. 221– 55.

—— (2009), 'Jonah Jang and the Jasawa: Ethno-Religious Conflict in Jos, Nigeria', in *Muslim Christian Relations in Africa*, <www.sharia-in-africa.net/pages/publications.php> (last accessed 2 February 2016).

Otayek, René (ed.) (1993a), *Le radicalisme islamique au sud du Sahara: Daᶜwa, arabisation et critique de l'Occident*, Paris.

—— (1993b), 'L'affirmation élitaire des arabisants au Burkina Faso: enjeux et contradictions', in René Otayek (ed.), *Le radicalisme islamique au sud du Sahara*, Paris, pp. 229–54.

—— and Benjamin F. Soares (2007a), 'Introduction: Islam and Politics in Africa', in R. Otayek and B. Soares (eds), *Islam and Muslim Politics in Africa*, New York, pp. 1–26.

—— and Benjamin F. Soares (2007b), *Islam and Muslim Politics in Africa*, New York.

Paden, John N. (1973), *Religion and Political Culture in Kano*, Berkeley.

—— (1986), *Ahmadu Bello: Sardauna of Sokoto*, Zaria.

—— (2005), *Muslim Civic Cultures and Conflict Resolution: The Challenge of Democratic Federalism in Nigeria*, Washington, DC.

Parkin, David (2000), 'Templates, Evocations and the Longterm Fieldworker', in Paul Dresch, Wendy James and David Parkin (eds), *Anthropologists in a Wider World*, New York, pp. 91–108.

Penrad, J. C. (1998), 'Madrassat an-Nur', in Colette Le Cour Grandmaison and Ariel Crozon (eds), *Zanzibar aujourd'hui*, Paris, pp. 307–20.

Pérouse de Montclos, Marc-Antoine (2014), 'Nigeria's Interminable Insurgency? Addressing the Boko Haram Crisis', Chatham House Research Paper, London.

—— (ed.) (2015), *Boko Haram: Islamism, Politics, Security and the State in Nigeria*, Los Angeles.

Peters, Ruud (2003), *Islamic Criminal Law in Nigeria*, Ibadan.

Peterson, Brian (2011), *Islamization from Below: The Making of Muslim Communities in Rural French Soudan, 1880–1960*, New Haven.

Petterson, Don (2002), *Revolution in Zanzibar: An American's Cold War Tale*, New York.

Piga, Adriana (2002), *Dakar et les ordes soufis: Processus socioculturels et développement urbain au Sénégal contemporain*, Paris.

—— (2007), 'Un parcours guide dans le Sénégal islamique', *Islam et sociétés au sud du Sahara (nouvelle série)*, 1, 13–42.

Pontzen, Benedikt (2014), *Islam in the Zongo: An Ethnography of Islamic Conceptions, Practices and Imaginaries among Muslims in Asante (Ghana)*, PhD Thesis, Free University of Berlin, Germany.

Pouwels, R. L. (1987), *Horn and Crescent: Cultural Change and Traditional Islam on the East African Coast, 800–1900*, Cambridge.

Prunier, Gérard (1989), 'Les Frères musulmans au Soudan: un islamisme tacticien', in Marc Lavergne (ed.), *Le Soudan contemporain*, Paris, pp. 359–80.

—— (2010), 'Benign Neglect versus La Grande Somalia: The Colonial Legacy and the Post-colonial Somali State', in Markus Höhne and Virginia Luling (eds),

Milk and Peace, Drought and War: Somali Culture, Society and Politics, London, pp. 35–50.

Purpura, Alison (1997), *Knowledge and Agency: The Social Relations of Islamic Expertise in Zanzibar Town*, PhD Thesis, The City University of New York.

Quinn, Charlotte A. and Frederick Quinn (2003), *Pride, Faith and Fear: Islam in Sub-Saharan Africa*, New York.

Quṭb, Sayyid (1981 [1966]), *Ma^{c}ālim fī-ṭ-ṭarīq*, Cairo.

Rabasa, Angel (2009), *Radical Islam in East Africa*, Santa Monica.

Rajab, Khatib (2001), *Sheikh Abdullah Saleh al-Farsy*, <http://www.islamtz.org/nyaraka/farsy.htm> (last accessed 31 July 2009).

Redfield, Robert (1956), *Peasant Society and Culture*, Chicago.

Reese, Scott (1999), 'Urban Woes and Pious Remedies: Sufism in Nineteenth-Century Benaadir (Somalia)', *Africa Today*, 46: 3–4, 169–94.

—— (2004), *The Transmission of Learning in Islamic Africa*, Leiden.

—— (2008), *Renewers of the Age: Holy Men and Social Discourse in Colonial Banaadir*, Leiden.

Reichmuth, Stefan (1998), *Islamische Bildung und soziale Integration in Ilorin (Nigeria) seit ca. 1800*, Münster.

Die Religion in Geschichte und Gesellschaft (RGG) (1986), 3rd edition, Tübingen.

Religionswissenschaftlicher Medien- und Informationsdienst e.V., 'Boko Haram – neue Semantiken im Spiegel ihrer Mediendeutungen', <http://www.remid.de/blog/2011/07/boko-haram> (last accessed 29 May 2012).

Rémy, Jean-Philippe (2012), 'Les liens troubles entre Boko Haram et AQMI au Nigeria', *Le Monde*, 12 March.

Renders, Marleen (n.d.), 'Islam and Islamism in a Collapsed State: The Case of Somalia/Somaliland', unpublished conference paper.

—— (2007), 'Global Concerns, Local Realities: Islam and Islamism in a Somali State under Construction', in Benjamin F. Soares and Réné Otayek (eds), *Islam and Muslim Politics in Africa*, New York, pp. 47–64.

Renne, Elisha (2012), 'Educating Muslim Women and the Izala Movement in Zaria City, Nigeria', *Islamic Africa*, 31: 1, 55–86.

Reusch, Richard (1931), *Der Islam in Ost-Afrika mit besonderer Berücksichtigung der muhammedanischen Geheim-Orden*, Leipzig.

Reyna, Stephen P. (1990), *Wars without End: The Political Economy of a Precolonial African State*, Hanover.

Rialland, Maélle (1998), 'Hypothèses sur les origines d'un mouvement fondamentaliste en pays soninke', *Islam et sociétés au sud du Sahara*, 12, 75–88.

Riesebrodt, Martin (2007), *Cultus und Heilsversprechen: Eine Theorie der Religionen*, München.

Ritchie, J. M. (1966), 'Islam in Politics: East Africa', *The Muslim World*, LVI, 296–304.

Robinson, David (1993), 'Malik Sy: un intellectuel dans l'ordre colonial au Sénégal', *Islam et Sociétés au sud du Sahara*, 7, 183–92.

—— (2000), *Paths of Accommodation: Muslim Societies and French Colonial Authorities in Senegal and Mauritania 1880–1920*, Oxford.

—— (2004), *Muslim Societies in African History: New Approaches to African History*, Cambridge.

Roné, Beyem (2000), *Tchad: L'ambivalence culturelle et l'intégration nationale*, Paris.

Roy, Olivier (2002), *L'Islam mondialisé*, Paris.

Sadouni, Samadia (1998), 'Le minoritaire sud-africain Ahmed Deedat: une figure originale de la da^{c}wa', *Islam et Sociétés au Sud du Sahara*, 12, 149–72.

—— (2002), 'Tentative d'une construction régionale de la oumma en Afrique australe', in Dominique Darbon (ed.), *L'Afrique politique 2002: Islams d'Afrique: entre le local et le global*, Paris, 101–10.

—— (2007), 'New Religious Actors in South Africa: The Exemple of Islamic Humanitarianism', in Réné Otayek and Benjamin Soares (eds), *Islam and Muslim Politics in Africa*, New York, pp. 103–20.

—— (2011), *La controverse Islamo–Chrétienne en Afrique du Sud: Ahmed Deedat et les nouvelles formes de débat*, Aix-en-Provence.

Said, Behnam T. and Hazim Fouad (eds) (2014), *Salafismus: Auf der Suche nach dem wahren Islam*, Freiburg.

Said, Mohamed (1998), *The Life and Times of Abdulwahid Sykes (1924–1968): The Untold Story of the Muslim Struggle against British Colonialism in Tanganyika*, London.

—— (2015) 'Kumbukumbu: Sheikh Yahya Hussein na Alhaj Abdallah Tambaza', *JamiiForums*, 4 June, <JamiiForums.com/threads/kumbukumbu-sheikh-yahya-hussein-na-alhaji-abdallah-tambaza.862605> (last accessed 26 September 2015).

Salim, Ahmad I. (1973), *The Swahili Speaking People of Kenya's Coast, 1895–1965*, Nairobi.

—— (1987), 'Sheikh al-Amin bin Ali al-Mazrui: Un réformiste moderne au Kenya', in F. Constantin (ed.), *Les voies de l'islam en Afrique orientale*, Paris, pp. 59–72.

Salim, Swalha (1985), *A Modern Reformist Movement among the Sunni Ulema in East Africa*, MA Dissertation, McGill University, Montreal.

Salomon, Noah (2009a), 'The Salafi Critique of Islamism: Doctrine, Difference and the Problem of Islamic Political Action in Contemporary Sudan', in Roel Meijer (ed.), *Global Salafism: Islam's New Religious Movement*, London, pp. 143–68.

—— (2009b), 'Shaykh Muhammad Hashim al-Hadiyya (1910–2007): A Spiritual Biography', in Roel Meijer (ed.), *Global Salafism: Islam's New Religious Movement*, London, pp. 433–4.

—— (2013), 'Evidence, Secrets, Truth: Debating Islamic Knowledge in Contemporary Sudan', *Journal of the American Academy of Religion*, 81: 3, 820–51.

Salvatore, Armando (1997), *Islam and the Political Discourse of Modernity*, Reading.

—— and Dale Eickelman (2004), *Public Islam and the Common Good*, Leiden.

Salzbrunn, Monika (2002), 'Hybridization of Religious and Political Practices among West African Migrants in Europe', in Deborah Bryceson and Ulla Vuorela (eds), *The Transnational Family: New European Frontiers and Global Networks*, Oxford, pp. 217–29.

Samatar, Said S. (1992), 'Sheikh Uways Muhammad of Baraawe, 1847–1909: Mystic and Reformer in East Africa', in S. S. Samatar (ed.), *In the Shadow of Conquest: Islam in Colonial Northeast Africa*, Trenton, pp. 48–74.

Samson, Fabienne (2002), 'Une nouvelle conception des rapports entre religion et politique au Sénégal', in Dominique Darbon (ed.), *L'Afrique Politique: Islams d'Afrique: Entre le local et le global*, Paris, pp. 161–72.

—— (2005), *Les marabouts de l'islam politique. Le Dahiratoul Moustarchidina Wal Moustarchidaty un mouvement néo-confrérique sénégalais*, Paris.

—— (2007), 'Islam social ou Islam politique? Le cas de Modou Kara Mbacké', *Islam et sociétés au sud du Sahara (nouvelle série)*, 1, 43–60.

—— (2009a), 'Islam, Protest and Citizen Mobilization: New Sufi Movements', in Mamadou Diouf and Mara Leichtman (eds), *New Perspectives on Islam in Senegal: Conversion, Migration, Wealth, Power and Femininity*, New York, pp. 257–72.

—— (2009b), 'Nouveaux marabouts politique au Sénégal: lutte pour l'appropriation d'un espace public religieux', in Gilles Holder (ed.), *L'islam: nouvel espace public en Afrique*, Paris, pp. 149–72.

Sanusi, Lamido Sanusi (2005), 'The West and the Rest: Reflections on the Intercultural Dialogue about Shari^{c}ah', in Philip Ostien, Jamila M. Nasir and Franz Kogelmann (eds), *Comparative Perspectives in Shari^{c}ah in Nigeria*, Ibadan, pp. 251–74.

—— (2007), 'Politics and Sharia in Northern Nigeria', in Réné Otayek and Benjamin Soares (eds), *Islam and Muslim Politics in Africa*, New York, pp. 177–86.

Savadogo, Matthias (2005), 'L'intervention des associations musulmanes dans le champ politique en Côte d'Ivoire depuis 1990', in Muriel Gomez-Perez (ed.), *L'islam politique au sud du Sahara. Identités, discours et enjeux*, Paris, pp. 583–600.

Schacht, Joseph (1965), 'Notes on Islam in East Africa', *Studia Islamica*, XXIII, 91–136.

Scharrer, Tabea (2013), *Narrative islamischer Konversion: Biographische Erzählungen konvertierter Muslime in Ostafrika*, Bielefeld.

Scheele, Judith (2012), *Smugglers and Saints of the Sahara: Regional Connectivity in the Twentieth Century*, Cambridge.

Schielke, Samuli (2007), *Snacks & Saints. Mawlid Festivals and the Politics of Festivity, Piety and Modernity in Contemporary Egypt*, PhD Thesis, University of Amsterdam, the Netherlands.

Schmid, Bernhard (2014), *Die Mali-Intervention: Befreiungskrieg, Aufstandsbekämpfung oder neokolonialer Feldzug?* Münster.

Schritt, Jannik (2015), 'The Protests against Charlie Hebdo in Niger: A Background Analysis', unpublished conference paper.

Schulz, Dorothea (2003), 'Charisma and Brotherhood Revisited: Mass-Mediated Forms of Spirituality in Urban Mali', *Journal of Religion in Africa*, 33: 2, 146–71.

—— (2012), *Muslims and New Media in West Africa: Pathways to God*, Bloomington.

Schulze, Reinhard (1990), *Islamischer Internationalismus im 20. Jahrhundert*, Leiden.

—— (1993), 'La da^{c}wa saoudienne en Afrique de l'Ouest', in René Otayek (ed.), *Le radicalisme islamique au sud du Sahara*, Paris, pp. 21–36.

Seck, Abdourahmane (2007), 'Politique et religion au Sénégal: Contribution à une actualisation de la question', in Jean-Louis Triaud (ed.), *Islam, sociétés et politique en Afrique subsaharienne. Les exemples du Sénégal, du Niger et du Nigeria*, Paris, pp. 23–50.

—— (2010), *La question musulmane au Sénégal: Essai d'anthropologie d'une nouvelle modernité*, Paris.

Seesemann, Rüdiger (2005a), 'Islamism and the Paradox of Secularization: The Case of Islamist Ideas on Women in the Sudan', *Sociologus*, 1, 1–30.

—— (2005b), 'The Quotidian Dimensions of Islamic Reformism in Wadai (Chad)', in Muriel Gomez-Perez (ed.), *L'islam politique au sud du Sahara. Identités, discours et enjeux*, Paris, pp. 327–46.

—— (2006a), 'African Islam or Islam in Africa? Evidence from Kenya', in R. Loimeier and R. Seesemann (eds), *The Global Worlds of the Swahili: Interfaces of Islam, Identity and Space in 19th and 20th Century East Africa*, Berlin, pp. 229–50.

—— (2006b), 'Between Sufism and Islamism: The Tijāniyya and Islamist Rule in the Sudan', in Paul L. Heck (ed.), *Sufism and Politics: The Power of Spirituality*, Princeton, pp. 23–58.

—— (2007), 'Kenyan Muslims, the Aftermath of 9/11 and the War on Terror', in Benjamin Soares and Réné Otayek (eds), *Islam and Muslim Politics in Africa*, New York, pp. 157–76.

—— (2011), *The Divine Flood: Ibrāhīm Niasse and the Roots of a Twentieth Century Sufi Revival*, Oxford.

Shanono, Shehu Muhammad (1976), *Abubakar Mahmoud Gummi as a Mujaddid in Nigeria in the 20th Century*, BA Thesis, Bayero University Kano, Nigeria.

Sharkey, Heather (2003), *Living with Colonialism: Nationalism and Culture in the Anglo-Eygptian Sudan*, Berkeley.

Shehu, Abdullahi Hamisu (2013–2014), 'Chibok Girls Abduction: Too Many Unanswered Questions', *Annual Review of Islam in Africa*, 12: 1, 23–30.

Sheriff, Abdul (2001), 'Race and Class in the Politics of Zanzibar', *Afrika Spectrum*, 36: 3, 301–18.

—— and Ferguson, Ed (eds) (1991), *Zanzibar under Colonial Rule*, London.

Sidahmed, Abdel Salim (1997), *Politics and Islam in Contemporary Sudan*, Richmond.

Sieveking, Nadine (2005), Negotiating Development in Senegal: Women Organizations, Issues and Strategies, unpublished conference paper.

Simone, T. Abdou Maliwalim (1994), *In Whose Image? Political Islam and Urban Practices in Sudan*, Chicago.

Smith, Gina Gertrud (2008), *Medina Gounass: Challenges to Village Sufism in Senegal*, Copenhagen.

Soares, Benjamin F. (2005a), *Islam and the Prayer Economy. History and Authority in a Malian Town*, Edinburgh.

—— (2005b), 'The Muslim Public Intellectual, the Media Star and Satan: Changing Modalities of Religious Expression in West Africa', unpublished conference paper.

—— (2007), 'Islam in Mali in the Neoliberal Era', in Benjamin F. Soares and Réné Otayek (eds), *Islam and Muslim Politics in Africa*, New York, pp. 211–26.

—— (2009), 'The Attempt to Reform Family Law in Mali', *Die Welt des Islams*, 49: 3–4, 398–428.

—— (2012), 'On the Recent Mess in Mali', *Anthropology Today*, 28: 5, 1–2.

—— (2013), 'Saint and Sufi in Contemporary Mali', in Julia Day Howell and Martin van Bruinessen (eds), *Sufism and the Modern in Islam*, London, pp. 76–91.

Sohier, Estelle (2011), *Portraits controversés d'un prince Éthiopien: Iyasu 1897–1935*, Paris.

Solomon, Hussein (2013), 'Islam vs. Islamism: The South African Dimension', in Pade Badru and B. M. Sackey (eds), *Islam in Africa South of the Sahara*, Plymouth, pp. 355–66.

Souley, Abdoulaye Niandou (1993), 'Les « licenciés du Caire » et l'État au Niger', in René Otayek (ed.), *Le radicalisme islamique au sud du Sahara*, Paris, pp. 213–28.

Sounaye, Abdoulaye (2005), 'Les politiques de l'Islam au Niger dans l'ère de la démocratisation de 1991 à 2002', in Muriel Gomez-Perez (ed.), *L'Islam politique au Sud du Sahara*, Paris, pp. 503–28.

—— (2007), 'Instrumentalizing the Qur'ān in Niger's Public Life', *Journal for Islamic Studies*, 27, 211–39.

—— (2009), 'Izala au Niger: une alternative de communauté religieuse', in Laurent Fourchard, Odile Goerg and Muriel Gomez-Perez (eds), *Lieux de sociabilité urbaine en Afrique*, Paris, pp. 481–500.

—— (2011), 'La « discothèque » islamique: CD et DVD au cœur de la réislamisation nigérienne', in *Revue Éthnographique de l'Institut d'Éthnologie de l'Université de Neuchâtel*, 22, 1–20.

—— (2012a), 'Heirs of the Sheikh Izala and its Appropriation of Usman dan Fodio in Niger', *Cahiers d'Études Africaines*, 206–7, 427–47.

—— (2012b), 'Les clubs des Jeunes Musulmans du Niger: Un cadre de formation et un espace intergénérationnel', in Muriel Gomez-Perez and Marie Nathalie LeBlanc (eds), *L'Afrique des générations: entre tensions et négotiations*, Paris, pp. 217–58.

—— (2013), 'Alarama is All at Once: Preacher, Media "Savvy" and Religious Entrepreneur in Niamey', *Journal of African Cultural Studies*, 25: 1, 88–102.

—— (2014), 'Mobile Sunna: Islam, Small Media and Community in Niger', *Social Compass*, 61: 1, 21–9.

—— (2015), 'Irwo Sunnance yan-no! 1: Youth Claiming, Contesting and Transforming Salafism', *Islamic Africa*, 6, 82–108.

Sow, Fatou (2005), 'Les femmes, l'État et le sacré', in Muriel Gomez-Perez (ed.), *L'islam politique au sud du Sahara. Identités, discours et enjeux*, Paris, pp. 283–309.

Stauth, Georg (2005), *Ägyptische heilige Orte: Konstruktionen, Inszenierungen und Landschaften der Heiligen im Nildelta: Abdallah b. Salam*, Bielefeld.

Steinberg, Guido (2013), *Regionaler Jihad in Ostafrika*, Berlin.

—— and Annette Weber (eds) (2015), *Jihadismus in Afrika: Lokale Ursachen, regionale Ausbreitung, internationale Verbindungen*, Berlin.

Stolz, Fritz (1988), *Grundzüge der Religionswissenschaft*, Göttingen.

Stuke, Oliver (2011), *Islamismus am Horn von Afrika: Al-Shabaabs Rolle für die Entwicklung Somalias*, Frankfurt.

Sulaiman, Muhammad Dahiru (1993), 'Shiaism and the Islamic Movement in Nigeria 1979–1991', *Islam et Sociétés au Sud du Sahara*, 7, 5–16.

Taguem-Fah, Gilbert L. (2001), 'Le facteur peul, l'islam et le processus politique au Cameroun', *Islam et Sociétés au Sud du Sahara*, 14–15 : 81–98.

—— (2007), 'The War on Terror, the Chad–Cameroun Pipeline, and the New Identity of the Lake Chad Basin', *Journal of Contemporary African Studies*, 25: 1, 101–17.

Tahir, Ibrahim (1975), *Scholars, Sufis, Saints and Capitalists in Kano, 1904–1974*, PhD Thesis, University of Cambridge.

Tajo, ᶜAmeir (n.d.), *ash-Shaykh al-ᶜālam al-ᶜulamāᵓ Ḥassan b. ᶜAmeir, 1300–1399*, Zanzibar.

Tamari, Tal (1996), 'L'exégèse coranique (*tafsīr*) en milieu Mandingue', *Islam et Sociétés au Sud du Sahara*, 10, 43–80.

Tayob, Abdulkader (1995), *Islamic Resurgence in South Africa: The Muslim Youth Movement*, Cape Town.

—— (1999), *Islam in South Africa: Mosques, Imams, and Sermons*, Gainesville.

Thurston, Alexander (2009), 'Why is Militant Islam a Weak Phenomenon in Senegal?', *Institute for the Study of Islamic Thought in Africa (ISITA) Working Paper Series, 09-005*, Evanston.

—— (2014), 'Muslim Politics and Shariᶜa in Kano, Nigeria', *African Affairs*, 114: 454, 28–51.

—— (2015), 'Nigeria's Mainstream Salafis between Boko Haram and the State', *Islamic Africa*, 6, 109–34.

—— (2016), '"The Disease is UnBelief": Boko Haram's Religious and Political Worldview', The Brookings Project on U.S. Relations with the Islamic World, Analysis Paper, No. 22, January 2016, 1–28.

—— (forthcoming), *Debating Islam in Nigeria: The Salafi Canon in Preaching and Politics*, London.

El-Tinay, Hashim (2005), 'Review of Haydar Ibrahim Ali's "The Downfall of the Civilizational Project 1"', *Sudan Studies Association Newsletter*, 24: 1, 18–22.

Touati, Jasmin (1997), *Ethnizität und Nationalismus in Somalia (1890–1991)*, PhD Thesis, Free University of Berlin, Germany.

Touré, Cheikh (1957), *Afin que tu deviennes un croyant*, Dakar.

Traoré, Alioune (1983), *Cheikh Hamahoullah: homme de foi et résistant*, Paris.

Traoré, Bakary (2005), 'Islam et politique à Bobo-Dioulasso de 1940 à 2002', in Muriel Gomez-Perez (ed.), *L'islam politique au sud du Sahara: Identités, discours et enjeux*, Paris, pp. 417–48.

—— (2010). 'Ã la recherche d'une voie africaine de la laicité: Islam et pluralisme religieux au Burkina Faso', *Islam et sociétés au sud du Sahara (nouvelle série)*, 2: 9–54.

Triaud, Jean-Louis (1981), 'Le mouvement réformiste en Afrique de l'Ouest dans les années 50', *Mémoires du CERMAA, Institut National des Langues et Civilisations Orientales, Paris, 1*, 207–24.

—— (1986), 'ᶜAbd al-Rahman l'Africain (1908–1957): Pionnier et précurseur du wahhabisme au Mali', in O. Carré and P. Dumont (eds), *Radicalismes Islamiques, Vol. 2: Maroc, Pakistan, Inde, Yougoslavie, Mali*, Paris, pp. 162–80.

—— (1988a), 'L'Université islamique du Niger', *Islam et sociétés au sud du Sahara*, 2, 157–65.

—— (1988b), 'Bamako, la ville aux deux cents mosquées, ou la victoire du « secteur informel » islamique', *Islam et sociétés au sud du Sahara*, 2, 166–78.

—— (1995), *La légende noire de la Sanusiyya: Une confrérie musulmane saharienne sous le regard français (1840–1930)*, 2 vols, Paris.

—— and Leonardo Villalon (2009), 'Introduction thématique', *Afrique contemporaine*, 231: 3, 23–44.

Trimingham, J. S. (1952), *Islam in Ethiopia*, London.

Triulzi, Alessandro (1981), *Salt, Gold and Legitimacy: Prelude to the History of a No-man's Land: Bela Shangul, Wallaga, Ethiopia (ca. 1800–1898)*, Naples.

Tull, Denis and Annette Weber (2015), *Nigeria: Boko Haram und die Regionalisierung des Terrorismus*, Berlin.

Umar, Muhammad Sani (1988), *Sufism and Anti-Sufism in Nigeria*, BA Thesis, Bayero University Kano (BUK), Nigeria.

—— (1993), 'Changing Islamic Identity in Nigeria from the 1960s to the 1980s: From Sufism to Anti-Sufism', in Louis Brenner (ed.), *Muslim Identity and Social Change in Sub-Saharan Africa*, London, pp. 154–78.

—— (2002), 'Islamic Arguments for Western Education in Northern Nigeria: Muᶜazu Hadejia's Hausa Poem, Ilmin Zamin', *Islam et Sociétés au Sud du Sahara*, 16, 85–107.

—— (2004), 'Islamic Education and Emergence of Female Ulama in Northern Nigeria: Background, Trends and Consequences', in S. Reese (ed.), *The Transmission of Islamic Learning in Africa*, Leiden, pp. 99–120.

—— (2006), *Islam and Colonialism: Intellectual Responses of Muslims of Northern Nigeria to British Colonial Rule*, Leiden.

Utvik, Björn Olav (1997), 'Islamism – Cromwell's Ghost in the Middle East', in Stein Tönnesen, Juhani Koponen, Niels Steensgard and Thommy Svensson (eds), *Between National Histories and Global History*, Helsinki, pp. 129–42.

Vahed, Goolam (2009), 'Ahmed Deedat and Muslim–Christian Relations at the Cape', *Journal for Islamic Studies*, 29: 2–31.

van de Bruinhorst, Gerard (2001), 'Islamic Literature in Tanzania and Kenya', *ISIM Newsletter*, 8, 6.

—— (2007), *Raise your Voices and Kill your Animals: Islamic Discourses on the Idd el-Hajj and Sacrifices in Tanga (Tanzania)*, Amsterdam.

van Hoven, Ed (1999), 'Medina Gounass: The End of Religious Isolation', *ISIM Newsletter*, 4, 25.

Vérin, Emmanuel and Pierre Vérin (1999), *Histoire de la révolution Comorienne: Décolonisation, idéologie et séisme social*, Paris.

Villalon, Leonardo A. (1995), *Islamic Society and State Power in Senegal: Disciples and Citizens in Fatick*, Cambridge.

—— (1999), 'Generational Changes, Political Stagnation, and the Evolving Dynamics of Religion and Politics in Senegal', *Africa Today*, 46: 3–4, 129–48.

—— (2000), 'The Moustarchidine of Senegal: The Family Politics of a Contemporary Tijan Movement', in Jean Louis Triaud and David Robinson (eds), *La Tijāniyya: Une confrérie musulmane à la conquête de l'Afrique*, Paris, pp. 469–98.

—— (2004), 'Senegal', *African Studies Review*, 47: 2, 61–72.

—— (2007), 'Senegal: Shades of Islamism on a Sufi Landscape', in William Miles (ed.), *Political Islam in West Africa: State–Society Relations Transformed*, London, pp. 161–82.

Voll, John O. (1969), *A History of the Khatmiyya Tariqah in the Sudan*, 2 vols, PhD Thesis, Harvard.

—— (1983), 'Renewal and Reform in Islamic History: Tajdid and Islah', in John L. Esposito (ed.), *Voices of Resurgent Islam*, New York, pp. 32–47.

—— (2005), 'Afrikanischer Localism und das islamische Weltsystem', in R. Loimeier, D. Neubert and C. Weissköppel (eds), *Globalisierung im lokalen Kontext: Perspektiven und Konzepte von Handeln in Afrika*, Hamburg, pp. 277–310.

de Waal, Alex (1994), 'Turabi's Muslim Brothers: Theocracy in Sudan', *CovertAction*, 49, 13–21.

—— and A. H. Abdel Salam (2004), 'Islamism, State Power and *Jihad* in the Sudan', in Alex de Waal (ed.), *Islamism and its Enemies in the Horn of Africa*, Bloomington, pp. 71–113.

Wagemakers, Joas (2009), 'The Transformation of a Radical Concept: al-wala' wa-l-bara' in the Ideology of Abu Muhammad al-Maqdisi', in Roel Meijer (ed.), *Global Salafism: Islam's New Religious Movement,* London, pp. 81–106.

—— (2012), *A Quietist Jihadi: The Ideology and Influence of Abu Muhammad al-Maqdisi*, Cambridge.

—— (2014), 'Salafistische Strömungen und ihre Sicht auf *al-wala' wa-l-bara'* (Loyalität und Lossagung)', in Behnam T. Said and Hazim Fouad (eds), *Salafismus: Auf der Suche nach dem wahren Islam,* Freiburg, pp. 55–79.

Walker, Iain (2007), 'What Came First? The Nation or the State? Political Process in the Comoro Islands', *Africa,* 77: 4, 582–605.

Wandera, Joseph M. (2013), *Public Preaching by Muslims and Pentecostals in Mumias, Western Kenya and its Influence on Interfaith Relations*, PhD Thesis, University of Cape Town, South Africa.

Wane, A. M. (2003), *Le Senegal entre deux naufrages? La Joola et l'alternance*, Paris.

Warburg, Gabriel (2003), *Islam, Sectarianism and Politics in Sudan since the Mahdiyya*, Madison.

—— (1985), 'Islam and State in Numayri's Sudan', in J. D. Y. Peel and C. C. Stewart (eds), *'Popular Islam' South of the Sahara,* Manchester, pp. 400–13.

Ware, Richard T. III (2014), *The Walking Qur'an: Islamic Education, Embodied Knowledge and History in West Africa,* Chapel Hill.

Warms, Richard (1992), 'Merchants, Muslims and Wahhabiyya: The Elaboration of Islamic Identity in Sikasso, Mali', *Canadian Journal of African Studies*, 26: 3, 485–507.

Weber, Max (1988 [1920]), *Gesammelte Aufsätze zur Religionssoziologie* I, Tübingen.

Weimann, Gunnar (2010), *Islamic Criminal Law in Northern Nigeria: Politics, Religion, Judicial Practice,* Amsterdam.

Weingrod, Axel (1990), 'Saints and Shrines, Politics and Culture: A Morocco–Israel Comparison', in Dale Eickelman and James Piscatori (eds), *Muslim Travellers: Pilgrimage, Migration and the Religious Imagination*, London, pp. 217–35.

Weiss, Holger (2006), 'Political Islam in Ghana: Muslims and their Position in a Secular West African State', in Michael Bröning and Holger Weiss (eds), *Politischer Islam in Westafrika: Eine Bestandsaufnahme*, Berlin, pp. 47–80.

—— (2008), *Between Accommodation and Revivalism: Muslims, the State and Society in Ghana from the Precolonial to the Postcolonial Era,* Helsinki.

Weissköppel, Cordula (2005), '"Hybridität": die ethnografische Annäherung an ein theoretisches Konzept', in R. Loimeier, D. Neubert and C. Weissköppel (eds),

Globalisierung im lokalen Kontext. Perspektiven und Konzepte von Handeln in Afrika, Hamburg, pp. 311–47.

Werenfels, Isabelle (2015), 'Im "glokalen" Spannungsfeld: Jihadisten in Algerien und Tunesien', in Guido Steinberg and Annette Weber (eds), *Jihadismus in Afrika: Lokale Ursachen, regionale Ausbreitung, internationale Verbindungen*, Berlin, pp. 55–72.

Westerlund, David (2003), 'Ahmed Deedat's Theology of Religion: Apologetics through Polemics', *Journal of Religion in Africa*, 33: 3, 263–78.

Wiktorowicz, Quintan (2004), *Islamic Activism: A Social Movement Theory Approach*, Bloomington.

—— (2006), 'Anatomy of the Salafi Movement', *Studies in Conflict & Terrorism*, 29, 207–39.

Wild, Stefan (2005), 'Alle Tage ist kein Freitag. Bemerkungen zu Freitag, Feiertag und Alltag in der islamischen Welt', in Thomas Bauer and Ulrike Stehli-Werbeck (eds), *Alltagsleben und materielle Kultur in der arabischen Sprache und Literatur*, Wiesbaden, pp. 399–409.

Wimmelbücker, L. (2001), 'Die sansibarische Revolution von 1964: Widersprüche und Unzulänglichkeiten offizieller Geschichtsschreibung', in L. Marfaing and B. Reinwald (eds), *Afrikanische Beziehungen, Netzwerke und Räume*, Münster, pp. 295–308.

Woldeselase, Woldemichael (2010), *Terrorism in Ethiopia and the Horn of Africa: Threat, Impact and Response*, Addis Ababa, Ethiopia.

Wolf, Susanne (1993), 'Die islamische Bewegung im Sudan bis 1989', in Sigrid Faath and Hanspeter Mattes (eds), *Wuquf 7–8: Sudan*, Hamburg, pp. 205–22.

Woodward, Peter (1990), *Sudan, 1898-1989: The Unstable State*, London.

—— (2013), *Crisis in the Horn of Africa: Politics, Piracy and the Threat of Terror*, London.

Yacoub, Mahomat Saleh (1992), 'L'Islam et l'État en Republique du Tchad', in Jean-Pierre Magnant (ed.), *L'Islam au Tchad*, Talence, pp. 93–8.

Yahaya Hashim and Judith-Ann Walker (2014), '"Marginal Muslims": Ethnic Identity and the Umma in Kano', in Abdul Raufu Mustapha (ed.), *Sects and Social Disorder: Muslim Identities and Conflict in Northern Nigeria*, Woodbridge, Suffolk, pp. 126–46.

Zakari, Maïkoréma (2007a), 'La naissance et le développement du mouvement Izala au Niger', in Jean-Louis Triaud (ed.), *Islam, sociétés et politique en Afrique subsaharienne: Les exemples du Sénégal, du Niger et du Nigeria*, Paris, pp. 51–74.

—— (2007b), 'Shaykh Shaibu Ali. Un soufi au cœur de la capitale nigérienne', *Islam et sociétés au sud du Sahara (nouvelle série)*, 1, 101–16.

—— (2013), 'Niger: la laïcité contestée', *Islam et sociétés au sud du Sahara (nouvelle série)*, 3, 9–18.

Zaman, Muhammad Qasim (2002), *The Ulama in Contemporary Islam: Custodians of Change*, Princeton.

Zappa, Francesco (2015), 'Between Standardization and Pluralism: The Islamic Printing Market and its Social Spaces in Bamako, Mali', in Rosalind Hackett and Benjamin Soares (eds), *New Media and Religious Transformations in Africa*, Bloomington, pp. 39–62.

el-Zein, Abdul Hamid (1974), *The Sacred Meadows: A Structural Analysis of Religious Symbolism in an East African Town*, Evanston.

Zeltner, Jean-Claude (1988), *Les pays du Tchad dans la tourmente 1880–1903*, Paris.

—— (2002), *Histoire des Arabes sur les rives du lac Tchad*, Paris.

Zenn, Jacob (2014), 'Nigerian al-Qaedaism', *Current Trends in Islamist Ideology*, 16, 99–118.

Zerihun A. Woldeselassie (2013), 'Venerating Practices, Identity Politics and Islamic Reformism among the Siltie', in Patrick Desplat and Terje Østebø (eds), *Muslim Ethiopia: The Christian Legacy, Identity Politics and Islamic Reformism*, New York, pp. 139–62.

Ziddy, Issa (2001), *Athar minhaj at-tarbiya al-islāmiyya ᶜala ṭullāb. Al-marḥala ath-thānawiyya fī Zinjibār fi-l-fatra 1964–1999*, PhD Thesis, University of Khartoum, Sudan.

—— (2002), 'Wāqiᶜ al-madāris al-thānawiyya li-l-lajna al-muslimī ifrīqī tanzānia', unpublished conference paper.

—— (2003a), 'Shaykh Ḥassan b. ᶜAmeir ash-Shirāzī: His Life and Legacy', unpublished conference paper.

—— (2003b), 'Shaykh Ḥassan b. ᶜAmeir ash-Shirāzī: His works', unpublished conference paper.

Zitelmann, Thomas (1994), *Nation der Oromo: Kollektive Identitäten, Nationale Konflikte, Wir-Gruppenbildungen*, Berlin.

—— (2011), 'Soziale Strukturen, Organisationsformen und Konfliktverhalten unter Somali', in Walter, Feichtinger and Gerald Heinzl (eds), *Somalia: Optionen – Chancen – Stolpersteine*. Wien, pp. 29–54.

Zobel, Clemens (2013), 'Le Mali postcolonial', in Patrick Gonin, Nathalie Kotlok and Marc-Antoine Pérouse de Montclos (eds), *La tragédie malienne*, Paris, pp. 57–82.

Archival Sources

Public Record Office (PRO) (London)
PRO DO 185/68 (Political Situation in Zanzibar)
Zanzibar National Archive (ZNA) (Zanzibar)
ZNA AB 86/136 (Abdallah Salih al-Farsy)
ZNA AB 70/7 (Disturbances Report)
ZNA BA 5/9 (Annual Report for the year 1935)

Journals

Africa Confidential
Africa Today
an-Nuur (Tanzania)
Dira (Zanzibar)
Études Islamiques (Senegal)
ISIM Newsletter
iz3w (informationszentrum dritte welt)
Jeune Afrique
L'Abreuvoir des assoiffés (Senegal)
La voix du Touba (Senegal)
Le Musulman/al-Muslim (Senegal)
Le Soleil (Senegal)
Maarifa (Tanzania)
Mouride (Senegal)
Nasaha (Tanzania)
Neue Zürcher Zeitung (NZZ)
New York Times International Weekly
Newswatch
rewmi.com
Sahara Reporters
Sauti ya Zanzibar Huru
Süddeutsche Zeitung
The Guardian (Tanzania)
The Guardian (UK)

The Pen (Nigeria)
The Reporter (Nigeria)
The Triumph (Nigeria)
This Day (Nigeria)
Wal Fadjri (Senegal)
Zanzibar Leo (Zanzibar)

INDEX

EU representative:
Easy Access System Europe
Mustamäe tee 50, 10621 Tallinn, Estonia
Gpsr.requests@easproject.com

www.ingramcontent.com/pod-product-compliance
Lightning Source LLC
Chambersburg PA
CBHW050622280326
41932CB00015B/2491
9781474432191